Social Work Practice

Editor-in-Chief, Social Sciences: *Karen Hanson*
Series Editor, Social Work and Family Therapy: *Judy Fifer*
Series Editorial Assistant: *Alyssa Pratt*
Marketing Manager: *Jackie Aaron*
Composition Buyer: *Linda Cox*
Manufacturing Buyer: *Julie McNeill*
Cover Administrator: *Brian Gogolin*
Production Administrator: *Rosalie Briand*
Editorial-Production Service: *Trinity Publishers Services*
Electronic Composition: *Omegatype Typography, Inc.*

Library of Congress Cataloging-in-Publication Data

Johnson, Louise C., 1923–
    Social work practice : a generalist approach / Louise C. Johnson and Stephen J.
Yanca. — 7th ed.
      p. cm.
    Includes bibliographical references and index.
    ISBN 0-205-31701-4
    1. Social service. 2. Social case work. I. Yanca, Stephen J. II. Title.

HV40.J64 2000
361.3'2—dc21

                                00-028862

Printed in the United States of America
10 9 8 7 6 5 4 3 2 1   05 04 03 02 01 00

Credits are on p. 447, which constitutes a continuation of the copyright page.

SEVENTH EDITION

Social Work Practice

A Generalist Approach

Louise C. Johnson

Professor Emeritus
University of South Dakota

Stephen J. Yanca

Saginaw Valley State University

Allyn and Bacon

Boston ▪ London ▪ Toronto ▪ Sydney ▪ Tokyo ▪ Singapore

CONTENTS

Preface   xiv

PART ONE   Perspectives on Social Work Practice   1

1 Social Work as a Response to Concern/Need   3

From Concern to Need   4

Need   4

Cause-Function Debate   6

Common Human Needs   7
 Human Development Perspective   8
 Human Diversity   9
 Social Systems Theory   11
 Ecological Perspective   12
 Strengths Perspective   13

Social Functioning   14

Summary   14

Questions   15

Suggested Readings   15

Notes   16

2 Social Work as a Developing Profession   17

Social Work as a Profession   18

Development of Social Work Knowledge   19
 Pre-1920   19
 1921–1930   21
 1931–1945   22
 1946–1960   24
 1961–1975   25
 1976–1990   28
 1991–2000   29

Summary   31

Questions   32

Suggested Readings   32

Notes   33

3 Social Work as a Creative Blending of Knowledge, Values, and Skills   39

Knowledge   40

Values   45

Skills   52

Creative Blending of Knowledge, Values, and Skills   54

Summary   57

Questions   57

Suggested Readings   58

Notes   59

4 Social Work as a Process of Facilitating Growth and Change   61

Blending an Ecosystems Strengths Approach with the Problem-Solving Process   62

The Natural Process of Growth and Change   65

Process   66

The Stages of the Change Process   66

Social Work Practice and the Change Process   73

Summary   74

Questions   74

Suggested Readings   75

Notes   75

5 Social Work as Intervention into Human Transactions   76

Intervention   77

Transactions as the Focus for Change   80

Influence   82

Changes Sought by the Social Worker   85

Summary   87

Questions   88

Suggested Readings   88

Notes   89

PART TWO   The Interactional Process   91

6 The Worker   93

Knowledge of Self   94
Lifestyle and Philosophy of Life   95
Moral Code and Value System   95
Roots   98
Life Experiences   98
Personal Needs   99
Personal Functioning   102

The Helping Person   107
Characteristics of a Helping Person   107
Responsibility and Authority   109
Helping Skills   111

The Multiperson Helping System   112

Summary   116

Questions   117

Suggested Readings   117

Notes   118

7 The Client   119

Becoming a Client   120

Understanding the Individual Client   124
Vital Roles   126

Human Diversity   126
Motivation, Capacity, and Opportunity   131
Stress and Crisis Determination   132
Strengths and Uniqueness of Clients   132

Understanding the Multiclient System: The Family   137

Summary   148

Questions   149

Suggested Readings   149

Notes   150

8 Environment   152

Person in Environment as an Ecosystem   153

The Community as a Social System   153

Understanding the Agency   163

Transactions between Person and Ecosystem   170

Working in a Bureaucracy   172

Summary   176

Questions   177

Suggested Readings   177

Notes   179

9 Interaction with Individuals   180

Formation of a One-to-One Action System   181

Relationship   190
The Helping Relationship   190
Special Influences on the Helping Relationship   193

Communication   199

The Interview: An Interactional Tool   203
Preparing for an Interview   205
The Stages of an Interview   205
Skills Used by the Worker during the Interview   207

Summary   212

Questions   212

Suggested Readings   213

Notes   214

10   Multiperson Interaction   215

**The Family as the Fundamental Experience
with Multiperson Interaction**   218

The Family as a Multiperson Client System   220

The Small Group as a Social System   225
Structure   225
Function   229
Development   230

The Social Worker as a Group Member   237
Group Enabling   237
Issues in Group Participation   240
Use of the Team   240
Leadership   242
Conflict   243
Social Work Tasks   243

The Worker and the Multiperson Client   244
The Worker and Group Interaction   245
Group Formation   247
Discussion Leadership   249
Structuring Group Activity   250

The Family Group as a Social System   251
Structure   251
Function   252
Development   253

Summary   253

Questions   254

Suggested Readings   255

Notes   256

PART THREE   **The Social Work Process**   **257**

11 **Assessment**   **259**

The Content of the Assessment Phase   **260**
Judgment   263

The Use of the Change Process in Assessment   **268**
Identification of Need   269
Identification of Blocks to Need Fulfillment   270
Formulation of the Concern or Need   272
Preliminary Assumptions about the Nature of the Concern
or Need   274
Preliminary Assumptions about Potential Strengths and Resources
in the Ecosystem   275
Selection and Collection of Information   276
Analysis of the Information Available   276
Assessment of Small Groups   277

Transactional Assessment   **278**
The Dual Perspective   279
Mapping   280
Social Support Network Analysis   281

Needs Assessment   **282**

Summary   **286**

Questions   **287**

Suggested Readings   **287**

Notes   **289**

12 **Planning**   **290**

Components of a Plan   **292**
Goals and Objectives   292
Units of Attention   296
Strategy   296

Planning with Multiperson Client Systems   **303**

Factors Affecting a Plan of Action   **305**
The Community   305
The Agency   306
The Social Issue   307

The Worker   308
The Client   309
Diversity and Populations at Risk   310
Strengths and Limitations of the Systems Involved   311

Agreement between Worker and Client   312

Summary   313

Questions   314

Suggested Readings   315

Notes   315

13 Direct Practice Actions   317

Action to Enable Clients to Use Available Resources   319
The Service Delivery System   320
Referral   323
Broker and Advocate Roles   324
Empowerment and Enabling   326

Action in Response to Crisis   330
Recognizing Crisis   331
Responding to Crisis   332

Action That Is Supportive   334

Use of Activity as an Interventive Strategy   337

Action as Mediation   341

Summary   344

Questions   345

Suggested Readings   345

Notes   347

14 Indirect Practice Actions   349

Environmental Change   350

Involvement of Influentials   354

Coordination of Services   356
Case Management   358
Networking   360

Program Planning and Resource Development   363
   Developing a Volunteer Program   367
   Self-Help Groups   368

Changing Organizations from Within   369

Cause Advocacy   373
   Community Organization   375
   Influencing the Political Process   375
   Social Action Organizing   377

Summary   378

Questions   379

Suggested Readings   379

Notes   381

15 Evaluation   383

Accountability   384

Kinds of Evaluation   387

Techniques for Use in Evaluating   389
   Recording   389
   Research   393
   Program Evaluation   400
   Use of Computers   401

Issues Related to Evaluation   402
   Client Participation   402
   Confidentiality   402
   Effect of Privacy and Open-Access Laws   404

Summary   404

Questions   405

Suggested Readings   405

Notes   406

16 Termination   408

Kinds of Termination   409

Planned Termination   **413**
   Individuals   413
   Families   415
   Small Groups   415

Components of Termination   **417**
   Disengagement   417
   Stabilization of Change   418
   Evaluation   419

Summary   **422**

Questions   **422**

Suggested Readings   **423**

Notes   **423**

Appendix: Models of Social Work Practice   **425**

Glossary   **440**

Author Index   **449**

Subject Index   **451**

PREFACE

Written from a generalist perspective, *Social Work Practice: A Generalist Approach,* Seventh Edition, synthesizes historical and current understandings into a logically developed sequence for learning about and teaching the practice of social work. As a textbook for beginning students, it should be particularly useful for undergraduates in introductory practice or methods courses. The material can be used on a one-semester basis or in a two-semester sequence.

Generalist social work, as developed in this text, begins with the need of an individual or a social system. The social worker explores or assesses the situation in which the need exists with the client and significant others. Based on the findings of this exploration, a plan for work to alleviate the situation is developed and an agreement contract between the worker and the client is drawn up. The focus of the plan can be an individual, a small group, a family, an organization, or a community. Once the plan is developed, the worker and client, and perhaps other persons, work to carry out the plan. At some point, the worker and client decide whether to terminate their relationship or continue to work together on further plans.

Students should have certain prerequisites before using the material covered in this book. These include:

1. At least one introductory course covering the history and development of social welfare and an introduction to the profession.
2. A broad liberal arts base providing a wide variety of knowledge pertaining to the human situation, an appreciation of history, and some understanding about the nature of knowledge.
3. Courses providing an understanding of human behavior and the social environment such as those in psychology, sociology, anthropology, political science, and economics. Courses that include understandings of human development and human diversity, including racial and ethnic differences, are particularly important.

A course on human behavior in the social environment taken in a social work program is *not* a prerequisite or a corequisite. This book provides the content needed for integration of social science content into the social work practice frame of reference. Examples of concepts and how they are used in practice situations are given as one means to assist students in applying this knowledge to practice.

The book does not attempt to present any one model or approach to social work but rather synthesizes material from a number of sources into a coherent whole. Although at points it may seem that the major focus is on work with individuals, this is not the case. It is often easier, however, for students to grasp concepts when their application to work with individuals is presented. These examples can then be used as a base for considering applications to other systems (family, small group, organization, and community). Also, no attempt is made to consider practice with any particular population or social problem area. Rather, the assumption is made that the generalist approach can be used in a wide variety of situations, such as with older people, those who have medical and mental health problems, those who are discriminated against because of lifestyle, and those who suffer because their social situation does not provide for their basic needs. This focus, then, includes service to discrete groups such as homosexuals, the homeless, and veterans.

Plan for the Text

Part One develops five perspectives on social work practice and a framework on which the other two parts are based. Parts Two and Three consider two processes essential to the social work endeavor: the interactional process and the social work process—which is conceptualized as assessment, planning, action, evaluation, and termination.

Social work background material about minority groups and women has been emphasized in the text, which specifically addresses issues of working with these groups. The material on minority groups is not focused on working with a particular minority group but on providing the student with a framework from which to view all persons of minority status. It seeks to provide an understanding of what knowledge and attitudes are needed if a social worker is to work effectively with persons of minority status. It is expected that the learning environment will then provide specific materials for those minority groups that students are most apt to encounter in their practice of social work. Readings that are useful in the development of understanding about practice with minorities and women are suggested. In order to enhance readability, yet maintain a nonbiased gender content, the pronouns *he* and *she* are used alternately throughout the book.

The organization chosen for this text seems most appropriate to the authors, who have based it on years of experience in teaching generalist social work practice. As the concepts are developed, attention is given to building on material presented in earlier sections of the book. Repetition is used to reinforce learning. The authors assume that the present cannot be understood apart from the past; thus historical as well as contemporary aspects of the material covered are noted.

Since this is a book for beginning students, it was written with their needs in mind and does not attempt to detail all aspects of the concepts introduced. It does develop concepts so that students will have more than a superficial introduction yet not be overwhelmed by material for which they have no experiential knowledge. An attempt has been made to minimize the use of jargon yet to introduce the student to professional language. Charts and schemas are provided to help students organize considerable amounts of information into a coherent whole to maximize understanding.

The book contains many case examples. Most major sections of each chapter contain vignettes that depict the major concepts in action. In addition, longer case examples are provided. In some chapters, a case may be provided in several parts, illustrating several major concepts. An attempt has also been made to use case examples from practice in a wide variety of settings. In choosing case material, dimensions of size and kind of community, client age and needs, and agency purpose and source of sanction have been considered. Although much can be learned from a textbook, thorough learning takes place only as the conceptualizations are applied in actual practice experiences. Each chapter contains a summary, a statement of learning expectations for that chapter, study questions, and suggested readings for use by students and teachers. An appendix, with summaries of models of social work practice, as well as a glossary of key terms, are included at the end of the text.

Acknowledgments

Thanks are due to the reviewers of various editions of this text, whose suggestions were greatly appreciated and were incorporated into this revision wherever possible: Jean Brooks, Jackson State University; Margaret R. Calista, Marist College; Shirley M. Clark, Chattanooga State Technical Community College; Jean E. Daniels, California State University, Northridge; Diane Dwyer, State University of New York–Brockport; Ralph J. Gilmore, Westfield State College; Susan Grettenberger, Michigan State University; Kenneth J. Herrmann, Jr., SUNY, Brockport; Patricia Hunter, California State University, Chico; Lillie C. Kirsch, Marion Technical College; Anna Martin-Jearld, Bridgewater State College; Christine McGill, San Francisco State University; Barbara L. McGregor, Saginaw Valley State University; Judy Norman, Brigham Young University; Jean L. Nuernberger, Central Missouri State University; Art Preciado, California State University, Chico; Emma Quartaro, Seton Hall University; Jeanette Simon, Upper Iowa University.

L. C. J.
S. J. Y.

Social Work Practice

Perspectives on Social Work Practice

Part One provides an overview of the nature of social work practice. When the reader has an understanding of the complexity of the practice situation and has developed a framework in which to place the details, study of practice specifics can follow. The reader likely will wish to return to the concepts presented to develop a greater depth of understanding.

Social work is complex, having a wide variety of applications. Because of this, there are a number of *perspectives* regarding its nature. Five descriptions or perspectives are presented here to provide the overall framework of generalist social work practice. These are most often those referred to in social work literature and that best explain the nature of contemporary generalist social work practice. No attempt has been made to identify a particular ideology or model as the approach of this book. However, a specific approach has developed with each subsequent edition and is referred to as an *interactive-transactional* approach to generalist social work practice using ecosystems and strengths perspectives. Concepts, ideas, and understandings gained from a wide variety of practice literature and experiences are synthesized to describe the realities of generalist social work practice.

A *generalist approach* requires that the social worker assess the situation with the client and decide which systems are the appropriate *units of attention,* or focus of the work, for the change effort. As the units of attention may include an individual, a family, a small group, an agency or organization, a community, or the transactions among these, the generalist approach emphasizes knowledge that can be applied to a variety of systems. Each of the five perspectives discussed in Part One has application to all these units of attention.

Each perspective describes social work practice from contrasting but complementary views. Each may be seen as a different facet of a complex way of thinking, feeling, and doing, and each provides a way of understanding the activity that has come to be known as generalist social work practice. Together, they provide a description of the essential nature of generalist social work practice.

In the first two chapters, the first two perspectives address the "why" of social work practice. Chapter 1, "Social Work as a Response to Concern/Need," discusses the basic reason for the social work endeavor. It focuses on the desirable outcome of the combined work of worker and client and develops the concepts of need, common human needs, human diversity, social systems needs, social functioning, ecosystems, and the strengths perspective. Chapter 2, "Social Work as a Developing Profession," examines practice historically in order to understand why practice exists in its current form. Contemporary practice has many vestiges from the past. Thus, some understanding of the development of practice theory, as contrasted with social welfare history, is important for understanding the major concepts that underlie practice. Chapter 2 also introduces the concepts of profession, assessment, person in the situation, relationship, process, and intervention. These topics were chosen because of their common usage in many conceptualizations of social work practice.

The last three chapters cover the remaining perspectives—the "how" of social work practice. Chapter 3, "Social Work as a Creative Blending of Knowledge, Values, and Skills," discusses how knowledge, values, and skills are used in understanding and taking action in relation to social-functioning needs. The concepts developed are knowledge, values, skills, and creative blending. Chapter 4, "Social Work as a Process of Facilitating Growth and Change," presents a way of thinking about the process of social work and the steps used in responding to need. It develops the concept of facilitating growth and change from a strengths perspective. Chapter 5, "Social Work as Intervention into Human Transactions," discusses the way in which the social worker seeks to bring about growth and change. It develops the concepts of intervention, transaction, and influence.

The assumption is made throughout the book that the reader is bringing a knowledge base developed through previous social work courses and experiences. Also, it is assumed the reader has some basic understanding of social science concepts, especially those from psychology and sociology. These will be developed in Part Two, which considers the interactional processes present in the social work endeavor, and Part Three, which describes the ongoing process undertaken by worker and client as they seek to respond to need and reach commonly set goals.

1 Social Work as a Response to Concern/Need

LEARNING EXPECTATIONS

1. Understanding the concept of need and the difference between concern and need.
2. Ability to identify common human needs.
3. Understanding of how concepts about human development are used in identifying need.
4. Some understanding of the relationship of powerlessness to human need.
5. Understanding the concept of human diversity and its use in identifying human need.
6. Understanding the concepts of social systems and ecosystems and their use in identifying human need.
7. Understanding of social functioning and strengths as the focus of social work.

The "why" of social work practice is addressed when social work is viewed as a response to concern or need. This perspective helps identify appropriate goals for service and considers the appropriate target for change given the context of the concern or need. It allows thinking about social work practice to "start where the client is," at the point a concern is felt or a need is identified. Additionally, it begins to provide the means for integrating knowledge about human behavior and the social environment with the social work practice approach to meeting human need.

This chapter explores some conceptualizations that clarify this facet of social work practice. These understandings are derived from classical and contemporary themes used by social workers to describe the nature of human need. Students will have encountered most of these themes in previous learning experiences, for example, in a sociology course or a human behavior in social environment course.

From Concern to Need

To begin to understand the complexity of a situation, it is helpful first to identify some of the possible ways concern may be felt in one situation. For example, a parent may be concerned because his child is not learning in school; a teacher, because a student is disruptive in the classroom; a merchant, because an adolescent boy is taking merchandise without paying for it. A student may be concerned because his family seems to be falling apart. An agency may be concerned because there are no resources to help families with communication problems. A community group may be concerned that so many young people are in trouble with the law. Each of these concerns may exist around the same situation, and each indicates some difficulty in the relationship between people and social systems.

Human situations, and thus human need, are complex. The social worker must develop a frame of reference for understanding the reasons behind the behaviors of people. She must also understand the environmental factors that influence these behaviors and how the environment is influenced by the behavior. Each situation must be viewed as multifaceted and unique.

Concern is a feeling that something is not right. It is interest in, regard for, and care about the well-being of oneself or other individuals. A feeling of concern is often the result of some behavior that affects the relationship between the individual and other individuals or a social system. All behavior has meaning, and people express and fulfill need through behavior. Need also generates feelings. As a part of understanding what is causing a concern and why the concern is important, feelings relative to the concern should be identified and explored. The social work response to such behavior and related feelings identifies need and discovers alternate ways of need fulfillment so that the needs of each party in a situation may be met.

Need

Need is that which is necessary for either a person or a social system to function within reasonable expectations in a given situation. Need is not a want for something that would be nice to have but, rather, is important to the development or functioning of the person or system. For example, if a boy is caught taking merchandise without paying for it, an unreasonable expectation would be that he keep the stolen items because he felt he needed them. A reasonable expectation would be to identify the reasons behind his desire for the items and to find alternate ways of meeting the related need in a socially acceptable manner.

"They need"—need that is identified by others—has often been a focus of social work. This outside identification of need sometimes leads to people being told what they need. But **felt need**—need identified by the client—is just as relevant. Often the "they need" and the felt need are different or are expressed in different ways. Social workers, using their expert knowledge and professional value system, can sometimes identify need that does not seem relevant or realistic to clients. The felt need of the client and the concerned persons must always be considered. This practice is consistent with a basic social work principle: "start where the client is." In using this principle, the social worker starts with the concern or felt need of the client and other concerned persons; identifies various needs (felt needs or "they needs") in the situation; and with the client determines goals based on both kinds of need. In the case example below, the debate would be whether services should focus on John and his family or on conditions that interfere with family functioning. Questions to be investigated might be: Are the father's working hours too long? Is there insufficient income to meet the family's needs? Is there a problem of alcoholism in the family?

Case Example

Mrs. A comes to a mental health center. She tells the social worker that her thirteen-year-old son, John, is not getting along very well in school. His last report card had all D's and C's. Last year he had B's and two A's. She talked to the teacher and learned that John does not pay attention in class and disturbs the other students. After some time, she tells the worker her husband got a call from Mr. W at the local drugstore telling him John had stolen a candy bar. Mrs. A thinks that John "did that awful thing" because he is so upset about not learning. She says that her husband works long hours in the store he owns and is not home very much. She states that the store is having problems competing with the large national chain stores and they do not know if it will remain open.

The worker suggests that he talk with John, and Mrs. A agrees. John confirms that he is doing poorly in school; he says he just cannot do the work. He thinks the teacher expects too much and yells at him too often. He is just "fooling around." He says he doesn't want to talk about the candy bar incident. The worker asks about things at home. His reply is, "Okay, I guess." The worker notes a sad tone in his voice and so asks about what he does with his dad. From this they talk about his dad not being home, and eventually John talks about feeling stress from the uncertainty of his dad's business.

With these facts, the worker begins to speculate about the needs of John in this situation. He thinks about the developmental needs of a thirteen-year-old boy. Important is John's lack of security, which could in part explain his behavior in school and his stealing from the drugstore. The worker knows the teacher cannot teach John—that is, carry out her assigned function—if John is so concerned about the situation at home that he is unable to pay attention at school. Also, if he is bothering others, their learning may be disrupted as well. The worker knows that the storekeeper cannot allow his goods to be stolen and that John's father needs to be well thought of by fellow merchants. The most important system is the family. There seems to be a need for improved communication and ways for coping with the stress related to Mr. A's job. This family is a third-generation Italian-American family. The worker needs to consider how cultural factors affect its functioning. He is not yet sure of other needs involved.

In this simplified situation we see the worker converting the explicit concern of Mrs. A and John and the implicit concern of other systems into an identification of need. He is identifying which systems and individuals have needs and the needs of each. While the worker is focusing on the needs of John and his family, the need to modify

(continued)

Case Example   Continued

John's behavior in the school and in the community is also considered, for John's behavior is disruptive to these systems.

The components of this situation are the people involved—the child, each parent, the teacher, the merchant, and the child's classmates and peers—and the social systems of the family and the classroom group. The situation also involves the concerned agency, the school, Mr. A's business, and community groups and reflects the culture and expectations of the community. As the needs of each component in relation to the situation are identified, the interdependent and reciprocal nature of these needs becomes apparent. This is the beginning of the social work endeavor.

Cause-Function Debate

A social worker needs to consider whether the response to need should be on a person-to-person basis or should address societal problems that help create the person's unmet needs. This issue has often been referred to as the **cause-function debate.** In 1929, Porter Lee, in a classic paper, defined a **cause** as "movement directed toward the elimination of an entrenched evil...(or) a new way of meeting human need."[1] He went on to say that once the evil was eliminated, the new response to need became a "function of well-organized community life." He saw social work seventy years ago as moving from cause to function. At that time social work was concerned with response to need and with whether one profession could respond to both societal problems and individual need. This issue continues to be of concern to a profession that includes both clinical social workers and community organizers and reflects their different approaches to meeting need. There is still considerable debate about whether the same profession can respond to human need on an individual, case-by-case level and also be involved in changing a society that is frequently the cause of individual problems.

The sociologist C. Wright Mills refers to these two kinds of need as **private troubles** and **public issues.** Private troubles have to do with "the individual and... the range of his immediate relations with others...issues have to do with matters that transcend these local environments."[2] William Schwartz saw this issue of the "social vs. the psychological...[as] responsibility for social reform on one hand and individual help to persons in trouble on the other," as the "grand daddy of dilemmas of social work." He believed that these two positions should not be polarized. Since personal troubles (needs) arise out of relationships with the larger society, the social worker must address the needs of both the individual and the larger systems that are a part of contemporary society.[3] This approach recognizes not only the need of an individual client but also the needs of others who may be significant in the situation. In addition, it may call for examination of significant systems (families, small groups) of which the individuals may be a part, for consideration of community or societal institutions, and for awareness of how situations sometimes prevent the meeting of individual needs.

Common Human Needs

In *Common Human Needs*, a social work classic, Charlotte Towle discusses need in relation to the factors that affect human development. Towle contends that the following elements are essential if people are to be motivated toward social goals:

1. Physical welfare—food, shelter, and health care
2. Opportunity for emotional and intellectual growth
3. Relationships with others
4. Provision for spiritual needs[4]

She also points out that need is relative to a person's age and life situation. For instance, the infant must have physical care, an opportunity to learn, and a relationship with a loving adult. Adults must have survival opportunities in the form of food, shelter, and clothing, but ordinarily they do not need physical care. They do need human relationships, but these can be of varying nature.

Abraham Maslow developed a hierarchy of needs that supports Towle's thinking and expands the understanding of need. In his expanded list, needs are placed in ascending order; in order to meet each need one must have met the previous ones. With the most essential need at the top, the list includes:

1. Physiological needs—food, water, air
2. Safety needs—avoidance of pain and physical damage through external forces
3. Need for belonging and love—feeling secure when in close, intimate contact with others
4. Esteem needs—having status and acceptance in one's group
5. Needs for self-actualization—expression of potentialities and capabilities
6. Need for cognitive understanding—understanding of self and the external world[5]

According to Maslow's hierarchy, a person must first satisfy primary physiological needs, such as the need for food, before social needs can be considered. Yet it must be remembered that, particularly with a young child, the need for food cannot be satisfied without a relationship with another person.

Social workers are aware of the need for individuals and groups to feel that they have the power or the control necessary to meet their needs or to change situations that are affecting need fulfillment. The literature has been particularly focused on the need for *empowerment* of discriminated-against groups (persons of color and women). The nature of contemporary American society can lead many individuals and groups to feel helpless and hopeless. Thus, consideration of feelings of hope for quality of life and control of resources and situations that impact need fulfillment are important aspects of contemporary social work practice.[6] This theme will be explored throughout this book.

To identify and understand human need in any situation, five knowledge bases are helpful: human development, human diversity, social systems theory, ecosystems, and the strengths perspective.* Each considers human need from a different point of view and together provide the base for a response that considers the complexity of human situations.

Human Development Perspective

Human need from a human development perspective indicates that people develop physically, cognitively, socially, emotionally, and spiritually over the life cycle.[7] There are benchmarks that can be used to measure growth in each area. Physically, there are such measures as the age of beginning to walk or the age of onset of puberty. Cognitively, the work of Jean Piaget is often used to examine how a person deals with concepts, or IQ tests are given to measure intelligence. In the social-emotional area, the work of Erik Erikson is often used as a reference point. His "eight stages of man,"[8] based on the mastery of psychosocial tasks relevant to each age, are useful in determining whether expected psychosocial growth has taken place.

From a developmental perspective, human need may be identified in two ways. First, at each stage of life individuals should be developing in certain age-specific ways, and for this development to take place, certain conditions must be present. The infant needs love and physical care as well as sensory stimulation. The school-age child still needs physical care, though not to the same degree as the infant. This child needs protection but also the freedom and opportunity to learn skills and develop creativity. The adolescent needs opportunities to resolve the normal conflicts of growing up, to find out who she is, to deal with sexuality, and to make vocational decisions. Adults need opportunities in which they can feel a sense of accomplishment, fulfill their nurturing needs, and participate in group life and the society in which they live. Older adults need economic security; provision for health needs; and the opportunity to deal with feelings arising from retirement, failing health, and impending death.

A second way to identify human need would be to note development that would be expected at a particular life stage but that has not taken place. This includes needs from the past that have not been met and are contributing to difficulties in present social functioning. It also includes identification of developmental lags or situations in which there is a danger that the expected development will not take place.

---

*It is assumed that readers will have knowledge of each of these areas from courses in the social sciences. The focus of this discussion is on the translation of that knowledge into action. No attempt will be made to list all possible needs to be considered or all the knowledge included in each area. The focus will be on the complexity of human need based on knowledge of the five areas.

In working with John, the boy who stole merchandise, a social worker would be aware that John is entering the developmental stage of adolescence, a time of confusion for many boys. John is probably trying to discover who he is in relationship to others. He is experiencing new sexual feelings. He is probably testing out various value systems. The insecurity of his father's job may undermine John's ability to work through these issues.

The response to need from a developmental point of view is to provide the necessary conditions that will allow development to progress and to eliminate those that block development. These conditions are heavily dependent on social interaction between individuals and their environment. In responding to these common human needs, the social worker should have a thorough understanding of human development in all its aspects throughout the life span.

Human Diversity

Though there are common human needs, people fulfill those needs in different ways. The way in which needs are fulfilled is greatly influenced by cultural factors, as well as by physical disabilities, socioeconomic factors, gender or sexual preference, and discriminatory practices against certain groups in our society. The human diversity perspective is useful in considering human need in a multicultural society.

The **human diversity** approach brings together understandings about the nature of culture and its effect on the development and functioning of human beings. Given the power differential inherent in a structured society, this perspective is specifically concerned with the effects of social institutions on human behavior.

The concept of human diversity is based on the premise that American society is composed of a wide variety of cultures. Some cultural groups have difficulties in meeting needs because they differ from the dominant cultures of U.S. society. Some of these groups have experienced prejudice and discrimination; some have experienced poverty and institutional racism—the built-in characteristics of societal institutions that have a negative effect on certain segments of society. These segments of society are further impacted because they tend to be rendered less powerful in modifying societal institutions to better provide culturally congruent means for meeting human need.

The human diversity approach considers human behavior from the stance of cultural relativity. It sees normal behavior as an irrelevant concept and behavior as appropriate or inappropriate relative to the social situation in which a person is operating. What may be appropriate in one situation may be inappropriate in another. Differences in developmental patterns found in different cultures should not be considered as necessarily abnormal. According to this approach, the response to need is not to measure norms but to determine the meaning of perceptions, experiences, and events as they affect the growth and functioning of individuals in their own cultural context.

Ronald Federico, in discussing the concept of human diversity, sees behavior as being influenced by three factors: (1) genetic, (2) cultural, and (3) societal. Genetic influences include both mental and physical growth potential, the ability to tolerate stress, and ways of responding to stress. Cultural influences include life goals, behavior patterns, resource utilization patterns, self-concepts and attitudes, and ways of perceiving events. Social influences include the social institutional structure, which comprises systems of socialization, social control, social gratification, and social change. These three sets of influences—genetic, cultural, and social—interact in a complex manner.[9] This conceptualization can also be applied to conditions that are not cultural in source, such as developmental disability, blindness, or chronic physical illness.

Dolores Norton, who has developed a similar concept, "the dual perspective," sees each person as part of two systems: (1) the nurturing system, which includes the family and immediate community environment (the culture of an individual), and (2) the sustaining system, which includes the organization of goods and services, political power, economic resources, educational system, and larger societal systems. If the perspective of the two systems is such that there are broad areas of incongruence between the two, then individuals are prone to difficulties in functioning.[10] Such individuals will have unique needs. In our society this incongruence is particularly evident in the situation of women and racial minority groups. The dual perspective provides another way of considering human development and functioning in a diverse society. The response to need lies in helping individuals and groups find ways of living together in such a way that opportunities to meet the needs of all are maximized.

In order to understand human need, the social worker must also have significant knowledge about the role of environmental factors as they affect the development and functioning of individuals. Environmental factors include social, economic, and geographical and climactic conditions that are a part of the immediate surroundings of the individual. Discriminatory attitudes toward the person, extremes of climate, and sociocultural expectations all influence individual behavior. The worker should also understand the effect of disabling conditions on individual functioning and development, including physical and mental disabilities as well as prejudice and discrimination. The causes as well as the nature and effects of prejudice and discrimination should be understood, as should differences in lifestyle patterns among socioeconomic groups.

For example, if John and his family (see the case example) are African American, issues of discrimination and culture must be considered. The community might tend to react to his stealing by involving the police. He might be arrested. The social worker would need an understanding of John's culture, specifically of the particular African American culture of John, his family, and his peer group. All of these factors would be important in determining need in this situation.

To understand such environmental factors, a social worker needs to have considerable knowledge of the culture of the ethnic and racial groups with which he is working. This involves knowledge of a cultural group's history, values, mores, family and community patterns, attitudes and thinking patterns, religious traditions, child-rearing practices, and ways of coping with change and stress. Also important are the group's experiences in relating to the dominant culture, which involves social and economic factors and acculturation experiences and their results. The worker needs to be cognizant of the different subgroups that exist within any cultural group. This knowledge may be used to identify special needs of individuals and groups of individuals that arise in relation to their development and functioning because of human diversity.

Some workers substitute the term **special populations** for human diversity. There is a risk that such designation can result in stereotyping people according to the population groups to which they belong. In contrast, the concept of human diversity encourages social workers to look at diversity in an individual manner and recognizes that diversity is more than identification with a specific population group.

Social Systems Theory

Human need cannot be considered apart from the larger systems in which humans function. These larger systems include the family; the small group; the community; and various social institutions, such as the school, the church, and the social agency. All people belong to several larger systems, which often make conflicting demands. These systems are a part of each individual's environment. Some social workers call the demands of these systems **environmental demands.** Social systems theory provides a means of understanding these systems and identifying their needs.*

Ann Hartman describes the social systems approach as a "means of ordering the…world in terms of its relatedness.… A system would be a whole composed of interrelated and interdependent parts.… It has boundaries."[11] The system of focus also has a relationship to individuals and systems outside its boundary. The relationships across the boundary are not as intense as those within it and do not have the strength of influence that the parts (subsystems) have on one another. The environment nevertheless does affect the social system. A social systems approach calls for a kind of thinking that considers parts, wholes, and environments and the relationships that exist among them.[12]

Social systems theory is useful to social workers by providing a means for conceptualizing linkages and relationships among seemingly different entities—individuals, families, small groups, agencies, communities, and societies. This theory notes similarities and differences among different classifications of systems and aids social workers in considering private troubles and public issues within both the nurturing system and the sustaining system of the situation being assessed.

For a **social system** to be able to maintain itself and fulfill its function, the subsystems or parts (individuals and groups of individuals) must make adjustments in their own functioning to meet the needs of the larger systems. When

*Special understandings about each of these systems are also needed. It is assumed that this knowledge is available to the reader. Some of the specific knowledge will be considered later in this book.

these adjustments are supportive of the need fulfillment of individuals, no problem exists. However, often this is not the case. The task of the social worker then is to focus on both the personal trouble (individual need) and the public issues (system need). The response identifies the needs of all persons and systems involved and seeks to enable each to function in such a manner that need fulfillment is complementary and the needs of all are fulfilled. This response calls for identification of all the component parts (systems) of a situation in which need exists. It also calls for consideration of the need of each system in relation to the situation under consideration. A social systems analysis of human functioning demonstrates the great complexity of that functioning and thus leads to responses that take this complexity into consideration.

Ecological Perspective

Closely related to systems theory is the **ecological perspective.** The term *ecology* comes from the biological theory that studies the relationship between organisms and environment. The ecological perspective includes the environment in the change process and encompasses the areas of human development, human diversity, and social systems theory. This approach bridges some of the gap between cause and function in the cause-function debate. In the ecological view, the function or societal side is made more relevant to people's everyday lives by including the environment in a comprehensive manner. Carol Meyer and Carel Germaine are generally seen as the major contributors to the development of this perspective.[13]

From an ecological perspective, need is viewed as a condition of the relationship between a person or people and the environment. People as well as the environment are seen as having needs and resources. Needs are met when the environment responds to the person in a way that satisfies her need and the person responds to the environment in a way that satisfies needs in the environment. A mutually beneficial interaction between person and environment is the desired state of affairs. When needs are met, then a state of **congruity** exists. That is, there is agreement or harmony—a "fit"—between the person and the environment.

Unmet need arises out of an imbalance between the responses of the person and the environment to each other. Sometimes needs are not met because there are insufficient resources available to the person and/or to the environment. More often, the interaction between the person and the environment is not balanced in a way that can sustain the needs of either one or both over time. This results in a state of **incongruity**—that is, a lack of agreement or harmony between the person and the environment.

An **ecosystems perspective** is a subset of the ecological perspective and involves all the systems in a person-in-environment approach, including the surrounding physical environment. This approach examines the exchange of matter, energy, and/or information among these systems over time, including past, present, and future. Changes in these exchanges in one part of the ecosystem will influence other parts of the ecosystem.

In planning for change, the ecosystems approach considers the impact of change on all the systems involved. Meeting needs is not simply a matter of meeting the needs of one person at one moment in time. If needs are met at the expense of other people or systems in the environment and if transactions between systems are not balanced in a way that results in mutual benefit, then the client will have difficulty in maintaining over time any benefits from the social work endeavor. If a balance is not found, there is the likelihood that the situation will either return to its previous state or perhaps worsen. Using this perspective to assist clients in meeting needs means facilitating changes in the person, the environment, and the transactions between person and environment in a way that ensures a balance between needs and resources over time.

Strengths Perspective

In the **strengths perspective** the worker moves from looking at deficits to looking at abilities and assets. This approach recognizes the importance of empowerment, resilience, healing, and wholeness in working with people. Membership (or belonging) is seen as essential to well-being. The development of this approach has been led by the social work faculty at the University of Kansas, in particular Dennis Saleeby.[14] Two of the basic tenets of this approach are that (1) "every individual, group, family, and community has strengths"[15]; and (2) "every environment is full of resources."[16]

In responding to need, social workers should assist the client in identifying strengths and resources in herself and in her environment and then use these strengths to create an appropriate response to the need. There are some critical reasons for incorporating the strengths perspective into the process of meeting needs. Policy changes in health care, mental health, and public assistance have resulted in limitations on the length of service and an emphasis on brief, solution-focused intervention. Interventions that focus on deficits and dysfunction and look at the past to understand pathology do not lend themselves well to brief intervention. The strengths perspective is focused on the future and fits much better with shortened time frames. This approach builds on strengths and capacities that the client and the environment already have rather than relying on the acquisition of new skills and resources. Thus, a more solid foundation for changes that do occur is ensured. In addition, the worker can identify and build a support system in the existing environment designed to maintain a new balance in the person-in-environment ecosystem.

In this text, the ecosystems and strengths perspective are combined with the problem-solving process to form an approach in which the social worker facilitates growth and change as a response to need. The focus will be on the concerns and needs of the client in interaction with her environment. In responding to need, the worker develops an understanding of the person in environment and then assists the client in developing and carrying out a plan for meeting her needs. In accomplishing this, the strengths, abilities, assets, and capacities of the person, family, neighborhood, and community are included.

Social Functioning

Social workers become involved when individuals are having difficulty living in relationship with other people, growing so as to maximize their potential, or meeting the demands of the environment or when there is a relatively high potential that any developing needs will not be met. It is then that concern and need become apparent. Harriet Bartlett has described this situation as "people coping" and "environmental demands." The bringing together of these two aspects of living in society can be termed **social functioning.**[17] The core of the social work endeavor is the worker and the client interacting to promote healthy social functioning and to alleviate concern over unmet need. The response is one in which the worker and client *together* assess the need in all its complexity, develop a plan for responding to that need, carry out the plan, and evaluate the results of their work together. Both the worker and the client have a responsibility for the work. Since the roles are reciprocal, both must carry out their roles if the process is going to work.

This is, in essence, the meaning of **generalist practice.** In developing a plan, the focal system for change may be any system experiencing or contributing to a lack of need fulfillment. The change strategy is chosen from a repertoire of strategies that the generalist worker possesses. This repertoire contains strategies appropriate for work with a variety of systems (individuals, families, small groups, agencies, and communities).

The **social work process** usually begins with a **feeling** of concern about something. This concern arises because a need is not being met. After **thinking** about the situation in a particular way—a process called assessment—some **action** is taken. This response—feeling, thinking, acting—is cyclical in nature. As the worker and client think and act together, new feelings of concern arise and new needs become apparent. As they act, they think about what is happening and gain new insights into the situation. The worker's knowledge about human development, human diversity, social systems theory, ecosystems, and the strengths perspective is used in thinking about the situation. (See Figure 1.1.)

Summary

One perspective of social work sees social work practice as a response to concern and need. Concern derives from a feeling that all is not right. Social workers respond to concern by identifying any unmet needs in the situation. In doing this they use knowledge about human development, human diversity, social systems, ecosystems, and strengths. They identify not only the unmet needs and the strengths of a particular client but also the needs and strengths of significant individuals and systems in the situation. When people attempt to meet their needs (to cope) and when the environment makes demands on people in response to environmental needs, a process of social functioning exists. Social functioning is a major focus of social work practice.

The focus of the social work endeavor is on helping individuals to cope and on the environmental factors impinging on social functioning. The decision on what

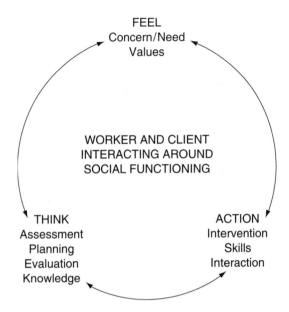

**FIGURE 1.1   The Social Work Process: A
Feeling, Thinking, Acting Endeavor**

the focus of service is to be relates to what is causing the difficulty (the barrier to
need fulfillment) and on what can be changed—the client, the situation, or both.

QUESTIONS

1. What do you consider to be the minimal need level for a person to function in contemporary American society? What would be the ideal need level?

2. Discuss the relationship of the conceptualization of need as encompassing both
private troubles and public issues and the nature of powerlessness in contemporary American society.

3. How can the developmental perspective and the human diversity perspective be
integrated into social work practice? What are the differences between the two
perspectives?

4. Describe the coping behaviors and the environmental demands in a situation related to your present functioning.

SUGGESTED READINGS

Cox, Enid O. "The Critical Role of Social Action in Empowerment Oriented Groups." *Social Work
with Groups* 14 (1991): 77–90.

DiNitto, Diana, and McNeece, C. Aaron. *Social Work: Issues and Opportunities in a Challenging Profession.* Boston, MA: Allyn and Bacon, 1996 (Chapter 15).

Edwards, Richard L., Ed. *Encyclopedia of Social Work,* 19th ed. Washington, DC: NASW Press, 1995 ("Ethnic Sensitive Practice"; "Generalist and Advanced Generalist Practice"; and "Human Development").

Erikson, Erik H., Erikson, Joan M., and Kivnick, Helen Q. *Vital Involvement in Old Age.* New York: W. W. Norton, 1994.

Erikson, Erik H., Erikson, Joan M., and Kivnick, Helen Q. *The Life Cycle Completed.* New York: W. W. Norton, 1998.

Gutierrez, Lorraine M. "Working with Women of Color: An Empowerment Perspective." *Social Work* 35 (March 1990): 149–153.

Minahan, Anne, Ed. *Encyclopedia of Social Work,* 18th ed. Silver Spring, MD: National Association of Social Workers, 1987 ("Generalist Perspective," pp. 660–669; "Human Development: Biological Perspective," "Human Development: Psychological Perspective," "Human Development: Sociocultural Perspective," pp. 835–866).

Norlin, Julia, and Chess, Wayne. *Human Behavior in the Social Environment: Social Systems Theory.* Boston, MA: Allyn and Bacon, 1996 (Chapters 2 and 3).

Norton, Dolores G., Ed. *The Dual Perspective.* New York: Council on Social Work Education, 1978 (Chapter 2).

Saleeby, Dennis, Ed. *The Strengths Perspective in Social Work Practice,* 2nd ed. New York: Longman, 1997 (Preface, Chapter 1).

Serzoff, Joan. "From Separation to Connections: Shifts in Understanding Women's Development." *Affilia: Journal of Women and Social Work* 4 (Spring 1989): 45–58.

Williams, Sharon E., and Wright, Dolores G. "Empowerment: The Strengths of Black Families Revisited." *Journal of Multicultural Social Work* 2 (1992): 21–36.

NOTES

1. Porter R. Lee, "Cause and Function," *Proceedings of the National Conference of Social Work, 1929* (Chicago: University of Chicago Press, 1930) pp. 3–20.

2. C. Wright Mills, *The Sociological Imagination* (New York: Grove Press, 1959), p. 8.

3. William Schwartz, "Private Troubles and Public Issues: One Social Work Job or Two?" in *Social Welfare Forum 1969* (New York: Columbia University Press, 1969), p. 25.

4. Charlotte Towle, *Common Human Needs* (Washington, DC: National Association of Social Workers, 1945), p. 37.

5. Adapted from Abraham H. Maslow, *Motivation and Personality* (New York: Harper and Row, 1954).

6. One of the best discussions of the empowerment perspective is Lorraine M. Gutierrez, "Working with Women of Color: An Empowerment Perspective," *Social Work* 35 (March 1990): 149–153.

7. Anne Minahan, Ed., *Encyclopedia of Social Work,* 18th ed. (Silver Spring, MD: National Association of Social Workers, 1987), "Human Development: Biological Perspective," "Human Development: Psychological Perspective," "Human Development: Sociocultural Perspective," pp. 835–866.

8. Erik H. Erikson, *Childhood and Society* (New York: W. W. Norton, 1950), chap. 7.

9. Ronald C. Federico, "Human Behavior and the Social Environment Within a Human Diversity Framework," in *Educating the Baccalaureate Social Worker: A Curriculum Resource Guide,* vol. 2, Betty L. Baer and Ronald C. Federico, Eds. (Cambridge, MA: Ballinger, 1979).

10. Dolores G. Norton, *The Dual Perspective* (New York: Council on Social Work Education, 1978).

11. Ann Hartman, "To Think About the Unthinkable," *Social Casework* 58 (October 1970): 467–474.

12. Genevive Dehoyos and Claigh Jensen, "The Systems Approach in American Social Work," *Social Casework* 66 (October 1985): 498–497.

13. See Carel B. Germaine, Ed., *Social Work Practice: People and Environments* (New York: Free Press, 1976); Carol H. Meyer, Ed., *Clinical Social Work in the Eco-Systems Perspective* (New York: Columbia University Press, 1983); and Carel B. Germaine, *Human Behavior in the Social Environment: An Ecological View* (New York: Columbia Press, 1991).

14. Dennis Saleeby, Ed., *The Strengths Perspective in Social Work Practice,* 2nd ed. (New York: Longman, 1997).

15. Ibid., p. 12.

16. Ibid., p. 15.

17. Harriet M. Bartlett, *The Common Base of Social Work Practice* (New York: National Association of Social Workers, 1970), chap. 6.

2 Social Work as a Developing Profession

LEARNING EXPECTATIONS

1. Understanding of the nature of professions and of social work as a profession.
2. Some understanding of the following concepts and how they developed: assessment, person in situation, relationship, process, and intervention.
3. Some understanding of how earlier conceptualizations of social work practice affect the nature of contemporary practice.
4. A beginning understanding of current and future issues that impact social work practice.

Social work as a developing profession is a second major theme of social work practice. In order to understand social work as it is conceptualized and practiced today, it is necessary to have some idea of how it developed. Contemporary social work practice is the product of a heritage of responses to need and concern in other times and situations. The response to need has always been influenced by the events of the times and by the current philosophical stance, knowledge base, and social welfare concerns and events.

Although the development of the social work profession, including the development of its theory base, is related to the development of social welfare in the United States, the two are not the same.[1] Any understanding of contemporary generalist social work practice is enhanced by an understanding of the development of the profession, particularly the way in which practice theory developed. This understanding includes some attention to the earlier conceptualizations of practice.

Social work, which began in the life and thought of the late nineteenth and early twentieth centuries, is a fairly new profession, although its roots are firmly planted in the Judeo-Christian heritage. All professions must change to meet constantly changing times. Social work, as a young profession, has experienced growth not only relative to the concerns and climate of changing times but also relative to the process of developing its knowledge, value, and skill bases.

Social Work as a Profession

There is no clear, consistent definition of the term *profession*.[2] Many attempts have been made to develop frameworks for describing the attributes of a **profession.** Although some continue to question whether social work is a profession, by most definitions and criteria social work does seem to meet the requirements of a profession. Ernest Greenwood has stated that "all professions seem to possess (1) systematic theory, (2) authority, (3) community sanction, (4) ethical codes, and (5) a culture."[3] These are the attributes most often referred to in social work literature when discussing social work as a profession.

Leslie Leighninger has referred to Greenwood's approach as a "trait-attribute" approach. She points out that a "process model" focuses on movement toward professional status, particularly the development of professional organizations and professional education.[4] Another approach might be a power/control approach, which looks at the status of a profession. Authority and monopoly of service delivery are considered as indicators of professional status.[5] Elizabeth Howe has pointed out that some professions, such as medicine and law, operate from a "private practice model." She suggests that other professions, such as social work, in which the vast majority of practitioners are employed in agencies, probably should operate from what she identifies as a "public model." The difference between the two models relates to issues of autonomy. Public professions are subject to a greater degree of control by the public. Not only do professionals in the public professions have less autonomy but they are also responsible to clients, the agency, and those to whom the agency is responsible.[6]

When considering social work as a profession, it seems most appropriate to begin by considering Greenwood's attributes. First among these is the possession of a systematic theory. Social work has struggled long and hard to develop this attribute. Because of the complexity of the human situation and other factors, which will be discussed later in this chapter and in Chapter 3, this development is incomplete. It is at this point that thinking about the process of knowledge development by the social work profession (process model) becomes useful. This approach allows for considering social work as a developing profession and leads to consideration of the influence of the past on the present.

When thinking about the attributes of authority and community sanction, the power/control model becomes useful. The social work profession has not established a monopoly over the delivery of services relative to social functioning. It is only one of many professions (such as education, nursing, and substance abuse treatment) concerned with social functioning. In addition, it has been possible, especially in public social welfare agencies, for employees who carry out certain functions to carry the title of social worker even though they have not had professional social work education. Licensing laws have been most helpful in identifying who is a social worker. That identification is strongly tied to educational qualifications (BSW or MSW degrees). Through licensing and other types of regulations, there now is some authority, community sanction, and recognition of an area of expertise and its services. An ethical code and a culture are provided through the National Association of Social Workers (NASW). The NASW *Code of Ethics,* which was revised in 1996 (see Figure 3.1), is discussed in Chapter 3 as a part of the values system a social worker must consider when making practice decisions.

One important area in understanding the nature of social work practice is an appreciation for how its knowledge base has developed over time. Understanding how the profession's knowledge base has developed also helps to explain how contemporary practice, particularly generalist practice, is in part a continuous development of the practice of the past.

Development of Social Work Knowledge

As social work developed, several concepts became important in expressing the nature of its practice. Five of these concepts are useful in developing an understanding of how the knowledge base developed, not in isolation but in the social climate of the day and in the contemporary social welfare scene. These five concepts are assessment, person in situation, relationship, process, and intervention.

It is not possible to present here all the details either of social history and its effects on the development of social welfare institutions or of the history of the profession itself.[7] (See Appendix 2.1 at the end of this chapter for an overview of this historical material.) The focus here is on the development of the five concepts of social work practice theory during each particular historical era. These five concepts are important for the explication of generalist practice and will be further developed in subsequent chapters of this book.

Pre-1920

The early practice of social work can generally be characterized as pretheoretical. Workers saw needs and responded. They were caught up in the pragmatic philosophy of the times. They had preconceived views of the causality of pauperism and poverty from individual defects such as laziness, mismanagement, or alcoholism. Workers felt that by using a "friendly visitor" approach they could help people overcome the causes of their difficulties.

The first major statement of social work practice theory was Mary Richmond's *Social Diagnosis*[8] in which she developed the original framework for the assessment construct. However, rather than the term *assessment,* she used the term **diagnosis,** borrowing from medical terminology for what was to become known as the **medical model.**

Richmond's work reflects a period when social sciences, particularly sociology, were highly influential on social work practice. Psychology had not yet developed to the point at which personality could be explained in any but global, imprecise terms. Emphasis was on a broad study, as there was still a great deal of uncertainty about which factors were most important for diagnosis. It was assumed that a cause-effect relationship existed; in other words, the social worker was looking for the cause of the problem. The cause was generally assumed to be either moral inadequacy or lack of appropriate use of social resources. The process of careful, thorough, systematic investigation of the evidence surrounding those in need of service and then the putting together of that evidence so that the worker gained an accurate picture of the situation were the heart of the social work process. This was **scientific philanthropy,** the study of the social situation.

The description of the information to be gathered was comprehensive and meticulously specific. The sources to be used included not only the client but also the family, other relatives, schools, medical sources, employers, neighbors, and pertinent documents. The guiding principles were sociological in nature. Richmond defined diagnosis as

> the attempt to make as exact a definition as possible of the situation and the personality—that is, in relation to other human beings upon whom he [the client] in any way depends or who depends on him, and in relation also to the social institutions of his community.[9]

There seems to have been an assumption that the painstaking gathering of information would lead to an understanding of the cause of the problem. Further, it was assumed that if the cause were known, the remedy would be simple to apply. This idea, which grew out of the Charity Organization Society, assumed that the problem lay primarily within the individual. For example, poverty was considered a result of immorality, misuse of money, and excessive drinking.

Settlement houses, the originators of the group work method, responded to the same social conditions differently. This approach saw the source of problems as lying in the environment and in a lack of understanding about how to cope with one's surroundings. Workers at settlement houses used educational and enriching group activities and worked within the political system to bring about needed change.

Because the Charity Organization Society saw the cause of poverty as lying with the person, it represents the conservative perspective. Settlement houses recognized that people who were poor were often caught in situations that were not of their own doing. Economic and political conditions, including discrimination, oppression, and exploitation, left many people powerless to change their circumstances. Settlement workers sought to empower people through collective action to bring about change in the system. The radical version of this view was that a complete change in the system, particularly with regard to capitalism, was needed. The liberal view held that radical change was unlikely but that amelioration of some social problems was possible by making the system more humane and responsive to people's needs.

The beginning of professional social work was a response to the social milieu of the early twentieth century, a time when new immigrants, with their different cultures and lifestyles, were of concern to the larger society. It was also a time when progressives were working for reforms they believed would eliminate poverty. This era saw the development of the social sciences, which were rooted in the belief that application of a scientific method could identify the causes of poverty and deviance. It was felt that if these causes could be identified, solutions would be apparent and social ills eliminated.

The early articulation of theory about the *practice* of social work (as opposed to theory regarding understanding of person in situation) reflected efforts to work with the new immigrants in ways that would enable them to live "moral lives" and thus avoid pauperism. This theory was strongly based on the new sociological understandings and called for meticulously searching for facts that would illuminate the causes of deviance. This reflected the conservative perspective of the Charity Organization Society, which also sought to make helping more scientific. Science was seen as based on facts; facts led to answers. Thus, the answers as to how to help lay in the collection of facts. A strong emphasis on diagnosis (assessment) developed and remains an important legacy in contemporary social work practice.

1921–1930

By 1930, changes had taken place in the understanding of diagnosis. Much has been written about the adoption of the Freudian psychoanalytic view of man by social workers during this period.[10] Though it has been shown that this adoption was not as complete or dramatic as often depicted,[11] the Freudian influence was nevertheless considerable and long lasting. The psychological aspects of social behavior became an influential aspect of the *social case history.*

The report of the Milford Conference (a group representing casework agencies that met to seek commonalities in different settings, for example, hospitals or schools) reflected the development of social casework theory during the 1920s. This theory identified the common elements of social study from the various fields of practice. It also noted that whereas special knowledge specific to a field of practice existed, such as understanding medical terminology in medical social work, the social history component of each field demonstrated an essential unity.

This report also began to develop the concept of intervention, though it used the medical concept of **treatment.** At this time in history, treatment was aimed at assisting the client to "adjust" and assumed deviance from normal social standards. Three fundamental processes were (1) use of resources, (2) assistance of the client in self-understanding, and (3) assistance for the client to develop the ability "to work out [his or her] own social program."[12]

Rather than focusing on the social situation, the worker was far more concerned about "value and meaning as individual experience."[13] The focus of attention was on the individual and included a detailed study of behavior, attitudes, and relationships. Particular emphasis was placed on early childhood experience. The emphasis on the source of information also shifted. No longer was a wide variety of information sources used; rather, it was felt that the individual must be primarily depended on for information if the meaning of experiences to him was to be obtained. Through careful interviewing of the client, a full picture necessary for understanding could be obtained. Assessment or diagnosis was better organized than in the past, when cause and effect were emphasized.

The concept of treatment (intervention) changed from "impulsive action on the client's behalf" to "respecting the client's individuality which leads to identification with the client's experience." Little knowledge about treatment existed at this time.

Considerable emphasis was placed on the relationship between client and worker. Meaningful interaction between worker and client was seen as a sharing experience vital for developing the worker's understanding of the client and for treatment to take place.[14] This understanding marked a movement away from attitudes of "doing for" or "doing to." This theoretical development of the 1920s reflected both the individualism of the times and a decreased emphasis on social problems. Psychology, particularly psychoanalysis, which offered a theory useful in explaining individual functioning in a manner not possible until this time, was becoming a viable tool. As society turned inward, so did social work. It sought a theory base; it sought to clarify itself as a profession by looking for the common knowledge base used in diverse settings; and it sought a function broader than working with poverty groups, no longer a popular cause. As the knowledge base began to develop, so did the need for means to convey that knowledge. Thus, attention was given to education and theory development.

During this era, group work placed more emphasis on people than it did on conditions. The growing informal education movement and the work of John Dewey were particularly influential. Youth service organizations and recreation developed, thus placing considerable emphasis on the use of activity and on group process as a means to enhance growth, democratic functioning, and change. The heritage of this era for today's practice might be characterized as the movement from doing *to* or *for* to working *with* the client.

1931–1945

During this period, Gordon Hamilton, an important theorist of the diagnostic approach to practice, clarified the term *diagnosis*. In 1940, Hamilton described diagnosis as a "working hypothesis for understanding the person with the problem as well as the problem itself."[15] This concept of diagnosis included the client's subjective version of the situation. The diagnostic statement was seen as interpretative and always tentative.

This view of diagnosis led to the development of the concept "person in situation"—an interpretation of the way a person meets the situation (as has been noted). Hamilton saw this interpretation as being evaluative rather than diagnostic. Evaluation considered the resources available to the client and recognized that problems are both individual and social.

The helping process was conceptualized as "study, diagnosis, and treatment." These three aspects of the helping process were not performed in logical, step-by-step sequence but wove in and out, often paralleling one another.[16]

The treatment relationship was seen as important in helping. Its nature and intensity depended on both the client's need and the service being provided.

Hamilton defined *treatment* as "furnishing a service" or "behaving toward some-one."[17] It might involve meeting deficiencies with social resources, program mod-ification, or resource adjustment as well as counseling or therapy.

Hamilton's statement of social casework theory in *The Theory and Practice of Social Casework* (both the 1940 and the 1951 editions) remained for many years an important statement of one approach to social work practice and is known as the **diagnostic approach.** Hamilton's classic formulation greatly influenced subse-quent practice and underlies much of the subsequent practice theory develop-ment. It was based on psychoanalytic thinking and thus was a factor in the continued use of that frame of reference in thinking about the personality.

Another approach to practice was developing during this era. The **func-tional approach** considered the client not as sick or deviant but rather as a person requesting a specific service. It was largely based on the work of Otto Rank. Jessie Taft and Herbert Aptekar are sources for early statements of this approach.[18]

The term *diagnosis* had a different meaning in the functional approach from its use in the diagnostic approach. It was seen as an attempt by the worker and the client to discover whether there was a common ground for working together. It led not to treatment but to working together, and this relationship was seen as professional when the worker was carrying out an agency function and was ap-plying her professional knowledge to the work at hand. It recognized a process in the relationship that was expressed as beginning, middle, and ending. As the rela-tionship developed and individuals came to affect one another, the opportunity for change developed.

A third important theory development of the 1931–1945 era was the recogni-tion of social group work and community organization work as methods of social work. Hamilton has noted the importance of group process as a means of under-standing the family. The actual theoretical development of these new methods was, however, only in the preliminary stage.

The rich development of theory during the late 1930s and early 1940s was at least partly a result of the tremendous impact of the Depression era on social work. Older theories about personal deficiencies as the cause of poverty and devi-ance no longer held up. Rather, the influence of a person's situation was seen in terms of how it affected his well-being. Psychological knowledge, particularly that based on Freud's work, provided understandings of deviance that looked at cause for deviance in the intrapsychic part of the personality and provided a usable, or-ganized theory for assessing the personality.

The interest in the psychological sphere was also furthered, as government agencies took over much of the work of relief and social provision during the Great Depression. Private agencies had freedom to focus on psychological factors as well as on new groups of clients. Although the early 1930s found social workers far too busy with the realities of people in need to engage in much theory develop-ment, they later had time to reflect on those experiences, which resulted in rich theory development. One important outgrowth still present in contemporary practice is the notion that the individual must be seen in a situation (a context or an environment) and that assessment must include this dimension.

1946–1960

During the early part of this era, the diagnostic-functional controversy continued. Social workers used either Freud's psychoanalytic approach and were adherents of the diagnostic school of practice or the Rankian approach that underlay the functional school. Most theory development was in the form of statements of one position or the other, and these statements clarified the details of the two positions. In 1951, a revised edition of Hamilton's 1940 book was published.[19] This revision reflected new understandings developed in psychoanalysis and clarified differences between psychoanalysis and social work. Considerably more attention was given to the content of the diagnostic statement. The material on treatment was explicated, and attention was paid to intrapsychic factors.

In his 1957 book, *The Casework Relationship*,[20] Felix Biestek defines the casework relationship as "the dynamic interaction of attitudes and emotions between the caseworker and the client, with the purpose of helping the client achieve a better adjustment between himself and his environment." He also identifies seven principles of that relationship:

1. Individualization
2. Purposeful expression of feeling
3. Controlled emotional environment
4. Acceptance
5. Nonjudgmental attitude
6. Client self-determination
7. Confidentiality[21]

Biestek's work is an example of the development or fleshing out of the social work theory that was taking place during this period.

Near the end of this era, a new statement of casework was presented by Helen Harris Perlman in *Social Casework: A Problem-Solving Process*.[22] In many ways this new statement was a blending of the diagnostic and functional approaches, and essentially it marked the end of the diagnostic-functional controversy. Perlman saw the casework endeavor as "a person with a problem comes to a place where a professional representative helps him by a given process."[23]

Perlman continued using the term *diagnosis,* but her meaning seems closer to that of the term *assessment,* as used in contemporary social work literature. She saw diagnosis as dynamic, as "a cross-sectional view of the forces interacting in the client's problem situation."[24] Diagnosis was seen as an ongoing process that gives "boundary, relevance, and direction"[25] to the work. It was considered to be the thinking in problem solving.

Perlman's book reflected a focus on the ego functions of the personality. This is in contrast to the diagnostic approach of the earlier era in which the id, ego, and superego were each considered equally important. Adaptation was viewed as one of the important ego functions. In Perlman's work one begins to see the concept of "coping" used relative to adaptation, which would seem to be an aspect of the view of person in situation. Perlman saw casework as a process—a problem-solving process—and she developed the process or movement idea throughout her book. She held that the caseworker-client relationship was essential to the movement or work of problem solving. The professional relationship was perceived as being purposeful, accepting, supportive, and nurturing. Underlying Perlman's work is the assumption of human competence, with a goal of developing this competence. Problems are seen not as pathological but as part of all life. The social-functioning focus of social work began to emerge.

Another trend of this era deserving of mention is the emergence of literature that began to identify and specify the theory base underlying practice. This emerging theory base included not only the casework method but also group work and community organization methods. These two methods drew heavily from a sociological theory base. Knowledge of small-group process was a major interest, and the assessment of group interaction was a major concern. The focus of these two methods was in part on growth as a process. Relationship with non-clients began to be considered. The groundwork was being laid to identify the common base of social work practice—those concepts that applied to practice regardless of the system being worked with.

Social work, like the society of which it was a part, was expanded during the 1946–1960 period. This was not a time of great unrest or change but rather a period of conformity and of acceptance of sometimes superficial answers. There was a belief that poverty was being eliminated and thus was not an issue of concern. Much social work energy went into the development of the professional organization and professional education. The majority of clients focused on were not poor but middle-class people who had adjustment problems. This orientation reflected societal demands for conformity and the illusion of an affluent society. It was also a time in social work when the search for a unified profession reflected the spirit of the times. Theory was developed by stating a position (diagnostic or functional) and then defending that position. This expanded the existing theory and led to new theory development in the search for a unifying approach. Two legacies of this era are a major concern for the relationship of worker and client and the notion that there is a process aspect of practice.

1961–1975

This era was indeed rich in theory development, just as it was rich in the development of new service possibilities, concern for new problem areas and new client groups, and the use of old methods in new ways. A review of theory development in this era focuses on three areas: (1) the continuing development of traditional methods, (2) the development of generic or integrated approaches to practice, and (3) the development of new approaches to practice using new underlying assumptions for use in service to specific groups of clients.

During the 1960s, both the diagnostic approach (now called the **psychosocial approach**) and the functional approach were further expanded and updated.[26] Both of these formulations were approaching the stage of well-developed theory. These new formulations took the five concepts (assessment, person in situation, process, relationship, and intervention) and incorporated new theory development from the social sciences. Use of social systems theory and communications theory began to appear.[27]

During the early part of this period, important formulations of group work and community organization work became available. These formulations not only continued to develop the practice theory of these methods but also made it possible to identify the concepts that were universal to casework, group work, and community organization. Thus, the theoretical commonalities of all types of social work practice could be distilled.

Of particular interest is the movement from the use of the medical terms *diagnosis* and *treatment* to the more general terms *assessment* and *intervention*. As community organization theory developed, the use of the terms *assessment* and *intervention* was given additional support as commonalities were found.

Examination of the concept of problem-solving process during the early part of the era indicates that it was being used in all three traditional methods of social work: casework, group work, and community organization. The casework use of the problem-solving process is reflected in the continued importance of Perlman's approach during this era. Process came to imply movement through time.

The concepts of person in situation and client-worker relationship were again expanded somewhat later in the era by the application of new social science theory. The 1970s saw a rapid rise in the use of social systems theory as important supportive knowledge for all social work.

The concept of relationship also enlarged. Not only was relationship seen as important for work with the client, but also the importance of many other relationships was noted in group work and community organization literature. During this era there began to be discussion of **interactional skill,** an idea that was very close to the idea of relationship and that enlarged the scope of the meaning of relationship.

In 1970, two early attempts to conceptualize social work from an integrative point of view were published. Carol Meyer's *Social Work Practice: A Response to the Urban Crisis* stressed the need for a new conceptual framework because of limitations of current theory in relating to urban turmoil in the 1960s.[28] Harriett Bartlett's *The Common Base of Social Work Practice* was written out of the need of the social work profession for specification about the nature of practice.[29] Both books reflected the development of the five concepts being discussed. Although the books focused on the problems of integration rather than on the development of theory, they did introduce several useful concepts. Bartlett identified *social functioning, professional judgment in assessment,* and *interventive action.* Meyer noted *process of individualization, interventive points,* and *plan of action.* She saw the diagnostic process as a tool of assessment and intervention as having a variety of possibilities known as the **interventive repertoire.** These two books marked a turning point in theory development. No longer was theory to be developed for the traditional methods of casework, group work, and community organization. It was to be developed for the unified social work profession and to respond to particular problems and needs.

During the early 1970s, several textbooks appeared that presented conceptualizations that were integrative in approach.[30] A text by Allen Pincus and Anne Minahan received the widest acceptance. In their approach, social work was seen as a planned change, with the intervention plan being based on problem assessment. The assessment "identified problems, analyzed dynamics of the social situation, established goals and targets, determined tasks and strategies, and stabilized the change effort."[31] One major aspect of the approach was the use of influence—"effecting the condition of development of a person or system."[32] The use of relationship was seen as part of this process. In the Pincus and Minahan approach, the five concepts are used, but they are put together in new ways and new concepts are added. The developing profession was moving toward new ways of thinking about practice, toward new practice conceptualizations.

Given the growing commonality of social work practice, it is not surprising that an important contribution of this era was the effort to develop what came to be known as *integrated methods* or *generalist practice*. New services were evolving and new groups of clients were being served. It was discovered that these clients did not fit nicely into traditional casework, group work, or community organization categories. Instead, a combination of methods was needed to respond to the complex problems and situations these clients presented. The efforts of the National Association of Social Workers and others toward the unification of the profession provided a milieu in which efforts toward identifying the commonality of theory could go forward. The federal legislation of the Great Society and the War on Poverty provided training funds that increased the capacity for knowledge building. The rediscovery of rural social work called for a generalist approach. The time was right, both in a societal and a professional sense, for this forward movement in the development of the theory base of social work.

A third trend of this era was the development of many new approaches to practice, most of which focused on specific needs. This trend began in the 1960s as the family became a unit of attention and as approaches for work with the family developed. At about the same time, interest in short-term casework, particularly crisis intervention, also contributed to this trend. As social workers began to work with new problems and new client groups, approaches with a more specific focus were needed for action with and for clients after a generalist approach had been used in the early stages of service. Concurrently, examination of current group work and community organization practice yielded the understanding that more than one approach had developed in each of these traditional methods.[33] The 1969 Charlotte Towle Memorial Symposium was a presentation of major theoretical approaches to casework practice.[34]

In the late 1960s and early 1970s, there was not as much agreement about practice approaches as there once had been. For example, social workers no longer agreed that the conceptual framework of the person in situation underlay professional practice. Some of the important new practice approaches that evolved were crisis intervention, task-centered casework, and social-behavioral social work. (See Appendix 2.1 for a summary of these and other contemporary approaches of social work practice.)

A social work practice was emerging in which a general theory base was used for the original response to need and for the assessment of client in situation. Then, using a relationship developed in the process, an intervention based on one of the more specific approaches was chosen from the intervention repertoire. This practice reflects the needs and concerns of the times—broadened client groups and new problems. The essence of generalist practice began to appear.

1976–1990

This era saw a societal disenchantment with the social welfare system. This was a period of inflation, unemployment, and concern with defense. Within the social work profession, issues that received considerable attention were the differential roles of the BSW and the MSW worker, the development of specialization at the MSW level, and the conceptualization of generalist practice. Considerable attention was paid to identifying the foundation or core that underlies all social work practice. It was a time of concern about the social problems of homelessness, AIDS, substance abuse, and peace and justice.

Assessment was seen as the process that develops the understanding of person in situation and as the basis for the action to be taken. Assessment was ongoing and made use of knowledge developed from a number of different sources. Of particular importance was assessment of the effect of cultural and ethnic factors on the behavior of individuals and on the capacity of the individual and family to use help. Also, attention was paid to the effect of gender on individual development and behavior.

The **person in situation** (now referred to as **person in environment**) construct received considerable attention with the development of the ecological approach to practice.[35] Personal support networks were identified, developed, supported, and used as a part of the helping process. Persons and social systems were both seen as significant in problem solving. The social systems approach was almost universally accepted. This period also saw the beginning of the feminist perspective, which emphasizes acknowledging the client system's social and political stressors, empowering the client, and working to change her environmental systems.

Relationship, both its professional and helping qualities, continued to be seen as the cohesive quality of the action system. Relationships seen as important were not only those with clients but also relationships with significant social systems and with influential persons in those systems.

Process continued to be seen as a recurrent patterning of a sequence of change over time—that is, various stages of the work were specified in the order in which they were the primary focus of practice. Process was conceptualized in different ways by different theorists. Intervention was also conceptualized differentially, but there was a growing tendency not to accept any one intervention or approach to practice as appropriate for all situations.

In 1986, James K. Whittaker, Steven P. Schinke, and Lewayne D. Gilchrist suggested that social workers had moved to a new paradigm, or way of thinking, about practice. They further stated that this new way of thinking, the ecological paradigm, is based on "improving social supports through various forms of environmental helping and on improving personal competencies through the teaching of 'life skills.'"[36] This way of thinking is congruent with generalist practice, as discussed in Chapter 1. In this framework, generalist practice likely would also suggest focusing intervention on environmental change. Subsequent trends seem to confirm this idea.

1991–2000

During the 1990s, practice theory was influenced by several policy changes. The first was the limitation or reduction of funding for various social welfare programs. In the public sector, the decade saw the end of the original public assistance program enacted under the Social Security Act (Aid to Dependent Children, or ADC, later modified and called Aid to Families with Dependent Children, or AFDC). The welfare reform that was enacted by the conservative Congress during the 1990s changed the fundamental principle of public assistance from an *entitlement* program under which people were guaranteed assistance based on need. The new law, titled the Personal Responsibility and Work Opportunity Reconciliation Act, includes a program called Temporary Assistance to Needy Families (TANF), which limits eligibility to five years or less, allows states to set their own income limits, and imposes work rules along with encouraging greater regulation of the behavior of the poor, including childbearing decisions. These changes clearly represent the conservative perspective of holding individuals responsible for dealing with the conditions of poverty. Another change was made in the way public welfare is funded. Under AFDC, states received a federal match ranging from 50 to 80 percent of expenditures. When need increased due to recession, population growth, and the like, a portion of the cost was offset by a guaranteed increase in federal aid. Under TANF, states receive block grants that are frozen at a certain level, with no guarantee of increased aid if need increases. TANF also allows states to contract out their programs to private corporations, including those who operate for profit.[37] During the decade, the United States experienced an extended period of prosperity, with low inflation and low unemployment. It remains to be seen what will happen to children and families when the economy contracts and the lifetime limits on eligibility for assistance begin to run out.

In the private sector, managed care has dominated the agenda in health care, mental health, and substance abuse treatment. While the professed goals of managed care are to control costs and ensure quality service, it seems apparent that controlling costs is the primary concern. Managed care basically means that all potential recipients of service must be screened prior to service and referred by the managed care organization for that service. The service then must be monitored by the screening organization for effectiveness of service provision. Managed care organizations have increased the demand for concrete evidence that the services provided have been effective. Many managed care organizations operate on a capitation basis, in that they will allocate a certain amount of funds for a specific service no matter how long it may take to provide it. Other managed care organizations may operate on a fee-for-service reimbursement basis, whereby they pay for each session of service but limit the number of sessions for the client.[38]

Either managed care approach poses some inherent problems for social workers who serve clients with long-term issues or disabilities. These populations are most likely to need service over an extended period of time and yet are more likely to be at risk of not receiving adequate services under managed care. Further, several states are now in the process of turning many, if not most, of their social welfare programs over to managed care corporations. It remains to be seen how this will affect social work's clients in the long run, but it is an issue that all social workers need to keep in mind as they work with their clients and in their communities.

As a result of these policy changes, social workers have been called upon to do more with less. Practice has increasingly come to depend on brief interventions that are solution focused. There is more emphasis on connecting clients with other resources in the community. This includes greater use of social support networks and self-help groups for ongoing support.

Partly because of the limitations in service that result from a managed care system, there is an emerging trend to provide what is termed **solution-based interventions** with an emphasis on actions that historically have been successful. "The basic premise...is that exceptions to problems offer keys and clues to solving problems and that it is more profitable to pay attention to the activities that center around successful solutions."[39] In this focus, a solution to the challenges faced by clients is defined very quickly, and all efforts are designed to attain this goal.

The ecological perspective (see Chapter 1) has gained widespread acceptance, particularly at the BSW level, given its emphasis on both person and environment as well as the interactions between them. "Ecological thinking" is not linear. It examines exchanges that shape and influence or change both the person and the environment over time. With its focus on the interaction between person and environment, this approach has the potential to become the overarching theory that can bridge the gap between individual and environmental change.[40]

The strengths perspective (see Chapter 1) has contributed to practice theory by reducing the emphasis on deficits and pathology and focusing on strengths that can be used to facilitate growth and change.[41] The ecological and strength perspectives combine with the problem-solving approach to form a powerful tool in serving the needs of clients. In this text, this approach will be called the **ecosystems strengths approach.** It is a fundamental aspect of the generalist approach that is developed in Part Three. It provides a comprehensive assessment of person in environment and allows the worker to use a variety of interventions in facilitating growth and change. Keeping the emphasis on the strengths of the clients and the strengths to be found in their environment conveys a consistent message that change is possible and that clients can empower themselves.

A paradigm that is suggested by some social workers as applicable to many populations is the **feminist perspective.**[42] This paradigm is based on five principles: (1) the elimination of false dichotomies and artificial separations, (2) the reconceptualization of power, (3) the valuing of process equally with product, (4) the validity of renaming, and (5) the personal is political. In other words, this approach calls for a holistic view, a wide distribution of power, attention to how goals are implemented, the renaming of action so as to purge discriminatory language, and the recognition that personal problems are often the result of political injustice and require that the focus of intervention be on change in large systems. This paradigm seems useful in any situation in which discrimination is of major concern, for example, in work with women or minority groups.

Feminist social workers stress the need for teaching clients how to empower themselves as well as how to work with systems that impact them. They also emphasize the importance of working with clients as equals in order to avoid replicating the "one-up" position common in other environmental interactions. Feminist workers also attempt to link clients with others who face similar issues in order to build systems that can be used for networking, support, and education.

A major concern of social workers is working with people who experience social injustice or who are considered to be at risk. The feminist perspective and method seem particularly relevant in addressing these populations in that it acknowledges that many of the difficulties faced by these populations are a result of their interactions with the environment or with the surrounding systems rather than within the clients themselves.

There is also increasing interest in international social work practice as the profession recognizes the interdependence of nations and the reciprocal learning that can occur through dialogue with other countries. Although social work practice issues in developing countries may be different than those in, for example, the United States or Canada, the challenges these developing countries face in providing service to disadvantaged populations and populations at risk and the ways in which these needs are addressed can provide guidelines for social workers faced with diminishing resources and increased needs. Further, sharing what works and what does not work across nations increases the likelihood that solutions can be found to common problems that affect all clients, whatever their nationality. Focusing on international social work also provides education about various cultures and ethnic groups, which can enrich the knowledge base and be helpful for working with first- and second-generation client systems from other countries.[43]

Generalist practice, then, reflects the evolutionary response over the past century to societal concerns and needs and to events and thinking. Generalist practice reflects the theoretical heritage of the profession: assessment, person in situation, relationship, process, and intervention. Social work is an ever-changing and ever-developing professional endeavor. However, its strong emphasis on assessment, a concern for intervention through working *with* rather than doing *to* or *for* a client, its emphasis on person in situation, the importance of relationship, and the concern for the process of practice all remain at the heart of social work practice today and into the twenty-first century.

Summary

This chapter discusses the nature of a profession and the development of its theory. Social work does meet the criteria of a profession, although it is sometimes not recognized as such because of some of its characteristics. The development of a knowledge base is one criterion of a profession. Five concepts (assessment, relationship, person in situation, process, and intervention) are used to trace the development of social work's knowledge base. This knowledge base developed in response to historical and cultural conditions. An understanding of the historical basis of social work practice provides one way of understanding contemporary practice.

Q U E S T I O N S

1. Why is social work not given the respect other professions receive?

2. How has the social welfare system been affected by societal trends and events? How has this affected social work practice?

3. How has a changing clientele changed the manner in which social work is practiced?

4. What problems do you see for the social work profession because of the lack of agreement about practice theory? What are the advantages?

5. How has the development of social work practice enhanced contemporary practice? How has this development inhibited response to the contemporary situation?

6. How does the feminist perspective enable social workers to work with people of color, populations at risk, and persons with disabilities?

S U G G E S T E D   R E A D I N G S

Brieland, Donald. "The Hull House Tradition and the Contemporary Social Worker: Was Jane Addams Really a Social Worker?" *Social Work* 35 (March 1990): 134–138.

Chesler, Phyllis, Rothblum, Esther D., and Cole, Ellen. *Feminist Foremothers in Women's Studies, Psychology, and Mental Health.* New York: Haworth Press, 1995.

Doel, Mark, and Shardlow, Steven. *Social Work in a Changing World: An International Perspective on Practice Learning.* Brookfield, VT: Ashgate, 1996.

Dorfman, Rachelle A., Ed. *Paradigms in Clinical Social Work.* New York: Brunner/Mazel, 1988.

Edwards, Richard L., Ed. *Encyclopedia of Social Work,* 19th ed. Washington, DC: NASW Press, 1995 ("Ecological Perspective"; "Ethnic Sensitive Practice"; "Managed Care"; "Person-in-Environment"; "Social Welfare History"; "Social Work Practice: History and Evolution"; "Social Work Practice: Theoretical Base"; "Social Work Profession Overview"; "Social Work Profession: History").

Edwards, Richard L., Ed. *Supplement to the Encyclopedia of Social Work.* Silver Springs, MD: NASW Press, 1997 ("Federal Social Legislation from 1994–1997"; "Managed Care: Implications for Social Work Practice"; "Temporary Assistance to Needy Families").

Garvin, Charles D., and Cox, Fred M. "A History of Community Organizing Since the Civil War with Special Reference to Oppressed Communities." In Fred M. Cox, John L. Erlich, Jack Rothman, and John E. Tropman, Eds., *Strategies of Community Organization,* 4th ed. Itasca, IL: F. E. Peacock, 1987, pp. 26–63.

Germaine, Carel B., and Gitterman, Alex. *The Life Model of Social Work Practice: Advances in Theory and Practice,* 2nd ed. New York: Columbia University Press, 1996.

Greene, Roberta R., and Watkins, Marie, Eds. *Serving Diverse Constituencies: Applying the Ecological Perspective.* New York: Aldine De Gruyter, 1998.

Hokenstad, Merl C., Khinduka, S. K., and Midgley, James. *Profiles in International Social Work.* Washington, DC: NASW Press, 1992.

Jimenez, Mary Ann. "Historical Evolution and Future Challenges of the Professions." *Families in Society: The Journal of Contemporary Human Services* 71 (January 1990): 3–12.

Johnson, Louise C., Schwartz, Charles L., and Tate, Donald S. *Social Welfare: A Response to Human Need,* 4th ed. Boston: Allyn and Bacon, 1997.

Kondrat, Mary Ellen. "Concept, Act, and Interest in Professional Practice: Implications of an Empowerment Perspective." *Social Service Review* 69 (September 1995): 405–428.

Morales, Armando T., and Sheafor, Bradford. *Social Work: A Profession of Many Faces,* 8th ed. Boston: Allyn and Bacon, 1998.

Pardeck, John T. *Social Work Practice: An Ecological Approach.* Westport, CT: Auburn House, 1996.

Payne, Malcolm. *Modern Social Work Theory.* Chicago, IL: Lyceum Books, 1991.

Perlman, Helen Harris. *Looking Back to See Ahead.* Chicago: University of Chicago Press, 1989, pp. 211–228.

Rank, Mark R., and Hirshl, Thomas A. "The Likelihood of Poverty across the American Adult Life Span." *Social Work,* 44 (May 1999).

Reamer, Frederic, Ed. *The Foundations of Social Work Knowledge.* New York: Columbia University Press, 1994.

Reisch, Michael, and Gambrill, Eileen, Eds. *Social Work in the 21st Century.* Thousand Oaks, CA: Pine Forge Press, 1997.

Saleeby, Dennis, Ed. *The Strengths Perspective in Social Work Practice,* 2nd ed. New York: Longman, 1997.

Sands, Roberta G., and Nuccio, Kathleen. "Post-Modern Feminist Theory and Social Work." *Social Work* 37 (November 1992): 489–494.

Simon, Barbara Levy. *The Empowerment Tradition in American Social Work: A History.* New York: Columbia University Press, 1994.

Specht, Harry. "Social Work and the Popular Psychotherapies." *Social Service Review* 64 (September 1990): 345–357.

Van Den Bergh, Nan, Ed. *Feminist Practice in the 21st Century.* Silver Spring, MD: National Association of Social Workers, 1995.

Witkin, Stanley, L., Ed. "Special Centennial Issue." *Social Work* 43 (November 1998).

Witkin, Stanley, L., Ed. "Special Centennial Issue 2." *Social Work* 44 (July 1999).

N O T E S

1. For one view of the development of the social welfare system, see Louise C. Johnson, Charles L. Schwartz, and Donald S. Tate, *Social Welfare: A Response to Human Need,* 4th ed. (Boston: Allyn and Bacon, 1997).

2. June Gary Hopps and Pauline M. Collins, "Social Work Profession Overview," in *Encyclopedia of Social Work,* 19th ed., Richard L. Edwards, Ed. (Silver Springs, MD: NASW Press, 1995), p. 2266.

3. Ernest Greenwood, "Attributes of a Profession," *Social Work* 2 (July 1957): 45–55.

4. Leslie Leighninger, *Social Work Search for Identity* (New York: Greenwood Press, 1987).

5. Gary R. Lowe, Laura Rose Zimmerman, and P. Nelson Reid, "How We See Ourselves: A Critical Review of Text Versions of Social Work's Professional Evolution" (unpublished paper).

6. Elizabeth Howe, "Public Professions and the Private Model of Professionalism," *Social Work* 25 (May 1980): 179–191.

7. For an in-depth study of this material, see June Axinn, *Social Welfare: A History of the American Response to Need,* 4th ed. (White Plains, NY: Longman, 1997); Walter I. Trattner, *From Poor Law to Welfare State: A History of Social Welfare in America,* 6th ed. (New York: Free Press, 1999); Bruce S. Jansson, *The Reluctant Welfare State: American Social Welfare Policies—Past, Present, and Future,* 3rd ed. (Pacific Grove, CA: Brooks/Cole, 1997); Phyllis J. Day, *A New History of Social Welfare* (Englewood Cliffs, NJ: Prentice Hall).

8. Mary E. Richmond, *Social Diagnosis* (New York: Russell Sage Foundation, 1917; reprint, Free Press, 1971).

9. Ibid., p. 357.

10. See Herman Borenzweig, "Social Work and Psychoanalytic Theory: An Historical Analysis," *Social Work* 16 (January 1971): 7–16.

11. Leslie B. Alexander, "Social Work's Freudian Deluge: Myth or Reality?" *Social Service Review* 46 (December 1972): 517–538.

12. *Social Casework: Generic and Specific* (New York: American Association of Social Workers, 1929).

13. Virginia P. Robinson, *A Changing Psychology in Social Case Work* (Chapel Hill: University of North Carolina Press, 1930).

14. Ibid.

15. Gordon Hamilton, *The Theory and Practice of Social Casework* (New York: Columbia University Press, 1940), p. 153.

16. Ibid., p. 35.

17. Ibid., p. 167.

18. Jessie Taft, Ed., *A Functional Approach to Family Casework* (Philadelphia: University of Pennsylvania Press, 1944); and Herbert H. Aptekar, *Basic Concepts in Social Casework* (Chapel Hill: University of North Carolina Press, 1941).

19. Gordon Hamilton, *Theory and Practice of Social Casework*, 2nd ed. rev. (New York: Columbia University Press, 1951).

20. Felix P. Biestek, *The Casework Relationship* (Chicago: Loyola University Press, 1957).

21. Ibid., p. 17.

22. Helen Harris Perlman, *Social Casework: A Problem-Solving Process* (Chicago: University of Chicago Press, 1957).

23. Ibid., p. 4.

24. Ibid., p. 171.

25. Ibid.

26. Florence Hollis, *Casework: A Psychosocial Therapy* (New York: Random House, 1964); and Ruth Elizabeth Smalley, *Theory for Social Work Practice* (New York: Columbia University Press, 1967).

27. Florence Hollis, *Casework*, 2nd ed. (1971).

28. Carol H. Meyer, *Social Work Practice: A Response to the Urban Crisis* (New York: Free Press, 1970).

29. Harriett M. Bartlett, *The Common Base of Social Work Practice* (New York: National Association of Social Workers, 1970).

30. Max Siporin, *Introduction to Social Work Practice* (New York: Macmillan, 1975); Beulah Roberts Compton and Burt Galaway, *Social Work Processes* (Homewood, IL: Dorsey Press, 1975); Howard Goldstein, *Social Work Practice: A Unitary Approach* (Columbia: University of South Carolina Press, 1973); and Allen Pincus and Anne Minahan, *Social Work Practice: Model and Method* (Itasca, IL: F. E. Peacock, 1973).

31. Pincus and Minahan, *Social Work Practice*, p. 103.

32. Ibid., p. 247.

33. See Catherine P. Papell and Beulah Rothman, "Social Group Work Models: Possession and Heritage," *Journal of Education for Social Work* 2 (Fall 1966): 66–77; and Jack Rothman, "Three Models of Community Organization Practice," in *National Conference on Social Welfare Social Work Practice* (New York: Columbia University Press, 1968), pp. 16–47.

34. Robert W. Roberts and Robert H. Nee, Eds., *Theories of Social Casework* (Chicago: University of Chicago Press, 1970).

35. Carel Germaine and Alex Gitterman, *The Life Model of Social Work Practice* (New York: Columbia University Press, 1980).

36. James K. Whittaker, Steven P. Schinke, and Lewayne D. Gilchrist, "The Ecological Paradigm in Child, Youth, and Family Services: Implications for Policy and Practice," *Social Service Review* 60 (December 1986): 483–503.

37. Mimi Abramowitz, "Temporary Assistance to Needy Families" in *Supplement to the Encyclopedia of Social Work,* Richard L. Edwards, Ed. (Silver Springs, MD: NASW Press, 1997), pp. 311–330.

38. Golda M. Edinburg and Joan M. Cottler, "Managed Care," in *Encyclopedia of Social Work,* 19th ed., Richard L. Edwards, Ed. (Silver Springs, MD: NASW Press, 1995), pp. 1635–1642; Kevin Corcoran, "Managed Care: Implications for Social Work Practice," in *Supplement to the Encyclopedia of Social Work,* Richard L. Edwards, Ed. (Silver Springs, MD: NASW Press, 1997), pp. 191–200.

39. Insoo Kim Berg, *Family-Based Services: A Solution-Focused Approach* (New York: W. W. Norton, 1994), p. x.

40. Carel B. Germaine and Alex Gitterman, "Ecological Perspective," in *Encyclopedia of Social Work,* 19th ed., Richard L. Edwards, Ed. (Washington, DC: NASW Press, 1995), pp. 817–824.

41. Dennis Saleebey, Ed., *The Strengths Perspective in Social Work Practice,* 2nd ed. (New York: Longman, 1997), pp. 12, 15.

42. Nan Van Den Bergh and Lynn B. Cooper, Eds., *Feminist Visions for Social Work* (Silver Springs, MD: National Association of Social Workers, 1986), Introduction, pp. 1–28; and M. Bricker-Jenkins and N. Gottlieb, *Feminist Social Work Practice in Clinical Settings* (Newberry Park, CA: Sage, 1991).

43. Richard Estes, Ed., *Internationalizing Social Work Education: A Guide to Resources for a New Century* (Feasterville, PA: Americor Press, 1992).

APPENDIX 2.1   The Development of Social Work in the United States

Societal	Social Welfare	Social Work
1885–1900		
Immigration (new groups); population increase. Industrialization-urbanization puts populations at risk. Closing of the frontier. Big business influence on politics. Agragarian revolt; beginning of trade unions. Beginnings of federal control (commerce and trusts). Social Darwinism vs. Puritan ethics.	Search for cause of poverty and individual breakdown. Emphasis on moral behavior and on affecting individual through personal influence and "neighborliness." Search for improved methods of government responsibility for care of special groups—children, the insane, etc. Emphasis on the "deserving poor." 1873—National Conference of Corrections and Charities.	Concern for urban situations in response to religious motives. Movement from volunteer to paid employment. 1863—First state social welfare board. 1866—First settlement house in the United States. 1887—Charity Organization Society comes to the United States.
1901–1919		
Age of progressives; liberalism; Social Darwinism. Emphasis on the real rather than the ideal. Development of the social sciences as a body of knowledge. Rise of the "Social Gospel." Growth of the Muckrakers. Growth of labor movement— concern for work conditions. Influence of John Dewey and "progressive education." World War I—"Make the world safe for democracy."	Age of philanthropy. Emphasis on environmental improvement and social reform with emphasis on poverty. Concern for labor conditions, safety, hours, wages. Establishment of programs in highly specialized and fragmented form. Concern for the care of dependent children; institutional vs. foster care; establishment of juvenile courts, widows' pensions, child labor laws. Social welfare legislation for special groups. 1909—First White House Conference (Children). 1912—Establishment of the Children's Bureau. Country life movement. Welfare programs for military personnel. Reform legislation: Restriction of immigration. Prohibition (of alcoholic beverages). Women's suffrage.	Beginnings of social work education with emphasis on method. Age of scientific philanthropy. Attempts to establish knowledge base, clarify goals, and establish itself. Social science theory predominant; sociology emphasis. Beginning attempt to establish practice theory with Richmond's *Social Diagnosis*. Development of practice in specialty areas. 1905—Medical social work. 1906—School social work. 1907—Psychiatric social work.
1920–1929		
Conservatism returns; disillusionment and dissatisfaction prevalent. Emphasis on production and distribution; responsiveness to corporations.	Disillusionment with political solutions to social problems. Marked increase in philanthropic foundations. Multiplication of service clubs.	Emphasis on function of social work rather than on the social cause. Withdrawal from social responsibility and placing of emphasis on the adjustment of individuals.

(continued)

APPENDIX 2.1   Continued

Societal	Social Welfare	Social Work
1920–1929 (continued)		
"Return to normalcy"; individualism. Prosperity—national income high, unemployment low. Reduction in immigration—deportation of alien radicals. Antisocialism, racial intolerance, upsurge of Ku Klux Klan. Era of laissez-faire and intolerance. Urbanism—indifference to social reform, sensationalism, skepticism. Development of psychology.	Formation of community chests—reorganization of private charities. Rise of public administration, state agencies, institutions. Change from "charity and corrections" to "public welfare." Rise of "child guidance," "mental hygiene," character-building agencies, concern for the prevention of delinquency. Some state laws on unemployment compensation, mothers' pensions, old-age pensions, help for the blind. County-level organization of rural child welfare services in some states.	Use of casework with middle-class clients. Milford Conference of 1923–24; search for generic aspects of casework, definition of social casework. Development of specialized professional organizations; medical, school, and psychiatric social workers as well as the American Association of Social Workers. Search for a body of knowledge and theoretical framework led to adoption of psychoanalytic theory by an increasing number of workers and educators. By 1930 twenty-eight schools of social work had been established.
1930–1945		
Depression—solutions for economic and social ills in action by the federal government. Social experimentation—pragmatism. New Deal; federal regulation of business. Rise of organized labor. Mass movement from rural to urban settings. Collectivist mood for building a new social order. World War II; revolt against totalitarianism, but an emphasis on unity. Rise of communism—fear of communism.	Federal government becomes heavily involved in social welfare, relief programs, and public works programs. Social Security Act of 1935. Federal funding—state administration of categorical assistance for the unemployable (children, aged, blind). Federal administration of social insurance against old age. State-administered unemployment insurance. 1939—Social Security amendment includes survivor's insurance.	Concern over public-private functions as the major responsibility for relief becomes public. Redefinition of role of family agency. In search for casework theory, two approaches develop—diagnostic and functional. Group work becomes a part of social work; formation of the National Association for the Study of Groups, 1936. Lane Report on Community Organizations, 1939. Formation of many national planning organizations; rise of community chests. Continued growth and development of social work education; minimum curriculum requirements, formal accreditation, need for university affiliation, strong concern that it be graduate education. Debate over uniqueness of rural social work.

APPENDIX 2.1 Continued

Societal	Social Welfare	Social Work
1945–1960		
Postwar prosperity; partnership of business and government.	1946—Hill-Burton Act (hospital survey and construction).	Time for introspection, cooperation, and search for unity.
Threat of nuclear war—fear of communism.	1946—National Mental Health Act.	Development of methods of group work, community organization, and research; continued diagnostic-functional dichotomy.
"New conservatism," McCarthyism.	1950—expansion and strengthening of Social Security; addition of aid to the disabled.	
Korean War; Cold War.	Growth of interest in services and their delivery.	Expansion into new settings; new problem areas.
Farm problems; decline of family farm.	Business corporations' and labor unions' support of private philanthropy.	1946—establishment of the National Council on Social Work Education to resolve problems of educational standards.
Gains for labor; higher wages and welfare packages.	Growth of community chests and councils.	1952—Hollis-Taylor Report, *Social Work Education in the United States.*
Population explosion.	1953—establishment of Department of Health, Education, and Welfare.	1952—formation of Council on Social Work Education, MSW the professional degree; development of curriculum policy, accreditation standards, 85% of social work students in casework sequence.
Growth of metropolitan communities; migration of minorities to cities.	1955—Joint Commission on Mental Illness and Health.	
Television.	1956—amendments to Social Security Act call for services as well as income maintenance.	
"Happy home" illusion; *Growing Up Absurd;* affluent society.	1956—Federal Housing Act.	1955—NASW formed; adoption of *Code of Ethics;* establishment of ACSW.
	Growth of national institutes of health.	1958—eight-volume curriculum study.
	Concern about juvenile correctional institutions and delinquency.	
1961–1975		
High unemployment; growth slowed.	Discovery of poverty; *The Other America.*	Growth in number of social workers, in areas of concern, and in knowledge development.
Cold War; Cuban Missile Crisis; Vietnam War.	War on Poverty; Great Society.	Knowledge base expanded; use of social systems theory, lessening of psychoanalytic influence.
Space program.	Drift toward "universalism."	
Desegregation.	Growing ADC roles; AFDC (1962).	Return to concern for multiproblem, difficult-to-serve client.
Growth of government bureaucracy.	1962—Social Security amendments implement service provision.	
Kennedy assassination.	1962—Manpower Training Act.	Proliferation of new practice modalities.
Concern with consumerism.	1965—Medicare-Medicaid.	Involvement in social reform, social action, and social policy activity.
From civil rights to Black Power; minority rights.	1965—Office of Economic Opportunity.	
Women's Liberation Movement.	1965—Older Americans Act.	Emphasis on research and theory development.
Counterculture; New Left.	Concern for health care; discussion of income distribution; preoccupation with rehabilitation and accountability.	Concern with manpower and deployment issues.
Federal support for education.		Development of integrated or generalist methods.
Family farm declines.	Federal Grants-in-Aid Program; intermingling of public and private sectors; revenue sharing; purchase of service.	Reappearance of rural social work.
Concern for law and order.	Rent supplement program; food stamps; WIN.	Rise of "clinical social work" movement and private practice.

(continued)

APPENDIX 2.1   Continued

Societal	Social Welfare	Social Work
1961–1975 (continued)		
	Separation of income maintenance and services.	Tremendous growth in social work education.
	Rebirth of rural concerns.	Accreditation of BSW programs; development of doctoral programs; considerable diversity of educational programs.
	1970s—time of doubt about effectiveness; reorganization and accountability themes.	
	1972—SSI replaces AA, AB, and AD; federal administration of programs.	NASW accepts BSW for membership.
	1975—Title XX of Social Security Act; decentralization of services; child support enforcement.	Proliferation of new practice modalities including planned short-term approaches.
	1975—original passage of fairly liberal entitlements.	
1976–1991		
Inflation.	1980s—restrictions that crippled entitlement programs.	Generalist at BSW level; specialization at MSW level.
Fiscal retrenchment.	1981—block grants restrict Title XX.	Continued tension between BSW and MSW levels.
Conservatism prevails.		
New Realism; New Federalism.	Block grants.	Rise of social work in industrial and rural settings.
High unemployment.	Revenue sharing.	
Changing family structure.	Civil Service declassification.	Clinical Register; growth of private practice.
Changing role of women; defeat of ERA.	Deinstitutionalization.	New *Code of Ethics*.
Aging of the population.	Curtailing of social welfare budget; cost containment.	Emphasis on political involvement.
Escalation of health care costs.	Third-party payments.	Concern with:
New technology, age of computers.	Health care planning mechanisms.	Child and spouse abuse,
Concern about nuclear energy, defense, and peace issues.	"Workfare" and other "welfare reform."	displaced homemakers, use of community resources,
Farm crisis.	1983—introduction of prospective payment for health care costs for Medicare recipients through Diagnostic Related Groups (DRGs).	homelessness, AIDS, substance abuse, and peace and justice.
		Growing support for an ecological paradigm.
		Education:
		New curriculum policy statement.
		New accreditation standards
1992–2000		
Low inflation.	Family Leave Act.	Private practice by MSWs expands.
Low unemployment.	Downsizing of government.	Continued tension between BSW and MSW.
Economic globalization.	End of Aid to Families with Dependent Children (AFDC).	New *NASW Code of Ethics*.
Conservatism dominates.	Personal Responsibility Act.	Brief solution-focused interventions.
Republicans gain control of Congress.	Temporary Assistance to Needy Families (TANF); block grants replace federal aid formulas.	Education:
Welfare reform.		New curriculum policy statement.
Continued aging of the population.	Total federal funding for welfare frozen.	New accreditation standards.
Continued escalation of health care costs.	Managed care.	Increased use of ecological and strengths perspectives.
The Internet rapidly expands.	Concern over aging population.	
President Clinton impeached but stays in office.	Debates about saving Social Security and Medicare.	
Budget surpluses.	Concern over increasing violence.	

3 Social Work as a Creative Blending of Knowledge, Values, and Skills

LEARNING EXPECTATIONS

1. Understanding of the range of knowledge used by the social worker.
2. Understanding of the nature of values.
3. Knowledge about the value base underlying social work.
4. Understanding of the nature of skills and beginning knowledge of the skills of a generalist social worker.
5. Understanding of the manner in which knowledge, values, and skills are used together in social work.

Social work as a creative blending of knowledge, values, and skills is the third major perspective of social work practice. It relates to the "how" of social work practice. As discussed in Chapter 2, important characteristics of any profession are systematic theory and ethical codes. The development of systematic theory on which to base practice implies that the practice is grounded in a knowledge base and that practioners are using that knowledge base in their practice decision making. This practice also is based in an ethical code that in part delineates the value base for practice. The value base must consider societal, client, and worker values.

Soon after the formation of the National Association of Social Workers (NASW), it became evident that there was a need for definition and clarification of social work practice in order to codify the unifying elements of the profession. The Commission of Social Work Practice of NASW, through the work of a subcommittee chaired by Harriet Bartlett, developed the "Working Definition of Social Work Practice."[1] From this work and the subsequent work of Bartlett and William Gordon,[2] understanding began to evolve about the necessity for further identifying the body of knowledge (ways of knowing) and the set of values (attitudes toward people) that guide practice and are operationalized through a set of skills. This constellation of knowledge, values, and skills is one important means of describing the nature of social work practice. It is used to operationalize the five concepts discussed in Chapter 2: assessment, relationship, person in situation, process, and intervention. It provides an organizing framework for practice regardless of situation, system of focus, worker role, or context of practice. It is the foundation of professional relationships and of the helping process and gives substance to the concepts of concern and need with which a social worker is confronted.

In some ways knowledge, values, and skills are related to the feeling, thinking, and doing construct introduced in Chapter 1 (see Figure 1.1). Knowledge is a part of the cognitive or thinking component of practice; values are a part of the feeling or emotional component of practice, though in some ways they are also a part of the thinking component. Skills are action, or the doing of social work; they are part of the behavioral component. However, it must be recognized that skills may also be cognitive in nature. Development of the capacity to think about a practice situation—that is, to utilize the broad knowledge base and choose those aspects appropriate to the situation, determine relevant values for consideration, and identify appropriate action—is included in the realm of skill as discussed in this book.

It is important to examine the nature of each of these components of social work practice as well as the content of each component. It is also important to consider how these three components are used together in practice. This gives rise to the notion that the connection among the three results from a *creative blending*.[3] Other issues that must be considered are the use of both science and art in considering the relationship of knowledge, values, and skill and the importance of creativity in combining the three into a coherent practice assessment and plan.

Knowledge

In *The Common Base of Social Work Practice*, Bartlett makes a strong case for the need for social work action to be founded on a strong knowledge base—to be guided by knowledge.[4] **Knowledge** is a term with a broad and varied meaning. Gordon defined knowledge as "the picture man has of the world and his place in it."[5] Max Siporin gives a definition that enhances Gordon's: "Knowledge is cognitive mental content (ideas and beliefs) concerning reality that we take to be true (perceive with certainty, based on adequate evidence), or that we decide is confirmable and has a high probability of truth."[6]

Social work has placed increasing emphasis on knowledge that is scientific as opposed to beliefs in unconfirmed ideas. An attempt has been made to develop a knowledge base that begins to move toward the hardness characteristic of the sciences. Yet the very nature of the social sciences, with their concern for the complex phenomenon of the human being in his social environment, tends to make this difficult and gives a quality of softness to the knowledge base.[*]

---

[*]It is assumed that students will be exposed to the concept of scientific knowledge in a research course. It is also assumed that they will understand such terms as *concept, theory,* and *hypothesis.* It is not the purpose of this book to consider this material in any depth. This book is concerned with application of knowledge after a judgment is made about its reliability and validity.

In their struggle to develop the science of sociology, sociologists have experienced problems similar to those of social work. Paul Reynolds identifies a scientific body of knowledge as designed to "describe things and identify why events occur."[7] He perceives this body of knowledge as providing a method for organizing or categorizing things, predicting future events, explaining past events, and giving a sense of understanding about what causes events and the potential for control of events.[8] He goes on to state that knowledge that is accepted as scientific has these attributes:

1. *Abstractness*—independence of time and space.
2. *Intersubjectivity*

   a. *Explicitness*—description in necessary detail and with terms selected to ensure that the audience agrees on the meaning of the concepts.
   b. *Rigorousness* (logical rigor)—use of logical systems that are shared and accepted by relevant scientists to ensure agreement on the predictions and explanations of theory.

3. *Empirical relevance*—the possibility should always exist that other scientists can evaluate the correspondence between theory and the results of empirical research.[9]

Other sociologists have demonstrated how society determines the presence and content of ideas—how social values define the phenomena to be studied and color interpretations of these phenomena.[10] This leads to the understanding that although knowledge can be tested—can be developed in a scientific manner—the content developed and tested is strongly influenced by the social context in which social work practice takes place. For example, societal values about individuals have influenced the development of knowledge that emphasizes the needs of individuals.

Social work knowledge, particularly the foundation knowledge used for understanding, has been largely borrowed from the social sciences, particularly psychology and sociology, though anthropology, political science, economics, and history as well as the natural sciences of biology and physiology also contribute. This knowledge base is complex, requiring a breadth of knowledge in various disciplines as well as a depth necessary for more than superficial understanding.

Social work knowledge is what is known about people and their social systems. It is relative to the situation in which it was developed. It is descriptive of the phenomena of persons in situations and explains the functioning of individuals and their social systems. It is used to gain understanding of persons in situations and of larger social systems and to guide the actions of social workers as they seek to enhance individuals' social functioning. It includes knowledge of human development, human diversity, social systems theory, the ecological perspective, and the strengths perspective as discussed in Chapter 1. It is knowledge that directs the response to need and includes knowledge about assessment, relationships, the social work process, and intervention.

The knowledge used to guide the action of the social worker with clients has usually been developed by social workers. Much of this knowledge has not been rigorously tested in a scientific manner. However, a small body of practice knowledge can be identified. Task-centered social work is an example of this type of knowledge.[11] However, the use of only scientifically developed knowledge in social work practice fails to account for much that the practioners know about human beings and how change takes place. Reality is much more than that which has been proven and observed in concrete ways. Ways of knowing other than the narrowly scientific have been referred to as *practice wisdom.* Howard Goldstein has referred to this as "that which we learn from the lives of our clients and from the experiences we share with them."[12] Goldstein also noted that recognition of this knowledge as valid for practice opens up a new range of what are known as generative theories for use in practice.[13]

Practice wisdom must include the ability to appreciate diversity and individuality and to see the strengths in people and their environment. Workers need to value and be open to learning from the lives of clients and from shared experiences. In this way workers grow and strengthen their knowledge base as well as empower their clients. Clients are helped to experience their strengths and capacities rather than focusing on weaknesses or limitations. The focus moves from what is missing to what is possible. A word of caution is offered. In the process of learning from clients, it is important to avoid using those experiences to create stereotypes or generalizations. If anything, practice wisdom conveys that uniqueness and individuality are what really characterize human beings.

Thus, the knowledge base developed for social work is eclectic, interdisciplinary, tentative at best, complex, and often subjective. Social work continues to search for the acceptance of common concepts and common frames of reference and to test hypotheses about the nature of practice in the effort to become more scientific. By its very nature, this knowledge base is problematic. Some of these problems include:

1. Problems that come from borrowing knowledge from another discipline. This borrowing often provides yesterday's knowledge rather than the current thinking of the discipline developing the knowledge. Often, such knowledge is given much more certainty by the borrowing discipline than it is given by the developing discipline. Also, borrowing tends to be of a simplified nature.[14] Questionable assumptions may result when borrowed knowledge is improperly used.

2. Problems that arise from separating the knowledge and value elements of practice. Value considerations so influence one's view of reality that observations and facts that conflict with these values are often overlooked. The manner in which knowledge is developed and used contributes to this difficulty.[15]

3. Problems that develop because practice wisdom has often been conceptualized insufficiently to separate fact, perception, ideas, and values. Practice wisdom has often not been tested by applying it to different situations in a controlled manner. Its validity and reliability with respect to different situations has not been examined. Thus, it is difficult to determine if knowledge gained from practice wisdom is appropriate in a given situation.

4. Problems that develop because of the many variables involved in the human situation and in the worker-client interaction. These make it difficult to generalize knowledge for use in determining intervention possibilities. Of particular concern are cultural factors that change perceptions about human behavior and helping situations.

5. Problems that result from a tendency to use terms and concepts without sufficient definition or without agreement as to definition. Without this agreement, the same terms and concepts are sometimes used with different meanings.

6. Problems that result from a tendency to develop insufficient relationships among terms and concepts. Social systems theory has given a framework for doing this, at least in part, with the knowledge used for understanding—person in situation. The practice theory knowledge is still very difficult to place in an organized framework except at an abstract level.

Although many problems are inherent in the social work knowledge base, it has a major strength. Because social work takes a broad view of person in situation and of social functioning, there is a vast amount of knowledge that can be called on to inform practice. Knowledge that workers have gained from life experiences, observations made about other's life experiences, and understandings developed from a broad liberal arts education are all available.

If a worker is to base practice on a knowledge base, she must have the ability to evaluate the knowledge available, to use judgment in the choice of knowledge to apply to specific situations, and to keep an open mind as to the tentativeness of the knowledge base and the knowledge about the client in the situation. The worker must be able to think theoretically, systematically, critically, and creatively. Goldstein states that this is far more an art than an applied science. He further states: "Reflectively, creatively, and imaginatively, the mind of the practioneer strives to blend and incorporate fragments of theory, information, intuitions, sensations, and other perceptions into something ambiguously called 'understanding.'"[16]

The sources of knowledge used by the social worker are wide and varied, coming from a variety of disciplines. The choice of which understandings to use in which situations is always problematic, and connecting knowledge bits from a variety of sources is difficult. The human condition is a complex phenomenon. It has been explained in a variety of ways. To have a sufficiently broad knowledge base, a social worker needs the following:

1. *A broad liberal arts base*—This includes a knowledge of the social sciences (sociology, psychology, anthropology, history, political science, and economics) to provide explanations about the nature of human society and the human condition. Study of the natural sciences provides tools for scientific thinking and an understanding of the physical aspects of the human condition. Study of the humanities aids in the development of the creative and critical thought processes; it provides an understanding of the nature of the human condition through the examination of creative endeavors and of the cultures of human society. A social worker is a person with a developed and expanded personal capacity gained by exposure to a broad, liberal educational experience.

2. *A sound foundation knowledge about persons, their interactions, and the social situations within which they function*—This includes knowledge about persons from emotional, cognitive, behavioral, and developmental points of view. Such knowledge must consider the diversity of the human condition and the effect of diversity on functioning and development. Understanding of human interaction in depth is also essential. This knowledge includes one-to-one relationships, family relationships, and small-group relationships. It also includes understanding of the societal organizations and institutions that are a part of contemporary society and of the social problems that affect human functioning.

3. *Practice theory, with concern for the nature of helping interactions, of the process of helping, and of a variety of intervention strategies appropriate for a variety of situations and systems*—This includes knowledge of professional and societal structures and institutions for delivery of service to individuals in need of help and methods of adapting and developing the service structure for more adequate need fulfillment.[17]

4. *Specialized knowledge needed to work with particular groups of clients and in particular situations*—The choice of knowledge each worker includes in this area is dependent on the practice situations and on career aspirations.

5. *The capacity to be reflective, imaginative, and creative in the use of knowledge obtained from a variety of sources*—It is especially important to be able to see the strengths in people and in their environment and to be able to use those strengths to build a vision for the future.

Case Example

When working with an older person, over age 65, there is a great deal of specific knowledge that will help the social worker in understanding the needs of such a client. Biology and physiology will provide knowledge about the physical aging process. In the field of gerontology, a number of theories relative to the aging process have emerged. These include disengagement theory, activity theory, and developmental theory. Developmental theory is particularly congruent with the emphasis of this book and identifies specific tasks that the older person needs to complete if the older adult stage of life is to be a fulfilling one. It is important to have basic knowledge about the many health problems of older persons as well as an understanding about death and dying.

Sociological knowledge provides understanding of the meaning of retirement to individuals as well as the role and function of older persons in our culture. It provides understandings about the social context of both the individual and institutional situations. Cultural and gender differences regarding the view of the aging process are also important. Knowledge about family structure and functioning as they relate to older persons is a needed understanding. Another valuable concept is that of cohort (age group) differences. This is particularly important as societal changes have speeded up to the point that different cohorts have experienced life in very different ways. Knowledge of various social problems that often affect older persons, such as limited financial resources, age discrimination, and isolation and loneliness is also necessary. The social worker should acquaint herself with the various societal and community resources that have been developed to help older persons deal with these problems. An in-depth understanding of social policy as it has developed is another needed knowledge for working with older persons. This knowledge all helps the worker to understand person in situation. In order to help that person, knowledge about a wide range of interventive strategies that have proven useful in the past is also needed.

Values

Knowledge and values are often confused. It is important to distinguish between these two important components of social work practice. Knowledge is at least potentially provable; it is used to explain behavior and to conceptualize practice. **Values** are not provable; they are what is held to be desirable; they are used to identify what is preferred. This includes preferable assumptions about human behavior and preferable ways of helping. Knowledge assumptions and value assumptions are used in different ways in the helping endeavor.

Several definitions of the term *value* are useful for developing an understanding of the term. Muriel Pumphrey has defined values as follows: "Values are formulations of preferred behavior held by individuals or social groups. They imply a usual preference for certain means, ends, and conditions of life, often being accompanied by strong feeling."[18] Herbert Aptekar refines the meaning of value: "A standard or standards held by a significant portion of a society reflected in patterns of institutionalized behavior, and predisposing the participants to act in relation to one another within the framework of commonly understood although not consciously controlled or logically consistent referential system."[19] This definition might be questioned for its requirement that the value be held by a "significant portion of society." It is useful, however, in pointing out the societal aspect of values, or the influence of others in the development of values.

It is also questionable whether in the contemporary diverse society of the United States there are, in fact, any generally agreed-on societal values. What does seem to exist are groups of values that various segments of society *believe* should be the societal values and which they tend to want to impose on everyone.

A source from outside the field of social work is also useful in the search for understanding the term *value*. The literature of values clarification sees values as (1) guides to behavior, (2) growing out of personal experiences, (3) modified as experiences accumulate, and (4) evolving in nature.[20] This literature provides additional understanding about the nature of values by noting that the conditions in which values operate often have conflicting demands; that is, several values are functioning in the same situation, and each calls for conflicting modes of functioning or end states. One social work example of this is working with a frail older woman. In such a case, the worker is confronted with values of physical safety and self-determination. The older person wants to remain in her own home, but it is not safe as presently set up. Which value should take precedence? A value judgment is called for.

Milton Rokeach defines value as "an enduring belief that a specific mode or end state of existence is personally or socially preferable to an opposite or converse mode or end state of existence."[21] He goes on to state that values, rather than standing alone, exist in systems; that is, individual values are organized in such a manner that they have a relative importance to other values. He construes values as being relatively enduring, as beliefs upon which persons act by preference, and as modes of conduct or end states of existence. Value beliefs are conceptions of what is desirable; there is an emotion or feeling aspect to them; and they lead to action.

There are several types of values. *Ultimate values* are the most abstract and tend to be those most easily agreed on by large groups of people. They include such values as liberty, worth, and dignity of people, progress, and justice. *Proximate values* are more specific as to the desired end state. The right to an abortion on demand, freedom to determine how one will do the assignments in a course, and the right to punish one's child in a specific manner are examples of proximate values. There is apt to be disagreement regarding these values. *Instrumental values* are those values that specify the desired means to the ends; they are modes of conduct. Self-determination and confidentiality are examples of instrumental values. They are means for operationalizing the worth and dignity of individuals.

Values originate, in part, from the society of which a person is a part. If individuals are thought of as evil, it is difficult to believe that individuals have worth and dignity. Factors that influence the values individuals hold include (1) their cultural heritage, (2) values held by individuals and groups with which they are associated or to which they aspire to associate, (3) personal experience, and (4) the views they hold about human beings and the nature of the human situation.

Social workers have often ignored the importance of religious or spiritual values in the lives of people, but religious beliefs and spiritual frameworks are important sources for the development of beliefs. They strongly impact the value systems of both individuals and cultural groups. To respect truly a client's values, a worker must not only recognize the role of religion and spirituality in the development of those values but also how beliefs are important components of human functioning.

Value conflicts develop as individuals are exposed to the differing value systems upon which they are expected to act. The *societal value system* contains values generally held by the dominant segment of society. In American society, some of these values that have been articulated are achievement and success, activity and work, moral responsibility, concern for people who are victims of natural disaster and temporary distress, efficiency and practicality, progress, material comfort, equality, freedom, external conformity, science and secular rationality, nationalism and patriotism, democracy, worth of the individual, and superiority of the dominant group.[22] These values have had their origin in a combination of sources, including (1) the capitalistic-Puritan ethic; (2) the Judeo-Christian heritage; and (3) humanistic, positivist, utopian thinking.[23] Conflicts, tensions, and inconsistencies exist among these various sources as well as among societal values, professional values, and personal values of clients and social workers. Tensions and conflicts become more apparent as one moves from ultimate values to the choice of specific goals and means, that is, as one moves from the abstract to the concrete. Some of these tensions arise because of differences between values about needs of individuals and values about needs of groups of which individuals are a part.

Social work practice is based on a set of values that is often expressed in such principles as the worth and dignity of the individual, the right to self-determination, and the right to confidentiality. Gordon expresses these values in the following manner: "It is good and desirable for man to fulfill his potential, to realize himself and to balance this with equal effort to help others fulfill their capacities and realize themselves."[24] Aptekar has expressed these same ultimate values in a slightly different manner: "Worth and dignity of a man as related to the well-being and integrity of the group.... Progress and development of individual and society as related to the security of individual and the society."[25] Armando Morales and Bradford Sheafor, using Charles Levy's scheme for organizing values,[26] have identified values held by the social work profession:

Preferred Conceptions of People
1. Social workers believe in inherent worth and dignity.
2. Each person has an inherent capacity and drive toward change that can make life more fulfilling.
3. Each person has responsibility for himself and his fellow human beings—including society.
4. People need to belong.
5. There are human needs common to each person, yet each person is unique and different from others.

Preferred Outcomes for People
1. Society must provide opportunities for growth and development that will allow each person to realize his fullest potential.
2. Society must provide resources and services to help people meet their needs and to avoid such problems as hunger, inadequate education, discrimination, illness without care, and inadequate housing.
3. People must have equal opportunity to participate in the molding of society.

Preferred Instrumentalities for Dealing with People
People should be treated with respect and dignity, should have maximum opportunity to determine the direction of their lives, should be urged and helped to interact with other people to build a society responsive to the

needs of everyone, and should be recognized as unique individuals rather than put into stereotypes because of some particular characteristic or life experience.[27]

Codes of ethics flow from values; they are values in action, and as such they are preferred instrumentalities for dealing with people. Werner Boehm has stated that values are behavioral expectations and preferences associated with responsibility; they represent consensus regarding the preference in specific situations.[28] Ethical codes specify what ought to be done in professional practice. At the 1996 Delegate Assembly, NASW adopted a new *Code of Ethics*, replacing a code of ethics adopted in 1960 and amended in 1967 and 1979. Growth and change in the profession of social work as well as shortcomings in the old code made it desirable to develop this new code of ethics. The new code includes issues such as use of electronic media and more specific guidelines for worker behavior in relationships with clients. It also ties ethical principles directly to social work values. Figure 3.1 gives the preamble of the code as well as the core values and ethical principles on which the code is founded. All social workers should have a copy of the *Code of Ethics* for reference and should be familiar with its contents.

As the social worker attempts to base practice on these values, it is soon apparent that this is not an easy or simple matter. The basing of practice on values leads to several problems:

1. The abstract statements of values are the subject of conflicting interpretations. As the abstract value is operationalized, the guidelines must take into consideration not just one value but several. It is often difficult to decide what action will fulfill the value's imperatives. For example, does a worker enhance a person's worth and dignity by allowing a choice that will clearly lead to the consequence of imprisonment? Can such a client be allowed self-determination in that choice?

2. The balance between individual rights and societal responsibility is difficult to maintain. Potential elements of conflict and tension in maintaining this balance are (a) the need to reform the social structure yet help persons cope with the imperfect social structure that exists; (b) the responsibility to the consumers of service and at the same time to those who pay for the service; (c) the providing for the good of the group and the community; and (d) equality for all yet the need to meet individual needs, for in American culture individual self-sufficiency provides a sense of dignity; using help often lowers self-esteem.[29]

3. Henry Miller points out another problem in the application of values to practice: "How is one to minister to man's suffering without robbing him of his dignity?"[30] This is an ongoing question that is always present in social work practice.

4. Alan Keith-Lucas points out yet another problem: How is it possible to use the scientific approach and at the same time use a humanistic approach?[31] Roland Warren looks at this same problem in a somewhat different way. He sees two values that operate in relationship to social change: truth and love. Each seems to

---

FIGURE 3.1 **NASW *Code of Ethics*—Summary of Core Values and Ethical Principles**

Preamble

The primary mission of the social work profession is to enhance human well-being and help meet basic human needs, with particular attention to the needs of people who are vulnerable, oppressed, and living in poverty. A historic and defining feature of social work is the profession's focus on individual well-being in a social context and the well-being of society. Fundamental to social work is attention to the environmental forces that create, contribute to, and address problems in living.

The mission of the social work profession is rooted in a set of core values. These core values, embraced by social workers throughout the profession's history, are the foundation of social work's unique purpose and perspective. Core values, and the ethical principles that flow from them, must be balanced within the context and complexity of the human experience.

Core Values and Ethical Principles

Value: *Service*

Ethical Principle: *Social workers' primary goal is to help people in need and to address social problems.*

Value: *Social Justice*

Ethical Principle: *Social workers challenge social injustice.*

Value: *Dignity and Worth of the Person*

Ethical Principle: *Social workers respect the inherent dignity and worth of the person*

Value: *Importance of Human Relationships*

Ethical Principle: *Social workers recognize the central importance of human relationships.*

Value: *Integrity*

Ethical Principle: *Social workers behave in a trustworthy manner.*

Value: *Competence*

Ethical Principle: *Social workers practice within their areas of competence and develop and enhance their professional expertise.*

Source: Reprinted with permission from NASW *Code of Ethics,* 1997. Copyright 1997, National Association of Social Workers, Inc. The above is an extract of the NASW *Code of Ethics* approved by the 1996 Delegate Assembly. The complete text is available from the National Association of Social Workers, 750 First Street, NE, Suite 700, Washington, DC 20002-4241.

lead to different assumptions as to how to bring about change. Truth seems to call for knowing about, reasoning, a task orientation. The relationship with people in this value seems to be that of I-It. It carries the stance of the prophet. Love seems to call for knowledge by acquaintance of intuition and a process orientation. The relationship with people is more in an I-Thou manner. It carries the stance of the reconciler. This is the problem raised by valuing both the use of the scientific method and the worth and dignity of each individual. In his recognition of this dilemma, Warren calls for a stance that seeks to persuade but never to coerce the conscience, that does not love but respects, that is concerned with task but not oblivious of process, that seeks to understand but also to experience directly, that has a trace both of the prophet and of the reconciler.[32]

Dealing with values is central to social work practice. The social worker must be concerned with both societal and personal values, with the client's and with her own. The worker also must function within the framework of social work values and ethics. The worker must be comfortable with discomfort as the search continues for congruence between believing and doing and for resolution of conflict among values. This calls for tolerance and humility.

Some of the contemporary issues confronting social work and about which there are conflicting value judgments are abortion, homosexuality, treatment for AIDS victims, extreme health care measures, and treatment of the chronically mentally ill.

When dealing with ethical issues, there is often not a clear-cut answer to determining the ethical action in a particular situation. For instance, when does a client have a right to privacy in a situation in which a child may be at risk of abuse? If there is a clear indication of abuse, most legal jurisdictions mandate that the abuse be reported. But what about when there is only an *indication* of risk? Or what about the client who makes threats against another person in the course of service? What about the mentally ill person who makes threats on her own life? All of these situations call for a professional judgment as to the seriousness of the situation. Another contemporary dilemma may arise when working with a person who is HIV positive or one who suffers from AIDS. If that person has not informed a sexual partner of the risk, does the social worker have an obligation to do so? The landmark case of *Tarasoff v Regents of the University of California* (1976) is often cited regarding the liability of a social worker for failure to warn.[33]

There are no clear-cut answers to any of these situations. The NASW *Code of Ethics* requires the social worker to maintain confidentiality except for compelling professional reasons. It would then follow that the worker must be sure that a real danger to another person exists before breaching the confidentiality ethic. Yet, when a real danger exists, the worker must intervene on behalf of the at-risk other. A first step would be a careful and fully documented assessment of the situation. Next would be an attempt to persuade the client to self-reveal to the at-risk other. If this fails to occur in a timely manner, the worker, usually after informing the client, should take steps to ensure that the other is protected.

Clients should always be aware that there are limits to confidentiality and be informed regarding those limits. The worker should be aware of laws protecting and limiting confidentiality. They also must be aware of liability risks and standard guidelines for informed consent.

Valuing is a common human experience. It allows persons to identify what they hold in high esteem—the objects, instruments, experiences, conditions, qualities, and objectives that are worthy of human effort and interest. It is particularly important for the social worker to engage in the process of valuing. Each worker has developed an individual value system that at least in part is related to the societal and cultural value system of which he is a part. The social work values are also similar to the societal value system in some respects, but there are differences. Social workers must recognize these differences and develop ways of dealing with the tensions and conflicts that result from them. They must be aware of their own values so that unexamined values do not influence their practice.

In valuing, it is important to recognize and value diversity. Too often when people see differences, they fall into the trap of constructing false dichotomies— that is, the tendency to see two things that are different as if one is superior and the other is inferior. As a result, value judgments are made that lead to perceiving differences as good and bad instead of just different. Perceiving differences in this way provides a rationale for treating people as inferior and leads to prejudice, discrimination, and oppression.

When we value diversity, we open ourselves up to new experiences and to different ways of perceiving and valuing. It allows us see the richness and the strengths in variety. It is like watching a rainbow through a black-and-white lens and then seeing it for the first time in full color. Valuing diversity is also fundamental to being able to value and respect each individual and to appreciate the uniqueness of each human being.

The social work endeavor is based on the dual values of the worth and dignity of individuals and of social responsibility. These values can be expressed in these principles for action:

1. People should be free to make choices.
2. Individuals are important; individual needs and concerns cannot be totally subjected to community needs.
3. Workers should use a nonjudgmental approach to persons and their concerns, needs, and problems.
4. The social work role is helping or enabling, not controlling.
5. Feelings and personal relationships are important.
6. People have responsibility for others, for their needs and concerns.

Case Example

Understanding one's values is particularly important when working with older persons. In our society, which almost worships youth, health, athletic ability, and beauty in the young body, the negative attitudes toward the aging process and toward aging persons are very prominent. This often affects the older person's feelings of self-worth. A worker may be so influenced by these societal values that she is unaware of how negative feelings toward older people affect her relationships with older clients. Social workers also need to be vigilant that they do not accept the common myths about old age, such as old people are alike, they are not dependable, they cannot learn. *Ageism,* or discriminatory behaviors toward older people, has its roots in values. This discrimination is counter to the NASW *Code of Ethics.*

The worker must constantly watch that he does not take away the client's rights to self-determination, to confidentiality, that he does not place institutional rules and

(continued)

Case Example   Continued

family desires as more important than the wishes of the client. Quality-of-life issues are often difficult to sort out, but there must be an assessment as to what the client considers to be quality of life, and whenever possible that must be a guide in service provision.

When working with older persons, values about death and dying often come into play. Many younger workers attempt to avoid this area, but dealing with the process of aging calls for a person to come to grips with their mortality. For a worker to be helpful to older persons around this issue, she needs to have considered it in her own life and have come to some comfort with this topic, which is extremely value laden.

Thus, we see that in working with older people the social worker needs to consider not only social work ethics but societal values, her own values, and the client's values. These values may not be congruent. Strong feelings are often raised because of the discrimination experienced by older people or because of acceptance of societal myths. Often the worker's first task in working with an older client is to identify the value issues that are present in the situation.

Skills

Skill is the practice component that brings knowledge and values together and converts them to action as a response to concern and need. A sociological definition of **skill** is also useful in understanding the meaning of the term: a complex organization of behavior (physical or verbal) developed through learning and directed toward a particular goal or centered on a particular activity.[34]

Bartlett uses the term *interventive repertoire* to describe the bringing together of knowledge and values to respond to problems of social functioning. She describes this interventive repertoire as being made up of methods, techniques, and skills. Skill is seen as technical expertise, the ability to use knowledge effectively and readily in performing competently.[35] This formulation seems to encompass two important attributes of this particular component of practice. First, it is necessary to make choices from a variety of possibilities based on knowledge and value considerations. Second, the choices are in regard to action to be taken in relation to a concern or need.

The more recent literature seems to use the term *skill* rather than *interventive repertoire* in discussing the action component of practice. Morales and Sheafor see the skill of social work as the appropriate selection of techniques for a particular situation and the effective use of those techniques. They discuss how this selection is based on a conscious use of knowledge and state that social work values filter this knowledge in determining appropriate skills for use in providing service. They believe that skill is needed both for the selection of appropriate techniques and for the ability to use techniques effectively.[36] They define skill as the social worker's capacity to set in motion—in a relationship with the client (individual, group, community)—guided psychosocial intervention processes of change based on social work values and knowledge in a specific situation relevant to the client. The change that begins to occur as the result of this skilled intervention is based on the strengths and capacities of the client.[37] This would seem to point to a consideration of how to enable the client to use these strengths and capacities not only in the helping situation but in other areas of human functioning.

Social work does not have one skill but a wide variety of skills useful for many different situations. It would seem appropriate to use the term *skills* for the action component of practice and to use the term *skillful* in discussing the competent manner in which skills are used.

Several attempts have been made to identify the core, base, or basic skills needed by all social workers. Betty Baer and Ronald Federico have organized the skills component of practice into four areas: (1) information gathering and assessment; (2) the development and use of the professional self; (3) practice activities with individuals, groups, and communities; and (4) evaluation. They listed the needed skill cluster in each of these areas and translated these skills into ten competencies.[38] Included in these competencies are skills in working with and on behalf of oppressed and disadvantaged populations. This requires an appreciation for and valuing of diversity and an ability to see strengths in those who are different. Given the amount of prejudice in our society, it takes a great deal of skill to overcome the barriers among various groups. This includes skill at recognizing barriers within ourselves as well as those our clients may bring with them. It means being open and creative in building bridges and tolerating complexity rather than seeking simplicity. To do so social workers need to develop skills in self-awareness, empathy, and relationships, especially as these relate to race, culture, gender, age, sexual orientation, and disabilities. Based in part on this formulation as well as numerous other statements about the nature of social work practice, other formulations have been developed.[39]

The "Curriculum Policy Statement" of the Council on Social Work Education[40] provides the official statement of the skill level expected of baccalaureate- and master's-level social work graduates. This is a complex document, but two types of skills are called for (although it is impossible to completely separate them): cognitive skills and interactive or relationship skills. *Cognitive skills* are those used in thinking about persons in situations, in developing understanding about person and situation, in identifying the knowledge to be used, in planning for intervention, and in performing evaluation. *Interactive skills* are those used in working jointly with individuals, groups, families, organizations, and communities; in communicating and developing understanding; in joint planning; and in carrying out the plans of action. A social worker must be proficient in both types of skills.

Skillfulness develops over time as a result of practice in the use of the various techniques and methodologies. The development of skillfulness involves not only the application of knowledge and the operationalization of values but also the use of the worker's individual attributes and the development of a personal style of work. A useful analogy in understanding the development of skillfulness (and thus competence and personal style) is the musician. Musicians develop their skills and competence only after long hours of practice, practice that starts with learning such simple basics as fingering, note reading, and time concepts and then progresses to more and more complex techniques and music. The musician's personal style develops in the interpretation of the music. Similarly, it is only as the social worker learns to blend the cognitive and interactive skills that skillfulness develops.

Case Example

The skills a worker might use in working with older persons are many and varied. Certainly all situations will call for assessment skills, problem-solving skills, skill in identifying strengths in the person and her ecosystem, planning skills, and relationship skills. Different situations may call for skill in working with the individual older person or with a group of older persons, with a family group or with a community group on behalf of older persons, as well as working to develop services for older adults. Some older persons work best through use of activity, such as storytelling or painting to express their feelings and thinking; others may be in crisis; some may need support. The worker will choose which skills to apply in each situation depending on the needs, the resources, and the client's desires.

Creative Blending of Knowledge, Values, and Skills

The ability to combine appropriately and creatively the elements of knowledge, values, and skills in the helping situation is indeed an important characteristic of the social worker. This characteristic calls not only for choosing and applying appropriate knowledge, values, and skills but for blending the three elements in such a manner that they fit together and become a helping endeavor that is a consistent whole. This ability involves more than the blending of knowledge, values, and skills; it involves identifying and choosing appropriate, often unrelated bits of knowledge and using not only social work values but also those of the client and the agency in order to screen the knowledge tentatively chosen for use. It involves skillful application of the knowledge and interactional skill to the situation. Because each person in a situation and each need for help is different, the knowledge, values, and skills to be used are also different. There can be no cookbooks, no standardized procedures that must be adhered to in great detail, though there can be generalized ways of approaching persons in situations. The application of knowledge, values, and skills can be approached only from a creative stance.

The creative stance is often expressed as the *art of social work* as opposed to the *science of social work.* This art is based on hunches and intuition, on previous experience, on very personal attributes of workers that are difficult if not impossible to identify. It is the social worker encountering the knowledge, values, and skills elements and choosing and applying them that makes the helping endeavor indeed a unique work of art. Beulah Compton and Burt Galaway have described this art as having an emphasis on feeling, an empathic quality, and a high degree of subjectivity and of self-consciousness. This art allows for the creation of new vistas and new perspectives.[41] It should be the essence of each worker's individual style.

Much of Lydia Rapoport's description of creativity is useful for understanding the blending of knowledge, values, and skills. She identifies qualities that creative people possess. These include a kind of nonconformity in opinion and judgment; high motivation and persistence in task performance; openness and receptivity to new information and ideas; a liking for complexity; a high tolerance for ambiguities; a capacity not to seek premature closure; a tolerance for contradiction, obscurity, and conflict; not too deep a commitment to particular theoretical positions; and thorough familiarity with, and knowledge of, all aspects of the problem.[42]

The blending of the ecosystems and strengths perspectives with problem solving to form a change process greatly enhances the social worker's ability to be creative and allows her to organize the complex array of knowledge into a cohesive whole. This approach calls for moving from understanding needs to identifying assets, abilities, and capacities of all of the systems involved in the situation. The worker needs to be open and creative when doing this. She then uses her creativity to assist the client in developing a plan based on his strengths and those of the ecosystem. This perspective avoids the view that the individual is the "carrier of the problem" and must change if the situation is to be resolved. The ecosystems strengths perspective expands the focus to all the systems involved in the person's life and looks for assets, abilities, and capacities in the systems and the individual. While expanding the focus may initially seem overwhelming, the ecosystems approach is a way of organizing one's understanding of the various systems involved. Enlarging the possible resources available for growth and change brings creativity to the social work endeavor. This perspective also respects the client's ability to control his own life and recognizes that people have the capacity to function well in most areas of their lives even though they may have unmet needs in some areas.

Rollo May has said that creativity is the "encounter of the intensively conscious human being with his world"[43] and that it "occurs in an act of encounter and is to be understood with this encounter as its center."[44]

The science and art aspects of social work, rather than being in conflict with one another, are complementary. As science and art are blended creatively in the use of knowledge, values, and skills, the essence of professional social work is expressed.

Case Example

Mrs. Abbott, an eighty-six-year-old woman, has been admitted as a resident to the Sunnyside Assisted Living Facility. She is recovering from a broken hip and displays some confusion. Her family and doctor have decided that she can no longer live alone and needs assistance and care the family cannot provide. The social worker is responsible for helping Mrs. Abbott become comfortable in her new situation and for developing the psychosocial aspect of her care plan. To do this, the social worker will draw on knowl-

(continued)

Case Example   Continued

edge, values, and skills to develop a relationship with Mrs. Abbott and an understanding of her needs.

First, the social worker will look to knowledge of human behavior with particular concern about knowledge of older individuals. The worker knows that potential sources of strength in older individuals includes their ways of coping with change; the ways they relate to other persons, including family members and friends; and how they are functioning in dealing with the psychosocial tasks of aging. The worker will need to determine Mrs. Abbott's coping patterns, values, and skills; the nature of her interpersonal relationships; and her psychosocial development status.

The worker will also look to understandings about crisis and particularly the crisis of needing to leave a home and familiar surroundings. This yields the knowledge that older persons may become confused in new situations. When moving to a new living situation, they need support and help in finding their place. In Mrs. Abbott's situation she is also faced with limited mobility because of the broken hip, which adds to the crisis of change. This knowledge not only gives some understanding about Mrs. Abbott's behavior, it also informs the worker about the way to work with her. Knowledge about crisis intervention says that the worker needs to be actively involved with the client as quickly as possible after the onset of the crisis and that the client needs to know that someone cares about her.

The worker also knows from experience in working with older persons adjusting to the same basic situation that certain tasks need to be accomplished. Mrs. Abbott needs to know what the routine of the home will be and what will be expected of her. She needs to know who will be taking care of her and what resources and activities will be available to her. Mrs. Abbott needs to maintain her relationships with family and friends, and the family may also need help in this new situation in order to maintain their relationships. The worker knows how Sunnyside Assisted Living Facility functions and what resources it offers its residents. The worker also knows from experience that it is best not to try to gather too much information for the social history in one interview. Several short interviews are usually preferable to develop the plan.

The worker applies a social work value base in the work with Mrs. Abbott. It is important that Mrs. Abbott feel that she is still able to make choices about her life, that she maintain as much self-determination as possible. Ways in which this can be done include giving Mrs. Abbott the choice of which of her personal belongings can be brought from her home to have in her room and by allowing her a choice of which activities she will take part in from the total program available to Sunnyside residents.

The worker will recognize Mrs. Abbott's worth and dignity in the way in which past experiences and present feelings are discussed with her. These discussions will take place in a quiet, private area so that confidentiality can be preserved. The worker will strive to understand Mrs. Abbott's feelings and behavior rather than make judgments of "good" and "bad" and rather than plan for Mrs. Abbott before sufficient understanding is gained.

The worker will use skill in relating to Mrs. Abbott so that she will feel comfortable in expressing concerns and feelings. As information is gathered, the worker will skillfully develop a social history that will yield the understanding needed for planning. The worker will use skill in involving Mrs. Abbott and her family in the planning process. The worker will present the psychosocial plan to staff in such a way that they can become a part of the integrated care plan.

The preceding example provides only a portion of the knowledge, values, and skills needed by a social worker in this situation. It does, however, depict the creative blending of knowledge, values, and skills needed in carrying out the task of the social worker in meeting the needs of a client.

Summary

Knowledge, values, and skills are all used in the social work endeavor. Knowledge is that part of reality that is confirmable. The knowledge base of the social worker is complex, being partly borrowed from other disciplines. It explains the functioning of persons and social situations. It also directs the response to need. Values are what is preferred or can be considered as a guide for behavior. Values that concern social work are those of the client, the social worker, the profession, as well as the general cultural and societal values of the situation. These values can conflict with one another; in fact, a value system usually has conflicting parts. Social work values contain preferred conceptions of persons, preferred outcomes for persons, and preferred instrumentalities for dealing with persons. The NASW *Code of Ethics* expresses what ought to be done in professional practice. Skill brings knowledge and values together and converts them into action. Skills must be developed through use over time. Social workers should have a variety of skills for use in practice. Choices are made as to which knowledge, values, and skills are applied in each practice situation. The bringing together of these elements calls for creative blending. This creativity is the art of social work.

QUESTIONS

1. Identify the knowledge you now have that you believe may be helpful to you as a social worker. How did you attain that knowledge? Identify knowledge you believe you should gain at this time.

2. What values do you hold about people and their relationship to each other? Do these values seem congruent with social work values and with its code of ethics? How will your values affect the manner in which you work with clients?

3. How are your values congruent or incongruent with societal values as you understand them? How do you deal with situations in which your values and societal values are different?

4. What is the usual manner in which you develop skills in your daily living? How can you use this method in learning social work skills?

5. Discuss the concept of "creativity" as it is used in meeting clients' needs.

SUGGESTED READINGS

Abramson, Marcia. "Keeping Secrets: Social Workers and AIDS." *Social Work* 35 (March 1990): 169–173.

———. "Reflections on Knowing Oneself Ethically: Toward a Working Framework for Social Work Practice." *Families in Society* 77 (April 1996): 195–202.

Canda, E. R. "Conceptualizing Spirituality for Social Work: Insights from Diverse Perspectives." *Social Thought* 14 (1988): 30–46.

Congress, Elaine. *Social Work Values and Ethics: Identifying and Resolving Ethical Dilemmas.* Chicago: Nelson Hall, 1999.

Davidson, Jeanette R., and Davidson, Tim. "Confidentiality and Managed Care: Ethical and Legal Concerns." *Health and Social Work* 21 (August 1996): 208–215.

DeRoos, Yosikazu S. "Development of Practice Wisdom Through Human Problem Solving Processes." *Social Service Review* 64 (June 1990): 276–287.

Dickson, Donald T. *Confidentiality and Privacy in Social Work: A Guide to the Law for Practioners and Students.* New York: Free Press, 1998.

Gelfand, Bernard. *The Creative Practitioner: Creative Theory and Method for the Helping Services.* New York: Haworth Press, 1988 (Chapter 2).

Gelman, Sheldon. "Risk Management through Client Access to Case Records." *Social Work* 37 (January 1992): 73–99.

Gelman, Sheldon R., Pollack, Daniel, and Weiner, Adele. "Confidentiality of Social Work Records in the Computer Age." *Social Work* 44 (May 1999).

Goldstein, Howard. "The Knowledge Base of Social Work Practice: Theory, Wisdom, Analogue, or Art." *Families in Society: The Journal of Contemporary Human Services* 71 (January 1990): 3–12.

———. "The Neglected Moral Link in Social Work Practice." *Social Work* 32 (May–June 1987): 181–186.

Hartman, Ann. "Many Ways of Knowing." *Social Work* 35 (January 1990): 3–4.

Klein, Waldo C., and Bloom, Martin. "Practice Wisdom." *Social Work* 40 (November 1995): 799–807.

Kopels, Sandra, and Kagle, Jill D. "Do Social Workers Have a Duty to Warn?" *Social Service Review* 67 (March 1993): 101–126.

Linzer, Norman. *Resolving Ethical Dilemmas in Social Work.* Boston: Allyn and Bacon, 1999.

Lowenberg, Frank M. *Ethical Decisions for Social Work Practice.* Itasca, IL: F. E. Peacock, 1992.

Middleman, Ruth R., and Wood, Gale Goldberg. "Seeing/Believing/Seeing: Perception-Correcting and Cognitive Skills." *Social Work* 36 (May 1991): 243–246.

Morales, Armando, and Sheafor, Bradford W. *Social Work: A Profession of Many Faces,* 8th ed. Boston: Allyn and Bacon, 1998 (Chapters 7 and 8).

Peile, Colin. "Determinism versus Creativity: Which Way for Social Work?" *Social Work* 38 (March 1993): 127–134.

Proctor, Enola K., and Davis, Larry E. "The Challenge of Racial Difference: Skills for Clinical Practice." *Social Work* 39 (May 1994): 314–323.

Reamer, Frederic G. *Ethical Dilemmas in Social Service,* 2nd ed. New York: Columbia University Press, 1990.

———. "AIDS, Social Work, and the 'Duty to Protect.'" *Social Work* 36 (January 1991): 56–60.

———. "AIDS and Social Work: The Ethics and Civil Liberties Agenda." *Social Work* 38 (July 1993): 412–419.

———. *The Foundations of Social Work Knowledge.* New York: Columbia University Press, 1994.

———. *Ethical Standards in Social Work: A Critical Review of the NASW Code of Ethics.* Washington, DC: NASW Press, 1998.

———. *Social Work Values and Ethics,* 2nd ed. New York: Columbia University Press, 1999.

Rhodes, Margaret. "Gilligan's Theory of Moral Development as Applied to Social Work." *Social Work* 30 (March–April 1985): 101–113.

Robison, Wade L. *Ethical Decision Making in Social Work.* Boston: Allyn and Bacon, 2000.

Rock, Barry, and Congress, Elaine. "The New Confidentiality for the 21st Century in a Managed Care Environment." *Social Work* 44 (May 1999).

Scott, Dorothy. "Practice Wisdom: The Neglected Source of Practice Research." *Social Work* 35 (November 1990): 364–368.

Sheafor, Bradford W., Horejsi, Charles R., and Horejsi, Gloria A. *Techniques and Guidelines for Social Work Practice,* 5th ed. Boston: Allyn and Bacon, 2000 (Chapters 1, 2, and 3).

Shulman, Lawrence. "Developing and Testing a Practice Theory: An Interactional Perspective." *Social Work* 38 (January 1993): 91–97.

Siegel, Lorraine. "Cultural Differences and Their Impact on Practice in Child Welfare." *Journal of Multicultural Social Work* 3, 3 (1994): 87–96.

Siporin, Max. "Clinical Social Work as an Art Form." *Social Casework* 69 (March 1988): 177–183.

Torczyner, Jim. "Discretion, Judgment, and Informed Consent: Ethical and Practice Issues in Social Action." *Social Work* 36 (March 1991): 122–128.

Weick, Ann, and Pope, Loren. "Knowing What's Best: A New Look at Self-Determination." *Social Casework* 69 (January 1988): 10–16.

Wells, Carolyn Cressy, and Masch, M. Kathleen. *Social Work Ethics Today: Guidelines for Professional Practice.* Prospect Heights, IL: Waveland Press, 1991.

Wetzel, Janice W. "A Feminist World View Conceptual Framework." *Social Casework* 67 (March 1986): 166–173.

Witkin, Stanley L., and Gottschulk, Shimon. "Alternative Criteria for Theory Evaluation." *Social Service Review* 62 (June 1988): 211–224.

Yu, Muriel M., and O'Neal, Brenda. "Issues of Confidentiality When Working with Persons with Aids." *Clinical Social Work Journal* 20 (Winter 1992): 421–443.

Ziefert, Marjorie, and Brown, Karen. "Skill Building for Effective Intervention with Homeless Families." *Families in Society* 72 (April 1991): 213–219.

NOTES

1. Harriett M. Bartlett, "Toward Clarification and Improvement of Social Work Practice," *Social Work* 3 (April 1958): 3–9.

2. Harriett M. Bartlett, *The Common Base of Social Work Practice* (New York: National Association of Social Workers, 1970); William E. Gordon, "A Critique of the Working Definition," *Social Work* 7 (October 1962): 12; and idem, "Knowledge and Value: Their Distinction and Relationship in Clarifying Social Work Practice," *Social Work* 10 (July 1965): 32–35.

3. For another early formulation of this perspective, see Werner W. Boehm, "The Nature of Social Work," *Social Work* 3 (April 1958): 10–18.

4. Bartlett, *The Common Base,* chap. 5.

5. William E. Gordon, "Notes on the Nature of Knowledge," in *Building Social Work Knowledge* (New York: National Association of Social Workers, 1964), p. 70.

6. Max Siporin, *Introduction to Social Work Practice* (New York: Macmillan, 1975), p. 363.

7. Paul Davidson Reynolds, *A Primer in Theory Construction* (Indianapolis, IN: Bobbs Merrill, 1975), p. 4.

8. Ibid.

9. Ibid., p. 18.

10. Peter Berger and Thomas Luckmann, *The Social Construction of Reality* (New York: Doubleday, 1967).

11. For examples of this, see William J. Reed, "Task-Centered Approach," in *Encyclopedia of Social Work,* 18th ed., Anne Minahan, Ed. (Silver Springs, MD: National Association of Social Workers, 1987), pp. 757–765; Scott Briar, "Incorporating Research into Education for Clinical Practice in Social Work: Toward a Clinical Science in Social Work," in *Sourcebook on Research Utilization,* Allen Rubin and Aaron Rosenblatt, Eds. (New York: Council on Social Work Education, 1979); and Martin Bloom, *The Paradox of Helping: An Introduction to the Philosophy of Scientific Practice* (New York: John Wiley, 1975).

12. Howard Goldstein, "The Knowledge Base of Social Work Practice: Theory, Wisdom, Analogue, or Art?" *Families in Society* 71 (January 1990): 41.

13. Ibid., pp. 38–41. Included as humanistic alternatives are Narrative Theory, Social Constructionism, Cognitive Theory, Moral Theory, Faith and Spirituality, and Feminist Theory.

14. Based on material in Alfred Kadushin, "The Knowledge Base of Social Work," in *Issues in American Social Work,* Alfred J. Kahn, Ed. (New York: Columbia University Press, 1959), pp. 67 ff.

15. Note Berger and Luckmann, *Social Construction of Reality,* and Gordon, "Knowledge and Value."

16. Goldstein, "The Knowledge Base," p. 41.

17. For another formulation of the knowledge base, see Betty L. Baer and Ronald Federico, *Education of the Baccalaureate Social Worker: Report of the Undergraduate Curriculum Project* (Cambridge, MA: Ballinger, 1978), pp. 75–78.

18. Muriel W. Pumphrey, *The Teaching of Values and Ethics in Social Work Education,* vol. 13 of the Curriculum Study Council on Social Work Education (New York, 1959), p. 23.

19. Herbert Aptekar, "The Values, Functions and Methods of Social Work in an Integrated Report of the Honolulu Seminar," in *An Intercultural Exploration: Universals and Differences in Social Work Values, Functions, and Practice* (New York: Council on Social Work Education, 1967), pp. 3–59.

20. Lewis Raths, Merrill Harmin, and Sidney B. Simon, *Values and Teaching* (Columbus, OH: Charles E. Merrill, 1966).

21. Milton Rokeach, *The Nature of Human Values* (New York: Free Press, 1973), p. 5.

22. From Robin Williams, *American Society: A Sociological Interpretation,* 2nd ed. (New York: Alfred A. Knopf, 1967), as discussed in Charles S. Prigmore and Charles R. Atherton, *Social Welfare Policy: Analysis and Formulation* (Lexington, MA: D.C. Heath, 1979), chap. 2.

23. Alan Keith-Lucas, *Giving and Taking Help* (Chapel Hill: University of North Carolina Press, 1972), chap. 8.

24. Gordon, "A Critique of the Working Definition," p. 7.

25. Aptekar, "Values, Functions, and Methods of Social Work," p. 17.

26. Charles S. Levy, "The Value Base of Social Work," *Journal for Education for Social Work* 9 (Winter 1973): 34–42.

27. Armando Morales and Bradford W. Sheafor, *Social Work: A Profession of Many Faces,* 4th ed. (Boston: Allyn and Bacon, 1987), pp. 205–207.

28. Werner Boehm, "The Nature of Social Work," *Social Work* 3 (April 1958): 10–18.

29. For a discussion of balance, see Mary McCormick, "The Role of Values in Social Functioning," *Social Casework* 42 (February 1961): 70–78.

30. Henry Miller, "Value Dilemmas in Social Casework," *Social Work* 13 (January 1968): 27–33.

31. Keith-Lucas, *Giving and Taking Help.*

32. Roland Warren, *Truth, Love and Social Change* (Chicago: Rand McNally, 1971), pp. 273–299.

33. For further discussion, see Frederick G. Reamer, "AIDS, Social Work, and the 'Duty to Protect,'" *Social Work* 36 (January 1991): 56–60; Marcia Abramson, "Keeping Secrets: Social Workers and AIDS," *Social Work* 35 (March 1990): 169–173; and Sandra Kopels and Jill Doner Kagle, "Do Social Workers Have a Duty to Warn?" *Social Service Review* 67 (March 1993): 101–126.

34. George Theodorson and Achilles Theodorson, *A Modern Dictionary of Sociology* (New York: Crowell, 1969), p. 382.

35. Bartlett, *The Common Base,* pp. 80–83.

36. Morales and Sheafor, *Social Work,* chap. 9.

37. Ibid., p. 140.

38. Baer and Federico, *Education of the Baccalaureate Social Worker,* chap. 9.

39. One of the more important statements of social work functions and tasks is found in Allen Pincus and Anne Minahan, *Social Work Practice: Model and Method* (Itasca, IL: F. E. Peacock, 1973), chap. 1.

40. Found in *Handbook of Accreditation Standards and Procedures,* 4th ed. (Washington, DC: Council on Social Work Education, 1994), pp. 96–104, 134–144.

41. Beulah Roberts Compton and Burt Galaway, *Social Work Process* (Homewood, IL: Dorsey Press, 1979), p. 28.

42. Lydia Rapoport, "Creativity in Social Work," in *Creativity in Social Work: Selected Writing of Lydia Rapoport,* Sanford N. Katz, Ed. (Philadelphia: Temple University Press, 1975), pp. 3–25.

43. Rollo May, *The Courage to Create* (New York: W. W. Norton, 1975), p. 51.

44. Ibid., p. 77.

4 Social Work as a Process of Facilitating Growth and Change

LEARNING EXPECTATIONS

1. Knowledge of the nature of the process of growth and change.
2. Understanding of how the change process is used in social work.
3. Understanding of the contributions of the ecosystems strengths perspective to the helping process.

The fourth approach to describing generalist social work practice is as a process of facilitating growth and change, one of the "hows" of social work practice. It is one of the ways of approaching concern and need and of organizing and applying knowledge, values, and skills. It is an organized way of thinking about assessment, the person in situation, relationship, process, and intervention.

In many ways this chapter is an introduction to Part Three of this book, in which the change process is considered in much more depth. This chapter is placed in Part One to give the reader a sense of the overall process in relationship to the other perspectives considered in this part. It prepares the reader to consider Part Two, "The Interactional Process," as embedded in the change process.

As social work searched for its commonalities in the 1960s, problem solving was one of the concepts found in casework, group work, and community organization. Helen Harris Perlman, in *Social Casework: A Problem-Solving Process*, states: "The casework process is a problem-solving process in that it employs the orderly, systematic methods which are basic to any effective thinking and feeling toward action."[1]

Murray Ross, in *Community Organization: Theory, Principles, and Practice*, discusses the planning process as a key concept in his formulation of community organization.[2] As one examines Ross's formulation, it is evident that the planning process is indeed an adaptation of the classic problem-solving process. Helen

Northen, in *Social Work with Groups,* discusses the problem-solving theme in group work.[3] Wide applicability and its use by the diverse parts of the profession seeking unification caused problem solving to become one of the earliest identified commonalities of social work practice. It also became an important concept in developing integrative or generalist practice theory.[4]

Problem solving, of course, is not unique to social work but is an important approach to human need in many helping endeavors. The **problem-solving process** is the scientific process, being a means of addressing the science component of social work practice as contrasted with the creative process, or art, of social work (see Chapter 3). The scientific process in one of its many formulations is used almost universally by scholars from all disciplines as they seek to develop new understandings of the material they study, to conduct or set up formal research studies, or to answer questions in their discipline.

Two emerging social work approaches—the strengths and the ecosystems perspectives—have added important dimensions to the change process that create a positive, comprehensive approach to meeting needs. In the current formulation of the strengths perspective, the problem is given little attention and the focus is on the overall goals and aspirations of the client. The ecosystems perspective offers a way to organize and understand the environment and the transactional nature of person in environment. In this text, the strengths and ecosystems perspectives are blended with the traditional problem-solving process to form an ecosystems strengths approach to change. This approach views problem solving as meeting needs in a way that facilitates natural growth and change in the person and the environment. It sees the social work endeavor as aimed at identifying and utilizing the assets that are available in the person and the environment to bring about change that fits with what the client desires and the reality of his situation.

The ecological and the strengths perspectives have a health-based orientation. Both see growth and change as a natural part of human development over time and consider healthy functioning as a goal and as a reality for most areas of the client's life. It is not necessary to change everything about the person or the situation, only the area in which need is not being met. In general, people are able to meet the majority of their needs in socially accepted ways. Blending these two approaches into assessment, planning, implementation, and evaluation allows the worker and the client to build on environmental and personal strengths in discovering ways to meet unmet needs.

Blending an Ecosystems Strengths Approach with the Problem-Solving Process

Even though problems and participation in the problem-solving process are a normal part of life for everyone (as individuals and as members of families, small groups, organizations, and communities), there is increasing concern that a focus on problems highlights deficits while devaluing the strengths of the systems involved. This concern has led to new ways of viewing the problem-solving process.

In the field of organizational development, for example, David Cooperrider and Suresh Srivasta have developed the concept of "appreciative inquiry" as an alternative to traditional problem solving in organizational development. This affirmative approach to change begins with valuing those aspects of the organizational system that work well and proceeds to develop collaborative dialogue in exploring possibilities and directions for further development and growth.[5]

In social work, the concern with focusing on the problem is related to the tendency, even on the part of the professional social worker, to blame the victim.[6] This process identifies the ways in which the victim of a social problem differs from those who do not experience the problem and then suggests that these differences help make that person a victim of social problems. In this process there is a tendency to ignore environmental factors responsible for social problems and to also ignore the strengths that have enabled individuals to survive in oppressive environments. Ultimately, there is a concern that a focus on problems may lead to labeling the client as the problem.[7]

The social work response to these concerns is the **strengths perspective.** This perspective refocuses the traditional problem-solving process by emphasizing the involvement of the client in a solution-focused process that builds on client strengths. This perspective respects the uniqueness and strengths of the client, collaborates with the client in the helping process, recognizes the resources and possibilities within the environment, and supports people's inherent capacities for growth and well-being. Instead of viewing clients as victims of circumstances beyond their control, the strengths perspective focuses on "the client's values, hopes, and desired goals."[8]

Even within the strengths perspective, there is an acknowledgment of the realities of the problems often faced by clients—for example, schizophrenia, child sexual abuse, cancer, violence.[9] In accepting the realities of such problems, the strengths perspective refuses to view psychopathology, especially as expressed in diagnostically oriented assessments, as the major focus in the lives of clients. Instead, this perspective points out that the strengths of clients have allowed them to survive and perhaps thrive in the face of adversity and encourages maximal involvement of clients in focusing on the possibilities for "choice, control, commitment and personal development."[10]

Interventions based on most theories from psychology or psychiatry overemphasize the psychological aspects of behavior and have led to interpreting the client's situation in terms of symptoms that represent pathology or disease. This leads to seeking to discover deep-seated causes within the person and then treating him to "cure" the problem. Traditional problem-solving processes used in social work risk considering the client in a similar way by first looking at what is wrong. This makes it difficult to transition from problem to solution. The approach being used in this text defines the **problem** in terms of need. The strengths perspective considers meeting needs as a normal part of everyone's life. It recognizes that people are able to meet their needs in most areas of their lives. Instead of focusing on causes of unmet need, this perspective focuses on marshalling talents and resources to reach goals that will meet needs.

The strengths perspective avoids the hazard of "blaming the victim." By searching for abilities, capacities, and assets, the strengths perspective shifts attention away from finding deficits and limitations in the person and toward discovering the positive aspects of the person in environment. It attributes the problem to the person in situation rather than attributing the problem to the person alone. Adding the ecosystems perspective gives the worker a means of assessing the entire person in situation rather than limiting the assessment to the "person" side of the equation. This approach also opens up a vast array of possibilities that can contribute to meeting the needs of all involved.

When the worker interprets the situation as needing to fix something that is wrong, it gives the worker the status of expert in the helping process. This stance also carries with it the expectation that the worker will be able to bring about meaningful change in the life of the client. The reality is that only the client can do this. The real work must be done by the client, otherwise it either does not get done or the change is temporary. However, when the worker is able to combine forces with the client in a positive way, the momentum for change can be significant and long lasting. The ecosystems strengths approach is aimed at accomplishing long-term change.

In a deficit approach, the client is less likely to feel valued because the focus is on what is missing. This approach also raises doubt about his ability to exercise control over his own life. If the client is given the message that only he needs to change, rather than bringing about a change in the situation, his confidence in his ability to exercise self-determination is undermined. However, when the social worker works with the client to set goals that are consistent with his aspirations and to search for abilities, capacities, and resources in the client and his environment, the message is that the client is competent and that his environment has the resources to meet his needs. This instills hope, probably the most important commodity the worker has to offer in the helping process.

The ecosystems approach sees need as arising out of an imbalance or incongruity in the transactions among systems. The person in environment is viewed as a system of systems in which the client and his natural environment are all a part of one ecosystem. The social worker and the client work together to identify the transactions that are out of balance. Using a strengths approach, they seek to rebalance the transactions based on the abilities, capacities, and resources available within both the client and the environment. The knowledge, values, and skills of social work, along with the strengths and resources within the client and the client's environment, are used in understanding the situation and in identifying possible goals.

Contributions from the strengths perspective can become an integral part of the problem-solving process used in social work practice when (1) the focus of the helping process is on the unique individual or client system involved and on the possibilities for positive growth and change, rather than on the identified problem; (2) the strengths and competencies of the client system are respected and valued by the social worker and utilized as a major resource in the helping process; and (3) the client is involved in all phases of the helping process and is given maximum opportunity for self-determination in that process. Social workers who incorporate these principles in their work with client systems will discover that the problem-solving process is a useful tool to help the client reach the goals and objectives.

The Natural Process of Growth and Change

Social workers recognize that growth and change are a natural part of the life cycle. Needs and meeting needs are a constant part of life, and so are changes in needs and meeting needs. As pointed out earlier, our needs as infants are different from our needs as adults. At each stage of life there are some needs that remain constant, while there are others that change. At the same time, how we get our needs met frequently changes during the course of our life. In addition, the demands and needs that come from our environment also change. Needs tend to be common in global terms but are felt in a very unique and personal way by each individual. The challenge for the social worker is to be able to see the commonality of needs while empathizing with the uniqueness of felt need for each client.

Instead of seeing unmet need as a sign of unhealthy or retarded growth and development, the ecosystems strengths approach assumes that there is a natural drive toward growth and development of one's potential and that unmet needs are challenges to be faced in realizing that potential. In helping clients to meet needs, the social worker seeks to incorporate the work into the goals and aspirations of the client. Instead of trying to change the client to fit what the worker believes she should be or become, the worker brings out what the client wants to be or become. In this way change becomes part of natural growth and development. By tuning in to the drive toward growth and development as the client is experiencing it, the worker ensures that change becomes a part of the natural life cycle. The worker also is able to be sensitive to the cultural aspects of development experienced by the client instead of imposing his own expectations.

Incorporating meeting unmet needs into the process of growth and change means that the social worker takes on the role of facilitator rather than of "fixer" or problem solver. This approach gives the role of expert to the client when it comes to her own life. The worker is recognized as having knowledge and expertise or skills that can be used by the client to create a situation in which unmet needs are being met. The worker uses his knowledge and skill in reaching an understanding of person in environment or the ecosystem, in identifying strengths and resources in the ecosystem (which includes the client), in assisting the client in reaching a decision and developing and implementing a plan, and in evaluating the results of the endeavor.

For example, a neighbor calls the child protection agency because she is concerned that a young single mother leaves her four-month-old baby crying in her crib for long periods of time (thirty or more minutes). On talking to the mother, the social worker discovers the baby is indeed left to "cry it out." The worker also discovers that this mother has little understanding of how to care for a young baby. The child needs her mother to respond to her and the mother needs knowledge about childcare.

It is still uncertain if these are the only needs. Are there other factors—such as the personal needs of the mother, lack of material resources, or community expectations and attitudes—that might be blocks to meeting the child's needs?

Process

The term *process* also needs definition. In a social work context, Sal Hofstein states: "Process refers to the recurrent patterning of a sequence of change over time and in a particular direction."[11] It is important to note three qualities of this process: (1) occurring in recurrent patterning or stages, (2) taking place over time, and (3) moving in a particular direction. However, this description does not completely explain the nature of process, for there is also a cyclical aspect.

The change process involves making decisions and taking actions to carry out those decisions. In the process of doing this, adjustments are needed in order to successfully implement a decision. New information becomes available either about the situation or about the path taken to meet the unmet need. Sometimes new information results in changing the decision and/or the plan. Sometimes a more serious need is uncovered that requires more immediate attention. In any case, the process is rarely linear or step by step, but rather is cyclical in that the worker and the client return to earlier stages in order to make any adjustments that are needed.

In the example of the young mother who allows her small baby to "cry it out," the worker would use a change process to decide what should be done in the situation. First, information must be gathered. The worker would talk with the mother, examine the child, and perhaps talk to the neighbor or other concerned persons. He would seek to identify the strengths and competencies of the mother as well as the resources within the environment. He would determine which needs of the child were not being met and also determine whether the mother, with help, could meet those needs. Plans would be made with the mother about how best to meet the most immediate needs. As this plan is implemented, the worker would continue to gather information such as: What resources (personal, interpersonal, organizational, or societal) could best help this mother meet the needs of her child? What are her goals as a mother? What competencies does the mother have to enable her to carry out her part of the plan? What other needs exist in this situation? The result will be further explanation of the situation and more planning. The process will be carried out in an orderly yet cyclical manner, moving toward a goal of meeting the needs of the young child.

The Stages of the Change Process

It should certainly be recognized that all persons face perplexing situations and reach solutions in a variety of ways. However, the social work process is related to a highly organized and reliable manner of reaching solutions.

People in different disciplines have discussed the change process for various usages and have specified the steps in a variety of ways. The process for meeting needs that is presented in this text is an ecosystems strengths approach to change that includes steps in reaching a decision about change and in developing and carrying out a plan to implement the decision. The basic process is as follows:

1. Preliminary statement of the concern or need
2. Statement of preliminary assumptions about the nature of the concern or need
3. Statement of preliminary assumptions about potential strengths and resources in the ecosystem
4. Selection and collection of information
5. Analysis of information available
6. Development of a plan
7. Implementation of the plan
8. Evaluation of the plan

The change process is somewhat different from the overall social work process. Change is a part of the social work process, but the social work process is broader and contains work that is focused on developing and maintaining a relationship and on beginnings and endings. It should also be noted that at each step of the process creativity is an important ingredient. Looking at situations in new ways and examining many ideas and possible plans before reaching a decision and defining plans for action are two ways creativity is used in problem solving. Before discussing the social work process, each of the steps in the change process is examined more closely below.

1. *Preliminary statement of the concern or need*—A clear statement of the need is necessary before proceeding to subsequent steps. Often statements of need tend to be vague, global, and lacking in precision. This happens when the social worker fails to sufficiently examine a concern and to identify the nature of need or needs involved. For example, school dropouts or unwed mothers are often referred to as problems, but in this vague formulation nothing is said about the needs of individuals or other human systems, and nothing is indicated about how need fulfillment is being blocked. Furthermore, this perspective views the person as the problem, contrary to the belief of the professional social worker in the inherent worth and dignity of individuals and in their innate capacity and drive for change.

In this example, a more accurate formulation of the problem concerning unwed mothers might be: "Pregnant teenage girls in this community need support and educational resources in order to continue to progress in school during and after their pregnancy." In this statement, the individual and societal need is for education. The population having the need is clearly defined, not by a vague term *unwed mother* but by an age group in a particular situation, pregnant teenage girls. The need can be met by providing adequate educational resources. The manner in which the need is stated gives direction to all the stages that follow. Often the key to successful change lies in what is known as **reframing,** or stating the concern or need in a new way and from a different point of view. The social worker's skill in reframing can help the client view the problematic situation not as a personal deficit but as a result of the interaction of multiple systems within the environment. The more precise the statement and the more individualized the situation, the more relevant and salient can be the goals and desired solutions. Usually, as one proceeds to further steps, the need and opportunity for greater precision of the statement of need arises, and this step is returned to for restatement of the concern or need.

2. *Statement of preliminary assumptions about the nature of the concern or need*— This step is necessary to help make explicit the type of information needed for understanding, decision making, and planning. As the need is stated, implicit assumptions are made about its nature, which provide indications of the need in the situation and the block to need fulfillment. It is especially important at this stage to consider the client's views of the situation, including the challenges and obstacles perceived by the client. If the assumptions prove untrue, it usually leads to new assumptions. A return to an early step is called for, and new assumptions are made explicit so that direction can be established for the information to be sought.

Identifying the nature of the need helps to prioritize goals and focuses the change process so that it is effective and efficient. Knowledge of Maslow's hierarchy of needs helps to determine if the nature of the need involves a threat to life or well-being that would require more immediate attention or if the need involves an issue of quality of life that can be addressed after basic needs are met. The social worker should be cognizant of the need to be efficient and effective, especially in this era of limited resources and managed care. By focusing on the nature of the need, the worker and the client can move more quickly toward a successful resolution of the situation.

There are times when the nature of the need requires intervention beyond the professional preparation of the BSW social worker. When this is the case, then the worker should refer the client to someone who can assist him. Sometimes the worker remains involved to assist in meeting certain needs. Other times the client may need a comprehensive service from another agency that includes specialists who can meet his needs. For example, it is beyond the scope of generalist BSW practice to engage in therapy with clients who are experiencing a major mental health condition. If the condition requires therapy, then the worker should refer the client to an MSW who is able to engage in therapy. Treatment may also require the involvement of a psychiatrist. In some cases the responsibility of serving the client is assumed by the MSW and her agency. In other cases, the MSW may provide therapy while the BSW continues to provide services in other areas of need, such as assisting in setting up appointments, ensuring that basic needs are met, and the like. This process is case management, which is covered in more detail in Chapter 14.

3. *Statement of preliminary assumptions about potential strengths and resources in the ecosystem*—Identifying potential resources and strengths involves looking beyond the need and searching for a positive outcome to the situation. Dwelling on what is going wrong does very little to bring about change. In fact, it can interfere with the change process by discouraging the client and the worker and reducing the energy needed to rebalance the ecosystem. The quicker the process moves from identifying need to building a positive change process, the sooner the client will experience having her need met.

This step in the change process is very important to the steps that follow. In addition to moving the process from need to the resources available to meet the need, it also provides direction to the gathering of information necessary to reaching a decision and developing a plan. As the worker and the client look for strengths and resources in the whole ecosystem, areas for exploration begin to emerge. The assumptions that are made about potential strengths and resources provide direction for the information that is gathered in the next two steps of the change process. The worker and the client will gather and analyze information to determine if these assumptions are correct. If they are, then a plan can be developed that is based on them. If the assumptions are not supported by the information that is gathered, then new assumptions are developed for exploration.

4. *Selection and collection of information*—Determination of what is important to know about any specific situation is a skill. The identification of significant systems in a situation and of the need of each in relation to the other gives some indication of the information needed. Sources for information should include a variety of perspectives that may be chosen from historical, social-psychological, biological, economic, political, religious, and ethical understandings.

Both the facts of the situation itself and the meaning of it to those concerned are important. Information should test the validity of the preliminary assumptions regarding the nature of the need and potential strengths and resources. The information collected should be based on a breadth of knowledge and related to theory appropriate to the situation. The worker's preliminary understanding of the client's perspective, as well as the general knowledge base and value systems of the social work profession, are influential in determining information to be sought. The worker should explore the unique strengths and capacities of the client and the potential resources within the client's environment, along with those factors that appear to contribute to the problematic situation. Hence, the worker's capacity for perception of situations as they really are and his awareness of his own prejudices and values are very important.

Skill in the collection of information also calls for skill in communication and social interaction with those who are sources of the information. The validity of such information is determined in part by the nature of both the communication and the social interaction. Creativity should be used in determining information sources. The values of social work call for the client to be a primary source. There is a need to determine and accumulate relevant evidence about the situation. This evidence needs to be related to the salient features of the situation and to the presented concern or need and to the strengths and resources available in the ecosystem to meet the need.

Together, the worker and the client explore all areas of the ecosystem for strengths and resources. Some of these are within the client. Some will lie in various systems in the client's natural environment, such as family, neighbors, friends, relatives, church, school, and various community organizations with which the client interacts. A relationship with any of these systems that meets the needs of the client and members of the system is a strength that may be used directly or indirectly to meet the current need. Some potential strengths and resources can be found in what the worker brings to the process. These include his knowledge and skills along with resources of the agency and of the human service system in the community. Adding the ecosystems approach to the strengths approach makes the overall process much more comprehensive. It adds the vital ingredient of considering the environment not only as a target for change but also as a means of bringing about change. To the extent that strengths and resources can be found outside of the client, the potential for success in meeting needs is greatly increased.

5. *Analysis of information available*—Analysis of information is influenced and directed by the purpose for which the analysis is to be used. Some of these purposes are (1) identification and assessment of the various systems involved in the situation, (2) further definition and explanation of the nature of the need, (3) identification of additional information needed, and (4) identification and formulation of relevant policy.

Other purposes include (1) determination of feasible goals and possible outcomes, (2) determination of possible plans of action, (3) interpretation of the meaning of the information gathered, and (4) evaluation. The cyclical nature of the process becomes apparent, for one returns to analysis as an ingredient of each step of the process. The carrying out of the process generates new information. Additional information is often called for at each step.

The worker must be careful to avoid leaving the client out of this process. The client's view of the situation is much more likely to be accurate than the worker's because it is based on the client's own life. After all, the worker can never really know everything about the client and her situation. The process of building a trusting relationship with the client is a two-way street. As social workers we are asking the client to trust us. It is only fair that we trust our client. Besides, "reality" is more a matter of perception than of fact. Ultimately, the client will take what is offered in the social work endeavor and fit it to her perception of her situation. Therefore, the worker is better off knowing what this perception is and accepting it. Then the final outcome will more likely fit with the client's life as she lives it. The client should be recognized as being the expert when it comes to her own life. The strengths perspective calls for a belief that the client will perceive her situation more accurately than the worker can. Too often, professionals are skeptical of their client's perceptions. This tendency to disbelieve clients assumes that the worker is the expert and knows what is really going on and that the client is incapable of adequately describing or understanding her situation. This position is inconsistent with social work values, which call for us to treat people as valuable and worthwhile and respect their right to make their own decisions.

In analyzing the information available, the worker and the client consider the entire ecosystem, with a focus on the strengths and resources available. If other resources are needed, a means of locating or developing them should be included in the plan and the necessary information should be sought. Thus, it is necessary to continuously move back and forth between the steps of the change process.

There are general considerations in analysis, regardless of outcome desired. First, it is important to determine the nature of the information. Is it fact or opinion? How reliable is the source of the information? Does it agree or disagree with other information that has been gathered? Conclusions are only as reliable as the information on which they are based. Thus, conclusions remain tentative and additional information must be analyzed as the process proceeds.

The determination of salient parts and of the relationship of the various parts to each other and to the whole constitutes another important aspect of analysis. The human situation is complex in even a seemingly simple problem. Considerable skill is involved in determining what is important in any particular situation. As the human situation is seldom of a cause-effect or linear nature, a systematic approach to analysis is desirable. This is assessment in social work practice.

6. *Development of a plan*—Information and analysis provide a basis on which the worker can assist the client in reaching a decision about meeting the identified need. However, reaching a decision does not guarantee that it will be carried out. In the change process based on the ecosystems strengths approach, either a restoration of an old way of meeting the identified need takes place or a new way is found or the old way is combined with a new way. In any case, a plan is necessary to ensure that the decision will result in the need being met. Planning is a joint process involving worker and client and is based on the strengths and resources that were identified in the ecosystem during the assessment and that are relevant for the situation at hand. The plan should be feasible and should describe the desired state of affairs in specific, positive terms. The plan includes goals, objectives, and tasks that are designed to bring about the desired change. Goals and objectives are best stated in behavioral terms that describe a desired outcome in as specific a manner as possible. For example, a goal might be stated as "The family can discuss conflict and resolve it in a manner agreeable to all members" rather than "The family can get along better." Since the goal should be achievable, analysis of constraints and feasibility is called for.

Plans develop from a consideration of a variety of possible strategies and techniques. As a plan becomes more specific, the social worker will return to early steps in the process to gather and analyze new information needed for the specifics of planning. Consideration of a variety of plans is important in creative planning. Each plan should be evaluated for possible outcomes, not only in terms of goal fulfillment but also in terms of other possible implications for the functioning of the systems involved. The final plan is typically a synthesis of several of the possibilities. The worker uses creativity in developing the synthesis and evaluative strategy.

7. *Implementation of the plan*—In social work, implementation involves interaction between people and is interventive in nature. It is action based on thinking that has its source in feelings about concern or need. In addition, it is action based on substantial knowledge from many sources that explain and predict behavior of people in the situation.

8. *Evaluation of the plan*—This step may result in redefinition of the need, expanded information gathering and analysis, or reformulation of the plan. If the goal has been reached, evaluation is an appropriate and necessary climax to the process. Regardless of the outcome of the plan, evaluation of what happened can lead to an understanding that can be transferred to other situations and to more effective problem solving in those situations.

Case Example

1. *Preliminary statement of the need:* The child needs adequate care to meet her needs.

2. *Preliminary assumptions about the needs of the mother and child:* (a) The mother needs to know how to care for the child. (b) The mother has needs of her own that are not being met. (c) The mother needs sufficient income or access to other essential resources within her environment to meet the child's needs. (d) There are cultural differences between the mother and concerned others in specifying what constitutes adequate childcare.

3. *Preliminary assumptions about potential strengths and resources:* (a) The mother is able to meet her own needs and those of her infant the majority of the time. She has shown resilience and creativity in struggling with the challenges of being a young, single parent. The mother desires to be a good mother and is able to meet her infant's needs if provided with adequate knowledge about how to do so along with the necessary resources. (b) If the mother has her needs met, then she will have the capacity to respond more appropriately to her infant's needs and will do so. (c) There are sufficient resources available in her natural environment or through the worker and community organizations to meet the mother's needs for sufficient income and other resources necessary to meet her infant's needs. (d) The mother's culture has values and norms that are appropriate for adequate child-rearing.

4. *Brief summary of the available information:* The social worker now proceeds to check out the validity of each of these assumptions. He finds that not only does the mother not know how to care for the child but also that she is frustrated by "being cooped up" all the time with no social outlets. She does love the baby and wants to care for it. Her own mother died when she was very young, and her grandmother, now dead, raised her. The worker finds that the mother is on Temporary Assistance to Needy Families (TANF). The neighbor reporting the situation is truly concerned for both the child and the mother but does not know how to help them. She is afraid of interfering. The mother is of mixed European descent and has a strong cultural support for positive child-rearing but limited access to family and friends who can help her with her child.

5. *Brief analysis of the available information:* In discussing the information that has been gathered, the worker finds that this mother is motivated to give proper care to the baby. She needs instruction in childcare. Some provision is needed for time away from the baby so the mother can socialize with friends. Budgeting help is needed. The mother's relationship with the neighbor needs to be explored (and more information gathered about that). It may prove to be an important resource in this situation. The major need does seem to be more knowledge about childcare. A secondary need is the mother's need for meaningful relationships with others. Regulations that place limits on her continuing eligibility for TANF will eventually require the mother's participation in the work force and may pose additional problems. However, the opportunity to receive more education or training and to develop a skill or trade along with receiving assistance for childcare might be used to assist the mother in becoming more financially independent in the future.

6. *Decision making, planning, implementation, and evaluation:* The worker and client work together in developing a plan. First, the worker suggests a homemaker or public health nurse to provide childcare instruction. He also investigates the young mothers' club at a nearby community center (gathering and analyzing information), and the client agrees that this group would be appropriate in this situation. The group provides an opportunity for young single mothers to receive instruction in childcare and discuss the issues involved; childcare is provided during the meetings. This group is chosen because it meets not only the instructional need but also to some extent the socialization need. The worker helps the mother and neighbor recognize that they can be of help to each other. The neighbor is older and cannot do heavy chores. The mother is willing to do these in return for babysitting one night a week. As the neighbor has come to understand the situation, she has been able to give the mother suggestions and provide support and companionship. The mother says the neighbor is good to her like her grandmother was. The plan also includes the worker continuing to see the mother once a week for a three-month period to coordinate services, help with budgeting, and provide support. The neighbor will be involved in these meetings once a month to clarify any concerns. At the end of three months, the situation will be evaluated to see if further help is needed.

Social Work Practice and the Change Process

The outstanding characteristic of the change process in social work practice is the inclusion of the client as much as possible in the work at each step of the process. The client expresses the need or concern. The client also furnishes much of the information needed in the process, validates information sought from other sources, makes a decision, participates in developing the plan of action and in implementing and evaluating it, and develops problem-solving skills to use in coping with other life situations. Most important, it is the client's unique strengths and competencies that have enabled the client to have her needs met and that can be mobilized to meet both present and future needs.

Social work practice includes the change process but also involves much more. The change process is part of the cognitive aspect of practice, but there are also other aspects that are essential to good practice. These include the ability to interact with a variety of different people and systems. This will be the focus in Part Two of this text. The worker must establish a working relationship with his client and with people involved in the situation along with those who are needed to provide resources to meet needs. There are often obstacles to doing this, especially those associated with such diversity factors as race, gender, ethnicity, age, or sexual orientation. Other barriers might be the fact that the client has been coerced into meeting with the social worker. This may result from a referral from another organization, such as a court or protective services, or from a member of the client's family environment, such as a parent or spouse. Establishing a working relationship requires skills in communication, listening, empathy, and establishing trust.

If the worker is able to establish enough of a relationship to obtain an initial assessment of the situation and the needs or concern, then a decision must be made as to whether the work will continue. Sometimes the client may need to be referred to another agency that is better suited to her needs. Sometimes the match between client and worker is not right (perhaps as a result of one or more of the diversity factors identified above). If differences cannot be resolved, then the client may need to see another worker. Sometimes the client may only need to clarify the situation and then can proceed without further assistance. Or the client may decide not to accept the help she has a right to. If she is mandated to participate, then she may choose to face the consequences of not doing so. Alternatively, she may decide to meet, but will need assistance in defining what help she will accept in dealing with her situation. If the decision is to continue the work, then the change process is implemented. This will be studied in greater detail in Part Three.

Summary

The change process is a means of responding to concern and need and of applying knowledge, values, and skills to work with clients using the concepts of assessment, person in situation, relationship, process, and intervention. The change process is a means of proceeding over time through stages in a cyclical manner to meet needs. In social work practice the client is involved in the process to the maximum extent possible. Worker and client together proceed from an initial statement of the need through information collection to assessment, planning, implementation of the plan, and evaluation of what happened in the work together. Throughout this process, the worker focuses on the unique strengths and competencies of the client system and the environment and the possibilities for growth and change inherent in that ecosystem.

QUESTIONS

1. What is the usual manner in which you meet your needs? What strengths and resources have assisted you? How is your experience in changing and growing similar to or different from the process described in this chapter?

2. Think of a need of which you are aware. Use the social work change process to develop a plan for meeting that need.

3. Contrast the change process presented in this chapter with problem solving you have been presented with in another course.

4. What are the advantages of using the ecosystems strengths approach with a client? What are the disadvantages?

5. How can the ecosystems strengths approach to change be used in helping to promote growth and change in a community?

6. Can the social worker always share all of her own cognitive processes with the client? If not, why not? How should such a situation be handled?

SUGGESTED READINGS

Compton, Beulah Roberts, and Galaway, Burt. *Social Work Processes,* 6th ed. Belmont, CA: Wadsworth, 1999 (Chapters 2 and 3).

DeRoos, Yosikazu. "The Development of Practice Wisdom through Human Problem-Solving Processes." *Social Services Review* 64 (June 1990): 278–287.

Gelfand, Bernard. *The Creative Practitioner: Creative Theory and Method for the Helping Services.* New York: Haworth Press, 1988.

Germaine, Carel B., and Gitterman, Alex. *The Life Model of Social Work Practice: Advances in Theory and Practice,* 2nd ed. New York: Columbia University Press, 1996.

Goldstein, Eda G., and Noonan, Maryellen. *Short-Term Treatment and Social Work Practice: An Integrative Perspective.* New York: Free Press, 1999.

Greene, Roberta R., and Watkins, Marie, Eds. *Serving Diverse Constituencies: Applying the Ecological Perspective.* New York: Aldine De Gruyter, 1998.

Kemp, Susan P., Whittaker, James K., and Tracy, Elizabeth M. *Person-Environment Practice: The Social Ecology of Interpersonal Helping.* New York: Aldine De Gruyter, 1997.

Miley, Karla Krosgrud, O'Melia, Michael, and DuBois, Brenda L. *Generalist Social Work Practice: An Empowering Approach.* Boston: Allyn and Bacon, 1995 (Chapter 4).

Pardeck, John T. *Social Work Practice: An Ecological Approach.* Westport, CT: Auburn House, 1996.

Payne, Malcolm. *Modern Social Work Theory.* Chicago, IL: Lyceum Books, 1991.

Saleeby, Dennis. *The Strengths Perspective in Social Work Practice,* 2nd ed. New York: Longman, 1997.

NOTES

1. Helen Harris Perlman, *Social Casework: A Problem-Solving Process* (Chicago: University of Chicago Press, 1959), p. 3.

2. Murray Ross, *Community Organization: Theory, Principles, and Practice* (New York: Harper and Row, 1955).

3. Helen Northen, *Social Work with Groups* (New York: Columbia University Press, 1969).

4. See Kurt Spitzer and Betty Welsh, "A Problem Focused Model of Practice," *Social Casework* 50 (July 1969): 323–329. See also Beulah Roberts Compton and Burt Galaway, *Social Work Processes,* 3rd ed. (Homewood, IL: Dorsey Press, 1984), chap. 8.

5. For further information regarding this approach, see David L. Cooperrider and Suresh Srivastva, "Appreciative Inquiry in Organizational Life," *Research in Organizational Change and Development* 1 (1987): 129–169.

6. William Ryan, *Blaming the Victim,* rev. ed. (New York: Vintage Books, 1976).

7. Dennis Saleeby, *The Strengths Perspective in Social Work Practice,* 2nd ed. (New York: Longman, 1997), p. 3. This book provides a thorough analysis of the philosophical basis of the strengths perspective and its application in social work practice and research.

8. Ibid., p. 35.

9. Dennis Saleeby, "The Strengths Perspective in Social Work Practice: Extensions and Cautions," *Social Work* 41 (May 1996): 296–305.

10. Ibid., p. 298.

11. Sal Hofstein, "The Nature of Process: Its Implications for Social Work," *Journal of Social Work Process* 14 (1964): 13–53.

5 Social Work as Intervention into Human Transactions

LEARNING EXPECTATIONS

1. Understanding of the concept of intervention.
2. Understanding of the nature of human transactions.
3. Understanding of the concept of influence.
4. Understanding of the nature of the change sought by the social worker.

Intervention into human transactions is the fifth and last of the perspectives on generalist social work practice to be considered. It is another way of discussing the "what" of social work practice. Discussion of this perspective calls for (1) consideration of the meaning of intervention, (2) discussion of transactions as the focus of change, (3) influence as a means of intervention, and (4) consideration of the change sought in social work practice.

When using an ecosystems strengths approach to change, social workers consider the transactions between the client system and the environment to be the primary focus of attention. The assessment involves developing an understanding of these transactions, identifying needs in the client system and the environment, and identifying strengths and resources available to meet those needs. Planning develops goals and objectives designed to balance these transactions and meet the needs of the client system and the environment, based on strengths and resources. Intervention into transactions is the practice activity related to the process of influencing for change. The worker uses influence with various parts of the ecosystem to assist the client in carrying out the plan or when barriers to success arise. Using influence in the change process calls for the creative blending of knowledge, values, and skills.

This perspective describes a contemporary view of the nature of practice based on a social systems approach and practice wisdom.[1] The interventive approach seems particularly useful when practicing within a generalist framework with a multisystem focus.

Intervention

The term *intervention* began to appear in the social work literature in the late 1950s and early 1960s. At first there was little explanation of the meaning of the term. It was substituted for the term *treatment* as used in the "study, diagnosis, and treatment" description of the social work process. Usually, the use of *intervention* was accompanied by the term *assessment,* which replaced the more traditional word *diagnosis.*[2]

The change in usage came about because of a variety of influences and marked the beginning of the contemporary conceptualization of social work practice. Some of the more important influences include the following:

1. The use of newer conceptualizations of ego psychology, which emphasized coping and social functioning, raised questions regarding continued employment of the medical model. *Diagnosis* and *treatment* are terms that have strong connotations of medicine and illness.

2. Attempts to find the commonality in the practice theory of casework, group work, and community organization increased. Community organization practice and some types of group work practice did not fit into the concept of treatment; thus, different terminology became necessary to capture the commonality of practice.

3. The growing diversity of practice modalities, many of which rejected the medical model, entailed new ways of approaching practice situations and new terminology. *Intervention* was a term used in other helping professions that social work adopted for its own use.

4. The use of social systems theory grew. When considering a person or persons in a situation from a social systems point of view, the notion of change arising from "intervention into social systems" seemed a logical progression.[3] Intervention is congruent with systemic thinking. The social systems framework highlights the importance of relationships among systems and the influence of change in one subsystem on the need for change in other subsystems. Thus originated the notion that change in relationships between systems (or subsystems of the larger system) is a valid target for change.

5. A more aggressive practice stance developed. During the 1960s, social work became involved with new problems, new groups of clients, and new situations. Many of these called for new aggressive strategies and techniques that encouraged clients to develop insight or to think logically and then make their own changes.

6. The strengths perspective, with its emphasis on client strengths, is a holistic approach for change that acknowledges positive areas to build on rather than focusing exclusively on problems and needs.[4] Another contemporary emphasis is the importance of diversity and the identification of commonalities and differences within and between groups. This emphasis recognizes the role that power inequity and dominance play in the oppression of minority groups.[5] Both the strengths perspective and the recognition of diversity factors call for the use of transactional assessment.

7. The ecological perspective, or ecosystems approach, expanded and modified the person-in-environment perspective. The client and the environment are not viewed as separate but as part of a whole called an ecosystem. All of the systems, including the client, transact with and influence each other.[6] This approach focuses on these transactions as both the source of unmet need and the solution to meeting need. Whether or not needs are met is dependent on whether or not the transactions are balanced or not balanced. Thus, assessment is focused on transactional assessment rather than assessing individual systems, and intervention is aimed at developing a balance in the transactions among systems so that the needs of each are met.

The change to intervention represented not just one of terminology but a change in the way of looking at person in situation. It was an indication of the new paradigm discussed in Chapter 2. Assessment began to focus on roles, relationships, and interactions rather than on intrapersonal aspects of the client's life. It began to deal with environmental factors to a much greater extent than had previously been the case. A great deal of new knowledge was available for use by social workers, and this knowledge was ordered in new ways. The focus came to be on relationships of systems rather than on systems as separate entities. This shift in focus called for a new kind of analysis, one that was multidimensional in nature.[7]

Intervention is the activity of the worker in bringing about change in a systemic sense. It represents a leap in social work thinking from understanding a person in a situation to purposefully bringing about change in the person-situation phenomenon. *Intervention*, as conceived of in this text, is specific action by a worker in relation to human systems or processes in order to induce change. The action is guided by knowledge and professional values as well as by the skillfulness (competence level) of the worker. Intervention is purposeful, goal directed, and makes use of the worker's helping repertoire (including his creativity, knowledge, values, and skills).

As used in social work, intervention does not assume control of either the client or the situation. Not only is absolute control impossible in most human situations, but it is also contrary to social work values. What is expected is that the worker will move with the "stream of life," the developmental process of the systems in the relationship, and that the worker, by means of actions and other input into the situation, will influence that stream of life. This influence will change the course of events to be expected if there were no intervention. The course of events is also changed by the reactions and interactions of the client and others in the situation. The change in the course of events can be of a preventive as well as ameliorative nature. The social work input consists of perceptions and understanding about what is happening, identification of needs in a situation, enhancement of necessary skills, recognition of strengths, and knowledge of specific resources the worker can bring to bear to meet needs. This approach to intervention places considerable stress on enabling clients not only to engage in the helping endeavor but also to become heavily involved in change-producing behaviors of their own. It also expands the change process to include any relevant system in the environment and the transactions among systems.

Intervention, then, is action guided by the worker's knowledge, values, and skill directed toward the achievement of specific ends. Intervention encompasses the concepts of treatment, planned change, and social intervention as they have been used in social work literature.

Case Example

A social worker in a small rural hospital, on finding that a patient who has AIDS is not receiving needed routine care, decides that intervention is called for. First the social worker, John, asks the patient, Bob, for detailed information about the care he has received in the last twenty-four hours. John also asks who on the staff has come into his room. He finds that Bob has not been given a bath and his room has not been cleaned. Bob is on complete bed rest and yet has been given a urinal to keep by his bed, which has only been emptied twice in the last twenty-four hours. Bob has been given no meal choice, though this would be indicated according to orders on his chart. Based on his knowledge of the usual care given to patients, John believes he now has sufficient information on which to determine that Bob is being discriminated against regarding the provision of care.

John decides that his social work value system indicates that he has a responsibility to intervene so that Bob receives the care that he needs. John knows that Bob is the first AIDS patient who has been admitted to this hospital. John decides that his next step is to question discreetly the head nurse about the situation. The nurse states that they are very busy on the floor with many critically ill patients. Because of this they are having to cut corners; some routine care is just not getting done. John senses that the head nurse is resentful of his questions and not comfortable in caring for Bob. He decides that to probe further might cause more difficulty for Bob.

He next seeks out Bob's doctor and shares his findings. Dr. Blue says he is aware that the staff are afraid of Bob. He says he has no patience with people who believe the scare stories about the dangers of treating an AIDS patient. They just have to take care of him.

John next seeks out the administrator of the hospital and shares his knowledge about Bob's care with him. The administrator states that it is evident that the staff are scared of this patient and that there needs to be in-service training that will reinforce their knowledge of safe treatment techniques and also deal with their fears. He asks John

(continued)

Case Example   Continued

to help him plan for this. John suggests they call the head nurse and ask her help with planning the needed in-service. John believes that this is one way to involve her in the problem and minimize her resistance.

In deciding how to intervene in this situation, John used knowledge he had about the hospital system and the interactions of the various subsystems. He saw his goal as obtaining better care for Bob as well as developing attitudes in the staff that would enable them to care not only for Bob but for future AIDS patients without fear of contagion. To do this he knew that he had to work with the dual-authority system of doctor and administrator. John also skillfully gave the message that he was not blaming anyone for the situation but was trying to find out why the situation existed and how he could help in resolving it. His intervention was focused on changing relationships among subsystems in the hospital system. He also knew that this approach would enable the staff to look at their own caregiving and make changes they determined helpful.

Transactions as the Focus for Change

A major consideration of the interventive approach is determining what change is to be sought. More specifically, what change is possible in any given system or between systems? Careful consideration of this question in light of knowledge from social systems and ecosystems theories and from practice wisdom led to the conclusion that change of systems is not the target for change; rather, the target is change in the relationships among systems. The relationships among the parts of the systems affect the whole. The person in situation is a system, a part, and a whole. Parts are systems in their own right. This targeting of relationships of systems (persons and groups of persons) is also valid when the focus of social work is on social functioning strengths and enabling. Social functioning implies relationships, interactions, and ways of functioning with other persons and with social groups and institutions. If social functioning is the focus of social work, the target of social work intervention should then be the relationship among systems.

Gordon expresses this central focus of social work as "the interface between the meeting place of person and environment.... The phenomenon of concern is the interface in the transaction between persons and environment."[8]

Transaction denotes the nature of relationships in the person-situation phenomenon—not just a simple interaction but an interaction influenced by other interactions in the situation. Interactions, then, are affected by other interactions. For example, a mother-child relationship is influenced by a number of factors: the mother's relationship with the father and with other children in the family; other relationships she may have had in the past, particularly with her mother; the relationship of the father with the child and with other children in the family; and a variety of relationships outside the family (see Figure 5.1).

In considering the nature of the family, John Spiegel has described transactions as the interplay among individual, family, and society. His thesis—that

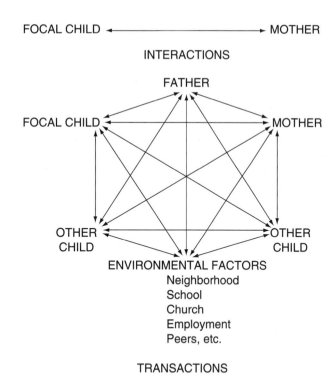

FIGURE 5.1 **Interactions and Transactions**

everything is connected to everything else—implies that there is a mutual interrelatedness affecting action between any two members of a family. This interrelatedness is also affected by environmental factors and by the mutual interrelatedness as it has extended over time. The individual is seen as filling social roles, having impact on the system, and having impact on other individuals.[9] Spiegel says that "any act of a person in a role must fit into the reciprocal and complementary actions of his role partner."[10] Problems in social functioning develop when these role patterns do not fit.

These understandings about the nature of transactions within the family system are applicable to transactions within any system and among any systems. By focusing on the transactions (the relationships) among systems, the social worker finds a realistic means to influence for change. Social functioning is problematic when the needs of one or more systems in the transaction are not being met. Thus, a transactional focus cannot be on any one system in the transaction but must be on the interplay among the systems in relation to needs. The desired change is one that brings the systems into harmony as they function together. This usually brings about change in the relationships among the systems. These relationships may be affected by issues of power, energy, communication, or motivation as well as by external impingements on one or more of the systems in the relationship. Obviously, then, the intervention needs to take the transactional nature of relationships into consideration.

The transactional nature of relationships becomes especially important when the practice is with a person from a disadvantaged or oppressed group. These may include groups that are identified by race, ethnicity, social class, age, gender, sexual orientation, disability, or recent immigration or dislocation. Members of such groups may be influenced in their decision making by the predominant culture of their reference group. They may not understand or trust the messages coming from a member of a different culture or see the importance of any expectations from institutions that reflect the values of the dominant culture. They may be reluctant to seek services from traditional service organizations that represent the majority culture.

Case Example

The Chicana mother of an eight-year-old girl has been urged by the school nurse to seek medical help for her daughter's skin rash. The mother has not followed up on this recommendation, and the school social worker has been asked to see what can be done. The social worker should consider cultural attitudes toward health care; the family's experiences with the school, school nurse, and local health care system; the family's relationships; and the family's decision-making process. The difficulty or inability to follow through on the recommendation may be influenced by factors arising from any of these areas. Difficulties can also arise from a language barrier, a lack of knowledge of health care and financial resources, or other family problems. The relationship of the mother and the school nurse or school social worker should be seen as transactional in nature.

Influence

"Reality demonstrates influence, not control" best describes the worker's impact on a situation. As has been stated, the social worker does not have complete control and cannot guarantee a specific outcome when working from an interventive-transactional stance. Clients and others involved in the situation maintain the ability to decide what their behavior will be in the situation. This ability makes control by the social worker impossible except in those areas in which he has been given the authority to control certain aspects of the client's behavior, such as in some institutional situations, some work with children, protective service work, and probation and parole work.

Influence has been defined as "the general acts of producing an effect on another person, group, or organization through exercise of a personal or organizational capacity."[11] Influence is powerful. It can produce change, persuade or convince, overcome obstacles, motivate, and bring about attitudinal changes. The social worker's input is to create a climate favorable for the needed work, heighten the motivation of those needing to do the work, "provide a vision"[12] for the work to be done together, and reduce the resistance involved.

An important base for influence is the skill and knowledge of the social worker in developing and using relationships with a variety of persons in a variety of situations. Influence can be exerted by those who know about and can use a planned change process. Influence derives from understandings about human development, human diversity, the variety of social problems, and the availability of services and resources.

Social workers use not only their own base of influence but that of other people with whom they are working. When working for change in situations, in organizations, and in communities, people with influence are very useful. Influential people may be elected or appointed to positions of authority, are respected and looked up to, have control over resources and information, and are involved in important decision making. They often are people who control from behind the scenes. Values are another important factor to consider in relationship to influence. People are more apt to be influenced for change when the change is within their value system and provides something that is important to them.

Workers need to be aware of the nature of the power and influence they wield in relationships with clients. Influence can be an inherent outgrowth of the power differential in the worker-client relationship. Every effort needs to be made to guard against the potential for abuse of power with clients. In addition to professional expertise, which workers possess by virtue of their skill, values, and knowledge base, certain personal characteristics may also contribute to a worker's influence with a client.

Clients do have some choice of whether they will be influenced or not. To be influenced, clients must have at least some motivation for change. Some factors that affect willingness to be influenced include discomfort with the situation and a belief that it can be changed, a desire to gain position or resources, and a desire to change the situation for someone else.

Nora Gold states, "Social workers can be very useful as motivators to their clients by increasing their sense of competence and control and helping them to recognize the power in 'seeing oneself as a potential force in shaping one's ends; and changing oneself with making whatever changes must come about.'"[13] Gold's quote is from none other than Helen Harris Perlman, the originator of the problem-solving approach in social work. This statement is very close to describing a process of enabling.[14]

Resistance is the opposite of motivation and is sometimes a sign that other influences on a person are stronger than the need for change. The Chicana mother, for example, may be influenced by her culture and family to such an extent that the influence of the school has little effect. There may be practical barriers of family responsibilities or lack of money influencing the situation. Using knowledge and skill, the social worker may be able to discover what is preventing the mother from seeking the needed medical care for her daughter and, using the change process, find a way of having that need met.

Barriers to change—to accepting influence—can be cultural in nature. Ideologies, traditions, and values are all part of cultural influences on situations. Barriers also may be social in nature. The influence of a person's family or peer group, the norms of the situation, or the reputation of the change agent can be social barriers to change. Or the barrier may be organizational in nature: a competitive climate or an organizational climate that considers procedure rather than individuals. Family communication patterns can be another barrier to change. Personal barriers such as fear, selective perception, or lack of energy and skill also affect an individual's capacity to accept influence and to change. All of these barriers may be part of the transactive nature of relationships in a helping situation.

The influence process is carried out in a relationship with one or more of the systems involved in the transaction. This relationship is transactional in nature, in that it is affected by other relationships. The relationship between the social worker and the system being influenced is a major source of a social worker's influence. A major task in the social work endeavor is to foster the kind of relationships that allow the worker to bring other sources of influence to bear on the situation. As the worker applies these various sources of influence to the situation, change takes place in the relationships among the subsystems involved. The worker's knowledge and skillfulness as well as social work values guide the decisions about what sources of influence to use and how to use them.

There are also ethical considerations regarding the use of influence. Of particular importance is concern about the difference between influence and manipulation, control, or abuse of power. Clients and others typically do not understand the limits of the social worker's span of control and ascribe more authority to the worker than is legally allowed. Clients may believe that the worker can withhold an income maintenance check if they do not do what they think the worker wants them to do. Such situations can become complex when the client acts according to what she believes the worker wants rather than what the worker has said. Workers can use their ascribed authority to control clients. However, this negates the value of self-determination and also raises concerns about who has the right to do what and on what grounds.[15] In the contemporary situation, social work values, such as the right to self-determination and confidentiality, are often limited by agency mandates, statutory reporting laws, or other constraints of practice.

All three of the following questions can be used to determine if influence is being used within social work values:

1. Whose needs are being met by the use of the influence? If it is the client's needs, it is within the social work value system. If it is the worker's needs, it is not.
2. Have the goals been established by the worker and client together as part of a collaborative process?
3. Has freedom of choice for all concerned been considered and maintained to the maximum extent possible?

Influence is a major consideration for the social worker to take into account in planning and implementing interventions in transactions among people and their systems. Because a power differential often exists between social workers and their clients, attention must be given to prevent misuse of influence. Influence, or use of self, when used within the social work value system serves as an enabling function.

Case Example

In the earlier example of the eight-year-old Chicana girl, the worker can influence the situation in several ways. She can discuss the cultural implications with the school nurse to see if the nurse's recommendations can be given in a manner more congruent with the Chicano culture. In doing this she is changing the situation by working for a change in the relationship between the nurse and the mother, thus changing the transactional nature of the situation. The social worker could influence the mother to follow the nurse's recommendations by either explaining their importance or by enabling the mother in seeking the health care needed, perhaps making a referral to an affordable health clinic or even taking the mother and daughter to the first appointment. If a Chicano aide is available, the worker could explain to this aide why the care is needed and ask her to work with the mother in obtaining the care, thus influencing a third party, who in turn will influence the mother. If the worker has seen several similar situations, she might work for change in the school system by such means as staff education about the Chicano culture or by influencing the health care system as to ways to make that system more usable by these clients. The social worker could also influence the educational system to be more responsive to the needs of all Chicano children and their parents.

Changes Sought by the Social Worker

Over the course of its history, the focus of social work in its role of enabling social functioning has been the subject of much discussion and debate. One of the earliest of these debates is referred to as cause-function.[16] This debate can be translated as: Is the change to be sought that of the larger social system, or is it the change of individuals from within? In discussing the change sought and social functioning, Harriett Bartlett has used the terminology "people coping" and "environmental demands." She states that "these ideas must be brought together within the same dimension and it is the idea of 'social interaction' that the writer thinks accomplishes this."[17] The ecosystems approach unites these dimensions by focusing on the transactions among systems and using the change process to balance those transactions to meet needs of the client and his environment.

People must cope within an environmental context. In coping they engage in relationships with the environment or, more specifically, with people in their environment. Thus, by changing relationships or enabling the development of new relationships, the desired change takes place. In the example of the Chicana mother, the social worker may find that the mother does not understand the seriousness of her daughter's skin rash. The mother may not be able to explain the situation to other family members, especially her husband, who must be involved in the decision to seek help. She also may need to become aware of resources available for medical treatment. Here the social worker might use a teaching/learning strategy to influence the situation. She could do this by telling the mother about two or three specific resources and explaining to her procedures for obtaining service from each resource or helping her to relate appropriately to the environment.

Whereas change in relationships is the major focus of intervention, change in individuals and systems involved in the relationship must also be considered, for the means of change in relationships—the desired end state—is often change in individuals and in systems. Genevieve Oxley has identified five ways in which positive individual growth takes place: (1) maturation, (2) interaction, (3) action, (4) learning, and (5) crisis.[18] This formulation is helpful for the purposes of this discussion because it looks to the **life processes** of individuals and the change that takes place over time as an individual lives and participates in relationships. The interventive-transactive approach looks at the life process, or relationships, and seeks to influence that life process for change. Enabling or enhancing maturation, interaction, action, learning, and crisis management are means of influencing relationships (the life processes).

Change in larger systems takes place through change in the roles of people and the structure of their relationships in the system. This includes change both in communication patterns and in the decision-making process. Change also takes place as subsystems are added or taken away from the larger system. Change takes place as new ways of functioning or carrying out tasks develop. All these changes call for individuals to change and involve the life process of the larger system. The social worker can be involved by enabling, enhancing, supporting, facilitating, and managing change in relationships. The decision to choose a specific intervention is made by determining which changes within both the individuals and the larger systems involved can enable the needed relationship change.

Schwartz has described the role of the social worker as that of mediator. In his view, the worker's function is "to mediate the process through which the individual and his society reach out for each other through a mutual need for fulfillment."[19] It is through relationships that people grow, learn, meet their needs, and resolve crises and that larger systems carry out their functions in society. The relationships among people and systems are important aspects of the helping process in mediating or enabling the resolution of problems of social functioning. Also important are the relationships between the social worker and the people and systems involved. As the social worker fills the mediation role, she strengthens and supports the efforts of individuals and systems to function in a mutually fulfilling manner. This enables not only more effective social functioning but also the growth of individuals as well. In intervening in the transactions among persons and situations, the social worker must be concerned with change in the nature of relationships, which involves individual and larger system change.

The National Association of Social Workers Publication Committee and the Editorial Board of *Social Work* sponsored a project for study and debate about the purpose and objects of social work. One product of this debate was a "Working Statement on the Purpose of Social Work" (see Figure 5.2). The transactional nature of social work practice is supported by this statement, which also specifies the kinds of change the social worker seeks when working with clients and significant others.

Summary

Intervention is purposeful and goal-directed action by a social worker in relation to human systems or processes in order to induce change. Intervention does not assume worker control of any situation but rather implies moving with and influencing the stream of life. Human interaction is transactional in nature; that is, all

---

FIGURE 5.2 Purpose of Social Work

Working Statement on the
Purpose of Social Work

(Developed by participants at the second meeting on conceptual frameworks)

The purpose of social work is to promote or restore a mutually beneficial interaction between individuals and society in order to improve the quality of life for everyone. Social workers hold the following beliefs:

— The environment (social, physical, organizational) should provide the opportunity and resources for the maximum realization of the potential and aspirations of all individuals, and should provide for their common human needs and for the alleviation of distress and suffering.
— Individuals should contribute as effectively as they can to their own well-being and to the social welfare of others in their immediate environment as well as to the collective society.
— Transactions between individuals and others in their environment should enhance dignity, individuality, and self-determination of everyone. People should be treated humanely and with justice.

Clients of social workers may be an individual, a family, a group, a community, or an organization.

Objectives
Social workers focus on person-and-environment *in interaction*. To carry out their purpose, they work with people to achieve the following objectives:

— Help people enlarge their competence and increase their problem-solving and coping abilities.
— Help people obtain resources.
— Make organizations responsive to people.
— Facilitate interaction between individuals and others in their environment.
— Influence interactions between organizations and institutions.
— Influence social and environmental policy.

To achieve these objectives, social workers work with other people. At different times, the target of change varies—it may be the client, others in the environment, or both.

Source: Reprinted with permission from *Social Work*, Volume 26, Number 1, p. 6, January 1981. Copyright 1981, National Association of Social Workers, Inc.

interactions are affected by other interactions. Social work intervention focuses on these transactions in order to encourage change when social functioning is problematic in meeting the needs of one or more elements in the transactions. Influence brings about change by the exercise of the social worker's capacity. This capacity is based in the worker's knowledge, skill, and reputation, among other factors. Particular attention is given to identifying and using clients' strengths.

The interventive-transactive approach calls for the social worker to identify needs; to apply knowledge, professional values, skills, and creativity; and to influence the ongoing transactions relative to the needs so as to bring about a change in the transactions. The change sought is the development of relationships that are need-fulfilling for all parties of the relationship. This development may result in new relationships or in a change in existing ones. In order to participate in the change process, the worker engages in two types of activity: (1) the development of helping relationships with the transactional system that is the focus of change (Part Two) and (2) the carrying out of the helping process with the transactional system that is the focus of change (Part Three).

QUESTIONS

1. Think about a situation in which you interacted with someone else. Identify all the influences that affected that interaction.

2. List value considerations that the term *influence* brings to your mind.

3. What do you think are ways you influence situations in your own life?

4. How is the view of social work presented in this chapter similar to your present understanding of social work practice? How is it different?

SUGGESTED READINGS

Anderson, Joseph D. "Toward Generic Practice: The Interactional Approach." *Social Casework* 65 (June 1984): 323–329.

Cimmarusti, Rocco A. "Family Preservation Practice Based on a Multisystems Approach." *Child Welfare* 81 (May–June 1992): 241–256.

Garvin, Charles D., and Seabury, Brett A. *Interpersonal Practice in Social Work: Promoting Competence and Social Justice,* 2nd ed. Boston: Allyn and Bacon, 1997.

Germaine, Carel B., and Gitterman, Alex. *The Life Model of Social Work Practice: Advances in Theory and Practice,* 2nd ed. New York: Columbia University Press, 1996.

Gold, Nora. "Motivation: The Crucial but Unexplored Component of Social Work Practice." *Social Work* 35 (January 1990): 49–56.

Greene, Roberta R., and Watkins, Marie, Eds. *Serving Diverse Constituencies: Applying the Ecological Perspective.* New York: Aldine De Gruyter, 1998.

Kemp, Susan P., Whittaker, James K., and Tracy, Elizabeth M. *Person-Environment Practice: The Social Ecology of Interpersonal Helping.* New York: Aldine De Gruyter, 1997.

Lee, Judith, A. B. *The Empowerment Approach to Social Work Practice.* New York: Columbia University Press, 1994.

Lum, Doman. *Social Work Practice and People of Color: A Process Stage Approach.* Pacific Grove, CA: Brooks/Cole, 1992.

Meyer, Carol. "The Ecosystems Perspective: Implications for Social Work Practice," in Carol Meyer and Mark Mattaini, *The Foundations of Social Work Practice.* Washington, DC: NASW Press, 1995 (pp. 16–27).

Miley, Karla Krogsrud, O'Melia, Michael, and DuBois, Brenda L. *Social Work Practice: An Empowering Approach,* 2nd ed. Boston, MA: Allyn and Bacon, 1998.

Monkman, Marjorie McQueen. "Outcome Objectives in Social Work Practice: Person and Environment." *Social Work* 36 (May 1991): 253–257.

Pardeck, John T. *Social Work Practice: An Ecological Approach.* Westport, CT: Auburn House, 1996.

Saleeby, Dennis. *The Strengths Perspective in Social Work Practice,* 2nd ed. New York: Longman, 1997.

Shulman, Lawrence. *Interactional Social Work Practice: Toward an Empirical Theory.* Itasca, IL: F. E. Peacock, 1991.

Simons, Ronald L. "Strategies for Exercising Influence." *Social Work* 27 (May 1982): 268–274.

Social Work 26 (January 1981). Second Special Issue on Conceptual Frameworks.

NOTES

1. See readings for examples of this view.

2. See Carol H. Meyer, *Social Work Practice: The Changing Landscape,* 2nd ed. (New York: Free Press, 1976), chap. 5, for a discussion of the change in the use of terms.

3. For early formulations using this notion, see Gordon Hearn, Ed., *The General Systems Approach: Contributions Toward an Holistic Conception of Social Work* (New York: Council on Social Work Education, 1969); and Charles R. Atherton, Sancha T. Mitchell, and Edna Biehl Schein, "Locating Points of Intervention" and "Using Points of Intervention," *Social Casework* 52 (March and April 1971): 131–141 and 223–228.

4. Dennis Saleeby, *The Strengths Perspective in Social Work Practice,* 2nd ed. (New York: Longman, 1997).

5. Doman Lum, *Social Work Practice and People of Color: A Process Stage Approach* (Pacific Grove, CA: Brooks/Cole, 1992).

6. See John T. Pardeck, *Social Work Practice: An Ecological Approach* (Westport, CT: Auburn House, 1996).

7. For a practice model that has this multidimensional focus, see Carel B. Germaine and Alex Gitterman, *The Life Model of Social Work Practice: Advances in Theory and Practice* (New York: Columbia University Press, 1996).

8. William E. Gordon, "Basic Constructs for an Integrated and Generative Conception of Social Work," in Hearn, *The General Systems Approach,* p. 7.

9. John Spiegel, *Transactions: The Interplay Between Individual, Family, and Society* (New York: Science House, 1971). For another view of these ideas, see also Roy H. Rogers, *Family Interaction and Transaction* (Englewood Cliffs, NJ: Prentice-Hall, 1973).

10. Ibid., p. 96.

11. Irving Spergel, *Community Problem Solving* (Chicago: University of Chicago Press, 1969), p. 106.

12. William Schwartz, "The Social Worker in the Group," in *The Social Welfare Forum Proceedings* (New York: Columbia University Press, 1961), p. 157.

13. Nora Gold, "Motivation: The Crucial but Unexplored Component of Social Work Practice," *Social Work* 35 (January 1990): 49–56.

14. Helen Harris Perlman, *Social Casework* (Chicago: University of Chicago Press, 1957).

15. See Charles S. Levy, "Values and Planned Change," *Social Casework* 53 (October 1972): 488–493, for another discussion of these factors.

16. Porter R. Lee, "Social Work: Cause and Function," *Proceedings of the National Conference on Social Welfare, 1929.* See also the section entitled "Cause-Function Debate" in Chapter 1 of this text for a previous discussion of this idea.

17. Harriett M. Bartlett, *The Common Base of Social Work Practice* (New York: National Association of Social Workers, 1970), p. 100.

18. Genevieve B. Oxley, "A Life Model Approach to Change," *Social Casework* 52 (December 1971): 627–633.

19. Schwartz, "The Social Worker in the Group," pp. 154–155.

PART TWO

The Interactional Process

Based on the overview of generalist practice presented in Part One, specific processes integral to the social work endeavor will be considered. In Part Two, the interactional process is explored.

In the simplest sense, the generalist social worker is a provider of services that vary in nature. These include provision of concrete services (such as income maintenance), facilitation of growth and change, developmental services (such as group work in a settlement house), intervention into crisis situations (such as illness or loss of loved ones), and certain therapeutic services. It is not the service but the focus of the service and how that service is given that defines generalist social work. The service focuses on social functioning—the interaction of persons and social systems in meeting human needs.

In order to provide services that focus on social functioning, the worker must interact with individuals and social systems. How the service is provided has two dimensions: (1) the interactions of the worker and other people and social systems as service is provided and (2) the process of service provision. The interactions and service provision are simultaneous, intertwined processes. In this text they are artificially separated to enable students to develop in-depth understanding of each process. Part Two focuses on interactions. It also considers development of understanding of individual, group, agency, and community functioning as each affects the interactional process. In-depth understanding of these systems and their functioning usually has been obtained from courses in sociology, psychology, economics, political science, anthropology, and human biology as well as from courses titled Human Behavior in the Social Environment or something similar. Discussion in Part Two focuses on the use of this knowledge, including means of organizing it in service of the interactional process. In other words, understanding of the system both from a global and a particular frame of reference is deemed essential for professional relationships. Part Three will treat the process of service provision.

A basic interactional approach is used regardless of the service being offered, although there are modifications and adaptations of that interactional approach depending on the service.

In its simplest form, the components of the interactional process are the worker and client interacting in an environment. However, the generalist social worker often is part of a multiperson worker system (e.g., a team) and often works with a multiperson client system (e.g., a small group or family). Thus, Part Two will also explore these kinds of interactions.

Chapter 6 discusses the worker component and considers five concepts: knowledge of self, the helping person, responsibility and authority, helping skills of the worker, and the multiperson worker. This chapter further develops the concept of common human needs.

Chapter 7 discusses the client component and considers three concepts: becoming a client, understanding the individual client, and understanding the family as a multiperson client. The concept of human diversity is expanded.

Chapter 8 discusses the environment and the interaction and transactions that take place between the client and systems in the environment. This environment includes the community from which the client comes and the community where the service takes place, as well as the agency offering the service. Also discussed is the worker as an agency employee and working with organizational and community systems as the focus for change.

Chapter 9 discusses the interaction between one worker and one client by considering formation of a one-to-one action system, relationship, communication, and the interview as interactional tools.

Chapter 10 discusses the interaction when a multiperson worker or client is involved. The focus of this chapter is on the family and the small group as social systems. The chapter also discusses the social worker as a member of a group, with a multiperson client, and with a family group. In addition, transactions between clients and their ecosystems are examined.

6 The Worker

LEARNING EXPECTATIONS

1. Development of a framework for a continuous process of developing knowledge of self.
2. A beginning of the process of self-knowledge needed in the practice of social work.
3. Understanding of human need at various stages of the human development process.
4. Identification of personal needs that arise from human development, human diversity, and membership in social systems.
5. Knowledge about the characteristics of a helping person.
6. Identification of the motivation for being a helping person and of the attitudes and knowledge needed to become a helping person. Identification of some of the helping skills that need to be developed.
7. Understanding of concepts of authority and responsibility and their relationship to the values of self-determination and social responsibility.
8. Understanding of the term *multiperson worker* and of its various manifestations.
9. Identification of the knowledge and skills that need to be developed in order for the social worker to function in the multiperson worker situation.

In the interaction of generalist social worker and client, the social worker is first a person with life experiences, human needs, and a personal lifestyle and value system. The worker is also a helping person with skills for interacting with individuals and groups and for developing relationships.

The worker brings to the helping situation a knowledge base that provides understanding about persons in situations, knowledge of helping methods and of means for implementing those methods, and knowledge gained from other helping situations. The worker also brings a value system based on professional values, agency and community values, and his own personal values.

In a complex society with complex social problems and multiple human needs, it is sometimes advantageous for the worker to become part of a **multiperson**

helping system. A multiperson helping system consists of several workers who are involved in providing the needed service in a collaborative manner. Each worker has special knowledge or skill that is necessary for goal attainment. To explore the meaning of the concept of worker, three topics will be considered: (1) the worker as a person, or knowledge of self; (2) the helping person; and (3) the multiperson helping system.

Knowledge of Self

It has been said that the most important tool a social worker possesses is herself. To use that tool skillfully and knowledgeably, a worker must have considerable self-knowledge. It is important that the worker know herself so that she can better understand the differences between herself and her client. For instance, it is essential that she be able to differentiate between her own personal needs or concerns and those of her client. This calls for a kind of introspective stance that seeks to bring personal concerns, attitudes, and values into the area of conscious thought. It calls for a continuous search for self-understanding and for a reasonable degree of comfort with the discovered self.

Social workers develop this self-knowledge in a variety of ways. The process of supervision or discussion of practice situations and problems with peers has always been an important means of developing self-knowledge. Others can often see how our unrecognized concerns, attitudes, and values affect our interaction with others and our helping capacity. Social workers need to be open to help from others as a means of developing self-understanding.

Another way social workers develop self-understanding is through the study of human behavior. Psychological, sociological, anthropological, and biological knowledge that explains human functioning can be the source of considerable self-understanding. It is important to recognize oneself as having imperfections, but it is equally important to keep such awareness within the limits of reality. Medical students tend to believe that they have the disease they are studying. The study of psychology and sociology includes examining human behavior that is labeled as pathological, dysfunctional, or deviant. Social work students sometimes believe that the situations they are studying are operational in their own functioning and see symptoms, pathology, or a deviance in themselves. If this identification is realistic, it can be helpful to self-understanding. Care needs to be taken, however, not to become overly introspective and to assume dysfunction that is not really there. A balance needs to be reached in which introspection is sufficient to gain needed self-knowledge but not so much as to become overwhelming. Self-knowledge cannot be developed all at once; it needs to grow over a period of time. It is also important to learn to deal with the recognition of one's imperfection in a manner that supports self-worth and dignity.

Another useful way for a beginning social worker to develop self-knowledge is to conduct an organized self-study. This entails thinking about one's lifestyle and philosophy of life, moral code and value system, roots, life experiences, personal needs, and personal functioning.

Lifestyle and Philosophy of Life

People are different because of heredity, life experiences, and environment. Such differences affect the manner in which life is lived and how life's problems are dealt with. Some people are more practical and matter of fact; others are more sympathetic and friendly; others are enthusiastic and insightful; still others are more logical and well organized. Some people prefer to deal with technical facts and objects; others prefer to give practical help and services to people; some like to understand and communicate with people; others like to deal with technical and theoretical developments.[1] Some people are physically strong with no visible disabilities; others may have limited sight or physical stamina or other disabilities. People differ according to gender, socioeconomic class, cultural group, and religious beliefs. People differ in the ways they learn and in their capacity for learning. They have different energy levels. All these factors affect lifestyle. **Lifestyle is the manner in which we function in meeting our human needs; in interaction with others; and in our patterns of work, play, and rest.** It is important not only to describe lifestyle but also to be aware of why a particular lifestyle is preferred.

A philosophy of life—which is related to lifestyle in that lifestyle is affected by philosophy of life—is even more basic to self-understanding. One's **philosophy of life** includes beliefs about people and society and about human life, its purpose, and how it should be lived. In identifying one's philosophy of life, some questions to be asked are: What are my beliefs about the nature of humanity? Is humanity innately good or evil? What should be the relationship between men and women? What is the place of work, family, and recreation in a person's life? When is dependence on another person acceptable? What responsibility does each person have for the well-being of his or her fellow human beings? What is the relationship of persons to a higher being, to God? What is the relationship of persons to the natural world? One's philosophy of life affects all we are, feel, think, and do. A philosophy of life is often strongly dependent on religious teachings or beliefs to which a person has been exposed. It also depends on culture and on family influences. The influence of these early beliefs can result in their rejection or in adherence or commitment to them. It is important that a philosophy of life be well thought out and reflect the person each of us is. One's philosophy of life changes with growth and new experiences.

Moral Code and Value System

A moral code and value system are closely related to one's philosophy of life. A **moral code** is a specification of that which is considered to be right or wrong in terms of behavior. One's *value system* includes what is considered desirable or preferred. The actions and things we consider valuable are also prioritized so that a system of values exists. A person's moral code and value system are affected by cultural heritage, family influences, group affiliations (including religious affiliation), and personal and educational experiences. For some people, the moral code is prescribed and fixed regardless of the situation. For others, the moral code is determined by a set of principles that guides moral and value decisions but that allows for some degree of flexibility; for still others, these decisions are dependent on the situation.[2]

Florence Kluckholm and Fred Strodtbeck have discussed value orientations and identified several dimensions along which people develop a value system:

1. *Human nature:* Is it evil, neutral, mixture of good and evil, or good?
2. *Relationship of individual to nature:* Should it be subjugation to nature, harmony with nature, or mastery over nature?
3. *Time orientation:* Is the emphasis placed on past, present, or future?
4. *Activity:* Should activity focus on being, being in becoming, or doing?
5. *Relationality:* Should its nature be one of lineality, collaborability, or individuality?[3]

Identifying one's position on each of these five dimensions can give some indication of basic values—one's way of responding to needs and situations. For example, if a person sees people as basically evil, her response to behavior she does not like may be to punish in order to exact "good" behavior. Such a presupposition carries a belief that people's inclination is to be bad and punishment is needed to curb undesirable behavior. On the other hand, seeing people as good carries a belief that people will try to do what is right, consider others and their needs, and work for what is right. The stance that human nature is good seems more in keeping with social work values than the stance that human nature is bad.

Value conflicts that exist between the dominant society and an ethnic group can often be identified through examining the value orientation of the ethnic group. Some Hispanic people believe that a person's relationship to nature is one of subjugation to nature. Natural disasters such as floods or hurricanes are seen as indications that God or the forces of nature are punishing them for some misdoing. Most Native Americans have a value system based on harmony with nature. For them, natural disasters may be an indication that in some way they are out of harmony with the forces of nature. For example, floods may be the result of misuse of the land. The response of the dominant American culture tends to reflect a belief in mastery over nature. The response to a flood is to attempt to control future floods with dams and other flood-control mechanisms. These differences often explain why individuals view the same situation differently.

Since many social workers are members of the dominant society, they may experience substantial value conflicts when working with clients who are members of diverse, disadvantaged, or oppressed populations. Some value conflicts occur between the worker's personal values and those of the client. Some conflicts can occur between the values of the social work profession and the values and beliefs of the client. In addition, the worker can experience conflicts between their personal values and beliefs and the values of the social work profession. Some examples of these situations might be working with gays and lesbians, abortion, differences in child-rearing practices, mistrust of the police and authority figures, illegal activities, and so on.

Self-awareness and a commitment to social work values are critical factors when there are substantial differences between the worker and the client. It takes courage to look at oneself and realize one's inability to accept everyone. Supervision from peers and supervisors is also important. In general, if workers do not discuss and resolve these conflicts, it will affect their ability to form a helping relationship. What is not or cannot be discussed frequently becomes a barrier.

Time orientation also is responsible for value conflicts. Some people are heavily influenced by how things have been done in the past and tend to make decisions based on "how it has always been done." Others are focused on the future. These people place considerable emphasis on planning ahead, "saving for a rainy day," and the needs of their children and grandchildren. Still others focus on the here and now. They tend to live a day at a time, to not save money, and to expect children to make their own way. Often those who must use all their energy providing for their basic needs—the poverty-stricken—will have this orientation, since they are so overwhelmed by their circumstances that it is difficult for them to think about the future. Again, differences in decisions about similar situations often can be explained by the value difference of time orientation.

Many Americans emphasize activity that results in observable accomplishment. However, some people see value in *being,* that is, in activity that is not outcome oriented. This stance places more emphasis on the person than on the outcome or the production. *Being in becoming* also places emphasis on the person but stresses activity as a vehicle for the growth of individuals. A social worker's belief about the purpose and value of activity will have an important influence on how she practices social work and on her goals with clients. It is important to employ methods and to identify beliefs so that approaches can be chosen that are congruent with the worker's value system.

Another way in which people view the world is how they see relationships among various events or parts of the situation. This relates to the Kluckholm and Strodtbeck dimension of rationality. Relationships are sometimes explained in a cause-effect, or linear, manner. This explanation is not congruent with contemporary generalist social work thinking, which calls for a transactional approach (see Chapter 5). The transactional approach emphasizes collaborability, that is, seeing the interaction of factors as influencing behavior in a situation. Others see each situation as unique and do not see a relationship with other situations, past or present. This can be considered the individuality approach to reaching conclusions about the nature of situations. These varying views of relationships among events can be due to different value orientations.

Often people operate from moral codes and value systems of which they are only partly aware. They may have accepted these without fully exploring the meaning or implications of a particular code or system. Sometimes one's beliefs are in contradiction with one another and one is not aware of the value priorities. Social worker self-knowledge calls for specification and understanding of one's moral code and value system. This understanding includes identification of the source of one's moral code and values as well as recognition of and the degree of flexibility regarding priorities.

Roots

As a person thinks about lifestyle, philosophy of life, moral code, and value system, the importance of roots—cultural and family background—should become clear. Individuals have different reactions to their roots. Some feel comfortable continuing the traditions and lifestyle of past generations; others reject all or a part of that way of life. Many become confused and are uncertain about what should be continued and what should be rejected; others find a balance between using the part of their roots they find useful and making adaptations and changes necessary to function in their present life situation.

One method of gaining understanding about one's cultural heritage is to spend time studying that heritage. This can be done through formal courses; by reading books about people who belong to that culture or about cultural heritage; and by talking with family members about family customs, lifestyle, and beliefs. An attempt should also be made to understand cultural heritage as a response to historical events and situations. Many people find that a journey into their cultural heritage is rewarding and yields considerable self-understanding.

The **genogram,** a family tree that specifies significant information about each individual for at least three generations, is a useful tool for gaining understanding of one's family (see the case example). From studying a genogram one can identify the effect of such things as death, size of family, birth position in family, naming patterns, and major family behavior patterns, to name a few. This method of studying the family as a system can yield much previously unrecognized information and help a person see not only the place he has filled in a family but also how he has been influenced by the family.[4]

There are other ways of considering family influence that aid in the quest for self-knowledge. The study of the family from a sociological and psychological point of view provides insight into the family. Discussions with family members about important events in the life of the family are another useful method for gaining deeper understanding about the family and its ways of functioning.

The search for one's roots can be a lifelong journey, yielding many fascinating facts. It can also open old wounds and thus be painful. Yet recognizing and dealing with the pain can often result in a person becoming more sensitive to others' pain and a more effective helper. Most of all, it can lead to greater understanding of self, to knowledge of who one is and why one is unique.

Life Experiences

The study of roots yields some understanding of experiences important in shaping the person. In addition to experiences within the family, other experiences are important, including educational experience—the experience of learning, the knowledge learned, and attitudes toward learning. Other meaningful experiences include those with one's peers and those in one's community and neighborhood and involve all kinds of people—those who are different because of age, race, ethnic background, and mental or physical disabilities. Experiences in organized group situations and in religious activities and experiences related to illness, disability, poverty, or abundance of economic resources are also important.

Identification of life experiences that have significant personal impact is yet another way of developing self-knowledge. It is also helpful to evaluate how each of these significant life experiences relates to other life experiences and how each affects ways of thinking, feeling, and acting. Also to be considered is how an experience results from a particular set of previous life experiences.

Personal Needs

Another area of self-knowledge is understanding one's needs and how they are dealt with. This includes personal needs as related to common human needs, needs that result from human diversity, and needs that arise from relationships with social systems (see Chapter 1).

In thinking about common human needs, the focus is on the need for food, clothing, shelter, care, safety, belongingness, and opportunity for growth and learning. An understanding of personal need includes how needs are met and the adequacy of the need provision. It is also useful to consider personal developmental patterns in the area of physical development. An understanding of human development provides information about expected development at a specific age; it is important to consider the development expected in relation to preceding development. Also involved are biological needs, which encompass such issues as health and wellness, disease and disability, physical strengths and limitations, changes in the body and its functioning due to aging, and the need for physical closeness.[5]

Identification of the current developmental stage is necessary before consideration can be given to the needs of individuals. For example, during the period of rapid physical growth and development in early adolescence, a person has a need for additional food to support the growing body.

 Erik Erikson and others have identified psychosocial need at various stages of human development. Identification of these needs gives rise to developmental tasks that must be accomplished if psychosocial need during each stage is to be fulfilled. See Table 6.1 for a summary of these tasks. For example, as the young child develops cognitively, there is a need for activities that allow for the exploration necessary for learning.

Some have questioned the validity for women of Erikson's formulation of human development.[6] New formulations about differences in male and female development continue to emerge, and these theoretical developments should be taken into account. There have also been questions raised about the validity of Erikson's theory for women and for people of color, since it is based on males of European descent. However, there do not seem to be any substantial alternative

TABLE 6.1   Psychosocial Tasks to Be Accomplished in the Stages of Human Development

Stage I   Trust vs. Mistrust (Infancy)

Development of a sense of being cared for through the provision of food, comfortable surroundings, and adult care.

Development of feelings that basic needs will be met and that the adult caretaker can be trusted.

Stage II   Autonomy vs. Shame and Doubt (Early Preschool Child)

Development of a sense of self as a separate individual.

Development of the realization that self can assert itself and control parts of personal functioning yet still need adult control because of limited ability to care for self.

Stage III   Initiative vs. Guilt (Late Preschool Child)

Development of the ability to plan and carry out activities. To do this there must be opportunities to try new things and to test new powers.

Development of the capacity to maintain a balance between joy in doing and responsibility for what is done.

Stage IV   Industry vs. Inferiority (Grade-School Child)

Development of skills necessary to function in a particular culture and society. To do this there needs to be opportunities to produce and to feel good about the production.

Development of a positive self-image and friendships with other persons.

Stage V   Identity vs. Role Confusion (Adolescence)

Opportunity to integrate and consolidate psychosocial growth from earlier stages.

Development of a sense of personal identity.

Acceptance of sexuality and of self as an independent person with personalized needs and desires.

Development of a sense of self in relationship with other persons.

Time and opportunity to examine how the person (or self) fits into the world and opportunity to develop a personal value system.

Stage VI   Intimacy vs. Isolation (Young Adulthood)

Opportunity to make decisions about lifestyle and career.

Opportunity to make commitments and to develop relationships of an intimate nature with other persons.

Development of adult relationships with family of orientation.

Stage VII   Generativity vs. Stagnation (Middle Adulthood)

Involvement in establishing and guiding the next generation and in concern for others.

Development of an outlook on life that values wisdom rather than physical power.

Development of relationships that are socializing rather than sexualizing.

Development of flexibility and openness in thinking about life.

Stage VIII   Ego Integrity vs. Despair (Older Adulthood)

Development of some order in own life in a spiritual sense.

Acceptance of life as lived without regret for what might have been.

Differentiation of self from work role.

Acceptance of physical decline.

Separation of self-worth from body preoccupation.

Opportunity to deal with the reality of own death.

Sources: Based largely on work of Erik Erikson, *Childhood and Society* (New York: W. W. Norton, 1950). Stages VII and VIII are also based on the work of Robert C. Peck, "Psychological Developments in the Second Half of Life," in Bernice L. Neugarten, Ed., *Middle Age and Aging* (Chicago: University of Chicago Press, 1968).

theories that have gained widespread acceptance. Nonetheless, the application of Erikson's formulation should be done with some flexibility and openness to other possibilities. In considering psychosocial need, it is useful not only to determine need at the present stage of development but also unmet need in earlier stages. Present functioning is in part affected by the way need has been met in the past. Thus, identification of unmet need is one means of gaining self-understanding.

Another dimension of human functioning from which needs arise is the spiritual dimension. This area is often ignored by social workers because there is little agreement about its nature and content and because there has been little research in this area. Spiritual development has often been considered a part of religious development; although this is frequently the case, there are broader implications. Carlton Cornett defined spirituality as "the individual's understanding of and response to meaning in life; time and morality; expectations regarding what, if anything, follows death; and belief or non-belief in a 'higher power.'"[7] It follows, then, that spiritual development is the process a person goes through in developing as a spiritual being. Although social work has paid little attention to this area, it is one that is extremely important in understanding the formation of a value system and philosophy of life. It is of particular importance to the self-knowledge a social worker needs to develop a professional value base. Some of the most helpful materials are those concerning moral development by Lawrence Kohlberg and Carol Gilligan[8] and faith development by James W. Fowler and Sharon Parks.[9]

It is also useful to reflect on how one's cultural group meets the psychosocial needs of its members. Doing so can yield some understanding as to whether personal experience has been typical or atypical for one's cultural group.

A second area of personal need arises because of human diversity. Need because of diversity relates to how identification or affiliation with a particular group has affected the person. Institutional racism, prejudice, and discrimination all have a serious impact on human functioning. Because of this impact, individuals who are a part of certain groups (racial minorities, persons with disabilities, etc.) have distinctive needs. Differences in language, physical appearance, and mental ability tend to separate people from some resources and opportunities for meeting need. Responses to societal expectations and responsibilities are different, as are coping mechanisms. Any understanding of personal need should take into account needs that arise because of different lifestyles and the stresses that accompany such differences.

A third area of personal need arises because of each person's interrelatedness with other persons—his or her membership in social systems. Systems such as the family, peer groups, institutions of work and education, organizations, the neighborhood and community, and cultural groups all place expectations and responsibilities on their members. People have a need to respond to these expectations and responsibilities. Individuals can accept expectations and responsibilities and can negotiate with the system to modify expectations and responsibilities.

Making an inventory of personal needs is another way of developing self-knowledge (see Table 6.2). As one comes to understand personal needs, an understanding of behavior, feelings, and responses to a variety of life experiences also

TABLE 6.2   A Guide for Thinking about Personal Need

My Common Human Needs

1. What are my needs for food, shelter, and clothing? How do I meet these needs?
2. What are my needs for safety so as to avoid pain and physical damage to self? How do I meet these needs?
3. What are my health care needs? How do I meet these needs?
4. What are my needs for love and belongingness? How do I meet these needs?
5. What are my needs for acceptance and status? How do I meet these needs?
6. What are my needs for developing my capacity and potentiality? How do I meet these needs?
7. What are my needs for understanding myself and the world in which I live? How do I meet these needs?
8. What other biological needs do I have?
9. How do I describe my spiritual development? What are major sources for this development? What are my present needs in this area?

My Developmental Needs

1. What are my needs because of my experience in developing physically? How do I meet these needs?
2. What are my needs in relation to my cognitive development? How do I meet these needs?
3. What is my present stage of psychosocial development?
4. What are my needs because of the development tasks of my current stage of development?
5. How well have I accomplished the tasks of earlier developmental stages?
6. What present needs do I have because of challenges related to not accomplishing these tasks?

My Needs Arising from Human Diversity

1. What in my lifestyle is "diverse" from the dominant lifestyle of my community?
2. What is the basis of the diversity—race, cultural group, gender, religion, disabling conditions, other?
3. What is the meaning of this diversity to me? How do I feel about myself in relation to this diversity?
4. What is the meaning of this diversity to my immediate environment? How does the environment deal with me as a diverse person?
5. How do I deal with the stresses and strains that exist because of diversity?
6. What strengths or special needs do I have because of my diversity?

My Needs Arising from Social Systems of Which I Am a Part

1. What expectations do the various social systems of which I am a part have of me? (These include family, peer group, school or work, organizations of which I am a member, neighborhood or cultural group, etc.).
2. What do I see as my responsibility toward the social systems of which I am a part?
3. What needs do I have in relation to these social systems, including the expectations and responsibilities related to them?

develops. This is a necessary aspect of true self-knowledge that not only has psychosocial dimensions but biological and spiritual dimensions as well.

Personal Functioning

Self-knowledge includes not only identification and understanding of one's lifestyle, philosophy of life, moral code, value system, roots, and personal needs, it also includes an understanding of how these affect day-to-day functioning. This understanding involves identification of how one learns, how one shares self with others, how one responds to a variety of situations, and how one's biases and prejudices play a role. Also important is how one feels about oneself and how this affects day-to-day functioning. Self-knowledge also includes understanding of how one meets personal needs; how one deals with freedom and restrictions; how one accepts change, both in oneself and in one's environment; how one views one's responsibility toward the social system of which one is a part; and what one's roles are in those systems.

Fundamental to self-knowledge is a healthy self-image or a sense of positive self-worth or self-esteem. When the worker is able to achieve self-esteem, self-knowledge in the areas mentioned above becomes more accessible. Negative self-worth leads to defensiveness and a greater likelihood that both self-image and one's view of others will be distorted. Positive self-worth is linked to the cardinal social work belief in the innate value and worth of all human beings. This belief is predicated on the realization that human beings are not perfect and that we all have flaws and make mistakes. However, by making mistakes, we prove that we are human. Accepting oneself as worthwhile in spite of one's flaws and mistakes allows one to view oneself and others more genuinely.

If the worker feels inadequate as a person, this will have a negative effect on the way in which help is delivered. The worker may feel good about being needed by the client, and she may yield to the temptation to foster dependency. This may meet her need to be needed, but it undermines the client's need to gain more control over his life and makes it difficult for him to become more independent. On the other hand, if the worker has a healthy self-image, she will be able to be more genuine in her care and concern for the client. This care and concern will be based on the client as a human being, not on her own needs. She will be able to work with her client without expecting something in return and can feel good about facilitating his growth and development. She can find gratification in providing a high quality of service rather than taking credit for what the client has achieved. The worker is better able to seek out strengths in the client and in herself, since she begins with the basic assumption that both she and her client have value and worth as human beings.

Awareness of one's interactions with the social systems around oneself is important to developing an appreciation for the ecological approach to helping. The more the worker becomes aware of the impact of her environment on herself and her impact on her environment, the more confidence she will have in broadening her work with her client to include the environment. Experiencing a supportive environment is fundamental to growth and change for human beings. Seeking out the strengths in the client's environment provides support for growth and change that is beyond the limited time and scope of the helping relationship.

The kind of self-knowledge discussed here is not easy to develop. It takes time for introspection, for observation of self in a variety of circumstances, for seeking out others' observations about self. It also requires risk taking. There may be a cost for self-knowledge: dissatisfaction with the self that is found, pain about past experiences, or anger about one's place and role in society. It is a lifelong journey toward self-knowledge and self-acceptance. It is also a necessary journey if the helping person is to be able to use a major tool—the self—skillfully, fully, and with maximal results.

Case Example

I am Janie Bryan, a twenty-year-old junior social work student. I grew up in a small town of 10,000 in a midwestern state. I am the middle of five children in a family that has lived in the same community all of my life. My oldest brother is five years older than I am, married, and a news announcer in a nearby city. My twenty-two-year-old sister married her high school boyfriend, lives in our hometown, and has a three-year-old daughter and a one-year-old son. My sister Mary, who is four years younger than I am, is moderately mentally retarded and is still at home, as is our younger brother, who is now eleven years old.

I see myself as enthusiastic and insightful. I really get excited about a lot of things and seem to have the ability to sense what is happening in many situations. I seem to understand my friends and their needs and problems. I think I am also logical and ingenious. I like to have time to think about things and to decide what is the logical way to do something, step by step. I guess I like to see where I am going when I start something, but I also like to brainstorm about what can be done and come up with new ideas about how to reach my goals.

It's very easy for me to talk to people. People seem to like me. I have to be careful, however, that I don't try to second-guess where others are coming from based on my experiences. I'm learning to find out from them why they think and feel as they do. In fact, right now I'm trying to learn as much as I can about a lot of different kinds of people. They have really interesting stories and seem to enjoy telling them to me. Also, I'm fascinated with the different kinds of experiences some of my fellow students have had. I am finding I really need to know something about other people to understand why they think the way they do.

I don't consider myself to have any disabilities, though some of my friends think being a woman is a handicap. I am very optimistic that my generation will not have to put up with all the old hangups, so I just plan that I can do anything I want to do. My family has always been middle class, never a lot of money but always comfortable. We have had what we needed. Dad has owned a small business for as long as I can remember. He is respected by everyone, and I have always been respected as his daughter. We are Methodists, and the church and its activities are important to our family.

I have always done well in school. I was usually on the honor roll in high school as well as being active in cheerleading, drama, and music. When I got to college, my first semester was not too good. I was not used to the kinds of assignments and tests given here at college. But then I seemed to kind of get the hang of it. I did some structuring of my time and organizing myself, and now I'm getting A's and B's with a C once in a while. I learn best when I am exploring new ideas and when I'm challenged to think and express my own thinking. This year I'm living in an apartment with three other girls. This is great after living in the dorm, but we did have some trouble at first keeping the place livable and getting the cooking done.

I am a positive thinker, optimistic. People are good. I think if you really work at it you can get along with almost anyone. I do like some people better than others, though. I hate to spend too much time discussing all the bad things that are happening and hearing about people's worries over things like tests next week, et cetera. I want to be independent, and it bothers me that I'm still financially dependent on my family. Yet I wonder if I'm not also dependent on my friends, too. I do hope it's in a way that they can count on me when they need it. I really care about other people and want to help them feel good about themselves. So many students seem to not have a lot of self-confidence or feel good about what's happening to them. I wish I could help them.

I guess I see the relationship of man and nature as one of harmony. I am a doer and seem to focus on the present rather than the past or future, though I am concerned about what I will do when I get out of school. I want to see some of the world, maybe work in a big city, though that is scary too. I would rather work alone but know some things must be done with others. Guess I should develop more skills for working with others.

I've never thought much about my family. Dad's side came from Germany about four generations ago, and Mother's people just moved out from the East about the same time. We seem to have sort of taken each other for granted. My mother's brother is really angry at my mother for letting my grandmother live in a nursing home, but Mom just can't handle her and my sister Mary. Dad is so busy at the store that he can't be much help. He really was the one to insist that Mom can't care for Grandma now. The folks really worry about what is going to happen to Mary. I've learned some things in my social work classes that might help. Last time I was home we talked about this, and I felt real good that the folks said it sure helped. I don't know much about Dad's family. That's something I want to find out more about.

The genogram (see Figure 6.1) helps me see that as a middle child I seem to have been more of a helper than the other children. I think this may be because Mary does need special

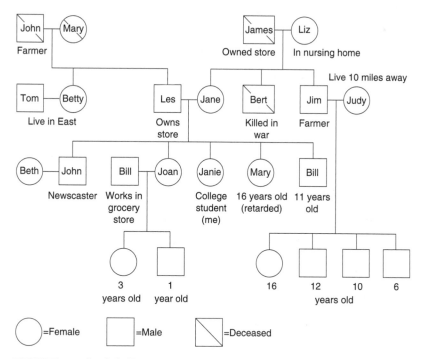

FIGURE 6.1 Janie's Genogram

(continued)

Case Example   Continued

attention and my little brother is so much younger. Mom has had her hands full with them. My older brother and sister sort of left home and got out of the helping. I think maybe I'm more mature because of this experience in my family. These family experiences and the real good experience I had in high school seem to have really prepared me for dealing with college life. I had to learn to use time well if I wanted to do all I did in high school.

As I look at my "common human needs," they all seem to have been met by my family. Mom and Dad still provide part of the money I need to go to school, and I've gotten loans and worked in the summer. Now I have to plan for myself how to deal with the day-to-day needs like eating right; sometimes I don't do so well here. Also, I never thought about health care. Mom has always sent me to the dentist and doctor. I think it's time I took some responsibility for this. I'm going to school to develop my ability to earn money and take care of myself but also to help others. I'm meeting that need by using the opportunities here at school.

I think I've developed normally, but with my sister's problems I understand that this can be a problem for her. I've just never thought about having needs in this area. I'm moving into Stage VI. I'm not yet ready to make any long-term commitments with a man. I want to live a bit and see some of the world first. But I do feel real close to my roommates and sometimes have wondered if they were taking the place of my family. I'm not sure where I am in this area. Maybe this is a sign I am struggling with a developmental task. I guess I need to test myself out as an independent adult person. I'm not sure I really have completed all the tasks of Stage V. I never thought of it, but I've known some role confusion. At home I play mother to my little brother, and I'm not sure what my relationship with Mary should be. I need to think about this and perhaps talk with Mom about it. Otherwise I seem to have gone through the other psychological stages pretty well. I trust people (usually); I feel good about myself; I like to do things and am fairly responsible; I have lots of friends.

I've never thought about diversity. I seem so average. Yet maybe that is my "diversity." Almost everyone I know is different in some way. They have had bad growing-up experiences and now have problems. I've really been lucky. Also, I don't know many people of different races. I need to think about what it means to be different in this way.

Because I'm so fortunate I have a lot of responsibility. Maybe that's part of my reason for wanting to be a social worker. Social systems do expect things of me. My parents want me to come home more often than I really want to. I need to talk with them about this rather than just let the problem go on. My instructors place lots of expectations for reading and papers on me. My friends want me to spend time with them. Sometimes it's hard to handle all this and still have the time I need to be alone. I need to work for a good balance. Maybe I need to set up some kind of a schedule for myself.

Overall I see myself as doing pretty well, but there are some things I need to do:

1. I need to continue to find out where others are coming from and to realize everyone has not had the opportunities and experiences I have had. I need to listen.
2. I need to plan for some alone time so I can get to know myself better. This means I need to structure my time better so I can meet all my obligations.
3. I need to get to know more about my extended family. I don't seem to know them very well.
4. I need to talk to my parents about my feelings of growing up and being independent. I'm not at all sure of my role in the family. We need to discuss this.
5. I need to increase my capacity for working cooperatively with others.

The Helping Person

The generalist social worker is a helper who can effectively use self with other persons to enable them to meet needs or solve problems more adequately. This helping focuses on needs and interactions between the person and the systems that make up the environment. Thus, the generalist social worker must develop the interactional skills necessary for productive interaction with individuals and groups of individuals.

As the social worker approaches the helping situation, he brings first and foremost self. This self brings concern for others; a knowledge base, both substantive and experiential; values, those of the profession and those of self; a view of the nature of change; and skills, both cognitive and interactive. The self is the major tool for working with others.

Many of these skills are characteristic of the helping person. There is a distinction between a helping person and a helping professional. The social work professional is a helping person, and the helping is done in the context of using the knowledge, values, and skills of the social work profession. One major difference between helping and professional helping is that the help given is based firmly in and with conscious use of an identifiable knowledge and value base. Another characteristic of professional helping is that the help is nonreciprocal. That is, help is given with no expectation that the helped will in turn provide help for the helper.

Characteristics of a Helping Person

There have been many descriptions of the helping person. Arthur Combs, Donald Avila, and William Purkey, in a research study, found that the belief system of the worker was an important characteristic of helping. The effective helper believes that people are

1. More able than unable
2. Friendly rather than unfriendly
3. Worthy rather than unworthy
4. Internally motivated rather than externally motivated
5. Dependable rather than undependable
6. Helpful rather than hindering

They found that the worker's beliefs about self were also important. The effective worker sees self as (1) identified with people, (2) adequate, (3) trustworthy, (4) wanted, and (5) worthy. Some additional traits of the helping person, according to these researchers, are (1) freeing rather than controlling, (2) being concerned about larger issues rather than smaller ones, (3) self-revealing rather than self-concealing, (4) being involved rather than alienated, (5) being process oriented rather than goal oriented, and (6) being altruistic rather than narcissistic. Effective workers approach a task in terms of people rather than things and from a perceptual rather than an objective viewpoint.[10]

Beulah Compton and Burt Galaway see maturity as another characteristic of helping persons. In their view, maturity consists of the capacities to be creative and to observe self in interaction with others, of a desire to help, and of having the qualities of courage and sensibility.[11] This mature person would seem to be one who is free enough of his own life problems to experiment, to risk, and to give of self in service of another. The quality of sensibility can be expressed as good judgment. Used in this sense, good judgment means the ability to make good decisions that serve the client and her needs rather than the worker's.

David Johnson sees the helping person as having another set of attributes.[12] First is the ability to self-disclose while being self-aware and showing concern for what the other person feels about what the worker says or does. This attribute has a quality of honesty, genuineness, and authenticity. Second is the capacity to trust, which entails warmth, acceptance, support, and the capacity to check for meaning. Third is skill in communication. This includes the ability to send messages so that the other can understand, to listen, to respond appropriately, and to clarify what is misunderstood. Fourth is the ability to express feeling; fifth is the ability to accept self and others; sixth is the ability to confront others constructively; and seventh is the capacity to reinforce and model appropriate behavior.

The helping person can be described as one who

1. Has a generally positive view of individuals and their behavior
2. Is concerned about others and their well-being for the sake of the other, not for self-centered purposes
3. Is open, trusting, warm, friendly, and honest
4. Works with persons being helped, not for them
5. Responds to people rather than supports the use of a particular technique
6. Is mature, has good judgment, and is willing to risk in the service of others
7. Is realistic about human situations, the amount of change possible, and the time it takes to change

Anthony Maluccio has reported research that examined the factors influencing outcomes of treatment from both the client's and the worker's perspectives.[13] He found agreement between the workers' and clients' perspective with respect to the following as desirable worker characteristics: acceptance, interest, warmth, and supportiveness. In addition, the clients saw these characteristics as helpful: being human and understanding; being caring, trusting, and friendly; encouraging work together; looking for solutions; giving advice and suggestions; and releasing anxiety.

In discussing worker styles, Edward Mullen describes the helping person as one who exerts personal influence rather than as one who applies techniques.[14] This indicates that it is the worker, as he uses self, that is the major factor in helping. Thus, a primary task in becoming a helping person is a fine-tuning of characteristics that are a part of everyday human interaction. Techniques can be useful tools, but only when used by a person who knows how to use personal influence (self).

The worker is not a cold, objective student of humanity who knows about rather than feels with; nor is he one who has a strong personal need to control, to satisfy his own conscience, to feel superior to other persons, or to be liked. The worker is not an overly confirmed optimist or a person who has solved his own problems but forgotten the personal cost, or a person whose own solutions to life problems are so precarious that the solutions take on a moralistic character. The worker is not afraid of feelings, his own or others. The worker uses knowledge and experience for understanding. This understanding is more than intellectual; it has emotional, or feeling, aspects as well. It is an understanding that leads to sensitive and realistic response to human need.

The helping worker is one who can defer his own needs and both recognizes and is not afraid of those needs; is not impulsive and is aware of his own feelings so they do not cause impulsiveness; is responsible for self and his own tasks in the helping endeavor; is growth facilitating and empathic; and is able to communicate clearly and effectively—concretely and specifically. This worker can clarify roles, status, values, and intentions with the client.

Responsibility and Authority

Two characteristics of a helping person—responsibility and authority—are particularly troublesome to the social worker. These two characteristics are related because each is a part of the personal influence aspect of the helping situation. They are also related in that they often become confused with value judgments related to the right of self-determination. Each worker must learn to manage these two characteristics in relationships with clients.

It is very easy for the social worker to take on responsibilities that do not belong to her. Often the worker perceives that self-destructive behavior is a client's way out, and the client is unwilling or unable to change the behavior or to take another way out. The worker begins to feel inadequate because she cannot "get the client to see what is best for him." Societal pressures also place a worker in a position of feeling responsible for the client's behaviors. Friends, public officials, and the person on the street ask why the social worker does not "make clients" do something. The worker again begins to accept inappropriate responsibility. Often the worker can see the consequences of a client's behavior and has a great desire to "save the client from self. The right of self-determination includes not only the right to make one's own choices; it also includes the right to suffer the consequences of those choices.

If the worker is not responsible for the client's choices in the helping situation, what, then, is the nature of the worker's responsibility? The worker is responsible for self in the helping situation, which includes:

1. Understanding person in situation as far as possible, given the circumstances of the helping situation
2. Using self in the way that will be most helpful to this client in this situation
3. Creating a climate that makes it possible for the client to use the help

4. Providing a perspective to the client's need, based on the worker's knowl-
    edge and experience
5. Providing a structure for thinking about the need, including focusing on,
    and skillful use of, the process of facilitating growth and change
6. Providing assistance in identifying strengths and information about needed
    resources along with assistance in obtaining those resources

The worker and client share responsibility for the outcome of the work together. The worker provides resources and opportunities for work on the problem
of meeting need. The client must make use of the opportunities and resources. If
the worker carries out the responsibility for providing the opportunity and resources and the client chooses not to use those opportunities and resources, this is
not the worker's responsibility.

Regardless of the nature of the worker's responsibility, the client views the
worker as a person with authority. Robert Foren and Royston Bailey, in discussing
the authority clients ascribe to workers, identify the following as aspects of that
authority:

1. Power to enforce standards of childcare
2. Personal attributes, social class, education
3. Association with parental figures
4. Knowledge and skill
5. Fantasy-magical power[15]

It is important for social workers to recognize that such authority has been
ascribed to them. In accepting the value of the right of self-determination, many
workers will deny this authority or be very uncomfortable with it. They see the
right to self-determination and the exercise of authority as contradictory, but an
in-depth examination of the nature of social work authority reveals that this is not
necessarily true. Denial of authority is not useful; the helping person must recognize and become comfortable with the ascribed authority. For example, a worker
can examine with a client the exact nature of the worker's authority so that a client
knows that the worker will not impose inappropriate standards.

It is also important to help the client become aware of unrealistic authority
expectations and free him to be self-determining. Some functions performed by
social workers carry a kind of legal authority, which is the means by which certain
of society's social control functions are carried out. These areas include protective
service for children, the mentally impaired, and the aged and probation and
parole work. The needs of social systems must be recognized; people cannot be allowed to act destructively toward others, particularly those who cannot protect
themselves. The worker needs to learn to be comfortable with the ascribed authority. There are limits to self-determination.

It is important to help clients understand not only their right of self-determination but also their social responsibility (another social work value). Self-determination, or choice, is limited by social responsibility. If people decide not to be

socially responsible, then they choose to take the consequences of their behavior. Social workers must use their authority in helping clients understand the consequences of behavior so that their choices regarding social responsibility are truly self-determining. Workers also must accept responsibility for those who cannot protect themselves, such as children, the frail aged, the abused, and the victims of crime.

To be helping persons, social workers must accept responsibility for those areas of the situation for which they are responsible but not for responsibilities that belong to the client. Social workers also must accept the realistic authority that goes with their role. In exercising this ascribed authority, they must constantly be guided by the values of both self-determination and social responsibility.

Helping Skills

The effective social worker develops helping skills. These skills are not mystical or esoteric; they are the skills of well-functioning human beings. The worker uses these skills with people who have difficulties in social functioning and cannot fulfill the usual responsibilities in human interaction and with people whose sociocultural context for interaction may be different than that of the worker. These factors place greater responsibility for the interaction on the worker than is usual for interaction with people of similar backgrounds. Thus, the skills for human interaction must be fine-tuned and be brought into the conscious awareness of the worker. The skills that need to be developed include the following:

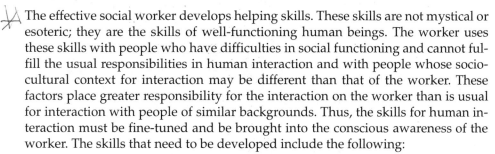

1. *Skills needed for understanding, including understanding of person in situation and helping other people understand themselves in the situation*—Skills in this area are listening, leading the person to express self, reflecting on what has been said, summarizing what has been said, confronting the person with the realities of situations, interpreting the facts as presented, and informing the person of facts.

2. *Skills needed for developing a climate that encourages helpful interaction*—Skills used in making people comfortable in strange or new situations include skills in supporting people, in crisis intervention, in focusing the area of concern to ease a sense of being overwhelmed, and in constructing a comfortable physical and emotional climate.

3. *Skills needed in acting on the needs of the client*—These include skills in problem solving, decision making, planning, referring, modeling, teaching, enabling, identifying strengths and resources, and using activity as well as the skills necessary to any practice strategy the worker may be using.

4. *Skills used in communicating and relating to others*—These include skills in listening and attending to the communication of others; in paraphrasing, clarifying, and checking perceptions; in getting started, encouraging, elaborating, focusing, and questioning; in responding to feelings and to others' experiences; in summarizing and pulling thoughts together; and in interpreting and informing.[16]

This summary of skills is not meant to be all-inclusive but rather gives some idea of the breadth of skills the social worker needs. Skill development is a continuous task for all social workers if they are to grow as helping persons.

Case Example

Janie Bryan thinks of herself as a helping person. After her experience in a social work program in college, she knows that sometimes the help she gave in the past contained too much advice and that she often jumped in to do for others before she adequately understood the situation. Sometimes she had difficulty understanding why a person might not take her advice and yet seemed to solve the problem in another way. Now she understands that help is not telling someone what she would do in that situation.

Janie now has a firm knowledge base on which to base her helping. She has become aware of her value system and of many different lifestyles and the value bases they reflect. A part of her value base now is the ethical code of the social work profession. She has developed skills for developing understanding of people and their situations, for relating to a wide variety of people, and for influencing for change. She has a sense that she has developed into a helping professional person, though she knows this development will be a lifelong experience.

The Multiperson Helping System

The social work endeavor is usually discussed from the perspective of one worker helping a human system, which can consist of an individual, family, small group, organization, or community. In a complex society characterized by the knowledge explosion along with increasing specialization, providing such help is not always possible. The worker is often part of a multiperson system. Susan Lonsdale, Adrian Webb, and Thomas Briggs have stated: "Individual problems [are] interconnected, do not always neatly divide along discipline lines and…the expertise required for effective interaction may elude the solo practitioner, or a single profession for that matter."[17] Contemporary social work often requires the coordinated work of several persons—several social workers, a social worker and paraprofessionals or volunteers, or social workers and those from other professions.

Allan Pincus and Anne Minahan define several systems involved in the social work endeavor: the client system, the change agent system, the target system, and the action system. The action system is made up of those involved in the change process. The target system is the system toward which the change activity is aimed. The conceptualization of change agent system carries the implication that the change agent, or worker, can be a multiperson system.[18]

The *multiperson helping system* manifests itself in a number of ways. In a sense, the worker-supervisor activity is a multiworker system. The supervisor is generally an experienced person who can provide the worker with technical assistance, a perspective for considering the worker-client interaction, and help that the worker may need in order to deliver the service. Other manifestations of the multiworker system are the use of consultation, collaboration, or referral. In each of these situations one worker is using the expertise of another worker to meet client needs. In **consultation,** the worker uses the help of another social worker or a person of another professional background to better understand the client and the client's needs to consider possible interventive strategies or to enable the worker to carry out the interventive strategy more adequately. Although the worker is free to accept the help given or to reject or adapt it, the consultant is nevertheless a part of the action system. **Collaboration** is a situation in which two or more helping persons are each responsible for certain aspects of service to a client. They may represent a single agency or several agencies, may all be social workers, or may come from several professional disciplines. The collaboration is a means of integrating the various services being delivered, of defining roles and services to be offered by each participant, and of ensuring that conflicting messages are not given to clients.

Referral is the process by which a client is enabled to use additional services, either in conjunction with, or instead of, services being provided. It calls for sharing of information about the client and the client's needs, interpreting the nature of the new service to the client, and enabling the client to use resources. Ideally, the initial worker should also follow through to ensure that the new service is meeting the client's needs. Referral when the worker will continue to provide some service to the client might be thought of as a special case of collaboration.

Often the multiworker system is formalized so that it serves more than one client. It then becomes an ongoing system and is often called a **team.** Lonsdale, Webb, and Briggs have identified four kinds of teams with which social workers are involved: (1) a team in which the workers represent different organizations and agencies, (2) a team composed of persons from different professions, (3) a team of social workers employed in the same agency, and (4) a team that includes not only professional workers but also clients and community members.[19]

The team that represents different organizations and agencies is used when these institutions tend to serve many of the same individuals. Such would be the case when health or mental health agencies and the public social service agency are serving clients from a particular area. Agencies that are often concerned with services for children may include not only public social services, health, and mental health agencies but also the school, the juvenile justice agency, and a community recreation center. Cooperative planning and collaborating for specific clients are goals of this kind of team. Sometimes such a team also considers preventive and program-planning issues. The team often functions through what is known as a **case conference,** in which members of the team share knowledge about clients or the nature of the service to a particular client that agencies are providing. In addition, a case conference can result in joint planning for service to the client. Another version of this are "wraparound" services, which have been developed to serve the needs of families who are overwhelmed and may be at risk of having their children placed in care outside of the home.

Use of a team of members from different professional disciplines first occurred in mental health settings, in which psychiatry, psychology, nursing, and social work collaborated in provision of service to clients. Medical settings also make use of the interdisciplinary team approach in providing for both the psychosocial and the physical needs of the patients; diagnostic centers also employ this type of team. The range of professions that may be represented on the team is broad and depends on the setting and the client's needs.

Interdisciplinary practice calls for the social worker to gain knowledge about, and to develop understanding of, the disciplines being worked with. This knowledge and understanding should include:

1. The role and function of that profession from its point of view, including the normal way of carrying out the tasks of the profession
2. The profession's value system or code of ethics
3. Something of that profession's knowledge base
4. How the profession is sanctioned—its educational levels and specialties
5. Current issues that face that profession
6. Areas of overlap and tension with social work

This knowledge and understanding can be gained in several ways: by talking with representatives of the profession, by working together on teams, and by reading the literature of the professions. Rosalie Kane has identified two types of interdisciplinary teams: the coordinative and the integrative. On the *coordinative team* the professions maintain distinct professional roles; there is designated leadership, nonconsensual decision making, little concern for the process of the team, formal communication, and an emphasis on the assessment phase of service. On the *integrative team* there is deliberate role blurring, consensual decision making, high interdependence among the team members, and much attention to process.[20] Most interdisciplinary teams probably combine elements of the coordinative and integrative teams along a continuum, being nearer one type or the other.

The team made up of employees of a social service agency is known as a *social work team*. The team can include paraprofessional and nonprofessional persons who are carrying out parts of the social work task. It may be led by a worker with a master's degree or by an experienced worker with a bachelor's degree. It may be a group of social service workers who divide the tasks of providing service to clients. For example, in a mental hospital one worker may be responsible for geriatric patients and nursing home placements, another for a specific ward or group of patients from a particular geographic area, another for group services, and so on. Briggs says of this type of team: "Every agency has varying types-levels of personnel and must deploy a rational scheme for division of labor that delivers service consistent with goals and priorities while maintaining adequate standards and levels of accountability."[21]

The team made up of professionals and community persons resembles the change agent system described by Pincus and Minahan. It is used when these persons work together to change something within a community or institution, to develop a new resource or programs, or to influence policy or legislation. The child protection team found in some communities is an example of this type of team.

There has been considerable discussion about the use of teams. Gene Hooyman, in discussing the reasons for and problems with using teams, says that most of the problems seem to come about because of poorly functioning teams.[22] Teamwork can be time consuming. Teams differ from each other just as people do. Because of the complex needs and concerns of clients and the complex social systems that impact them, participation on teams must often be a part of the service delivery of social workers. The worker must develop skill in functioning on a team.

In utilizing an ecosystems strengths approach, the worker actively supports the development of a partnership involving herself, her client, and her client's natural helping system. The natural helping system is composed of supportive people and includes family, friends, coworkers, and other members of the client's ecosystem who are able to assist in the effort to meet the client's needs. These individuals do not have professional training or assigned helping roles, but nonetheless are critical to supporting the efforts of the client and the worker. In an ecosystems strengths approach the multiperson worker is the social worker, who interacts with the informal, often primary group system. The worker represents the formal, often bureaucratic system. It is essential that the social worker and the client be able to mobilize and support the efforts of the client's ecosystem. Identifying the strengths within the ecosystem and building a plan for growth and change that is based on these strengths ensures meeting needs in a way that is both efficient and enduring.

A problem that can develop when using a multiperson worker is the exclusion of the client in the helping endeavor. The worker must spend time developing the relationship with the system, and this can easily lead to excluding client input or participation. Planning can develop as planning for, rather than planning with, the client. This is a particularly difficult issue when working with other professionals who do not value working with the client but prefer doing to or for the client. One solution has been to include the client on the team, but this is not always effective. Clients who are overwhelmed with needs and who have low self-esteem do not feel comfortable in a group of professionals.

Another problem in using a multiperson worker is the amount of time involved in developing the worker system. Some teams lose sight of their primary purpose—service to the client—and focus on team functioning as the goal, rather than as a means to an end. Time needs to be used in developing the team and monitoring its function, but time spent on team-functioning activity should be kept to a minimum and, when possible, carried out as a part of the task focus of the team. Despite the fact that working as a team is often difficult and time consuming, in some situations a team can provide service to a client that is not possible for one worker to give.

In these circumstances, the social worker's choice is to empower the client and encourage his active participation. If this is not effective, then the worker might seek to have a member of the client's natural helping system participate with the client for support or advocacy. The social worker should also advocate for the client with other members of the multiperson worker/team. In cases where the client is disabled to the point that his participation is seriously impaired, a guardian or advocate should participate.

In any multiworker situation the individual social worker is in an interdependent situation. In order to function in service of the client in multiworker situations, the individual must have developed a set of knowledge, values, and skills specific to such situations. Knowledge needed includes considerable understanding of small-group process and of group problem solving. (See Chapter 10.) This includes knowledge of methods of working with others in a cooperative and collaborative manner and an understanding of other disciplines and of the natural helping system. The worker must incorporate into his value system a positive attitude toward cooperative and collaborative efforts and be comfortable in interdependent situations. Willingness to share and trust other workers is important, as are flexibility and tolerance for disagreement. Skills that are important include the ability to facilitate team process and to develop and maintain cooperative and collaborative relationships.

Summary

The interactions of worker and client are at the center of the social work endeavor. The worker must develop a high level of self-understanding and healthy self-esteem if she is to maximize helping interactions. The development of self-understanding, which is never complete, is an ongoing endeavor that involves assessing one's values, lifestyle, roots, personal needs, and culture.

The worker's use of self is a major tool in the helping endeavor. Some of the characteristics of the helping person are concern for others, acceptance of others, warmth, supportiveness, and maturity. The helping professional person is one who is grounded in a knowledge base and who uses a professional code of ethics as a guide to the helping endeavor. Good judgment also is a very important factor. The helping person needs to develop skills for understanding clients and their situations, for creating a climate that encourages interaction, for acting on the client's needs, and for communicating with and relating to others. The social worker also needs to develop a degree of comfort with the authority and responsibility inherent in the professional helping role.

Sometimes more than one person or worker needs to be involved in the helping situation. This may take the form of consultation, referral, or collaboration. Functioning in a team situation is an important skill for social workers. Teams take many forms: sometimes they are made up of persons from different professions; sometimes, of social workers from a variety of agencies or with a variety of skills. Regardless of the type of team, functioning with others in a cooperative, collaborative manner is imperative.

QUESTIONS

1. What areas of self-knowledge should you examine in order to develop greater helping capacity?

2. What is the difference between a philosophy of life and a value system?

3. What do you see as your strengths as a helping person? Your limitations? What can you do to mitigate your limitations?

4. How well do you believe you have dealt with issues of authority in your life experience? With issues of responsibility? With healthy self-esteem?

5. What do you see as problems you may have in working in a multiworker situation?

SUGGESTED READINGS

Abraham, Julie S. "Making Teams Work." *Social Work with Groups* 12, 4 (1989): 45–63.

Abramson, Marcia. "Reflections on Knowing Oneself Ethically: Toward a Working Framework for Social Work Practice." *Families in Society* 77 (April 1996): 195–202.

Bissell, Gavin. "Personal Ethics in Social Work With Older People." *International Social Work* 39 (July 1996): 257–263.

Brammer, Lawrence M., and MacDonald, Ginger. *The Helping Relationship: Process and Skills,* 7th ed. Boston: Allyn and Bacon, 1999.

Chau, Kenneth L. "Educating for Effective Group Work Practice in Multicultural Environments of the 1990's." *Journal of Multicultural Social Work* 1, 4 (1992): 1–15.

Cornett, Carlton. "Toward a More Comprehensive Personology: Integrating a Spiritual Perspective into Social Work Practice." *Social Work* (March 1992): 101–102.

DePoy, Elizabeth, and Miller, Monte. "Preparation of Social Workers for Serving Individuals with Developmental Disabilities: A Brief Report." *Mental Retardation* 34 (February 1996): 54–57.

Erikson, Erik H., Erikson, Joan, M., and Kivnick, Helen Q. *The Life Cycle Completed.* New York: W. W. Norton, 1998.

Gummer, Burton. "Stress in the Workplace: Looking Bad, Telling Lies, and Burning Out." *Administration in Social Work* 20 (January 1996): 73–88.

Johnson, David W. *Reaching Out: Interpersonal Effectiveness and Self-Actualization,* 7th ed. Boston: Allyn and Bacon, 1999.

Joseph, M. Vincentia. "Religion and Social Work Practice." *Social Casework* 69 (September 1988): 443–452.

McPhatter, Anna R. "Cultural Competence in Child Welfare: What Is It? How Do We Achieve It? What Happens Without It? *Child Welfare* 76 (January 1997): 255–278.

Scott, Dorothy. "Meaning Construction and Social Work Practice." *Social Service Review* 63 (March 1989): 39–51.

Sheafor, Bradford W., Horejsi, Charles R., and Horejsi, Gloria A. *Techniques and Guidelines for Social Work Practice,* 5th ed. Boston: Allyn and Bacon, 2000 (Chapter 2, 3, 5, and 10).

Soderfeldt, Marie, Soderfeldt, Bjorn, and Warg, Lars-Erik. "Burnout in Social Work." *Social Work* 40 (September 1995): 638–646.

Sotomayer, Marta. "Language, Culture and Ethnicity in Developing Self-Concept." *Social Casework* 58 (April 1977): 195–203.

NOTES

1. Adapted from the work of Isabel Briggs Myers, *Introduction to Type* (Gainsville, FL: Center for Application of Psychological Type, 1976).

2. For development of this idea from a Christian viewpoint, see Joseph F. Fletcher, *Situational Ethics: A New Morality* (Philadelphia: Westminster Press, 1966).

3. Florence Rockwood Kluckholm and Fred L. Strodtbeck, *Variations in Value Orientations* (Evanston, IL: Row Peterson, 1961), pp. 10–20.

4. Ann Hartman and Joan Laird, *Family-Centered Social Work Practice* (New York: Free Press, 1983), chap. 10.

5. See Dennis Saleeby, "Biology's Challenge to Social Work: Embodying the Person-in-Environment Perspective." *Social Work* 37 (March 1992): 112–117.

6. See Carol Gilligan, *In a Different Voice* (Cambridge, MA: Harvard University Press, 1982); Jean Baker Miller, *Toward a New Psychology of Women* (Boston: Beacon Press, 1976); and Alice S. Rossi, "Life-Span Theories and Women's Lives," *Signs* 6 (Autumn 1980): 4–32.

7. Carlton Cornett, "Toward a More Comprehensive Personology: Integrating a Spiritual Perspective into Social Work Practice," *Social Work* 37 (March 1992): 101–102.

8. For a discussion of moral development in a social work frame of reference, see Wayne A. Chess and Julia M. Norlin, *Human Development and the Social Environment,* 2nd ed. (Boston: Allyn and Bacon, 1991), pp. 231–237; Charles Zastrow and Karen Kirst-Ashman, *Understanding Human Behavior and the Social Environment* (Chicago: Nelson-Hall, 1997), pp. 283–288; and John F. Longres, *Human Behavior in the Social Environment* (Itasca, IL: F. E. Peacock, 1990), pp. 474–481.

9. James W. Fowler, *Stages of Faith* (San Francisco: Harper, 1995); and Sharon Parks, *The Critical Years: Young Adults and the Search for Meaning, Faith, and Commitment* (San Francisco: Harper and Row, 1991).

10. Arthur W. Combs, Donald Avila, and William W. Purkey, *Helping Relationships: Basic Concepts for the Helping Professions* (Boston: Allyn and Bacon, 1971).

11. Beulah Roberts Compton and Burt Galaway, *Social Work Processes,* 3rd ed. (Homewood, IL: Dorsey Press, 1984), pp. 245–248.

12. David W. Johnson, *Reaching Out: Interpersonal Effectiveness and Self-Actualization,* 7th ed. (Boston: Allyn and Bacon, 1999).

13. Anthony N. Maluccio, *Learning from Clients: Interpersonal Helping as Viewed by Clients and Social Workers* (New York: Free Press, 1979).

14. Edward Mullen, "Differences in Worker Style in Casework," *Social Casework* 50 (June 1969): 347–353.

15. Robert Foren and Royston Bailey, *Authority in Social Casework* (Oxford, England: Pergamon Press, 1968), p. 19.

16. Based in part on Lawrence M. Brammer and Ginger MacDonald, *The Helping Relationship: Process and Skills,* 7th ed. (Boston: Allyn and Bacon, 1999).

17. Susan Lonsdale, Adrian Webb, and Thomas L. Briggs, *Teamwork in the Personal Social Services and Health Services: British and American Perspectives* (Syracuse, NY: Syracuse University School of Social Work, 1980), p. 1.

18. Allen Pincus and Anne Minahan, *Social Work Practice: Model and Method* (Itasca, IL: F. E. Peacock, 1973), chap. 3.

19. Lonsdale, Webb, and Briggs, *Teamwork in the Social Services.*

20. Rosalie A. Kane, "Multi-Disciplinary Teamwork in the United States: Trends, Issues and Implications for Social Workers," in Lonsdale, Webb, and Briggs, *Teamwork in the Social Services,* pp. 138–150.

21. Thomas L. Briggs, "Social Work Teams in the United States of America," in Lonsdale, Webb, and Briggs, *Teamwork in the Social Services,* pp. 75–93.

22. Gene Hooyman, "Team Building in the Human Services," in Compton and Galaway, *Social Work Processes,* pp. 465–478.

7

The Client

LEARNING EXPECTATIONS

1. Understanding of the term *client* and familiarity with other terms used that convey a similar meaning.
2. Understanding of the meaning of seeking help from a social agency in U.S. society.
3. Understanding of the process a person must go through in becoming a client.
4. Understanding of and the beginning ability to develop a social history of an individual.
5. Understanding of the influence of diversity on the needs of individuals.
6. Development of knowledge of what factors about any culture a social worker must understand in providing service to a client of that culture.
7. Knowledge about the family as a social system.
8. Appreciation of the need to focus sometimes on the multiperson system as client.

The term **client** in social work usually refers to a person, family, or group that is the focus of the social worker's helping activity. In the generalist approach, this term may be somewhat inaccurate, because as the social worker assesses the situation and develops plans, the focus may not be on an individual or system that has requested help. The focus for change may be on a system that is blocking the need fulfillment of an individual(s) or family(s); the focus for change may be on groups, communities, or institutions/agencies. Nevertheless, the generalist social worker's knowledge base contains understandings about all of the systems on which change might be focused. This chapter focuses on the individual and family as client, on people seeking help. Later in the book, material on engaging larger systems in the helping process and on assessing those systems is developed.

The person seeking help brings to the helping situation concerns, needs, and strengths. She comes to the helping situation sometimes seeking help, sometimes being required to use help, and sometimes not realizing the nature of the help offered or the reason it is being offered. She has concerns and unmet needs. Although she comes from a societal and cultural milieu, a set of life experiences, and a set of transactions with other persons that make her unique, yet she shares the commonalities of humankind.

Regardless of the reason for coming for help, the client brings much more than concern or need to the helping situation. She also brings the total self as a biological, psychosocial, cultural, and spiritual being. This includes the resources of self and the personal environment and also environmental constraints. Also included are perceptions of self and the situation and patterns of coping with stress and patterns of interpersonal relationships. The present need is affected in part by the way developmental needs have been met and by needs arising from the diverse aspects of the client's lifestyle and from the expectations of the client's environment.

One of the major tasks of the worker-client interaction is to understand the client as a unique person in a unique situation. There can never be total knowledge about a client. The worker seeks knowledge about the client that is needed for giving the service to be delivered. The client is the major source of the facts used to develop the understanding of person in situation.

The social worker must also understand the meaning of seeking and using help, which is a first step to understanding the person seeking help. Understanding of the client also must include consideration of the multiperson client system. In this chapter, the family as a client is discussed as an example of a multiperson client system. Other multiperson systems will be considered in later chapters.

Becoming a Client

Emanual Tropp sees the client as one who seeks professional help, one who employs the help of another, or one who is served by a social agency or institution. In discussing each of these definitions, Tropp points out that there are inconsistencies. These inconsistencies also permeate the way workers, agencies, and community persons view clients. Several questions arise from these definitions: Is the client a customer or a dependent person? Is the client seen as a charge or ward, a person not worthy of respect? Is the client seen as a generally self-reliant person, able to make decisions? Must a client seek help, or may the person who is involuntarily referred be considered a client until she voluntarily seeks the help provided?[1]

Scott Briar and Henry Miller discuss the client in terms of his social role. A social role has normative expectations for the behavior of the person filling the role. These expectations are held by social agencies, reference groups, and the general public.[2]

Allen Pincus and Anne Minahan use the term *client* in a somewhat limited sense. The client system is the system that asks for help; the system that needs to change is known as the target system. The system asking for help may not be the system needing to change. A target system may become a client system by realizing a need for change and asking for help.[3]

In the context of this book, the client is one who has either sought the help of a social worker or is served by an agency employing a social worker. When the client has not sought the help, it is assumed that one of the tasks of the worker is to engage the client in a helping relationship that enables the client to understand the reason the help is offered and the implications for using the help or rejecting it. It is further assumed that the client's role calls for active participation in the helping endeavor, which includes furnishing appropriate information to inform the decision-making process, participation in the decision-making process appropriate to the client's ability and capacity, and the carrying out of mutually agreed-on tasks.

The client is either a person or a social system. Clients are of several types:

1. Those who ask for appropriate help for themselves
2. Those who ask for help for another person or system
3. Those who do not seek help but are in some way blocking or threatening the social functioning of another person (e.g., the neglectful parent in a child protection case)
4. Those who seek or use help as a means to reach their own goals or ends (e.g., a client the court has ordered to receive service in order to avoid more severe sanctions)
5. Those who seek help, but for inappropriate goals

Identification of client type is a first step in the delivery of service, for the worker-client relationship and interaction will vary depending on the type of client and the nature of the help sought.

The client is a person with both needs and strengths. The need may be related to a person the client has a responsibility for; for example, a parent becomes a client when seeking help for needs a child may have. The need may be related to interpersonal relationships, in negotiating with systems in the environment, or in role performance. The need may represent a lack of material means or personal capacity (temporary or permanent) or of the knowledge or preparation needed to carry out social roles. It may be due to disturbance or disorder resulting in intrapsychic turmoil, constriction, or distortion; it may be a result of discrepancies between expectations of a person and the demands of various segments of that person's environment or between environmental expectations and demands and personal needs.[4]

For example, a client may be having difficulty because of inadequate income due to a layoff at her place of employment; she is a victim of the problem of the workplace. Or she may be a single parent who needs assistance with parenting a young child but is still managing to cope with the help of a good childcare provider. When that provider suddenly becomes seriously ill and is no longer able to help, the parent's unmet need is aggravated by outside conditions over which she has no control. Or the client may not be able to hold a steady job due to excessive use of alcohol and thus be the cause of the need not being met.

The need may rest in interpersonal relationships; for example, a parent may be unable to understand an adolescent child's needs and thus be so strict that there is open rebellion and an inability to discuss the situation between parent and child. The need may rest in an inability to negotiate with systems in the environment; for example, a patient in a hospital may be unable to ask the doctor the questions that bother him or to make his concerns known to the doctor. Or the need may rest in improving role performance; for example, the parent does not meet the nutritional needs of the child or maintain a suitable home for the child.

The need may be one of deficiency; that is, an individual does not have either the material means or the personal capacity (temporary or permanent) to carry out the tasks needed for coping with a situation. Or an older person with a limited income and limited physical capacity may not be able to maintain a home or fix nutritious meals. The need may also be related to not having the preparation needed to carry out a social role. The mother who did not have adequate mothering as a child and has received no instruction in childcare may not be able to properly care for her child because she does not know how to care for small children.

Some needs are due to disturbance or disorder resulting in intrapsychic turmoil, constriction, or distortion. In these situations, the person may be mentally ill or have some perceptual difficulty that results in using inappropriate or ineffective means for coping with life situations. There may be discrepancies between expectations of a person and the demands of various segments of that person's environment. For example, an individual may expect that food, clothing, and shelter will be provided by a community social agency without work on his part, but the agency can only provide partially for those needs and then only if work is performed for the community. Other needs may be due to discrepancies between environmental demands and personal needs. For example, a teenage girl whose mother is ill may be expected to care for younger siblings, but she needs time for completing her education and for socialization with her peers.

In practice, a number of terms are used for the client role. The term used depends in part on the setting for practice and carries with it additional meanings. Social agencies generally use the term *client,* but in medical and mental health settings the term **patient** is often used. When using the term *patient,* a social worker might see the client in a more traditional patient role, that is, as sick and dependent rather than as an interdependent person. In a school setting and certain institutions for youth, the client is called a *student.* This can lead the worker into an instructor-learner or a superordinate-subordinate relationship. Social workers in advocate roles sometimes see clients as victims. The relationship may then be based on compensating for the wrongs of others and on doing for the client. Whatever term is used, the client should be seen not in a subordinate position but in a collaborative role, as having specific tasks and responsibilities that result in more effective social functioning when carried out in cooperation with the worker.

The worker, the client, and the environment all have expectations about how the client will fill the client role. The worker and the agency supplying the service have expectations about appointments, use of the time during helping sessions, time and place of these sessions, and the client's sharing of information and involvement in the helping process. The community's expectations of clients often center around the client's being grateful for the help provided. The community also has expectations concerning drinking, sexual behavior, childcare practices, and money management concerns. Clients often do not understand what is expected of them in the helping situation. They may expect to be told what to do or to receive certain kinds of advice and help or to be treated as second-rate persons because they need help. Clients usually come for help at times of powerlessness and a lowered sense of self-worth and with anxiety about the unknown helper and the helping situation. Seeking help and taking on the client role can add to the stress of an already stressful situation.

Before a person seeks help from a social agency, he has usually attempted to meet the need in a way that has worked with previous needs. But if this is not successful, a person may then turn to his natural helping network. Going to a social agency is generally a last resort. Thus, individuals often come to the agency after a period of unsuccessful attempts to meet their needs. Going to an agency or being unable to **cope** can result in anxiety and in feelings of low self-worth or of anger.

When clients from a culture different from those providing service come for help, another stress is added. For example, when a black person must seek help from an agency staffed by white people, the black person may bring feelings of resentment and anger toward whites because of discriminatory practices she has experienced in other situations. She may be unsure that a white social worker can understand her or her situation because the white worker does not have sufficient knowledge about black culture.

Before coming to a social agency, most people will have attempted to meet the need first with their own resources and then with the resources of their natural support system (e.g., friends, relatives, associates). If this has not been successful, they may have sought advice or help from a familiar helping person such as a pastor, teacher, or doctor.

People come to agencies in varying ways. F. M. Lowenberg has identified the pathways to help as (1) an informal referral by a neighbor or acquaintance, (2) knowledge of the work of the agency in one's social circle, (3) self-referral, (4) a formal request or referral from another professional or agency, (5) outreach the agency has done to identify persons with needs and encourage these persons to accept service, and (6) mandated participation by a court or some other authority.[5] Lowenberg goes on to note that becoming a client requires a person to admit that he has a problem and to express willingness to give up a behavior if necessary and to cooperate with a relatively unknown person in an often-misunderstood process in an unknown place.

People may resist the acceptance of help from a social agency because of discomfort with strange people and strange or new situations. They may resist because of cultural norms regarding the use of help. Cultural groups prescribe helping mechanisms, attitudes toward the use of help, and the kinds of situations for which one may receive help. People also may resist asking for help because they feel that no help is possible.

David Landy has identified the process a person goes through in seeking help or in becoming a client:

1. The help seeker must decide something is wrong.
2. The help seeker must face the probability that family, friends, and neighbors will know of his disability.

3. The help seeker must decide to admit to a helper he is in distress, failed, or is not capable of handling his own problem.
4. The help seeker must decide to surrender enough sovereignty and autonomy to place himself in a dependent role.
5. The help seeker must decide to direct his search for help among persons and resources unknown to him.
6. The help seeker must decide whether to take time off a job or from other responsibilities to receive help.
7. The help seeker may realize that in receiving help other of his relationships may be threatened.[6]

In a study of farm families and the use of social services, Emilia Martinez-Brawley and Joan Blundall explored attitudes and preferences in help seeking. They note that help seeking and help acceptance are very complex processes. The study found that some of the major barriers to seeking or receiving help are concern about community reputation, lack of knowledge about services, feelings about the use of help that originate in the community culture, distrust of workers, and pride.[7] Although the study is limited in size of the population studied, it does provide information about the importance of culture and context in understanding help-seeking feelings and behaviors. It also leads to a conclusion that it is important for workers to consider not only the present context or situation of a client but also the client's historical context. For example, many farm families have had to migrate to metropolitan areas because of problems in agricultural communities. In the new setting, stresses and strains often affect the social functioning of individuals and families. Although there may be a need for social services, attitudes and ways of functioning brought from the rural setting are apt to be present, which affect the capacity to seek help.

The role of client is not an easy one to take on. Social and cultural groups have norms that mitigate against easy assumption of the role. Personal feelings of adequacy and self-worth are often threatened in assuming the role. There usually exist considerable discomfort, anxiety, and stress; there may even be a state of crisis when a person enters a social agency. The acceptance of this role also calls for energy when the personal system may have already depleted its energy supply in attempting to meet the need. The worker must understand the phenomena of asking for help and be ready to support the person through the process of becoming a client.

Understanding the Individual Client

Before a worker can adequately respond to an individual's need, develop a working relationship, or engage in decision making and planning with a client, it is necessary to understand that client and his situation. Although there are commonalities among people, there are also differences. These differences include ones that are related to the developmental stage and to present and past adequacy in meeting the individual's common human needs and developmental needs. Differences are the result of hereditary and environmental factors.

The human condition is very complex. Each person is a unique bio-psycho-social-spiritual being. When person in situation is examined from a systemic point of view, the various aspects—of both the person and the person's situation—are seen to interact with each other. The outcome of these transactions is a unique person who perceives the world in a unique manner, who reacts to common human needs and developmental needs in an individualized way. The understanding of person in situation is crucial to all of social work practice.

Just as the worker must develop knowledge of self, the worker must also develop knowledge of the client. Some of the same tools used for self-knowledge are useful in gaining understanding of the client. The identification of a client's lifestyle, philosophy of life, moral code, and value system is possible only insofar as the client is willing to share of self with the worker and as the worker is able to make assumptions based on her knowledge of the client's background, cultural identification, and life experiences and share these assumptions with the client for confirmation. The extent to which the worker needs to understand these factors about a client depends to a degree on the client's needs and the service to be offered.

Understanding the client's roots, that is, his cultural background, is often crucial in providing service. The worker can use some of the same tools available for understanding her own culture to understand the client. It is most important that the client not be stereotyped because of membership in a particular racial or ethnic group; there are many variations within each of these groups. To gain the needed understanding of any member of a racial or ethnic group, it is necessary to individualize that person.

An understanding of the client's family structure and functioning and of the client's place in the family is very important. Family factors are some of the strongest influences in a person's life. Sometimes the person reacts to these influences by accepting and conforming to the family's lifestyle; other times the person rejects what the family expects. In both situations, understanding of a client's family is necessary to understand the client's needs, desires, and strengths. The genogram is a useful tool to use with clients when developing an understanding of family influences for both worker and client.

It is important to develop an understanding of client needs and ways of functioning to the extent necessary for providing the needed service. Thus, the worker should be selective about the information to be sought and should individualize the nature and depth of the understanding, depending on client need and the service being provided. It is especially important to set the stage for helping by identifying the strengths of the client and of the ecosystem. This provides an essential foundation for the work to be done. Planning that is based on strengths has a much greater chance of success. The ecosystem strengths perspective has the potential for meeting the need more quickly than do approaches that emphasize altering the client's skills or lifestyle. This approach brings hope by providing a positive approach to difficult situations.

The method used for attaining an understanding of client needs and strengths is often referred to as a **social history.** Table 7.1 is a schema for the development of a social history of an individual. Not all of the material called for will be important or available for all clients. In some agencies, for some situations, and with some clients, other information will be relevant. For example, in a nursing home it is important for the social worker to have information about the resident's avocational interests and friendship ties to enable the resident to remain active and involved with other people. Often, religious ties and experiences will be important. In working with an adolescent who was adopted at age 7, it is helpful to know something about the adoption and the client's attitude and feelings about the adoption. The schema in Table 7.1 is meant not as a fixed outline of what must be included in all social histories but as a guide to be modified and adapted depending on agency practice, client need, and the service being sought. The schema has three major parts: (1) a description of the person in situation; (2) an identification of the concern and needs; and (3) a description of the strengths and challenges of client in situation. The social history should be descriptive rather than evaluative. For example, family relationships should be described in terms of who relates to whom and in what manner rather than by merely stating that the family relationships are "good." Strengths and challenges should be stated as facts rather than as value judgments.

Vital Roles

Any social history should pay particular attention to vital roles—the roles of work, marriage, and parenting.[8] With children and youth, attention should be paid to how they are being parented and how they are preparing for their work role (education). With older persons past retirement age or after the loss of the mate, attention should be given to how past functioning affects present functioning. Difficulty in one or more of these vital roles underlies most social-functioning difficulties that come to the attention of social agencies and social workers.

Human Diversity

Human diversity is another factor that merits special attention in developing an understanding of individuals. Before a worker can understand the influence of culture on any specific client, he must understand that person's cultural group generally. It takes special effort to gain such understanding, but social workers are responsible for having a knowledge of the general characteristics of any group with which they are working. Acquiring this knowledge can be accomplished in several ways. One approach is to undertake formal study through coursework or books and articles about a cultural group. Another way to gain understanding is to seek out members of the group or people with expertise. However, the most important approach is to recognize that the client is an expert, not only with respect to her culture, but also in how she has experienced her culture. The worker should

TABLE 7.1   Schema for Development of a Social History: Individual

I. The Person
  A. Identifying information (as needed by agency): name, address, date and place of birth, marital status, religion, race, referred by whom and why
  B. Family
    1. Parents: names, dates of birth, dates of death, place or places of residence
    2. Siblings: names, dates of birth, places of residence
    3. Spouse: names, ages, dates of marriages and divorces
    4. Children: names, ages, dates of birth, places of residence
    5. Resources in the family for client—expectations for client
  C. Education and work experience
    1. Last grade of school completed, degrees if any, special knowledge or training; attitudes toward educational experiences; resources and expectations of educational system for client
    2. Work history—jobs held, dates, reasons for leaving; attitudes toward work experiences; resources and expectations of work system for client
  D. Diversity
    1. Disabling factors—physical, mental health history, current functioning
    2. Cultural and ethnic identification, importance to client
    3. Other diversity factors (include religious affiliation or spiritual factors, if any)
    4. Resources and expectations related to diversity characteristics of client
  E. Environmental factors
    1. Significant relationships outside family; resources and expectations for client
    2. Significant neighborhood and community factors; resources and expectations for client
II. The Concern or Need
  A. Reason for request for service
  B. History of concern or need; onset of concern or need; nature and results of coping attempts; factors that seem to be contributing to concern or need
  C. Capacity to carry out "vital roles"
  D. Needs of client (general)
    1. Needs based on common human need/development
      a. Stage of physical, cognitive, and psychosocial development
      b. Adequacy of need fulfillment in previous stages
      c. Present needs (needs for developmental stage and compensation for previous stage deficiency)
    2. Needs based on diversity factors
      a. What dominant societal factors and attitudes affect the way people of this diversity meet common human/developmental needs?
      b. What cultural group factors affect the way people of this diversity meet common human/developmental needs?
      c. Individualize client within the diverse group. What are this client's attitudes toward diversity, means of coping with diversity, adaptation or lifestyle within diverse group, coping or adaptation relative to dominant societal expectations?
      d. What incongruities exist between this client's way of functioning and the societal expectations due to diversity?
      e. What needs does this person have because of dominant societal attitudes and expectations, because of cultural factors related to common human need/human development, because of individual factors of attitudes toward the diversity and dominant societal expectations and impingements, or because of incongruities between the client's way of functioning and societal expectations due to diversity?
    3. Needs based on environmental expectations
      a. Client's responsibilities toward family, peer group, work, organizations, community
      b. Other environmental expectations of client; client's attitudes toward these expectations

(continued)

TABLE 7.1   Continued

      c. Are responsibilities and expectations of the client realistic?
      d. Client needs because of the responsibilities and expectations
   4. Needs of client in relation to the request for service
      a. What general needs of the client have bearing on the request for service?
      b. What is the specific need of the client in relation to the request?
      c. What factors seem to be blocking the fulfillment of that need?
III. Strengths and Challenges for Helping
   A. What does the client expect to happen during and as a result of the service to be provided?
   B. What are the client's ideas, interests, and plans that are relevant to the service?
   C. What is the client's motivation for using the service and for change?
   D. What is the client's capacity for coping and for change? What might impinge? What are the individual's internal resources for change?
   E. What are the client's strengths?
   F. What are the environmental resources and the environmental responsibilities and impingements that could support or mitigate against coping or change?
   G. Are there any other factors that affect the client's motivation, capacity, or opportunity for change?
   H. What is the nature of the stress factor?
   I. Are the client's expectations realistic?
   J. Summary of strengths and the challenges of client in situation as they relate to meeting need

encourage the client to teach him about her culture. It is also important to understand the individuality of each person in the context of her diversity. Table 7.2 outlines the cultural factors that should be considered to understand a client from a particular cultural group.[9] As important as this understanding is, it is not sufficient; the worker must also understand how the dominant society has impacted on individuals of a particular group. A person's needs arise from the expectations of the cultural group and from the attitudes of, and relationships with, the dominant society. In addition, restrictions on the diverse group that arise from the dominant society must be understood. It is also important to consider the range of differences that exist in any cultural group. Cultural understanding recognizes that persons in situations operate uniquely within the diverse group just as they operate uniquely in the larger social setting.

    The influence of social class is another factor that must be taken into account in understanding the individual within a culture. In considering an ethnic culture, it is important to separate culture from social class. In other words: How much of the diversity is due to membership in a cultural group, and how much is due to the fact that the person lives in poverty? John Longres has stated that minority status is not just a matter of cultural difference but also is related to relative power, privilege, advantage, and prestige of a group within society (social class is an important consideration here). He also points out that these factors lead to the individual's perception of her place in society and her identity. This leads to help-seeking and help-using behaviors and influences the ways people of minority status perceive

TABLE 7.2 Human Diversity: Factors That Should Be Considered in Identifying Needs and Strengths Related to Diversity

A. Cultural factors
  1. Values
     Attitudes about: things, time use, dominant culture, authority, work, display of feeling or emotion, etc.
     Past, present, future orientation
     Taboos
  2. Relationships—ways of relating
     With other persons
     To the physical world
     To the spiritual world
  3. Family structure
     Nature of family relationships
     Content of family life
     Variety and change possible
     Decision making
     Generational factors—age, sex considerations
     Child-rearing and housekeeping practices
  4. History—migrations
     Of relationship to dominant culture
     Of change-development-meaning to the group
  5. Communication patterns—language
     Usage, idioms, colloquialisms, labels, dialects, symbols, grammar, breadth of expression
     Nonverbal aspects
     Patterns—use of small talk, time, etc.
  6. Community structure
     Political, economic, educational, religious
     Means of mutual assistance, socialization, social control
     Social, cultural, and religious activities
     Health care
     Resources for individuals and families
  7. Coping mechanisms
     Adaptation, compensation, reaction to stress, adjustment to new situations and environments
B. Factors related to dominant societal attitudes and behaviors
  1. Issues of prejudice, discrimination, stigmatization, stratification, and stereotyping
  2. Ethnic consciousness
  3. Relationship to majority culture
     Amount of distance, majority expectations, exploitation, minority hypersensitivity, pain and suspicion, power relationships
  4. Quality-of-life issues
  5. Group identity and expectation of group relative to majority group
  6. How difference is valued
  7. Opportunity provision or restriction
C. Individual differences
  1. Orientation—traditional, assimilated, adapting, confused relative to culture
  2. Attitude toward self, others of same minority, difference minorities, and dominant groups
  3. Self-concept, coping and adaptation mechanisms, use of language and other communication mechanisms
  4. Relationships with family and/or cultural groups, responsibility or resources in the relationships
  5. Significant life experiences as a member of the cultural group
  6. Dynamics of self affected by diverse status, impact of diversity on self

problems.[10] Kenneth L. Chau notes that unless "impediments to individual progress are taken into consideration in needs assessment, the meaning and significance of the client's attempt to solve problems may not be properly understood."[11]

Human diversity is not only ethnic or racial; we are diverse because of age, gender, physical or mental ability, physical appearance, religious affiliation, sexual orientation, and socioeconomic standing. When diverse persons form an identifiable group with a common culture, factors of cultural diversity exist, and worker understanding of that culture is important.

Some types of diversity do not exist as a cultural group. For example, a person with a physical disability may not identify with other persons with physical disabilities; nevertheless, that person may be subject to discrimination, stereotyping, expectations, exploitation, opportunity restriction, and the like. The societal attitudes and behaviors toward the person with diversity are important in identifying need because of diversity; also important is the person's attitude toward self as a person with diversity. It is important to consider the impact labels can have on people with diversity. It is preferable to say the word *person* or *people* first so that the emphasis is on the fact that this is a person rather than on the "differentness" or diversity. Thus, it better to say "person with a disability" as opposed to saying "disabled person" or "handicapped person."

One group that has received considerable attention in terms of diversity is women. Women are not a cultural group, though there is a sense of culture in subgroups of women such as feminist groups. It is important to see women as having a particular kind of diversity and as having been impacted by social factors that can undermine their capabilities, opportunities, and self-perceptions.[12] During times of social change it is particularly important to determine an individual's orientation toward that change by identifying attitudes and self-image in relation to change issues. Major social change has been taking place with respect to the role and function of women. Thus, social workers should be aware of a particular female client's orientation toward this change, of how she perceives society impacting her as an individual, and of her view of her role and function as a woman. It is especially important that female social workers not assume that all women have or should have the same attitudes toward the women's movement that they may hold.

Two other groups that have experienced considerable discrimination and oppression are gays and lesbians. There is generally a moralistic or religious basis used to rationalize this discrimination. The assumption is that gays and lesbians have chosen to be attracted to the same sex. Given the overwhelmingly negative attitude of the dominant society toward homosexuality, one might wonder about using the word *choice* or *preference*. Increasingly, research is indicating that human sexuality is much more complex and cannot really be dichotomized into heterosexual and homosexual. Biological and genetic factors seem to play an important role, along with environment. Even if it were legitimate to use the term *choice* in regard to sexuality, there is no room in social work or in a truly democratic society for discrimination against or oppression of gays and lesbians.

Motivation, Capacity, and Opportunity

In determining a client's strengths and challenges, a useful framework is one that assesses a client's motivation, capacity, and opportunity.[13] Motivation is influenced by what a person wants and how much the person wants it. It is assumed that for a person to meet a need or to use an offered service that person must want to work on the situation or use the service. Factors that can be important for motivation include the push of discomfort, the pull of hope that something can be done to meet the need or accomplish a task, and internal pressures and drives toward reaching a goal.

Capacity can be broken down into three categories: relationship, capacity for growth and change, and physical capacity. In considering relationship capacity, the factor to be determined is the ability of the client to form relationships with a worker or other persons who might be used as resources for helping. Capacity for growth and change is related in part to the cognitive development of the client. The ability of the client to engage in growth and change either independently or with the assistance of a worker should be determined. A person's physical capacity is affected by certain conditions and age.

Opportunity refers to two factors. First is whether the client's environment will allow the client to use the service or to change. A part of this opportunity would be whether the client has sufficient energy for the change activity after the energy expenditure required to satisfy environmental and personal responsibilities. For example, a woman who is a single parent and the breadwinner in a family may not have sufficient energy to engage in an after-work educational activity that would prepare her for work that would yield a higher income. Opportunity also refers to the availability of resources and services needed to support the change. Attention needs to be paid to whether the particular client can use available resources and services. Cultural or other factors may preclude the usability of resources and services by clients. This results in a lack of opportunity even though the resources or services exist. This conceptualization can also relate to workers' motivation (to work with this client), capacity (in terms of knowledge, skill, and energy), and opportunity (size of caseload, agency sanction, etc.).

Nora Gold has pointed out the importance of considering motivation when developing an understanding of clients. She notes that two factors seem to be of prime importance. One is **locus of control.** This concern is whether motivation comes from within (an internal process) or from influences in a person's environment (an external process). Also of importance and related to locus of control is the capacity of the individual for self-determination. Here the concern is whether the individual desires or is given the opportunity to make decisions based on internal factors (personal preferences) or external factors (situational imperatives and controls). According to Gold, motivational considerations affect the manner in which people select and define goals, which in turn are influenced by value issues.[14] An emerging goal for change is empowerment (see the section entitled "Empowerment" in Chapter 13). If the worker is concerned with empowering the individual, then understanding that individual's motivations can be very important. It is equally important that the worker be committed to assisting the client to maximize her ability to exercise self-determination and be guided by her wishes to do so.

Stress and Crisis Determination

In considering a client's strengths and challenges, another factor to take into account is the degree and nature of the stress the client is experiencing. Stress exists when any internal or external event or condition impacts a person or social system so as to upset its usual steady state or way of functioning. Usually, coping and problem-solving mechanisms are used, and the steady state is reestablished. If these mechanisms do not result in some modifications that enable reestablishment of the steady state, or if the severity of the problem or the number of events to be coped with becomes too great, a state of crisis may result.

The crisis state is marked by disequilibrium and disorganization.[15] A true crisis exists when a person who has usually functioned and coped relatively well is rather suddenly in a state of disequilibrium and disorganization. It is important to differentiate between a state of crisis and chronic disorganization. Another factor to examine is how previous crises have been resolved. Sometimes a crisis is resolved in a manner that presents challenges for later social functioning. Inappropriate resolution of a crisis may stifle growth or cause negative relationships or feelings to develop.

Strengths and Uniqueness of Clients

Before leaving the discussion of the person as a client, there are two more considerations. All people have strengths that must be identified and called into play in the helping endeavor, some of which have already been discussed with regard to motivation, capacity, and opportunity. Other strengths become apparent when past problem-solving or coping mechanisms are examined. Strengths also exist in the individual's surrounding network. Elizabeth M. Tracy and James Whittaker have developed an assessment instrument relative to the social supports of individuals and families.[16] With this instrument, they determine the components of a network, its capabilities, and its nonsupportive aspects, among other factors.

Focusing on strengths is an approach that is often difficult for the worker and the client to achieve or maintain. Because the goal of the helping process is to help clients address unmet needs, this tends to focus the process on what is deficient or missing. Earlier social work interventions used problem-focused approaches in working with clients. In using a strengths approach, the worker needs to resist the temptation to look for deficits or signs of dysfunction. Instead, she should seek out the strengths within the client and the various systems that make up his ecosystem. The strengths perspective takes a positive "can do" approach that builds a solid foundation for growth and change. The first step is to develop a social history that provides an understanding of the assets, resources, and capacities of the client and the various systems within his ecosystem. There are two fundamental purposes for developing an individual social history. The first should be to gain a better understanding of and appreciation for the client as a unique human being, along with an understanding of the environment and the interaction between client and environment. The second is to develop potential ways in which the client can meet needs that have not been met.

When using a schema such as the one presented in this chapter (Table 7.1), it is easy to miss the unique qualities of a particular individual or family. Jackie E. Pray declares that it is important to assume "at the outset that the client will differ from all others." She also calls for the use of the practitioner's practice wisdom and tacit knowledge in considering client uniqueness.[17] Also of importance is the development of mutual understanding between worker and client about the situation and the client, particularly the meaning of the experience to the client based on the client's personal beliefs and life experiences. Thus, the worker must be sensitive to information and understandings not called for in the schema and allow for the inclusion of this material when developing understanding about clients.

Social workers often become involved with clients after they have made considerable effort to cope with a situation, solve a problem, or meet a need. The client may be experiencing a high level of stress, be in danger of a crisis, or even be in crisis. Social workers should determine the stress level so that appropriate responses to need can be made.

Case Example

Social Study: Individual

I. **The Person**
   A. **Identifying information**
      1. **Personal information**

      Name: Rachel Smith   Address: 204 Main, Any Town
      Sex: Female   Date of birth: May 8, 1970,
      Ethnic identification: Mixed Irish,   Detroit, Michigan
         German, and English   Date of marriage: April 1990
      Marital status: Divorced 1993   Religion: Catholic, nonpracticing
      Husband's name: Michael Smith

      2. **Referral information:** Rachel was referred to Community Mental Health (CMH) from the inpatient unit at Any Town Hospital. She had been hospitalized for a psychotic episode during which she had attempted suicide by cutting herself. Rachel has a diagnosis of paranoid schizophrenia. She claimed that voices had told her to do this. Rachel has been under the care of a local psychiatrist who feels that she needs assistance from CMH because she has become alienated from her family and is unable to live independently without some assistance.

(continued)

Case Example   Continued

B. **Family**
1. **Parents:** William and Sarah McDougal (ages 68 and 63, respectively) are retired due to Mr. M's disability. Mr. M suffers from a lung condition related to
work and years of smoking that makes it impossible for him to live in a cold
climate. For several years they have lived in Michigan during the warm
months and in a mobile home in Florida during the winter. For a number of
years, they have allowed Rachel to live with them, but last year they were
forced to move to Florida full time because of Mr. M's health.
2. **Siblings:** Rachel has a younger brother, Bob, who lives in the area with his
family. Bob is married, with two young children, and works long hours in
construction.
3. **Spouse:** Mike and Rachel met each other at college. When Rachel became
pregnant, they married in 1990. Rachel had her first psychotic episode
shortly after the birth of their daughter, Jennifer. Mike tried to maintain the
marriage, but eventually decided to seek a divorce, which took place in 1993.
He has since remarried and has another child with his second wife.
4. **Children:** Rachel has a nine-year-old daughter, Jennifer, who lives with her
former husband, Mike, and his second wife. Mike has custody due to Rachel's
unstable mental health. Rachel is allowed supervised visits every other weekend, which have generally taken place with a member of her family.
5. **Resources and expectations of the family:** Until recently, Rachel had a
strong relationship and the support of her family in managing the challenges
of her mental illness. However, with her parents' move to Florida, she has
lost much of that support. They are willing to have her come live with them,
but she is reluctant to move to a strange place and would also not be able to
see her daughter very often. Her brother tries to help as much as possible,
but his work and family obligations limit him. In the past, he would check on
Rachel to make sure she was taking care of herself during the times when
their parents were away. Since their move, he has not been able to devote sufficient time to ensure that Rachel stays on her medication. Rachel's increasing paranoia resulted in her unwillingness to let him in her apartment. Her
former husband has tried to cooperate but is very protective of their daughter. He has stated that if Rachel does not stay on her medication, he may
decide to seek further restrictions on visitation.

C. **Education and work experience**
1. **Education:** Rachel completed high school at Any Town High and attended
two years of college, studying art at the state university.
2. **Work history:** Rachel worked at a fast food restaurant during her senior year of
high school. She is a talented artist and worked at an art supply store during the
first two summers out of high school. She has not worked for an employer since
becoming pregnant but has sold paintings regularly when she is stable.

D. **Diversity**
Rachel is a woman who suffers from a major mental illness. Her mental disability prevents her from being employed on a full-time basis and has severely limited her ability to parent her daughter. When she is stable, she looks fairly
healthy, although the medication slows down her thinking a great deal. As a result, some members of the community look down on her as a negligent mother.
They also wonder why she is not working. As a woman, she feels very de-

pressed about not being able to be a full-time mother to her daughter, which she would very much like to do.

E. Environmental factors

While Rachel has a supportive family, there are limitations on their ability to assist her. Rachel had an extensive network of friendships, but she has not maintained these since the onset of her illness. The community has an excellent mental health system, with a strong commitment to maintaining consumers independently in the community and maximizing the quality of life. The community has a strong economy, with many employment opportunities. There is an extensive human service delivery system, with good cooperation and collaboration among agencies. Rachel receives SSI and food stamps along with some income from selling her paintings.

II. Concern or Need

A. Reason for request for service

As mentioned above, Rachel suffers from paranoid schizophrenia and is in need of support if she is to maintain herself independently in the community. She needs to comply with her medication regimen and will need some assistance with completing daily living tasks on a regular basis. Rachel needs assistance in restoring and maintaining relationships with family and friends.

B. History of concern or need

Rachel's first decompensation occurred as she was trying to cope with a new marriage and the birth of her daughter. Prior to that time she had not shown any signs of developing a mental illness, although she had always been somewhat susceptible to experiencing stress. She tended to worry more than the average person but enjoyed a typical childhood, which she describes as happy. Since the first episode, she has been hospitalized three more times. Each time she had stopped taking her medication and had decompensated. When on medication she appears healthy, but her thinking is slowed down so it takes her a little longer to process things. Rachel does not like how she feels on the medication and wishes she could "be like everyone else" and not have to take it. Prior to her illness she was very active with many friends; however, now she feels some stress when she has to interact with others on a regular basis. She would like to socialize more and often feels lonely.

C. Capacity to carry out vital roles

Rachel's ability to engage in the roles of wife and mother has been seriously impaired. She also has difficulty in engaging in work that is stressful or requires a lot of interaction with others. When on her medication, she is able to cook and clean and take care of herself but needs encouragement and monitoring to maintain compliance with her medication. Her income is meager, and there are times that she runs out of money for food and some of her bills.

D. Needs of client

1. **Needs based on common human need/development:** Rachel's developmental needs were adequately met up until the time she suffered her first decompensation. Since that time it has been an up-and-down struggle. She needs an income sufficient to support herself along with budgeting that would allow her to pay her bills. Rachel would like to have a job, but is somewhat fearful of losing her SSI and insurance. She needs opportunity for socializing but also needs to be able to have time to herself when this becomes too stressful. Part of Rachel realizes that her daughter is better off with her father, but she wants very much to be as good a mother as she can be under the circumstances. She

(continued)

Case Example   Continued

wants her daughter to understand her illness and accept her even though she is not able to live with her. She is very fearful that her daughter will pull away from her as she gets older. Rachel has always regretted dropping out of college and dreams about becoming a full-time artist some day.

2. **Needs based on diversity factors:** Most of Rachel's needs in this area relate to community attitudes toward people with mental illness. While some people are enlightened about schizophrenia, many do not understand it and are fearful or negative. People who do not know about her illness wonder if she is mentally retarded or antisocial because her medication slows down her thinking. Rachel has also seen people stare at her and heard their derogatory comments at the supermarket checkout when she uses her food stamps. As a mother, Rachel needs an opportunity to form a meaningful relationship with her daughter.

3. **Needs based on environmental expectations:** Rachel expects to be able to live independently in the community. She realizes that in order to do so, she needs to maintain her mental stability, since the community reacts negatively to her when she experiences psychotic episodes. Her family expects her to show cooperation and appreciation when they do things for her. If Rachel wants to attend college or be employed, she will have to meet the expectations of instructors or employers.

4. **Needs of client in relation to the request for service:** Rachel needs to maintain herself on medication that provides her with maximum benefit in controlling her symptoms while reducing side effects. She needs to be safe from her suicidal impulses, which only occur when she has decompensated. Rachel might be able to benefit from a supported independent living program at CMH along with joining the clubhouse program. She may also benefit from either the supported employment program or the supported education program that is available.

III. **Strengths and Challenges for Helping:** Rachel is very hopeful that receiving services from CMH will help her to overcome the challenges she has faced since her parents moved to Florida. She would like to live in her own apartment and support herself. She would also like to go back to college to complete her education. In terms of her relationship with her daughter, she wants to resume regular visits, with the hope of eventually being able to have unsupervised visitation. Rachel realizes that she needs to give herself some time and should not try to do too much at once. She is not currently suicidal but could become so again if she decompensates. At this point, Rachel is highly motivated to take advantage of any opportunity she can. She is very bright and creative and has a good deal of artistic talent. Given her artistic talent and motivation, Rachel has the potential to further her education and perhaps develop a source of income for herself through her painting. Her family is supportive although limited in their ability to help her. The community has many job opportunities, an extensive human service delivery system, and an excellent mental health system. CMH is progressive and has several fine programs that could meet Rachel's needs. However, she will need support in taking advantage of these and will need to try one thing at a time so she does not get overwhelmed. Rachel has expressed some interest in practicing her religion on a regular basis and may benefit from some of the social groups and events in the church.

Understanding the Multiclient System: The Family

When the client is a multiperson system, the worker must understand not only the persons who are members of the system but also the subsystems that exist within the system and the system itself. This includes understanding the relationships among the individuals and subsystems. Social systems theory provides one means for describing multiperson systems. All social systems have structural, functional, and developmental aspects. An analogy from photography helps to differentiate these three aspects. Structure may be seen as a snapshot; it describes the parts and their relationship to one another at a given point in time. Functioning may be seen as the movie; functioning describes the nature of the process of the system. Development may be seen as time-lapse photography; development describes stages of family functioning and is also concerned with roots and history and with significant past events in the life of the system.

Systems that may be multiperson clients are the family, the small group, organizations, institutions, agencies, neighborhoods, and communities. Each of these kinds of systems has unique characteristics that must be considered in understanding the worker-client relationship with a specific system of that kind. In this chapter, the understanding of the family system is developed. (Chapter 10 will discuss the small group; Chapter 8 will discuss the agency and community.)

The family is the system most apt to influence the functioning of the individual; it is the primary system responsible for providing for needs of individuals. Challenges to individual functioning often arise from family functioning, past or present. Often, without change in the family system, the needs of individuals cannot be provided for and the challenges that the individual faces cannot be met. To bring about this change in the family system, it is necessary to understand the family as a social system. Knowing about an individual's place in his family system is also often necessary for understanding that individual. When the change needed is in transactions among members of the family system, the family becomes the unit of attention, or the client. The social worker determines the family system's strengths, motivation, capacity, and opportunity for change and engages the family system in the helping process. The family goes through the process of becoming a client.

Just as the use of a social history is useful in gaining an understanding of individuals, so a family social history is also useful in achieving an understanding of the family system. (See Table 7.3 for a family schema.) The family schema contains four parts: (1) necessary identifying information; (2) a description of the family as a system; (3) the identification of concerns and needs of the family system; and (4) identification of the strengths and challenges of the family system and the environment for meeting needs.

In studying the structure of the family, it is useful to understand each family member in considerable depth. Use of appropriate parts of Table 7.1 would be a helpful tool for development of such understanding. The family should be considered as a system. System members are those persons who have stronger relationships among themselves than with other persons. The boundary of the family—

TABLE 7.3   Schema for Development of a Social History: Family

   I. Identifying Information (as needed by agency)
     A. Names and birthdates of family members, dates of death
     B. Dates of marriage, dates of previous marriages
     C. Religion, race, cultural background
     D. Language spoken in the home
     E. Date of first contact, referred by whom
  II. The Family as a System (note the strengths, resources, and challenges for each section)
     A. Family structure
        1. Identify all persons within the functioning family system. Include members of extended family and nonrelated persons if they function as part of the system. Describe each person using appropriate parts of "Schema for Development of a Social History: Individual" (Table 7.1).
        2. Subsystems—Describe the relationships and functioning of the marital, parental, sibling, and parent-child subsystems or other subsystems.
        3. Family cohesiveness—Describe the manner in which the family maintains its system, boundary, and relatedness. Include the issue of connectedness and separateness among family members, specification of family rules and norms, and emotional climate.
        4. The family's environment—Describe the family's
           a. Living situation
           b. Socioeconomic status
           c. Nature of community or neighborhood and the family's relationship with the community or neighborhood. Include community organizations and institutions important for the family and the nature of the relationship with these. Describe community and neighborhood resources and responsibilities and impingements for this family in this community.
           d. Extended family: involvement with; significant persons in the extended family; strength of the influence of this family system; and resources, responsibility, and impingements from it.
     B. Family functioning
        1. Communication patterns
        2. Decision-making patterns
        3. Role performance
           a. Work and housekeeping standards and practices
           b. Parenting and childcare standards and practices
           c. System member support; growth encouragement, care, and concern
        4. Family's customary adaptive and coping mechanisms
        5. Construct an eco-map for the family. (See example on page 146.)
     C. Family development—history
        1. Roots, influence of cultural group and previous generations on the family system
        2. Significant event in the life of the family
        3. Developmental stage of family life
        4. Construct a genogram
 III. The Concern or Need
     A. Why did this family come to the agency? What service is requested?
     B. Needs of individual family members (see Table 7.1).
     C. Needs of subsystems within the family. (Particular attention should be paid to the marital system and the parental system.) Identify resources and other assistance or change needed for appropriate functioning.
     D. Needs of the family system. Consider how the needs of individuals and subsystems impact on the family system. Also consider environmental responsibilities, expectations, and any diversity factors that impact on the family as a system. Identify blocks to the family system's meeting these needs.

TABLE 7.3   Continued

IV. Strengths and Challenges for Meeting Needs
   A. What does this family want to happen as a result of the service provided?
   B. What are the family's ideas, interests, and plans that are relevant to the service?
   C. What is the family's motivation for using the service or for change?
   D. What is the family's capacity for coping and change? What might impinge?
   E. What are the family's resources for change (internal to the system)?
   F. What are the environmental resources, responsibilities, and impingements on this family that could support or mitigate against change?
   G. Are there any other factors that affect the family system's motivation, capacity, or opportunity for change?
   H. Are the system's and the environment's expectations realistic for this family?
   I. What are the strengths and challenges for family in situation as they relate to meeting need?

the separation of the family from the environment—should be drawn so as to include other significant persons and reflect the family's view of itself.

Thus, the family system may include some members of the extended family who may or may not be living in the home, such as a grandparent or an aunt. It may include an unrelated person living in the home or a neighbor. The children who have left the home for whatever reason need to be considered, depending on the nature of their functioning with the family system. Attention should be paid to absent family members—those who have died or left the family through divorce. Their influence on the family system and its functioning should be ascertained. The determination of who is in a family system is particularly difficult in the case of a blended family. The **blended family** is one in which the parents have had previous marriages and have children from these marriages. Often in blended families, custody and visitation of children from previous marriages create a changing mix of individuals and relationships that results in a state of flux. In addition, relationships between stepparents and stepchildren and between stepsiblings may be tenuous or conflicted. These family relationships may be even more complicated by multiple divorces, live-in partners, and children born out of wedlock.

Another part of the structure of the family is its subsystems—the marital, the parental, the sibling, and the parent-child subsystems. The marital subsystem includes the husband and wife as marriage partners. Their relationship should be described in terms of separation from each partner's family of origin and the ability of each partner to support and validate the other partner. The parental subsystem includes the mother and father and their interactions as parents of a child or children. The understanding of the sibling subsystem is concerned with how the children relate to one another. The parent-child subsystem is intergenerational in nature; of particular concern is how limits of authority and responsibility are drawn between the generations.[18] Other subsystems may exist in a family, and these should be identified and the nature of relationships in these subsystems described. Ann Hartman and Joan Laird have pointed out that an intergenerational perspective is very helpful in developing understanding of the family system. To do this, they suggest the use of a genogram.[19] (This technique was introduced in Chapter 6.)

A third consideration in describing family structure is cohesiveness. This is the stuff that binds the family together. It involves the emotional or feeling tone of the family, the we-ness of the family; it is the connectedness of family members with one another. Healthy family relationships allow for both connectedness and separateness.[20] The mechanisms for both connectedness and separateness should be described. Family rules and norms (the way this family does things or behaves) are means of expressing cohesiveness. Description of what is allowed and under what circumstances is another means of discovering the interrelatedness of family members.

The family system is part of a larger environment. That environment has expectations for the family, which involve both those for the functioning of the family as a system internally and for responsibility toward other systems in the environment. In a society of cultural diversity, there are often conflicting expectations, and these conflicting expectations should be identified. Impacts such as prejudice and discrimination because of family diversity should be identified. It is important to determine the nature and extent of the influence of systems such as church, school, cultural group, extended family, and the like that impinge on the family or have expectations of responsibility for the family. It is also useful to identify environmental systems that may be a resource to the family. As one way of gathering this information, Hartman and Laird have developed the technique of developing an eco-map. (An illustration of this technique is found in the case example.)[21]

Important features to consider with regard to the ways a family functions are the communication patterns, the manner in which decisions are made, and the way in which roles delegated to family members are carried out. Families having difficulty often have communication patterns that do not serve the needs of their members. Some of these patterns may involve parents communicating through children, lack of freedom to communicate, and conflicting messages.[22] Identification of these communication patterns is important in understanding the functioning of the system.

In understanding the functioning of any social system it is important to know how decisions are made in that system. This includes identifying which decisions are individual ones, which are made in the subsystem, and which belong to the total system. It also includes influences on the decisions and how those decisions are communicated, performed, and enforced. In most families, there are communication patterns that meet the needs of various members; however, these patterns may be limited to certain relationships. For example, a child may have a pattern of positive interactions with one parent but may not have such a relationship with the other parent. Or the child may have a pattern of positive communication with a sibling but experience strained communication with parents. A positive pattern of communication is a strength, and the goal is to extend this pattern to other relationships in the family.

The family is one of the major institutions of society. For any society to be functional, families must carry out the roles delegated to them by society. These functions include the primary provision of common human needs for individuals, the care and nurturing of children, and the continuance of the culture. In order to perform these functions, the adult members of the family perform work roles, including the homemaking role, the income-providing role, the parenting role, and the childcare role. These are vital roles in meeting the common human needs and the developmental needs of all family members. Through the carrying out of work, parenting, and marriage roles, the family provides the support, encouragement of growth, and the care of and concern for all family members. Knowing how these roles are filled provides an understanding of family functioning. These roles are often an important source of strength in the family, even when one or more of these roles present challenges. In fact, meeting challenges in fulfilling these roles is a sign of resilience and strength.

Change is a part of all human functioning. The family is subject to change in several ways: (1) growth of family members; (2) birth, children leaving the family home, death, and divorce; (3) changed functioning of family members due to illness or disability; and (4) changed environmental resources, impacts, or responsibilities. All systems develop mechanisms for coping with changes or for adapting to changing conditions. These adaptive and coping mechanisms should be identified and examined for their contribution to appropriate flexibility of the family system in meeting changes both within the social system and in the environment. Again, these are important indications of strength and resilience.

A final area for understanding the family as a social system is the development of the family, which begins in a family's roots. Current structure and functioning are in part a product of its roots. Again, the genogram is a useful tool to use with a family in considering these roots. Also important is an understanding of the family's cultural background (see Table 7.2). Events that have called for significant change, adaptation, and coping within the family system are also important in understanding a family's development. Family culture is part of a family's roots, and pride in one's culture and family heritage can be a foundation for growth and change. Self-knowledge begins with knowing where we came from and how our values, beliefs, and lifestyle reflect our past and that of our family and our culture. Understanding and appreciating family and cultural heritage strengthen the family and its members.

All families go through stages as the composition and needs of family members change. Sonya Rhodes has identified seven stages of family life:

1. *Intimacy vs. idealization or disillusionment*—The dyadic relationship of husband and wife is formed. Developmental task involves developing a realistic appreciation of one's partner.

2. *Replenishment vs. turning inward*—The stage between the birth of the first child until the last child enters school. Developmental task involves developing nurturing patterns for family members.

3. *Individualization of family members vs. pseudomutual organization*—The stage where the family has school-age children. Tasks include parents separating their own identity from that of the child and the enabling of the development of support and opportunities for individual family members outside the family system. Another task is the individualization of each family member.

4. *Companionship vs. isolation*—The stage of teenage children in the family. Important themes are separation and sexuality. The tasks are development of parent-child relationships based on the knowledge of the child's growing independence and a marital relationship based on companionship.

5. *Regrouping vs. binding or expulsion*—This is the stage of the children leaving home. The task is a regrouping on generational lines and development of an adult-to-adult relationship between parents and children.

6. *Recovery vs. despair*—The couple renegotiates a relationship that does not involve parenting children in the home. Parent-child relationships are also changed. The task then is renegotiation of relationships.

7. *Mutual aid vs. uselessness*—Parents are now retired. Couples often are grandparents. The task is to develop a mutual-aid system among the generations.[23]

A study of the family as a social system also includes the identification of that system's concerns and needs. Though the needs of individual members and subsystems contribute to the family system needs, the needs of the family system are different than those of the parts. The needs of the family system relate to what will enable the family to maintain itself as a system and still fulfill its responsibility to its members and to its environment.

Of particular importance when working with families in which ethnicity and social class must be considered is use of a multisystem model. Here the focus is on the interacting level of family functioning (within the family, within the extended family, and with the various formal helping agencies involved). This type of approach will lead the worker toward more appropriate interventive strategies, whether they are strategies better suited to a particular ethnic situation or toward a choice that will bring about change in the larger system that negatively impacts the family's healthy functioning.[24]

It is important to identify the strengths and challenges of the family in situation as a base for developing a professional relationship and for considering intervention into the transactions among family members and between the family and its environment. Through intervention into these transactions the social worker can enable families to meet the needs of the family as a system, as well as those of the individual members, and can help families improve social functioning. The understanding of the family as a social system is a means of identifying its strengths and challenges and of planning for intervention.

Case Example

Social Study: Family

In the situation of the A family discussed in Chapter 1, if the family is considered the client, an assessment of that family might look as follows:

I. **Identifying Information**

   A. **Names and birthdates of family members:**

Father:	Henry A	Born: June 12, 1963
Mother:	Sally A	Born: April 21, 1964
Children:	Henry Jr.	Born: November 3, 1984
	John	Born: September 10, 1986
	Mary	Born: February 16, 1989

   B. **Marriage:** June 24, 1982. First marriage for both parents. Parents had dated steadily in high school.

   C. **Religion:** Methodist; do not attend regularly.

   D. **Cultural/racial background:** Caucasian, mixed German and Scandinavian.

   E. **Language spoken at home:** English

   F. **Date of first contact with agency:** March 2000; referred by school because of concerns about John's behavior and learning needs.

II. **The Family as a System**

   A. **Family structure**

Henry finished high school and went to work full time in the hardware store that his father owned and that he now manages. Due to economic problems in the community and the growth of nationwide chain stores, this store is not doing as well as it once did, though, through hard work and long hours, Henry has managed to provide for his family and provide his widowed mother with an income. He says he has little time for his family but is looking forward to one of the boys coming into the business and lightening the load. Henry does belong to a local service club and is active in the businessmen's association. He says this is necessary if he is to stay in business. He says there was never any question but that he would work in the store. He just wants John to behave himself and stop upsetting his mother.

Sally is also a high school graduate. She and Henry were married soon after she graduated, and she has always stayed at home and cared for the children. Occasionally she helps in the store and enjoys getting out of the house to do this but believes her husband does not want her to become too involved in the business. It is her job to see that the children behave themselves. She has no trouble with Henry Jr. or Mary but has always found John a difficult child.

Henry Jr. is in high school. He has always been a good student. He has been active in Boy Scouts and is involved in clubs and athletics in high school.

John is in seventh grade and has always found school difficult. He thinks everyone wants him to be exactly like his big brother. He says he tries but he just can't do it and is giving up. He does not like Scouts and prefers to hang around with a group of friends. All these boys are entering adolescence and seem to be rebelling against school and parental control.

(continued)

Case Example   Continued

Mary is in fifth grade and is a good student. She enjoys helping her mother around the house and has one very close girlfriend. She wishes she could take dancing lessons but has not been able to because of the cost.

There seems to be little communication between the marital pair. Each has a well-specified area of responsibility in the family. Mr. A does not believe the family needs to be concerned with his business. He wants to find a clean house, well-cooked meals, and well-behaved children when he comes home. The couple have been hesitant to discuss their sexual life, though the worker suspects that this reticence could be overcome. Mrs. A would like some help with the children, especially John, but says, "He (Mr. A) is the way he is and won't change. I just have to find a way to get John to behave." There seem to be an increasing number of arguments between the couple, which seem to be related to John's behavior and to Mrs. A's desire to engage in some activity outside of the home.

The children seem to go their own ways. When the boys were younger, John tried to become involved with Henry Jr.'s activities, but Henry Jr. refused to have this. John seemed to give up and find his own friends. Now Henry Jr. is very critical of John's friends. Neither boy has much to do with Mary. When she was born, John had a very hard time for a while and seemed to feel he was being replaced. As the family seldom does anything together, the children have had little opportunity to form a close system.

The parent-child system is primarily focused on mother-children relationships. She seems to be having increasing difficulty understanding the needs of her growing sons. There is little father-son relationship. Henry Jr. seems to find role models in the men he knows through scouting. John seems to be seeking male attention but has not been successful in getting it; occasionally, if his behavior is particularly bad, his father gives him a yelling. Mary and her mother seem to have a very close relationship.

In this family there seems to be an expectation of traditional family roles and ways of functioning. No one seems free to discuss what any one member of the family wants. The cohesiveness that exists is related to this traditionalism, which seems to be questioned by at least John and to some degree his mother. There does seem to be considerable concern about what outsiders are thinking when one member of the family fails to function in expected ways. The economic difficulties in the business and John's recent problems have seemed to engender a tenseness in the climate of the family. Mr. A and Henry Jr. seem to deal with this by absenting themselves from family life. Mrs. A and Mary seem to find a great deal of satisfaction in their relationship and do not seem particularly distressed by the absences. John seems to be reacting to the tenseness in ways that are not acceptable to the family.

The family lives in a comfortable older house in a well-kept part of town. Each of the children has his or her own bedroom. The home looks lived in but is clean. The family is of lower-middle-class economic status.

The neighborhood is changing. In the past there were many older couples. Mrs. A used to spend time with these older women and enjoyed that very much. Now, she says, younger families are moving in, and the women work and have no time for neighborhood get-togethers. Also, some of these young couples are having loud parties and don't take pride in their home or neighborhood.

Mrs. A's parents died within four months of each other about two years ago. She states she was very close to her mother and misses her very much. She has one brother and one sister; they live at a distance and she is not close to either of them. Mr. A's father died four years ago after a long bout with cancer. He remained close to the business until his last days. Mr. A feels strongly that his father had a great influence on him and expected him to keep the business going so that it will provide an income for his mother, who lives in the community. She has recently moved into a housing complex for the elderly and is having difficulty adjusting. She often calls Mr. A at work about her needs. Mrs. A states that she tries to help her mother-in-law but finds that her help is not appreciated. Mr. A has one sister; he has never gotten along with her. She lives in town and is always telling him what he ought to be doing for their mother. She also has been very critical of John's recent behavior.

B. Family functioning (see Figure 7.1)

There seems to be minimal communication in this family around needs and desires of individuals. Mr. A communicates his desires to Mrs. A. He does not communicate his concerns about the business. He is annoyed that Mrs. A does not understand his mother and relate to her needs. There is good communication between Mrs. A and Mary. Communication among children seems primarily of a negative nature. Mr. A is distant from the children.

Mr. A makes all financial decisions. He also decides on the roles of each family member. Mrs. A is expected to make all decisions about the children and running of the household. There seems to be an expectation that each person will know what the other wants. Children are excluded from family decision making.

Housekeeping standards are high and carried out. Mr. A works hard and provides an adequate financial support for the family, although this is threatened by the economic problems that the business faces. Parenting is left to Mrs. A. She has high expectations for herself. The emotional aspect is missing except between Mrs. A and Mary. Mr. A shows approval for Henry Jr. and disapproval for John.

When adapting or coping with change, this family seems to revert to a set of guidelines that relate to traditional roles, hard work, and doing what is right. They seem to need more skill in adapting to change or individual needs.

C. Family development history (see Figure 7.2)

This couple seems tightly tied to their parents. They adhere to the lifestyle in which they grew up. However, the challenge of providing for a family with one income and the threat to the success of the business are creating tensions that could change this. There appears to be little conflict between the lifestyle of the two families of orientation. Neither partner seems to have a sense of their grandparents, as all died when they were very young; they had little contact with aunts and uncles. They cannot identify any specific cultural influences, saying they are just plain people who have always worked hard and kept to themselves. The death of parents seems to be a critical point of change for this couple.

They seem to be in the individualization of family members vs. pseudomutual organization stage. It appears that the balance is more toward pseudomutual organization. In earlier stages, it can be suspected that there was more turning inward than replenishment and that intimacy was not well established, but rather they may have used idealization.

(continued)

Case Example   Continued

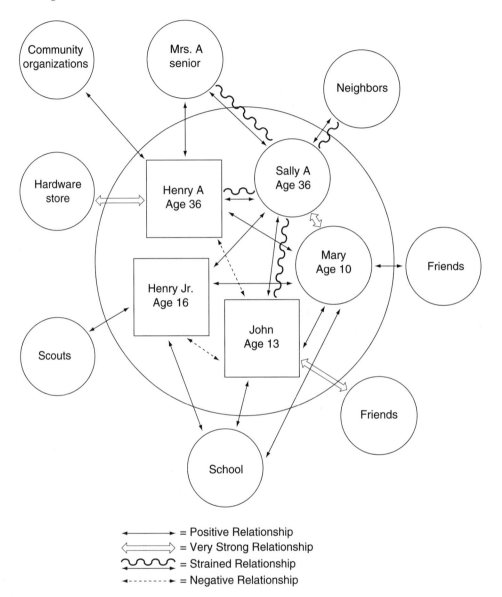

FIGURE 7.1   **Eco-Map**

III.   Concern or Need

Family was referred to agency for help because John had been involved in a minor stealing episode (candy bar at a local store) and because of increasing school difficulty. School suspects family difficulties. Mrs. A says she wants help in dealing with

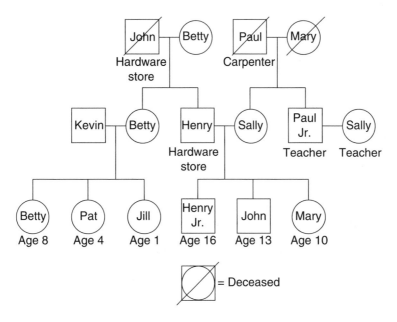

FIGURE 7.2   **Genogram**

John. Mr. A says he wants John to be straightened out. John says he wants to be allowed to be himself and not always be yelled at.

Mr. A seems to need help in understanding the needs of other family members. He also may need someone to talk to about concerns around the business and his relationship with his mother.

Mrs. A needs help in communicating her needs to her husband. She is very unsure of her parenting ability with her sons. She may need help in coming to grips with the death of her parents and of the changing nature of her community. She seems to need some interest or activity outside the home.

Henry Jr. appears to be the best-adjusted member of the family. He might benefit from greater interaction with his father. John needs a relationship with his father that focuses on his positive attributes. His behavior seems to be a call for help for this family; thus, he needs to be relieved of the role of troublemaker by having a better-functioning family. His school difficulty also may be an area to explore. Why has he always had difficulty in school? Does he have a minimal learning difficulty that could be corrected? He needs positive relationships with boys his own age and with other men. He also could use some help in understanding the adolescent process and how it is affecting him. Mary probably needs help in beginning to break away from the family and not being overly dependent on her mother.

This couple seems to need help with both the marital and parental relationship. There is a question as to how much intimacy exists in this relationship. They need help in learning to express needs to each other and in how to respond to these needs in a manner that brings satisfaction to the individual. They seem to have limited understanding of the needs of adolescent children. The children could use help in discovering their commonality and developing meaningful relationships with each other.

(continued)

Case Example   Continued

This family needs to explore their self-defined lifestyle to determine if it is meeting the needs of the family and its individual members. To do this it will be necessary to help them develop greater communication, particularly around feelings. Also, there should probably be emphasis placed on hearing about the needs of others. The family is very isolated from its environment, and greater participation, individually and perhaps as a family, seems indicated.

IV. **Strengths and Challenges in Meeting Needs**

The family seems to be asking that John's problems be solved. Mrs. A seems ready to participate in a treatment experience. Mr. A may be resistant. The children will take their cues from the parents. Both parents are responsible and hardworking. These characteristics could be strengths if the parents are committed to change. It would seem that pressure from the school to relate to John's needs might be something the parents could respond to. If they can begin to openly express feelings and needs, this experience could well motivate them to work on their needs. They seem very concerned about the children, and Mrs. A, at least, realizes she needs help in parenting. This may mean they would do well in a parenting group situation. This would also provide exposure to people outside the family. The community has a good family services system that could help meet this family's needs.

Summary

The client is an individual or social system requesting help or receiving service from a social worker. The client's capacity to request or use help is affected by his culture's attitudes toward receiving help, his past experiences in using help, and pressures and constraints of the context in which the help is given. It is important for a social worker to understand how attitudes about seeking and receiving help affect a client's capacity to function in the helping situation.

Understanding a client's past and present functioning and the various factors that affect functioning is a key skill of a social worker. This understanding is often expressed through the development of a social history. Factors that are particularly important to consider are how the client fills the vital roles of work, marriage, and parenting; how human diversity affects the social functioning of the individual; the motivation that the client brings to the helping endeavor; and the extent of the crisis and stress the client is experiencing.

Understanding a client also extends to understanding multiclient systems. Of prime importance is understanding the family as a client from a structural, functional, and developmental point of view. Understanding the client system is of vital importance when developing a professional relationship with that client.

QUESTIONS

1. What image do the terms *patient, client,* and *consumer* bring to mind? How do you think terminology may affect the way help is given?

2. What experiences do you believe help people seek assistance from social workers? What experiences make it difficult to seek help?

3. In what ways are people socialized to use or avoid using help by their culture?

4. Develop a social study for someone you have recently helped in some way.

5. Using a cultural group different from your own and with which you have had considerable contact, identify factors that you need to find out about to have sufficient knowledge to work as a social worker with people from that culture group.

6. Discuss the differences in the family structure and functioning in two families other than your own. Use families with whom you have had considerable contact.

7. Using the schema for individual social history, identify the strengths, needs, and challenges for you and your ecosystem.

8. Using the human diversity schema, identify your strengths, needs, and challenges related to your diversity.

9. Using the schema for family social history, identify the strengths, needs, and challenges for your family and its ecosystem.

SUGGESTED READINGS

Anderson, Joseph D. "Family-Centered Practice in the 1990's: A Multicultural Perspective." *Journal of Multicultural Social Work* 1, 4 (1992): 17–29.

Azzi-Lessing, Lenette, and Olsen, Lenore J. "Substance Abuse-Affected Families in the Child Welfare System: New Challenges, New Alliances." *Social Work* 41 (January 1996): 15–23.

Canda, Edward R. "Spirituality, Religious Diversity, and Social Work Practice." *Social Casework* 69 (April 1988): 238–247.

Carter, Elizabeth A., and McGoldrick, Monica. *The Expanded Family Life Cycle: Individual, Family, and Social Perspectives,* 3rd ed. Boston: Allyn and Bacon, 1999.

Chau, Kenneth L. "Social Work with Ethnic Minorities: Practice Issues and Potentials." *Journal of Multicultural Social Work* 1, 1 (1991): 23–39.

Cimmarusti, Rocco A. "Family Preservation Practices Based upon a Multisystems Approach." *Child Welfare* 71 (May–June 1992): 241–256.

Cox, Carol, and Ephross, Paul. *Ethnicity and Social Work Practice.* New York: Oxford University Press, 1998.

Daly, Alfrieda, Jennings, Jeanette, Beckett, Joyce O., and Leashore, Bogart R. "Effective Coping Strategies of African Americans." *Social Work* 40 (March 1995): 240–248.

Devore, Wynetta, and Schlesinger, Elfrede. *Ethnic Sensitive Social Work Practice,* 4th ed. Boston: Allyn and Bacon, 1996.

Ewalt, Patricia, and Mokuau, Noreen. "Self-Determination from a Pacific Perspective." *Social Work* 40 (March 1995): 168–176.

Freeman, Edith M. "Welfare Reforms and Services for Children and Families: Setting a New Practice, Research, and Policy Agenda." *Social Work* 41 (September 1996): 521–532.

Gold, Nora. "Motivation: The Crucial but Unexplored Component of Social Work Practice." *Social Work* 35 (January 1990): 49–56.

Green, James. *Cultural Awareness in the Human Services,* 2nd ed. Boston: Allyn and Bacon, 1995.

Harrison, Dianne F., Wodarski, John S., and Thyer, Bruce A., Eds. *Cultural Diversity and Social Work Practice.* Springfield, IL: C. C. Thomas, 1992.

Hartman, Ann. "Diagrammatic Assessment of Family Relationships." *Families in Society* 76 (February 1995): 111–122.

Ivanhoff, Andre Marie. *Involuntary Clients in Social Work Practice: A Research-Based Approach.* New York: Aldine de Gruyter, 1994.

Kim, Yoon-Ock. "Cultural Pluralism and Asian-Americans: Culturally Sensitive Social Work Practice." *International Social Work* 38 (January 1995): 69–78.

Lee, Mo-Yee. "A Constructivist Approach to the Help-Seeking Process of Clients: A Response to Cultural Diversity." *Clinical Social Work Journal* 24 (Summer 1996): 187–202.

Longres, John F. "Toward a Status Model of Ethnic Sensitive Practice." *Journal of Multicultural Social Work* 1, 1 (1991): 41–56.

Martinez-Brawley, Emilia E., and Blundall, Joan. "Farm Families' Preferences Toward Personal Social Services." *Social Work* 34 (November 1989): 513–522.

McGoldrick, Monica, Pearce, John, and Giordano, Joseph. *Ethnicity and Family Therapy,* 2nd ed. New York: Guilford Press, 1996.

McMahon, Anthony, and Allen-Meares, Paula. "Is Social Work Racist? A Content Analysis of Recent Literature." *Social Work* 37 (November 1992): 533–539.

O'Hare, Thomas. "Court-Ordered Versus Voluntary Clients: Problem Difference and Readiness for Change." *Social Work* 41 (July 1996): 417–422.

Papajohn, John, and Spiegel, John P. *Transactions in Families.* Northvale NJ: J. Aronson, 1995.

Pray, Jackie E. "Respecting the Uniqueness of the Individual: Social Work Practice within a Reflective Model." *Social Work* 36 (January 1991): 81–85.

Rooney, Ronald. *Strategies for Work with Involuntary Clients.* New York: Columbia University Press, 1992.

Saleeby, Dennis. *The Strengths Perspective in Social Work Practice,* 2nd ed. New York: Longman, 1997.

Sheafor, Bradford W., Horejsi, Charles R., and Horejsi, Gloria A. *Techniques and Guidelines for Social Work Practice,* 5th ed. Boston: Allyn and Bacon, 2000 (Chapter 11).

Tracy, Elizabeth M., and Whittaker, James K. "The Social Network Map: Assessing Social Support in Clinical Practice." *Families in Society* 71 (October 1990): 461–470.

Voss, Richard W., Douville, Victor, Little Soldier, Alex, and Twiss, Gayla. "Tribal and Shamanic-Based Social Work Practice: A Lakota Perspective." *Social Work* 44 (May 1999).

Weaver, Hilary N. "Indigenous People and the Social Work Profession: Defining Culturally Competent Services." *Social Work* 44 (May 1999).

Williams, Sharon E., and Wright, Dolores Finger. "Empowerment: The Strengths of Black Families Revisited." *Journal of Multicultural Social Work* 2, 4 (1992): 23–37.

Yamashiro, Greg, and Matsuoka, Jon K. "Help-Seeking among Asian and Pacific Americans: A Multiperspective Analysis." *Social Work* 42 (March 1997): 176–186.

NOTES

1. Emanual Tropp, "Three Problematic Concepts: 'Clients,' 'Help,' 'Worker,'" *Social Casework* 55 (January 1974): 19–29.

2. Scott Briar and Henry Miller, *Problems and Issues in Social Casework* (New York: Columbia University Press, 1971), chap. 6.

3. Allen Pincus and Anne Minahan, *Social Work Practice: Model and Method* (Itasca, IL: F. E. Peacock, 1973), chap. 3.

4. Helen Harris Perlman, *Persona* (Chicago: University of Chicago Press, 1968), p. 207.

5. F. M. Lowenberg, *Fundamentals of Social Intervention: Core Concepts and Skills for Social Work Practice* (New York: Columbia University Press, 1977).

6. David Landy, "Problems of the Person Seeking Help in Our Culture," in *Social Welfare Institutions: A Sociological Reader,* Mayer N. Zald, Ed. (New York: John Wiley, 1965), pp. 559–574.

7. Emilia E. Martinez-Brawley and Joan Blundall, "Farm Families' Preferences Toward Personal Social Services," *Social Work* 34 (November 1989): 513–522.

8. Perlman, *Persona,* pp. 207–211.

9. An excellent resource for the study of a diverse culture is Ann Templeman Brownlee, *Community, Culture, and Care* (St. Louis: C. V. Mosby, 1978). Also, Emelicia Mizio and Anita L. Delaney, Eds., *Training for Service Delivery to Minority Clients* (New York: Family Service Association of America, 1981).

10. John F. Longres, "Toward a Status Model of Ethnic Sensitive Practice," *Journal of Multicultural Social Work* 1, 1 (1991): 41–56.

11. Kenneth L. Chau, "Social Work with Ethnic Minorities: Practice Issues and Potentials," *Journal of Multicultural Social Work* 1, 1 (1991): 23–39.

12. Sharon Berlin, "Better Work with Women Clients," *Social Work* 21 (November 1976): 492–497.

13. Lillian Ripple, Ernestina Alexander, and Bernice P. Polemis, *Motivation, Capacity, and Opportunity: Studies in Casework Theory and Practice,* Social Service Monographs, Second Series (Chicago: School of Social Service Administration, University of Chicago, 1964).

14. Nora Gold, "Motivation: The Crucial but Unexplored Component of Social Work Practice," *Social Work* 35 (January 1990): 49–56.

15. Howard J. Parad, "Crisis Intervention," in *Encyclopedia of Social Work,* 17th issue, John B. Turner,

Ed. (Washington, DC: National Association of Social Workers, 1977), pp. 228–237.

16. Elizabeth M. Tracy and James K. Whittaker, "The Social Network Map: Assessing Social Support in Clinical Practice," *Families in Society* (October 1990): 461–470.

17. Jackie E. Pray, "Respecting the Uniqueness of the Individual: Social Work Practice within a Reflective Model," *Social Work* 36 (January 1991): 80–85.

18. For further discussion, see Curtis Janzen and Oliver Harris, *Family Treatment in Social Work Practice* (Itasca, IL: F. E. Peacock, 1980), pp. 6–12.

19. Ann Hartman and Joan Laird, *Family-Centered Social Work Practice* (New York: Free Press, 1983), chap. 10.

20. Janzen and Harris, *Family Treatment,* pp. 12–16.

21. Hartman and Laird, *Family-Centered Social Work Practice,* chap. 8.

22. Janzen and Harris, *Family Treatment,* pp. 15–20.

23. Based on Sonya L. Rhodes, "A Developmental Approach to the Life Cycle of the Family," *Social Casework* 58 (May 1977): 301–311.

24. See Joseph D. Anderson, "Family-Centered Practice in the 1990's: A Multicultural Perspective," *Journal of Multicultural Social Work* 1, 4 (1992): 17–29; and Rocco A. Cimmarusti, "Family Preservation Practice Based upon a Multisystems Approach," *Child Welfare* 71 (May–June 1992): 241–256.

8 Environment

LEARNING EXPECTATIONS

1. Understanding of the importance of the environment as a part of the client's ecosystem and its influence on the worker-client interaction.
2. Understanding of the community as a social system.
3. Beginning skill in studying a community.
4. Understanding of the social service agency as a social system.
5. Beginning skill in studying a social agency.
6. Understanding of the skill needed for working in a bureaucracy.
7. Beginning skill in understanding the impact of recent "reforms" such as managed care and privatization on human service delivery.

The environment of the helping interaction, that is, of the social work endeavor, is the community and the social agency. The client comes from a community or neighborhood, which has both expectations and resources that must be considered in the helping. The worker is usually an agency employee and thus has expectations and resources from that agency. The agency is also a part of a community. The community has expectations about the services being delivered by the agency. It also provides resources. The community of the client and agency may or may not be the same. In order to understand the influence of both the community and the agency on the helping endeavor, the worker can use a social systems approach as an organizing framework. The helping endeavor takes place not in a vacuum but in an environment. Because of the transactional nature of human interaction, understanding that environment and its impact is essential for effective service.

Sometimes the transactions between the community or the agency and clients are not congruent with the needs of the client, and so the community or the agency or the transactions with them might be considered as targets for change. As generalist social workers develop understandings and assess agencies and communities, they must be alert to identify when the agency or the community is the appropriate unit of attention and when the transactions between the community or agency and the client or clients is the appropriate unit of attention. The first part of this chapter will focus on the content of a community study and an agency study. The last part will look at the transactions between community and client and between the agency and client. Strategies for working toward change in these systems are discussed in Chapter 14.

Person in Environment as an Ecosystem

In ecological terms, person in environment represents an ecosystem. An **ecosystem** includes the person(s), all of the systems with which the person(s) interacts, and the larger environment, along with the transactions among the person(s) and systems.[1] Thus, people and their environment are seen as a unified whole in which the various parts are interdependent. People are influenced by their environment and in turn also influence the environment by their actions.

In using an ecosystems approach that encompasses person in environment, the *in* can serve as the focal point for social work services. The *in* can represent the *in*terface between the person as a system (or a multiperson client system) and the environment. **Interface** is the point of contact between two systems. At the *in*terface there are *in*teractions that occur. To the extent that both the person and the environment exchange resources, energy, or *in*formation via these *in*teractions, transactions take place. When these *in*teractions or transactions are balanced, both the person and the environment benefit. *In*terrelationships are formed and a certain level of *in*terdependence exists. Change in one part of the ecosystem will *in*fluence or impact on other parts of the ecosystem. When the *in*teractions or transactions are out of balance, an *in*congruity exists between the needs of the person and/or the environment and resources available to meet those needs. This imbalance or *in*congruity gains the attention of the social worker and is the reason for and focal point of social work *in*tervention.

The combination of the ecosystems and strengths perspectives gives the worker a powerful means to assist clients to meet their needs beyond the immediate situation. This approach also brings the environment into play in a positive way and dramatically expands potential resources for change well beyond the worker or the client. Instead of limiting the possibilities to whatever the worker or the client brings to the helping situation, the worker and the client can seek other possibilities by tapping into resources in the environment. In addition, as the client is able to experience this expanded range of resources with the worker, he is empowered to use this approach in working to meet other needs, now and in the future.

The Community as a Social System

The **community** is the environment of the worker, the client, and the agency. Different units of that community will have different impacts and influences on each.

The interaction of worker and client is influenced by the transactions of the community. Service delivery is a part of the community system. Understanding these impacts and influences is an important aspect of generalist social work knowledge. To gain this understanding, it is first necessary for the worker to see the community as a social system. This knowledge is important not only because the environment influences the worker-client interaction but also because the community may be the client or it may be the target for intervention. In either of these cases, the worker usually works with individuals and small groups to bring about change in the community structure and functioning. For the generalist social worker, effort is usually focused on changing or developing a community resource that will in turn enhance the functioning of individuals and families. Whether the community or some element of it is the client or is the target of change, it is important to understand the community as a social system so that its strengths and resources can be included in promoting growth and change. Particular attention needs to be paid to these elements as the worker studies the community.

At a minimum, such knowledge calls for awareness of the boundaries of the community, its component parts (individuals, families, associations, neighborhoods, organizations, institutions, etc.), and its environment. The worker also needs to be aware of the way the community functions and of its historical development.

The identification of a community's boundaries poses a substantial problem in a society of large cities and multiple institutional catchment areas. Is an agency's community a geographic place, the catchment area from which the clients come? Is a group of persons who support and sanction the agency its community? Is it the immediate geographic neighborhood in which it is located? Should the entire metropolitan area be considered a community? Or are community and neighborhood the same? Each of these questions may be answered affirmatively under certain circumstances.

There is also a time element in the concept of community. The *community system* functions in relation to issues and to provide services (e.g., education). The *community units* may interact only when dealing with those issues and in providing services. Community units are groups (both formal and informal), organizations, institutions, and other social systems that function within the boundaries of the community. Thus, the community system also has a time element; it exists only under certain circumstances.

The community may be seen as a geographic place. In addition, *community* is a term also used to describe "nonplace" associations such as the professional community or the religious community. When considering the kinship group, the extended family, or certain cultural groups, community is a related concept. The community system can have a wide variety of forms, all of which are relevant for social work in that all impact the transactions among individuals, families, and small groups.

Sociology furnishes us with several ways of considering a community. Ferdinand Tönnies saw a change in the relationships among people with the industrialization of society. He described this change as one from **Gemeinschaft** (rural "we-ness") to **Gesellschaft** (individuals related through structures in the community).[2]

These differences among communities still exist. Rural or small communities function rather informally; urban or large communities tend to function more through formal structures. In searching for understanding of a community, a worker will find it useful to determine the kinds of relationships that exist in the community. Usually there are different kinds of relationships, depending on the community functions involved.

Understanding the use of land adds another dimension to the study of a community. One method of using this concept is to draw maps of a community showing retail stores; wholesale businesses; industry (light and heavy); schools, churches, and other institutions; various types of residential dwellings; and the locations of various ethnic and socioeconomic groups.

Floyd Hunter's studies of community power are also useful.[3] The location of the community power structure is particularly important when trying to develop new services or to change existing services. This power structure may be formal or informal, elected or assigned. The impact of the power is varied depending on how the power holder and others perceive the power. It is exercised through initiating activity, legitimizing activity, giving approval to ideas and plans, implementing decisions, or blocking discussion of issues and of decisions. Usually, the impact of a particular power holder depends on the issue at hand. Some in power tend to have greater influence over economic issues than over social welfare issues. In larger communities, where power is more dispersed, there is a greater chance that power is related to specific segments of community life. In smaller communities, power tends to reside with one small group of people. Identification of not only the individuals in the power structure but also how they exercise that power and over what issues they have significant influence is another important ingredient of any community assessment.

Eugene Litwak's work on the significance of the neighborhood points out the neighborhood's importance for the individual in meeting need. He has identified several types of neighborhoods and their effectiveness in meeting need. The *mobile neighborhood* manages to retain its cohesion despite a rapid turnover of residents. The *traditional neighborhood* is one in which residents are long term and that maintains stability. The *mass neighborhood* is one in which there is no mechanism of integration.[4] Understanding the kind of neighborhood a client lives in helps a worker understand a client and the resources that may be available for that client.

Roland Warren's work, which considers the community as a social system, is especially useful. He identifies the locally relevant functions of a community as (1) production-distribution-consumption, (2) socialization, (3) social control, (4) social participation, and (5) mutual support. Each community has community units that carry out these functions. The business community has a major responsibility for production, distribution, and consumption. The schools are involved in socialization. Government is concerned with social control. Various clubs and organizations fulfill social participation needs. Social welfare organizations are involved in mutual support. Warren also notes that many community units have ties with structures and systems outside the community. These links are known as *vertical patterns;* relationships within the community are known as *horizontal patterns.* An example of this conceptualization as it relates to a church (a community unit) would be that the horizontal link would be a local council of churches or ministerial group; the vertical link would be to a denominational body. Warren sees the exploration of these patterns as a primary means for studying a community.[5]

There are differences among communities, just as there are among types of any category of social system. It is almost impossible to develop a scheme for classifying communities because of the many variables involved. Dennis Poplin has identified three areas that seem important when considering differences among communities: size, the nature of a community's hinterland, and social-cultural features.[6]

Differences in size usually have been discussed on a rural-urban continuum. The U.S. Census Bureau uses a population of 2,500 as the division point between rural and urban. This leaves many different types of communities in the urban category. Another division point frequently used is 50,000, or the population necessary for a Standard Metropolitan Statistical Area. In looking at nonmetropolitan community service delivery systems, Louise Johnson has identified four types of communities: the small city (15,000 to 20,000), the small town (between 8,000 and 20,000), the rural community (under 10,000), and the reservation community.[7]

In subsequent work, Johnson identified two additional types of small communities: the bedroom community and the institutional community. The bedroom community is found near a larger community that furnishes jobs and often a variety of services for residents of the bedroom community. The institutional community contains a large institution, such as a state mental hospital, an educational institution, or a government site (state capital), which is the major employer in that community. She also found that community characteristics are heavily influenced by the distance between communities that contain services (e.g., medical, social, and retail). In other words, small communities that are at considerable distance from services in another community have a richer service system than do communities of the same size that are near communities from which they can obtain services.[8]

Metropolitan areas contain communities that differ: there are the central city, the suburban community, and the satellite city. In addition, some communities are inhabited by the upper class (Grosse Point, Michigan, for example). Some may have a reputation for being inhabited by bohemian, intellectual, or artistic persons, such as Greenwich Village; others are middle-class communities. There also are the ghettos and the barrio communities that have always been a particular concern of social workers. Ethnic communities have particular characteristics that come in part from the culture of the groups occupying them. A social worker should possess an understanding of the characteristics of the particular kind of community with which she is working.

A community, then, can be considered as a social system that has a population, shared institutions and values, and significant social interactions between the individuals and the institutions. The institutions perform major social functions. A community usually but not always occupies space or a geographic area and has many forms. In modern society several communities may overlap. Communities differ in the amount of autonomy they have and the extent to which persons living in the community identify with their community. When considering the community as a social system, understanding from many sources can be used to provide a theoretical base or to point to characteristics that should be considered in specific communities. In other words, different communities, because of differing characteristics, often call for different choices as to what is important to include in a community study.

In trying to attain understanding about a community and its impact on people, agencies, and institutions, a social worker faces two major problems. First is the identification of the system itself, which varies depending on the situation. Often a political unit is the defined system; this is a fairly easy way to define boundaries, but it is artificial and does not really consider parts of the community system that may lie outside the political boundaries. When looking at the neighborhood system, it is difficult to define boundaries.

Understanding a community calls for identifying the boundaries of the unit to be considered. Too large an area makes the study unwieldy; too small an area makes it too limited. In nonmetropolitan areas the choice may be a small city or town. In metropolitan areas the choice may better be a neighborhood or some other manageable unit. Creativity is necessary in deciding how to define the community.

Social workers function in many different kinds of communities: large metropolitan areas, neighborhood settings, small cities, rural communities, large institutions, Indian reservations, and so on. Each kind of community has different characteristics. The study of any community as a social system provides understandings that can lead to greater degrees of client-congruent culture, to better use of available resources, to identification of when the community should be the focus of change, and to better identification of which work strategy is best suited to a particular situation.

Of special concern to social workers are diversity factors that exist in the community. The racial and ethnic makeup of the community are important to know. With regard to race and ethnicity, the worker should have knowledge about the degree to which various groups are integrated or segregated. She should note the attitudes of various groups toward each other. Is there respect or valuing of differences? Are there coalitions that have been formed? Are there adversarial relationships? How tolerant or intolerant are these groups toward each other? What groups hold power? Who has little or no power, and how does this reflect the general population? Similar questions should also be asked with respect to gender, age, and sexual orientation.

Some information about diversity can be obtained from census data or community surveys. However, much of this information is obtained more informally, through observation and discussion with key informants who know the history and have personal knowledge about various populations. For instance, knowledge about the gay or lesbian community may only be available from someone who is a member of the gay or lesbian community or from someone who works with these individuals.

Second, the information that can be collected about any community is vast. It is never possible to obtain complete information. Some decisions must be made as to when there is sufficient information for understanding. Care needs to be taken to ensure that the information is representative of all units in a community. Some information can be found in a library in local history books, census reports, directories, and the like. Other helpful written material can be obtained from chambers of commerce, local government units, and volunteer organizations. Some information is not as easy to obtain; it may be known within the community but not shared with outsiders. This includes information about relationships among people and institutions and the community's decision-making and power structure. Information about norms and values may be obtainable only after observing and being a part of the community for some period of time.

In order to understand community interaction, gathering information from many individuals and small groups is essential. The generalist social worker uses both formal and informal interviews and observes and participates in small groups. The worker carefully observes a wide range of community interactions in order to develop understanding about the community and its impact on the functioning of individuals, groups, and families.

Because of the amount of material, in terms of both volume and variety, it is helpful if an organized plan is developed for gathering such material. Social workers can begin to gather some material before entering a new community. They also need to add to this material as long as they work in the community. As with all social systems, the community system continues to change. In Table 8.1 one means of organizing a community study considers major subsystems related to Warren's locally relevant functions. The table provides a means to identify possible impacts, influences, and resources in the community system and looks for both horizontal and vertical relationships. Table 8.1 provides a social worker with a guide for developing a working understanding of a community.

Once a social worker has the necessary information, it becomes possible to identify and understand current concerns in the community, the community decision-making process, and the manner in which that community usually solves its problems. Issues relative to community autonomy become clearer, as do differing service areas for different community agencies and institutions. For instance, the school district, the political boundaries, and the shopping service area are often different. Also, at this point it is possible to identify strengths and limitations of the community system. Because of the size and diversity of the units (subsystems) within the community system, different parts of the system will show different strengths and different limitations. One way of focusing the consideration of strengths and limitations is to consider the overall quality of life as perceived by community residents.

A community study should include at least some consideration of the strengths and limitations of the community system, the manner in which that community solves its problems, and the capacity and motivation for change.

TABLE 8.1   **Schema for the Study of a Geographic Community**

I. Setting, History, Demography
   A. Physical setting
      1. Location, ecology, size
      2. Relationship to other geographic entities
         a. Ecological, political, economic, social
         b. Transportation, mass media from outside the community
   B. Historical development
      1. Settlement, significant events, change over time, cultural factors
   C. Demography
      1. Population
         a. Age and sex distribution
         b. Cultural, ethnic, racial groups
         c. Socioeconomic distribution
      2. Physical structure
         a. Who lives where?
         b. Location of businesses, industry, institutions
      3. Other
         a. Mobility
         b. Housing conditions
   D. Cultural setting
      1. Community norms, values, and expectations
      2. Community traditions and events
II. Economic System
   A. Employment
      1. Industry: nature, who employed, number of employees, influence from outside community, relationship to community and employees
      2. Distribution-consumption: retail and wholesale business, kind, location, ownership, employees, trade territory
      3. Institutions that employ large numbers of persons: nature, number of employees, types of employees, relationship to community, influence from outside community
   B. Other economic factors
      1. Stability of economy
      2. Leading business persons
      3. Organizations of business or organizations that influence the economic system
III. Political System
   A. Government units (structure and functioning)
      1. Span of control
      2. Personnel, elected and appointed
      3. Financial information
      4. Way of functioning—meetings, etc.
   B. Law enforcement, including court system
   C. Party politics: dominant party and history of recent elections
   D. Influence on social service system
   E. Services provided
IV. Educational System
   A. Structure and administration (all levels)
   B. Financing, buildings
   C. Students
      1. Numbers at each level or other divisions
      2. Attendance and dropout rates
   D. Instructional factors
      1. Teacher-student ratio
      2. Subjects available, curriculum philosophy
      3. Provisions for special-needs students

(continued)

TABLE 8.1   Continued

E. Extracurricular activity
F. Community relations

V. Social-Cultural System
  A. Recreational-cultural activities, events
    1. Parks, public recreation programs
    2. Cultural resources: libraries, museums, theaters, concerts
    3. Commercial recreation
  B. Religious institutions and activities
    1. Churches: kind, location, membership, activities, leadership
    2. Attitudes: values, concern for social welfare issues, concern for own members
    3. Influence on community
  C. Associations and organizations
    1. Kind, membership, purpose, and goals
    2. Activities, ways of functioning, leadership
    3. Intergroup organizations and linkage within and without the community
    4. Resources available
  D. Mass media in community
    1. Radio, TV, newspapers
  E. Ethnic, racial, and other diverse groups
    1. Way of life, customs, child-rearing patterns, etc.
    2. Relationship to larger community
    3. Structure and functioning of group
  F. Community persons
    1. Power persons; how power is manifest
    2. Leadership and respected persons

VI. Human Service System
  A. Health care services and institutions
    1. Doctors, dentists, and other professionals
    2. Hospitals, clinics, nursing homes
    3. Public health services
    4. Responsiveness of health care system to needs of people
  B. Formal social welfare system
    1. Agencies in community: function, persons eligible for service, how supported and how sanctioned, staff, location
    2. Agencies from outside that serve community: location, services available, conditions of service, control of agency
    3. Conflicts among, overlaps, complementary factors of social welfare agencies
  C. Informal helping system
    1. Individuals and organizations
    2. How help is given, to whom
    3. Relationship to formal system
  D. Planning bodies
    1. Fundraising, regulatory, consultative

VII. General Considerations
  A. Current concerns of community. Who is concerned? Why? What has been done about the concern?
  B. Customary ways of solving community problems. Who needs to be involved?
  C. Community decision-making process
  D. How autonomous is the community? Do various service areas coincide or are they different? How strong is the psychological identification with the community?
  E. Strengths of community in terms of "quality of life"
  F. Limitations of community in terms of "quality of life"

Communities that seem most able to fulfill their functions and meet people's needs have the following characteristics:

1. At least some primary relationships exist.
2. They are comparatively autonomous (not overly impacted by outside influences).
3. They have the capacity to face problems and engage in efforts to solve those problems.
4. There is a broad distribution of power.
5. Citizens have a commitment to the community.
6. Citizen participation is possible and encouraged.
7. There are more homogeneous than heterogeneous relationships.
8. They have developed ways of dealing with conflict.

It is difficult for a community to meet citizen need when (1) the problems lie beyond the capacity of the community to solve, (2) the organizations and institutions of the community lack sufficient autonomy, and (3) the citizens lack identification with the community. These community characteristics should be considered when identifying strengths and limitations of any community system.

The community can be a nebulous entity that is often understood only intuitively. It can also be a defined system understood through organized study. In fact, through organized study a social worker is most apt to grasp the impacts and influences the community has on the social work endeavor.

Skill in understanding a community includes

1. A framework to organize information
2. The ability to locate information and resources
3. The ability to identify the information needed in specific situations
4. The ability to analyze the information obtained and to identify linkages and relationships among information and among subsystems in the community system
5. The ability to interact with individuals and small groups for purposes of developing relationships and gathering information about a community
6. The ability for careful observation of community functioning

It is also through organized study that the social worker gains knowledge about the resources a community provides for all members of that community. Knowledge of impacts, influences, and resources leads to effective practice with individuals, families, and small groups. It also leads to a practice that considers interventions into the system of the community and/or its subsystems when these larger systems impact on individuals, families, and small groups. Negative impacts, then, may become legitimate targets for change.

One community-centered model of practice, described by Padi Gulati and Geoffrey Guest, is based on experience in Quebec, Canada. It grew out of a conviction that poverty could not be addressed apart from social justice and social rights and that alternatives to existing service delivery structures should be explored. It contains a strong preventative element and addresses the delivery of both community health and social services. Major features in the model include the use of multidisciplinary teams, universality of service provision, use of community networks, user participation in policy and service delivery, and egalitarianism in the workplace. Although this model developed using a community organization approach to improve services to individuals in a particular political and social environment, it also holds considerable potential for other settings. Generalist social workers with an understanding of community functioning might well consider the community delivery system to be an appropriate focus for change.[9] (Chapter 14 discusses specific strategies that might be used in such practice.)

The community is a social system. Like any social system, it has a structure, a way of functioning, and a history. It has energy and organization. The functioning of the helping system cannot be fully understood apart from the environment in which it functions, the community.

Case Example

Helen, a new BSW graduate, faced her first job with both anticipation and anxiety. She had been hired by the Family and Children's Division of a Department of Social Services in a state adjacent to the one where she had lived all her life and gone to school. Having done her field experience in a similar setting in her home state, she had some idea about how such an agency functioned. However, she was also aware of differences. In her home state the Department of Human Services was organized on a district basis. Her new job was in a state that had county administration.

She had spent about a week in Pringvale, the community where she would be working, getting settled in her new apartment. She was glad she could have this time to get settled and to begin to learn something about the community. It would be the community in which she would be living as well as working. She had discovered where the grocery stores were and how to get her utilities turned on. A neighbor who was also an employee of the department had told her about some groups she might want to join.

She had taken time to stop by the library. The librarian had been very helpful in providing her with the resources from which she could begin to develop her understanding of the community. She was really glad that her social work class had done a community study and that she knew what to look for and what to ask about. Census directories, community reports, and books about the community were all available. The librarian had recommended one good history, which she had brought home.

She had stopped by the chamber of commerce office and had gotten a lot of information, and the local tourist office also gave her some material. She had started to get the local paper. Now that she was settled in, she wanted to get going on her new job.

Helen knew she had made a good start in developing her understanding of the community. She also knew there was a great deal more she would have to learn about it. She knew it would take time, but she already had an outline of the information she needed, and by seeking out that information and asking questions of those she worked with or met at community activities, she would enhance her now sketchy understanding.

Understanding the Agency

Social work is an agency-based profession. The **agency** is the immediate environment of the worker-client interaction. This interaction often takes place in an office or building identified as "the agency." The influence of the agency is strong even when the interaction takes place elsewhere in the community. As an employee, the worker is a part of the agency system, and because of this the worker is accountable to the agency. The form and content of the service offered must be within the agency's purview and guidelines. The manner in which the agency is structured and functions greatly influences the nature of the worker-client interaction. The agency also provides resources for both the worker and the client. To work in and use the agency in service of the client, the social worker must first understand the agency and its way of functioning.

Social workers not only need to understand the agency in which they are employed, but they also need to be able to understand other social agencies. This is important if the worker is to help clients use the resources and services of other agencies. In addition, where needed resources are not available or usable, an understanding of the agency is a prerequisite to bringing about needed change. (See Chapter 14.)

From an ecosystems strengths perspective, the agency is a part of the worker's ecosystem and also becomes a temporary part of the client's ecosystem as the helping process develops. In addition, the agency has an ecosystem that is made up of the community. An important component of the agency's ecosystem is the human service delivery system within the community of which the agency is a part. Understanding the agency as a system and as a part of the larger ecosystem is essential to maximizing access to important resources for growth and change.

Agencies in which social workers are employed vary as to type and organization. Some are exclusively social work agencies. They provide social services delivered by professional social workers (MSW or BSW). A family service agency might be an example of this. The family service agency may, however, have a homemaker service or use other than professional workers in other ways. A family service agency is a voluntary agency; that is, it has a governing board of citizens and raises money for its support in the community (either separately or with other agencies). Once voluntary agencies did not use governmental funds, but since public funds have been used to purchase service from private agencies, this is no longer true.

Other social workers are employed by a variety of governmental agencies. They are in what is known as the *public sector.* These agencies are often state and/ or federally funded. The worker is regulated by law and by governmental policies and regulations. Other social workers are employed in what is known as *host* or *secondary* settings. In this kind of setting, the primary function of the setting is not social service; social services are used to enhance the primary service. The social worker in a hospital is an example of this kind of setting. In other settings the social worker is part of an interdisciplinary team. The prime focus may be social service, or it may be some other service. Work in a community mental health center is an example of this kind of setting.

It has been pointed out by Barbara Oberhofer Dane and Barbara L. Simon that social workers in host settings have predictable issues that they must address. These include value discrepancies between social workers and those who are the primary discipline in an agency; an often marginal status assigned to social work in such settings; devaluing social work as woman's work; and role ambiguity and role strain.[10] Thus, agencies vary with respect to several dimensions: size, means of support and governance, nature of the primary service offered, and range of people who are employed.

Another differential aspect of social service agencies is the **field of practice,** or the area on which the service focuses. Some fields are clearly identified, such as medical social work, school social work, and social work in corrections. Others are more difficult to differentiate. For example, where does child welfare end and children's and family services begin? The important differentiation in terms of understanding the agency is what field of practice the agency sees itself within. Related to this is how the community sees the problems with which the field of practice is concerned. Does it perceive people who experience these problems as sick, deviant, or inadequate or as persons who deserve some help over a rough spot? Community attitudes impact the agency and its capacity to deliver service.

These attitudes lead to another differential that can be described as people-processing, people-sustaining, or people-changing agencies.[11] At the people-processing end of the continuum would be the provision of an information-and-referral service with little follow-up. The goal is to give information. At the people-changing end of the continuum is the highly skilled social work clinician in a mental health agency. Many social service agencies are involved in varying amounts of both people processing and people changing. The people-changing focus of an agency may be seen as socialization or growth oriented, or it may be seen as rehabilitation or treatment oriented. One common problem of service delivery is when worker, agency, and community have different views of the mix of people processing and people serving. This leads to incongruent expectations for the outcome of the service.

The community provides financial and other support and sanction for the agency. It also has expectations of the nature and outcome of services. These resources and expectations vary depending on the nature of the agency structure and on the service the agency offers. These impacts also vary from community to community, because the agency is one unit in the community system. As changes take place in the larger system, change will be inevitable in the agency system. Social workers who understand this relationship of agency and community are better able to understand and use the agency system in service of the client.

The social service agency is an organization. In its larger forms it is a complex organization or a bureaucracy. This complex organization is made up of sub-units, small groups, and individuals. The agency is a social system with distinctive qualities that affect the way it functions:

1. The goals are external to the system. They are not primarily self-satisfying for those who are employed by the agency.

2. They are people serving, not product producing. This service function differentiates social agencies from organizations, the goal of which is the production and marketing of a product.
3. The goals are change in knowledge, beliefs, attitudes, and skills. The means to achieve these goals are complex, and the measurement of the outcome is also complex.
4. A major component of the agency is professional people. The professional functions with a degree of autonomy and a commitment to the client that often conflicts with the classic and efficient functioning of organizations.

Because of these distinctive characteristics of social service organizations, social workers find themselves functioning with two different kinds of expectations: the professional and the bureaucratic. The larger the organization, the greater the differences. Bureaucratic expectations call for loyalty to the organization; acceptance of authority from above; working within rules and regulations; formal relationships; and an emphasis on achievement of goals, specialization, and efficiency. Professional expectations call for commitment to professional values and to the service of clients; ability to have a broad span of decision-making power; collegial relationships; and an emphasis on meeting client need and allowing for client self-determination and individualization. These two kinds of expectations lead to tensions in service delivery and are manifest in such issues as (1) How is the competence of the worker to be determined? From a bureaucratic perspective or from a professional perspective? (2) Should workers specialize or be generalists? (3) Should the focus be client need or societal need? (4) What range of professional judgment is to be allowed workers? (5) Are certain services and tasks performed best by professional workers or by technicians? (6) Should service be a clearly identifiable activity, or is there a "mystical something" that happens?

Before a worker can effectively deliver service as a professional in a bureaucratic organization, the worker must first understand the organization. A social systems approach, again, is a means for developing that understanding.

The first task in understanding an agency is to define its boundaries. The entity that operates with a great enough degree of autonomy so that a unique structure and ways of functioning have developed—in which the influences within the structure are stronger than those without—might be identified as the agency. In a Veterans Administration hospital the social services department might be the choice as the primary system for focus if interaction among departments is limited largely to department heads. If the interaction is greater within a team of doctor, nurse, and social worker, then the unit team might be considered the agency. Because both kinds of interaction are important, however, the total institution might be the better choice. None of these answers is completely adequate. Whatever set of boundaries is used, it should be one that defines the entity with the greatest influence on the worker-client interaction.

The second task is to determine environmental factors that influence the structure and functioning of the agency. These influences involve other social systems and broad socioeconomic factors, including those that impact the agency either by providing resources or by placing expectations.

Some of the social systems that may need to be considered include:

1. Any organization or system of which the agency is part (e.g., a national membership organization, a statewide organization, or an institution of which the social services department is a part)
2. The community (or communities) from which clients come or that provides support for the agency
3. Professional organizations to which the workers belong
4. Foundations or other sources of support
5. Community planning and funding bodies
6. Governmental bodies that regulate or supply support for the services
7. Colleges and universities that educate for the professions employed
8. Other social agencies
9. Individuals and families who are clients or potential clients
10. Organizations such as churches and service clubs that may be resources to the agency or its clients

Socioeconomic forces that should be considered include:

1. Economic trends
2. Societal trends
3. Community expectations
4. Community need
5. Political forces
6. Governmental policies or regulations
7. Cultural diversity needs within the community

The third task is to understand the structure and functioning of the agency system. The factors involved include:

1. *The purposes, objectives, and values of the system*—These are spelled out in articles of incorporation, enabling legislation, agency handbooks, and other official documents. Also important is how these formal expressions are interpreted and implemented in actual service delivery. The agency's value priorities influence this interpretation and implementation. The history of the agency is important in determining how the purposes, objectives, and values developed.

2. *Agency resources, including financial resources*—Resources include the funds provided by the community, through either gifts or tax money; the building or other physical structures the agency leases or owns; and the people resources, both paid and volunteer, including professional and support staff.

3. *The traditional ways of working*—Each agency tends to use particular approaches in its service (such as long-term counseling, crisis intervention, provision of specific resources, group-work activity). This can also include specific theoretical approaches, such as task-centered, psychoanalytic, and so on. Agencies tend to work with particular systems, individuals, families, groups, or communities. They tend to hire workers with particular educational backgrounds for specific tasks (e.g., MSW, BSW, college graduates, persons indigenous to the community). They have particular patterns of work (e.g., teams, cotherapy).

4. *Boards or other governing bodies*—An important consideration is the method of sanctioning the agency (public or private). If public, the laws, policies, and other regulations that govern the agency and the organizational structure of the larger organization of which the agency is a part should be identified. If private, the structure and functioning of the board of directors is the focus. Members of the board and their motivations and needs are also important, as is the relationship of the governing body to the agency and its staff. Another element is the committee structure and functioning. This structure can be one of the board, the staff, or a combination of the two. It is often in committees that new ideas are formulated, that the work of the organization is carried out.

5. *The organizational structure*—This includes both the formal and informal structure, the administrative style, the accepted norms and values, the decision-making and communication processes, and the power and control patterns.

6. *The staff*—Important considerations include who they are as both persons and professionals; the relationships among staff (formal and informal); and the relationship of staff, clients, administration, and governing body. The professional identification and qualifications of staff should also be considered.

7. *The clients*—Often clients are overlooked as a part of the agency system. Without them the agency would have no reason for existence. In an age of consumer advocacy, this aspect of agency functioning takes on new importance. Consideration should be given to client needs, expectations, and ways of relating to the agency. The status, designation (patient or student, etc.), and values relating to clients should also be considered.

Each of these aspects of the structure and functioning of the agency system may overlap with other aspects. In developing understanding of an agency, workers should be aware of these overlaps and of the relationships and linkages between the various aspects. Workers also need to be aware of any special aspects of their agency that affect its structure and functioning. In order to gather the information needed for understanding an agency, an organized framework is often useful, such as Table 8.2.

It should now be apparent that there are several subsystems that function within the agency. First, there are *persons*. Each person in the system brings personal and sometimes professional attributes. As these persons interact in carrying on the work of the agency, their attributes influence interactions. Second, those persons fill *roles*. Some of the roles are defined in job descriptions. Roles imply relationships to other roles. This relationship structure also influences other interactions. Third,

TABLE 8.2   **A Schema for the Study of a Social Agency**

A. Identify the boundaries of the agency.
B. Discuss the history of the agency.
C. Discuss the structure and function of the agency.
   1. The purposes, objectives, and value priorities of the agency
   2. The agency resources: financial (sources and amount); physical property, staff (paid and volunteer)
   3. The traditional way of working with clients
   4. The sanctioning of the agency (public or private). If public, identify the laws, policy, and regulations that impact on the agency functioning. Identify the organizational structure of any larger organization of which the agency is a part. Note means of citizen involvement and input. If private, describe the structure and functioning of the board of directors. Who serves on the board? (Describe them as persons.) What are the roles and responsibilities of the board (both internal to the board and with the rest of the agency)? Describe committee structure and functioning.
   5. The organizational structure of the agency. Describe formal and informal functioning of the agency. What are the accepted norms and values? How are decisions made? What is the communication process? Describe power and control aspects.
   6. The staff, as persons and as professionals, their relationships, roles, and ways of working with each other, clients, administration, and governing boards. Identify formal and informal staff groups and describe their functioning.
   7. The clients, their needs, characteristics, expectations, role, and status
D. Identify the strengths and limitations of the agency.
   1. What are the strengths of the agency in terms of serving clients?
   2. What are the limitations of the agency in terms of serving clients?

there are *small groups.* These small groups may be formal work groups or informal social groups. The functioning of these small groups is another influence on interactions within the agency. Fourth, there is the *formal structure,* which includes the formal lines of authority outlined by the organizational chart. The chart defines the hierarchical relationships: who is responsible to whom and/or how the various parts of the organization are related. Fifth, there is the *power system*—the system of decision making.[12] It is important to know who makes decisions and how those decisions are influenced in understanding an agency. Each of these systems is important in the functioning of the agency. An understanding of all is necessary for understanding the agency as a social system. It is also necessary if the worker is to work effectively for needed changes in the agency's structure or way of working. (Specific strategies for working with agencies in an effort to change the agency will be discussed in Chapter 14.)

Recently, health care and mental health agencies have begun to be impacted by limitations on funding and on service provision. Various funding sources, including the government, have begun capping funds and services. In these settings especially, managed care is rapidly becoming the norm. Under managed care, the choice of making referrals to specialists or of continuing service is not left up to the client or the service provider. Instead, a third party is involved as "the manager of care." This may be the physician or an independent agency that contracts with funding sources to regulate services or an insurance company. Sometimes this management of care includes conducting an initial assessment and making a referral to a participating organization. It almost always includes a limitation on the amount of service and a requirement that approval be obtained to provide service beyond those limits.

While it may seem that other areas of human services are not affected by managed care, various forms of limiting and controlling service delivery are major aspects of the "reforms" that are sweeping through social welfare. Accompanying this reform is a movement toward increasing competition among providers of service and contracting out what traditionally were government services to private corporations, including for-profit organizations. Eventually, all human service providers will likely be impacted by these changes. For instance, in the latest version of "welfare reform," the limitation of five years of assistance, is basically a capitation of service. When work requirements are added, welfare reform begins to take on some of the aspects of a managed care system, especially since client choice is limited. Several states are looking at contracting out their state social service systems to private for-profit corporations, including major defense contractors.

These changes will have a major impact on how agencies function and how social workers function within agencies. Agencies will have to do more with fewer resources. The competition among agencies for funds will likely intensify, since some agencies will be fighting for survival. At the same time that competition increases, there will be a greater need for cooperation in order to coordinate services. To be successful, agencies will need to be able to adapt while walking a tightrope between competition and cooperation.

The emphasis for workers will be on efficiency and on working within limited time frames with clients. There will be a greater need for brief and solution-focused approaches as well as group work services. While workers will be asked to do more with less, opportunities for creativity and innovation will also be available. Prevention programs and early intervention will become more important, as will more informal support services such as self-help groups.

Another area that is in desperate need of reform is the amount of paperwork most social workers must do. Computerized records and computers that take dictation are gradually being introduced into the human services. However, what is really needed is fundamental change in the amount and type of information gathered. Much of the information gathered by human service agencies is never used or has little to do with resolving the client's situation. The social worker should take advantage of every opportunity to influence record keeping in their agency. This is not just the responsibility of a supervisor or administrator; workers should question the record-keeping systems under which they operate. Freeing more time from paperwork means having more time to devote to clients. Briefer forms of service should involve briefer records. If workers are expected to deliver services within shorter time frames, they will need to be much more efficient in collecting and recording information.

Transactions between Person and Ecosystem

In addition to understanding the community and the agency as social systems in the ecosystem, it is essential to understand the transactions that take place between the client and/or the worker and these systems. Sometimes fundamental change in the structure and functioning of the community or agency is necessary in order to improve opportunities for meeting clients' needs. However, most often it is not necessary to undertake such radical change. It may only be necessary to change the transactions so that the needs of clients and these systems can be met. Sometimes change is only needed in the transactions with the particular client system being served. Other times the community or agency's transactions with larger groups may need to be altered. In any event, the worker begins by gaining a thorough understanding of the relevant aspects of the community or agency through the schema presented. The worker then proceeds to evaluate the transactions taking place.

People have needs and strengths as do other systems in their environment. The transactions that take place within an ecosystem include exchanges of matter, energy, and information.[13] Matter is any tangible object. In the social work endeavor this generally represents the physiological or basic needs included at the first level of both Towle's and Maslow's hierarchies of need (see Chapter 1). These basic needs include air, water, food, clothing, shelter, and health. Food, water, and air are converted by the body into energy. The rest of Towle's and Maslow's needs are intangible and represent transactions that energize a person. These include social, emotional, intellectual, and spiritual growth. When the person's ecosystem supports meeting these "higher needs," he has more energy to meet other needs, both within himself and within other parts of his ecosystem. However, when basic needs are not being met, or the effort to meet those needs drains the person, then he has little energy to spend on meeting higher needs for himself or on responding to needs and demands from the environment.

Transactions that involve exchanging information are of particular interest to social workers. As people in an ecosystem exchange information, they are changed, as are their transactions. Human beings and their social environment are information-processing systems. We seek out information and use it to interpret our environment and to improve our opportunities to meet our needs. In fact, higher needs are met primarily by exchanging information. For instance, social needs are met by interacting with other people. However, as a society becomes more technological and complex, we become more interdependent. The exchange of information becomes the primary means by which even basic needs for food, clothing, and shelter are met.

The social work endeavor itself may involve direct exchanges of matter and energy, but most often it involves exchanging information. The worker seeks information from the client, as does the client from the worker. In an ecosystems approach, the worker and the client form a partnership in which they also seek information about other parts of the client's ecosystem. This information is then used to develop a plan that will meet the needs of the client and his environment.

Chapters 9 and 10 will take a closer look at these transactions involving the change of information.

It is clear that people are influenced by their environment while also having an influence on their environment. The ecological perspective seeks to provide a theoretical and conceptual base for incorporating both of these factors into the helping process, including the interactions between people and their environment. The addition of the strengths approach means that the focus is on assets, resources, abilities, and capacities that will meet the needs of the client as well as others in the environment. In the long run, it is not in the best interests of the client to have his needs met at the expense of other people or systems in his environment. This would leave the ecosystem out of balance, which means that various parts of the system would experience tension that would eventually be released. When this tension is released, the ecosystem will seek to rebalance itself. In the process, the client may end up in the same situation he was in to start with or he could even be worse off than he was.

The generalist social worker recognizes the need to examine the exchange of matter, energy, and information between the client and his ecosystem. She observes areas of strength where there is a mutually beneficial relationship that meets the needs of all involved. She also notes areas that need to be strengthened or changed because the transaction is out of balance. When clients experience a balance between the needs and expectations of their environment and having their own needs and expectations met, they are content with their lives and feel good about themselves and about their relationships with others. In addition, they feel competent and in control of their lives. This represents a state in which the client truly experiences as a reality the social work values of dignity and worth of the individual, self-determination, and having socially accepted needs met in socially accepted ways.

Case Example

The first morning on the job Helen dressed very carefully, for she knew that first impressions are very important. When she got to the office one of the secretaries showed her her desk and got her some office supplies—pencils, pens, paper, and so on. One of the workers stopped by her desk and introduced himself. About that time her supervisor came in and said she had an emergency and wouldn't be able to see her until about 10:30; she gave Helen the manual and five case folders for her to read and dashed off.

Helen looked at the manual first. She looked at the table of organization and began to find out how the department was organized. While she was reading, she also observed what was going on in the office and tried to identify who the various people were. As she read the manual she jotted down questions that she had. She was certainly glad for her social welfare policy course, for she at least knew what the programs were and the federal laws that related to them.

At 10:30 her supervisor came in. Helen got her pad with her list of questions and the case records. The supervisor told her that she could begin to work with these five cases immediately.

(continued)

Case Example   Continued

They proceeded to discuss each case. Then Helen asked her questions about the manual and the material she had read. She asked about supervision, what was expected of her, and how often she would see her supervisor. The supervisor said that for the first month or so she would try to see her twice a week but that sometimes it might not be at a set time. Then they would decide what to do about supervision. The supervisor told her that there would be more case assignments later that week. She said she wanted Helen to go with other workers two or three times on child abuse investigations before she went on one of her own. She should be prepared to do these as they came up. Then Helen was given a lot of employment forms that she was to fill out and give to the supervisor tomorrow.

Helen asked the supervisor if she had any suggestions for getting to know the community and the agency. The supervisor said, "Oh, that just happens, but maybe you would like to go to the interagency luncheon meeting with me on Wednesday." Helen asked if there were some kind of directory of the other agencies in the community. The supervisor told her that the one they had was really out of date but that one of the secretaries had a good list of the agencies and it might be a good idea to look at it. The supervisor told her she'd need a map too.

Just as Helen was returning to her office, Bob, another one of the unit workers, told her he had to investigate a child abuse report and asked if she would like to come along. As they drove out to the M home, Bob told her that this was a family the agency had worked with in the past. While they were driving to see this family, Bob pointed out a number of things to Helen and talked about the west side of town where many of the agency's clients lived. Helen asked questions about the kinds of problems these clients had and noted that many of them stemmed from lack of resources.

By the time they got back to the office it was almost 4:00. Helen spent the rest of the day reading records and thinking about how to approach each client. When she got home, she took stock of what had happened that first day and what she needed to do.

1. She was beginning to get a feel of the community. No one seemed to have all the information she wanted. She would just keep her eyes and ears open and jot down what she had learned each night.
2. The information about the agency was a little easier to get. She would continue to ask questions and sit back and watch until she got the hang of things.
3. She liked the way her supervisor was letting her get started. She intended to try to see all five of her cases this week. Then she would make plans about what to do with each one. She thought that this way she could preserve her power of discretion. She was glad she had some clients to work with right away and could go ahead on her own.

Working in a Bureaucracy

With the growth of a service society, many social workers find employment in bureaucratic settings. They are confronted with the conflict between professional and bureaucratic expectations—with human need, human pain, and societal injustices and with agency policy, rules, and regulations. They are confronted with the slowness of change, the seeming unresponsiveness of the system, and de-mands for accountability by the bureaucratic agency. They are also confronted with the need to find ways to use the agency and its resources to meet the needs of clients. This calls for a set of skills for functioning in a bureaucracy.

Ralph Morgan has identified five role conceptions that social workers have adopted in bureaucratic organizations:

1. *Functional bureaucrats*—These workers just happen to be working in a bu-reaucratic organization. Their major orientation and loyalty is toward the profes-sion and its values. They look for interaction with, and recognition from, professional peers. There is resistance to interaction in and with the bureaucracy. These workers are usually very competent practitioners whose services are valued by the agency, so that the agency overlooks their lack of bureaucratic loyalty.

2. *Service bureaucrats*—These workers are oriented toward the client but also see themselves as part of the bureaucratic structure. They maintain relationships with both professional peers and agency staff. They are ambivalent about their identification with the agency but believe the agency is the means to help clients reach their goals and to obtain needed resources.

3. *Specialist bureaucrats*—These workers attempt to reconcile "bureaucracy to humans and humans to the bureaucracy." They use the rules and regulations but are also guided by professional judgment. They understand that the human con-dition is so complex that it can never be encompassed by rules and regulations. They seek means of using professional discretion so as to make the system work in service of the client. They realize that, like all human endeavors, the agency is im-perfect. They have a strong professional identification.

4. *Executive bureaucrats*—These workers' major orientation is toward the exer-cise of power. They are innovators, infighters, and risk takers who tend to enforce bureaucratic norms. They like to manage people, money, and materials.

5. *Job bureaucrats*—These workers have a considerable investment in a bureau-cratic career. They seek job security. Their primary orientation is to the agency. They adhere to rules and regulations. They also live by the agency norms.[14]

When working in a bureaucratic setting, a combination of characteristics of the functional bureaucrat, the service bureaucrat, the specialist bureaucrat, and the executive bureaucrat seems most effective. This combination of characteristics would include a professional loyalty, a client orientation, a mediation stance, a sense of realism, a search for areas of discretionary freedom, a respect for rules and regulations, and an innovative approach to services. This is a tall order for a young, inexperienced worker but one that can be sought after. It would seem, then, that the issue is not professional versus bureaucratic but rather a search for means to combine the best of the professional with the best of the bureaucratic.

Robert Pruger has pointed out the necessity for learning bureaucratic skills at a time when it is increasingly impossible to deliver professional service without being a bureaucrat. He points out that one can be a "good bureaucrat." A first step to developing these skills is the realization and acceptance of the reality that a career in social work will involve work in and with bureaucracies. He sees the key to being effective in a bureaucracy as maintaining the greatest amount of discretion possible. To maintain this discretionary power a worker must be self-directive. The worker who expects to be told every move to make soon loses this power. The good bureaucrat also knows how to negotiate stresses, opportunities, and constraints. According to Pruger, the worker does this by:

1. Staying with it, not giving up on the first try
2. Maintaining vitality and independence of thought
3. Being responsible by understanding legitimate authority
4. Conserving energy, working only on some issues, and choosing issues that are worth the effort[15]

The bureaucracy, like all human institutions, is meant to serve society's needs. The social worker who can help the social service bureaucracy meet the needs of people can become a valuable employee. This can give the worker leverage to obtain the needed discretion. Another means of gaining this leverage is to gain the competence the agency sees as important. For example, if the agency is developing the case management approach to working with some clients, then the worker should seek information, go to workshops, and collect material about this way of working with clients. In order to maintain discretionary power it is important for a social worker to demonstrate good judgment. Part of this good judgment is the ability to make decisions that are in compliance with agency rules and regulations, that do not cause negative community reactions, and that lead to effective service to clients. Another part of good judgment is doing the right thing at the right time. The attributes of self-directedness and good judgment are possible when social workers have a realistic sense of their professional self, when they use a knowledge base in making decisions, and when they develop a repertoire of skills.

The following are a number of ways in which workers can enhance their effectiveness:

1. Don't seek blame; rather, spend the energy available on seeking solutions.
2. Learn to do a lot with a little. Be realistic about the resources available and make them stretch as far as possible.
3. Be comfortable with uncertainty, ambiguity, and inconsistency. When these are present discretion is necessary.
4. Be self-confident, creative, and responsible.

The use of supervision can be an effective means of becoming a good bureaucrat. The supervisor can provide a great deal of information about the agency, about what is happening, and about what is allowable. The worker can negotiate with the supervisor for a degree of discretion. The supervisor can be a sounding board for new ideas. To use the supervisory process effectively, the worker must take responsibility for bringing questions and problems to the supervisor. The supervisor needs to have some knowledge of the problems that exist for the worker and the ideas of the worker in order to defend him when questions arise from other parts of the system.

Social workers get into difficulty in a bureaucracy when they make unfounded decisions or do not determine the feasibility of plans they make. Problems also develop if their concerns are not focused but take the form of vague complaints. The expectation that change will take place overnight also can cause difficulty. An understanding of what the agency is trying to do and what is expected of the worker are a base on which to develop effective service. A thorough understanding of the agency as a social system is a prerequisite for being a good bureaucrat.

The development of managed care means adding another layer of bureaucracy to the service delivery system. Under these systems, decisions regarding the amount of service are no longer left to the worker and the client but are reviewed by another agency or entity. Managed care also has had an impact on how workers provide services and on how they document their work. Assessments may need to be reviewed prior to approving services, and justification is required if service continues beyond the allotted number of sessions. This means that documentation and service delivery are more closely tied together. The amount of service is usually prescribed by the diagnosis. Social workers in mental health typically have been reluctant to diagnose, since mental health care is based on a disease-based, medical model of service. This reluctance leads many workers to give the most benign diagnosis for the symptoms presented. Under managed care, this generally means briefer service. Thus it is important to obtain accurate assessment and diagnosis to ensure appropriate services are available.

Social workers are in a good position to adapt to changes brought about by managed care and various forms of limiting services. Their skills in negotiating systems, problem solving, and advocacy are needed by agencies and clients operating within this new environment. Social workers will need to promote the development of prevention approaches and adequate aftercare services in order to ensure that support for change endures beyond the formal intervention period.

Increasingly, managed care companies have employed social workers as service reviewers. Workers employed by companies that are committed to quality service as well as efficiency may find a comfortable niche in facilitating the maximum effective use of limited resources. However, those employed by a company that overemphasizes profits or limiting services will find that ethical dilemmas make it nearly impossible to survive with a commitment to social work values and ethics intact.

The development of managed care and the competition for scarcer resources have added to worker stress. Workers must account for their decisions and have external and sometimes arbitrary limits placed on the time for providing service. In addition, competition or limits on funding may threaten the survival of the agency. Workers also feel stress about not knowing if they will have a job or how their job might change.

One phenomenon that has received considerable attention is *worker burnout*. Christina Maslach has described it as "helping professionals losing positive feelings, sympathy, and respect for their clients or patients."[16] **Burnout** may be a symptom of stress in the agency system. It interferes with a worker's capacity to interact with clients and others in a professional capacity. Martha Bramhall and Susan Ezell have described some of the symptoms of burnout as feeling unappreciated, loss of the ability to laugh, being literally sick and tired (suffering from headaches, backaches, stomachaches), feeling exhausted, dreading going to work, or having trouble sleeping.[17] Some people seem particularly susceptible to burnout. They tend to be people who take on too much for long periods of time, in a very intense manner. They are often young and enthusiastic about their work. Another group susceptible to burnout are those who use relationships in the work situation to compensate for a lack of meaningful relationships in their private lives. Workers who feel they cannot achieve their objectives or believe they lack control over their activities also seem particularly vulnerable to burnout.

Social workers need to be sensitive to their functioning and to symptoms of burnout. If they are developing, they should engage in a plan to overcome the burnout. Although stress within the agency system can be a source of burnout, the worker can develop lifestyle changes that allow the worker to function within the system. Identification of the condition is the first step. Once burnout is identified as the source of the difficulty, the worker needs to pay attention to personal needs that have been slighted. A regimen that includes sufficient rest, exercise, good diet, and other self-care tasks needs to be undertaken. The worker should develop a network of personal resources that can help in meeting personal need. Having a person who can serve as a sounding board and help in analyzing the situation is particularly useful.[18]

Prevention of burnout should be a goal for all social workers. Preventive measures include providing time and energy for personal needs—the pacing of oneself so as to provide a time to work and a time for self is important. Developing the skills of a good bureaucrat is also important. This includes taking responsibility for maintaining and enhancing one's sphere of discretion.

Using the strengths perspective can help in reducing worker stress and the potential for burnout. It is a positive approach to helping clients and assumes that necessary resources to meet client needs can be found or developed within the client and the environment. Instead of focusing on deficits, it looks at assets, abilities, and capacities. Even though the worker may still feel stress, she is relieved from the burden of being an expert who is responsible for having answers to client problems. Instead, the client is recognized as an expert in his own life, and the worker uses her expertise as a resource for assisting the client in meeting his needs.

Summary

This chapter considers the environment of the helping endeavor, the community and the agency. Both can be understood from a social systems perspective. The transactional nature of human functioning makes it essential that social workers understand the strengths and resources of the community and the agency and the influence of these two systems on the functioning of both worker and client.

If the worker is to be a generalist, this understanding is essential in making decisions as to the target for change and the mode of intervention. If the target is to be the community or agency system, the worker needs in-depth understanding of that target. Communities and agencies are complex systems that must be understood in considerable depth before they become a target for change.

Most social workers are employed in bureaucratic settings. Conflicts between professional and bureaucratic demands are often confronted by the social worker in these settings. It is important that social workers develop skills for dealing with these conflicts and become "good bureaucrats." Social workers are also prone to burnout and need to develop means of protecting themselves against this occupational hazard.

QUESTIONS

1. How does conceptualizing the community as a social system enhance a social worker's understanding of any community? How might the community be conceptualized as an ecosystem?

2. Using a community with which you are familiar and the material presented in this chapter, identify information you should obtain if you are to develop greater understanding of the community. Pay special attention to strengths and resources. Where would you go to obtain that information?

3. What factors do you consider the most important influences on the manner in which an agency functions? What might be some potential strengths and resources?

4. What are the differences in agencies where social work is the primary profession and those in which some other profession is primary?

5. How would you go about gathering the information needed to understand any agency in which you might be employed?

6. Using Morgan's classification (see the section "Working in a Bureaucracy"), identify the preferred way for a social worker to function in a bureaucracy. Why did you make the choice?

7. What do you think are some of the ways a social worker can avoid burnout?

8. Identify the impact of social service "reform," privatization, and managed care on the human service delivery system in your state. What are the impacts on social workers now and in the future?

SUGGESTED READINGS

Abramson, Julie S. "Orienting Social Work Employees in Interdisciplinary Settings: Shaping Professional and Organizational Perspectives." *Social Work* 38 (March 1993): 152–157.

Arches, Joan. "Social Structure, Burnout, and Job Satisfaction." *Social Work* 36 (May 1991): 206–208.

Bailey, Darlyne, and Koney, Kelly McNally. "Interorganizational Community-Based Collaboratives: A Strategic Response to Shape the Social Work Agenda." *Social Work* 41 (November 1996): 602–611.

Cox, Fred M. "Communities: Alternative Conceptions of Community: Implications for Community Organization Practice." In Fred M. Cox, John L. Erlich, Jack Rothman, and John E. Tropman, Eds., *Strategies of Community Organization: A Book of Readings,* 4th ed. Itasca, IL: F. E. Peacock, 1987 (pp. 213–231).

————. "Community Problem Solving: A Guide to Practice with Comments." In Fred M. Cox, John L. Erlich, Jack Rothman, and John E. Tropman, Eds., *Strategies of Community Organization: A Book of Readings,* 4th ed. Itasca, IL: F. E. Peacock, 1987 (pp. 150–167).

Cox, Fred M., Erlich, John L., Rothman, Jack, and Tropman, John E. *Tactics and Techniques of Community Practice.* Itasca, IL: F. E. Peacock, 1977 (Chapter 1, "What's Going On: Assessing the Situation").

Dane, Barbara Oberhofer, and Simon, Barbara L. "Resident Guests: Social Workers in Host Settings." *Social Work* 36 (May 1991): 208–213.

Edwards, Richard L., Ed. *Encyclopedia of Social Work,* 19th ed. Washington, DC: NASW Press, 1995 ("Community"; "Community Needs Assessment"; "Community Organization"; "Community Practice Models"; and "Ecological Perspective").

Fellin, Phillip. *The Community and the Social Worker.* Itasca, IL: F. E. Peacock, 1995.

Finn, Janet L. "Burnout in the Human Services: A Feminist Perspective." *Affilia* 5 (Winter 1990): 55–71.

Fong, Lillian G., and Gibbs, Jewelle Taylor. "Facilitating Services to Multicultural Communities in a Dominant Culture Setting: An Organizational Perspective." *Administration in Social Work* 19, 2 (1995): 1–24.

Gibelman, Margaret, and Kraft, Steven. "Advocacy as a Core Agency Program: Planning Considerations for Voluntary Human Service Agencies." *Administration in Social Work* 20, 4 (1996): 43–59.

Gulati, Padi, and Guest, Geoffrey. "The Community-Centered Model: A Garden Variety Approach or a Radical Transformation of Community Practice?" *Social Work* 35 (January 1990): 63–68.

Gutierrez, Lorraine, Alvarez, Ann Rosegrant, Nemon, Howard, and Lewis, Edith A. "Multicultural Community Organizing: A Strategy for Change." *Social Work* 41 (September 1996): 501–508.

Homan, Mark S. *Promoting Community Change: Making It Happen in the Real World.* Pacific Grove, CA: Brooks/Cole, 1994.

Meyer, Carol. "The Ecosystems Perspective: Implications for Social Work Practice," in Carol Meyer and Mark Mattaini, *The Foundations of Social Work Practice.* Washington, DC: NASW Press, 1995 (pp. 16–27).

Moore, Stephen T., and Kelly, Michael J. "Quality Now: Moving Human Services Organizations Toward a Consumer Orientation to Service Quality." *Social Work* 41 (January 1996): 33–40.

Netting, Ellen F., Kettner, Peter M., and McMurtry, Steven L. *Social Work Macro Practice,* 2nd ed. New York: Longman, 1998.

Park, Katherine McMain. "The Personal Is Ecological: Environmentalism of Social Work." *Social Work* 41 (May 1996): 320–323.

Ratliff, Nancy. "Stress and Burnout in the Helping Professions." *Social Casework* 69 (March 1988): 147–154.

Rivera, Felix G., and Erlich, John L. *Community Organizing in a Diverse Society.* Boston: Allyn and Bacon, 1992.

Rothman, Jack. *Practice with Highly Vulnerable Clients: Case Management and Community-Based Service.* Englewood Cliffs, NJ: Prentice-Hall, 1994.

Rubin, Herbert J., and Rubin, Irene S. *Community Organization and Development,* 2nd ed. New York: Macmillan, 1992.

Ruff, Elizabeth. "The Community as Client in Rural Social Work." *Human Services in the Rural Environment* 14 (Spring 1991): 21–25.

Sheaford, Bradford W., Horejsi, Charles R., and Horejsi, Gloria A. *Techniques and Guidelines for Social Work Practice,* 4th ed. Boston: Allyn and Bacon, 1997 (Chapters 9 and 10 and Section B in Chapters 11, 12 ,13, 14, and 15).

Walsh, Joseph A. "Burnout and Values in the Social Service Profession." *Social Casework* 68 (May 1987): 279–283.

Weinbach, Robert. *The Social Worker as Manager,* 3rd ed. Boston: Allyn and Bacon, 1998.

NOTES

1. See Carol Meyer, "The Ecosystems Perspective: Implications for Social Work Practice," in *The Foundations of Social Work Practice,* Carol Meyer and Mark Mattaini (Washington, DC: NASW Press, 1995), pp. 16–27.

2. Ferdinand Tönnies, *Fundamental Concepts of Sociology* (Gemeinschaft und Gesellschaft), trans. Charles P. Loomis (New York: American Books, 1940).

3. Floyd Hunter, *Community Power Structure* (Chapel Hill: University of North Carolina Press, 1953).

4. Eugene Litwak and Ivan Szelenyi, "Primary Group Structures and Their Function: Kin, Neighbors, and Friends," *American Sociological Review* 34 (August 1969): 465–481; Phillip Fellin and Eugene Litwak, "The Neighborhood in Urban American Society," *Social Work* 13 (July 1968): 72–80; and Eugene Litwak, *Helping the Elderly* (New York: Guilford Press, 1985), chap. 8.

5. Roland L. Warren, *The Community in America* (Chicago: Rand-McNally, 1963).

6. Dennis E. Poplin, *Communities,* 2nd ed. (New York: Macmillan, 1979), chap. 2, "Community Types."

7. Louise C. Johnson, "Human Service Delivery Patterns in Non-Metropolitan Communities," in *Rural Human Services: A Book of Readings,* H. Wayne Johnson, Ed. (Itasca, IL: F. E. Peacock, 1980), pp. 55–64.

8. Louise C. Johnson, "Services to the Aged: Non-Metropolitan Service Delivery" (unpublished paper delivered at NASW Symposium, Chicago, IL, November 1985).

9. Padi Gulati and Geoffrey Guest, "The Community-Centered Model: A Garden Variety Approach or a Radical Transformation of Community Practice?" *Social Work* 35 (January 1990): 63–68.

10. Barbara Oberhofer Dane and Barbara L. Simon, "Resident Guests: Social Workers in Host Settings," *Social Work* 35 (January 1990): 63–68.

11. See Phillip Fellin, *The Community and the Social Worker* (Itasca, IL: F. E. Peacock, 1987), chap. 9.

12. This identification of systems is based on Armand Lauffer, Lynn Nybell, Carla Overbeiger, Beth Reed, and Lawrence Zeff, *Understanding Your Social Agency* (Beverly Hills, CA: Sage Publications, 1977).

13. See J. G. Miller, *Living Systems* (New York: McGraw-Hill, 1978); and Margaret M. Bubolz and M. Suzanne Sontag, "Human Ecology Theory," in *Sourcebook of Family Theories and Methods: A Contextual Approach,* Pauline G. Boss, William J. Doherty, Ralph LaRossa, Walter Schumm, and Suzanne K. Steinmetz, Eds. (New York: Plenum Press, 1993), chap. 17.

14. Ralph Morgan, "Role Performance in a Bureaucracy," in *Social Work Practice 1962* (New York: Columbia University Press, 1962), pp. 115–125.

15. See Robert Pruger, "The Good Bureaucrat," *Social Work* 18 (July 1973): 26–32, and "Bureaucratic Functioning as a Social Work Skill," in *Educating for Baccalaureat Social Work: Report of the Undergraduate Social Work Curriculum Development Project,* Betty L. Baer and Ronald Federico, Eds. (Cambridge, MA: Ballinger, 1978), pp. 149–168.

16. Christina Maslach, "Job Burnout: How People Cope," *Public Welfare* 36 (Spring 1978): 56–58.

17. Martha Bramhall and Susan Ezell, "How Burned Out Are You?" *Public Welfare* 39 (Winter 1981): 23–27.

18. These ideas are further developed in Martha Bramhall and Susan Ezell, "Working Your Way Out of Burnout," *Public Welfare* 39 (Spring 1981): 32–39.

9 Interaction with Individuals

LEARNING EXPECTATIONS

1. Understanding of the one-to-one action system as one context for delivering social work services.
2. Understanding of what goes into the formation of such a system.
3. Understanding of the concept of relationship and of its importance in the one-to-one action system.
4. Understanding of the specific characteristics of a professional relationship.
5. Understanding of the characteristics of a helping relationship.
6. Appreciation of the complexity of cross-cultural relationships.
7. Understanding of the communication process and of some common blocks to that process in the professional helping relationship.
8. Knowledge about the use of the interview as a tool in social work practice.
9. Knowledge about the ways to prepare for an interview and of the stages in an interview.
10. Knowledge about the skills needed when working in a one-to-one action system and the beginning ability to use some of these skills in everyday communication.

The social work endeavor takes place in an interpersonal interactional process. This interaction is more than an exchange between a worker and a client; the worker also interacts with colleagues, community persons, and any other professionals and people who are significant to the helping situation (significant others). The interaction can be one-to-one, between the worker and another person, or it can take place in multiperson situations such as a family, a team, or a small group. Although there are similarities between the process of interaction of one individual to another and the interaction with multiperson systems, there are also differences. This chapter considers the interaction of the social worker with one other person. Chapter 10 will consider the interaction in multiperson situations.

In the ecosystems strengths perspective, the work that is done by the worker and the client involves other relevant parts of the client's ecosystem. In most cases, the client mobilizes the strengths and resources available in his ecosystem. This approach empowers the client to take control of his life and get his needs met while meeting the needs of others in his environment. In some cases, the worker may need to assist the client in developing skills. When the client is unable to mobilize resources or there is a major obstacle to doing so, the client and the worker may decide that the worker should intervene more directly either with or on behalf of the client. Many of the skills covered in this chapter, Chapter 10, and Chapter 14 are important for such interventions. Because the worker-client interaction is the core of the social work endeavor, it will receive primary focus; however one-to-one interactions with members of the client's ecosystem also will be discussed. Much of the knowledge base relative to the worker-client interaction also applies to the interactions a worker has with other persons.

As discussed in Chapter 8, in the ecosystems approach there is an emphasis on the interactions and transactions that take place among systems. The client is considered a part of the ecosystem, and matter, energy, and information are exchanged among various systems that make up the ecosystem. When there is congruity or balance in these exchanges, all of the systems function in a manner that results in needs being met for the client and for other systems in his ecosystem. However, when there is an unmet need, there is imbalance or incongruity in the ecosystem. The work of the social worker and client focuses on restoring balance or developing a new balance. This does not necessarily mean that fundamental changes will be needed in the client or in systems in the environment. Instead, the emphasis is on bringing about a change in the interactions and transactions among systems (including the client). This approach is more realistic than approaches that hope to restructure or change a client's personality or change the basic structure and functioning of a family, organization, or community.

The social worker may temporarily provide needed matter or energy either directly or by linking the client with other human services. However, much of the work to be done represents exchanges of information. This includes information that flows from client to worker, from worker to client, from client to other systems in his ecosystem, from worker to other systems in the client's ecosystem, and from worker to other work-related systems in her ecosystem. The purpose of exchanging information is to influence growth and change in various parts of the ecosystem with the purpose of meeting needs and restoring balance. Much of this process involves changing one-to-one interactions.

Since the exchange of information is the focus of most of the social work endeavor, issues that are important in understanding the one-to-one interaction are (1) formation of a one-to-one system, (2) the nature of relationship, and (3) communication. Techniques to enhance relationship and communications are also important, as they can improve the quality of interactions.

Formation of a One-to-One Action System

 An **action system** is formed because of the work to be done and because the tasks to be carried out require more than one person. In addition, the ecosystem strengths approach is based on the theory that needs are met through interaction.

The worker collaborates with a colleague because each may have special areas of expertise relative to the work at hand or because the worker may profit from another view of the situation. The worker interacts with a significant other when that other person has some information needed for helping a client or can serve as a support or resource for the client's efforts in meeting needs.

In the worker-client interaction, the efforts of both are also necessary in the helping endeavor. The worker brings to the interaction a professional knowledge base and a professional set of values and skills for helping. The worker also brings the total self, finely tuned, to be used with the client as is appropriate to the needs of the helping situation and the worker's capacity. The worker brings skill in understanding situations, identifying needs, focusing on strengths, and facilitating growth and change. The client brings needs, a perception of the situation, life experiences that influence this perception, and capacity for growth and change. The client also brings motivational forces for work in meeting needs or for change of self or the situation. In the work to be done, the roles of the worker and of the client emerge from what each brings to the interaction.

Felix Biestek has identified seven needs of clients as they come to the helping situation:

1. To be dealt with as an individual rather than a type or category
2. To express feelings both positive and negative
3. To receive sympathetic understanding of and response to feelings expressed
4. To be accepted as a person of worth, a person with innate dignity
5. To be neither judged nor condemned for the difficulty in which the client finds himself
6. To make one's own choices and decisions concerning one's own life
7. To help keep confidential information about self as secret as possible[1]

The first encounter is crucial in forming the action system, since it determines much that will happen in subsequent sessions. The nature of the interaction, its kind and quality, begins to form at this point. The client will be making decisions as to whether the worker can provide the needed help, can be trusted, and has the capacity to understand the client in the situation.

The initial contact takes place when the person comes to the agency for help, either with regard to a need of her own or with a concern about someone else; or it occurs when the worker reaches out to someone to help with a need. In preparation for the first contact, it is helpful for the worker to collect and review any available information to determine what is known about the prospective client. Consideration of possible needs this client might bring as well as potential strengths in herself and her ecosystem is also useful. The worker can also get in touch with feelings he might have about the particular client in situation and about possible feelings of the client. Social workers disagree about whether new workers should read records of a previous worker before meeting the client. Records may present stereotypes or invalid assumptions that can color the thinking of the new worker. They may focus on problems or deficits rather than strengths and resources. But if records can be read with an open mind and an eye for facts, they can be good preparation for meeting with a client for the first time. The worker needs to be careful not to develop unsupported preconceptions about the client and the situation. Unsupported preconceptions can endanger the formation of the action system.

Based on the preliminary understanding of client in situation, the worker can structure the first encounter to make the client feel comfortable. This structuring will also involve environmental factors related to the time and place of the encounter—for example, the nature of the worker's greeting as the client enters the agency and meets the worker, the placement of desks so as not to be barriers between worker and client, and comfort in terms of temperature and privacy for the encounter. Choice of a time for the client is also important.

At the point of contact the worker will attempt to make the client as comfortable as possible. Cultural factors need to be taken into consideration. If the client comes from a culture in which small talk is used before getting on with the task at hand, the worker should engage in a bit of small talk. If, on the other hand, the client is anxious about the purpose of the interaction and comes from a culture that wastes few words, the worker will quickly explain what is to be done together. In other words, it is important to structure the initial contact from the interactional framework of the client, not from the worker's framework. The worker should demonstrate to the client what will happen in the work together as soon as possible and to the extent possible. The worker does this by

1. Being attentive to what the client is saying and being receptive to the client's feelings
2. Demonstrating a real desire to help the client and giving the client some indication that the worker knows how to help
3. Actively asking the client to share his perceptions of the situation (asking the client about the significance of the need, about the onset and attempts at meeting the need, and about the solutions desired are other ways to involve the client and demonstrate the way of working together)
4. Attempting to answer any unspoken questions the client may have (e.g., the client may not be sure of whether the information being shared will be available to anyone else)
5. Explaining something about the way the agency delivers service, the kind of help it gives, and the procedures for using that help
6. Focusing on strengths and potential resources within the client and within her ecosystem (this will reduce feelings of blame and of helplessness or hopelessness and will communicate a positive "can do" approach to meeting needs)
7. Trying to reach for the feelings the client is having about what is happening

In other words, the worker does as much as possible to enable the client to become engaged in helping herself in the need-meeting, problem-solving activity. In addition, attention should be given to supporting and developing self-esteem in the client. Partly, this can happen through the realization by the client that she is capable of participating in the search for solutions. Under no circumstances should the worker give unrealistic assurances about the outcome of the service.

As the worker is demonstrating to the client the way in which both can work together, he is also gathering information, understanding client functioning and the need as seen by the client, and enabling the client to think about the situation and perhaps see it in a new perspective. The social history is begun. The worker also encourages a climate of trust to develop. Until the client can trust the worker, the relationship is tenuous and the interaction is influenced by the client's concerns about the trustworthiness of the worker. As the client experiences the concern, understanding, and expertise of the worker, there is usually a reduction of these concerns and a strengthening of the relationship. This is further facilitated when the worker uses an ecosystems strengths approach, because the focus is on resolving the situation in a positive way rather than an examination of what has gone wrong. With this approach, a sense of trust develops between worker and client.

During this exploratory phase of the initial contact, the worker's task is to test out ideas about the nature of the need and the potential strengths; to gather information about client in situation, with an emphasis on the strengths of the client and his ecosystem; and to define expectations for the client about the nature of service, relationships, and behaviors. The worker is nonauthoritarian, genuine, accepting, and empathic. The client is gathering information about the agency, its services, and the helping process and is also providing information needed to give the worker understanding. The goal is to develop what Nick F. Coady identifies as a "therapeutic alliance." He defines therapeutic alliance as "an observable ability of the worker and client to work together in a realistic collaborative relationship based on mutual liking, trust, respect, and commitment to the work of counseling."[2]

Sometimes the client presents an angry, hostile, and resistive front. Carl Hartman and Diane Reynolds believe this front is used when the client is frightened and hurting and lacks trust in the worker and in the process of help. They suggest using an approach that they identify as confrontation, interpretation, and alliance. After searching for the source of the feelings and associated behaviors, the worker first confronts the client about the behavior with questions or other means that communicate that the worker recognizes the feelings and the resistance to help. This is not a hostile, personal confrontation, but one that lets the client know that the worker is willing to accept his anger and hear him out. Immediately thereafter the worker provides the client with an interpretation of the meaning or source of the feelings and associated behaviors. Then the worker provides the client with support and encouragement.[3] This approach often allows the client to feel accepted, which leads to a trusting and working relationship.

When the worker decides that sufficient understanding has been developed, he refocuses the discussion to negotiation concerning service delivery. During this next stage, the worker and the client discuss whether the need as the client sees it is one that the worker, agency, and client can work on meeting. They also discuss whether the client is willing to work on meeting the need in the way expected by the agency, if this seems appropriate. The worker and client will discuss other possibilities for need fulfillment. The worker attempts to break down the situation into parts for the client and identify potential strengths so that it does not seem overwhelming. The worker also outlines the realities of what the client can expect from the service.

During this phase the worker and client decide whether (1) they can work together on the concern or need brought by the client; (2) some other need should be worked on; (3) the service needed by the client is better delivered by another resource; and (4) the client desires not to use further services. There are times when all a client needs is to discuss a situation and gain a new perspective or knowledge of unthought-of resources. The client can then cope without further service.

In deciding whether to continue to work together (to form an action system), the worker and client need to make explicit the expectations of each person, the possible goals and expected outcomes of the service, the role of each person, and the ways of working together. The worker looks for feelings the client may have and brings negative feelings and disagreements out into the open so they can be examined and discussed. It is very important to discuss the limits of confidentiality connected with the service. Also, the worker should be sure that all terms being used are understood by the client.

If the decision is made to work together, an agreement or preliminary contract or agreement may be developed that states the next steps of the work as well as the responsibility of both worker and client and time frames for accomplishing the needed task. The contract or agreement should also indicate hoped-for outcomes of the service. (The concept of contract will be developed in Chapter 12.)

During the negotiation and contract stage, the worker openly faces and deals with resistance. Edith Ankersmit, in discussing contracting in probation settings, has suggested that in dealing with resistance it is useful to help the client discuss two questions: Why am I here? How do I feel about being here? This discussion will allow the client to ventilate hostile feelings. The worker must not deny the existence of such feelings; rather, the worker should actively listen and point out the reality of such feelings. Ankersmit also says it is important to point out the power the worker has in the situation and particularly note its limits and the power the client maintains. This discussion can communicate to clients that they do have responsibility for their own behavior.[4]

Charles Horejsi calls for a motivation, capacity, and opportunity approach in working with clients on probation. He points out that it is particularly important to try to identify the problem from the client's point of view and then decide with the client if the problem can be worked on together. He also points out that the client must believe that there is hope for a solution and recognize a feeling of discomfort about the problem. The balance between hope for relief and recognition of discomfort is very important; both must be present, yet neither should overwhelm the other. He points out that there is discomfort in change. This must be considered when determining the client's capacity for change. Workers should attempt to lessen the discomfort concerning change as one means of lowering resistance.

One source of resistance may be environmental factors. For example, if a person's peers are supporting delinquent behavior, it can be difficult for her to give it up. The discomfort of losing the companionship of one's peers may be so great that the change carries too great a price for the client.[5]

During this stage, the worker attempts to provide a climate that allows for productive discussion and a focus for the work together and to identify behavioral, cognitive, and emotional responses of the client to the work at hand and possible future work together. The worker also needs to keep in touch with her own feelings and to share these, as appropriate, with the client.

When agreement about the work together is reached, the worker should summarize what has happened in the previous stages of exploration and negotiation. It is also important to be sure that the next steps, the next session together, and any tasks to be accomplished before the next session are clearly understood.

The formation of the action system may be accomplished in one session, or it may take several sessions. During this formation the worker is attempting to bridge gaps in understanding; set the tone for the work; develop client involvement in the work to be done; maintain a focus on the work; tune in to the client's feelings, way of functioning, and concerns; and identify potential strengths and resources in the client and his ecosystem. In carrying out the worker role, the worker is sensitive to the readiness of the client to move from one stage of work to another.

Several blocks can prevent the formation of a functional worker-client system. The worker should be aware of these and attempt to prevent them from interfering with the system's functioning. First, there is the complexity of human functioning. Relationships between persons with different life experiences and cultural backgrounds are particularly difficult. Misunderstandings happen easily. Bias and prejudice are often present. These lead to differences in perception of what is happening in the work together.

A second block arises from the client's fears. He may fear depersonalization, powerlessness, being judged, or having irrelevant goals placed on him. These fears can lead to feelings of anger and may also cause the client to keep distance between himself and the worker or to avoid appropriate involvement in the work together. The fears may result from prejudices and unrealistic expectations on the part of the client.

A third block arises because the worker is often an employee of a bureaucratic organization. The complexity of rules and regulations and the inability of an organization to individualize clients often gets in the way of providing the needed service. The worker may have feelings of powerlessness and may not feel appreciated by the agency. This can lead to frustrations that hamper responding to the client appropriately.

A fourth block can be inadequate communication, which is also related to the differing cultures of worker and client. Because of poor communication, the client may not understand what is expected in the work together. The client also may not be able to sense the worker's interest and readiness to help or may see the worker as incompetent.

A fifth block relates to the worker's sense of purpose. If the worker has unrealistic expectations for self and clients, the client may sense this and avoid engagement in the tasks at hand. Workers sometimes aspire to heal all, know all, and love all; this leads to unrealistic expectations. Other workers have strong nurturing drives and tend to place clients in overly dependent relationships. Still other workers tend to avoid conflict, anger, and aggressive behavior. This may stifle the expression of feelings that need to be considered in the development of the action system.

A final block is the underlying assumptions or theory base chosen by the worker for explaining the situation. For example, if the assumptions label the client as sick, the worker may be hesitant to demand work from the client, and this may lead to more dependency in the relationship than is merited. If the assumptions assign blame, as might occur with a family of a child that is acting out at school, this will impact the worker's relationship with that family.

When working with the nonvoluntary client, it is particularly important to pay attention to these blocks. Unwilling clients often do not see the need for service, do not believe help is possible, or have difficulty in developing a relationship with the worker. In this situation, workers can sometimes overcome resistance by pointing out the reason for the concern or the consequences of a lack of change. A caring, nonjudgmental approach that focuses on the client's concerns and desires can often provide the nonvoluntary client with a unique helping experience and reduce resistance to help. The nonvoluntary client can be very sensitive to any hint of blame. Thus, using an ecosystems strengths approach can be very helpful in working with a nonvoluntary client, since the focus is on changing interactions and transactions in a positive way as opposed to looking for causes.

The worker has a responsibility to attempt to engage a resistant client when services have been mandated by a societal institution or when the client or a person for whom the client is responsible is in danger of significant harm. In doing this, the worker should try to relate as much as possible to the client's frame of reference. The worker should attempt to use the client's communication patterns and should not catch the client unaware. The worker should say why there is a concern and what the consequences of not resolving the situation might be. The worker should openly deal with either hostility or quiet inertia and should support the client's strengths. In working with a resistive client, the worker must be reasonably comfortable with the authority she carries and be reasonable and supportive in its use. Often the resistant client misunderstands the nature of the service, has unmet needs that mitigate against dealing with the situation, has inadequate cognitive capacity to deal with the situation, or is influenced by the environment in a way that prevents need fulfillment. In working with a resistant client, the worker should determine the source of the resistance and attempt to overcome it if possible; otherwise, a functioning action system may not form.

Often a bargaining strategy can be used; that is, the worker can make individuals who are resisting services aware of benefits they can receive from working with the social worker. For example, a neglecting mother can come to understand that cooperation with the worker may prevent removal of her children from her care. A juvenile delinquent can come to see that cooperation with the worker can prevent placement in an institution. An institutionalized youth can see that by adhering to certain rules and carrying out prescribed tasks she can gain desired privileges.

In using these strategies, it is important that the worker acknowledge the client's anger and resentment and develop with him a plan that incorporates the object of his concern. For instance, if a client has been ordered by a court to receive services, he is likely to be angry, hostile, and resistant. The worker might begin by asking the client how he feels about working with her. This will likely bring the client's anger to the surface. At some point, the client will express a desire to not be there. Instead of trying to talk the client out of his anger and into liking the situation, the worker should accept these feelings and seek to form an alliance by finding ways in which the client will not have to come for service. Of course, this generally means reaching a point at which the client is functioning at a level that will satisfy the court that the situation is resolved. The worker may also help the client to see that since he has to be there it is better to work on his concerns rather than waste his time.

The development of the action system may be limited by the time available to the worker and client, by the skill of the worker, by ethical considerations, by the agency function, and by the client's desires. The worker and client must decide together on the desirability and the ways of working together.

Another type of two-person action system that social workers are often involved in is one made up of a social worker and a nonclient person. This is a common arrangement when using an ecosystems strengths approach, since mobilizing potential resources and changing interactions and transactions are the focus of the work. The nonclient is generally a member of the client's ecosystem and can be a significant other in a client's life, a resource provider, or an individual who is or could be involved in a helping endeavor. In utilizing an ecosystems perspective, the worker uses resources in the community and within her work-related ecosystem. In this case, the individual might be a community influential, a person who is or could be involved in action plans focused on community or organizational change, or a person whom the worker is seeking to educate about some aspect of service delivery or the social welfare system.

Although worker-nonclient relationships are somewhat different, the worker still must pay attention to the formation of the action system. The same principles apply to these systems as apply to worker-client systems. If a worker uses the process of precontact, exploration, negotiation, and agreement, both parties are more aware of the reason for working together and of the responsibility of each party for that work. Nonclient individuals may also display resistance. Exploration of the reasons for resistance is a first step in overcoming it and in deciding if it is possible to form a functional action system. Taking a positive, strengths-based approach tends to result in less resistance than an approach that focuses on deficits or problems.

Case Example

Tim Brown is a BSW social worker in a community hospital. He has received a referral for Mrs. Hernandez. Protocol calls for a worker in this hospital to see the patient within twenty-four hours after the referral. Tim begins service to this client by reviewing the referral. It is from Dr. White, a resident physician who recently joined the staff at the hospital. Tim has not worked with him before so he does not know what his approach to this situation might be. He notes that Mrs. Maria Hernandez is an eighty-five-year-old Hispanic woman who is widowed. She is hospitalized because of pneumonia. Dr. White has requested that nursing home placement be made. No other information is given. He flags the request for nursing home placement, which seems extreme unless there are factors other than the illness to be considered.

Preparation

Next, Tim goes to the chart to review Mrs. Hernandez's medical history. She has been in the hospital two days. She was admitted after a neighbor found her lying on the floor of her home unable to get up by herself. The neighbor was able to assist her in coming to the emergency room, where Mrs. Hernandez was admitted. She is progressing nicely, and there seem to be no complications. Tim decides to consult with the head nurse on the floor. He knows this nurse can be very brusk and short with social workers and decides to anticipate resistance and try to overcome it by careful preparation for this interaction. He knows the head nurse is overworked and so chooses a time when she will be less busy. He formulates a few questions that, if answered, should give him the information he needs. First, he wants to know what the nurses have found out about Mrs. Hernandez and her living situation. Second, he wants to know who has been visiting Mrs. Hernandez. He is particularly interested in whether there have been any family members.

Tim finds that Mrs. Hernandez has been a very compliant patient but has shared little with the nurses; they do know that she lives alone. She speaks only limited English and is much more comfortable speaking Spanish. Her priest has been in to see her, but the only other visitor has been a neighbor, who brought her a few personal things she needed. There have been phone calls every day from a daughter who lives at some distance. The daughter is expected to arrive some time tomorrow. The nurse refuses to discuss whether she believes nursing home placement is appropriate for Mrs. Hernandez, saying the doctor's orders are to be followed. Tim decides not to push for more information, as he needs to maintain a working relationship with the head nurse and he senses that he has obtained all the information that she is willing to give at this time.

Tim then begins to plan his first visit with Mrs. Hernandez. He wonders about language and cultural barriers that may need to be overcome in working with Mrs. Hernandez. He considers the hospital schedule and chooses a time when patient care will not interrupt the interview. He knows he will have to conduct the interview in Mrs. Hernandez's room and that she has a roommate, so he plans to sit by her bed in a manner that will make the conversation as private as possible. Tim also considers how he might overcome some of the language and cultural barriers. Since a translator is not readily available, he decides that the best approach would be to acknowledge that Mrs. Hernandez is bilingual while he is not. He decides to apologize for his lack of bilingual skills and to ask Mrs. Hernandez for her assistance in making up for this gap. He decides that he needs to explore several areas with Mrs. Hernandez. She is probably very fearful of going to a

(continued)

Case Example   Continued

nursing home. He needs to get these fears out in the open and communicate to her that he is there to find out what she wants and what resources she needs when she leaves the hospital. Tim needs to show her that she indeed has some input into the decision-making process. He also needs to find out when the daughter is coming and get Mrs. Hernandez's permission to talk to her daughter. He needs to get a better feel for her present living situation and for her support network. With this preparation he is ready to meet with Mrs. Hernandez.

Relationship

Relationship is the cohesive quality of the action system. It is the product of interaction between two persons. *Relationship* is a term of considerable historical significance in social work practice (see Chapter 2). It has often been expressed as "good rapport" with the client. The development of a good relationship has been seen as a necessary ingredient of the helping endeavor. Helen Harris Perlman has provided a description of relationship and its importance: "Relationship is a catalyst, an enabling dynamism in the support, nurture and freeing of people's energies and motivation toward problem solving and the use of help."[6] She sees relationship as an emotional bond and as the means for humanizing help. She further states: "'Good' relationship is held to be so in that it provides stimulus and nurture.... [It] respects and nourishes the self-hood of the other.... [It] provides a sense of security and at-oneness."[7]

The social work relationship is both a professional and a helping relationship. A **professional relationship** is one in which there is an agreed-on purpose; one that has a specific time frame; one in which the worker devotes self to the interests of the client; and one that carries the authority of specialized knowledge, a professional code of ethics, and specialized skill. In addition, a professional relationship is controlled in that the worker attempts to maintain objectivity toward the work at hand and to be aware and in charge of her own feelings, reactions, and impulses.[8]

The Helping Relationship

A great deal has been written about the nature of *helping relationships*.[9] The characteristics that appear most often in these discussions include the following:

1. *Concern for others*—An attitude that reflects warmth, sincere liking, friendliness, support, and an interest in the client. It communicates a real desire to understand person in situation.

2. *Commitment and obligation*—A sense of responsibility for the helping situation. Dependability and consistency are also involved. The worker must have a willingness to enter into the world of others, with its hurts and joys, its frustrations and commitments.

3. *Acceptance*—A nonjudgmental, noncritical attitude on the part of the worker, as well as a realistic trust of the client and respect for the client's feelings. Belief that the client can handle his own problems and can take charge of his own life.

4. *Empathy*—An ability to communicate to the client that the worker cares, has concern for the client, is hearing what the client is perceiving, wants to understand, and is hearing and understanding.

5. *Clear communication*—The capacity to communicate to the client in ways that enable the client to fully understand the message being sent.

6. *Genuineness*—The worker's honesty about self and his own feelings. An ability to separate the experiences and the feelings of the worker from those of the client. Genuineness on the part of the worker allows the client to become what the client wants to be. It is present when the worker's communication is understood and comfortable for the client. The worker's personal style of helping should not be an inflexible use of technique.

7. *Authority and power*—The expectation that the client will work to fulfill needs and responsibilities and will want to resolve the situation. This expectation involves encouraging the client to go beyond the present level of functioning as well as providing guidance and resources so that goals can be reached. It involves insistence that the client do what she can for herself. The worker's knowledge and skills are a base for authority and power. The client must know that the worker's power and authority are not to be used to dominate or control the client but to assist the client in having his needs, and those of others around him, met in a positive, mutually beneficial manner.

8. *Purpose*—The helping relationship has a purpose known to, and accepted by, both worker and client. According to Beulah Compton and Burt Galaway, this is the most important characteristic of all.[10]

There is some disagreement about the place of advice giving in helping. Traditionally, social workers have thought it unhelpful to give advice; advice was seen as the worker's solution for the client and not the product of mutual problem solving and thus was not useful for the client. Clients, however, often indicate that they expect and are looking for advice.[11] Advice is tangible evidence of help. If advice is given selectively and as a result of mutual problem solving by worker and client and in a nondemanding manner as something that might be tried, leaving the final decision for its use to the client, advice may well be a useful tool for helping. However, it is essential that the advice be given by the worker and received by the client in a way that ensures that the client sees it as one of several options. Generally, it is best to use advice as a last resort, when the client is truly stuck or if he seems headed for a situation that is harmful to himself or others or if he is overwhelmed by a crisis.

Another characteristic of the helping situation is that help can be given by the client to the worker. When the client helps the worker understand the situation or culture, this is help and should be recognized as such. When the client evaluates the usefulness of various means of help and the appropriateness of various goals, this is help. Such a view of help enables the client to see the roles as interdependent rather than as superordinal to subordinal. An interdependent relationship encourages growth rather than dependency and is more helpful to the client.

Biestek's classic seven principles of a casework relationship and the worker's role in using each principle are one way of defining the responsibility of the social worker in a worker-client interaction or action system.

- *Principle I: Individualization*—This principle is "the recognition and understanding of each client's unique qualities and the differential use of principles and methods." The worker uses this principle when functioning from a nonbiased nonprejudicial stance; when applying knowledge of human diversity; when listening and observing to better understand the client; when moving at the client's pace; and when empathizing with the client.
- *Principle II: Purposeful expression of feelings*—This principle is concerned with "the client's need to express his or her feelings freely, especially negative feelings." The worker uses this principle when creating an environment in which the client is comfortable, when expressing the desire to be of help, when encouraging the client to express feeling and then listening to the expression of the feeling, and when avoiding providing advice and solutions before the client's situation is understood.
- *Principle III: Controlled emotional response*—This principle calls for "sensitivity to the client's feelings; an understanding of their meaning; and a purposeful, appropriate response to the client's feelings." The worker uses this principle when responding to the client on a feeling level in a purposefully selective manner, using her self-knowledge to direct her response to the needs of the client.
- *Principle IV: Acceptance*—This principle calls for perceiving and dealing with the client as he really is. It entails recognizing and using the client's strengths and limitations, congenial and uncongenial qualities, positive and negative feelings, and constructive and destructive attitudes and behaviors.
- *Principle V: Nonjudgmental attitude*—This principle "is based on a conviction that the [social work] function excludes assigning guilt, innocence, or degree of client responsibility for causation of the problems or needs" of the situation.
- *Principle VI: Client self-determination*—This principle recognizes the "right and need of clients to freedom in making their own choices and decisions in the [social work] process." The worker carries out this principle by helping the client see problems and needs clearly and with perspective, by acquainting the client with appropriate community resources, and by creating an environment in which worker and client can work together.

- *Principle VII: Confidentiality*—This principle asserts the right of the client to preservation of secret information concerning self that is disclosed in the professional relationship. It is the worker's role to explain the limits of confidentiality and rights of the worker and client within the framework of professional and legal obligations.[12]

These principles are used to guide the professional helping relationship. They help promote a climate in which the client-worker action system can work toward fulfilling client needs. The principles can also be applied selectively to other two-person action systems.

Special Influences on the Helping Relationship

There are a few situations in which a client's or worker's personal characteristics have a special influence on the action system's functioning. These include situations in which the worker and the client come from different ethnic or racial backgrounds and those in which the gender of the worker affects the interaction with the client and the environment in which the action takes place.

Several obstacles seem to be prevalent in cross-cultural helping relationships:

1. *Mutual unknowingness*—Because of a lack of knowledge about the other's culture on the part of both the worker and the client, there is a tendency toward stereotyping. Fear of the other is also a result of lack of knowledge and understanding. Inappropriate "good" or "bad" judgments may be made. Social distance that does not allow for the sharing and the trust necessary in the helping endeavor is often present. Of particular importance is lack of knowledge about a client's traditional communication patterns.

2. *Attitudes toward the other culture*—Negative attitudes may have developed from limited knowledge about a different culture. These attitudes may also have developed from negative experiences with persons who belong to the same cultural or ethnic group as the person being interacted with.

3. *Availability of different opportunities*—Members of different cultural groups have different opportunities. When the social worker does not understand this difference of opportunity, he can have unrealistic expectations about how clients should use the help offered. This fact can also relate to the use of appropriate resources. Some resources are not usable for a particular cultural group. For example, a culture that does not allow expression of feeling or that uses limited verbal expression and is action oriented will have considerable difficulty with traditional talk therapy. Some resources are available to, and traditionally useful for, particular ethnic groups. For example, Native Americans traditionally use the tribe's medicine man or elders as a resource. They also have the support and financial aid resources of the Bureau of Indian Affairs.

4. *Conflicts between societal and cultural expectations*—These often are difficult to resolve around the helping situation. Clients may have difficulty in identifying these conflicts, and the worker may not be aware of them.

In addition, minority clients may have a low sense of self-worth as a result of chronic and acute oppression and discrimination. This can result in low expectations for resolution of situations, in special relationship needs, and in lack of appreciation of their own culture. There may be a different world view, different expectations for the use of time, and different expectations of male and female behavior. These can get in the way of developing working relationships. The minority client may have a low trust level toward persons of other cultures; this may be the result of past relationships that produced pain and anger. A client with a low level of trust may use concealment mechanisms that hinder the helping endeavor. Different mechanisms for showing respect can result in misunderstandings. Different mechanisms for expressing ideas and feelings and different communication patterns can be particularly troublesome. Ann Brownlee has identified some of the areas in which communication differences may exist, including: situations appropriate for the communication of specific information, tempo of communication, taboos, norms for confidentiality, ways of expressing emotions, feelings, and appreciation, meaning of silence, form and content of nonverbal communication, and style of persuasion or explanation.[13]

In order to work effectively in cross-cultural situations, the worker should develop an understanding of diverse needs, of the complexities of cross-cultural communication, and of her own biases and prejudices and must also develop considerable skill in accurate perception and tolerance for difference.

In using an ecosystems strengths perspective, it essential that the worker be diligent, flexible, and creative in uncovering strengths and resources within the client and his ecosystem. Contrary to its professed belief in freedom and tolerance, the United States has a history of oppression and discrimination toward minorities, especially people of color. The basis of prejudice and discrimination is viewing other cultures as weak, inferior, and undesirable. Thus, members of the dominant culture, as well as nondominant cultures, are not accustomed to finding strengths in other cultures. In spite of the social worker's efforts to be nonjudgmental, it will be impossible to avoid all prejudice and stereotyping, since these are pervasive and imbedded in the dominant culture. Even if the worker has a predisposition toward seeing strengths, it is unlikely that she will thoroughly know these strengths unless she has had considerable exposure to or conducted research about other cultures. Nonetheless, if the worker and client make a real effort to see strengths and positive opportunities, they can overcome the negative effects of cultural bias.

Gender is another factor that affects relationships. Social work literature contains little discussion of the influence of the worker's gender on the helping endeavor. There seems to be an assumption that a skilled worker should be able to work with both male and female clients. Although this is probably true, social workers should become more aware of gender factors in professional relationships. One study has found that when male and female workers make assessments about female clients, male workers see these clients as less mature and less intelligent than do female workers. Female workers see women as having greater need for emotional expression and less need of home and family involvement than do male workers.[14] Differences in perceptions between male and female social workers, then, seem to exist. These different perceptions are probably a result of sex-role socialization and can affect professional relationships.

Joanne Mermelstein and Paul Sundet have found differences in client expectations in rural areas due to gender factors. In the female worker–female client situation, the client expects nurturing, mothering, and friendship. In the female worker–male client situation, the client sees taking help from a woman as going counter to his definition of manhood. The interaction is also affected by taboos about what is to be discussed with women. In the situation of male worker and female client, the male worker is seen as performing a traditional female nurturing role. The female client expects the male worker to support her, to give her moral guidance and clear direction. In the male client–male worker situation, the male client expects the male worker to prove his masculinity.[15]

Louise Johnson, Dale Crawford, and Lorraine Rousseau found that in traditional Sioux Native American culture it is a mistake for a male worker to go alone to a female client's home. The male worker should go through a male relative, for in traditional culture a female speaks through a male relative.[16]

Social workers should examine the expectations for male and female behaviors from the client's perspective and take these into consideration in developing action systems and in understanding and using relationships within these systems. Attention also must be given to the influence of gender of both worker and client on practice, that is, on the functioning of the action system. Workers also need to develop an understanding of how their own gender expectations influence their professional relationships.

Other differences that may exist between worker and client are young workers with old clients; unmarried workers with experienced parents; well-educated, middle-class workers with illiterate, poor clients; and upright, well-behaved workers with norm violators. These and other differences all influence the functioning of the action system—the helping relationship.

Little attention has been given to how the context of the social work endeavor affects practice, particularly the relationship factors of practice. A growing body of literature relative to the practice of social work in rural areas has pointed out the need to pay attention to the context of practice. Again, the work of Sundet and Mermelstein provides an indication of the influence of context on practice. They have found that social work roles that call for little risk on the part of the client are most effective when an outside worker enters a new rural community.[17] It may be that this experience provides a useful principle for situations in which cultural distance exists between the worker and the client. Confidentiality is an aspect of relationship that takes on new features when examined in a rural setting. People are more visible in rural settings. In some situations, it is in the client's best interest that certain aspects of the service be known so that misinterpretations about the service do not develop.[18] The effect of the context of practice on the social work interaction was explored in Chapter 8.

Social workers have given little attention to the understanding of the two-person relationship in an action system that does not involve a client—for example, relationships with other professionals such as a teacher or a pastor or relationships with community leaders. Yet workers often use this type of action system in serving clients, especially when using an ecosystems strengths approach. In discussing this type of system from an interactional viewpoint, Yvonne Fraley has suggested that mutual problem solving is more effective if this type of relationship is assessed using these six variables: (1) the position of the worker ("actor one")—that is, the location of actor one in an agency or community system; (2) the goal of actor one in the relationship; (3) the position of the other ("actor two"); (4) the goal of the other; (5) the form of communication being used (verbal, written, nonverbal media, etc.); and (6) the method of influence being used by each actor (problem solving, teacher-learner, helper-helpee, etc.).[19] This kind of analysis points out that in the nonclient action system there needs to be some reason for the two actors to work together. If the goals of each are compatible, if one actor does not feel threatened by the position of the other, and if the form of communication and the method of influence are carefully chosen, there is a better chance for gaining the desired outcome.

Regardless of the nature of the action system, the characteristics of the actors (worker-client or other), and the situation in which the interaction is taking place, the relationship of the two persons is a crucial factor in whether the work together produces the desired outcomes. Each person brings much to the system that can aid in, or detract from, the relationship and the work to be done. The social worker must be aware of these factors and use them to further the work by developing functional working relationships with other people. (See Figure 9.1.)

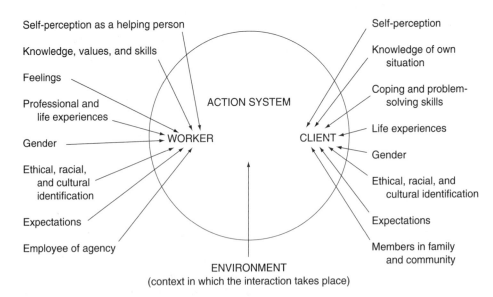

FIGURE 9.1 Relationship

Relationship is not the end-state goal of the helping endeavor or the action system; it is the glue that holds the action system together and as such is a necessary ingredient of a well-functioning action system. It is not a relationship in which there is no conflict and all is happiness and goodwill, nor is it an overly dependent relationship. It is a relationship in which conflict is open and examined and in which there is respect for the position of the other. It is a working relationship, and the purpose of the relationship is the accomplishment of tasks needed to fulfill client need and promote growth and change.

Case Example

Beginning Stage
Tim introduced himself and placed a chair near to the bed so that Mrs. Hernandez could see his face and so neither of their voices would project to the neighboring bed. He tested out Mrs. Hernandez's hearing ability by asking if she had had a good visit with the neighbor. (Here he individualized by finding out if Mrs. Hernandez had a hearing problem rather than assuming as much because of her age.) He found that she seemed very able to hear him if he spoke clearly.

He then told her who he was and that her doctor had asked him to see her and discuss plans for when she was able to leave the hospital. Tim apologized for his lack of skills in speaking Spanish and asked if she would be willing to help him understand what she needed. He said that if she could do this he would be better able to assist her in developing a plan that would meet her needs. (He did not want to bring up the nursing home or mention any specific date until the relationship was better formed.) Mrs. Hernandez agreed and then said her doctor had told her someone would be in to see her about going to a nursing home. She stated that she does not want to leave the home she has lived in for the past fifty years. She said that she would be fine if people would just leave her alone. Tim noted that her affect was somewhat sad, almost like she was giving up. He then said that a nursing home was certainly one possibility, but he needed to know more about what she wanted before he could say that a nursing home was the most desirable plan for her care after leaving the hospital. He told Mrs. Hernandez that he had not talked to the doctor and thus did not know why the doctor had decided she needed a nursing home. He wanted to talk to her first and find out a little about her and her desires. Then, if there were a better plan, he would suggest this to the doctor. He also told Mrs. Hernandez that she would have to make the decision about whether she went to a nursing home (client self-determination). Mrs. Hernandez said that she didn't think there was any choice. Tim responded by saying that maybe the nursing home would be recommended to her, but they needed to see if there were other possibilities. (During this conversation Tim was attempting to communicate to Mrs. Hernandez that she did have some choice in the matter and that he wanted to know how she felt about the situation. He was using this discussion to demonstrate the way the work together could proceed.)

After this, Mrs. Hernandez began to be less sad and in fact became somewhat agitated as she talked about her fear of going into a nursing home. She said that she was able to take care of herself and wanted to get back to her home. She told Tim how much her home meant to her. She and her husband had worked hard to save for the home. They had been migrant laborers until her husband had been able to get a job in a local

(continued)

Case Example   Continued

foundry. The home had been their only permanent residence, and they had raised six children in it. Unfortunately, the local economy had changed and the children had all moved away in search of work. She said she was upset that anyone might take her home away from her. After expressing these negative feelings for a while, she became quiet. (During this time Tim had tried to maintain a stance of accepting her negative feelings and listening to her concerns. He controlled his emotional response by not responding to her in a way that showed any displeasure with her agitation because he knew that at this point these feelings needed to be expressed before the work could proceed.)

Middle Stage
Tim then said that before he could make any suggestions he needed to know more about Mrs. Hernandez and her situation. He told her that there was also some information that he needed to get for the hospital records. At this point Tim asked for some factual information, but as Mrs. Hernandez gave this he explored to obtain more detail where it was needed. For instance, when he asked about the details of her living situation, he found that the neighborhood had become a high crime area of the city and that she had been a victim of several thefts. Mrs. Hernandez's children had been trying to get her to move in with them, but she had resisted because she was reluctant to leave her home and felt that she would be betraying her husband's memory if she left, especially since there would be no one left to visit his grave or to care for it. Mrs. Hernandez lives on a widow's pension from Social Security of only about $400 per month, along with money that she occasionally receives from some of her children. Last year, she had various utility shut-offs due to her inability to pay some of the bills. She has no phone. She currently has shut-off notices from the gas, electric, and water services, since she was not able to pay her bills while hospitalized. Mrs. Hernandez also owes a large bill to the hospital from the portion Medicare did not cover. She typically forgoes medication and medical treatment, since she cannot afford the deductible or the premiums for additional Medicare coverage. Many of her friends have died or moved away in the last few years, so she does not have friends around her as she once had. (During this discussion Mrs. Hernandez seemed much more involved in the work together. Tim sensed that the relationship had started to form. Even though they needed to repeat various parts of their discussion, Tim found that by respecting Mrs. Hernandez's culture and language he was able to form a bond that would support the work that needed to be done.)

He then began questioning her about her family. She was a little more reluctant to discuss this area, saying her children all had their own lives to live and she did not want to burden them. Tim asked about the daughter who was coming to visit. Mrs. Hernandez said that she was closest to her. The daughter had arranged things so she could spend several weeks and would help care for her when she was discharged from the hospital. Tim asked if she wanted some help in explaining to the doctor that this could be a short-term plan until Mrs. Hernandez and her daughter could discuss alternative future plans. Mrs. Hernandez brightened up and said, "Oh yes, I don't seem to be able to get him to listen to me." Then Tim asked her if he could talk to her daughter when she came. He told Mrs. Hernandez that perhaps the daughter also might need someone to talk to about her feelings regarding what was happening with her mother. Mrs. Hernandez said, "Yes, it was hard for her to talk about this, and I do want my daughter to help me think about what I should do."

Ending Stage

At this point Tim felt that he had developed a relationship sufficient for the work at hand. He had made a tentative assessment that Mrs. Hernandez did not need a nursing home placement, especially if her daughter was to stay with her for a time. He also suspected that the mother and daughter needed some help in discussing long-term plans for Mrs. Hernandez. He felt Mrs. Hernandez was almost ready to change her living situation but did not know what resources were available to help her maintain her independence in the community. He realized that she might be eligible for Medicaid, food stamps, and Supplementary Security Income (SSI) but might need assistance in accepting this and in applying for it. His next step would be to discuss the situation with the doctor and to make contact with the daughter to get her view of the situation.

Tim asked Mrs. Hernandez if she had any other concerns and she said, "No." He thanked her for being patient with his lack of language skills in Spanish. She said, "That's okay. You seem like a nice man." He told her that he would be following up on this visit and would see her later. She nodded and seemed satisfied with this.

Communication

Because effective communication is such an important ingredient of the functioning action system, it is important for all social workers to develop good communication skills. Communication is the sending and receiving of messages between two or more persons. Effective communication occurs when the persons involved in a situation accurately perceive the messages of the other person and in which the messages are sent in a way that allows the receiver to take action or respond to the sender in ways that facilitate the purposes of the communication. The purposes of communication in the social work interaction include:

1. Gathering information needed for the helping endeavor including strengths and resources
2. Exploring ideas, feelings, and possible ways to meet need based on the strengths and resources within the client and the ecosystem
3. Expressing feelings or thoughts
4. Structuring the work of the action system
5. Providing support, informing, advising, encouraging, and giving necessary directions

Communication is a process. The *sender* conceptualizes the message and through a *transmitter* (the voice or visual production) sends the message through a *channel* (sensory and modern technological means) to a *receiver* that interprets the message cognitively and affectively. This results in a *response*, another message and/or an action. The response may result in *feedback*, a means for the sender to evaluate the effectiveness of the message. One other factor of the process is *interference* or noise. Interference consists of those influences from outside the process that affect the message while it is in the channel and cause *distortion* of the message as it reaches the receiver. (See Figure 9.2.)

Each part of the process has a particular function and special problems that can interfere with the effectiveness of the communication. The sender must conceptualize the message in a way that is understandable to the receiver. This requires understanding how the receiver deals with and interprets ideas and information. The transmission of the message takes place not only through verbalization but also through nonverbal means. Nonverbal communication takes place through vocal tone and behaviors, such as gestures, facial expression, and body position. The motivation, needs, feelings, and attitudes of the sender influence the manner in which the message is transmitted. The message has content—the specific words used—and it has meaning—how that content is treated. The choice of words, the order of ideas and words, the use of humor and silence all contribute to the quality of the message.

Special attention needs to be paid to cultural and personal differences in the meaning of words. Different cultures can have different attitudes, values, and beliefs that influence how words are interpreted. Beyond the cultural aspect, each of us has unique and individual life experiences. For example, take the word *mother*. For someone who has had a warm, loving relationship with his mother, the word will evoke positive feelings. However, if a person had experienced the death of his mother at an early age, the word *mother* will probably be associated with grief and loss. Even siblings can have different ideas of their mother based on their individual perceptions.

As the message travels through the channel, the possibility of distortion is great. Previous experiences, cultural and societal demands, and attitudes and feelings of the receiver can distort the message. Distractions such as additional stimuli, concerns, and responsibilities can distort the message. The recognition of distortion and noise is a recognition of the transactional nature of communication.

The manner in which the message is received also influences the effectiveness of the message. The receiver may perceive or interpret the message in a

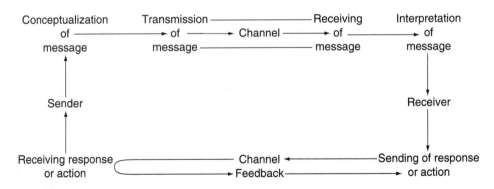

FIGURE 9.2 Communication

manner different than the intention of the sender. The receiver may not comprehend the meaning of the message as intended or may receive only a part of the message. Feedback is the means of ascertaining if the message received and the message intended by the sender are sufficiently similar to make the communication effective. Feedback is sending a message about a received message to the sender of that message. The feedback is also subject to the problems of the original message.

Effective communication is communication in which the outcome is the accomplishment of the purpose intended by the sender. Messages that have the best chance of being effective are those in which:

1. The verbal and nonverbal messages are congruent
2. The message is simple, specific, and intelligible to the receiver
3. The receiver can understand what is meant by the sender
4. There is sufficient repetition for the receiver to sense the importance of this message from among other messages being received simultaneously
5. There has been sufficient reduction of both psychological and actual noise
6. Feedback has been solicited from the receiver and sufficient time taken to ensure that the original message was received

Effectiveness in communication is affected by the credibility and honesty of the sender of the message. The receiver who has reason to trust the competence and reliability of the sender will tend to be receptive to the message and its expectations. Effective communicators tune into and are sensitive to the feelings and situations of those they are communicating with. They are assertive without being overly aggressive or confrontational.

Often the one-to-one communication is not with the client but with other professionals, with significant others in the client's environment, or with people who may in some way be involved in situations that are blocking client need fulfillment. These relationships are particularly important when the focus is on organizational or community change. The principles of communication discussed in this section (regarding clients) apply to interactions with nonclients even though communication may be of a bargaining or adversarial nature (discussed in Chapter 14). When social workers find themselves in situations where the viewpoint of the other may be different from their own, clear communication is imperative. Sometimes the differences can be resolved through clarification of messages. Other times a clear understanding of the differences allows work to progress.

Brett Seabury has identified several problems that confront social workers in their communications with clients and significant others:

1. *Double messages*—Two contradictory messages are received simultaneously or in close succession.
2. *Ambiguous messages*—These messages have little meaning or several possible messages for the receiver.
3. *Referent confusion*—The words have different meanings to each person, or they may be professional jargon not understood by the other person involved in the communication.

4. *Selective attention and interpretation*—This causes distortion of the message or confusion as to meaning.
5. *Overload*—This is the receiving of more messages than a receiver can interpret and respond to at any one time.
6. *Ritual or order incongruence*—This is the failure of the message sequence to follow expected or habitual behavioral patterns.
7. *Regulator incompatibility*—The use of eye contact and patterns of speaking and listening that regulate the communication of one party in the interchange are not known to, used by, or are unacceptable to another party in the interchange.[20]

Other barriers to effective communication are inattentiveness, assuming the understanding of meanings, and using the communication for purposes different than those of others in the interchange (having hidden agendas). Cross-cultural communication is particularly problematic because the structure of messages differs from culture to culture. Even if the same language is used, words are used differently or have different meanings. Each culture has its own idioms and expressions, and the syntax (form) of the language may be different. The differences make it difficult to listen to the messages and make the likelihood of misunderstanding great. The social worker must overcome the barriers to effective communication if the action system is to function to reach its goals. In social work, communication is dialogue. The worker and client openly talk together and seek mutual understanding. Floyd Matson and Ashley Montagu, in the introduction to *The Human Dialogue*, describe communication as

> not to "command" but to "commune" and that knowledge of the highest order (whether of the world, of oneself, or of other) is to be sought and found not through detachment but through connection, not by objectivity but by intersubjectivity, not in a state of estranged aloofness but in something resembling the act of love.[21]

This is the essence of communication in its most effective form. This kind of communication adds vitality to, nourishes, and sustains the process of working together, the interaction.

Case Example

Tim next sought out Mrs. Hernandez's doctor. He introduced himself as the social worker assigned to Mrs. Hernandez. The doctor immediately asked in a brusk, hurried manner, "When can she go to the nursing home?" (This manner of communication could have easily turned Tim off. He could have developed a block to listening. On the other hand, the doctor may be assuming that what Tim had to say to him related to sending Mrs. Hernandez to the nursing home. Thus, he was not ready to hear the message to be given.) Tim said that Mrs. Hernandez's daughter would arrive tomorrow and that it seemed as if she was prepared to care for her mother for a time. He wondered if Mrs.

Hernandez's condition was such that this would be a workable plan for now. (Tim could have told the doctor outright that he did not think a nursing home was the desirable plan. This could have set up further communication blocks as the doctor might see his authority as being challenged. Instead, Tim chose to give the doctor new information and involve him in deciding whether a different plan might be better in light of that new information.)

The doctor said, "Yes, if someone stays with her she can go home." However, he did not want her to live alone, as it was just too risky for eighty-five-year-old women to live alone. (This statement led Tim to suspect that the doctor's plan was not related to Mrs. Hernandez's specific medical condition but to his preconceived ideas about eighty-five-year-old women. This was interfering with the discussion about Mrs. Hernandez and her specific needs.) Tim then told the doctor that he was going to find out how the daughter was prepared to help her mother. He said he thought Mrs. Hernandez was ready to make a change in living situation and that he could refer the mother and daughter to someone who could help them make long-range plans. (Tim wanted to communicate to the doctor that there were resources other than nursing homes for eighty-five-year-old women living alone. He knew he would have to go slow in challenging the preconceived ideas, so he decided to just try to get Mrs. Hernandez home and help the mother and daughter find the assistance they needed.)

Tim then asked the doctor when he thought Mrs. Hernandez would be ready for discharge and what specific care she would need for the first few days after discharge. The doctor indicated she could go tomorrow and that she would need to continue some medication and have plenty of rest and a nutritious diet. Tim wondered if the day after tomorrow might not be better so the daughter would have a day to settle in and prepare for her mother's homecoming. The doctor reluctantly agreed. Tim said he would let the doctor know how his interview with the daughter went and if the plan was satisfactory to her. (Tim wanted to communicate to the doctor that he needed time to work with this patient and that he would keep the doctor informed. He felt that he had at least made a start in this direction. He hoped the daughter would indeed care for her mother for a time, but if that did not work, he had several alternatives that would avoid permanent nursing home placement. Tim also was aware that he needed to find a way to discuss with the doctor his concerns about inappropriate referrals for nursing home placement. He planned to discuss the issue with the other social workers in the hospital and urge that together they develop plans to address the problem.)

The Interview: An Interactional Tool

The **interview** is a primary tool of the social worker. It is the structure for operationalizing the interaction between a worker and a client. Each social worker develops her own interviewing style. Interviewing is an art and a skill, and learning how to interview is learned by doing it. Some guides to interviewing can be helpful to the person learning to interview. These guides include preparing for an interview, knowing the stages of an interview, and developing interviewing skills.

Each interview should have a specific purpose or goal. Generally, this purpose may be to obtain the information needed for carrying out some task or function or to work together to meet a client's need or solve a client's problem. The purpose of a specific interview will depend on the stage of work together, the agency function and the method of service, and the client's needs and/or the nature of the situation at hand. In addition to purpose, several types of variables, listed below, affect the nature of the interview:

1. *How the interview is initiated.* Is it a voluntary activity on the part of the client? Is it a formal, planned, regular interview or a walk-in request of the client? Or is it a life-space contact (one that takes place in the process of the client's daily activities)?
2. *Where the interview takes place.* Does the interview take place in an office, a home, a hospital room, or some other setting?
3. *The experience of the worker and client with each other.* Have this worker and this client had previous contact with each other? Is this encounter a part of a time-limited or long-term plan?

Each interview will be different. The worker needs to be flexible in structuring and guiding the interview, depending on the interview's purpose and the needs of the client. It should be carried out in a manner that encourages interaction and relationship.

Limited or shrinking resources and the advent of managed care have brought about a greater emphasis on brief and solution-focused intervention. The results are limitations on the amount of time available to work with a client. Some settings still provide unlimited and/or open-ended services. However, the wave of the future is clearly toward some form of time-limited service throughout the human service delivery system.

Time limits mean that the social worker must place a high premium on the efficient use of time in accomplishing maximum effectiveness. This applies to each interview that is undertaken with a client. It means that the worker must be focused on developing and accomplishing goals and objectives that will bring about necessary change. This might seem to be contrary to the idea of encouraging interaction and relationship. However, if the worker is able to empathize with the client, she would come to realize that the client's needs are met best by moving toward resolution of the concerns that brought the client to the worker. In the process, the client is also well served by learning to bring about change without assistance. This is in line with the social work value of maximizing self-determination for the client. Thus, clients can benefit from a solution-focused approach that builds on their strengths and that results in improved problem-solving skills. It is not so much the amount of time that is spent in building a relationship but the manner in which the worker interacts with the client. When the worker makes it clear to clients that they are valued and respected as human beings and that they are capable of making their own decisions, the foundation for a sound helping relationship has been established. This is not separate from the problem-solving process but rather a fundamental part of it.

Preparing for an Interview

In preparing for any interview the worker has three tasks: (1) planning the environment for the interview, (2) planning the content of the interview, and (3) "tuning in." Each of these tasks is carried out before contact with the client.

The worker thinks about the physical conditions of the interview. If the interview takes place in an office, the worker arranges the office so as to encourage the work together. This can be done by giving some thought to the placement of desk and chairs (sitting behind a desk may place a barrier between worker and client). An office that is comfortable and does not have too many distracting features is ideal. The worker tries to prevent interruptions such as phone calls and knocks on the door. If the worker plans to take notes or use a tape recorder, arrangements are made so this can be done with full knowledge of the client but in a manner that does not distract from the work at hand. The worker also tries to provide a place for the interview where the conversation will not be overheard by others. Attention is given to the time of the interview so that neither worker nor client will be hurried, but the interview will also not be overly long. The worker will think about the impact of his dress on the client. If the interview is held outside the office, the worker will choose a time that is convenient for the client and when the fewest interruptions are likely to take place. For instance, an interview with a mother in the home might best take place when the children are in school.

In planning for the content of the interview, the worker will recall the goal and the purpose of the service and will identify the goal for this particular interview. The tasks to be accomplished will be considered. Any additional knowledge or information needed will be obtained. The worker might review notes about the previous interview if there has been one. The structure of the interview and questions to be asked will be considered. This planning is done to give form and focus to the interview, but the worker is prepared to be flexible and make changes if the client has unanticipated needs.

In tuning in, the worker first tries to anticipate the client's needs and feelings in the interview and to think about his own response to those feelings and needs.[22] The worker tries to become aware of his own feelings and attitudes that might interfere with effective communication. Such awareness should minimize the impact of these feelings and attitudes on the interview. The worker also needs to prepare to help by dealing with personal needs and any work-related attitudes that might interfere with the work of the interview.

Preparation for the interview is one way to promote worker readiness, which communicates to the client that she is important and that the work to be done together is important. Worker readiness prepares the way for effective interviewing.

The Stages of an Interview

All interviews have three stages: (1) the opening or beginning stage, (2) the middle or working-together stage, and (3) the ending stage. Each stage has a different focus and different tasks. In each interview some time is spent in each stage, but the amount of time spent in each stage may differ depending on the work at hand and the relationship of the worker and client. The stages represent steps in what might be called a "mini" change process. In Part Three of this text, we examine the social work process as a change-oriented approach. The phases are assessment, planning, action, evaluation, and termination. However, these phases are not limited to the overall process but are included during each contact the social worker has with the client.

The opening, or beginning, stage of interviewing corresponds to the relationship-building and assessment phases. The middle, or working-together, stage involves evaluation, planning, and action. It includes evaluating success and barriers to success in carrying out the plan, deciding whether to continue with the plan or to modify it, and taking action to continue success or to remove barriers to success. The ending stage involves termination of the interview.

During the first few interviews with a new client, more emphasis might be needed on the first phases of relationship building and assessment with planning and action limited to meeting needs that require immediate attention. Likewise, the last few interviews might focus more on termination. However, elements of each phase of the change process should be built into each interview. Besides helping to maintain a focus on the work to be done, this has the added benefit of reinforcing the steps necessary for successful change.

The beginning stage starts when the worker greets the client by name and does whatever seems in order to make the client comfortable. In working with adults, it is important that the worker address the client more formally, using *Mr.*, *Mrs.*, or *Miss* unless the client asks to be addressed by his or her first name. This is especially important for people of color such as African Americans, who have experienced situations where the use of their first name is used as a sign of inferiority or control. Generally, in Hispanic culture, the use of first names with adults is reserved for those who have been accepted into the family system. The worker tries to reduce any tensions and discuss any hostilities that may exist and reaches out to the client to help him become an active participant in the interview. This can be done by asking the client to share any significant events since the last session. This keeps the worker in tune and current with the client and his concerns.

During the beginning stage, the worker defines the purpose of the interview or recalls plans made in a previous session. The client is given an opportunity to discuss this purpose and any special needs he might have at this time. The worker elicits the client's feelings about the work to be done and accepts the client's sense of purpose and need by modifying the purpose and plan of the interview if necessary. Thus, an assessment of the current situation is made while the worker also establishes or reestablishes a relationship by demonstrating care and concern and empathy.

If this is an initial interview, much of the time may need to be devoted to building a relationship and making an initial assessment of the situation. Diversity issues may be especially prominent during these first few interviews. The worker should communicate a respect for diversity and a valuing of difference while also seeking to learn about diversity from the client. However, some of the time should be spent in getting started with the work to be done. At the least, the worker should ask the client what they might do during the next week that might make a difference in meeting his need. A plan for carrying this out should be included.

When the worker senses that the client is ready to proceed with the work to be done, the worker changes the focus of the interview. According to Lawrence Shulman, the worker may have to "demand this work."[23] This is not done in a harsh or demeaning manner, but in a firm manner that helps the client accept the need to begin working on the situation at hand. The middle phase has then begun. The content of this phase depends on the task at hand but should include evaluation of the success of the plan, decisions regarding continuation or modifications of the plan, and actions needed to carry out the plan or to remove barriers. The worker needs to maintain a sense of timing attuned to the client's pace of work as well as time limits that may be relevant, to refocus if the content strays from the task, or to renegotiate the purpose if this is indicated. The worker also should monitor communication for its effectiveness.

Before the agreed-on time for ending an interview is reached or when the purpose of the interview has been fulfilled, the worker again shifts the focus. In bringing the interview to an end, the worker summarizes what has happened during the interview and how it fits into the service being offered. The worker and the client together plan the next steps, which include work to be done by each before the next interview and the purpose, goal, time, and place of the next interview. If this is a single interview or a final interview, the client is helped to say good-bye and given permission to come again if other needs develop.

If the worker has been successful in incorporating termination at the end of each interview, the client may be well prepared for the termination of service when it comes. However, even if the worker is able to do this, some clients may have difficulty with termination. This will be covered in greater detail in Chapter 16.

Skills Used by the Worker during the Interview

As a means of guiding and supporting the work together and of promoting relationship and effective communication, the worker uses five groups of skills during an interview: observation skills; listening skills, especially reflective listening; questioning skills; focusing, guiding, and interpreting skills; and climate-setting skills. The skill of interviewing is, in part, skill in selecting and using the appropriate response at the appropriate time. Like all skills, these must be developed through use over a period of time. The student or worker can improve her communication skills by using them in her everyday life. In addition, many exercises have been developed that are useful in beginning to acquire these skills, but it is only in actual client situations that skill development reaches the professional level. Again, each of these skills should be utilized in a way that is sensitive to cultural and individual differences.

Observation Skills.   Clients give information and express feeling in nonverbal, behavioral ways. They also provide information and express feeling in the way in which other information is given and discussed. Sensitivity to this nonverbal material is useful for tuning in to where the client really is in relation to the material being discussed, for checking the validity of the client's verbal expression, and for feedback purposes. Workers should observe the following:

1. *Body language*—What is the client communicating by the way she sits, by behaviors such as thumping on the desk with the fingers, by facial expression?

2. *The content of opening and closing sentences*—These sentences tend to contain particularly significant material. They also may give cues about the client's attitudes toward self and the environment.

3. *Shifts in conversation*—These shifts, particularly when always related to similar topics, can indicate that a particular topic is painful, taboo, or something the client does not want to discuss.

4. *Association of ideas*—Observing which ideas the client seems to associate with which other ideas can often give the worker an indication of unspoken feelings.

5. *Recurrent references*—When the client continues to bring up a subject, this indicates that it is a subject of importance to the client or one with which the client would like help.

6. *Inconsistencies or gaps*—When these are present, it is an indication either that the material being discussed is threatening to the client or that the client is unwilling to openly share in this area.

7. *Points of stress or conflict*—In cross-cultural action systems, stress and conflict may indicate areas of inadequate knowledge about cultural aspects of the client's functioning. This may also indicate misunderstanding on the part of the client or areas of client bias or prejudice.

Listening Skills.   Of vital importance in any interview situation is listening. The worker listens to what the client has to say and how the client responds to questions and responses. Beginning workers often place primary emphasis on what they have to say and on the questions to be asked. Good questioning enables clients to provide necessary information, consider alternatives, and work on the situation at hand. If the worker's listening skills are deficient, the full value of the interview will not be realized. Active listening—being with the client in her struggle to deal with difficulties and problems—is the appropriate response at many points in the interview.

Developing listening skills is also important because social workers often communicate with persons whose language expression is somewhat different from their own. In listening, it is important to try to understand what the client is attempting to communicate. To do this the worker seeks to understand what the words mean to the client. The worker maintains focus on what the client is saying even though there is a tendency to shut out the communication because it seems strange and is difficult to listen to. It is important to note feeling words and how they are expressed. Listening should reflect an attitude of openness and acceptance. Effective listening involves a sense of timing that allows the worker to focus on the client and what is being said and does not shut off communication by premature evaluation or advice.

Questioning Skills. The essence of this group of skills is knowing the various types of questions to ask and the usefulness of each type of question. A first category of questions includes open- and closed-ended questions. A closed-ended question calls for a specific answer. An example would be "What is your age?" These questions are used to gain factual information. An open-ended question is one that enables the client to define, discuss, or answer the question in any way he chooses. An example would be "What do you think is the reason your child is doing poorly in school?" The open-ended question allows expression of feeling and gives the worker the client's perception of the subject at hand. In developing a social history, it is usually advisable to mix open- and closed-ended questions; this allows for discussion between the worker and the client about the facts as well as about the client's life experiences.

There are also leading and responding questions. A leading question is used when it is desirable for a client to continue to explore the subject at hand. An example would be "You have tried to cope with this problem, haven't you?" A responding question follows the lead of the client's response. An example would be when a client has been discussing how he has tried to cope and the worker responds, "Tell me more about how you went about helping your child."

In an answer-and-agree question, the client is expected to answer in such a way as to agree with the worker. An example would be "You are feeling much better today, aren't you?" This usually is not a good form of questioning to use because it blocks discussion and imposes the worker's ideas on the client.

With most clients, it is better to ask questions so that they contain single, rather than several, ideas. A question with a number of ideas might be used when the worker is attempting to help the client recognize connections between the ideas. Whether to ask very broad questions or very specific ones depends on the work at hand and on the worker's style. Some workers like to gain a broad picture first and then explore details. Other workers believe it is more helpful for clients to consider small parts of the situation and then look at the broader picture later. Questioning is one of the means used by a social worker to enhance relationships and communication.

In general, it is better for the worker to avoid asking too many questions, otherwise the client may feel bombarded or put on the spot. Questions also tend to set an agenda that is worker-centered rather than client-centered. In many respects, questions can be used to control the interview in that the client can end up talking about what the worker wants to discuss, as opposed to discussing his concerns. In addition, questions tend to be one-sided and offer little opportunity for feedback, interaction, or give and take in the interchange. There are other ways to provide guidance or focus that do not use questions but do incorporate client concerns.

Focusing, Guiding, and Interpreting Skills.   This group of skills is used by the worker to enable the action system to accomplish the tasks necessary to reach the agreed-on objectives. It includes the capacity to paraphrase and summarize what has been said and to reflect feelings and ideas. These are skills that incorporate what the client says or does into the worker's response. Thus, they are client-centered, but they can be used to guide or focus the interview on what the worker decides to follow up on. The capacity to confront and to elaborate are important in terms of moving the work toward difficult areas and reaching an understanding of the situation or the work to be done. The effective use of these skills includes a sense of timing as to when to focus, when to interpret, and when to direct.

Paraphrasing and summarizing often clarify what has been said. Clarification and elaboration enhance understanding. With understanding of issues and facts, the work can progress as a truly joint effort.

Confrontation and silence are often difficult for the worker. Confrontation is the bringing out into the open of feelings, issues, and disagreements. It involves looking at these elements and attempting to find ways to deal with them. If feelings, issues, and disagreements remain hidden, they may interfere with the work at hand. Silence may indicate resistance, frustration, or anger, but it also can provide a time for worker and client to be reflective. Instead of being uncomfortable with silence, the worker can attempt to understand the nature of the silence and use it appropriately. Times of reflection are useful in the work together. Silence related to resistance can be used to develop sufficient discomfort on the part of the client so that she will have to do something. This can help in focusing on the work together. The worker who senses frustration and anger can bring it out into the open, confront the client, and thus deal with it so that the work can proceed.

It is the worker's responsibility to direct the interview but not to control it. The worker takes whatever material and expression of feeling are given by the client and, by focusing, guiding, and directing, enables the process of the work together to proceed toward the desired outcome.

Climate-Setting Skills.   Three attributes have been identified as characteristics of interpersonal situations that seem to produce understanding, openness, and honesty, which are enabling factors in the work of the action system. These three characteristics are empathy, genuineness, and nonpossessive warmth.[24]

Empathy is the capacity to communicate to the client that the worker accepts and cares for the client. Empathy communicates that at this point in time the client's welfare is to be considered before the worker's. Empathy is expressed by openly receiving and recognizing the feelings of the client, by accurately perceiving the client's messages, and by providing the client with concrete feedback about messages.

Genuineness is the capacity of the worker to communicate to the client that the worker is trustworthy. It is expressed by being willing to let the client know the worker as a person in ways that meet the client's need for such information. It also expresses congruence between the worker's verbal and nonverbal messages. In addition, genuineness involves informing the client when the worker disagrees with the client and when the client's behavior and communication are inconsistent. This skill calls for honesty but honesty communicated in a manner that is sensitive to the client's feelings and concerns.

Nonpossessive warmth is the capacity to communicate to the client both a concern and a desire for intimacy; this allows the client to make decisions, to have negative and positive feelings, and to feel worthwhile. It has qualities of non-blame, closeness, and nondefensiveness. A warmth that is nonpossessive is displayed through positive regard and respect for the client and through thoughtfulness and kindness as well as appreciation for, and pleasure at, the client's growth and well-being.

These three attributes are tied to social work values. One of the cardinal values of social work is the belief in the value and worth of every human being. This leads the worker to respect the client as an individual. This does not mean that the worker approves of all of the client's behavior. Some clients will have done things that are clearly wrong either morally or legally. Rather, the worker accepts the client as a human being even with her faults and mistakes. When the worker is able to do this, then he can listen to the client's story without judging her as a person. This helps the worker put himself in his client's shoes and leads to empathy. A genuine belief in the value and worth of every human being allows the worker to be more genuine in treating the client with dignity and respect. It allows the worker to care about the client as a human being even though he may find things about the client that he does not like.

The climate of all interpersonal endeavors greatly affects the nature of the relationship and the quality of the communication. Skills in developing and maintaining an accepting, growth-producing climate are an important part of the worker's repertoire.

Interviewing is just one form of communication. The skills used in the interview can also be used in less formal social work interactions. They are the same skills that encourage relationships to form and to be used and maintained. In the social work endeavor, in the one-to-one action system, it is the responsibility of the social worker to move toward the client so that relationships may form and a common ground for communication may be established. To do this the social worker must understand the client and be willing to work with the client in meeting the client's needs and in resolving the situation. Improved communication and relationships are central to success in the ecosystems strengths approach. The focus of growth and change is on the interactions and transactions among systems. Success is often determined by the client's ability to change her interactions with others and their interactions with her. Thus, the worker frequently will be in a position to assist the client to acquire these skills in order to bring about growth and change.

Summary

The emphasis in this chapter is on one-to-one (worker-client) interaction that takes place in an action system and with members of the client's ecosystem. The formation of the action system requires understanding of the client and skill on the part of the worker. Special consideration must be given in developing action systems with resistant clients.

Relationship is the cohesive quality of the action system and is for the purpose of helping clients. It is influenced by the life experiences of both the client and the worker. Cross-cultural relationships have special characteristics that the worker must understand.

Communication is an important ingredient of the action system. The process of communication can become blocked in a variety of ways. Social workers need to be aware of these blocks and of the means for dealing with them.

The interview is an important interactional tool for use in the one-to-one action system. It is important to prepare for interviews and to make them goal directed. Each interview has three stages: a beginning, a middle, and an ending. Workers use a variety of skills in the interview. These include observation; listening; questioning; focusing, guiding, and interpreting; and climate setting.

The same principles and skills used in one-to-one interaction with clients are also used when working with significant persons in the situation, with those who may be able to provide resources for the client, or with a variety of community persons. The capacity for forming and using one-to-one relationships is a core social work skill.

QUESTIONS

1. How can the client's needs best be met in the interview situation?

2. What are some of the ways to facilitate the development of a professional relationship?

3. Why is the development of a relationship so essential to the helping situation?

4. How do the three phases of interviewing differ?

5. What are some ways to encourage nonvoluntary clients to engage in the helping process?

6. How should resistance be viewed in any helping situation?

7. Discuss each of Biestek's principles of relationship relative to operationalizing them in the interview situation.

8. Why is it difficult to communicate across cultural boundaries? How can social workers facilitate such communication?

9. Discuss the needed balance between questioning and listening in a social work interview.

SUGGESTED READINGS

Brammer, Lawrence M., and MacDonald, Ginger. *The Helping Relationship: Process and Skills,* 7th ed. Boston: Allyn and Bacon, 1999.

Coady, Nick G. "The Worker-Client Relationship Revisited." *Families in Society* 74 (May 1993): 291–298.

Compton, Beulah Roberts, and Galaway, Burt. *Social Work Processes,* 6th ed. Pacific Grove, CA: Brooks/Cole, 1999 (Chapters 7, 8, and 9).

Cormier, Sherry, and Cormier, William. *Interviewing Strategies for Helpers,* 4th ed. Pacific Grove, CA: Brooks/Cole, 1998.

DeJong, Peter, and Miller, Scott D. "How to Interview for Client Strengths." *Social Work* 40 (November 1995): 729–736.

Devore, Wynetta, and Schlesinger, Elfrede. *Ethnic Sensitive Social Work Practice,* 4th ed. Boston: Allyn and Bacon, 1996.

Egan, Gerald. *The Skilled Helper,* 6th ed. Pacific Grove, CA: Brooks/Cole, 1998.

Green, James. *Cultural Awareness in the Human Services,* 2nd ed. Boston: Allyn and Bacon, 1995.

Hasenfeld, Yeheskel. "Power in Social Work Practice." *Social Service Review* 61 (September 1987): 469–483.

Hepworth, Dean H., Rooney, Ronald H., and Larsen, Jo Ann. *Direct Social Work Practice: Theory and Skills,* 5th ed. Pacific Grove, CA: Brooks/Cole, 1997 (Chapters 5, 6, 7, and 18).

Hutchinson, Elizabeth D. "Use of Authority in Direct Social Work Practice." *Social Service Review* 61 (December 1987): 581–598.

Ivanhoff, Andre Marie. *Involuntary Clients in Social Work Practice: A Research-Based Approach.* New York: Aldine de Gruyter, 1994.

Ivey, Allen E., and Ivey, Mary Bradford. *Intentional Interviewing: Facilitating Client Development in a Multicultural Society,* 4th ed. Pacific Grove, CA: Brooks/Cole, 1999.

Kadushin, Alfred. *The Social Work Interview,* 4th ed. New York: Columbia University Press, 1997.

Kerson, Toba Schwaber, and Michelson, Renee W. "Counseling Homebound Clients and Their Families." *Journal of Gerontological Social Work* 24, 3–4 (1995): 159–190.

Klein, Amelia R., and Cnaan, Ram A. "Practice with High Risk Clients." *Families in Society* 76 (April 1995): 203–212.

Leigh, James. *Communicating for Cultural Competence.* Boston: Allyn and Bacon, 1999.

Murphy, Bianca, and Dillon, Carolyn. *Interviewing in Action.* Pacific Grove, CA: Brooks/Cole, 1998.

Perlman, Helen Harris. *Relationship: The Heart of Helping People.* Chicago: University of Chicago Press, 1979.

Perloff, Janet D. "Medicaid Managed Care and Urban Poor People: Implications for Social Work." *Health and Social Work* 21 (August 1996): 189–195.

Raines, James C. "Empathy in Clinical Social Work." *Clinical Social Work Journal* 18 (Spring 1990): 57–72.

Rooney, Ronald. *Strategies for Work with Involuntary Clients.* New York: Columbia University Press, 1992.

Sheafor, Bradford W., Horejsi, Charles R., and Horejsi, Gloria A. *Techniques and Guidelines for Social Work Practice,* 5th ed. Boston: Allyn and Bacon, 2000 (Chapters 8 and 11).

Shulman, Lawrence. *The Skills of Helping: Individuals and Groups,* 4th ed. Itasca, IL: F. E. Peacock, 1999.

———. "Developing and Testing a Practice Theory: An Interactional Perspective." *Social Work* 38 (January 1993): 91–97.

NOTES

1. Felix P. Biestek, *The Casework Relationship* (Chicago: Loyola University Press, 1957).

2. Nick F. Coady, "The Worker-Client Relationship Revisited," *Families in Society* 74 (May 1993): 293.

3. Carl Hartman and Diane Reynolds, "Resistant Clients: Confrontation, Interpretation, and Alliance," *Social Casework* 68 (April 1987): 205–213.

4. Edith Ankersmit, "Setting the Contract in Probation," *Federal Probation* 40 (June 1976): 28–33.

5. Charles R. Horejsi, "Training for the Direct-Service Volunteer in Probation," *Federal Probation* 37 (September 1973): 38–41.

6. Helen Harris Perlman, *Relationship: The Heart of Helping People* (Chicago: University of Chicago Press, 1979), p. 2.

7. Ibid., p. 24.

8. Ibid., p. 62.

9. See Lawrence M. Brammer, *The Helping Relationship: Process and Skills,* 3rd ed. (Englewood Cliffs, NJ: Prentice-Hall, 1984); and Beulah Roberts Compton and Burt Galaway, *Social Work Processes,* rev. ed. (Homewood, IL: Dorsey Press, 1979), chap. 6.

10. Compton and Galaway, *Social Work Processes,* p. 224.

11. See Anthony N. Maluccio, *Learning from Clients: Interpersonal Helping as Viewed by Clients and Social Workers* (New York: Free Press, 1979).

12. Quoted material in this list from Biestek, *The Casework Relationship,* pp. 25, 35, 50, 72, 90, and 103, respectively.

13. Ann Templeton Brownlee, *Community, Culture and Care* (St. Louis: C. V. Mosby, 1978), chap. 3.

14. Joel Fischer, Diane D. Dulaney, Rosemary T. Frazio, Mary T. Hadakand, and Ethyl Zivotosky, "Are Social Workers Sexists?" *Social Work* 21 (November 1976): 428–433.

15. Joanne Mermelstein and Paul Sundet, "Education for Social Work in the Rural Context," in *Educating for Social Work in Rural Areas: A Report on Rural Child Welfare and Family Service Project of the School of Social Work,* Lynn R. Hulen, project coordinator (Fresno: California State University, June 1978).

16. Louise C. Johnson, Dale Crawford, and Lorraine Rousseau, "Understandings Needed to Work with Sioux Indian Clients" (unpublished paper).

17. Joanne Mermelstein and Paul Sundet, "Worker Acceptance and Credibility in the Rural Environment," in *Rural Human Services: A Book of Readings,* H. Wayne Johnson, Ed. (Itasca, IL: F. E. Peacock, 1980), pp. 174–178.

18. Janet Kirkland and Karen Irey, "Confidentiality: Issues and Dilemmas in Rural Practice," in *2nd National Institute on Social Work in Rural Areas Reader,* Edward B. Buxton, Ed. (Madison: University of Wisconsin—Extension Center for Social Studies, 1978), pp. 142–149.

19. Yvonne L. Fraley, "A Role Model for Practice," *Social Service Review* 43 (June 1969): 145–154.

20. Adapted from Brett A. Seabury, "Communication Problems in Social Work Practice," *Social Work* 25, 1 (January 1980): 40–44.

21. Floyd W. Matson and Ashley Montagu, *The Human Dialogue: Perspectives on Communication* (New York: Free Press, 1967), p. 6.

22. See Lawrence Shulman, *The Skills of Helping: Individuals and Groups,* 2nd ed. (Itasca, IL: F. E. Peacock, 1984), chaps. 2 and 4.

23. See ibid., pp. 65–72, for discussion of this task.

24. This triad is based on the work of C. B. Truax and R. R. Carkhuff, *Toward Effective Counseling and Psychotherapy* (Chicago: Aldine, 1967). For an excellent discussion of this material, see Eveline D. Schulman, *Intervention in the Human Services,* 2nd ed. (St. Louis: C. V. Mosby, 1978), chap. 8, "Traux Triad."

CHAPTER

10 Multiperson Interaction

LEARNING EXPECTATIONS

1. Understanding of group process so as to be able to recognize its various aspects in the functioning of a small group or a family.
2. Understanding of the importance of the small group in generalist social work practice.
3. Understanding of how the social worker can influence the work and process of any small group of which he is a member.
4. Beginning skill in small-group interaction as a member of a group.
5. Knowledge of the role and function of the generalist social worker with a multiperson client and with groups within the client's ecosystem.
6. Understanding of the nature of the generalist social worker's interaction with the family system in the various forms the family takes in U.S. society.

The social worker is often called on to interact with more than one person at the same time, particularly when working from a generalist approach. This happens when the client is a family, a small group, an institution, an agency, or a community. When the agency, institution, or community system is the client, the interaction is usually with groups of people within the system. When the focus is on the development of new resources, task groups are usually involved. In using an ecosystems strengths approach, the worker may interact with more than one person at a time when working with systems within the client's ecosystem, such as members of the client's family. The social worker works with more than one person at the same time when she is functioning on a team or a case conference or as a member of a committee or a planning group. These groups can have a fact-finding, evaluation, policy-making, planning, education, problem-solving, or therapeutic purpose; they can be casual, appointed, ongoing, or self-formed. Multiperson interaction is used when people share a common task or purpose and when the situation does not lend itself to one-to-one interaction. Situations that often call for the use of the group include the following:

1. Those in which individuals cannot reach their goal except by working with others (e.g., when a group of persons works for some environmental change)
2. Those in which individuals cannot function on a one-to-one basis with a professional person but can function with peers (e.g., a group of delinquent adolescents)
3. Those in which the group has considerable influence over the individual (e.g., the family influence on individual functioning)
4. Those in which the task or purpose needs the contribution of several persons (e.g., the interdisciplinary team)
5. Those in which persons are faced with similar needs or concerns (e.g., parents of developmentally disabled children)
6. Those in which working with systems in the client's ecosystem is more effective when it takes place with all of the system or with significant parts of the system (e.g., family, parents, etc.)

Much of what was discussed in Chapter 9 about one-to-one interaction also applies to group interaction. Relationships between individuals are important for the facilitation of the tasks to be accomplished. Group process and task accomplishment are also enhanced by effective communication. Relationships and communications become more complex when additional people are involved; in this case the transactional nature of the interaction must receive greater attention. In effect, the interview becomes group discussion. Thus, many of the techniques useful in facilitating the interview are also useful in facilitating group discussion.

In using an ecosystems strengths approach, the worker must keep in mind that clients hold membership in many different groups that are a part of their ecosystem. As a result, the worker may be directly involved in multiperson interaction when she works with systems in the client's ecosystem. In addition, she will need to assist the client in developing necessary skills in multiperson interaction as he comes into contact with various systems in his environment. This does not mean that the client needs to become skilled in leading groups or in working with families. It does mean that the client probably will find himself in groups and in interactions within his family system on a daily basis. When he does, he will need to know how to meet the needs of others while also meeting his own needs. This is often the very crux of the matter that brings the client to the agency for help. Relationships with others in the ecosystem may be out of balance or in conflict. Or relationships important to meeting needs may not be functioning in an effective way. These relationships may be one-to-one or multiperson. The client needs to have mutually beneficial interactions in both cases.

When social workers work with families and groups, they come into direct contact with interactions and transactions among people. Chapter 9 covered the worker's interaction with individuals. In working with individuals, the worker is a part of the interactional system. Thus, she is responsible for her part of the interaction. The worker needs to be aware of the direct influence she may have in these instances, since she is a major part of the interaction. When working with families and groups, the worker is a part of a much larger interactional system. Much of the interaction is not between the worker and individual members but among the members of the family or group. In fact, there is a great deal of interaction that goes on among family members outside of the time when the worker is meeting with the family. This can also be the case for many groups. As a result, although the worker may influence the interaction, her impact is much more indirect, since she cannot control the actions of others.

Because the worker may not be directly involved with all interactions among members, she usually has less influence on what is happening in working with families and groups. For the most part, the appropriate role for her is that of facilitator. The questions pertaining to this role are: What should the worker facilitate? When should she observe and when should she intervene? What should happen when conflict or difficulties arise? The answers to these questions are heavily influenced by values. The worker must always be aware of the experiences she brings with her from her own family and from groups to which she belongs. These experiences, especially those with her own family, are value laden. Since families are conduits for culture and values, it is important for the worker to respect the values of the family or group members with whom she is working while also being aware of her own values and those of her profession.

In addition to being aware of the impact of culture and values in relationships, the worker can also facilitate the development of relationship skills. Typically, the worker has knowledge and skills in communication, facilitating growth and change, conflict resolution, and behavioral change. Teaching these skills to the family or group is essential to improving individual, family, and group functioning. The use of these skills within a framework of social work values and within the cultural systems to which the family or group members belong can provide a basic foundation for meeting the needs of individuals, families, and groups.

In order for the social worker to be effective in multiclient and multiworker interactions, four kinds of understandings are important:

1. *The family as the fundamental experience with multiperson interaction*—The first group experience nearly everyone has is with one's own family. This experience comes first in our lives and is the most profound experience we will ever have, being extremely intense and lasting over an extended period of time. Most important, it occurs while we are growing and developing as a person and while we are learning to interact with others. As a result, our family experience influences who we are and how we interact with others throughout our lives.

2. *The family and the small group as a social system*—This chapter considers client groups (unrelated persons), community and professional groups, systems in the client's ecosystem, and families. The family is seen by some theorists as a special case of the small group. Because of the intensity and the long-term nature of its relationships, the family has qualities not found in other small groups.

3. *The social worker as a member of a small group*—When the social worker is a member of a team or participates in a community committee or an agency task force, the worker is a member of a small group. Although the social worker is not always the designated leader of these groups, he can use knowledge about small-group interaction and skill in interaction to influence group process so that the group can effectively carry out its function and tasks.

   4. *The social worker and the multiclient system*—Often the social worker does not become a member of the group when working with the multiclient system. Rather, the social worker influences the group process or the family interaction from a point outside the group or family system. Doing this entails a differential use of interactional skills.

The Family as the Fundamental Experience with Multiperson Interaction

Nearly everyone starts out life in a family. Generally, it is only when the parents are unable or unwilling to raise their child that this is not the case. Of course, families may look quite different from the nuclear family that has been the image of what a family is for white society in the United States. The absence of a family experience can be devastating for human beings unless a suitable replacement is provided. This discussion will center on the family as the first and most important multiperson interaction human beings have. Tables 7.1, 7.2, and 7.3 in Chapter 7 provide a guide for looking at the individual, diversity factors, and the family as this chapter explores the influence of the family on multiperson interaction.

   A basic assumption guiding this consideration of multiperson interaction is that the fundamental issue for all human beings is answering the question, Can I be an individual and still be loved and accepted by others? The tension between acting on one's own needs while preserving relationships with others is basic to human relations. Initially, this tension is played out in the family between the young child and his parents. The child vacillates between the search for autonomy and independence and the desire for meaningful attachment. When parents successfully communicate the message that the child is loved and accepted unconditionally for himself, then attachment is secure and provides a base from which the child can establish individual autonomy. When the message is something else or if it does not get through, then doubts begin to occur and self-confidence is more tenuous.

   In simple terms, if the answer to the question above is or seems to be "yes," then the child can internalize this answer and feel more secure about loving and accepting himself. This is the essence of self-image, self-esteem, self-worth, and self-respect. What does one think or feel about oneself? If the answer to the question above was a conditional "yes" (I love you if…or I love you when…), then the child begins to look outside himself for the approval of others and for his value and worth. If the answer was "no," then the child may conclude that he is not worthwhile or may reject others as the source of influence on his behavior.

   This last circumstance is what generally happens when children are abused or neglected. These children often have extremely low self-worth or learn to treat others as objects just as they were treated as objects. In the first case the person says to herself, "If my parent(s) did not love me, who will? I must be unlovable." In the second case, the person says, "If my parents did not care about me, why should I care about anyone else?" This is the reasoning of the majority of people who go to prison, who were abused or neglected as children. These individuals conclude that acting on self-interest is the only way to survive.

Whatever our experience was as a child, we carry it with us outside of the family and reflect it in our expectations of ourselves and others. This fact is fundamental to multiperson interaction and impacts the client, the social worker, and the people in the systems with whom we have contact. Understanding who we are means understanding the impact our family had on us. Before undertaking work with clients, especially with families, social workers should first have insight into their own backgrounds and how they influence their perceptions of themselves, their clients, and their world. (See Chapter 7.) Self-awareness and a healthy self-esteem are necessities in developing oneself as a competent professional social worker.

When working with individuals, families, and groups, it is important to keep in mind how the client's self-image and relationships with others have been shaped by family experiences. Working with clients in families or groups is an opportunity to help them to find a different answer to the above question regarding acceptance and individuality. In fact, the social work value of belief in the inherent value and worth of every human being represents a positive response to the question about acceptance of self and others. Thus, if the social worker is successful in communicating this value to others and in getting the family or group to experience it, then individuals can reexperience the question of self-worth in a more positive way. A more positive experience can have a profound impact on a client's future experiences.

Understanding the influence of family on self-esteem and on relationships with others is fundamental to assessment and intervention with individuals, families, and groups. The ways in which families influence individual development and relationships provide a key to what the worker needs to focus on in multiperson interaction. As indicated in Table 7.3 (Schema for Development of a Social History: Family), it is important to view the family as a system and understand its structure, functioning, and development or history. It is also important to understand the needs of each member and the system as a whole. Examining strengths and challenges provides a basis on which to build strategies for change.

When the social worker uses social work values to guide her work with families and groups, the answers to the questions raised about the facilitator role become more clear. The worker should facilitate interactions in families and groups that reflect dignity and respect for each person. She should support this type of interaction when it occurs and intervene when it does not. She should be aware of differences in culture and values and respect those differences. She should help members to work out their conflicts with respect and with the recognition that each person needs to have a voice in the final resolution. Win-lose situations will inevitably produce losers. If one feels like a loser or belongs to a family or group in which others feel like losers, then everyone in the system will eventually feel this impact. Win-win situations support all parties in having their needs met. Being open about the values that social work espouses reduces the chances that the worker will impose values or manipulate. The social worker supports valuing human beings and treating each other with dignity and respect whether she is working with a client or with members of the client's ecosystem.

The Family as a Multiperson Client System

Many approaches to working with the family as a system have been developed, several of which are summarized in the Appendix. It is beyond the scope of this book to consider any one of these in depth; rather, what will be presented about working with the family as a system will be understandings and principles of action that enable the worker-family interactional process to develop. A first principle of working with families is that the social history of the family unit be developed (see Table 7.3) so that the worker gains the necessary understanding of the family.

The family is seen as a system using knowledge of social systems, small-group processes, and family structure and functioning. The family group has many of the same characteristics as the small group (which will be covered later in this chapter). The family, however, is a special small group—one that is usually intergenerational, exists over an extended period of time, and has very strong bonds owing to the amount of time members have spent together and the strength of the influence a family has on its members. The family has its own developmental process that is related to the developmental stages of the family members.

A second principle is that a caring, understanding relationship be developed with the total family unit, not just with certain individuals within that unit. The social worker must recognize that the family is a well-established system. The social worker should not become entangled with that system; neither should the worker take sides with individual family members. The contribution of all family members is sought and valued, and each family member is respected as an individual.

A third principle is that responsibility for the situation is to be owned by the family, not blamed on individual family members. It is important to gradually confront families with the realities of the situation—that is, with the responsibility of the whole family for family-related problems. This can be done by conveying an explorative attitude toward the presented situation. It can also help if the worker explains to the family that problems are often an indication of a blockage in the growth of the family or may be a sign that family members are not meeting needs or having their needs met, either within the family or in interactions with the ecosystem. Anxiety can often be relieved by clarifying the situation. Most important, the family needs to understand that the helping situation is a safe place in which to work on meeting its needs. By demonstrating a nonblaming attitude that respects the rights of all family members, the worker provides them with a model of how they might begin to work together on the family's needs.

Next, he helps the family take responsibility for the situation as a total system rather than blame the situation on one family member. The family is then expected to develop and carry out plans for meeting unmet needs for the family as a system, for individual members of the family, and between the family (or members) and the ecosystem. The worker's role is to enable the family in this process.

A fourth related principle is that blame and guilt are to be avoided because they place responsibility on specific family members. When working with the family as the client, the focus is on how family structure and functioning contribute to the situation. In using an ecosystems strengths approach, the worker helps the family to realize that unmet needs may be related to interactions within the family system and to its interactions with the environment. The worker helps the family find ways of rebalancing these interactions and transactions. The influence of environmental factors and the need to develop skill in meeting family needs are also stressed, when appropriate.

When working with the family, the worker expects that all members be allowed to speak for themselves. The worker demonstrates to the family how the work will be done and how communication is to take place. This should be done in a way that is sensitive to the culture and value system of the family. Each family member is given the feeling that this is a safe place to work on concerns. Attention is paid to the physical setting in which the work takes place. If young children are involved, provision is made for them to move around and play quietly. The expectations and concerns of each family member are clarified so that each understands those of other members.

The worker seeks to help the family develop consensus about the nature of the needs or concerns. Negotiation among the family members about not only the nature of the needs or concerns but also about the purpose, goal, and strategy of the work together is very important. The worker helps the family develop a contract among the members as well as a contract with the worker about what needs to be done and who should do it. The worker uses an educational approach when members of the family lack understanding and skill necessary for effective family functioning. These skills include communication, problem solving, conflict resolution, positive reinforcement, cognitive restructuring, and the like. Skill in dealing with resistance to change is most important, because families often have entrenched ways of functioning that are not only the source of difficulties but also are very hard for individual members to give up.

When working with the family as the unit of attention, social workers often encounter difficulty because they either are not aware of or have not resolved some of their own concerns and feelings about their families of orientation (the families they grew up in). Workers may also make unfounded assumptions about the functioning of families based on their personal experience. Thus, an important prerequisite to working with family groups is recognition and resolution of how the worker has been affected by her own family.

Often the assumption is made that a family consists of two parents and two or more children. In contemporary American society this is often not the case. Many couples choose to remain childless; some parents have multiple divorces;

some have children outside of marriage; more couples are living longer after their children have left home; and the number of single-parent families, families with grandparents raising grandchildren, and blended families is growing. Social workers need to adapt models for work with family groups to these varied situations. Couple or marital therapy can provide a basis for working with a family made up of only a husband and wife. When working with older persons, either as couples alone or with their adult children and their families, consideration must be given to the developmental tasks of the later years. Role reversal of parents and adult children is to be avoided. Unresolved or poorly resolved issues from the past may need to be dealt with. Two tasks that often are important for families with older persons are (1) to help the family find and use community resources that will allow older persons to live in the least restrictive environment possible and (2) to help families maintain supportive, helpful relationships that do not overburden any family member.

When working with single-parent or blended families, it is important to consider the influence of the absent parent. Different concerns may be present if the absent parent is dead, a divorce has taken place, or there has never been a marriage. The father or mother may be the custodial parent, or there may be a joint-custody agreement. When working with the single-parent family, it is particularly important to consider role overload and the needs of the single parent. There may be unresolved feelings or issues resulting from death or divorce. Inappropriate expectations of family members may be present. Children may be filling the role of the absent parent in a way that places too much stress or responsibility on the child. This type of family often has a need for supportive community resources.

Blended families present special challenges for the social worker. There may be children from the current marriage or union, along with children from other relationships. Some of the children may be "half siblings." Everyone in the family has a "step" relationship with at least one other member. Some of the children may leave to visit their other biological parent. Some children may come to visit their noncustodial parent. All of this can be very confusing for the family as well as the worker. One of the fundamental issues that all blended families face is how to adjust to living together as a family, given all of these various types of relationships. Most second marriages fail because family members are not able to adjust. Thus, the work to be done generally revolves around the development of appropriate relationships in the face of what are often difficult circumstances. It is especially important that children be assisted in accepting their parents' decisions regarding divorce and remarriage. The work also should include helping the family to restructure itself around the current reality and to adapt its communication and functioning to meet each member's needs.

Many of the families that social workers work with may be seen as multi-problem or chaotic families. Child abuse, spousal abuse, and substance abuse are often what bring these families to the social agency. These families usually do not come to social workers voluntarily but are ordered by the court or some other authority to seek service. When working in these difficult situations, a first step must be the development of a relationship based on trust of the worker. To do this, the worker must be consistent and flexible and avoid any type of retaliation. The worker must be honest with the family about why they are there and what the consequences of lack of cooperation may be. Concern and empathy expressed in a nonjudgmental manner are very important. In many of these cases, the worker will find a history of difficulties that goes back to previous generations. In addition, the worker will generally find individuals who are unable to get their needs met in socially acceptable ways or who simply do not know how to get their needs met. Often the family's interactions with its ecosystem are limited or fraught with conflict. These families often need help in setting priorities and developing skills of social functioning. Their communication skills may be limited. It is most important that these families develop a sense of competency.

The worker must understand the differences in family functioning and structure within different cultural groups. When working with families from a minority cultural group, workers should not presume an understanding of family function until they have checked out with the family how it operates within its cultural group. Usually, meeting with families in their home and using short-term, action-oriented modes is a successful approach. The worker helps the family work out its own solution in a manner that is supportive of the extended family and immediate ethnic community system. Often, work with minority group families involves helping them deal with the external dominant society system and its institutions. This is when an ecosystems strengths approach is especially beneficial. Advocacy or mediation by individuals, groups, and institutions within the majority culture may be needed. An important goal when working with all families, but particularly with families who have experienced discrimination, is to enable the family and its members to take control of their own lives and work toward changing their situation by influencing the transactions with their ecosystem. (Enabling as a practice strategy will be discussed in Chapter 13.)

The social worker needs to develop understanding of the various forms families take in our society. Workers need to develop skill in assessing a family and its situation and then creatively developing means for working with the family. Skill is necessary in interacting with the family so as to provide the needed information and to enable participation in the planning and work necessary for need fulfillment and enhanced social functioning.

Finally, the Schema for Developing a Family Social History (Table 7.3) includes an assessment of the strengths of the family and of the systems in the family's environment. There is a tendency to see families that are different than the traditional nuclear family as being inferior. In reality, all families have strengths, regardless of their structure, function, development, ethnicity, or culture. Even chaotic families are able to provide for most of the needs of their members. There is also a tendency to focus on what is missing rather than what is already there. If the worker and the family are able to see the strengths of the family system and its ecosystem, then growth and change can be built on these strengths and on the transactions within the ecosystem instead of undertaking a major overhaul of the whole system. If people decide to make a change, they need to do so from a position of strength, not a position of weakness. It is more likely that change will occur and be sustained if it is based on existing strengths the system already possesses. It is up to the worker to identify and point out the strengths when the family is not able to do so.

Case Example

Summary of the First Session with the A Family

The worker had arranged the chairs in a circle. He had deliberately provided one more chair than there would be people involved to give some indication of separations in this family as they seated themselves. Mrs. A (from the Case Examples in Chapters 1 and 7) and Mary sat next to each other, Mr. A left one chair between himself and Mrs. A, and Henry Jr. sat on the other side of him. John hesitated for some time as to where to sit, and he sat next to Henry Jr. but moved his chair somewhat away from his brother. The worker chose to sit next to John with Mary on the other side. Mr. A immediately seemed to try and take over the situation by announcing that he had to get back to work at 3:00 and he didn't see why all of them had to be involved because John couldn't behave himself. The worker replied that in order to understand the family situation, he preferred to talk to the entire family together. He also stated that when one member of a family is having difficulty there is a family difficulty. Mr. A responded, "That is true, each of us is being affected by John's behavior." (The worker chose to ignore this as he did not think Mr. A was ready for further confrontation at this time.)

The worker then said that he would like to know what each family member saw as the way in which the family solved problems. He would like to start with John. In going around the circle, the worker noted that the children commented that Mr. A decided how things should be and expected Mrs. A to see that things went that way. Mrs. A stated that she tried to handle as many of the problems as possible, but that the boys (particularly John) were just beyond her capacity, so she asked her husband for help. Mr. A stated that he had to make decisions in his business and that he felt comfortable that he knew what was best for the family, but he did not want to have to make all the day-to-day decisions. He thought his wife knew what he wanted and should be able to see to it that things were done that way. The worker noted that the children were uneasy but he needed to probe further in order to understand how the family functioned.

Next he asked each family member what they would like to see happen in the family. Henry Jr. was first to answer, and he began to blame John for all the trouble. The worker interrupted and said he did not ask what was wrong and he did not think it would help to blame anyone; rather, it would be more useful to talk about what the family wanted for itself. Henry said, "Well, I just wish the fighting would stop." The worker asked for clarification about the fighting. This led to a discussion of the parents' arguing and the fact that it wasn't always over John. The worker then returned to having family members tell what they wanted for the family. The following areas were brought up: Mary wished Henry Jr. would stop teasing her. John wished they could do some things together. Mrs. A said that she wished they could discuss things calmly and that people would listen to each other. Mr. A then launched into a monologue about how hard he worked for his family and how no one seemed to appreciate his efforts. The worker let this go on because he felt these feelings had not been expressed before and needed to be heard by other family members. Henry then said, "But Dad you never give us a chance to help and you never listen to us, you just talk."

At this point the worker noted that time was almost up. He thought that sufficient issues had been raised for discussion in another session and that it was time to plan ahead. He told the family that they seemed to have some issues that needed discussion and wondered if they would be willing to come back for three more sessions, after which the family would decide if they wanted further help. Mr. A said he guessed they had better come back; he hadn't realized how unhappy the family members were and would like to talk more about it. The rest of the family agreed with him.

The Small Group as a Social System

The term *group* is often used in an imprecise, broad sense. The designation of *small group* as a social system places some limitation on the term. As a social system, a **small group** is composed of three or more persons who have something in common and who use face-to-face interaction to share that commonality and work to fulfill needs and solve common problems, their own or others. An effective small group allows each person in the group to have an impact on every other person in the group. The group is an entity or system that is identifiable, and it is more than the sum of its parts. For best results, the group should not exceed eight to ten members. A task group may require more members to accomplish its tasks. Support groups may be larger, but membership fluctuates. Groups, like all social systems, have structure (the form of a system at any point in time); a way of functioning or behaving in order to accomplish tasks; and development that takes place in stages over time.[1] (See Table 10.1.) To develop sufficient understanding for effective interaction in and with a small group, a social worker needs to assess all three of these dimensions.

In addition, the group has an ecosystem, and each group member has an ecosystem unique to that member, although members of certain systems may overlap, such as systems in the community in which group members share membership. The purpose of most groups is generally to assist members in getting their needs met from their ecosystems and meeting the needs of others in those systems. In other words, members are expected to use what they gain in the group to bring about growth and change in their lives outside the group. In a task group, the purpose is to bring about change in the ecosystem of the group. Thus, the worker needs to develop skills in facilitating the group in accomplishing its goals and objectives, both within and outside of the group.

Structure

Three major dimensions of structure are boundary, relationship framework, and bond. **Boundary,** in a social system, is the point at which the system of interaction around a function no longer has the intensity that the interaction among the

TABLE 10.1 A Schema for the Study of the Small Group as a Social System

I. Structure
   A. Boundary
      1. What is the purpose, mission, or task of this group?
      2. Identify members of the group. Describe them as persons. (Use appropriate parts of Table 7.1.)
      3. What are the factors that separate these persons from other persons? How were the members chosen? Under what circumstances would a person no longer be a member of this group?
      4. What is the history of this group? How and why was it formed? How long has it been meeting?
      5. What is the position of the worker with this group?
      6. What is the influence of the environment on this group and its functioning? Include environmental expectations, impingements, and resources.
      7. Describe the open/closed character of the boundary. Include communication and energy exchange and openness to new ideas and ways of functioning.
   B. Relationship framework
      1. Describe any rating/ranking of group members.
      2. Draw a sociogram.
      3. Describe the manner in which members fill roles. Are all needed roles filled? Are any roles overfilled? Which members fill several roles?
   C. Bond
      1. What is it that holds members of the group together? Note common interests and friendships.
      2. Describe the climate of the group.
      3. What are the goals of the group? Are they explicit and known to, and accepted by, all group members?
      4. What are the norms or rules for functioning in this group? How did they develop? Are they known to, and accepted by, all group members?
      5. What are the rewards of membership in this group?
      6. What priority do members give to the group?
II. Functioning
   A. Balance/stability
      1. How does this group adapt to changing conditions? Consider change both in the environment and within the group.
      2. How much time is spent on group maintenance and how much on group task? Is this balance appropriate?
   B. Decision making
      1. How does this group make decisions about norms, goals, and plans for work?
      2. Describe group problem-solving mechanisms. Do any members engage in diversionary or blocking tactics that inhibit problem solving?
      3. Describe leadership as it facilitates or inhibits the group's decision making.
      4. How do group members influence group decisions?
      5. How is conflict resolved? Is it recognized and kept in the open?
   C. Communication
      1. Describe communication patterns of the group.
      2. Does the group have adequate feedback mechanisms? Is attention paid to nonverbal communication?
      3. Do all group members have adequate opportunity to communicate? Do any members tend to overcommunicate?
      4. Are there any content areas that seem to be troublesome when communicating?
      5. Is attention paid to communication difficulties that arise from cross-cultural or cross-professional interaction?

TABLE 10.1 Continued

    D. Task implementation

        1. Describe the manner in which the group carries out its tasks. Describe the quality of interaction in carrying out tasks.

        2. Do any members engage in diversionary or blocking tactics that inhibit the carrying out of plans?

III. Development

    A. Identify the stage of development in which the group is operating.

    B. Describe any factors that may be inhibiting continued group development.

IV. Strengths and Limitations

    A. What are the strengths of the group?

    B. What are the limitations of the group?

members has. Sometimes membership in a group is clearly defined; at other times, the determination of boundary may be difficult to establish. For example, a community group may have sporadic attendance. There may seem to be a real involvement in the task at hand by only a few persons. People who only occasionally attend meetings probably are not members of the group but may be quietly influencing the group's action in ways other than attending meetings. However, these people may be thought of as group members. When considering boundary, it is important to take into account who the group members are. All members have a personal history, current needs, and responsibilities toward other systems of which they are a part. These affect each person's functioning in the group. Each group member receives certain rewards for participating in the group, and these need to be identified. The history of the group, how and why it was formed, and any change in focus, membership, or way of functioning as it influences current structure is important for a group assessment.

The worker's role in the group is another component of relationship. Henry Maier has identified three orientations to member-worker interactions. A Type A relationship has a strict boundary between the work of the group and larger life situations. The worker is considered an expert; as such he functions from a position of separation from the rest of the group yet exercises considerable control over the functioning of the group. In a Type B relationship, the worker is more a part of the group yet has the distinctive role of facilitator of group functioning. In a Type C relationship, the worker is a member of the group, and there is no role differentiation. The Type C relationship would likely include such groups as community groups or interdisciplinary teams.[2]

The environment of the group also affects the group's functioning. The environment places expectations on, and furnishes resources for, the group. The boundary may be relatively open or closed. When a group has an open boundary, it is fairly easy for individuals to join the group, and the group is open to new ideas and other communication from the environment. When the boundary is more closed, membership is restricted, as is communication from outside. However, as mentioned earlier, the purpose of the group is to either act on the environment as a group or for members to act on their environment as individuals in order to bring about balance in meeting needs. The boundary helps to define the group, but members continue to have a life outside the group that influences their functioning in the group and that is influenced by their functioning in the group.

The relationships among the members can be examined in several ways, three of which include:

1. *The rating-ranking pattern*—In some groups one (or more) member clearly has higher status than the others. When examining relationships from this perspective, it is important to look not only at the status hierarchy but at the reason for members' status as well.

2. *The sociogram*—The **sociogram** shows patterns of liking and nonliking.[3] It can also show subgrouping and strength of relationships in a group. Figure 10.1 describes a group of delinquent boys in a group home. Reggie and Isiah have a very strong relationship, as do Gary and Eddie. There are mixed relations among others.

3. *The role structure*—Kenneth Benne and Paul Sheats have identified three categories of roles that may develop in groups: group task roles, group-building (or group maintenance) roles, and individual roles.[4] **Group task roles** are related to the accomplishment of the function or task of the group. In discussion groups, roles include the initiator or contributor of ideas, the information seeker, the clarifier of ideas, the information giver, the opinion giver, the opinion seeker, and the orienter. **Group-building (group maintenance) roles** are those that focus on the maintenance of the group as a system. Roles that fall into this category include the encourager, the harmonizer, the compromiser, and the gatekeeper. The gatekeeper is the one who controls the flow of communication by allowing, encouraging, and blocking messages from the various group members. The third category is com-

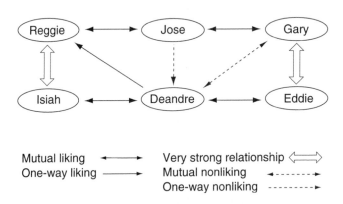

Mutual liking	← →	Very strong relationship ⟺
One-way liking	→	Mutual nonliking ◄ - - - - - ►
		One-way nonliking - - - - - - ►

FIGURE 10.1   Sociogram of a Group of Delinquent Boys in a Group Home

posed of the **individual roles** that satisfy individual need but detract from the work of the group. These roles include the dominator, the special-interest pleader, and the blocker.

Often, leadership is considered to be a role. **Leadership** can be thought of as the attribute of filling a number of roles, particularly of those needed for effective group functioning. The identification of who fills which roles, which roles are not being filled, and which members tend to carry many or crucial roles clarifies group structure.

Bond is the cohesive quality of the group; it is a "we feeling" as opposed to an "I-he-she feeling." It is expressed in common group goals, in norms for group behavior, and in common values held by group members. In systems terms, steady state is a related concept. *Steady state* is a particular configuration of parts that is self-maintaining and self-repairing. In other words, it is a state of systems that leads to both stability and adaptability. The functional group needs to maintain stability while still being adaptable to changing conditions and situations.

Description of the bond existing in a group identifies what holds the group together: common interests or tasks, friendships, desire for relationships, and the like. Also important is the identification of group goals, norms, and values as well as the ability of the group to adapt to changing conditions and situations.

The structure of the group is described by identifying the aspects of boundary, relationship structure, and bond. The structure changes as the group interacts and carries out its function over time. The social worker strives to enable the group to develop a structure that enhances the quality of the interaction of its members while also enhancing the group's ability to achieve its purpose. Generally, this involves either balancing the interactions between the group and its ecosystem (as in a task group) or enhancing the ability of members to meet their own needs as well as the needs of their ecosystem (as in counseling or support groups).

Function

Group interaction is a complex process influenced by the actions of group members and by the interactions among the various members. These actions and interactions in turn are influenced by group members' needs and responsibilities. The process is also influenced by the needs of the group as an entity accomplishing tasks and maintaining itself. The situation or environment in which the group functions also influences the functioning. This functioning, which is quite complex, is transactional in nature.

One way of describing group functioning is in terms of the *use of energy*. Every system has a limited amount of energy, and there is always a state of tension as to the way the energy will be used. Tensions may be expressed in terms of energy allotted to group tasks or to group building. They may be expressed in terms of stability versus change or adaptability issues. Each group develops ways of dealing with these energy issues.

Another way to describe group functioning is in how it uses information. As mentioned earlier, much of the social work endeavor involves the exchange of information. Group members share information within the group and use information from outside the group. They also take information from the group and use it in their interactions with their ecosystem. The bulk of the work in groups involves exchanges of information designed to achieve goals and objectives for the group and its members. Members are expected to use what they learn to either act on the group's ecosystem (task groups) or to act on their own (counseling or support groups). The need for confidentiality can restrict the flow of personal information from the group. (See Chapter 15 for more on confidentiality.)

Another aspect of the group's functioning is its *decision-making* and *communication processes*. Groups make decisions about which roles and tasks belong to which team members, about how to communicate and implement group decisions, and about the use of energy. Decisions are made in different ways in different groups. Sometimes a rational or problem-solving process is used; sometimes compromise is a method; sometimes one or more group members impose their will on the rest of the group. Often groups merely function on the basis of past experience.

Closely related to decision making are issues of leadership, power control, and conflict. **Conflict** is often viewed as a negative ingredient of group interaction. Properly managed, however, it can be a force that enhances group creativity and problem solving. Conflict is expected in a situation in which people of varying backgrounds seek to work together. Conflict is the struggle for something that is scarce. In a group this may be attention, power, status, influence, the right to fill a role, and so on. Groups make decisions about how conflicts will be resolved. One of the tasks of a social worker in fostering group interaction is to identify conflict areas and help the group work toward healthy resolution of the conflict.

Communication is the heart of the process of group interaction and thus a most important aspect of its functioning. Information, decisions, and directives are distributed through communication among group members. Communication is the means of forming and modifying opinions and attitudes. The *communication process* is described by focusing on who communicates to whom and about what.

Another way of describing the group's functioning is to note the *task implementation process*, that is, how the group accomplishes its task. The task implementation process is concerned with who does what and whether or not individuals carry out delegated tasks.

The functioning of the group is simply movement in carrying out the group's function. The structure changes as the movement takes place. This change is related to the development of greater organization, which results in specialization and stabilization. As the worker in and with the group strives to influence the group's interaction, he enables the group to carry out its function and tasks.

Development

As the group functions and the structure changes, it passes through a series of expected identifiable stages. At each stage, the group has differing group maintenance needs. The capacity for the group to fulfill its function grows as it progresses through the stages of development. Groups develop at different rates. Factors that encourage group development include:

1. The strength of the members' commitment to the group's function, tasks, and goals
2. The satisfaction of the mutual needs of the members
3. The liking or caring that the members feel for one another
4. Reciprocation rather than competition for roles
5. Respect for diversity among group members
6. The amount of time the group spends together
7. Interaction that encourages individual growth
8. A degree of homogeneity that allows group norms and goals to form
9. A degree of heterogeneity that provides different ideas and points of view among the members

The stages of group development may be conceptualized as follows:

1. *The orientation stage*—Members come together for the first time, seek similarities in interest, and make an initial commitment to the group. There is also an approach-avoidance mechanism at work. Patterns of functioning around tasks begin to develop. Task roles begin to emerge. Emphasis is on activity and orientation to the situation. Individuals make decisions about the desirability of belonging to the group and whether to become dependent on other group members.

2. *The authority stage*—There is challenge to the influence and control of the group by individual members. Conflict develops; members rebel and search for individual autonomy; power control is an issue; there may be dropouts. Structure and patterns of functioning are revised. Members share ideas and feelings about what the group should do and how the group should function. Norms and values develop through this sharing.

3. *The negotiation stage*—The group confronts, differs, and engages in conflict resolution. Goals, roles, and tasks are designated and accepted. Group traditions are stronger, norms develop, personal involvement intensifies. Group cohesion is stronger, and members are freer in sharing information and opinions.

4. *The functional stage*—A high level of group integration is reached. There is little conflict about structure, and ways of functioning have been established. Roles are differentially assigned to members and accepted by all. Communication channels are open and functional; goals and norms are known and accepted. The group has the capacity to change and adapt. Conflict and tension are managed with minimal energy use; a problem-solving capacity develops. Members are interdependent. Plans are implemented, tasks are completed, and goals are reached. The group can evaluate itself and its work. Few groups reach this stage in its ultimate form.

5. *The disintegration stage*—At any of the first four stages, a group may begin to disintegrate. Signs of disintegration include the lessening of the bond. There is a reduction in the frequency and strength of group interaction, in common norms or values for group members, and in the group's strength of influence on members. At the same time that this is occurring within the group, members will generally be strengthening and increasing their interaction with their ecosystem outside of the group.

Identifying a group's stage of development allows a worker to respond to that group with greater understanding about the structure and functioning of the group. It also provides an informed response to that group's functioning, which is a means for enhancing the interactional processes of the group.

Understanding the small group as a social system is a prerequisite to effective work as a group member or to working with the multiclient system. This understanding is a guide for the worker's interactions and interventions when working in and with groups.

Case Example

Group of Delinquent Boys in a Group Home

I. Structure
   A. Boundary
   1. Purpose: The boys in the group have all been placed in the group home by various courts around the state. Each of them has a history of mainly property crimes or involvement with drugs. The purpose of the group is to work on the life skills needed to resolve situations that are barriers to success in the home, at school, and in the community. The group also plans and carries out community service projects.
   2. Group members: There are six members in the group.
   Reggie is a sixteen-year-old African American who has been in the home for eleven months and is nearing discharge. Reggie was living on the street before being sent to the home and had a series of thefts and drug possession charges. He claims that his mother's live-in boyfriend was abusive toward him so he left home. He is uncertain where he will go after discharge, but he is hoping that his grandparents might agree to take him.

   Isiah is a fifteen-year-old African American who has been in the home for eleven months and is also nearing discharge. Isiah had a long history of delinquency, including burglary and drugs. He and his two older half-sisters were raised by his grandmother.

   Jose is a sixteen-year-old Mexican American who has been in the home for eight months. He was sent there for assault and car theft, which he committed with members of a gang. His girlfriend was pregnant when he was placed and has since given birth to a boy. Jose wants to marry her when he leaves and get a job.

Gary is a fourteen-year-old Caucasian who has been in the home for three months. He was sent by the court for a series of burglaries, which he committed with a group of friends. His parents are divorced and have married other partners.

Eddie is a fourteen-year-old Caucasian who has been in the home for three months. He is the youngest of six children and was sent to the home for a series of car thefts.

Deandre is a fourteen-year-old African American who has been in the home for a month after he was caught working in a drug house as a guard. Deandre had run away from home after being released on probation from the youth home.

3. **Why these boys constitute a group:** This is a nonvoluntary group that is a part of the boys' rehabilitation program. Failure to complete the program will likely mean placement at the state boys' training school or some restricted setting. The boys will not leave the group until they are discharged.

4. **History of the group:** The group is an ongoing group based on admission and discharge from the program. The group must unanimously recommend members for discharge. Candidates must present a thorough assessment of the difficulties that resulted in their placement, an assessment of their strengths and challenges, and a comprehensive discharge plan that includes a place to live and educational, vocational, and community service plans. The group meets daily Monday through Saturday. The current group membership has been together for a month since Deandre arrived.

5. **Workers and the group:** The workers are two BSW social workers who facilitate the group either jointly or on a rotating basis to cover Saturdays. The workers in this group have a combination of A and B characteristics (see Maier's typology). They are definitely in a professional role, which would be Type A, but they allow the group to do much of the work. They also spend a great deal of time with the boys outside of the group, especially with community service projects, family work, and individual counseling sessions. This makes them more Type B in the group members' view of them.

6. **Environmental influences:** Group members have what amounts to two ecosystems: the one they left when they were removed from their families and the one they share with each other in the group home. Since most of their time is spent together in the group, they share many of the same experiences with the environment. The situation is somewhat different at school, since they either attend the middle school or the high school and have different classes. The group home has been operating for ten years, and the local community has become accustomed to it. The community service projects that the group undertakes have had a very positive influence, but the boys are still seen as outsiders and regarded warily by some parts of the community since they are delinquents. The local Boys and Girls Club has welcomed them, and the group members have established a relationship with the YMCA. Some of the boys participate in athletics and clubs at school.

7. **Meeting arrangements:** The group meets in the living room daily from Monday through Saturday after dinner for ninety minutes.

8. **Open/closedness:** The group is characterized as having a closed boundary, since membership is determined by admission and discharge from the program.

(continued)

Case Example   Continued

B. Relationship framework

1. **Ranking:** There is no rating and ranking in this group. All are seen as equal, and ideas from all are accepted. However, boys who are preparing for discharge are expected to take a positive leadership role to demonstrate their readiness for life outside of the home.

2. **Sociogram** (see Figure 10.1): It should be noted that there is a generally positive relationship among all group members but that there is a tendency for the boys to pair up based on race or ethnicity and age.

3. **Roles:** Reggie is the organizer and a natural leader in the group. He is serious and reminds everyone of their responsibilities when they forget and is also most active in organizing community service projects. In the meetings, he is quick to point out unsuccessful behaviors in group members and participates in finding positive alternatives.

   Isiah is probably the most popular member. He is very humorous and always seems to have a smile on his face. Sometimes his humor takes the group away from their task, but he is also very adept at pointing out difficulties in a humorous way that seems to put members more at ease in terms of accepting responsibility.

   Jose is a listener. He makes his contribution by working on his own agenda but sharing his work with the group for their comments. In some ways he models for the rest of the group the work to be done in that he is making an effort to take the responsibility that parenthood has thrust on him.

   Gary is a follower who seems to be willing to go along with whatever the group wants. Recently, however, he has been distracting the group at times from their task by making funny sounds or changing the subject. While this is a blocking activity, it seems like it is a sign that his individuality is coming out. It also seems to relate to subjects with which he may be uncomfortable.

   Eddie is a questioner. He often seems to be stalling group discussion, but what he is really doing is asking the group for some direction and at times this helps the group to look at itself and how it is functioning.

   Deandre is still being rebellious by challenging positive activities in the group and refusing to accept responsibility for his actions. He has not found a positive role with the group as yet and feels like he is being picked on.

C. Bond

1. **What it is:** The commonality of their situation of being adolescent boys who are living together in a group home is a major component of the bond. The desire to return home is of major importance, especially since they must have approval from all of the members of the group before a release goes to the staff for approval.

2. **Climate:** The climate is most comfortable when planning a project or an outing in which everyone participates. It is less comfortable when the group is working on life skills, especially when an unsuccessful behavior or attitude has been identified in a member.

3. **Goals of the group:** The group goal is for each member to learn to make successful decisions that result in positive life outcomes. This includes learning life skills such as social skills, conflict resolution, decision making, planning, and personal and social responsibility.

4. **Norms of the group:** Most group norms are explicit in terms of the program and the expectations for individual and group behavior. The following are norms of the group: members must attend all meetings, which last an hour and a half; members must be on time; the material discussed is confidential and must not be discussed elsewhere; the group will spend part of the time focusing on individual situations and part of the time planning group projects or outings.

5. **Priority of the group:** Group members give high priority to the group, since it is important to their success in the program and their eventual discharge.

II. Functioning

A. Balance/stability

1. **Adaptation:** Recently, the group has not had a stable environment and stable membership due to turnover. The most recent member, Deandre, took the place of a member who was removed by the court when he eloped and broke into a home and stole a car. Deandre is having some difficulties in adjusting to placement. However, before that time there had been several successful discharges. The group spent a lot of time discussing its most recent failure, and this seems to have helped it to regain some stability. Most of the boys were able to admit that they had thought of doing the same thing at various times when things got tough or they were homesick. Thus, they seem to have been able to turn a negative into something positive. Members have been very patient with Deandre and seem determined to help him to become part of the group.

2. **Maintenance vs. task:** During the first meeting with Deandre, the group spent considerable time on maintenance. There was much discussion as to how the group works together. A contract was developed detailing some of the work to be done with Deandre, although this is still in progress. For most meetings, minimal time is spent on group maintenance, since the group meets so frequently. Usually, either at the beginning or end of each meeting, there is some discussion about projects and how well the group is fulfilling its contract with one another. As the group is working well together, the balance can be deemed appropriate.

B. Decision making

1. **Method:** Decisions are made by consensus. For example, when discussing projects or outings, members discuss several possibilities and, as a group, decide on the specific plans.

2. **Problem solving:** Problems considered tend to relate to a particular group member's struggle to make successful decisions. The pattern of problem solving is for members to throw out ideas as to possible solutions and then together consider each solution. Group solutions are then implemented after consensual decision making.

3. **Leadership:** Reggie and Isiah tend to share the leadership role. Both tend to be facilitative leaders. At times Jose calls for the worker to take this role by asking the worker to be more directive and tell them what to do.

4. **Influence on decision making:** Group members all have influence on the decisions through their contributions to discussion. Reggie and Isiah seem to have the most influence because of the quality of their contributions.

5. **Conflict:** Conflict is either denied by group members or is taken as a challenge. The worker notes that when group members recognize a conflict, they

(continued)

Case Example   Continued

tend to ask for input from him as to a decision or task. They refuse to recognize this as a mechanism of avoiding conflict, even when this is pointed out by the worker. However, after this denial, they work as a group in a problem-solving mode to resolve the differences.

C. **Communication**

1. **Patterns:** The group gives each person an opportunity to discuss each issue. There are some blocks, as mentioned above. Older or more veteran group members are aware of the communication process and of the need for listening as well as talking. Occasionally, newer or younger members will get into a side conversation. Other members will call attention to this, which ends the intrusion into the work of the group.

2. **Feedback:** Older or more veteran group members often ask each other for feedback. Younger members do not solicit feedback but are given it by older members.

3. **Opportunity:** Each group member is encouraged to add his thinking to the group discussion. If one member gets off on a tangent and holds the floor too long, someone will step in and bring the discussion back to the subject at hand.

4. **Troublesome content areas:** Personal responsibility is the biggest trouble area for the group. The older, veteran members have come to realize the importance of this area, not only for graduating from the program, but also for life afterward. Newer and younger members are very evasive and much more willing to blame others for any difficulties.

5. **Cross-cultural factors:** There is a tendency for the group to pair up by race and ethnicity. Much of this has been reduced by sharing experiences with each other. Members seem to have come to the realization that underneath their skin, they are all human beings. However, there is still some separation that appears in the group.

D. **Task implementation**

1. **How tasks are carried out:** Projects and outings seem to bring about the most enthusiasm. Discussing personal responsibility is usually met by some denial, with more veteran members moving quickly to acceptance. The group tends to get down to business on its own unless there has been a recent conflict. Discussing chores and daily living concerns generates a lot of complaints initially, but the group tends to find ways of resolving issues without too much intervention from the workers.

2. **Blocking tactics:** Denial is a primary blocking tactic that all members use at some time, and newer members use it frequently. Deandre's rebelliousness and Gary's distractions may also be seen as blocking, but are predictable, given their circumstances.

III. **Development**

A. **Stage:** The group demonstrates elements of various stages depending on the circumstances. With the recent addition of a new member, there has been some orientation and authority stage elements when working with Deandre. Overall, it seems to be primarily in the negotiation and functional stages, with newer members setting goals and veteran members fulfilling goals.

    B. **Inhibiting factors:** Denial and projection have been such basic defense mechanisms for members for so long that it is very difficult to give these up. Veteran members do so fairly quickly, but these responses still occur as an initial reaction to most difficulties.

IV. **Strengths and challenges**

    A. **Strengths:** The group is self-organized with well-focused tasks, especially with projects. The relationship framework, bond, decision-making process, and use of the problem-solving process are all very functional for the group tasks at hand.

    B. **Challenges:** The group itself is functioning well; however individual members face obstacles to success, especially when they return home. The immaturity of younger members is frustrating for those who are approaching graduation.

The Social Worker as a Group Member

The responsibility for the interactions of a small group rests with the members of that group. This is particularly true when members are professional and the focus is on the concerns and needs of clients. This responsibility for the interaction cannot be carried by any one member; it is a responsibility shared by all. Persons who understand small-group process and the factors that contribute to effective group functioning, however, can be quite helpful to groups of which they are members. Social workers can use their knowledge of human interaction in both one-to-one and small-group situations in fulfilling this responsibility of group membership. When enabling teams and other agency and community groups to reach their goals and accomplish tasks that relate to client service, the social worker is also serving the client.

Group Enabling

Four factors are particularly helpful in enhancing interaction so as to enable the group to reach its goals and to carry out its tasks or functions: (1) member involvement; (2) decision making about norms, goals, and roles; (3) group discussion skills; and (4) structuring of meetings.

    Member involvement is a prerequisite to effective decision making and problem solving. The climate of the group is a major contributor to member involvement. The ideal group climate encourages participation; is friendly and accepting; and is supportive of, and sensitive to, the needs of individual members. The group climate is one in which effectiveness is expected and self-actualization and innovation are encouraged. There is a stress on inclusion and trust. Members seek to collaborate with each other. The ideal group distributes influence and power among the members rather than relying on an authoritarian power figure. Influence and power rest in the knowledge and skills of the members. Conflict is not suppressed but is dealt with in the discussion process. Members engage in periodic evaluation of the work of the group.

A troublesome area in relation to involvement is bringing a new group member on board. An effective group does this in an organized manner so that the new member understands how the group functions, what its goals are, and what is expected of the new member. The new member needs time to get to know the group and its members, and the group needs time to get to know the new member.

A second contributor to effective functioning is the *decision-making process.* In making decisions about norms, goals, and roles, it is important that all members be involved in the decision-making process and that consensus be reached whenever possible. Not all group decisions must be made in this way. After norms and goals are set, some decisions can be made by individual members with permission from the group.

The process of developing norms is known as **norming**—the process by which implicit norms or expected ways of behaving are made explicit. The norms are examined to discover if they are appropriate to the task. Periodically, the norms should be evaluated to determine their usefulness. Changes are made in the norms as necessary. Norms that are most useful to group functioning are those that allow recognition in decision making and that support individuals and the cohesiveness of the group. Another important norm is that feelings are valid information.

The *development of goals* is another shared responsibility. Goals should be clear to, and accepted by, all group members. Whenever possible, a match should be sought between individual and group goals. Goals should not be imposed on the group. It is helpful if the goals are prioritized.

Role definition also belongs to the total group. No member should automatically take on a specific role without permission from the group. Messages should be clear to all members about the acceptability of members filling roles. A conflict over roles—the desire of two or more persons to fill the same role—should be openly negotiated and alternatives sought. Compromise is an appropriate mechanism in resolving role conflict. No one person should have a role overload, that is, be filling too many of the needed roles. One means of encouraging participation is to spread the roles among the members. Periodic evaluation to determine how roles are filled is helpful.

A third characteristic of good group functioning is *group discussion skill.* Group discussion is to the small group what interviewing is to the one-to-one action system: a means of structuring communication. One definition of group discussion is "Two or more people talking with one another in order to achieve mutually satisfactory understanding of each other's images or beliefs or a solution to a problem."[5] Cooperative interaction is influenced by each individual's perception of the topic under discussion and the group process. Two factors are particularly important for good group discussion: good communication and the use of the problem-solving process as a guide to group thinking.

Good communication calls for skill in sending messages and receiving messages so that all can know what is happening. No one person monopolizes the conversation. The feedback is:

1. Descriptive rather than evaluative
2. Specific rather than general
3. Such that it considers the needs of all persons involved
4. Directed toward that which the receiver has control over
5. Well timed

Group thinking involves several different people, each of whom may be at different stages in considering the situation. Use of the change process in group discussion is a means of structuring the group thinking so that each member is aware of the stage of the discussion. In order to use this means, all members of the group should understand the change process and be aware of which step in the process the group is using. In this way, group thinking can progress from need identification and formulation to analysis of the situation, to identification of possible goals, to analysis of the possibilities, and to choice of a plan. Thus, the plan becomes the property of the group rather than the contribution of an individual member.

Several areas that often give groups difficulty as they attempt to change are:

1. Lack of clarity in stating the need
2. Lack of necessary information
3. A critical, evaluative climate
4. Pressure for conformity
5. Premature choice of a goal or plan

If a plan for implementation is a result of group thinking, there is a better chance that the plan will be carried out than if the plan is imposed by a group member.

Some attention should be paid to the structure of group meetings to further enhance the group's capacity. There should be preparation for group meetings, just as there is preparation for an interview. Various members should be responsible for bringing needed information to the meeting. Someone should take the responsibility for ensuring that the meeting room is comfortable and arranged so that each member can have eye contact with each other member. Someone should also be responsible for seeing that agendas and other needed printed materials are available and for keeping minutes or recording decisions in some way.

The planned agenda should be reviewed and revisions made, if necessary, at the beginning of each meeting. Everyone should know what the meeting is intended to accomplish and what the time limitations are.

The middle part of the meeting is spent on the task of the day. When necessary, the group should deal with any group maintenance issues that seem to be impeding the work at hand. An indication that group maintenance should be attended to is when it does not feel good to the members. Discussion should focus on tasks or goals or on the process of carrying out these tasks or goals. All members should be urged to participate. One member of the group should be responsible for keeping the group on task and helping it move through the change process in an orderly manner. Before the allotted time is over, the group should review what has been accomplished at the meeting, and plans should be made for the next meeting.

In helping the group involve members, make decisions, have productive discussions, and structure the discussion, social workers can be a valuable resource for the group. Knowledge of group process and of the problem-solving process and skill in group discussion form the base of effective membership as a group member.

Issues in Group Participation

Several issues of group participation are of particular concern to social workers when they participate as members of small groups, including (1) the use of the team, particularly the interdisciplinary team, as a means of service; (2) leadership in its delegated form; and (3) conflict management. Each of these issues confronts the social worker and, if not understood, can block effective group functioning.

Use of the Team

Although the well-functioning team can be very effective in providing service to clients, there are often problems that cause some social workers and agency administrators to question the team approach. These problems need to be understood and some ways for overcoming them considered.

The team has been defined as "joining the essentially dissimilar skills which colleagues in diverse occupations bring to bear upon different aspects of a common problem."[6] This definition is most applicable to the interdisciplinary team, and it is the interdisciplinary team that presents the greatest hazards for working together. Dissimilarity of backgrounds and work expectations are a major cause of these hazards, as is overlap of the expertise of the various helping professions. This can lead to conflict over turf.

Some of the most frequent problems encountered by teams are

1. *The time and energy needed for team building*—The task of the team is to provide service to clients. Often, the immediacy of the need for service and number of clients needing service place expectations on the team that militate against the use of team time and energy for team building. These expectations may come from within the team or from the agency within which the team or any of its members operate. Yet effective team functioning requires time and energy from the team members. The allocation of time and energy for team building can be problematic.

2. *Communication*—The use of technical language by any member of the team that is not understood by all other members of the team blocks communication. Persons from different disciplines often use the same terms but with somewhat different meanings. When this happens, there are problems in communication.

3. *Decision-making traditions*—Professions and agencies develop traditions as to how decisions are made. In bureaucratic organizations decisions are often made from above, and lower-status persons are expected to implement the decisions. A team in such an organization may have a leader appointed by the administration; the appointed leader may assume an authoritative stance. In health care, the doctor, as the high-status professional, has traditionally used this authoritative stance. This stance is needed in an operating room, but it is not helpful in a protective service situation. Other decision-making models may call for everyone to have equal decision-making power about all aspects of service. All team members may not have equal knowledge or understanding of certain aspects of the team's service. One of the purposes of a team is to accommodate differing types of expertise to be used in service of the client. The decision-making process needs to allow for this diversity of understanding yet facilitate the process so that it is reasonably expedient.

4. *Use of the change process*—As with all small groups, goals need to be accepted by all. Differences in goals among team members can arise from inadequate need identification. If different team members see the situation differently and do not understand or accept the team goals, hidden agendas can develop. Also, if different team members are functioning at different stages of the change process, confusion in planning results.

5. *Implementation of plans and carrying out tasks*—Team members usually have other tasks and other influences on how they prioritize their work. Often this results in assigned tasks not being carried out, particularly when those tasks are imposed on team members.

6. *Functioning within a complex organization*—Sometimes organizations institute or sanction the use of the team approach without full understanding of the implications of teamwork. The organization may not allow sufficient time for team functioning, may impose leadership that does not enable team functioning to develop, or may interfere with the team's ability to function in other ways.

Each team is unique and must discover its own best way of functioning. Some teams will function in a cooperative manner in which an integrated approach to client service is the mode. Other teams will use a collaborative approach in which the team decides on the services needed; appropriate team members then provide those services in an autonomous manner. Other teams will use various combinations of the two approaches.

Regardless of approach, teams that function best have members who are dedicated, share a common ideal, and have confidence in one another. Members also have a willingness to work together, to learn from one another, and to share clients. They have a cooperative rather than a competitive climate, flexibility, and good communication and problem-solving processes. They also have the support of the agency of which they are a part.

Social workers who are members of teams can contribute to the enhancement of the decision-making process by helping the team to identify the issues confronting the team so that it can work for resolution.

Leadership

Because leadership has differing meanings for different persons, it is often the source of problems in group functioning. Some people perceive a leader as being one who tells everyone else what to do. Other people see the leader as one who consults with the other group members but in the end makes the decisions. Still others see the leader as the one who enables the group to function. Some people who carry the title "leader" are appointed, some are elected, and others emerge from the group. Some people resent leadership or leadership by certain people or professions. Others expect the leader to take full responsibility for the group or expect a member of a particular profession to automatically be the leader.

More and more, leadership is being understood as "interpersonal influence"; in this sense the meaning of leadership, as used here, is captured. Such influence can be exerted in a variety of ways, some of which are more helpful in furthering the functioning of the group than others. The idea that only one person, elected or emergent, carries the entire leadership responsibility is fallacious.

If group members understand leadership as a shared responsibility, much interpersonal conflict can be avoided. The group can then use the knowledge and skills of all group members, for the leadership can change from person to person, depending on the task at hand.

As a group member, the social worker can influence, or enable, the group to carry out its task and function. Some of the tasks involved in this enabling include:

1. *Seeing that decisions are made* (but not making them for the group).

2. *Being sure the group knows what it is doing:* Are there goals? Are they known to all the members? Does the group know its reason for being? Are group norms explicit?

3. *Making certain the group knows how it is doing:* What stage of the change process is the group functioning in? Are the essential roles in the group being filled? Are all group members' contributions accepted? Is communication open and understood by all?

4. *Being sure that when things are not going well or feeling good, the group stops to evaluate what is wrong.*

Social workers with a knowledge of group process can carry out these tasks for any group of which they are members, regardless of their position in the group. To do this they must use good judgment about how and when to exercise this kind of influence. In this way they exercise leadership and influence the outcome of the group's functioning.

Conflict

For many people conflict is frightening. There is a feeling that disagreements can lead to fighting, and the fear of uncontrolled fighting explains, in part, the fear of conflict. Other people believe that conflict can result in nothing positive and thus attempt to avoid it. Conflict does not need to result in uncontrolled fighting, and it can result in the development of new ways of functioning that give rise to new ideas.

Conflict is to be expected when people of different backgrounds and differing experiences interact with one another. Conflict in small groups is not to be avoided; it is to be managed. Differences about what the task and function of the group is, who will fill roles, and what the norms of the group will be should be discussed and negotiated. Negotiation is a process in which all parties to a conflict state their points of view and the reasons for them. These points of view are then examined to discover if there is any faulty thinking and if there are any aspects the parties are willing to accommodate; attempts are then made to reconcile the disagreement. Often, faulty communication is a part of the disagreement. Usually, each point of view has something that can contribute to the work of the group. Conflict is not to be avoided but rather to be brought into the open and dealt with by the group.

Following are some aids to the resolution of conflict:

1. Define the conflict not as one person's problem but as belonging to the group.
2. Listen to all points of view and seek to identify similarities as well as differences among them.
3. Seek clarification so that each point of view is fully understood.
4. Try to avoid win-or-lose solutions.
5. Do not ignore cues that conflict exists; check them out.
6. Work for a cooperative rather than a competitive climate.

Because social workers have skills in understanding people and their behavior, the worker who is a group member can often help the group recognize conflict. The recognition of conflict is the first step toward its management and resolution. When conflict is not recognized, it can be most destructive to the group's interaction.

Social Work Tasks

Social workers who are group members are qualified to carry out three tasks that can be very useful for the group in its functioning: consultation, facilitation, and coordination. The *consultation task* calls for the worker to ask for and offer information and suggestions; there is no demand that the suggestions be accepted. Consultation provides an expectation that all group members will examine the information and suggestions in light of their particular perspective and provide feedback on the usefulness and validity of the social worker's contributions. This type of consultation is a means of enabling the group to engage in a joint process of thinking about clients and situations to identify strengths and resources and to develop plans for action. Through consultation, the social worker contributes the expertise she brings to the group. This expertise can be in the area of group functioning, or it can be in the form of contributions to the task of the group.

Facilitation is the process of enabling others to function. Facilitation of the group process is one form of the *facilitation task*. Social workers can carry out this task in a number of ways. They can support helpful behaviors of other group members, model useful behaviors, ask appropriate questions, or provide appropriate observations and feelings about the group. They can teach other group members information about group process and functioning. Other means of facilitating are helping members stay on the topic, summarizing what has been said or decided, and letting other members know their feelings are accepted. Because of their skills, social workers can help the group state problems so that they can be worked on. Workers can partialize problems, which is done by breaking a problem into parts, prioritizing which part should be worked on, and/or deciding the order for working on the various parts. They can identify strengths and resources.

Some behaviors to avoid are criticizing others or their values, forcing ideas on the group, making decisions that belong to the group, and talking too much. The social worker studies the group and its functioning and decides what will most help the group at any point in time.

A third task, the *coordination task,* calls for monitoring to assess whether all members are carrying out their assigned tasks and whether, in carrying out the tasks, the work of each group member is done in a way that complements that of other members. Coordination ensures that the work of various members does not conflict but rather complements the work of other group members. Social workers are especially able to perform this role because of their broad view of personal and social functioning. They can view the various parts of a plan, ascertain how the parts fit together, and when misfit exists, identify means of modifying misfitting plans.

Much of this coordination is done by building relationships. The social worker attempts to understand the position of every other group member and to gain an appreciation of the needs of each member in relation to the group's task. Through relationships with group members, the social worker can attempt to mediate differences and provide observations about group functioning. In this way, the social worker assists the group in its work together and helps the group coordinate its work.

Social workers can contribute a great deal to groups of which they are members. Knowledge of group process; understanding of issues that can inhibit group functioning; and skill in carrying out the tasks of consultation, facilitation, and coordination provide the social worker with a firm base for making this contribution.

The Worker and the Multiperson Client

In many multiperson situations the social worker interacts as a worker with the system rather than as a member of the system (see the forgoing section "The Small

Group as a Social System"). When working in and with a group, the worker's interaction with the group depends on the situation. When the situation is clearly a multiclient one, the worker is usually not seen as a part of the group but rather as a professional helper. In other situations, such as when serving as a staff assistant to a board or a committee, the worker is seen more as a resource person who helps group members carry out the work of the group.

In order to function as a worker with a group, the social worker must understand group process and must develop interactional skills for working with groups. The worker employs many of the enabling skills used in working as a member of a group.

The Worker and Group Interaction

When a social worker works with a group of unrelated people, the focus is on group interaction. Because the system may not have formed, in the early stages the worker may be involved in interaction that enables the group system to form. Again, the interactions are to enable individuals to become part of the group and to function in the group. The major focus is on group interaction, not on worker–individual member interaction; otherwise, the worker is not working with the group system but with individuals in the presence of other individuals.

The worker influences the process of the system in a number of ways, including:

1. *Acceptance*—The worker accepts individual members with their feelings, attitudes, ideas, and behaviors. Through such acceptance, other members come to see the member's contribution, realize that their feelings can be respected, and appreciate difference. In being accepted by the worker, group members gain strength to carry out their roles in the group.

2. *Relationships*—The worker helps each group member relate to other members and gain interactional skill. The worker also uses relationship to help members find their commonalities.

3. *Enabling and supporting*—The worker helps members accept themselves and others, express themselves, have a feeling of accomplishment, and involve themselves in the activity and decision making of the group. In addition, the worker helps the group and its members gain understanding of their group process and how it may be modified. The worker contributes facts and understanding that enable the group to function.

4. *Limiting behavior*—When behavior of individual members is harmful to themselves and particularly to others or is destructive of property or relationships, the worker helps the group or the individual member to limit such behavior.

5. *Guiding*—The worker helps the group by providing guidance for the discussion process, such as helping the group keep on focus or task, and teaching effective decision-making and planning skills. The worker also guides the activity and the movement of the group in its process.

6. *Alleviation*—The worker relieves tensions, conflicts, fears, anxiety, or guilt that may be interfering with group functioning.

7. *Interpreting*—The worker helps the group understand the function of the agency and of the worker in relation to the group's task. The worker may also interpret the meaning of the feelings or actions of the group or its members.

8. *Observation and evaluation*—The worker constantly tries to understand what is happening in the group and why it is happening.

9. *Planning and preparation*—The worker plans for the group as needed to enable the group to function and carry out its purposes.[7]

Throughout the process, the worker helps the group to identify strengths in themselves and in their ecosystem. The worker also facilitates the ability of members to assist each other in identifying these strengths. Thus, the role of the social worker with the group is to help the members reach out to one another in such a way that they can help one another in meeting their needs or in some way influencing their environment so that group and individual needs are better met. Helping the group as a system to carry out its task is the focus of the social worker when working with a multiclient system.

The social worker's role is influenced both by the stage of group development and by the stage of individual development of group members. During the orientation stage the worker is very active with the group. The worker helps group members to share their needs and concerns relative to that function; structures group meetings so the members can get a vision of how the group can function; enables group members to maintain distance while making decisions about the group and their role in the group; and attempts to maintain a comfortable, accepting climate.

As the group moves to the authority stage, the worker allows members to challenge ideas and ways of functioning. The worker helps members recognize and deal with conflict. The worker supports the group and its members as they struggle to find ways to work together.

As the group begins to negotiate differences, the worker supports this negotiation and continues to assist the group in dealing with conflict. The group is helped to identify norms and values, establish goals, and negotiate roles. The worker clarifies feelings and ideas.

In the functional stage, the worker allows the group to function as independently as possible. The worker serves as a resource person and as an observer and helps the group evaluate its process. During this stage the worker's contribution to the group's process and work depends on what will be useful as the group engages in its work together.

When a worker senses the onset of disintegration, a decision should be made with the group as to whether the group has served its purpose; then the disintegration should be allowed to progress or an attempt should be made to help the group reverse the disintegration. If the decision is to reverse, the worker's role is to help the group determine the reasons for the disintegration and take the steps needed to restore the group to an appropriate level of functioning. A change process is used with the group. If the group has served its purpose, then the worker helps the group understand what is happening and feel good about the group's accomplishments.

Three areas of understanding are needed by the social worker in working with groups. These are the process of group formation, group discussion leadership, and the use of structure and activity to facilitate group functioning.

Group Formation

Although social workers sometimes work with already formed systems or groups, at times it is necessary to form a group. People considered for group membership may not be acquainted with one another. The handling of the formation process is an important factor in whether or not the group will be able to function to meet its goals. There are four stages to the formation of a group: (1) establishing the group's purpose, (2) selecting members, (3) making the first contacts with prospective members, and (4) holding the first meeting of the group.

The group's purpose may develop from client request or from an agency staff decision that there is a need that can be met through developing a group. Some of the reasons for forming a group are (1) when several people facing similar situations can benefit from sharing their experiences; (2) when group influence on individuals is great, such as during the teenage years; (3) when the target for change is in the environment, such as the development of a new community service; (4) when a natural group exists; (5) to improve relationships with others; and (6) to aid those experiencing social isolation. The group is an excellent vehicle to use for reality testing, for it is a social microcosm of the larger society. Groups should not be used to save workers' time when a common goal or purpose does not exist, when an individual is in danger of being overwhelmed by the group, when there is insufficient commonality for a cohesive climate to develop, or when the environment impinges on the group's functioning or prevents it from reaching its goals. Groups can work together on individual needs, on relationships within or outside of the group, on decision making or task achievement, or on targeting for change in the larger community.

For a group to be functional, group members must have some commonality (in part, the purpose and function provide the commonality). At this stage of the formation process, the worker and agency identify a common need and translate the need to the purpose for the prospective group. The worker formulates tentative group goals. Based on the purpose and the tentative goals, the worker begins the selection of members. Consideration is given to how many people should be in the group. When members have good interactional skills, the number can go as high as ten or twelve and still allow for interaction among all members. For clients with little interactional capacity, the size of the group should be limited to four or five persons.

Group commonality is in part based on the attractiveness prospective members have for one another. People are attracted to other people because they admire them, hold common values with them, respect them, or support their functioning in some way. People feel most comfortable with those who are similar to themselves. For a group to be productive, however, it is necessary for the members to have sufficient difference so that unique contributions can be made by each group member. The worker must determine how much commonality is necessary for the group to be attractive to prospective members and how much difference is necessary to carry out the function of the group.

In choosing prospective members the worker must evaluate how well these individuals can be expected to function in the group and what their contributions to the group might be. The choice of individuals as prospective members is based on multiple factors that relate to the need for balance and the individual qualities of these members.

Other factors in forming a group are the resources and expectations that arise from the prospective group's environment. These factors affect the prospective member's ability to function in the group and also affect the manner in which the group can function.

When the worker has completed the process of choosing prospective members, the next step is an initial contact with each person. During the initial contact, the worker explains the purpose of the group and the reason for considering the person for group membership. Together they explore how the group may function and come to a decision about the prospective member joining the group. In many ways, this session is similar to the worker's initial interview with an individual client. The major purpose of the session is to begin to engage the member in the group and to orient the member to the group.

The first meeting of the group is crucial for group formation. The group function and the way of operating are discussed again. The worker enables members to share their reasons for joining the group and their individual goals with respect to the group. The worker facilitates communication among the members and helps them begin formulating group norms and goals. The group begins to work on the tasks of carrying out the function of the group. Every attempt is made for this first session to be a positive experience for all members.

Adequate group formation is time consuming, but if properly done it saves time later. It reduces the chances of having a mismatch of group members and prepares the members for functioning in the group. In this way, the time in the group can be spent on its function and tasks, not on unrelated individual needs.

When the group is ongoing and not time limited, the group must decide how it will add new members. If it is an open group, as are support groups and self-help groups, members can join or leave at any time. For these groups, a certain member or members should be identified who can quickly orient new members to the norms of the group and help introduce them to the group.

In closed groups that are ongoing, new members are usually only added when someone leaves the group. The worker generally takes responsibility for screening prospective members. In community groups with voluntary members, the group may be responsible for the decision of whether or not to accept a prospective member after the worker describes the person and his situation, or the worker may have responsibility for making a decision. In nonvoluntary groups, such as the one in the group home from the case study earlier in the chapter, the staff of the agency decide who to accept through an intake process. The worker should ensure that the group has resolved any termination issues and is ready to accept the new member. Termination will be discussed in more detail in Chapter 16. In either case, the worker typically will orient the new member prior to the group meeting and then facilitate having the group complete the orientation process during the first session the new member attends. This orientation should include introductions, a discussion of group rules, and a discussion of what is expected of the new member in terms of participation. Periodic checks should be made with the new member and feedback given for the first few sessions to facilitate having him join in the group process.

Discussion Leadership

Discussion is the means of communicating within the group. The worker carries the task of enabling the discussion to develop until such time as leadership emerges in the group. This enabling takes place through

1. *Climate setting*—The worker pays attention to the physical atmosphere. Placement of chairs so that all members can have eye contact and are neither too close nor too far apart is important. The atmosphere should be warm, friendly, and relaxed.

2. *Stimulating*—The worker knows that encouragement of the sharing of ideas is important. The worker also helps group members disagree without developing hostility.

3. *Encouraging mutual respect and understanding*—The worker helps members understand their commonalities and differences. The right of people to be different is considered. The worker demonstrates respect for all members and their ideas. This modeling often helps members respect one another.

4. *Reducing overdependence*—The worker encourages the group to develop its way of functioning. The worker seeks ideas and facts from the members and helps group members fill the essential roles.

5. *Drawing in nonparticipants*—The worker helps a member who is not active in the discussion to contribute by asking questions or suggesting information she may have.

6. *Checking overaggressive participants*—The worker points out to the group the need for each member to have an opportunity to participate.

7. *Helping the group define and verbalize goals and needs or concerns*—The worker stimulates group thinking and helps the group in making decisions and developing plans.

8. *Helping the group in other ways*—The worker clarifies issues, analyzes problems, discovers and describes possible solutions, evaluates solutions, and carries out decisions. Also, the worker helps the group focus when it gets off course and summarizes as appropriate.

9. *Helping the group deal with conflict*—The worker points out symptoms of conflict, helps individuals clarify viewpoints and state positions, and seeks commonalities.

In providing discussion leadership to a group, the worker is also teaching members of the group how to take responsibility for their own leadership. The worker needs to help the group avoid placing undue pressure for conformity or dependency on its members, allowing harmful and unsupportive responses to vulnerable members, and tolerating assertive and talkative members to receive all the attention. As soon as group members are able to carry any part of this responsibility, the worker encourages the discussion leadership to begin to rest in the group members and then assumes the enabler role.

Structuring Group Activity

The group can be enabled to function through the use of activity. Activity can be tasks the group does together, such as games, crafts, or other program materials, or it can be structured exercises. The way in which a worker structures these activities can affect the group's development. Activity can also give the group data on which to make decisions about its functioning. Another part of structuring is the use of the physical facility and the time and place of the meeting. (See the section entitled "Use of Activity as an Interventive Strategy" in Chapter 13 for further discussion of this kind of action.)

When working with the multiperson client, the worker has four primary tools: (1) the worker and the way he uses self, (2) the use of group process, (3) discussion as a means of communication, and (4) structures and activity. Through the use of these tools the worker enables the group to function and carry out the tasks that lead to goal fulfillment.

The generalist social worker's interactive repertoire includes skill in working in and with small groups as well as in one-to-one interaction. To develop this skill the worker needs knowledge of group process, means for influencing groups of which she is a member, and means for enabling the functioning of the multiperson client group.

Case Example

Session Summary of a Group of Delinquent Boys in a Group Home

January 18: Today was Deandre's first day in group, replacing an earlier member, Frank. While Deandre had met everyone earlier, the group spent some time telling him why they were in placement, what they were working on, and where they were at in terms of progressing through the program. When asked about his situation, he bragged about working as a guard in a drug house and about how he and another boy had shot up a guy's car. Reggie challenged him on this and asked Deandre where that had gotten him. Deandre tried to act tough by saying that it didn't bother him to have to do some time. Jose asked him what would have happened if he had killed the guy. Deandre admitted that he could have faced life in prison. When asked by Reggie if that would have been worth the twenty dollars the man owed, Deandre was very quiet. He did not say very much for the rest of the session. The group spent some time discussing their last community service project, which was singing Christmas carols at some nursing homes and at an activity center for developmentally disabled adults. They decided that they wanted to do something at one of the local nursing homes for Easter but would also like to follow up with the developmentally disabled adults, especially when the weather got better.

The Family Group as a Social System

The family is considered by some practitioners and theorists as a special form of small group. As such, most of the skills and approaches for working with small groups are relevant to working with families. However, there are some differences. These differences can be seen in the areas of structure, function, and development (as outlined in the Schema for the Development of a Family Social History, Table 7.3).

Structure

A major difference between families and groups is structure. Most groups are assumed to be made up of peers. Even in groups in which there are officers, these are generally elected by the membership and serve only if a majority of the group's members continue to support them. The group is intended to meet certain needs of all of its members or to accomplish a task. Often these needs are similar and are encompassed in the purpose of the group.

Families have a much different structure, which generally includes the marital, parental, parent-child, and sibling subsystems. Different relationships, roles, and responsibilities are associated with membership in each of these subsystems. Some of these are somewhat universal, but most of them are culturally related. It is essential for the worker to be sensitive to these cultural expectations in order to work within the family system. At the same time, some cultural mores appear to be in direct conflict with social work values. For instance, Charles Garvin and Brett Seabury, drawing on the work of Amy Urry, point out the imbalance of power between genders in most family systems. They espouse the use of a feminist perspective in offering alternatives and new choices for families who are locked into a gender-based system.[8] Whether the worker or the family subscribes to this approach or not, the worker needs to help the family become more aware of its structure and make conscious choices that will meet the needs of all of its members.

Function

There are also differences between families and groups in how they function. Most of these come out of the fact that families are made up of subsystems. The family schema includes communication patterns, decision-making patterns, and role performance under this category. Each of these have some differences for families. The process of communicating effectively is basically the same for individuals, families, and groups (see the discussion in Chapter 8). However, there are differences in the appropriate manner and content of the communication based on membership in various subsystems. In general, members of the same subsystem will communicate more as peers. The exception to this is the parent-child system, in which the roles and status of parent and child dictate otherwise. The content of the communication within subsystems tends to relate directly or indirectly to the roles being played within that particular subsystem. For example, communication between a husband and a wife will tend to be peerlike and will likely involve sharing aspects of their daily lives with each other. When acting in the parental subsystem, the discussion will likely concern roles as parents and will include child-rearing practices. In the former case, the interaction is focused on each other as individuals and as a couple. In the latter, the focus is on child-raising roles.

Decision making tends to be much different in families than in groups. Whereas consensus is what the worker strives for in a group, there are limited areas in which consensus can be applied in families. This is usually limited to family goals, which will be covered in Chapter 12. In families, primary responsibility for making decisions rests with the parents. However, sound child-rearing practices involve helping children to make age-appropriate decisions so that they can become independent adults. This is often one of the focuses of family work, especially when the presenting problem involves behavior of the children. Families with an autocratic decision-making style often have difficulty assisting children to separate and emancipate. Families with an excessively permissive style may predispose their children to difficulty with limits and authority figures outside the family. A balance needs to be struck that will serve the needs of the family system while also preparing children for life in society.

Roles in the group tend to be temporary or even transferable among members. They are usually determined mutually between the individual and the group. They are generally categorized as either maintenance or task oriented. In families, roles tend to be longer term and associated with membership in a subsystem. In fact, when a member of another subsystem takes on a role that is not associated with that subsystem, it is usually described in terms of a "dysfunction." For example, if a child takes on a nurturing or caregiving role toward a parent, this is called "role reversal" and tends to be seen as not serving the long-term needs of either the parent or the child.

Development

Stages of development are much different for families and groups. Sonya Rhodes identified seven stages of family development (see Chapter 7). The stages of development for groups have been identified above. The similarities between families and groups revolve around the issue of attachment versus separation. Family development is long term and recognizes the fact that family relationships last a lifetime, whereas group membership is temporary. Group development is seen in terms of the development of relationships within the group (attachment) along with the eventual termination of those relationships (separation). For families, attachment and separation are issues that last throughout each individual member's life. These issues, along with the stage of family development, have profound influences on the behavior of family members within the family system and in groups outside of the family.

Another difference in development is that families share a common history and culture, and groups have members who have differences in these areas. Families also share the same ecosystem, whereas group members generally share only parts of each other's ecosystem. Families already share a common bond, but group members must establish common ground in order to identify themselves as a group.

Working with families and groups has both similarities and differences. It is important for the worker to be able to function in both of these multiperson systems. Although some skills can be readily utilized in either system, specialized skills are also needed that are specific to each system.

Summary

Multiperson interaction is an important part of generalist social work activity. In order to be effective in multiperson interaction, a social worker should understand the small group as a social system. Understanding the structure, functioning, and development of any small group gives the social worker direction for effective interaction.

Social workers participate as members of small groups as they carry out tasks and serve clients. They can enable these groups to function by (1) helping all group members participate in the group, (2) clarifying the decision-making process, (3) stimulating the discussion process, and (4) structuring group meetings.

One type of group in which social workers often participate is the team. Teams have special characteristics and problems in functioning. Social workers with knowledge of small-group functioning can help to resolve team problems.

Leadership and conflict are also important aspects of small-group functioning. Three tasks are key to enabling small-group functioning: consultation, facilitation, and coordination.

Generalist social workers also work with multiperson clients (groups and families). The social worker is not a member of the system but rather enables the system to function. In doing this, the social worker helps groups to form and uses group discussion techniques and activities to facilitate group functioning.

The tools a social worker uses to work in and with small groups are self, group process, discussion, and activities. It is important for social workers to have skill in using these tools.

A family group is a system that already exists. Thus, when a social worker works with a family group, she does not become a part of the system but remains outside the boundary. Interactions with an individual family member are for the purpose of enabling that person to interact with other family members more adequately. The focus is on the family interaction.

Q U E S T I O N S

1. Using the schema for study of a small group, describe a group of which you have been a part. How does this kind of analysis help you understand what was happening in that group?

2. Think about groups of which you are now a part. How do you think you might enable that group to function more effectively?

3. Identify a conflict situation in a group with which you are familiar. What was the cause of the conflict? How did the group handle the conflict? Was there a better way to handle the conflict?

4. How would you justify to an agency administrator the amount of time needed for good group formation?

5. Identify ways that you can develop your skill in group participation and in group leadership. What do you see as the difference between group participation and group leadership?

6. What issues do you think you should consider when working with a family group? Identify those issues that may be unresolved or important to you personally in your own family situation and that may get in the way as you work with a family.

7. Discuss the differences when working with the family as a system as contrasted with working with individuals who may be family members. Why is it important to work with the family as a system rather than work with individuals in a family?

SUGGESTED READINGS

Anderson, Joseph. *Social Work with Groups: A Process Model.* New York: Longman, 1997.

Anderson, Stephen A., and Sabatelli, Ronald M. *Family Interaction: A Multigenerational Developmental Perspective,* 2nd ed. Boston: Allyn and Bacon, 1999.

Beavers, W. R., and Hampson, R. B. *Successful Families: Assessment and Intervention.* New York: W. W. Norton, 1990.

Becvar, Dorothy Stroh, and Becvar, Raphael J. *Family Therapy: A Systematic Integration,* 4th ed. Boston: Allyn and Bacon, 2000.

Berman-Rossi, Toby. "The Tasks and Skills of the Social Worker Across Stages of Group Development." *Social Work with Groups* 16, 1 (1993): 69–71.

Boyd-Franklin, N. *Black Families in Therapy: A Multisystems Approach.* New York: Guilford Press, 1989.

Brown, Leonard. *Groups for Growth and Change.* New York: Longman, 1991.

———. "Group Work and the Environmental Systems Approach." *Social Work with Groups* 16, 1/2 (1993): 83–95.

Carter, Elizabeth A., and McGoldrick, Monica. *The Expanded Family Life Cycle: Individual, Family, and Social Perspectives,* 3rd ed. Boston: Allyn and Bacon, 1999.

Chau, K. L. "Needs Assessment for Group Work with People of Color: A Conceptual Formulation." *Social Work with Groups* 15 (1992): 53–66.

Davis, L. E., and Proctor, E. K. *Race, Gender, and Class: Guidelines for Practice with Individuals, Families, and Groups.* Englewood Cliffs, NJ: Prentice-Hall, 1989.

Edwards, Richard L., Ed. *Encyclopedia of Social Work,* 19th ed. Washington, DC: NASW Press, 1995 ("Families: Direct Practice," "Group Practice Overview," and "Families Overview").

Farley, Joan E. "Family Developmental Task Assessment: A Prerequisite to Family Treatment." *Clinical Social Work Journal* 18 (Spring 1990): 85–98.

Fatout, Marian. *Models for Change in Social Group Work.* New York: Aldine, 1992.

Flores, Maria T., and Carey, Gabrielle. *Family Therapy with Hispanics: Toward Appreciating Diversity.* Boston: Allyn and Bacon, 2000.

Garner, Howard G. *Teamwork in Human Services: Models and Applications across the Life Span.* Boston: Butterworth-Heinemann, 1994.

———. *Teamwork: Parents and Professionals Speak for Themselves.* Washington, DC: CWLA Press, 1998.

Garvin, Charles. *Contemporary Group Work,* 3rd ed. Boston: Allyn and Bacon, 1997.

Garvin, Charles D., and Seabury, Brett A. *Interpersonal Practice in Social Work: Promoting Competence and Social Justice,* 2nd ed. Boston: Allyn and Bacon, 1997.

Gitterman, Alex, and Shulman, Lawrence. *Mutual Aid Groups and the Life Cycle,* 2nd ed. New York: Columbia University Press, 1994.

Gurman, Alan, and Kinskerm, David, Eds. *Handbook of Family Therapy,* Vol. II. New York: Brunner/Mazel, 1991.

Helton, Lonnie R., and Jackson, Maggie. *Social Work Practice with Families: A Diversity Model.* Boston: Allyn and Bacon, 1997.

Henry, S. *Group Skills in Social Work: A Four Dimensional Approach.* Pacific Grove, CA: Brooks/Cole, 1992.

Hepworth, Dean H., Rooney, Ronald H., and Larsen, Jo Ann. *Direct Social Work Practice: Theory and Skills,* 5th ed. Pacific Grove, CA: Brooks/Cole, 1997 (Chapters 10 and 11).

Horn, Arthur, and Passmore, J. Laurence. *Family Counseling and Therapy.* Itasca, IL: F. E. Peacock, 1991.

Janzen, Curtis, and Harris, Oliver. *Family Treatment in Social Work Practice,* 3rd ed. Itasca, IL: F. E. Peacock, 1997.

Kilpatrick, Allie, and Holland, Thomas. *Working with Families: An Integrative Model by Level of Functioning.* Boston: Allyn and Bacon, 1999.

Logan, Sadye, Freeman, Edith, and McRoy, Ruth. *Social Work Practice with Black Families: A Culturally Specific Perspective.* Boston: Allyn and Bacon, 1990.

Lum, Doman. *Social Work Practice and People of Color: A Process-Stage Approach,* 4th ed. Pacific Grove, CA: Brooks/Cole, 2000.

McGoldrick, Monica, Giordano, Joe, and Pearce, John K., Eds. *Ethnicity and Family Therapy,* 2nd ed. New York: Guilford Press, 1996.

Nichols, Michael, and Schwartz, Richard. *Family Therapy,* 4th ed. Boston: Allyn and Bacon, 1998.

Papajohn, John, and Spiegel, John P. *Transactions in Families.* Northvale, NJ: J. Aronson, 1995.

Reid, Kenneth E. *Social Work Practice with Groups: A Clinical Perspective,* 2nd ed. Pacific Grove, CA: Brooks/Cole, 1997.

Ronnau, John, and Poertner, John. "Identification and Use of Strengths: A Family System Approach." *Children Today* 22 (1993): 20–23.

Saleeby, Dennis, Ed. *The Strengths Perspective in Social Work Practice,* 2nd ed. New York: Longman, 1997.

Shulman, Lawrence. *The Skills of Helping: Individuals, Families, Groups, and Communities,* 4th ed. Itasca, IL: F. E. Peacock, 1999.

Toseland, Ronald W., and Rivas, Robert F. *An Introduction to Group Work Practice,* 3rd ed. Boston: Allyn and Bacon, 1998.

Walsh, William M., and McGraw, James A. *Essentials of Family Therapy: A Therapists Guide to Eight Approaches.* Denver, CO: Love, 1996.

Zastrow, Charles. *Social Work with Groups,* 4th ed. Chicago: Nelson-Hall, 1997.

N O T E S

1. This discussion of the small group as a social system is a synthesis of knowledge about small groups primarily based on three schools of thought: (1) Field theory or group dynamics. The work of Kurt Lewin is the original source. Darwin Cartwright and Alvin Zander, *Group Dynamics: Research and Theory* (Evanston, IL: Row Peterson, 1960), is another source. (2) Interactional process analysis. Paul A. Hare, Edgar F. Borgotta, and Robert E. Bales, *Small Groups: Studies in Social Interaction* (New York: Alfred A. Knopf, 1965), is a source for this school of thought. (3) Homans's systems theory. George Homans, *The Human Group* (New York: Harcourt, Brace and World, 1960), is the third primary source. Another excellent source on group process is Margaret E. Hartford, *Groups in Social Work* (New York: Columbia University Press, 1972).

2. Henry W. Maier, "Models of Intervention in Work with Groups: Which One Is Yours?" *Social Work with Groups* 4 (Fall/Winter 1981): 21–34.

3. For a full description of this technique, see Mary L. Northway, *A Primer of Sociometry,* 2nd ed. (Toronto: University of Toronto Press, 1967).

4. Kenneth D. Benne and Paul Sheats, "Functional Roles of Group Members," *Journal of Social Issues* 4 (1948): 41–49.

5. John K. Brilhart, *Effective Group Discussion* (Dubuque, IA: Wm. C. Brown, 1974), p. 5.

6. John J. Horwitz, *Team Practice and the Specialist* (Springfield, IL: Charles C. Thomas, 1970), p. 10.

7. Based on a formulation developed by Henriette Etta Soloshin, "Development of an Instrument for the Analysis of Social Group Work Method in Therapeutic Settings" (Ph.D. diss., University of Minnesota, Minneapolis, March 1954). Also see William Schwartz, "The Social Worker in the Group," in *Social Welfare Forum 1961* (New York: Columbia University Press, 1961), pp. 146–171.

8. Charles D. Garvin and Brett A. Seabury, *Interpersonal Practice in Social Work: Promoting Competence and Social Justice,* 2nd ed. (Boston: Allyn and Bacon, 1997).

PART THREE

The Social Work Process

The content of the service process—the process of the work of the client and worker in meeting need—is the focus of Part Three. This process of the work can be separated from the interactional process only for purposes of study. Interaction and service are two ways of looking at the professional response to need. The generalist social work process, as developed in this book, is a change process based on knowledge, values, and skill. It is intervention into the transactions of human systems. Part Three will build on material presented in Parts One and Two, offering more depth regarding already-introduced concepts. It will present another facet of the social work endeavor.

The process can be conceptualized as having four major components: assessment, planning, action, and termination. Although assessment precedes planning, planning precedes action, and action precedes termination, the process is cyclical in nature. Planning often leads to the need for a new or different understanding of person in situation (assessment). Action often produces new information for use in understanding or demonstrates the need for additional planning. Evaluation, the assessment of what has happened as a result of action, is ongoing in the process and leads to new understanding and sometimes to new plans and action. Thus, all four stages are always present, but at various points in the work one or more may be the focus and receive the most attention.

All four stages as well as the interactional process constitute intervention. All can influence change in the transactions between clients and the systems in their environment. All can influence the social functioning of individuals and social systems. Figure 1 depicts the social work process.

Chapter 11 considers the content of the assessment phase. In addition, attention is given to the place of the change process in assessment, to the nature of transactional assessment, to strengths and resources available in the ecosystem, and to the strategy of needs assessment.

Chapter 12 discusses planning, including the means for developing a plan of action that includes goals and objectives based primarily on strengths and resources in the ecosystem, units of attention, strategy, roles, tasks, and techniques. Planning with multiperson client systems is also covered. Factors that affect the

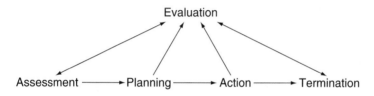

FIGURE 1 **The Social Work Process**

plan of action are explored, including diversity and at-risk populations. In addition, there is a discussion of the agreement between worker and client about the plan and consideration of the use of a contract.

Chapter 13 identifies and discusses important actions used in direct practice with clients by the generalist social worker. The specific actions identified and discussed are (1) use of resources, including a discussion of the nature of the service delivery system, referral, broker and advocate roles, and empowerment of clients; (2) crisis intervention; (3) supportive social work; (4) use of activity; and (5) mediation.

Chapter 14 discusses indirect practice, that is, actions taken by social workers on behalf of clients. Actions discussed include (1) work with influentials; (2) coordination of services, including the strategy of case management; (3) program planning and resource development, including development of a volunteer program and work with self-help groups; (4) environmental manipulation; (5) work toward changing organizations from within; and (6) cause advocacy.

In Chapters 13 and 14 the focus is on presenting a variety of strategies so that the reader gains a sense of the array of actions available for use by social workers. The strategies are developed so that the reader can gain an understanding of their more important aspects and of situations in which these strategies might be useful. Generally, strategies are used to carry out the plan or to remove barriers to successful completion of the plan. No attempt has been made to present a comprehensive discussion of the strategies, which can best be done by study of the primary sources for each strategy.

Chapter 15 discusses evaluation and its importance in contemporary American social work practice, which places considerable emphasis on accountability. This chapter presents issues related to evaluation as well as tools used by social workers for evaluation.

Chapter 16 considers termination and discusses various situations in which termination takes place with various size client systems. It discusses planned termination, the components of the termination process, and the relationship of termination to evaluation.

11 Assessment

LEARNING EXPECTATIONS

1. In-depth understanding of assessment as a complex process.
2. Beginning skill in assessing individuals, families, small groups, organizations, and communities.
3. Appreciation for the need to involve the client in the assessment process.
4. Ability to choose and apply appropriate knowledge to the assessment process.
5. Ability to tolerate the uncertainty of incomplete assessment.
6. Skill in judgment or decision making.
7. Skill in identifying needs and blocks to their fulfillment.
8. Skill in choosing assessment tools most useful in a given situation.
9. Skill in identifying strengths and resources in the ecosystem.
10. Skill in transactional assessment.
11. Understanding of the needs assessment process.

The first step in the generalist social work process is *assessment,* historically referred to as *diagnosis.* Interviews (discussed in Chapter 9) are a very important source of information in assessing the situation. The assessment phase of the social work process also includes "study, diagnosis, and treatment," the classic description of the social work process. Assessment is the phase being discussed when the term *analysis* is used. The development of understanding about individuals, families, small groups, agencies, and communities is an important aspect of assessment. The understanding about a system requisite for professional interaction with that system is the core of the assessment stage of the interventive or service process. Assessment includes identifying strengths and resources that exist within the client, within the systems that make up the client's environment, and in the transactions within this ecosystem. A social study is an assessment. The content of group meetings (discussed in Chapter 10) is another important source of assessment information, as are observations of individual and group behavior in the community. Questionnaires and other research tools as well as psychological tests can be used to gather information. Assessment is an essential ingredient for the individualization of people and social systems.

Max Siporin defines *assessment* as "a process and a product of understanding on which action is based."[1] It is the collection and analysis of information, the fitting together of available facts so that they yield meaning. Within the perspective of this book, assessment does not include planning, which is seen as a separate step.

Mark A. Mattaini and Stuart A. Kirk reviewed various assessment approaches used by social workers, including the psychosocial, classification systems, and behavioral approaches often used in clinical social work as well as computerized assessment instruments, the ecosystems perspective, and expert systems. The approach that most nearly approximates the one presented for use in generalist social work is the ecosystems approach. Mattaini and Kirk characterize this approach as a way of organizing complex assessment data and suggest that it significantly expands the breadth of assessment without a loss of depth.[2]

Four ideas will be discussed in the further development of the concept of assessment: (1) the content of the assessment phase, (2) the use of the change process in assessment, (3) transactional assessment, and (4) needs assessment.

The Content of the Assessment Phase

Assessment is a complex process at the core of the service process. The need for development of an understanding of clients, whether they are individuals, families, or small groups, and of the systems in the client's environment was discussed in relation to the interactional process in Part Two. These schemas are tools for gathering information, but care must be taken that relevant information that falls outside the schema is not overlooked. Assessment, although a creative process, is also scientific in that it is a manifestation of the scientific method. Some of its most important characteristics follow:

1. *Assessment is ongoing.* Assessment takes place throughout the life of the helping endeavor. During the early stages it is a primary focus. However, during later stages, when the work of doing something about need and of intervening into transactions among systems takes place, assessment is also a concern. As the client and worker engage in their work together, new information becomes available and new understandings emerge. These then become a part of the ongoing assessment.

2. *Assessment is twofold, focusing both on understanding client in situation and on providing a base for planning and action.* Information must be gathered about the people and systems involved, about their interrelationship and their environment. Information should be collected about the need, blocks to need fulfillment, the situation, and the people and systems significant to the need. It is also important to determine strengths, challenges, motivation for change, and resistance to change that are applicable to the persons and systems involved. When dealing with large systems, it is important to gather information about the demography of the system and the situation being considered. Also it may be important to gather information about interagency relationships, coordination, and cooperation; funding and other resources available or potentially available; and attitudes, values, and cultural factors that may affect the work to be done.

This information is gathered in many different ways. Of prime importance are the client's perceptions and feelings about the need or concern and the situation. Carefully attending to the client's story conveys respect and acknowledges that the client is the "expert" regarding his history. The manner in which the client tells the story, including observation of nonverbal communication, provides important information.

Other sources of information may be previous case records and reports from other interested persons. If a worker uses information sources other than the client, the client should be aware of the use of the resources and give suggestions about sources for such information and permission for the worker to obtain the information from other people. When gathering information about large systems, such as a community, both key persons in the community and those involved with the situation should be used as informants. The information being collected should always be clearly connected to the concern or need being worked on.

In addition, understanding the actual and potential resources, the expectations held by various concerned systems about the outcome of service, and the challenges to or encroachments on the client's environment are also important, especially for effective planning.

3. *Assessment is a mutual process involving both client and worker.* The client is involved in all aspects of assessment to the maximum of her capacity. The primary content to be assessed arises from the worker-client interaction in the interview or in group discussions. One source of content is the information provided as the worker observes the client in the interview or in group discussion. Content also derives from observations of the client in life situations. The worker discusses observations and other information with the client to establish the meaning of the facts or to gain an understanding of person in situation. The use of a mutual process in assessment is one means of empowering clients, for it provides them with a sense of self-worth and demonstrates that what they think and believe is important. They come to realize that they are not passive recipients of help but important partners in the work to be done.

4. *There is movement within the assessment process.* This movement usually occurs from observation of parts of the service situation to identification of information needed for understanding. This is followed by collection of facts about parts of the service situation and an explanation of the meaning of the facts collected. The facts and their meanings about various parts are put together in order to understand the total situation.

5. *Both horizontal and vertical exploration are important.* In the early stages of assessment it is usually helpful to look at the situation horizontally; that is, the situation is examined in breadth to identify all possible parts, interactions, and relationships. The purpose of this horizontal exploration is to determine the block to need fulfillment and the strengths and resources in the ecosystem that can be used to meet the need. Later, those parts identified as most important to the situation or to meeting needs are examined vertically, or in depth. The information-gathering process can move from horizontal to vertical and back to horizontal several times as the worker and client explore the need and the situation. Social workers should develop skill in determining when a horizontal approach is most appropriate and when a vertical approach is the one to use.

6. *The knowledge base is used in developing understanding.* The worker uses his knowledge base as one means for developing understanding of client in situation. An understanding of an individual takes into consideration factors of human development and diversity. An understanding of a family is related to what is known about family structure and process. For example, an understanding of a family with a developmentally disabled child requires knowledge about mental disability and family reactions to the child. An understanding of an agency considers knowledge of bureaucratic structures. An understanding of community functioning calls for knowledge of economics and political science. An understanding of the ecosystem requires knowledge of systems theory and the exchange of matter, energy, and information among systems. When appropriate, the social worker uses research techniques to gather needed information.

7. *Assessment identifies needs in life situations and explains their meaning and patterns.* Assessment makes use of the process of growth and change throughout the life cycle in specifying the need and what is blocking need fulfillment. (This idea is discussed more fully later in this chapter.)

8. *Assessment identifies client and ecosystem strengths with an eye toward building on those strengths during intervention.* Individuals grow from their strengths, not their limitations. A thorough assessment of physical, mental, emotional, and behavioral assets must occur in order to work with the client system to set goals, objectives, and tasks that have a high likelihood of success. Identification of client strengths requires identifying resources present in the client system and the environment or situation that can be used to meet needs.[3]

9. *Assessment is individualized.* Human situations are complex; no two are exactly the same. Each assessment is different and is related to the differential situation of the client. Assessment takes into consideration the different parts of the situation and relates these to the unique whole that emerges. This is particularly true when working with populations that differ from the worker's ethnic or sociocultural orientation. It is critical to understand the situation and its meaning to the client system from the client's, not the worker's, perspective.

10. *Judgment is important.* Many decisions must be made regarding each assessment. Decisions include what parts to consider, which parts of the knowledge base to apply, how to involve the client, and how to define the concern or need.

The kinds of decisions that are made greatly affect the content and the interpretation of that content. The client system's view of the significance of events must be evaluated carefully; again, what the worker may consider unimportant from his frame of reference may be of great importance to the client system.

11. *There are limits to the understanding that can be developed.* No assessment is ever complete. Not only is it impossible to gain complete understanding of any situation, but it is also undesirable. Understanding takes time. Clients in need are seeking help, and this help often must be given quickly. The worker must decide what understanding is necessary to give that help and then be aware of new understandings that develop in giving the help. The worker also must be comfortable with the uncertainty of limited understanding and learn to trust in the ongoing process of assessment.

The tasks of assessment, then, are (1) identification of the need or concern as well as of client and ecosystem strengths and resources, (2) identification of the information needed to further understand the need or concern and to determine appropriate means for meeting the need, and (3) collection and analysis of information.

Decision making includes interpreting meanings and ordering information as well as discovering relationships among parts of the situation. Decision making considers persons, needs, situations, *client and ecosystem strengths*, and relationships.

Judgment

Judgment is an important component of assessment. Judgment is, in effect, decision making. According to Harriet Bartlett, "Professional judgment provides the bridge between knowledge and value, on one hand, and interventive action on the other. Assessment is its first application in practice."[4]

Although the discussion of characteristics of assessment may seem to focus on small systems (individuals, families, and small groups), the same characteristics apply to larger system (organizational and community) assessment. Because individuals, families, and small groups are subsystems of large systems, any assessment of a large system involves assessing the subsystems. The schema provided in Table 10.1 in Chapter 10 provides a framework for large system assessments. This schema should, of course, be adapted and individualized depending on the particular system and the understanding needed for the specific service at hand. It is also used to assess the community portion of the ecosystem when working with families, groups, organizations, or neighborhoods. The generalist social worker must have knowledge and skill in assessing both large and small systems.

Values are very influential in the decision-making process. Our perceptions and thinking are affected by our values, which influence how much of a situation and what parts of a situation we perceive. We tend to screen out that which is not congruent with our values or our thinking. Because of our biases about how things should be, we may miss the unfamiliar or the different. In particular, the perception of what constitutes strength may be very different in various cultures. When working with people from different backgrounds, it is particularly important for the worker to be aware of how her values influence her decisions. Interpretations of meaning from the worker's value perspective are often invalid from the client's perspective.

For example, a worker who adopts a personality theory emphasizing the individual may have difficulty working with a client who is Native American and whose orientation is toward the extended family and the tribe. The worker might determine that the client is not being given appropriate opportunities for self-determination, whereas the client might feel the worker is overlooking the client's responsibilities to family and tribe. The worker would be viewing the situation through her value perspective, which considers individual rights to be of prime importance. The client would be viewing self-determination as irrelevant and be more concerned with how he could better the lot of the collective group. Some resolution of such value-driven difference must take place before a worker and client can work productively together.

Harriet A. Feiner and Harriet Katz have pointed out how deeply held beliefs relating to women and family structure influence the judgments that are made in practice situations.[5] They note that commonly held myths, such as that women should not compete with men and women should assume the nurturing role, can be detrimental when working with female clients who are struggling to become independent individuals.

Decision making is an important ingredient in professional judgment. Judgments are decisions based on reason and evidence, with the goal of identifying what is a fact, what is an assumption, and what is an inference. The influence that values may have on assumptions and inferences is then considered and perceptions are analyzed.

In applying a knowledge base to explanations, it is important to check that the appropriate knowledge has been chosen. Florence Hollis has identified the following three criteria for choosing knowledge for social work education.[6] These criteria can also be used in considering knowledge for application to specific practice situations.

1. *The choice should be related to the phenomena being assessed and the situation being considered.* In working with a small task group, it would be inappropriate to use knowledge about groups that has been developed through work with a therapeutic group in a mental health situation unless that knowledge has been tested with the task group. (A task group is formed to accomplish a specific task, as contrasted with a group in which treatment issues are of prime importance.)

2. *The choice should be related to whether or not the knowledge is useful in a social work context.* Social work takes the view of the human situation that people are self-determining. Thus, knowledge that is deterministic in nature is not appropriate for social work because it provides little hope for change. Determinism negates the idea that people have choices and that by making different choices they can more adequately deal with situations and problems. Without hope for change or the possibility of choice, the social work process is unworkable.

3. *Consideration should be given to the nature of the power the knowledge possesses.* Knowledge developed from working with a small sample in one situation does not have the power that knowledge developed by testing a hypothesis under different circumstances with a large sample does. In other words, what has worked with one client may not work with another client, because the worker may fail to take into consideration the power of the knowledge being used.

Choices need to be made with the client's needs, preferences, and strengths as a primary consideration. Principles that can be used when making judgments in assessment include:

1. *Individualization*—Each person and system in a situation is different. In order to assess effectively, the unique aspects of the system need to be identified and understood. This understanding should be derived primarily from the client system.

2. *Participation*—Client participation in the assessment process is an important means of developing an assessment that recognizes the client's needs and preferences. Further, it is extremely difficult to assess client strengths without client participation in some manner.

3. *Human development*—Assessment recognizes the developmental process of an individual and a social system as a means to further the understanding of that person or system. One also needs to be aware of the impact of cultural and ethnic influences on developmental stages.

4. *Human diversity*—Recognition of the diverse aspects of individuals, systems, and cultural groups is another important component of assessment. This recognition should take into account socialization processes and perceptions of strength that are unique to various populations.

5. *Purposeful behavior*—Recognition that all behavior is purposeful leads to a search for understanding of the underlying meanings of behavior in the assessment process.

6. *Systemic transactions*—The assessment process identifies stressful and energizing life transactions, adaptive and maladapative interpersonal processes, and environmental responsiveness and unresponsiveness when seeking understanding of persons in situations.

7. *Strengths and resources*—Identification and acknowledgment of the strengths and positive attributes of clients and their environments are critical.

Through using the principles of individualization, participation, human development, human diversity, purposeful behavior, systemic transactions, and strengths and resources, the worker identifies with the client, the client's needs, and the client's preferences about what needs to be done. This, combined with an awareness of value influences and an appropriate choice of the knowledge to apply, leads to an assessment that yields a valid understanding of client in situation that is useful for planning intervention. Mary K. Rodwell, in presenting a model for assessment based on the naturalistic paradigm of research, describes a model similar to the one discussed in this chapter when she states, "The naturalistic framework frees social work to reach a deeper understanding of person-situation through a holistic assessment style and promotes a sophisticated inquiry into human relationships with social and physical environments."[7]

Case Example

A school social worker requests that Mrs. P, a Hispanic woman, meet with her. Of her three school-age children, two have school-related needs. Juan, age 10, is not performing up to his capacity and is displaying inappropriate behavior in the classroom. Angela, age 6, has excessive absences and gives the excuse that she is staying with her aunt. Jose, age 8, seems to be doing well. He is seen as a bright, well-adjusted child. The worker knows that the children's father died very suddenly about six months ago. In using the principles of assessment the worker:

1. *Individualizes*—Although she knows the children's needs may relate to stress from the father's death and the need for reorganization in the family, she also knows that the impact on this family is felt uniquely. She already is aware that the three children seem to be reacting in quite different ways. She wants to find out if there are other stresses that may be contributing to the situation. She is also aware that the Hispanic male head of household generally retains a great deal of power and control over the organization of the family. Loss of the husband and father in this case may represent the potential for major familial disorganization.

2. *Allows for client participation*—The worker asks Mrs. P to discuss the situation as she sees it. She also questions Mrs. P about the areas that are not clear. The worker is careful to find out from Mrs. P what kind of help she would like. She discovers that Mrs. P is overwhelmed by her responsibility for the family. She is working outside the home for the first time, feels guilty about neglecting her children, and needs to be able to grieve her husband's death while assuming many new responsibilities. The worker discovers that Mr. P had made most of the major decisions in the family and prided himself on his ability to care for them.

The worker also interviews each of the children, after receiving the mother's permission, to discover each child's perception of the situation. Angela has a great deal of difficulty talking about her absences from school. She becomes teary when the worker tries to draw out her feelings about her father's death and says she does not want to talk about it. When the worker suggests she must like her aunt a great deal, Angela smiles. The worker probes a bit to find out why. Angela finally quietly says that her aunt plays with her and takes care of her. The worker then says she wonders if Angela misses someone to play with her at home. Angela again withdraws and becomes restless. The worker decides not to probe further at this time.

In the interview with Jose, the worker asks how he sees things at home since his father's death. Jose says that his mother always seems either busy or sad and that she has so much to do now. He believes his mother misses his father a great deal, as he does. He tries to help his mother by "being good." He also says he wishes his brother would stop causing her so much trouble. When the worker asks what he means by this, he talks about how Juan seems to pick fights with everyone. He says he tries to stay out of Juan's way.

Juan proves to be difficult to interview. He ignores the worker's questions. Finally he tells her that it is none of her business. She assures him that she is interested in helping his mother and wants to know how he feels. As he still refuses to talk, she decides to terminate the interview.

3. *Considers human development*—Each member of the family is considered in relation to his or her developmental stage. Mrs. P (Maria), age 30, seems to still be in the Intimacy vs. Isolation stage of development. (See Table 6.1 in Chapter 6.) During her marriage she seemed to have almost completed this stage, but the death of her husband has upset this resolution and thrown her into a state of isolation. She has also lost her identity as a wife and has returned to the Identity vs. Role Confusion stage and to consider who she is as a person in her new state of widowhood and wage earner. There also appears to be no male in the immediate or extended family to assume the role of "head of household," a role that in Mrs. P's culture is traditionally carried by a man.

The three children are all in the Industry vs. Inferiority stage, but each is having different experiences in this stage. Six-year-old Angela is just moving into the stage, and her reaction to the death of her father is to cling more closely to her mother. The worker knows that Angela's situation needs careful consideration so that she does not regress and develop feelings of inferiority, thus endangering her ability to develop the skills she needs to function independently. Jose, 8, seems to be progressing through this stage in good fashion. He feels good about himself and is developing the needed skills, but he too may need help with the loss of his father.

Ten-year-old Juan is not doing so well, certainly a reaction, at least in part, to the death of his father, with whom he spent a great deal of time. But as she talks with Mrs. P, the worker discovers that Juan has never liked school. He had difficulty learning to read in first grade and still does not read very well. The worker notes that perhaps some testing should be done to find out the nature of the difficulty. Juan may also feel some anxiety about being the oldest male left in the family and may feel a need to fill the head-of-household role, despite his age.

The family development was in the stage of individualization of family members versus pseudomutual organization at the time the father died (see Chapter 7). His death not only upset the steady state of the family system, but it also removed an important source of support for both mother and Juan and forced the family to redefine itself without a male adult to assume the significant role of "head of household." This family is in danger of moving toward a pseudomutual organization.

4. *Considers human diversity*—This is a Hispanic, lower-middle-class family that seems to have no family member present who can assume the head-of-household role, which is traditionally filled by an adult male. The family also appears to have no significant religious ties. Important considerations are that this is a single-parent, Hispanic family that has no significant adult male in either the immediate or extended family on which the family can rely.

(continued)

Case Example   Continued

5. *Considers purposeful behavior*—The worker knows that both Angela's and Juan's behavior is purposeful and at least in part related to their reactions to the death of their father. Angela is probably clinging to her mother and her aunt because she is afraid she might also lose them. At this stage of her development her fears take the form of not wanting them out of her sight. Thus, she needs help in understanding that they will not intentionally leave her and that she will be cared for. Juan, however, is reacting to broken relationships and problematic behavior of important females in his environment (his mother, who would like him to become the man of the house to meet her needs, and his frustrated teacher). In the companionship of a group of boys, he can feel "free and male." To be accepted by this group he must participate in their sometimes antisocial behavior. He needs an alternative way to develop his maleness through positive relationships with male figures. Although Jose is not displaying any negative behaviors, he too may be reacting to his father's death by being too good. His need for help in dealing with his loss should also be explored.

6. *Considers systemic transactions*—At least a part of the difficulty in this family is due to the death of the father. This stress has impacted the mother and thus lessened her parenting capacity. Stress that was already present in the school situation for Juan has been exacerbated by the new stress.

7. *Identifies strengths and resources*—Mrs. P is very concerned about her children and wants to meet their needs. She has been able to obtain outside employment, despite the fact that this goes against her perception of being a "good mother." She is aware that her children are responding in a different manner to the loss of their father. She seems to be accepting of help. The aunt can also be considered another concerned adult and thus a resource for both the mother and the children. The family relationships seem to have been positive, for the most part, and the memories of the father are good ones.

The Use of the Change Process in Assessment

There are two ways the worker uses the change process in the assessment activities of the helping process. First, the worker uses the early steps of the change process with the client as they work together at the task of assessing the client's situation. The steps of the process (see Chapter 4) used in the assessment phase are:

1. Preliminary statement of the concern or need
2. Statement of preliminary assumptions about the nature of the concern or need
3. Statement of preliminary assumptions about strengths and resources in the ecosystem
4. Selection and collection of information
5. Analysis of information available

The worker must decide how the client is to be involved in the change process. This decision depends in part on how much energy and desire the client has for working on the situation. The client's involvement hinges on her capacity, both cognitive and emotional, to work. For example, in a crisis situation, when the need for action is great and when the client is already overwhelmed, the worker will take a more active role in the work than in a situation in which there is less pressure for an early solution. It is not that the client in acute crisis is not involved in resolving the crisis; rather, it is a matter of how the worker involves the client and to what extent the process is made explicit to the client. Teaching the change process can be a strategy for involving the client.

Another use of the change process by the worker is as a means of developing an assessment. This assessment is checked out with the client. This use will be discussed in the remainder of this chapter. The worker must develop skill in problem solving before using the process with or attempting to teach the process to clients.

A difficult task in the change process is the specification of the need or concern. The preliminary statement is often the need or concern the client system brings to the helping situation. Based on material discussed in the first few contacts with the client, the worker may realize that the presenting need is not the actual need. As the worker clarifies the reasons for formulating the preliminary need or concern, the underlying assumptions about the nature of the need or concern become more explicit. Identification of theoretical knowledge used in thinking about client in situation is another way in which assumptions become explicit. As assumptions are made explicit, it is possible to identify information needed to verify the preliminary formulation of the need or concern and to restate it if necessary. The need to be addressed is formulated after an understanding of client in situation is developed and after the available information has been analyzed.

Formulation of the need or concern is the basis for planning and assessment. Planning and action can be enhanced by thorough and appropriate formulation of the need or concern. Three steps of formulating the need or concern are (1) identification of need, (2) identification of blocks to need fulfillment, and (3) formulation of the need in terms of removing the blocks to need fulfillment. It should also be remembered that the needs that concern the social worker are those that relate to social functioning and that planned change needs to build on existing strengths and actual or potential resources in the client and his ecosystem.

Identification of Need

The first source of material for identifying need is how the client tells his story. The worker not only listens to the verbal content but also looks for nonverbal communication. The pronouns and words used, the tense of verbs, the tone and inflection all give clues to the meaning of the need. The worker also can note what is not said, what is omitted.

The skillful worker often has hunches about what is needed. These hunches are part of the art of social work, the creative nature of the work. Hunches are very useful, but they should be checked out with the client or the system before they are given the power of fact. Hunches are generally based on the worker's experiences rather than the client's; it is therefore important to evaluate these ideas in light of the client's reality before sharing them verbally with the client.

As the worker begins to identify the client's need by using the material provided by the client, hunches or ideas that derive from the knowledge base, and information available to the worker from other sources, other systems significant to the situation can be identified. The needs of these systems in relation to the situation being considered should also be identified. Systems that are significant to the situation are those that are affected by the lack of need fulfillment, those that impact the situation, and those that may have resources for meeting the need.

One of the areas that warrants attention is the agency and the service delivery system. If the function of the agency does not include services that can enable the client to fulfill the identified need or needs, the client should be made aware of this. The nature of the service delivery system is sometimes an important factor in the lack of need fulfillment.

When working with families, it is important to let members tell their own stories, without interruption from other family members. There is a tendency of family members, and sometimes of the worker, to identify the "problem" as embedded in one person rather than in the family system itself. It can be difficult for some members to say what they need without demanding change from other members. Thus, it is important for the worker to help individuals identify their needs without blaming or accusing others in the family. For example, a worker might help a child say that he needs to feel that his parents think he's special, rather than say that his parents often criticize him.

Identification of Blocks to Need Fulfillment

Once the need is identified, it is then possible to consider why that need is not being fulfilled. The social worker's past experience, values, and theoretical framework lead to assumptions about the reasons for the blockage. These preliminary assumptions must be checked.

Additional information about the client and the situation may be needed. The client and the significant systems should be given an opportunity to provide their points of view. Written materials such as case records or descriptions of social systems involved may be useful.

From an ecosystems strengths perspective, the location of the blockage is sought in the relationships among the significant systems. In this way, the needs of all systems are recognized and the problem is not considered the responsibility of just one system but is seen as interactive in nature. This is particularly critical when working with families. Families tend to have an "identified client" and resist the idea that blockages come from the family members' interactions.

Carel Germain and Alex Gitterman have identified three situations that seem likely to lead to problems in social functioning: (1) stressful life transitions, (2) communication and relationship difficulties, and (3) environmental unresponsiveness.[8] Assessment of client in situation to see if one of these conditions exists is one means of determining the nature of the blockage of need fulfillment.

Stressful life transitions can result from difficulties in carrying out the tasks of the developmental stages of individuals and other social systems. Thus, the assessment must be concerned with identifying the developmental stage as well as the tasks that are not being carried out. Difficulties may result from lack of opportunity, including opportunity to fulfill tasks in ways congruent with one's cultural group (recognition of human diversity).

Another potentially stressful life transition is status change. This includes such events as becoming a widow or widower, becoming unemployed, graduation from or dropping out of school, and becoming part of the work force. Change of status creates new role demands on people. Sometimes there has been no preparation for these demands. The widow with young children who returns to the work force confronts not only the demands of being a single parent and helping the family adapt to the loss of a father but also the demands of a job. Demands of the single-parent role and the work role may conflict or be overwhelming and thus cause stress.

Closely related to stressful situations are crisis situations. When change is so great that persons and systems cannot cope and maintain a steady state, a crisis can result. The need in such a situation is not only for a resolution of the situation but also for the system to regain its steady state in such a manner that it can meet the expectations of its environment.

Other social-functioning difficulties develop because a person or social system is not effectively communicating with or relating to other people and social systems. Some people from diverse cultures have considerable difficulty relating to the institutions of society. For example, a school's lack of awareness of the needs of children from diverse cultures can aggravate the inability of diverse parents to relate to the school and can result in unmet developmental needs of the children. The individual or family may not be able to use existing resources or they may not even know about them. Also the institution may not be able to identify the strengths of the individual or family because of lack of understanding of cultural factors. The underlying issue is lack of accurate communication, which can result in relationship difficulties.

The needs of children from diverse cultures can also result from the school's unresponsiveness to their needs. Environmental unresponsiveness is a third cause of stress and coping failure. Environmental unresponsiveness can take two forms: failure to provide the needed service or failure to provide the needed service in a manner in which it can be used by the diverse client. Examples of the latter failure include unrealistic expectations of the client on the part of the social worker, providing the service in a way that requires the client to violate cultural values and norms, and expecting clients to function with ease in a culturally foreign milieu.

Blocks to need fulfillment in families often arise from conflicting developmental stages, life transitions of family members, or status change. These events tend to upset the homeostasis of the unit, leading to impaired communication. There is often considerable energy expended in trying to "force" members to conform to previous behaviors in order to achieve the former steady state. For example, a child who reaches adolescence may keep her bedroom door closed, resist going on family outings, and generally act embarrassed about her parents. Parents who are unaware of these normal adolescent behaviors may view their daughter's changes as threatening to the family unit and attempt to force her to conform to previous behaviors they found more desirable and acceptable. Communication difficulties can arise from members not understanding others' needs or what the family must do to restore or maintain balance within the system and still acknowledge members' rights.

Formulation of the Concern or Need

Once the blockage to the need is identified, it is possible to formulate the concern. Formulation of the need or concern considers the need that is not being fulfilled, the block or blocks to the fulfillment of that need, and factors contributing to the block. It is important to be as specific as possible while still recognizing the transactional nature of social functioning.

The specification of need may be made in several ways. It may be a demonstration that a concrete resource or service is lacking, such as sufficient income to meet the needs of a nutritious diet or health care. Need can also be specified in terms of psychosocial development needs. An example would be a physically challenged ten-year-old child who does not have the opportunity to develop daily living skills. This might occur because of lack of understanding of the child's need to feel competent or because the mother compensates for her guilt over the child's condition by "overcaring." Need can also be specified in terms of inadequate role fulfillment in the realms of parenting, marriage, or work or in terms of difficulty in life transitions. Another way of specifying need is in terms of relationships among people and social systems. It is also the specification used when working with organizations and communities.

The next step in formulating the concern or need is a statement about what seems to be blocking the need fulfillment, including the recognition of relationships with potential resources. This statement needs to be clearly worded and must recognize the transactional aspects of the blockage.

To illustrate the formulation of the concern or need, the example of Mrs. P, the Hispanic widow with three school-age children, can be used. The need is a life-transition need arising from her need to grieve and to cope with the demands of work and parenting as a single parent without extended family members to fill vacated roles. The block is created by feeling overwhelmed by grief along with conflicting demands in carrying out the two roles. One of the children is in trouble in school; another does not want to go to school. The school demands that the client take time off from her job for conferences. She is employed in a low-paying secretarial job, and her employer is threatening to fire her for taking too much time off the job. When the cause of the blockage is examined, several factors seem to affect her ability to cope:

1. Since it has only been six months since her husband's death, she is still overwhelmed with grief.
2. She needs to know how to manage the family finances, which contributes to her tension and crankiness with the children.
3. She needs to know how to fill the role of the single parent. She appears overly demanding of herself and feels sorry for her children.
4. Because of financial deficiencies, she does not have adequate childcare.
5. She needs to know about resources available to her.
6. She needs skills that will lead to a higher-paying job.
7. One son, the oldest child, misses his father and is very difficult to manage. He also appears to need a significant male figure in his life.
8. The youngest child, a daughter, is not happy with the after-school babysitter who lives in the neighborhood. When she stays home from school, she is taken to her aunt's home across town, where she is happy.
9. The school is overcrowded and needs more resources to deal with children who are having difficulties.
10. The family does not appear to have any connection with the larger Hispanic community.

The source of a blockage may be in attitudes and values, knowledge and understanding, behavior, coping skills, role overload, environmental expectations, ignorance of available resources, or lack of usable resources. Usually the source of blockage is not just one but a combination of circumstances; this combination causes stress and blocks need fulfillment. Formulation of the concern or need should recognize this complexity in stating need and specifying blockage to need fulfillment. The change process is particularly useful in formulating the concern or need.

When working in a psychiatric setting, the classification of *DSM-IV* (*Diagnostic and Statistical Manual of Mental Disorders of the American Psychiatric Association,* 1994) may be used. Social workers have also developed a variety of classifications of problems and needs. Some social workers believe that the use of classifications leads to stereotyping and labeling and interferes with individualized assessments.[9]

Some believe that the use of a problem focus in assessment leads to individualistic assessment rather than social-environmental explanations, which can in turn lead to "blaming the victim." The focus on a problem creates the illusion of a solution or remedy that is based on individual change.[10]

Identifying resources and strengths in the collection and analysis of data is an important part of the assessment process. Instead of focusing on barriers to solutions, assessments that identify strengths, environmental resources, and ways in which clients have met needs in the past may help clients appreciate their own resources and abilities. This focus is increasingly important in today's managed care settings or when resources are limited. In many instances workers can only initiate the change process and then hope that the client system will continue work after services have been terminated.

This part of the assessment also depends on the situational and environmental factors involved. These factors may be a source of the need, may support the continuance of the problematic situation, or may be reframed as assets in the client system's environment.

Case Example

The needs of the P family can be formulated in different ways for the various members of the family. It can be seen as a widow not having the opportunity to properly grieve because of demands from family and job. It can be seen as a widow who needs knowledge to manage the family finances. It can be seen as a widow who needs skills necessary for obtaining employment that will adequately support the family. Alternatively, the need can be related to the oldest son and formulated as the son acting out his anger over his father's death. Or the need can be related to the daughter's not receiving care from her mother and babysitter. Alternatively, the need can be formulated relative to the total family. In this case it can be seen as an upset in family organization and functioning caused by the death of the father and what this loss represents to a family in the Hispanic culture. The need can also be formulated as the family needing the resources to function. The way the need is ultimately formulated will depend on which system is seen as the client and what is considered the system's most pressing need.

Preliminary Assumptions about the Nature of the Concern or Need

As the worker and the client proceed through the assessment phase, there are assumptions about the person in environment that play an important role in focusing the assessment. At the outset of assessment, the worker determines (1) what information is necessary to understand the situation and (2) what resources are available to meet the needs of the client and his ecosystem. In order to accomplish the first, the worker must make some assumptions about the nature of the concern or need. She uses her knowledge of human behavior in the social environment, of human development and diversity, and of Maslow's and Towle's systems of identifying needs to determine the underlying nature of the needs. For example, using Maslow's hierarchy, are the needs related to basic needs, such as food, clothing, shelter, or health care? Is the need related to safety and security, socialization, self-esteem, self-actualization, and/or cognitive understanding?[11] Using Towle's elements of need, does the need represent a need for emotional and intellectual growth, relationships, and/or spiritual well-being?[12]

As a next step, the worker combines knowledge and creativity in speculating about what might be creating the need in the specific situation. In the case example, the worker might assume that Mrs. P is overwhelmed by grief and may be looking for a way to honor the memory of her husband while also coping with the stress of new and unfamiliar roles. The worker might assume that Juan's behavior at school has been exacerbated by his father's death, but that he likely would have experienced some difficulties even if his father had not died, since there had been earlier incidents. The worker might assume that Angela's clinging to her mother represents a fear of losing her (safety and security). She might assume that Jose is stuck in the bargaining stage of the grief process and trying to be good as a way of defending against his fear that the loss of his father is punishment for having been bad. The worker could assume that the death of the father has resulted in family disintegration and has strained the ability of the family to cope with everyday stress.

Preliminary Assumptions about Potential Strengths and Resources in the Ecosystem

Moving to the third step in the process, the worker might speculate about what would bring about the changes necessary to meet the needs. She begins by identifying potential strengths, abilities, assets, capacities, and resources within the client system and his ecosystem. How does the person, family, group, organization, or community meet its needs? What is going well? What works now or has worked in the past? How does the present circumstance represent a deviation from the client system's typical pattern of meeting needs? The worker then formulates some assumptions about what is needed to develop, maintain, or restore the ecosystem to a steady state in which needs are met on a mutually satisfying basis. In the case of the P family, these assumptions might be formulated as follows:

1. Each family member is capable of expressing grief and adjusting to life without Mr. P.
2. Mrs. P will be able to fulfill her new roles if she has the necessary knowledge along with a support system. She is employed and is supporting the family.
3. Juan is intelligent and will have success at school if he has his academic needs met.
4. Jose is a good student and does well in school.
5. Angela loves her aunt and feels safe and secure when she is with her.
6. The family members love each other and have the capacity to meet each other's needs.
7. Community resources are available to assist the family with childcare, academic needs, counseling, etc.

In this part of the change process, the worker tries to be realistic while still allowing herself to speculate about what might be possible. One question that is invaluable in working with any size client system is: What would it take to meet this need? This leads the worker away from looking at limitations and deficits and toward a consideration of possibilities.

Selection and Collection of Information

The assumptions that are made about the nature of the needs and the strengths and resources available are important to setting the stage for collecting information. The worker should not collect information without a purpose. The two main reasons for having information should be to assist the client in meeting his needs and to meet the bureaucratic demands of the agency or regulatory bodies. In the latter case, certain information may be collected to identify clients, to bill insurance or other third-party payment systems, to meet eligibility criteria, to meet basic standards of accepted professional practice, and so on. Care should be taken that information is gathered in a way that respects the client's right to confidentiality. This will be discussed further in Chapter 15.

In order to achieve a thorough understanding of the situation, it is useful if the worker asks herself what she knows about who, what, where, when, and how. These five areas of questioning are typically used by reporters when they are covering a story. They are also useful to the social worker to ensure that she has covered all of the aspects of the situation. A sixth area relates to the question "Why," but this will be covered in the analysis portion of the process.

Based on the assumptions made, the worker is able to select the information needed to understand the situation and to lay the groundwork for developing a plan to meet the needs of the client and his ecosystem. Using the various schema presented in Part Two of the text, the worker selects relevant parts of each schema, depending on the size of the client system and the parts of the ecosystem being considered. For example, in working with individuals, the Schema for Development of a Social History: Individual (see Table 7.1) is used as an overall guideline. Relevant parts of the family history schema (see Table 7.3) are used as they relate to understanding the person's interactions with his family, if this is important to understanding the situation and meeting the client's need. Relevant parts of the community schema (see Table 8.1) are used to assess the systems in the community that are impinging on the situation or that might be accessed in meeting the need.

Analysis of the Information Available

There are four general areas the worker must analyze as the work proceeds: (1) what the worker understands about the situation given what is known, (2) what changes are needed given what is known, (3) what further information is needed to better understand the situation, and (4) what further information is needed to bring about successful change.

As the worker analyzes these four areas, she uses critical thinking along with her knowledge base to gain insight into the client and her ecosystem. Throughout the process, she checks out her analysis with the client and with relevant parts of her ecosystem. Paraphrasing and summarizing are particularly valuable in this process. The worker asks the client (or significant person, if it is not the client) if her perceptions about the situation are accurate and if there are other aspects that the client is aware of that might be important. In the case example, the worker might say, "Mrs. P, it appears to me that it is very important to you that you honor the memory of your husband in some way. Is that right?" She might follow up by asking, "Is there anything else you can tell me about how you feel about remembering your husband?"

The worker also asks the client for her input into what changes might be needed and how feasible they might be. A good question to ask is: "What would you like to see happen that would meet your needs in this situation?" Or: "If you woke up tomorrow and your needs were being met in this situation, what would it look like?"

The worker focuses on understanding the strengths and resources within the client and the ecosystem. This includes understanding the transactions that are taking place. As discussed earlier, the types of exchanges that occur among systems involve matter, energy, and information. In analyzing a situation, the worker needs to know what matter is needed and where it comes from. For instance, how does the family obtain food or clothing? Who is involved? What is obtained? Where, when, and how is it obtained? In terms of energy, the worker might consider which relationships the client finds energizing and which drain energy. In terms of information, using the case example, the worker might need to know what information the family has about the grief process. Who or what is the source of that information? Where and when did the family receive it? How does the information influence the way in which the family is grieving? What other information might the family need? Who might they get it from? Where, when, and how might they get it?

Assessment of Small Groups

There are two major types of assessment needed for small groups: product and process. Assessment as product includes collecting and organizing data on each potential group member prior to beginning the group. This involves utilizing the steps in the change process described earlier in this chapter. Data collected are similar to those described above, although the emphasis is on assessing the individual's "fit" with both the group's purpose and with other potential members. The worker who is forming a small group must conduct an individual assessment from two viewpoints at the same time: (1) What are the issues, needs, concerns, and strengths of the individual being interviewed? (2) How would this individual fit with the other potential group members and the overall purpose of the group?

Although the purpose of the group will influence member selection, it is generally desirable to have members who are somewhat similar in socioeconomic status, age, and level of concern regarding the group's purpose. An ethnic, cultural, and gender balance can also be important, again depending on the overall goals of the group. Because in small groups members learn from and use each other's strengths, diversity in this area can be an asset for group functioning. Diversity in members' experiences can also be helpful if the disparity is not too great, since members can learn from one another about how to deal with situations relevant to the purpose of the group. It is also important to determine how potential members might interact with others in a group setting and what role they might be expected to assume. Communication skills, social skills, and developmental level must also be assessed in light of potential group membership.

There are some instances in which commonalities rather than diversity, and diversity rather than commonalities, are preferred. For example, a group for people who have been sexually abused would probably function better if all members are of the same sex. A group for people who are dealing with the death of a family member, however, may benefit from members who are in various stages of the grieving process. Again, the purpose of the group determines the composition of its members.

Once the group has begun, group assessment skills may include utilization of the tools described in Chapter 10, such as "A Schema for the Study of the Small Group as a Social System" (Table 10.1) and the sociogram depicted in Figure 10.1. These provide information about the group at a particular point in time and may contribute to an understanding of group dynamics or indicate when the group leader should intervene. Ongoing periodic assessment of members' progress and interactions, as well as group dynamics, will also help the worker shape or reshape the structure and intent of the group.

Transactional Assessment

The transactional nature of human interaction is complex, and this complexity can cause difficulties in assessment. Transactional assessment depends to a great extent on the worker's creativity and ability to look at a complex situation and bring order and meaning to that complexity. Transactional assessment is particularly useful when considering possible plans of action and the effect those plans might have on the various systems involved in the situation of concern.

Some frameworks for transactional assessment have begun to appear. An example is the ecosystems framework developed by Paula Allen-Meares and Bruce A. Lane. They identify variables to be considered and place them in a three-dimensional framework that consists of kinds of data, data source, and the system to which the data are related. Examination of the framework leads to the conclusion that in order to obtain the breadth of understanding needed for assessment, it is important to collect and place a wide variety of data in a framework that shows some relationship among the data.[13]

In considering the nature of transactional assessment, the generalist social worker needs tools for assessing the functioning, needs, and concerns of individuals, families, small groups, organizations, and communities. Three tools can be useful in transactional assessment: (1) using a dual perspective, (2) mapping, and (3) social support network analysis. The use of genograms, as discussed in Chapter 6, is another transactional assessment technique.

The Dual Perspective

Dolores Norton has developed the concept of **dual perspective** to depict the plight of many minority people. The dual perspective is "a conscious and systematic process of perceiving, understanding, and comparing simultaneously the values, attitudes, and behavior of the larger social system with those of the client's immediate family and community system."[14] This conceptualization holds that every individual is a part of two systems: (1) a societal system, which functions within the norms and values of the dominant groups within society, and (2) a smaller system, which functions in a person's immediate environment. This latter system can be the cultural system. When the two systems are not congruent in terms of norms, values, expectations, and ways of functioning, conflicting expectations can lead to misunderstanding among individuals, families, and cultural groups.

In making an assessment from the dual perspective, the worker looks for points of difference, especially for conflicting expectations between the two systems. The degree of difference and the number of characteristics that are different are important factors in judging the incongruity between the systems. Also important is how the systems perceive the difference and how the difference affects their functioning. This kind of an assessment calls not just for a general intellectual understanding of a specific cultural group, but also for an understanding of the specific, immediate environmental system of the person or group of persons. The dual perspective is a particularly useful tool in assessing the transactions of any specific cultural group or of those from a minority culture within the larger, dominant society.

When dealing with clients and situations having values, culture, and ways of functioning different from the dominant culture, it seems wise to use a dual perspective approach as a part of the assessment process. Some determination of the extent and impact of the difference on individuals and systems should be made. When the difference is great or the impact significant, it is important to determine motivations, resistances, and appropriate interventive points to bring about adjustments in dominant social systems that impact the situation or affect need fulfillment. It is also important to determine with clients if there are coping mechanisms that would be helpful in situations in which incongruencies exist between the two systems.

Use of the dual perspective can be illustrated by considering the characteristics of Puerto Rican culture. Sonia Ghali has identified these as an extended family structure with kinship through godparents; the importance of virginity for an unmarried woman; an emphasis on individualism and inner integrity; a fatalistic, submissive-passive approach to life situations; use of family, friends, and neighbors as the first sources of help; high respect for the advice of pastors and teachers of their own group; use of spiritualism; expectation that helping persons will use authority; belief in mysticism; use of the Spanish language; and an expectation that the wealthy will be paternalistic and benevolent toward the poor.[15] It is, of course, important to determine if these characteristics hold true for a particular Puerto Rican client. When these characteristics are compared with the characteristics of

ə majority society, a number of incongruities become apparent, including differ-
t language, different expectations about respect, different usage of expression,
and so on. An assessment of the incongruities gives an understanding of the transactional influences on a Puerto Rican client.

Mapping

Mapping is a tool for pictorially representing the relationships of the significant
parts of any situation. (See Figure 11.1 in the following case example.) **Mapping** is
a variation of the sociogram discussed in Chapter 10. First, the client or focal point
of a situation is depicted with a circle. If this focal point is a multiperson system,
the relationships of the person in that system are shown in the circle just as they
are in the sociogram.

The other significant systems in the situation are placed around the circle
representing the focal system. Various kinds of relationships are drawn, noting
which individual in the focal system carries the relationship to these systems.[16]

Mapping can also be useful in assessing the role structure of a situation. The
map can be examined for incongruities in role expectations, either within the focal
system or with systems in the environment of that focal system. The map can be
examined for role overloads and for missing roles.

Use of mapping makes apparent the transactional nature of the situation. It
can also be useful in identifying strengths and resources available to the helping
situation. Mapping is particularly helpful in understanding the relationships
among the parts of an organizational or community system. It also can be used to
depict the relationships among key persons in these larger systems.

Case Example

Mapping yields several understandings about the P family and its transactions.
(See Figure 11.1.)

1. The mother seems to have only one supportive relationship, her sister. (Relationships with children and work ask more of her than they give.) She seems to be surrounded by negative, problematic, and broken relationships.
2. The oldest son, who was very close to his father, is also surrounded by problematic, negative, and broken relationships. There is concern that as the oldest male in
   this Hispanic family he may feel he needs to replace his father.
3. The daughter has a strong relationship with the mother and a good relationship
   with her aunt. Her relationships to the school and to the babysitter are negative.
   This relationship pattern may hold an answer to the school problem. It may be that
   the strong relationship to the mother and the dislike of the babysitter create her
   desire to go to her aunt's house rather than to school.
4. The middle son seems to have more positive relationships, and he does not exhibit
   problematic behavior.

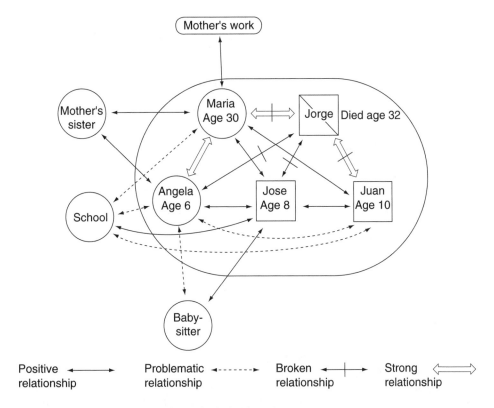

FIGURE 11.1 Map of a Family and Their Situation

The P family appears to be overwhelmed with grief over the loss of the husband and father. The members are attempting to handle their grief in their own ways. The results are that the family members feel more distant from each other and are not able to use the family system to alleviate the stress and other feelings. The family has been very resilient thus far in terms of meeting basic needs, with Mrs. P finding work and using some childcare alternatives. However, the emotional needs of family members must be met in order for the family to cope with the new demands they are facing. Assistance with grief work that is culturally sensitive might help the family to maintain the memory of the husband and father while it rebalances itself in terms of roles and responsibilities. Restoring ties with the family's church might help with this process.

Social Support Network Analysis

Closely related to the technique of mapping is the analysis of the social support network of an individual or family. Mapping aids the identification of significant social support resources. A **social support network analysis** helps in specifying the nature of the supports and complements the map in the assessment process.

Elizabeth M. Tracy and James K. Whittaker have developed a Social Network Grid for use in a research project. This grid can also be useful in assessing the social support network of an individual or family. Areas to be considered in such an assessment include the area of life in which the support is given (e.g., work, school, etc.), the kind of support (e.g., concrete, emotional, informational, etc.), how often the support is given, whether the support is critical of or problematic to the support receiver, whether the support is in a reciprocal relationship with the support receiver, the closeness of the support to the support receiver, how often there is contact between the provider and receiver, and how long the receiver has known the support provider.[17]

With the goal of identifying and using resources or social supports that are either available or potentially available to individuals, families, and groups, generalist social workers must develop assessment tools for analysis of social support networks.[18] This is particularly crucial when working with disadvantaged or oppressed populations, since locating, developing, and using support networks are avenues to empowerment. It is increasingly important in a time of managed care and resource constraints to develop practice knowledge in this area.

Needs Assessment

Assessment of a community and its resources, assessment of a group of people, or assessment of a client in a situation may result in the realization that needed resources are not available. Social workers have a responsibility for working toward the development of needed resources. One of the first steps in doing this is carrying out a **needs assessment.** Funding sources usually require that some data relative to the nature and extent of need are available before they are willing to support new projects or programs. Some governmental funding agencies and accreditation bodies also require a needs assessment as part of their ongoing review of programs. In addition, well-designed needs assessments are an excellent means for involving community members, users, and potential users of services in developing awareness of needs in a community.

The assessment can be carried out in several ways. First, general opinions about the service or the need for service can be obtained from various segments of the community, such as service providers, consumers, and community influentials. A major problem with this type of information gathering is that it represents opinions, not hard facts. However, this mechanism can provide information that may not be obtainable through other means. It can be a preliminary step in designing an assessment instrument that captures a complete picture of the problem and can be used to involve the community in the assessment. When obtaining information from service providers, it is important to recognize that they sometimes overlook the fact that some people do not want the services provided by the formal system and are able to meet their needs in other ways.

A second mechanism for needs assessment is to survey current users of service. Often professionals forget that the *I need* perspective is just as important as the *they need* perspective. Individuals and families are more apt to use services they believe are needed. Involving users in needs assessments may provide important information about the design of services. However, it is not always possible for users to articulate their needs, so the mechanism may not provide a complete picture of the need. For example, older people may have some difficulty admitting to need. They may feel that the admission of limitations would force them into a nursing home or to come to grips with the aging process in ways they prefer to avoid.

Another mechanism of determining need is through the use of statistical data. For example, if one community's population figures for the number of persons with disabilities are high compared with other similar-size communities, this would probably indicate a high level of need for services. If a community has a high percentage (compared to similar communities) of older people or people below the poverty level, it is likely that there are needs not being met. The worker must be careful in using statistical data, as the use of this mechanism may lead to assumptions that later prove unfounded.

Usually, in designing a needs assessment it is desirable to use several means for collecting data. Need can be identified in terms of gaps in services, redundancy of services, availability of services to various groups of people, accessibility of services to those who are in need, and usability of service (e.g., is it provided within a framework that can be used by various cultural groups?).

Before designing a needs assessment instrument, it is important to be thoroughly familiar with the community, the need area, and the population to be targeted. Involving community influentials or community organizations can also be very helpful in planning the assessment. These people can help interpret the need for the assessment, give it community sanction, and provide input to its construction; this will make the assessment acceptable to the community and thus result in a greater chance of accurate response. Other social systems significant to the study also need to be identified, as well as all possible data sources. The latter category includes demographic statistical profiles, key informants (those in direct contact with those experiencing problems), consumers of service, individuals experiencing difficulty or having potential for doing so, and the general public. A preliminary statement of the concern or need should be developed at this stage and assumptions about the nature of the concern or need and potential resources stated.

When the needed background information has been gathered, the worker is ready to begin the design of the needs assessment. Decisions must be made about the type of data needed, the individuals who can best provide the information, and the most appropriate means for gathering that information. Information can be gathered in person, by phone interviews, through mailed questionnaires, or through existing data such as agency or census records. Generally, it is wise to develop an instrument that will allow the collection of the same information from each respondent. Information sought may include demographic data, such as race, gender, age, marital status, educational level, and length of residence in the community; perceived problems; where information about services is obtained; factors that hinder the seeking of help; and services needed. The development of the needs assessment design requires creativity to individualize it for the situation.

As the needs assessment design is being developed, two other areas need attention. The first is the development of a publicity campaign. Public knowledge of the assessment and its purpose is necessary if people are to provide accurate information. A publicity campaign can include news releases, television and radio spots, posters, and announcements at meetings and community activities. It can also make use of the community members who have been involved in the development of the needs assessment. These individuals can give sanction and lend credibility to the effort. When considering a needs assessment that will involve the community, it is important to consider timing of the survey. The worker must be aware of other activities going on in the community and plan the assessment for a time when the community has the energy and time to be involved.

Another consideration relates to the confidentiality of information obtained, or the human rights concern. All publicity should indicate how the information obtained will be used, and assurances of confidentiality must be provided. Interviewers must be trained not only in confidentiality issues but also in how to conduct the interview. Often, it is helpful to first test an instrument with a small sample of people representative of those who will be contacted during the assessment. This test case can alert the designer to questions that are problematic and apt to be misinterpreted or not answered. This helps ensure that the outcome of the assessment will be accurate. The evaluation and interpretation of information are part of the assessment design and relate to the particular information. Once this stage has taken place, it is important to share the findings with those who have participated in the assessment. Needs assessment, when properly carried out, is an involved process but an important part of meeting the needs of individuals and families.

Case Example

Sally Jones is an adult services worker in a public social services agency in an area where about 18 percent of the population is over 65 years of age. The agency is concerned about the unmet needs of these older people and has developed a program that involves workers and communities working together to discover unmet needs and develop resources to meet those needs.

Sally has been working for about a year with this community, which has a population of about 5,000. She has already carried out a very thorough community study (see Table 8.1). She knows that it is important to find out if this community recognizes the needs and accepts responsibility for its senior citizens. She has found that there is an active senior citizens' center and several very active women's church groups that are interested in community projects. Because Sally does not live in this community, she needs sanction for the project from the community.

As a first step, Sally makes appointments with the president of the senior citizens' center and the presidents of three church women's groups. She learns these presidents are concerned, and they acknowledge that they have never thought of a formal or systematic means of trying to identify needs. Sally then introduces the idea of a formal needs assessment. She has some guidelines from the state office on carrying out an assessment. She also has some information on what other similar communities have done as a result of their needs assessment, and she shares these findings in each of the interviews. She states her belief that the community could benefit from such a process and asks if the organization each individual represents would be willing to help. Sally could have worked with just one organization, but she knows it will be important to have a broadly based community organization if plans for community projects are to be developed based on the needs assessment. She believes that establishing this broad base early in the process, through involving several groups in the needs assessment, will increase the chances of services being developed.

The group leaders express interest, as long as it does not involve too much time. The guidelines from the state office indicate that one hundred calls to senior citizens and one hundred calls to the general public will provide the information needed. She hopes for a total of twenty volunteers, five from each organization, so that each would only have to make ten phone calls in a two-week period. She also tells the president of the senior citizens' center that she will need some help in identifying those over age 60 in the phone book for the random sampling of that group. The president says they have a meeting in two weeks and asks Sally to come and talk to them about the project.

The first church group president wants to discuss the project with the members and get back to Sally. She does this in a month's time and says they are ready to help. The second church group president says she will have to talk to the pastor and see if he approves of the project, and she will then get back to Sally. She never does and is very evasive when Sally calls her back. Sally does not pursue this group, as she has found another group of ten women in the community who are anxious to be included in the project. The third church group president says that her group is too busy on their own projects to help right now, but she does want to be informed about the results.

The design for this assessment has been developed in the state office. Phone calls are made to a random sample of the general community and to those over age 60 in the community; an instrument has been developed for use with each group. The community sample is asked opinions about need in the community around five areas: loneliness and isolation, ability to care for a home, nutrition, transportation, and activities of daily living. Those over age 60 are asked about their needs in these areas. Respondents are also asked their age, whether they have family living within a thirty-mile radius, and how they would rate their health. Once the surveys are completed, they are sent to the state office for computer tabulation.

Sally goes over this procedure with the group of volunteers and asks if they would add any other questions unique to people living in this community. She explains that this assessment is their attempt to understand their own town and that it needs to reflect what they want to know. She says that any data they collect that are not appropriate for state office analysis will be gone over by her and any of the volunteers that want to help.

When it becomes apparent that community groups will be able to obtain the needed volunteers and when a date for the survey has been set, Sally begins a public relations campaign. This campaign is designed to inform the community of the upcoming survey and its purpose. The use of the information is carefully discussed, including the confidentiality of individual answers and how the findings will be shared with the community through news releases to the local weekly newspaper and public meetings. The campaign also uses announcements at meetings of various organizations.

When all the community respondents have been identified, when the senior citizens have completed their identification of those over age 60 in the community, and when Sally has chosen the random sample to be called, a meeting is held with the volunteers. At this

(continued)

Case Example   Continued

meeting Sally passes out the instrument to be used in collecting data during the phone call. She suggests that the telephone volunteers jot down any remarks or questions that respondents make about needs or present services. She tells the group that after the forms have been sent to the state office for tabulation, they will get together to discuss the experience and the remarks and questions of the respondents. She notes that this information may reveal additional needs in the community and of older persons as well as providing responses to the survey questions. She carefully goes over all details and stresses confidentiality of the information obtained. She discusses how to handle various situations that may be encountered and has the group engage in role-play of the phone call.

Each volunteer is then given ten names to call, with three alternates if they cannot complete the first ten calls. Sally stresses the need to get all the calls completed in a two-week period. She tells the volunteers to be sure to get in touch with her if they have any problems and that she will check with them at the end of a week and collect their forms at the end of two weeks. As a result of Sally's thorough knowledge of the community and her careful planning with community leaders and volunteers, all but five of the calls are completed in the two-week period. Two volunteers agree to complete the remaining calls that one volunteer, with unexpected family stress, could not finish. A month after sending the data to the state office for analysis, Sally receives the results. Sally is aware that the true meaning of the data will only be determined within the context of this specific community. She knows that the volunteers and club officers are the real experts on this community. Thus, she calls a meeting of the involved individuals so that they may begin the work of data analysis to determine the unmet needs of the elderly and move toward deciding what to do about those needs.

Summary

A social work assessment is a picture (however incomplete) made up of all available facts and fit together within a particular frame of reference for a particular purpose. It contains the following elements:

1. Identification of all the entities involved in the situation
2. Development of the needed understanding about each of these entities
3. Arrangement or ordering of these entities in such a manner that the role and relationship structure—the transactional nature in the situation—is seen
4. Identification of the need in the situation and of the blockage to need fulfillment
5. Identification of strengths and resources of individuals and systems present in situations, including previously successful efforts to meet needs
6. Identification of conflicting expectations of cultures in which the systems operate
7. Formulation of the concern or need from a transactional point of view

8. Identification of additional information needed, of the knowledge base to be used to enhance understanding, and of the values operating in the situation
9. Evaluation of the information available
10. Identification of relevant social policy, constraints in the situation, expectations of all involved, and actual and potential resources in the situation
11. Identification of possible impacts of potential change in the situation on all systems involved

Assessment is a core skill for any social worker. Like any other skill, it must be practiced if it is to be developed. Professional interaction and professional helping both are heavily dependent on skill in assessment.

QUESTIONS

1. Review the case example in Chapter 10. Identify all of the information you would seek if you were asked to make an assessment of this situation. What would you use as sources for each piece of information you have identified?

2. Review the material on interviewing in Chapter 9. How do you see the interviewing process used to assess the need or concern and situation with the client?

3. Consider the concept of professional judgment. What are the strengths you now have for operationalizing this concept? What are your current concerns about operationalizing this concept?

4. What is the place of "hunches" or "gut feelings" in the change process?

5. Think of someone you know who comes from a cultural background somewhat diverse from the commonly accepted majority group. Use the dual perspective to assess congruencies and incongruencies between that person's cultural or sustaining system and the societal system. Do you have any suggestions for dealing with incongruencies?

6. Use the mapping technique to develop a picture of some problematic situation of which you are aware. What did you learn from the map that might be of use in resolving the situation?

7. Discuss the advantages of using a strengths perspective rather than only identifying needs and problems in the assessment process.

SUGGESTED READINGS

Allen-Meares, Paula, and Lane, Bruce A. "Grounding Social Work Practice in Theory: Ecosystems." *Social Casework* 68 (November 1987): 315–321.

Anderson, Stephen A., and Sabatelli, Ronald M. *Family Interaction: A Multigenerational Developmental Perspective,* 2nd ed. Boston: Allyn and Bacon, 1999.

Castex, Graciela M. "Providing Services to Hispanic/Latino Populations: Profiles in Diversity." *Social Work* 39 (May 1994): 2882–2896.

Cheung, Kam-fong Monit. "Needs Assessment Experience Among Area Agencies on Aging." *Journal of Gerontological Social Work* 19, 3/4 (1993): 77–93.

Cowger, Charles D. "Assessing Client Strengths: Clinical Assessment for Client Empowerment." *Social Work* 39 (May 1994): 262–268.

Delva-Tauili'ili, Jorge. "Assessment and Prevention of Aggressive Behavior among Youths of Color: Integrating Cultural and Social Factors." *Social Work in Education* 17 (April 1995): 83–91.

DePanfilis, Diane, and Scannapieco, Maria. "Assessing the Safety of Children at Risk of Maltreatment: Decision-Making Models." *Child Welfare* 73 (May–June 1994): 229–245.

Devore, Wynetta, and Schlesinger, Elfriede G. *Ethnic-Sensitive Social Work Practice,* 4th ed. Boston: Allyn and Bacon, 1996.

Drachman, Diane. "Immigration Statuses and Their Influence on Service Provision, Access and Use." *Social Work* 40 (March 1995): 188–197.

Edwards, Richard L., Ed. *Encyclopedia of Social Work,* 19th ed. Washington, DC: NASW Press, 1995 ("Assessment" and "Diagnostic and Statistical Manual of Mental Disorders").

Flores, Maria T., and Carey, Gabrielle. *Family Therapy with Hispanics: Toward Appreciating Diversity.* Boston: Allyn and Bacon, 2000.

Helton, Lonnie R., and Jackson, Maggie. *Social Work Practice with Families: A Diversity Model.* Boston: Allyn and Bacon, 1997.

Hepworth, Dean H., Rooney, Ronald H., and Larsen, Jo Ann. *Direct Social Work Practice: Theory and Skills,* 5th ed. Pacific Grove, CA: Brooks/Cole, 1997 (Chapters 8, 9, 10, and 11).

Logan, Sadye, Freeman, Edith, and McRoy, Ruth. *Social Work Practice with Black Families: A Culturally Specific Perspective.* Boston: Allyn and Bacon, 1990 (Chapters 4, 5, and 6).

Marrow-Howell, Nancy. "Multidimensional Assessment of the Elderly Client." *Families in Society* 73 (September 1992): 395–406.

Mattaini, Mark A. "Contextual Behavior Analysis in the Assessment Process." *Families in Society* 71 (April 1990): 236–245.

Mattaini, Mark A., and Kirk, Stuart A. "Assessing Assessment in Social Work." *Social Work* 36 (May 1991): 260–266.

McPhatter, Anna R. "Assessment Revisited: A Comprehensive Approach to Understanding Family Dynamics." *Families in Society* 72 (January 1991): 11–21.

Meyer, Carol H. *Assessment in Social Work Practice.* New York: Columbia University Press, 1993.

Miley, Karla Krogsrud, O'Melia, Michael, and DuBois, Brenda L. *Social Work Practice: An Empowering Approach,* 2nd ed. Boston: Allyn and Bacon, 1998.

Paquin, Gary W., and Bushoni, Robert J. "Family Treatment Assessment for Novices." *Families in Society* 72 (June 1991): 353–359.

Pardeck, John T. *Social Work Practice: An Ecological Approach,* Westport, CT: Auburn House, 1996.

Ryan, Angela Shen, Ed. *Social Work with Immigrants and Refugees.* New York: Haworth Press, 1992.

Saleeby, Dennis, Ed. *The Strengths Perspective in Social Work Practice,* 2nd ed. New York: Longman, 1997.

Sheafor, Bradford W., Horejsi, Charles R., and Horejsi, Gloria A. *Techniques and Guidelines for Social Work Practice,* 4th ed. Boston: Allyn and Bacon, 2000 (Chapter 12).

Sherraden, Margaret Sherrard, and Martin, Judith Josiah. "Social Work with Immigrants: International Issues in Service Delivery." *International Social Work* 37 (October 1994): 369–384.

Siegel, Larry M., Attkisson, Clifford, and Carson, Linda G. "Need Identification and Program Planning in the Community." In Fred M. Cox, John L. Erlich, Jack Rothman, and John E. Tropman, Eds., *Strategies of Community Organization,* 4th ed. Itasca, IL: F. E. Peacock, 1987 (pp. 71–97).

Toseland, Ronald W., and Rivas, Robert F. *An Introduction to Group Work Practice,* 3rd ed. Boston: Allyn and Bacon, 1998 (Chapter 8).

Tracy, Elizabeth M. "Identifying Social Support Resources of At-Risk Families." *Social Work* 35 (May 1990): 252–258.

Vigilante, Florence Wexler, and Marlick, Mildred D. "Needs-Resource Evaluation in the Assessment Process." *Social Work* 33 (March–April 1988): 101–104.

Weick, Ann, Rapp, Charles, Sullivan, W. Patrick, and Kisthardt, Walter. "A Strengths Perspective for Social Work Practice." *Social Work* 34 (July 1989): 350–354.

Winters, Ken. "Clinical Considerations in the Assessment of Adolescent Chemical Dependency." *Journal of Adolescent Chemical Dependency* 1, 1 (1990): 31–52.

NOTES

1. Max Siporin, *Introduction to Social Work Practice* (New York: Macmillan, 1975), p. 219.

2. Mark A. Mattaini and Stuart A. Kirk, "Assessing Assessment in Social Work," *Social Work* 36 (May 1991): 260–266.

3. Ann Weick, Charles Rapp, W. Patrick Sullivan, and Walter Kisthardt, "A Strengths Perspective for Social Work Practice," *Social Work* 34 (July 1989): 350–354; and Florence Wexler Vigilante and Mildred Maileck, "Needs-Resource Evaluation in the Assessment Process," *Social Work* 33 (March–April 1988): 101–104.

4. Harriet Bartlett, *The Common Base of Social Work Practice* (New York: National Association of Social Workers, 1970), p. 159.

5. Harriet A. Feiner and Harriet Katz, "Stronger Women—Stronger Families," *Affilia* 1 (Winter 1986): 49–58.

6. Adapted from Florence Hollis, "And What Shall We Teach? Social Work Education and Knowledge," *Social Service Review* 42 (June 1968): 184–196.

7. Mary K. Rodwell. "Naturalistic Inquiry: An Alternative Model for Social Work Assessment," *Social Service Review* 61 (June 1987): 231–246.

8. Carel B. Germain and Alex Gitterman, *The Life Model of Social Work Practice* (New York: Columbia University Press, 1980), chap. 1.

9. Helen Northen, "Assessment in Direct Practice," in Anne Minahan, Ed., *Encyclopedia of Social Work*, 18th ed. (Silver Spring, MD: National Association of Social Workers, 1987), pp. 171–183.

10. Weick, Rapp, Sullivan, and Kisthardt, "A Strengths Perspective," pp. 350–354.

11. Abraham H. Maslow, *Motivation and Personality*, 3rd ed. (New York: Harper-Collins, 1987).

12. Charlotte Towle, *Common Human Needs*, rev. ed. (New York: NASW Press, 1957).

13. Paula Allen-Meares and Bruce A. Lane, "Grounding Social Work Practice in Theory: Ecosystems," *Social Casework* 68 (November 1987): 315–321.

14. Dolores Norton, *The Dual Perspective* (New York: Council on Social Work Education, 1978), p. 3. Also see Dolores G. Norton, "Diversity, Early Socialization, and Temporal Development: The Dual Perspective Revisited," *Social Work* 38 (January 1993): 82–90.

15. Sonia Badillo Ghali, "Culture Sensitivity and the Puerto Rican Client," *Social Casework* 58 (October 1977): 459–468.

16. Ann Hartman and Joan Laird, *Family-Centered Social Work Practice* (New York: Free Press, 1983), chap. 11.

17. Elizabeth M. Tracy and James K. Whittaker, "The Social Network Map: Assessing Social Support in Clinical Practice," *Families in Society* 71 (October 1990): 461–470; and Elizabeth M. Tracy, "Identifying Social Support Resources of At-Risk Families, *Social Work* 35 (May 1990): 252–258.

18. Also see Charles Froland, Diane L. Pancoast, Nancy J. Chapmen, and Priscilla J. Kimboko, *Helping Networks and Human Services* (Beverly Hills, CA: Sage Publications, 1981); and James K. Whittaker and James Garbarino, *Social Support Networks: Informal Helping in the Human Services* (New York: Aldine, 1983).

CHAPTER

12 Planning

LEARNING EXPECTATIONS

1. Understanding of the nature of strategic thinking in the planning process.
2. Skill in planning.
3. Understanding of the nature of goals in social work and skill in developing goals and objectives.
4. Skill in choosing units of attention.
5. Skill in identifying strategies to use in specific practice situations, including choice of roles and tasks.
6. Understanding of the factors that affect a plan of action and skill in identification of the impact of these factors on the specific practice situations.
7. Understanding of the nature of the contract in social work practice and of the skill needed to negotiate a contract.
8. Skill in identifying resources for use in planning.
9. Understanding of the importance of diversity factors in planning and the need for empowerment when planning with populations at risk of discrimination or oppression.
10. Skill in planning with client systems of various sizes.

Planning is the bridge between assessment and activity focused on change. Often it is seen as a part of the assessment process. Although planning considerations are important in assessment, the emphasis at this stage is on assessing possible planning resources. Planning and assessment are both such important aspects of the total process that each deserves separate consideration. Planning is based on assessment and is the outcome of assessment. It is part of the change process, and as such it cannot be separated from other aspects of the generalist social work process except for study purposes. Planning is based on deliberate rational choices and thus involves judgments about a range of possibilities.

The assessment process develops understanding of person in situation and identifies potential resources. The planning process translates the assessment content into a goal statement that describes the desired results. Planning also is concerned with identifying the means to reaching goals, which includes identifying the focal system or unit of attention and the strategies, roles, and tasks to be used. It sequences tasks, specifies a time frame, and considers the costs involved.

Planning, when related to social functioning, involves activity designed to enhance people's growth potential and adaptive capacity. It also is designed to increase the capacity of environments to respond to people's needs.

Strategic thinking is the cognitive source of the plan. This implies a complicated process of developing a plan with parts that fit together, not by chance, but by choice. This process considers alternatives, evaluates their usefulness, and predicts outcomes of each. The plan considers both process and outcomes by specifying intermediate objectives as well as end goals.

Planning is a skill. The work of the process calls for a complex set of decisions. These decisions are informed by a broad body of knowledge about the nature of human systems and their functioning and of possible interventive strategies. In addition, social work, client, and community values must be considered. The worker's experiences in similar situations also inform the decisions. Planning links purpose to action. Intervention into the transactions between people and social systems is the context of planning. The end goal is planned change. The plan is composed of specified, interrelated parts that have a logical relationship. The reason for each action is specified.

Because of the nature of the human condition and the complexity of the social situation, it is virtually impossible to predict with certainty the outcome of a plan. However, a well-developed plan—one developed with flexibility for change as the process develops—has a better chance of achieving the desired outcome than action not based on such a process.

In developing a plan, it is important to maintain a client-centered perspective and process. This is a phase during which it is easy to leave clients out of the process. Until now, the worker has relied heavily on the client for information. The development of a plan implies that enough information has surfaced to begin acting toward change. Thus, the worker may be tempted to take over and write the plan himself. This happens all too often in practice. Sometimes it occurs because workers feel pressured to complete their paperwork. In other cases, workers may be eager to start the change process, which tends to be their primary focus, since they see themselves as change agents. Inexperienced workers or students may desire either to demonstrate their skills and abilities or to compensate for anxiety over their developing skills. Also workers may feel uncomfortable with clients being in control of the helping process. However, when clients do not fully participate in the planning process, the chances of failure increase because they are deprived of an opportunity to become more empowered and to improve their problem-solving skills. In addition, their right to self-determination is undermined.

Plans should either be written with the client present or should be reviewed with them before being finalized. Of course, a plan should not be made without the agreement of the client. A plan that does not have the client's consent results in the need to manipulate the client into meeting the expectations of the worker. This would be against social work values and ethics. One way to tell if goals are being written by the worker instead of formulated with the client is to check for repetition. Over a period of time, workers who write goals for clients will use the same or similar goals over and over and have difficulty individualizing plans.

The plan should be sensitive to the background and circumstances of the client. Individual and cultural values need to be incorporated into the process. The best way to ensure that this happens is to have full participation by the client. In addition, the plan should build on the strengths of the client system and environment while seeking to overcome or strengthen areas in which there are barriers or limitations. Populations at risk of discrimination or oppression as a result of poverty, gender, race, ethnicity, age, disability, or sexual orientation are especially in need of planning that empowers them and that recognizes the need to change the attitudes and stereotypes of others. Assertiveness in interactions with others on the part of both the client and the worker is likely to be needed. This should be built into the plan by identifying targets for change in the environment. Helping members of these groups to adapt to discrimination or oppression is not acceptable. Confronting discrimination and oppression through empowerment and advocacy is generally what is needed for true change to take place.

Components of a Plan

Because a **plan of action** relates to a complex human situation to be dealt with over time, identification of the components of a plan helps in managing the complexity of the plan. One formulation of a plan specifies three components: goals and objectives, units of attention, and strategies that include the roles of worker and client and the tasks to be performed.

Goals and Objectives

The **goal** is the overall, long-range expected outcome of the endeavor. Because of the complexity of the overall plan, this goal is usually reached only after intermediate goals or **objectives** have been attained. These objectives may relate to several different persons or social systems involved in the situation. Goals and objectives develop out of assessment related to the needs of the various systems involved and the identification of the blockage or blockages to need fulfillment. They are generally related to the removal of a blockage or to developing new means of need fulfillment.

Students and new workers often find it challenging to write appropriate goals and objectives using an acceptable format. Social workers are prone to qualify or hedge their statements to allow for flexibility or individuality. Much of this comes from a desire to respect client self-determination and to allow for unforeseen difficulties. However, planning calls for direct and definitive statements so that expectations and outcomes are clear and progress can be accurately measured. Otherwise, confusion will occur about who is responsible for what, and measuring progress and outcomes will be impossible. Although goal statements must be definitive, there is room for flexibility in that plans can be changed. When it is obvious that something is not working, the plan needs to be changed. However, the need for flexibility in planning should not obscure the need for clearly defined goals, objectives, and tasks.

Many social workers will see a variety of things that might be improved or changed as they assess the person in environment and will want to fix everything. Clients can easily become overwhelmed by what may be received as a negative message about their well-being. It is best to keep things less complicated and focus on the main areas the client wishes to change and where change will likely make the biggest difference. A general guideline in working with individuals is to limit the number of goals to no more than three at any given time during the process. For individuals facing multiple barriers or difficulties, more goals may be necessary. However, the likelihood that a client will remember to work on more than two or three goals at a given time is very low. Families and groups may need more than three goals, depending on the size of the membership. However, no single member should be asked to keep track of more than two or three goals. For children and those who are under stress or have limitations, one or two goals may be the most they are able to handle at one time.

Goals should also be based on the strengths of the client system as well as the strengths of the environment. A strengths perspective ensures that the plan is built on the existing capacities of the client system and environment. Without this perspective, the plan might be based on skills the client has not mastered or cannot master or on resources that may not be readily available. The result would be a plan with a great deal of uncertainty, one that depends on too many "if's." It can be like "a house of cards," ready to tumble down at its weakest point. The more uncertainty, the greater the chances of failure. Although building on strengths does not guarantee success, it increases the odds for success and provides the client with opportunities to act more immediately rather than waiting to acquire skills and resources.

There is a danger in setting goals that are too broad and general. Broad goals do not lead to the precision that is possible when the objectives are more specific. It is helpful to specify a general goal that is a statement of the desired end and then develop specific short-term objectives. These short-term objectives can be placed in a time order to facilitate a plan; that is, the first objective must be reached before working on the second objective, and so on. Objectives can relate to a specific desired change of individuals or social systems involved in the total situation. In effect, a miniplan, or a plan within a plan, is developed. This approach allows for evaluation of the progress toward the general goal and for adjusting the plan in progress when there is a change in the situation or because of previously unrecognized influences and consequences.

Care must be taken to express the objectives in terms of the behavioral outcome desired rather than of how the goal will be reached. In other words, receiving a service is not a goal but rather a task designed to meet a need or achieve the goal or objective. Also, each goal and objective should have a specified date for its accomplishment. Objectives should be specific, concrete, and measurable. Goal statements are usually broader and more general than objectives. If objectives have specific statements about frequency, duration, and time frame, then the goal statement can be more broad. For example, the statement "The interaction between Bob and John and their school system will result in successful academic progress" is broad in that it does not specify how much positive behavior or the time frame for completion. In developing more specific, measurable statements for objectives, it is helpful to think in terms of a sequence of questions—namely, who, what, how, where, and when. The "who" refers to the person or persons taking action and the targets of change. The person(s) taking action should appear first in both the goal statement and the objectives. The next word should be *will*, which conveys a positive, unequivocal statement about the desired state of affairs. Next comes a description of "what" and/or "how" the situation will appear if the goal or objective were accomplished or the need were to be met. Identifying "who" is the target of change may come next, if appropriate. "When" describes the time, frequency, and/or duration in which the action is to take place and the time frame for completion. "When" may also refer to an if-then relationship of reciprocal goals. An example of a goal written using these guidelines follows:

> Goal: Bob and John will follow the rules while at school 100 percent of the time for one week by April 15.

"Bob and John" are the "who." "Follow the rules" represents the "what." "At school" refers to both "where" and "when." The expected frequency is "100 percent of the time." "For one week" is the duration, and "by April 15" is the time frame. It is clear from this statement who will do what and where and when they will do it. There should be no confusion about expectations; both progress and outcomes are readily measurable.

Goals should be reasonably feasible; that is, there should be a good chance of reaching them. In thinking about feasibility, consideration needs to be given to time and energy factors. Some of the questions that should be asked are: Do the worker and the client have the time available to work toward the specified goals? Is sufficient energy available to work toward the goals? Are the needed resources available?

Wherever possible it is wise to state goals and objectives in terms of a positive outcome rather than in negative terms. That is, goals should be stated as "John will" rather than "John will not." When goals and objectives are positive, they help to focus on the desired outcome instead of being problem focused. This reinforces behavior that is needed to bring about change. In addition, a positive focus gives the client more hope that the situation can be resolved. Finally, it creates a "self-fulfilling prophecy" that is more likely to result in success than failure. People tend to engage in behavior that is based on a prediction or "prophecy" of what they expect to have happen, not necessarily what they want to have happen.

"Self-fulfilling prophecy" means that one's own behavior contributes a great deal to the outcome. When clients are focused on behavior that is likely to bring about the desired change, they are more likely to succeed and are also more likely to receive positive reinforcement from their environment.

Clients can often be most helpful in evaluating the feasibility of a goal; thus, they should be involved in setting goals. The setting of goals can motivate a client for the work needed to reach that goal. As clients see small goals reached, they gain hope for reaching the overall goals.

As with all decisions in the social work process, decisions regarding goals are influenced by value judgments. The choice of goals or end states is based on what is desirable. What is desirable is a value judgment. Social work values also influence the means to the end, or the process and objectives involved in the process. Because people are seen as having the right to make decisions about themselves, workers should not use means in reaching goals that go against the client's desires and values. Workers should respect lifestyle and cultural factors in the development of goals and objectives. The worker should constantly evaluate whether or not the chosen goals are appropriate. There also must be flexibility in adjusting goals to changing situations as the plan is implemented.

Different situations call for different kinds of change and different kinds of goals. Kinds of change that should be considered are:

1. *A sustaining relationship*—used when it appears that there is no chance to change the person in situation and when the person lacks a significant other who can give needed support

2. *Specific behavioral change*—used when a client is troubled by a specific symptom or behavior pattern and is generally otherwise satisfied with her situation

3. *Relationship change*—used when the issue is a troublesome relationship

4. *Environmental change*—used when it is recognized that a part of the need is a change in some segment of the environment or in the transactions between person and environment

5. *Directional change*—used when values are conflicting or unclear, when a client system is unclear about goals or direction of effort, or when aspirations are blocked in a manner that makes unblocking very difficult or impossible

When setting goals, it is important to consider expectations of the client, of significant others in the client's environment, and of the worker. These three sets of expectations may be different, because each party may see the situation differently or may have identified the need differently. The consistency and inconsistency among these goals must be identified and some reconciliation obtained. The client's goals are to be considered of prime importance, and the worker should point out to the client the environmental expectations and the consequences of not meeting these expectations. The worker's goals can be discussed and incorporated or discarded as jointly determined by the worker and the client.

In summary, goals and objectives should relate to meeting a need. They should be stated in terms of an outcome, be specific, and be measurable. They should be feasible and positive in direction and developed with the client to reflect the client's desires.

Units of Attention

The **unit of attention,** or focal system, is the system being focused on. This is generally in relation to the overall goals, but there may be different units of attention in relation to specific objectives. A unit of attention is either a person, a social system, or the transactions between them. It may be the client or a significant influence on the situation. In other words, units of attention are systems that are the focus of the change activity.

The unit of attention can be an individual client; it can be several clients (a small group) working on meeting a common need or on similar individual needs; it can be an individual who in some way impacts the client and her situation; or it can be a group of persons in a community concerned about services to meet the needs of a category of clients.[1] The interactions and transactions among various parts of the ecosystem can be a unit of attention. For instance, in the case study in this chapter there is an incongruity in the relationship between Bob and John Jones and the school system. While the unit of attention for specific change may be the boys or the school, ultimately it is the interaction between them that needs to be changed.

As the change process is divided into activity related to more specific objectives, several objectives and miniplans are often worked on at the same time. It is important to specify the specific unit of attention related to each miniplan. For example, the overall goal may be a desirable living situation for a client. It may be necessary to have an objective that relates to understanding the client's situation. To develop this understanding, the focal system may be the client or the present landlord as a source of needed information. Another objective may be that a potential landlord be prepared to meet the special needs of the client. The potential landlord then becomes a focal system. Other objectives may relate to the provision of service by certain community service agencies. These agencies also become units of attention.

Units of attention may be individuals, family groups, small groups of unrelated persons, organizations, or communities. Table 12.1 gives some indications and counterindications for the choice of each kind of system. It is important to specify appropriate units of attention for every goal and objective. Units of attention may be clients or other persons and social systems involved in the situation.

Strategy

Strategy is an overall approach to change in the situation. It involves roles for worker and client, tasks to be done by each, and methods and techniques to use. It has been defined as "an orchestrated attempt to influence persons or systems in

TABLE 12.1   Indications and Counterindications with Units of Attention

	Indications	Counterindications
Individuals	Information giving Information gathering Concrete service Referral service Need relates primarily to an individual without significant family No other involvement feasible Intrapsychic difficulties Individual who with help can involve significant systems in the change process Individual choice	Cannot function in a one-to-one helping relationship Action-oriented service needed Focus on interactional aspects of family or peer group needed Need fulfillment best reached by change in larger system
Family	Major difficulties seem to exist in family interaction One family member undercuts change efforts of other members Family needs to respond to individual need Need for understanding family interaction to understand individual functioning Family needs to examine role functioning or communication Chaotic families where there is a need to restore order Family choice	Irreversible trend toward family breakup Significant impairment of individual family member prevents participation Need for individual help precludes work with family No common concern or goal Worker cannot deal with destructive interactions
Small group	Individuals face similar situations and can benefit from interchange Group influence on the individual is great Development of socialization skills is indicated Use of activity is desirable Focus on environmental change Usable natural groups	Individual overwhelmed by the group Individual destructive to group A common purpose or goal does not exist Sufficient cohesive factors do not exist Environment will not allow the group to function Environment will not allow the group to reach its goal to at least some extent
Organization	Difficulty related to organizational functioning Number of individuals are affected and needs not being met because of organizational factors Workers are overconstrained from providing service to clients	Dangers of further negative results to clients are great Client service will be neglected or negated
Community	Lack of needed resources and services Lack of coordination of services Community influence on organization or family prevents meeting of need Community functioning affects a large number of individuals and families negatively	Same as organization

relation to some goals."[2] The term originated in a military context and relates to a battle plan. It also is used in a game context. Action in the game depends on the action of others, as contrasted with "games of chance." Strategy implies multiple cause. Action is dependent on the action of others; that is, there is anticipation and assessment of the actions and reactions of others rather than reliance on independent action. There is a recognition of the transactional nature of human social functioning.

When a general strategy is used in many situations, it becomes a category of strategy. Some categories that have been identified are *consensus strategy, conflict strategy, demonstration strategy,* and *bargaining strategy.* Social work has developed a variety of approaches to practice. These may be called theories of practice or models of practice. These conceptualizations of practice (e.g., crisis intervention, conjoint family therapy, locality development) provide an overall approach to practice and thus may be considered as strategies.

Some strategies provide a philosophical approach to the situation. For example, a social action approach assumes a lack of balance in the power structure and recommends that a conflict strategy be used to redistribute power. Value judgments as to the desirability of power redistribution often guide the choice of this strategy. Other strategies have a theoretical base. The socialization model, which is based in socialization theory, is an example. Most strategies have both value assumptions and knowledge assumptions as well as identifiable practice theory. Strategies are one means of tying the knowledge and value aspects of practice to the action. (See the Appendix for summaries of commonly used strategies or models of practice.)

In choosing strategies it is important for the worker to decide if the value and knowledge base of a particular strategy are congruent with his own values and world view. It is also important for the worker to determine if he possesses the knowledge needed for using the strategy. The worker must also determine if the values, explicit and implicit, in the strategy are congruent with those of the client and her situation.

Strategies should not only apply to the client's need but also should be in keeping with the client's lifestyle. Much has been written about the necessity of understanding minority clients and their culture and of applying this understanding to service delivery with minority clients. This literature recommends decisions that match the helping style to the lifestyle of the client.

For example, in discussing services for blacks and Puerto Ricans, Emelicia Mizio and Anita Delaney indicate that it is important to use strategies that recognize how racism and discrimination impact the lives of minority people. They recommend the use of advocacy as a core strategy and the use of counseling strategies based on ecological and systems knowledge.[3] The authors' Native American students indicate that Siporin's situational approach and the functional approach are appropriate for their culture. (See the Appendix for summary of these two approaches.)

Different strategies and different kinds of service call for the social worker to fill different roles. The term *role* is used here in a somewhat different manner than in the strict pattern-of-behaviors sense. Rather, the definition used is that of Robert Teare and Harold McPheeters: "A cluster of altruistic activities that are performed toward a common objective [goal]."[4] The **role** is the way the worker uses self in the specific helping situation. Role is further dependent on the function of the worker and the particular agency offering the service and its function. For example, in short-term, crisis-focused service, the caregiver role will be minimally used, whereas in a nursing home this may be an often-used role.

Teare and McPheeters have identified twelve roles that may be part of the generalist repertoire that social workers fill:

1. *Outreach worker*—identifying need by reaching out to clients in the community; usually involves referral to services
2. *Broker*—enabling persons to reach appropriate services by providing information, after assessing need of individual and nature of resources; also includes contact and follow-up
3. *Advocate*—helping clients obtain services in situations in which they may be rejected; helping expand services to persons having a particular need
4. *Evaluation*—gathering information and assessing client and/or community needs; considering alternatives and planning for action
5. *Teacher*—teaching facts and skills
6. *Behavior changer*—activities aimed at specific behavior change
7. *Mobilizer*—helping to mobilize resources to develop new services or programs
8. *Consultant*—working with other professionals to increase their skill and understanding
9. *Community planner*—helping communities to plan for ways to meet human need
10. *Caregiver*—providing support and/or care to persons when problems cannot be resolved
11. *Data manager*—collecting and analyzing data used in decision making
12. *Administrator*—planning and implementing services and programs[5]

There seems to be one additional role, that of coordinator. The coordinator enables several social workers, other professionals, or other service providers to function so that services are provided in a synchronized manner. The coordinator sees that all involved are aware of and take into consideration the work of all others as they provide service. This role may also be identified as the case manager role. (This will be discussed in Chapter 13.) Another role is the enabler role. (See Chapter 13 for a discussion of enabling as a strategy.)

Ronald Simons and Stephen Aiger have discussed role choice in terms of client characteristics and needs.[6] The four client characteristics they see as important to consider when choosing the worker role are (1) the needs and desires of the client, (2) the resources of the client, (3) the expectations of the client and of the worker regarding the client, and (4) the client's perceived expectations of the worker. Although they define *role* somewhat differently than do Teare and

McPheeters, they identify particular situations and clients' difficulties in which particular roles are important. A lack of resources calls for the broker role; a lack of opportunity, the advocate role; role inadequacy, the teacher role; unrealistic role expectations or behavior, the confronter role; conflicting role expectations, the mediator role; role transition stress, the empathic listener role; role indecision, the clarifier role.

Usually, role and task are discussed in relation to the worker and the worker's functioning. However, role implies action and interaction by and with the client—a reciprocal relationship. Thus, in carrying out the plan attention needs to be paid to the client's functioning and tasks. The plan should specify the role or roles of the worker and consider the reciprocal role of the client. The tasks to be completed by the client and the worker should be specified. Task is a specific action or activity; it is the specification of what needs to be done.

The strategy, including the role and task specification, is developed after tentative goals and units of attention relative to the goals have been identified. After the strategy has been identified, it is possible to develop the operational goal or goals and objectives and to become more specific about tasks. Tasks and objectives are often related.

Tasks represent the steps that are necessary to achieve the objectives and ultimately the goal. Tasks may be used to describe events that occur only once or that are ongoing. They should also cover the "who, what, how, where, and when" for the actions that are planned. This is generally the first place the worker appears in the plan. The exception would be cases in which workers might be part of an objective by monitoring, prompting, or rewarding clients to assist them in accomplishing objectives.

The tasks that have been identified should be sequenced and a time for the completion of each established. This results in an overall time frame or time line for the service. It is also important to specify the resources needed to carry out the plan and to indicate how those resources are to be obtained. This would include the time investment of the worker and client. Any fiscal investment, such as client fees or agency funds, should be specified. Other needed resources could be the use of an agency or community facility or service or the inclusion of other persons in the action system.

The plan is always based on the information collected and the assessment of that information. It is always developed with the fullest possible participation of the client. The plan often results in a contract with the client outlining what the worker will do and what the client's responsibility in the endeavor is.

All plans of action should contain some mechanism for evaluating how well the goals of the plan were met. Evaluation, which is ongoing in the entire interventive process, is the focus of Chapter 15.

Plans should also contain some mechanism for specifying when various objectives are to be met or when specific tasks are to be completed. This can be as simple as specifying a date for the completion of each objective. When working on complex goals it is often useful to use a task-flow mechanism. Figure 12.1 shows an example of this type of time line.

	Week 1	Week 2	Week 3	Week 4	Week 5
Task 1	X------------------------- X				
Task 2		X-------------X			
Task 3			X------------------X		
Task 4					X-----X

FIGURE 12.1 **Time Line**

The plan must be flexible. As the implementation of the plan progresses, new information or assessments may be added, which may result in a change of plan. The development of the plan calls for a great deal of specificity. Specific plans are more likely to lead to service that is directed toward client needs and desires and that enhances accountability. Such plans allow for a breadth of possible decisions about the components of the plan, a mark of generalist social work as presented in this text.

When developing plans of action, it is usually advisable to consider several different plans and make choices based on an analysis of each plan and its suitability for the specific situation. This involves considering strengths and limitations of each plan. The chosen plan may be a synthesis of parts of several of the considered plans.

Case Example

I. Background

The school contacted the community services office because of behavior problems they were having with Bob and John Jones. There were also several instances in which negative racial epithets had been exchanged between the boys and the other children.

Bob and John are Jane and Jerry Jones's children. They have four more children, ages 6 months to 5 years. The family is African American, and they live in a neighborhood with a mixture of lower- and working-class households. They are also one of only two African-American families in the area. Mr. Jones is employed as a laborer. Because of the immediate need to sustain Bob and John in school, this was the immediate focus of the plan. Another focus was the negative racial attitudes on the part of the school and the community.

II. Plan of Action

A. **Goal A:** The interaction between Bob and John and their school system will result in successful academic progress.

1. **Objective 1:** Bob and John will follow rules while at school 100 percent of the time for one week by April 15.

a. **Client task:** Bob and John will be able to recite three basic rules for classroom behavior by March 15.

(continued)

Case Example   Continued

>   **b. Worker task:** By March 10, the worker will arrange for Bob and John's teachers to give them verbal feedback on their behavior each hour and written feedback at the end of each day.
>   **c. Parent task:** Mr. and Mrs. Jones will keep track of the written feedback and reward the boys for positive behavior at the end of the week according to the number of positive reports they receive.
>
>   **B. Goal B:** The school will reinforce a more positive attitude toward African Americans by incorporating diversity into the curriculum.
>   **1. Objective 1:** Teachers will develop and implement an assignment focused on the contributions of African Americans to each part of the curriculum.
>   **a. Worker task:** By March 10, the worker will meet with the faculty to discuss the development of assignments for students that involve contributions by African Americans to art, literature, science, history, and mathematics.
>   **b. Teacher task:** By April 1, teachers will develop and implement a curriculum with assignments that incorporate contributions by African Americans to art, literature, science, history, and mathematics.

III. Unit of Attention

The school is the client in many ways, as it requested help with the children and for the family. It is also the target of change in that racial tensions have arisen between Bob and John and their classmates. The school and the community have had little contact with members of diverse populations, and racial prejudices and stereotypes have surfaced. The school, as it is in many small communities, is one of the systems the town functions around and so follows the expectations and norms of the community. The school has a good staff that can be used as a resource. The worker may be able to act on behalf of the family by offering a means of sensitizing the staff and the students to African Americans in a positive way while also stressing a strengths perspective. The worker may need to be prepared to act more assertively if this plan meets with resistance.

Bob and John are also the clients, or units of attention, as they are part of the conflict. In some ways, the boys may be bringing to school behavior that they use at home to get attention. They may also be acting defensively because they are used to going to a school with predominantly African-American students. The boys are average students and have responded to adults working with them before. Their parents care for their children very much and are willing to help with the boys. In fact, the family moved to the smaller town in the hopes of providing a better education and environment for the children.

IV. Strategy

The social services worker, Maria, is an advocate for John, Bob, and their family at the school. Maria is using knowledge of child rearing to get the parents and the school to try some new approaches with the children. Maria is using a teaching strategy and is also a mediator between the parents and the school. She is enabling the parents to act in a positive way to change the boys' behavior. She is also enabling the school to respond favorably to the immediate situation while also expanding its curriculum to include valuing diversity.

Maria's tasks are to contact the school personnel and talk with them about the problems at school, to encourage them and give them suggestions about how they might work with the boys while also providing a more appropriate environment that values diversity. Maria also can explain a little of the boys' background without violating the Joneses' right to privacy to help the teachers better understand the situation. It is Maria's task to encourage Jane and one of the teachers to get together and talk about the misbehavior at school. It is also her job to keep in touch with the school and Jane each week in case anything comes up that they can work on together. Maria feels she can influence the guidance counselor and teachers to have a more realistic understanding of the family's strengths and limitations and that this will affect how they treat the boys.

Mr. and Mrs. Jones's tasks are to find out from the children what is happening at school, to encourage them to behave, and to reward them when they do.

The teachers' tasks are to keep trying to motivate the boys, to keep track of positive behaviors, and to support any improvement they make in behavior. They also have the task of incorporating the diversity assignment identified above as a beginning toward establishing a learning environment that values and respects diversity.

The guidance counselor's tasks are to work with the boys at school when they misbehave and to support them when they are doing well. It is also his task to help the boys trust him as an adult and a friend, to meet with Jane and talk with her about the boys, and to initiate some activities for Bob and John.

Bob and John's tasks are to behave for their teacher and to go to the guidance counselor or teacher when they need to talk.

The principal's tasks are to let Maria and/or Jane know if anything important happens in regard to the boys' classroom and schoolyard behavior, to support the teachers' efforts with the boys, and support development and implementation of diversity in the curriculum.

The plan will be evaluated by observing whether the goals and objectives are met within the time framework noted in the objectives.

Planning with Multiperson Client Systems

In developing a plan with a family system or a small group, the challenge is to balance the needs and goals of each individual with each other and with those of the system. The first task is to identify individual or personal goals for each member. Although the worker may have discussed these beforehand, it is important for members to state their goals to other members of the family or group.

The next step is for the worker to assist the family or group in articulating a common goal that includes everyone in the system. This inclusion process helps to establish and reinforce a sense of belonging and teamwork and increases a sense of cohesion. It is sometimes difficult to develop an all-encompassing goal, thus, the worker should keep the goal simple and straightforward. For example, for a family a common goal might be to get along better with each other. For a group, the goal is usually related to the purpose of the group. For example, in a support group the common goal would be to give each other support in coping with situations related to the focus of the support group. For a hospice support group, this would include coping with death and dying. Sensitivity to diversity and to at-risk populations is essential when planning with families or groups, as is building on the strengths of the individual, the system, and the environment.

Once the family or group members have established a common goal, the task is to assist them in finding ways to help each other achieve individual goals as well as to identify roles in helping the family or group to achieve its overall goal. The worker will need to use mediation and negotiation in helping the family or group in this process. Goals should build on the strengths of individuals and the family or group as a whole, as well as the strengths and resources available in the larger ecosystem.

In addition to personal or individual goals and a common goal for the group or family, there are two other types of goals that are important: mutual, or shared, goals and reciprocal goals. Mutual goals require two or more members to participate or act in certain ways regardless of the actions of others. An example would be a goal in which everyone agreed to use "I" statements when talking to each other in order to improve communication. If one person forgets, it does not excuse others from using the word *I* as a reminder. The respondent should not say, "You forgot to use 'I'!" Instead, they would need to say something like, "I would like to hear that in an 'I' statement."

Reciprocal goals require different actions on the part of two or more members. An example would be a goal in which a parent agrees to cook the family's favorite meal and the family members agree to make a commitment to sit together as a family for that meal. Reciprocal goals may also be contingent. This is usually stated as "if-then." For example, parents can agree to give each child an allowance based on completion of certain chores. This might be stated as "If Joe cuts the grass when requested, then Mr. Brown will pay him $20.00."

Planning on an organizational or community level generally involves some kind of task group. The planning process may take up a considerable amount of the group's time. Just as in small groups, it is important to establish a common goal that is inclusive and relates to the purpose of the group. Initially, the common goal may be stated in very broad terms. However, care should be taken to avoid stating the goal in terms of solutions. Task groups are usually made up of factions or representatives of organizations who may have a considerable investment in the outcome. For example, a community task force on juvenile gangs is likely to be made up of representatives from law enforcement, the juvenile court, the schools, substance abuse agencies, and youth organizations. Each of these brings its own perspective on the problem and is invested in solutions related to that perspective. Usually, the solution is viewed as a need for more resources for that particular organization or a need for a different response from one of the other organizations. Thus, law enforcement is likely to see the problem as related to not having enough police officers or of the courts not being tougher on juveniles. The juvenile court may see the problem in terms of needing more court workers or more money for placement options. The schools may see the goal as the need for a new program in the schools or for the court to be stricter with school truants. The substance abuse agencies and youth organizations are likely to see a need for more programs to treat substance abuse or to keep young people off the street. Generating a common goal that involves a community response is the key to holding these groups together. For example, the group could be encouraged to adopt a community goal of reducing gang membership by half. To accomplish this goal, each organization would have to do their part and make a collaborative effort.

In planning change within an organization, it is important for the administration to be inclusive. Often, there is a temptation to bring about change by issuing memos or directives. This can lead to resentment, resistance, and even sabotage by those employees who are affected by the change. How change occurs is as important as what gets changed. Getting input from those affected ensures greater investment in carrying out the change and helps to avoid unforeseen barriers. Getting input from clients should be done whenever applicable and feasible. At the least, client needs and concerns should be considered as primary, and "proactive advocacy" should be used by the social worker. "Proactive advocacy" means advocating for clients before barriers are encountered by avoiding policies that are not in the best interests of clients.

In a small agency, it may be possible to include everyone in the planning process. When major change is planned in larger agencies, it is usually wise to establish a *task group* made up of representatives of employees from various levels of the agency. The representatives should solicit input from the groups they represent. The task group is generally given responsibility to recommend changes to the executive. Generating several options, along with an analysis of the advantages and disadvantages of each, will allow the administrator to retain her decision-making role while incorporating input from other levels of the agency.

Factors Affecting a Plan of Action

Plans of action reflect the differential nature of social work. Each plan is specific to a situation and to the persons involved. Each plan of action, with its component parts, should be different than every other plan of action. It is important to specify not only the components of a plan but also the various factors that affect the development of that plan. Seven factors that have considerable influence on the plan are (1) the community in which it is being carried out; (2) the agency sanctioning the plan; (3) the social need that the plan is a response to; (4) the worker involved in the plan; (5) the client involved in the plan; (6) diversity issues among members of all of these systems, along with issues related to disadvantaged or oppressed populations; and (7) the strengths and limitations of all of the above.

The Community

The community as a system is an important influence on the differential plan of action. The client is a part of a community; as such, the client reflects its characteristics. The community has expectations for the client. Any plan of action needs to consider the environment in which the plan takes place. What is feasible in one community may not be feasible in another.

The culture of a community is important to consider in planning. Attitudes about receiving help are particularly important, as are accepted coping mechanisms. In communities in which self-help and neighborliness are highly valued, the chosen plan of action may be one that strengthens and enables the natural helping system to function well rather than an extended casework service.

The community's service delivery system is another factor to be considered. An assumption is often made that the ideal service delivery system should be that of a large urban community with many specialized services. This assumption has led to the development of strategies specific to such situations. However, these strategies are sometimes inappropriate for small nonmetropolitan settings in which the service delivery system is different.[7]

The Agency

In considering the influence of the agency on the plan of action, the worker is influenced by constraints and resources within the agency. Constraints may take the form of the kinds of service that can be offered, fiscal considerations, time priority factors, and the manner in which the agency is organized. Resources to be considered include people (staff expertise), structures, money, and expendable supplies that can be used by the worker and client to enhance the social work process or goal realization. Skillful use of the agency system in service of the client is an important attribute of planning.

The agency is a component part of the community, and as such it is an integral subunit of the community system. It is sanctioned by the community and thus must, at least in part, express its will. The agency is dependent on the community for resources. Social agencies seldom function without financial support from the community, which may be in the form of contributions or taxation. Other kinds of resources and support are also vital to providing services to clients. Planning must take into consideration the influence of community needs, values, and intentions for the service being delivered by the agency. It is important that the planning process recognize the influence of agency structure and functioning on service to clients. This recognition gives both the worker and client a sense of the realities involved in the provision of service.

An additional factor to consider with respect to some organizations is the impact of managed care on how the agency and its workers function. Although managed care is currently most relevant for health care, mental health, and substance abuse, this approach may eventually be applied to other areas of human services. There are two primary situations in which social workers may be affected by managed care in their practice. The first is when the agency provides services that are reimbursed by a managed care organization under a prescribed insurance plan. The other is when a social worker is employed by a managed care provider. In the first case, the worker can be affected by the length of service that is approved for reimbursement and by the type of service considered reimbursable. In the second case, the worker may be responsible for assessing, referring, and monitoring the implementation of a managed care plan. Some managed care providers recognize that social workers possess valuable assessment and referral potential, especially as regards mental health and substance abuse treatment.

An important consideration is that the *NASW Code of Ethics* requires that the social worker regard the client's concerns as primary. This means that regardless of the interests of themselves or their employers, social workers must do what is in the best interests of the client. A major criticism of managed care is that managed care plans may limit what is available to clients or encourage less care by discouraging more expensive services. Social workers must not allow themselves to be influenced by any policies that do not allow the worker to act in the best interests of clients regardless of the circumstances. Facing the challenges of these situations requires courage. Any organization that employs social workers can be subjected to sanctions by the NASW if their policies or practices are deemed to be unethical. Social workers should report violations to the local NASW chapter.

The Social Issue

Societal attitudes and expectations about social issues vary. By sanctioning or developing means for control, amelioration, or prevention, these attitudes and expectations influence the task assigned to the agency. Some social issues are seen as a sign of illness or deviance, and some, as the result of environmental influences.

Elliot Studt has expressed this idea in her conceptualization of the field of practice. She sees "three organizing dimensions for describing a field of practice: social problem, social task, and social service system."[8] In thinking about the social issue it is helpful to consider why the issue concerns the community and other social systems. Important are such questions as: How does the issue affect the general welfare of the community? Why does a community see a need for action? What is the condition of central concern? Also important is how the issue affects the social functioning of individuals and families. As these questions are answered and as social policy and programs are developed, the social tasks related to the specific social issues develop. The social task is what the community sees as needing to be done in order to control the social issue. Social tasks also include work needed to help the individual affected by the social issue. These tasks develop in part from the expectations of the various segments of the community— taxpayers, professionals, legislators, agents of social control, commercial interests, and so on. Thus, the social task is often unclear and subject to conflicting expectations. This is one of the reasons that accountability is difficult and that goal expectations are unclear.

For example, quite different attitudes are held about someone with a difficulty in social functioning that leads to breaking the law and someone whose difficulty in social functioning is the result of sudden illness. The former enters the corrections field of practice; the latter, the health care field. Social control concerns are greater in the corrections field, because the strategy used must protect the community from further threat of danger from lawbreaking. Thus, punishment is often the strategy used. Treatment of illness is the prime concern in the medical setting, and concern with social functioning is always in relationship to the illness.

Society has considerable compassion for the person whose social-functioning difficulties arise from sudden illness. The strategy chosen must allow for the treatment of the illness and provide means for coping with the resulting difficulties in social functioning. Social policy is often a reflection of societal concerns and attitudes about social issues. Relevant social policy must always be considered in developing plans of action. Societal and individual attitudes as they relate to the issue being worked on by the worker and client are important influences on the planning process.

The Worker

Each worker is first a unique person. The worker's primary tool is the self. The worker brings herself as a person, as a professional, as an agency employee, and as a member of the community to the social work endeavor. The self is another factor influencing the plan of action.

Because of workers' individuality, because there is no one theory about the human situation, and because there is no one way to achieve social work goals, workers have preferences about explaining the human situation and practicing social work. One worker may find ego psychology a helpful theory and use psychosocial casework extensively. Another worker may use a more eclectic theory base and find problem-solving social work and remedial group work useful. A third worker might find that an ecosystems strengths approach provides the most positive and comprehensive approach. Plans of action, though developed by worker and client together, reflect the worker's preferences, priorities, and skills.

As an agency employee, the worker is both constrained and supported. The worker is responsible and accountable to the agency for her work. The worker must function within the agency structure and is interdependent with others employed by the agency. As a member of the community, the worker is subject to pressures from that community. The worker's preferences and influences on the worker from both the agency and the community also affect the planning process.

When a social worker is employed by a managed care organization, it is essential that the worker be aware of relevant social work values and ethics. The *NASW Code of Ethics* includes a statement that the social worker should adhere to commitments made to the organization that employs him. However, another section refers to the fact that the social worker's primary responsibility is to clients. This can present a serious ethical dilemma in cases in which the client's needs are not being met by the organization. If the organization has responsibly informed participants of the limits on coverage for various services, then the client participated in the plan with knowledge of what would or would not be reimbursed. However, this requires the client to be an astute consumer, which may not always be the case. It is the obligation of the social worker to inform clients of all of their benefits and rights under the plan as well as those that might be applicable by law. For instance, if a client is entitled to appeal a decision either within the organization or to regulatory bodies, the social worker must inform the client of this and assist in the appeal process. If the organization takes a formal or informal position that discourages full disclosure, the social worker has an ethical and, in many cases, a legal responsibility to report this to the appropriate authorities. Besides regulatory bodies, the NASW itself has a process for investigating violations of ethics by individuals and by organizations. In addition, the social worker has an obligation to be knowledgeable about alternative resources that may be available to assist the client in obtaining the needed service.

When working in a system in which reimbursement is controlled by a managed care plan, the worker must know how to maximize client benefits to fit the needs of the client and to ensure that the client receives needed services. Besides being knowledgeable about the coverage the client has, the worker needs to be ready to advocate for the needed services. The worker also should be creative about linking the client to other community services that can make up for some of the shortcomings of the insurance plan. The worker must be efficient in planning and delivering services within the agency's mandate. Frequently, this means developing time-limited plans that are designed to maximize the impact of the intervention. The worker should be task oriented and outcome focused so that tasks are completed within the limited time frames imposed by the covered services.

Managed care situations necessitate very careful planning to ensure an effective outcome within the limited time frames generally imposed by the insurance plan. This requires accurate assessment and the development of a plan that is task and solution focused. The restricted time frame can severely undermine the ability of the worker to develop and maintain a helping relationship that will carry the process through to a successful completion. It is imperative that clients be made aware of the limitations of their coverage and the need for immediate action. Otherwise, the client may misinterpret the worker's urgency as a lack of caring. In addition, a limited time frame is no excuse for ignoring the need to include the client in planning and decision making. Client self-determination is still relevant and must be central to any approach used by a professional social worker. Helping clients make choices within the context of their situation, advocating for maximum use of their benefits, and using all of the resources at their disposal are the keys to successful planning in managed care situations. Including the client in this process will ensure that the worker and the client are working together rather than working against each other. As mentioned previously, an ecosystems strengths approach can be an effective and efficient means of delivering services. It emphasizes using the client's own natural helping and support systems. Developing existing strengths and resources is the focus rather than seeking to change the overall structure. However, a potential drawback in using this approach is that some managed care systems may not recognize certain worker activities as reimbursable. Again, advocacy and connecting tasks to an approved plan may be necessary to achieve reimbursement.

The Client

The client in his uniqueness brings much to the worker-client interaction. The client comes from a community, a neighborhood, a particular diverse group, and a particular family. The client brings the biological, psychosocial, spiritual being. The client has a self-image, roles in family and community, values, hopes, and expectations. The client has rights—the right to service, the right to participate, the right to fail. The client carries a reference group's expectations as well as the results of interactions with meaningful persons in meaningful situations. The client has strengths, modes of adaptation, and ways of coping. The client brings a particular set of motivations, capacities, and opportunities. This uniqueness will support some interventive strategies and eliminate others. Even more important, the client will have unique expectations and goals for the service. The client may have preferences about the way of working on the need with the worker. The client's need is unique, and the plan must be unique in its response to that need.

The client's role in the plan depends on several factors. Among these factors are the client's roles in his life situation (parent, child, employee, etc.), the client's role in the agency or organization (patient, inmate, student, etc.), and the role the worker has chosen (the client's role must be reciprocal to it). The client is a vital part of the factors influencing the plan of action.

Diversity and Populations at Risk

Important considerations in developing a plan are the similarities and differences among members of the various systems involved. (The discussion of diversity in Chapter 7 should be reviewed for a better understanding of its implications for planning.) Diversity is an important factor in planning because it permeates the process and impacts the worker, client, and agency. For instance, the family might find it difficult to accept help from an agency that has a negative reputation among members of their ethnic or racial group. Alternatively, overcoming this barrier might represent an even stronger commitment on the part of both the family and the agency. Both may realize a benefit in forging a relationship with each other. The agency may see the experience as an opportunity to build a bridge to a part of the community that has felt alienated from its services. The family may see it as a new resource that until now was not accessible.

Diversity factors in the community at large also can play an important role in planning. The more homogeneity there is in the culture of a community, the more expectations tend to be standardized. The positive side is that homogeneity creates cohesion and community pride in common heritage and traditions. The negative side is that there often is less tolerance for those who are "different." However, valuing "sameness" does not mean that "differentness" is bad. People can come to realize that there is strength in variety and diversity, but overcoming fear and prejudice is not easy. When the community is relatively homogeneous, there will likely be options for planning that are influenced by community expectations. These expectations may require certain expected behaviors but not tolerate others that deviate from the norm. Similarly, certain behaviors may not be tolerated because they are outside of the bounds of what the community will accept. This situation is probably more common in rural communities and in neighborhoods that have a strong ethnic identity.

Communities that are more heterogeneous may be more tolerant of a wider range of behaviors, but only to the extent that its citizens have been able to overcome their prejudices. Unfortunately, the gap between many ethnic and racial groups and the dominant Caucasian culture in America more often has resulted in devaluing diversity, even to the extent of open prejudice and oppression. When there is a gap between the expectations of the dominant culture and those of the person's ethnic or familial system, the client can feel he is in a double bind: no matter what he does he will be judged in a negative way by someone. In planning, the worker needs to discuss the implications of diversity and of prejudice and oppression so that the client is not set up for failure.

Strengths and Limitations of the Systems Involved

Each of the systems described above brings both strengths and limitations to the work to be done. A primary consideration in good planning is the concept of building on strengths while addressing limitations. Sometimes, limitations constitute barriers that need to be circumvented or overcome. However, the place to begin is with a strengths perspective. The worker needs to identify the capacities and potential of the agency, the community, the situation involving the social issue, the worker, the client and his immediate environment, and the diversity factors that might come into play.

To be successful in using a strengths-based perspective, the worker must be highly self-aware and sensitive to her own perceptions as well as those of the other systems involved in the situation at hand. When utilizing a problem-focused approach, there is a tendency to perceive the situation in terms of what is going wrong. This can easily lead to blaming, especially blaming the client for having the problem. The implication is that since the situation is caused by the client, all that is needed is for the client to change. Besides, changing a system seems a more daunting task than individual change.

The person-in-situation and the strengths perspectives dictate that all aspects of the situation need to be considered during assessment. Similarly, all aspects of the situation need to be incorporated in planning for change. A strengths-based perspective involves basing a plan on the abilities and capacities of clients and systems. Instead of requiring clients and systems to develop new skills and abilities as a prerequisite for change, the plan is based on what the client and systems are already able to do. In the case example, Maria was able to identify what Mr. and Mrs. Jones and their children were capable of doing. She also identified the fact that a strength for the school was its ability to develop and provide a good quality curriculum. Maria assessed that the boys were capable of displaying appropriate behavior, since they had done so in their other school. Maria saw the school as playing a vital role in sending a message of valuing diversity by recognizing the contributions of African Americans to the curriculum. Thus, each party was able to contribute to change by using skills they already possessed.

Finally, the strengths perspective is clearly the approach that fits best with two of the cardinal values of social work, namely, the belief in the value and worth of every individual and the belief in client self-determination. In addition to valuing people inherently as human beings, the strengths perspective orients the worker and the client toward abilities, thus valuing the contribution clients can make toward bringing about change. The strengths perspective gives clients the tools they need to exercise self-determination and recognizes that clients are a major force in their own lives. As people are able to make decisions for themselves, they also need to see themselves as acting to make those decisions a reality. Highlighting their strengths helps them realize how they can make self-determination a reality rather than merely an abstract concept.

Agreement between Worker and Client

When the worker and client have worked together in assessment and in developing the plan of action, an agreement develops between them as to what needs to be done and who should do it. This agreement may take the form of a **contract.** The contract may merely be an understanding between worker and client, or it may be a formal, written, signed agreement. The form the agreement takes will be dependent in part on what is best for a particular client and in part on agency practice and policy.

Contracting is an accepted part of the worker-client interaction in many agencies. However, the use of contracts has been challenged in two ways. Pamela Miller believes the use of contracts fails to recognize that the service provider is a professional using empathy as an important ingredient of the service. She calls for a covenant approach, which implies that the worker has a gift of service for the client.[9]

Tom Croxton has pointed out that the use of the term *contract* is inaccurate because it lacks an important ingredient—legal implications. He believes this inaccurate use can lead to misunderstandings, vagueness, and even conflict.[10]

Thus, instead of *contract*, the term *agreement* may better describe the worker-client decision. However, *contract*, as used in social work, has never been assumed to have a legal connotation. The concept of contract, as developed in social work literature, seems best to describe the agreement about the plan in the generalist social work sense. A contract can be thought of as an understanding between the worker and the client as to the work to be done. It is not necessarily a written document, though in some situations this is the case.

Contracts are easiest to develop with motivated, trusting clients. They are very useful with disorganized or forgetful clients who need reminding about the work to be done or about their responsibility for carrying out tasks. Contracts can be more effective if written, but sometimes this is not necessary or even desirable. For the resistant or distrustful client, a signed paper may be a barrier, whereas a verbal commitment might be helpful. For clients in crisis it may be best to quickly get to the work of helping and delay or eliminate the step of a formal contract. A quick verbal agreement may be all that is necessary. The contract should be flexible and appropriate to the specific client and situation. It should be a tool to enhance the work together, not a mechanistic procedure to fulfill some outside, imposed requirement. However, whether the agreement with the worker is written or not, the plan that is entered into the case file should still be reviewed with the client.

Planning and contracting are means for making clear the who, what, where, when, why, and how of the social work endeavor. They are means for individualizing the social work process to the person in situation and provide tools for accountability and evaluation. Planning and contracting tie knowledge about the person in situation to the work of doing something to change the situation for the client. Planning expands opportunity for accomplishing the desired change.

Summary

The following principles for developing a plan of action can give guidance to the planning process:

1. Each plan of action is a part of an overall social work process. This implies:

   - It is based on personal-social need.
   - It is developed through a change process that is based on a strengths perspective.
   - It recognizes the impact of diversity on all aspects of the planning process and incorporates into the plan the strengths of the individuals and systems involved.
   - It is dynamic, changing as new knowledge leads to reassessment of situations, reformulation of need, and development of new goals, strategies, and tasks.

2. Each plan of action clearly indicates

   - The goal toward which it is aimed. This goal should be directly related to personal-social need and should be stated in terms of a positive outcome. Objectives should be clearly stated in positive terms.
   - The unit(s) of attention that are included in the plan.
   - The strategy to be used and the role of worker, client, and others and the tasks to be performed by all concerned.

3. The plan of action takes into consideration the community in which the action system functions. This includes the awareness of community expectations, norms, values, service delivery system, and resources.

4. The plan of action reflects the agency or organization "way of doing business." Community influences and agency organization structure, functioning, and development all contribute to this "way of doing business."

5. The nature of the social issue is recognized as an important variable in the development of the plan of action.

6. The worker's contribution to the plan of action is based on professional knowledge, values, and skill. It involves ability to assess and determine the usefulness of various resources as well as the capacity for professional judgment and the ability to make appropriate choices from among various possibilities.

7. The client brings uniqueness to the situation. This includes a perception of the need, a set of values, unique motivation, capacity, opportunity, and goals.

8. The plan of action is the outgrowth of the worker-client interaction. Each contributes from his or her perspective regarding the person in situation. Planning sometimes results in a contract between worker and client.

9. The plan of action considers the availability of the resources needed to carry out the plan and the feasibility of reaching the goals.

10. The plan of action includes a time line.

11. The plan contains a means for evaluation.

QUESTIONS

1. Set a goal for yourself that you can reach in a week. Write it in outcome terms and identify three objectives that relate to the goal.

2. Discuss the difference between process, method, and goals.

3. What do you see as the advantages of being very clear about the identification of the unit of attention?

4. With three of the roles identified by Teare and McPheeters, discuss the complementary client role and possible tasks for client and worker.

5. In developing a plan of action for a client, discuss some considerations that exist in a community with which you are familiar.

6. Develop a shared, mutual, or common goal that you might use with a family. Develop a second goal that is reciprocal.

7. Develop a common goal that you might use for a group for adolescents experiencing difficulties being successful at school. Develop an individual goal for one of the group members who has poor attendance.

8. Identify how diversity might impact the plan and the planning process if you are working with someone who is a person of color? A woman? A person who is gay or lesbian? A person who is physically or mentally disabled?

9. Identify at least three strengths that could be considered in planning with someone who is a person of color? A woman? A person who is gay or lesbian? A person who is physically or mentally disabled?

SUGGESTED READINGS

Chau, Kenneth L. "Social Cultural Dissonance Among Ethnic Minority Populations." *Social Casework* 7 (April 1989): 224–230.

Cox, Fred M., Erlich, John L., Rothman, Jack, and Tropman, John E., Eds. *Strategies of Community Organization,* 4th ed. Itasca, IL: F. E. Peacock, 1987 (Part III, "Strategies" and "Community Problem Solving").

Croxton, Tom A. "Caveats on Contract." *Social Work* 34 (March–April 1988): 169–171.

Epstein, Laura. *Helping People: The Task Centered Approach,* 3rd ed. Boston: Allyn and Bacon, 1992 (Chapter 7).

Gambrill, Eileen. *Critical Thinking in Clinical Practice.* San Francisco: Jossey-Bass, 1990.

Hepworth, Dean H., Rooney, Ronald, and Larsen, Jo Ann. *Direct Social Work Practice: Theory and Skills,* 5th ed. Pacific Grove, CA: Brooks/Cole, 1997 (Chapters 12 and 13).

Horejsi, Charles. *Assessment and Case Planning in Child Protection and Foster Care Services.* Englewood, CO: American Humane Association, 1996.

Miley, Karla Krogsrud, O'Melia, Michael, and DuBois, Brenda L. *Social Work Practice: An Empowering Approach,* 2nd ed., Boston: Allyn and Bacon, 1998 (Chapter 11).

Miller, Pamela. "Covenant Model for Professional Relationships: An Alternative to the Contract Model." *Social Work* 35 (March 1990): 121–125.

Monkman, M. M. "Outcome Objectives in Social Work Practice: Person and Environment." *Social Work* 36 (March 1991): 253–258.

Netting, F. Ellen, Kettner, Peter M., and McMutry, Steven L. *Social Work Macro Practice.* New York: Longman, 1993.

Reid, William. *Task Strategies: An Empirical Approach to Clinical Social Work.* New York: Columbia University Press, 1992.

Rothman, Jack, and Sager, Jon Simon. *Case Management: Integrating Individual and Community Practice.* Boston: Allyn and Bacon, 1998.

Rothman, Juliet. *Contracting in Social Work.* Chicago: Nelson-Hall, 1996.

Saleeby, Dennis. *The Strengths Perspective in Social Work Practice,* 2nd ed. New York: Longman, 1997.

Seligman, Martin. *What You Can Change and What You Can't.* New York: Alfred Knopf, 1994.

Sheafor, Bradford W., Horejsi, Charles R., and Horejsi, Gloria A. *Techniques and Guidelines for Social Work Practice,* 4th ed. Boston: Allyn and Bacon, 2000 (Chapter 13).

Toseland, Ronald W., and Rivas, Robert F. *An Introduction to Group Work Practice,* 3rd ed. Boston: Allyn and Bacon, 1998 (Chapter 6).

Weinbach, Robert. *The Social Worker as Manager,* 2nd ed. Boston: Allyn and Bacon, 1994.

Zayas, Luis H., and Katch, Michael. "Contracting with Adolescents: An Ego-Psychological Approach." *Social Casework* 70 (January 1989): 3–9.

NOTES

1. This formulation is similar but not identical to a format developed by Ruth R. Middleman and Gale Goldberg, *Social Service Delivery: A Structural Approach to Social Work Practice* (New York: Columbia University Press, 1974), chap. 1, "A Frame of Reference."

2. Fred M. Cox, John L. Erlich, Jack Rothman, and John E. Tropman, Eds., *Strategies of Community Organization,* 4th ed. (Itasca, IL: F. E. Peacock, 1987), p. 258.

3. Emelicia Mizio and Anita J. Delaney, Eds., *Training for Service Delivery to Minority Clients* (New York: Family Service Association of America, 1981).

4. Robert J. Teare and Harold L. McPheeters, *Manpower Utilization in Social Welfare* (Atlanta, GA: Southern Regional Education Board, 1970), p. 34.

5. Ibid.

6. Ronald L. Simons and Stephen M. Aiger, "Facilitating an Eclectic Use of Practice Theory," *Social Casework* 60 (April 1979): 201–208.

7. For a discussion of nonmetropolitan service delivery, see Louise C. Johnson, "Human Service Delivery Patterns in Non-Metropolitan Communities," in *Rural Human Services: A Book of Readings,* H. Wayne Johnson, Ed. (Itasca, IL: F. E. Peacock, 1980), pp. 55–64.

8. Elliot Studt, *A Conceptual Approach to Teaching Materials* (New York: Council on Social Work Education, 1965), pp. 4–18.

9. Pamela Miller, "Covenant Model for Professional Relationships: An Alternative to the Contract Model," *Social Work* 35 (March 1990): 121–125.

10. Tom A. Croxton, "Caveats on Contract," *Social Work* 34 (March–April 1988): 169–171.

13 Direct Practice Actions

LEARNING EXPECTATIONS

1. Understanding of the need to match the action taken to the needs of the client.
2. Knowledge of the various kinds of action that may be used to help clients.
3. Understanding of principles that should be used in making choices about the action to be taken.
4. Understanding of how to enable clients to use available resources.
5. Understanding of strategies for empowering and enabling clients.
6. Knowledge of the range of resources that can be used to help clients.
7. Knowledge of the referral process.
8. Understanding of the nature of crisis.
9. Knowledge of the crisis intervention process.
10. Understanding of the nature of support.
11. Understanding of the place and use of activity in helping clients.
12. Understanding of the use of mediation in helping clients.

Following planning, the next step in the generalist social work service process is action. Different clients with different needs in different situations require different kinds of action on the part of the worker. For some situations the actions of the assessment and planning phase provide the help needed so that the client can then take action for change. Sometimes help comes through the development of the worker-client relationship. This relationship then frees the client to engage in problem-solving activity with the worker. In other situations, action on the part of the worker is required. This action can be helpful in the development of relationships and in assessment. Actions by the worker may be needed to implement the plan or when barriers arise. The social worker may also use various kinds of activity with people and with systems other than client systems as a part of the helping process.

Social workers need to be aware of the variety of theories available to guide their helping efforts. An in-depth study of the original sources of these theories is beyond the scope of this book. The Appendix, however, gives a short summary of the better-known theories, approaches, and models used by social workers.

One of the marks of a generalist practitioner is the capacity to choose from a wide variety of possibilities the action most appropriate for the specific situation. Social work action falls into two primary classifications: **direct practice** (action with clients) and **indirect practice** (action with systems other than clients). Direct practice primarily involves action with individuals, families, and small groups. Direct practice is focused on change in either the transactions within the family or small-group system or in the manner in which individuals, families, and small groups function in relation to persons and societal institutions in their environment.

Indirect practice involves those actions taken with persons other than clients in order to help clients. These actions may be taken with individuals, small groups, organizations, or communities as the unit of attention. This type of help will be discussed in Chapter 14.

Direct practice falls within the following categories:

1. Action taken to enable development of relationships
2. Action taken to enable development of understanding of persons in situations
3. Action taken in the planning process
4. Action taken to enable the client to know and use resources available
5. Action that empowers or enables clients
6. Action taken in crisis situations
7. Action taken to support the social functioning of clients
8. Action taken that uses activity with clients as the base of help
9. Action taken to mediate between clients and a system in their environment
10. Action taken in using a clinical model of social work

In this chapter, action related to the use of resources, to empowerment and enabling of people, to crisis intervention, to support, to the use of activity, and to mediating is discussed. Action taken to enable the development of relationships and of an understanding of person in situation and action taken in the planning process have already been discussed. Action taken in using clinical models of social work is beyond the scope of this book.

Action also depends on the skills of the worker. The *NASW Code of Ethics* mandates that social workers only practice in areas in which they have competence. Depending on the service goals and the usual ways the agency delivers service, workers more often use one kind of action than others. Skill in using the various types of action develops through use over time. In order to help diverse clients with various needs, social workers can be most effective when they are skilled in using a variety of actions and choose the action best suited to the client and the situation. The generalist practitioner's repertoire includes actions for working with individuals, groups, families, organizations, and communities. Often, several types of action are needed to reach identified goals. There is overlap among possible actions or strategies, and often the worker creatively combines strategies or makes alterations to better respond to specific situations. The art of social work comes into play when action becomes the focus of service.

In deciding which kinds of action to take in a particular situation, several principles can be used, including:

1. *Economy*—The action chosen should require the least expenditure of time and energy by both client and worker. Generally, a worker helps the client do for himself whatever is possible to do with help and does for a client only what the client cannot do for himself.

2. *Self-determination of clients*—The action that is most desirable to the client should be used whenever possible. The action of the worker is planned with the client during the planning phase of the helping process.

3. *Individualization*—Any action taken should be differentially adapted to the strengths, needs, and characteristics of the particular client system. The worker should creatively adapt the action to the client's characteristics and situation.

4. *Development*—The action of the worker depends, in part, on the developmental stage of the client system. Different kinds of help are appropriate at different stages of development of the individual, family, and small group.

5. *Interdependence*—The action of the worker depends in part on the action of the client. The activity of the client and the client's capacity to change should always be considered. The actions of the worker and client should be complementary.

6. *Focus on service goals*—The action should be related to the goals for the service as developed by the worker and client together during the planning stage.

Action to Enable Clients to Use Available Resources

For some clients the major block to meeting need is a lack of resources. Sometimes these resources are available but the client is not aware of or does not know how to use them. Sometimes the resource is not responsive to some clients. In a complex and diverse society all resources are not amenable to all clients. One part of the generalist social worker's understanding of a community is knowing which resources can meet the needs of which clients. An important part of the social worker's interventive repertoire is the ability to match client and resource and to enable the client to use the available resources.

To help clients use the available resources, workers should have knowledge and skill in four areas: (1) knowledge of the service delivery systems of the community in which they practice and the community in which the client lives and functions; (2) knowledge of and skill in the use of the referral process; (3) knowledge of the appropriate use of the broker and advocate roles and skill in filling these roles;

and (4) knowledge of how to empower clients to take charge of their life situation. The social worker takes action to enable clients to use available resources, with the purpose of enabling clients to meet their needs and thus enhance their social functioning and coping capacity.

The Service Delivery System

When identifying components of the service delivery system, workers usually begin by identifying social service agencies and services provided by other professionals. A far broader view needs to be considered. Within many neighborhoods, communities, and ethnic groups, a helping network outside the formal system exists. This **natural helping system** becomes known to social workers as they attempt to stretch the scarce resources of the formal system in a time of economic stress. There is, however, much to be learned about how to work cooperatively with this system.

The natural helping system is made up of a client's family, friends, and coworkers. These are the people to whom a person in need goes for help first. When clients come to a social worker, they have probably first tried to get help from these natural helpers. Social workers can sometimes strengthen or support the natural helping attempts rather than take over the helping function completely. The extended family has always been an important part of the helping system for many ethnic groups and in small towns and rural areas. For example, among Native Americans the extended family is so important that if a social worker fails to involve this system in the planning process, the client may not be able to use any help offered. Ross Speck and Carolyn Attneave have developed a method of working with extended families called network therapy, which involves and supports the extended family in helping a family member in need.[1] A **network** is an association of systems that operates through mutual resource sharing.

The work of Eugene Litwak and Ivan Szelenyi supports the use of family, neighbors, and kin as a helping resource.[2] They consider neighborhood ties to be useful because of the speed of response to need. With such ties, the person seeking help has personal, immediately available contact. The person in need is continually observed, and help is provided quickly when situations change. Family or kin are particularly helpful because of the long-term relationship that exists. For example, they are a resource for the care of children when a parent dies or when individuals face long-term medical care or institutionalization. Friendship networks are useful because of the strong emotional element and aspect of free choice.

Also part of the natural helping network are natural helpers in the community, community benefits, and self-help groups. **Natural helpers,** sometimes called indigenous helpers or healers, are those persons who possess helping skills and exercise them in the context of mutual relationships. These are usually individuals who make helping a part of their everyday life. They are hardworking people who are optimistic about being able to change; mature, friendly people who often have had the same needs as those they are helping; trustworthy people who keep confidences; and people who are available and share a sense of mutuality with others.

They usually have had similar life experiences and have similar values as the person they are helping. Members of neighborhoods, small communities, or ethnic groups usually know who these people are. For example, in the Hispanic community the *curandero* is considered the indigenous healer to be consulted when someone needs mental or medical treatment. However, it is often difficult for professional people to identify these healers without help from those who are a part of the community system.

Alice Collins and Diane Pancoast have discussed effective methods for working with natural helpers.[3] They believe that social workers should not try to train natural helpers or make them paraprofessionals. Rather, social workers should recognize natural helpers as valuable resources and support them in their unique ways of helping. This requires recognition of natural helpers' capacity and competence to help and calls for a consultative relationship.

Community benefits, fundraising events organized for someone who has had a catastrophe such as a fire, illness, or death of a family member, is another example of the natural helping system at work. Many cultural groups are more comfortable with this form of support than with support from a formal organization. The challenge to the worker is to use organizational skills in working with the client's native community while at the same time ensuring that leadership and responsibility for the benefit resides in the culture. Some of the guidelines suggested below concerning working with natural helping systems can be useful in this regard.

Self-help groups may also be considered a part of the natural helping system. Mutual aid is related to the responsibility people feel for one another. One means of carrying out this responsibility is the voluntary small group, often of spontaneous origin, that develops for people who have similar problems. Groups are important in developing connectedness to others at a time when isolation may be experienced. They are useful in encouraging growth and redefinition of self. Some also work for change regarding social issues that impact group members. In these groups those who have lived through problems help those who currently experience the problem. Help is given by modeling, positive reinforcement, and emphasis on the here and now. Examples of such groups are Alcoholics Anonymous, cancer support groups, and life-transition groups such as widow-to-widow groups.[4]

The relationship between self-help groups and formal human service organizations is often problematic because each has different ways of functioning. Such variables as the client group on which service is focused, the need for resources outside the system, and the relationship of helper and those receiving help usually differ significantly. Also, relationships among self-help groups and human service organizations vary. Yeheskel Hasenfeld and Benjamin Gidron have identified five relational patterns: competition, referral, coordination, coalition, and co-optation. The ideal relationship would be one of coordination and/or coalition.[5] Regardless of relational patterns, to maximize the use of self-help groups social workers must be aware of the relational pattern that exists and, when appropriate, work to facilitate a different pattern.

In working with all natural helping systems, social workers must be aware that these systems are primary groups that use an informal, personal means of interaction. Attempting to work with natural helping systems using the strategies and techniques of formal bureaucratic systems often blocks any meaningful interaction or coordination. Two results that can occur are: (1) The natural helping system may stop helping and allow the formal system to do the helping; in this situation the natural helping system is destroyed. (2) The natural helping system may withdraw from the formal system and go underground; in this situation the social worker is unable to coordinate and cooperate, and the two systems may offer help that does not allow the client to use both systems effectively. The consultative, enabling stance seems to be the most appropriate approach to functioning with natural helping systems. Social workers must be creative in linking formal and informal networks if the assistance of the natural helping system is to be maximized. It is most important to maintain communication without interfering with the functioning of either the formal or informal systems.

The formal service delivery system includes not only social service agencies but also organizations that either have an interest in specific projects or have resources for their members. The American Legion may be able to provide certain resources for a veteran or his family, particularly if that veteran is a member of the organization. The Lions Club has always concerned itself with visual problems and might help in obtaining glasses for a client. Other organizations may have resources, such as used clothing stores, that can provide necessary items for clients. The social worker should be aware of these organizational resources.

To help clients use the resources of various community institutions and professionals, the social worker needs a good understanding of the available services and resources and how clients can best avail themselves of these resources. Acquaintance with other professionals such as teachers, ministers, and doctors can help the worker learn of resources. Skill in coordination, consultation, and team functioning, as discussed in Chapter 14, is often important in helping clients use resources.

Service delivery by social service agencies takes different forms. Agencies use many kinds of workers to deliver different services. MSWs deliver clinical services; BSWs are used in many ways to support clients, to help with meeting needs, and to provide concrete services; paraprofessionals may also be used to provide some services. Indigenous workers, who can be skilled in working with their particular cultural groups, may be another resource. Although they often have no formal education relative to social work, indigenous workers have knowledge of the sociocultural group being helped. Homemaker or chore services may be provided by paraprofessionals or indigenous workers. Volunteers also provide some services.

Service may be provided in an agency office only, or workers may reach out to people in need. Agencies may provide only counseling or clinical social work, or they may provide concrete services or resources such as food or money. Some agencies station workers in small communities or in neighborhoods not easily accessible to the main office. Other agencies use a "circuit-riding" approach to servicing clients in remote areas. In this approach, the worker visits an area on a scheduled frequency to meet with clients. With limited populations or for some highly specialized services, the client leaves the community to obtain service. Social workers must have knowledge of how agencies deliver services and what resources they have if they are to help clients find needed resources. Some agencies may not deliver services in a manner that is usable by some clients. Workers need to be aware of agency limitations so that they do not further add to clients' frustration by referring them to services that are unattainable or institutions that are unresponsive.

The first step in enabling clients to use resources is a thorough knowledge of the resources available. The second step is choosing the appropriate resource for the client. This choice is based on matching client need and lifestyle with a resource that can meet the need and provide help congruent with the client's lifestyle. Client involvement in the choice is important for obtaining the desired match, for linking the client to the resource. In addition, workers may use indirect practice strategies to work for change in the relational patterns characterizing segments of the service delivery system so that client need can be better met. (See Chapter 14.)

Referral

Referral is the process by which a social worker enables a client to become aware of and make contact with another service resource. In addition, the referral process involves supplying the referral agency with information that may be helpful in providing service to the client and then following up on the usefulness of the service to the client. The worker must obtain written permission from the client or the client's guardian, usually called a release of information, before sharing any identifying information about the client system with an outside service. The referral service may be used in conjunction with the service a worker is providing or as the primary service.

Referral is used when the client's needs cannot be met by services provided by the agency that employs the worker or when a more appropriate service is provided by another agency. The worker uses knowledge of the potential resources and knowledge of the way service is delivered to match potential clients and potential services so that the service is acceptable to and usable by clients.

Referrals are made only with permission of the client. The worker and client together discuss the potential service, and the worker helps the client make the initial contact with the new agency, if necessary. This can be done by giving a phone number or directions for reaching the agency or by making suggestions about how to approach the agency. Sometimes it is helpful for a worker to call the agency for the client or go to the agency with the client for the first contact. It is important for the worker to make sure the client has the resources needed to access and utilize the service, including transportation, access to a telephone, financial resources, and daycare.

The worker and client also discuss the information that would be helpful to the agency. After receiving the client's permission and obtaining a written release of information, a worker provides this information to the worker at the new agency. It is often helpful if the two workers know each other and can discuss the client's needs.

A last and often overlooked step in referral is follow-up. In determining whether the client is receiving the services sought, the worker gains information about the appropriateness of the service for the client and others who may have similar needs. This enables the worker to make appropriate referrals in the future. If the client has not been able to use the service, the worker may need to follow up with the client to help her receive the needed service elsewhere or to determine why she was unable to use the service. Skill in referral is a necessary tool for all social workers.[6]

Broker and Advocate Roles

In enabling clients to use available resources, two primary roles are used: the broker role and the advocate role. It is important for the social worker to understand the difference between these two roles and to choose the one most appropriate to the situation. The **broker** helps a person or family get needed services. This includes assessing the situation, knowing the alternative resources, preparing and counseling the person, contacting the appropriate service, and ensuring that the client gets to the resource and uses it.[7] The goal is to expedite the linkage of client to the needed resource. This involves giving information and support, teaching clients how to use resources, and also negotiating with the agency.

The role of the advocate consists of "pleading and fighting for services for clients whom the service system would otherwise reject."[8] For example, a lesbian couple might be denied housing because of their relationship, or a person with HIV or AIDS may be denied medical treatment. The worker as advocate seeks different interpretations or exceptions to rules and regulations, points out clients' rights to services, and alerts clients to blockages in receiving or using an agency's services.

In the advocacy role, the worker speaks on behalf of the client. Before engaging in advocacy a worker must first be sure that the client desires the worker to intervene in this manner. Then the worker must carefully assess the risks involved for the client if advocacy is used. This includes consideration that any action taken might cause problems for the client or block access to the resources. The client should clearly understand the risks involved and be motivated to use the service if it is obtained. Case advocacy, advocacy for a single client, is most effective when used to obtain concrete resources for which the client is eligible. It is also useful when people and systems impinge on a client's functioning. To be a **case advocate,** social workers must be comfortable with conflict situations and knowledgeable about the means for conflict management. They must be willing to negotiate and be aware of the value of withdrawing application for service if the best interests of the client are not being served. Clients must have considerable trust in the worker before they will be willing for the worker to take an advocate role.

The worker uses the advocate role only when the broker role is not effective. Whenever possible, it is better for the client to act on her own behalf in order to strengthen her belief in self as well as gain a sense of empowerment. There are times, however, when an advocate stance must be taken in order to enable clients to obtain needed services. *Cause advocacy,* which serves groups with similar difficulties, will be addressed in Chapter 14.

Case Example

The social worker in a pediatric intensive care unit has been working with the Norton family since their prematurely born son, Bobby, was a few hours old and placed on the unit. Bobby is now three months old and is ready to be discharged to his home in a community one hundred miles away. The family is still having some emotional reaction to having a premature baby. The parents have been able to visit only once a week because of the distance and the fact that they have three other children, ages 2 to 6. Bonding is still somewhat of a problem, and Mrs. Norton seems frightened of what she sees as a very fragile baby. Bobby is showing more than the usual developmental delays of a premature baby and needs an infant stimulation program as well as continued monitoring of his physical condition.

The social worker knows that if this child is to continue to progress when he is discharged from the hospital, it is important that the Nortons use a variety of resources. Because they live in a small city, the social worker knows that she will have to be creative in finding what is needed. After receiving *written* permission from the Nortons, she calls the social worker in the small hospital that sent Bobby to the intensive care unit and finds that there is a local child welfare agency that can serve as a resource to help the Nortons with their feelings about Bobby, his prematurity, and his delayed development. The worker on the intensive care unit then discusses with the Nortons a referral to the agency. She shares her concern that they have the support they need in the next few months so that Bobby will be able to develop optimally. She informs them that the child welfare agency can also help the Nortons work with the school district to set up an infant stimulation program. The Nortons agree that they would like to have someone to talk to about their concerns regarding Bobby and agree that the social worker can call the agency and discuss the needs of the family and of Bobby.

When the social worker calls the agency, she finds that it is willing to work with the Nortons. The agency worker says she will get in touch with the Nortons before Bobby is discharged to help them in the transition period. (She feels it important to reach out now so that the relationship can develop before the Nortons become overwhelmed by their concerns about Bobby's care.) The worker also says that she is aware of several mothers of premature children she thinks would benefit from a group. She is willing to call them to see if they want to start a group. This group of mothers could also use resource persons to help them understand the needs of their children. The agency worker asks about the Nortons' extended family and finds that there are no relatives in the state. She suggests that the family use the services of an older woman in the community who is good in helping families who need a grandmotherly type of childcare.

The intensive care worker now feels she can work with the Nortons on the details of Bobby's discharge. She feels comfortable that the child welfare agency can meet the needs of this family, both through their own services and through referral to other community resources.

Empowerment and Enabling

Some clients need more than referral, brokering, or advocacy if they are to make use of available resources. Most clients can benefit from being able to take an active role in changing the situations impinging on their functioning.

Empowerment is "a process of increasing personal, interpersonal, or political power so that individuals can take action to improve their life situation."[9] **Empowerment** has been suggested as a strategy of choice when working with members of minority groups, populations at risk, and women.[10] Empowerment is particularly useful in the contemporary world in which power is an all-pervasive issue and in which the gap between haves and have-nots is growing dramatically. Empowerment means providing clients with the supports, skills, and understanding needed to allow them to take charge of their own lives and become powerful in situations in which they have felt powerless.

Those caught in feelings or situations of powerlessness often lack knowledge of how to negotiate systems, feel hopeless that any change is possible, and often lack the self-esteem necessary for engaging in change activity. Empowerment involves providing clients with assistance in negotiating systems. It also involves motivating, teaching, and raising self-esteem so that clients believe that they are competent individuals with the skills needed for negotiating community systems and that they deserve the resources necessary for healthy social functioning. Empowerment enables clients to receive the benefits of society and increases their capacity to work toward resolving the conditions preventing them from providing for their needs.

According to Ruth J. Parsons, a literature search confirms that the important ingredients of an empowerment strategy are support, mutual aid, and validation of the client's perceptions and experiences. When these ingredients are present, there is a heightened degree of client self-esteem, more self-confidence, and a greater capacity to make changes or take action. She believes that an empowerment strategy calls for building collectives; working with others in similar situations; educating for critical thinking through support, mutual aid, and collective action; and competency assessment, or identification of strengths and coping skills.[11]

Thus, the use of groups, particularly mutual aid groups, is necessary for this action strategy. Silvia Staub-Bernasconi points this out and calls for a focus on consciousness development, social and coping skills training, networking, and mediation. Also, she notes that empowerment calls for work with power sources and power structures.[12] This strategy is congruent with the generalist social work model presented in this text. The strong emphasis on maximal client involvement in assessment, planning, and action to meet goals is an important ingredient of empowerment. Teaching clients about meeting needs and about the nature of the systems in their environment is a part of empowerment.

A technique useful in an empowerment strategy is consciousness raising, which involves giving the client information about the nature of the situation, particularly the various environmental forces impacting client functioning. This work can heighten client understanding of self in relationship to others. Workers must feel comfortable with the anger that can result from using this technique and be able to help clients use anger in ways that further the work at hand. When the time is appropriate, it is also important for the worker to help the client move beyond anger into other responses. It is hoped that the client can gain a more realistic view of the situation and then take advantage of change possibilities.

Groups are a powerful adjunct to consciousness raising. It is helpful to the client to see others struggle with new understandings and the work of a group be of benefit. The group can be involved in collective action and thus enhance a sense of individual power. The group can also be a support system for mutual aid. Participation in a group can lead to enhanced self-esteem and can help clients learn new skills.

The nature of the relationship between the worker and the client is an important consideration when using this strategy. When using an empowerment approach, it is critical to establish mutual respect, build on client strengths, share information and knowledge of resources in a sense of partnership, and consider the client as the "expert" on his own situation. Because the worker may be viewed as yet another person with power over the client, the social worker needs to act as a colleague rather than as a detached professional. This requires the worker to shift her frame of reference from that of an expert to that of a collaborator.[13] As the worker demonstrates belief in the client and points out existing competencies, the client will gain a sense of self-worth and a belief that he has the ability to bring about change.

Another valuable technique that can be an adjunct to an empowerment strategy is work focused on reducing self-blame. The client needs to see that the difficulties he is facing often have their source in the functioning of systems in the environment. The worker can help the client take responsibility for changing the environment by teaching specific skills for environmental change. Although the worker may also work for environmental change through advocacy and mobilization of resources, it is important that the client accept major responsibility; otherwise, the feeling of personal inadequacy may be further reinforced.[14]

Empowerment is not a strategy that is used in isolation from other strategies. Instead it aims to reduce helplessness so that clients can take charge of their lives.

Enabling or helping clients and others do what they want may seem similar to empowerment, but there are subtle differences. **Enabling,** the broader term, refers to helping an individual or system carry out an activity otherwise not possible. This term recently has taken on negative connotations when used with regard to alcohol and other addictions. For example, a spouse whose actions support the addictive behaviors of the partner is often called an enabler. As used in this book, enabling has a positive connotation in that the action being supported is desirable.

Sometimes in the process of empowering or enabling the client, the worker may need to work directly with the client to enhance positive thinking and actions. Often, the client has had experiences that reinforce a negative view of himself or his situation. He may be frustrated or may have learned that it is safer to predict failure than to hope for success. The client may blame himself or others for the situation. He may engage in self-defeating thoughts or actions. When the worker senses that this is happening, she can assist the client in changing his thoughts or actions so that he can successfully meet his goals and carry out his plan. The thinking part of this strategy is called a cognitive approach or intervention and is outlined in the Appendix. The action part refers to behavior, and this is also outlined in the Appendix. Some theorists have combined these two approaches into what is called a cognitive-behavioral approach.[15]

The basic idea behind this approach is that thoughts lead to feelings and behavior. Negative thoughts lead to negative feelings and negative reactions, and positive thoughts lead to positive feelings and positive behavior. While the BSW-level social worker is not generally trained to use this approach as a clinical intervention with severely impaired clients, it is important to be able to work with the client to develop positive thinking and actions as he carries out his plan. The plan contains behaviors that the client has agreed to engage in. These behaviors are stated in the objectives and tasks. If the client does not think he can accomplish something, he is unlikely to do so. The worker asks the client what he is thinking about the situation and about the proposed goals, objectives, and tasks. She listens for thoughts that might be barriers to success. She helps the client to see how his thinking can have either a positive or a negative influence on carrying out the plan. A good set questions to ask are: (1) What do you think will happen if you do this? or What were you thinking when that happened? (2) What do you want to have happen? (3) What could you do to make that happen today? This week? This month? (or Next time?) (4) What could you tell yourself that would make you feel more confident in doing that? (5) What kind of payoff or reward could you give yourself that would help you to remember to do that?

An important technique in empowering or enabling clients that uses a cognitive-behavioral approach is assertiveness training. In this technique, the worker assists the client to become more assertive about meeting his needs. She will generally engage in practicing and role-playing assertive behaviors in situations in which the client needs to advocate for himself. It is important that the worker help the client differentiate between assertiveness and aggressiveness. Assertiveness is the positive expression of oneself and is marked by the use of statements that begin with "I." Aggressiveness is imposing one's thoughts or feelings on others and is generally marked by statements that begin with "You."

Sometimes clients need to be able to use a behavioral approach in their relationships with others. This is especially valuable for parents who need to influence their children's behavior. An example of this is contained in a case example of a single-system research project in Chapter 15. Social workers are uncomfortable with using negative reinforcement or punishment to modify behavior, because doing so usually violates social work values and ethics. In addition, clients may have experienced a great deal of punishment and negative reinforcement in their lives. The use of extinction and positive reinforcement tends not to be a violation of social work values and ethics. Basically, **extinction** involves ignoring undesirable behavior to eliminate it. The parent should be warned that the initial response of the child will be to increase the behavior in order to receive the customary attention. However, persistently using this technique does result in the desired goal.

Positive reinforcement is giving a reward for or in other ways recognizing the desired behavior. Parents can give positive reinforcement whenever they observe the desired behavior, or they can make an agreement beforehand with the child to reward certain behavior. The strongest reinforcements are those that are identified by the person receiving them. If a reinforcement is given too frequently, it is more likely to change the behavior more quickly, but the strength of the reinforcement tends not to last very long. On the other hand, if the reinforcement is infrequent or seen as unattainable, it will have little impact on changing behavior. Sometimes a smaller reward or a symbol can be used on a more frequent basis and a larger reward given less often. An example of this would be a star chart where the child receives a star that he can put on a chart for each day of the week. When he earns enough stars, he is rewarded with a toy. In this way the stars serve as positive reinforcement on a day-to-day basis, and the toy serves as a longer-term reward.

Positive feedback is a form of positive reinforcement that is extremely important in developing and maintaining positive relationships. Many clients may not have received much positive support in their lives. Thus, they may not be able to give much positive support. Whenever the worker sees dissatisfaction with a relationship, she should look for the absence of positive feedback. The worker then can suggest ways to give positive feedback and ways to receive it. Generally, giving positive feedback results in getting positive feedback in return, although this may take some time if the other person has become accustomed to negative feedback or no feedback at all. Feedback is an important part of parenting. Parents need to give consistent messages about the behavior they expect from their children and then follow up with positive or negative feedback. Positive feedback tends to be the strongest form of positive reinforcement that a parent can give a child.

Actions that assist clients to engage in positive thinking and positive behavior are important to empowering and enabling them. The ability to be assertive may be needed for the client to advocate or speak up for himself. Positive reinforcement and feedback are essential to good parenting and to developing and maintaining successful relationships. The worker incorporates these tools into her work in empowering and enabling clients to carry out their plans.

Generalist workers who have a thorough knowledge of available resources and skill in making referrals, filling the broker and advocate roles, and empowering clients are prepared to take action that enables clients to use needed resources. This can often be the strategy of choice.

Case Example

In the case example of the A family from Chapters 1 and 10, the worker uncovered several concerns that might be resolved using an enabling approach. During the family sessions in Chapter 10, John mentioned that he was upset about being blamed for everything and that it seemed like he could never do anything right, especially in the

(continued)

Case Example   Continued

eyes of his father. The worker explored this with John and his father and identified some positive behaviors of John's that generally went unnoticed, such as making his bed in the morning, mowing the lawn, cleaning his bedroom, attending school each day without any unexcused absences, informing his parents of his whereabouts, and abiding by his curfew. Mr. A commented that he did not see why any one should get recognition for "doing what you are supposed to do." The worker asked him if he would go to work if he did not get paid, and Mr. A said that he would not, especially since he needed to support his family. The worker pointed out that getting positive feedback from one's parent was like "pay day" for children. Mr. A nodded his head and said, "I never thought of it that way." The worker then turned to John and asked him what he would like to hear when he did something positive. John said that a "Thank you" would be enough or "Nice job on the lawn" would be great. The worker asked Mr. A if he would be willing to give John positive recognition for positive behaviors he saw. Mr. A said that he would try.

In working with John regarding his difficulties at school, the worker discovered that John felt that the teachers did not like him and so his effort was minimal at times. The worker asked for some specific examples of things John saw that indicated that a teacher did not like him. John described getting a D on a paper and the teacher writing a note that she felt John could do much better than this. The worker asked what John thought the message was from the teacher. He said that it made it sound like he was lazy or stupid. The worker challenged this and asked John if those were the teacher's words or if they were words that he was telling himself. John admitted that they were his own words. The worker then asked how John felt when he interpreted the teacher's comments this way. He said that the whole thing made him upset; he felt like there was nothing he could do to please the teacher so why try anyway. With some further discussion of the situation, John was able to see how his own negative thoughts were getting in the way of his desire to do well in school. The worker was also able to help John to see that the teacher may have been expressing her disappointment, but also may be attempting to get him to try harder by letting him know that such work was not an indication of his potential. The worker asked John what he could tell himself that would create a more positive attitude toward his work in that class. John initially could not think of anything, but with some assistance decided that telling himself that he could do it would make him try harder. He agreed to do this before he did his next assignment. He also agreed to ask the teacher for some assistance.

Action in Response to Crisis

Clients use many coping mechanisms as well as the resources of the natural helping systems and community institutions before coming to a social worker. They often are under considerable stress and may be in a state of crisis. If the client is in a state of crisis, it is important that the social worker be able to recognize this situation and respond appropriately. Crisis intervention is a model of social work practice that provides a knowledge base and guidelines for crisis response. All generalist social workers should develop some knowledge of and skill in working with people in crisis.

The major goal of action in response to crisis (*crisis intervention*) is resolution of the crisis and restored social functioning. If, after this goal is reached, the worker and the client then decide there is some other goal they want to work on together, another kind of action is taken.

Recognizing Crisis

A **crisis** exists when a stressful situation and/or a precipitating event causes a system such as an individual or family to develop a state of disequilibrium, or to lose its steady state. Coping mechanisms that have worked in past situations no longer work, despite a considerable struggle to cope. A person or family continually in a state of disorganization is not in crisis; working with such a situation requires a different kind of action.

Crisis can be and usually is a part of the life experience of all people. Workers seeing clients in crisis should assume that these people were functioning adequately before the crisis event and should view the helping role as restorative rather than remedial. It is important not to base an assessment of clients' normal ability to function on the behaviors and coping mechanisms displayed during the crisis.

A crisis situation can develop because of situational and developmental factors. Situational factors include illness of the individual or close family members, death of a close family member, separation or divorce, change of living situation or lifestyle, and loss of a job. These situational factors call either for assuming new roles and responsibilities or for changing the established way of functioning with others. Sometimes these factors cause considerable stress only temporarily; after a period of instability and trying new coping methods, the result is a new and comfortable way of functioning. At other times, an additional stressful situation precipitates the crisis situation.

Developmental stress arises from the unsettled or stressful feelings that may occur as individuals move from one developmental stage to another. This movement requires new ways of functioning. Adolescence is a time of stress, a time when new concerns and needs may not be fulfilled. As young persons learn to deal with their sexual drives, make career decisions, and develop new relationships with parents, they may become overwhelmed, and crisis can develop. Families also experience a crisis as they move from one stage to another. The birth of the first child calls for new patterns of social functioning, thus creating additional stress and sometimes crisis.

Figure 13.1 provides an overall view of the crisis process. The hazardous state, the vulnerable state, and increase in upset are precrisis states that are often resolved by the usual means of coping and help from personal support systems. When these means do not bring about resolution, individuals move into a crisis state, and crisis intervention becomes an appropriate strategy for action.

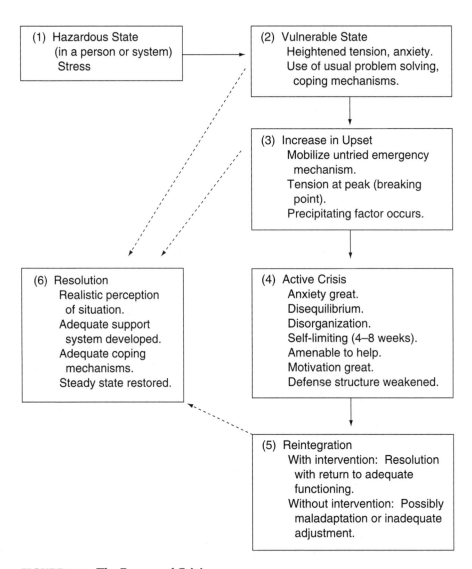

FIGURE 13.1   The Process of Crisis

Note: Dotted line indicates that Resolution can occur after states 2, 3, or 5.

Responding to Crisis

When working with individuals in crisis, the worker needs to be aware of the time element of crisis. The true crisis situation generally lasts from four to eight weeks. After that time individuals find new ways of coping. Without appropriate help during the crisis stage, the result may be a reduced capacity for effective social functioning. Thus, help for individuals in crisis must be immediate and sometimes fairly intensive.

The worker has two crucial tasks: (1) to develop an understanding about the person in crisis and what precipitated the crisis and (2) to develop the helping relationship. In developing an understanding, the worker searches for the precipitating event—the event that pushed the person into crisis—as well as the nature of the underlying stressful situation. The worker also determines what the client has tried to do to resolve the stress (the coping mechanisms used) and encourages the client to share how she feels about the situation.

The worker forms a helping relationship by actively responding to the client's concern and need. Together they explore the situation and determine the reality of the client's perceptions. The worker supports the client's strengths by acknowledging the coping attempts and makes specific suggestions for other means of coping. The worker shares with the client his understanding of the situation. The worker communicates realistic hope that the crisis can be resolved and that he will help the client through this difficult time. The client is encouraged to express feelings about the situation. The worker is sensitive to the client's anxiety and to the possibility of depression. If excessive anxiety or depression develops, the worker helps the client seek the services of a competent mental health professional. The worker also links the client to other needed resources.

Through the work together in the four- to eight-week period of crisis, the client usually discovers new coping mechanisms, and the crisis is resolved. In the latter part of this period, the worker can often enhance the client's problem-solving skills and thus prevent future crises. Working with clients in an intensive, fairly directive manner during the crisis helps prevent future social-functioning difficulties and restores the client to a state in which she can manage in an effective manner.

When family systems experience crisis, the use of crisis intervention is also appropriate. Sometimes it is possible to work with persons in crisis in small groups. When the worker has several clients in crisis situations, it can be helpful for these people to share perceptions and experiences as a part of the crisis response. Some crisis groups are open ended, with people in the later stages of crisis gaining help by helping those in the early stages of crisis.[16]

Case Example

When Mrs. Norton (in the first case example) came to see her newborn premature son for the first time, the social worker immediately noted that she was exhibiting considerable stress. She seemed unusually anxious, was hesitant to go into the nursery, and had to be encouraged to touch the baby. The social worker spent some time with the Nortons before they went in to see the baby. She tried to prepare them for the sight of the newborn, who had many tubes inserted into parts of his body. The social worker knew that the birth of a premature baby can be a cause of stress that leads to crisis.

After the Nortons had seen their son, the social worker invited them into her office. She first allowed them to talk about their reactions to seeing the baby. Mrs. Norton remarked that she felt like she was falling apart. She exhibited a great deal of guilt about not being able to carry the baby to term. Then she said, "This is really another piece of

(continued)

Case Example   Continued

bad luck." The social worker asked her what she meant. Mrs. Norton burst into tears and said that this year everything seemed to be going wrong. The worker asked what beside the premature birth had gone wrong. Mrs. Norton said it all started with the serious illness of her four-year-old child when she was three months pregnant. She had done a lot of lifting during that period and wondered if that could have led to the new baby being born prematurely. The social worker said she didn't know but wondered if Mrs. Norton should feel guilty about caring for her sick child. She then asked if there was anything else that had gone wrong. Mrs. Norton started to cry again and said that two months ago her mother had died very suddenly. She had planned to visit after the new baby was born and to help with the other children.

The social worker inquired about the functioning of the family prior to these stressful events and found that they had functioned adequately. She knew that at least Mrs. Norton, and perhaps the family, was now in a state of crisis. She sensed that prior to the time of the mother's death, Mrs. Norton was in a hazardous state due to the illness of her child and her pregnancy. She also believed that the death of the mother added to this stress and that Mrs. Norton was now vulnerable to crisis. The worker doubted that Mrs. Norton had recovered from the death of her mother when the new stress of premature birth occurred. Throughout the contact, the worker attempted to highlight Mrs. Norton's many strengths: her care for her family, her concern for her new son, her love of her mother, her ability to manage her household, and her willingness to work with the several systems involved.

In planning the work with the Nortons, the worker saw several tasks that needed immediate attention. Mrs. Norton needed an opportunity to talk about her feelings about the death of her mother and the birth of her child. She needed relief from the guilt she was feeling about her responsibility for the premature birth. She needed help in placing all of these stressful events in some perspective. The worker got the Nortons' permission to talk to the doctor who delivered the baby to see if he could discuss the reasons for the premature birth with the Nortons. She knew she needed to help Mr. Norton be aware of the reasons for his wife's distress and her need for support at this time. She asked if the family had a pastor they could talk to. They stated that they did and he had been helpful when Mrs. Norton's mother died. The worker suggested they get in touch with him, as she felt Mrs. Norton could still use some help around that event. She told them that it often takes time to deal with such a sudden death. She told them this was something they could work on while their son was in the hospital. She also discussed the need for frequent visits to the baby, and she set up an appointment for them to see the attending physician later that day to discuss the baby's progress. The Nortons stated they could only visit once a week as they lived at such a distance. The worker made arrangements for them to see her again on their next visit.

Action That Is Supportive

Support has been a universal part of helping. As Lois Selby accurately puts it, "It is as old as man's humanity to man."[17] Supportive means are a part of every generalist social worker's repertoire, yet support is a concept that has received little attention in social work literature. Beulah Roberts Compton points out that social work attitudes toward support historically have limited its use to chronic clients or to those for whom no other treatment is possible.[18] There is a prevailing notion that support is hardly worth the social worker's time. This notion seems to have developed as social workers emulated psychiatry and its world view.

Florence Hollis identifies sustainment as one of the procedures of social work practice.[19] Her usage of the term *sustainment* seems very close to the notion of support. She sees sustainment as primarily expressed by nonverbal means. Hollis identifies some of the components or techniques of sustainment as expression of the client's abilities and competencies, expression of interest, desire to help, understanding of a client's situation and feelings about that situation, and use of encouragement and reassurance. Reassurance should be realistic. Emphasis should be on the feeling component and support for the acceptability of having feelings about the situation of concern.

Contemporary social work sees support as an acceptable function. Social work literature recognizes the use of support as a means of helping people cope with difficult situations and thus to grow. However, little has been written that identifies the nature of support; there seems to be an assumption that social workers know what support is. The use of support seems to be an idea in the domain of practice wisdom of social work knowledge.

Judith Nelson has defined supportive procedures as "those intended to help clients feel better, stronger, or more comfortable in some immediate way."[20] She has also identified four kinds of support: (1) *protection,* which includes giving directions and advice, setting limits, and giving structure to complex or overwhelming situations; (2) *acceptance,* which includes making clients aware that the worker is with them in their struggles, confirming the worth of the person, and communicating understanding of clients' feelings and situations; (3) *validation,* which includes showing clients ways they are effective and competent persons, giving feedback, providing hope, communicating praise and approval, and encouraging clients in their coping efforts and role performance; and (4) *education,* which includes teaching clients how to cope and function effectively, providing clients with needed information, socializing clients to new roles, and helping clients develop self-knowledge. One of the ways of teaching is modeling effective methods of coping.

Not only is Nelson's classification useful for identifying what support will best meet a client's needs, it also is important in identifying which aspects of a client's functioning the worker desires to support. Selby and Compton discuss support as relating to a client's ego functioning. Two other useful ways to identify the specific area of social functioning that needs support might be in terms of coping tasks or life roles. Using the coping-task approach, the worker identifies the task or tasks a client confronts when coping with a life situation (e.g., acceptance of the limitations of chronic illness). Using the life-role approach, the worker identifies the client's limitations, difficulties, and strengths in carrying out a life role. For example, if the client has difficulty following through with disciplinary procedures as a parent, the worker might first note areas in which the client does follow through, such as meal preparation. The worker then helps the client determine what skills he uses to complete that task and teaches him how to use the same motivations and skills when disciplining his child. This approach builds on the client's strengths rather than weaknesses and reinforces the idea that the client has problem-solving skills useful in various situations.

When using support as an interventive strategy, the worker identifies the client's need (as in all social work practice). This assessment emphasizes the client's perception of the situation and the client's realistic experiences in attempting to fulfill the need. Feelings of threat or deprivation are particularly important to note. The assessment should also consider the client's capacity for hope, the client's strengths, and the support the environment can provide.

The worker then decides what behaviors and attitudes can be supported to enable the client to get the need met. A decision is made about the specific kind of support to provide. Sometimes it is useful to provide the client with concrete resources or tangible services as a means of demonstrating the worker's care and concern. Using a supportive approach, the worker tries to develop a climate for helping that is accepting, understanding, comfortable, and validating and in which the client feels free to discuss concerns and feelings openly. The worker expresses interest and concern, encourages and praises the client for appropriate efforts, expresses realistic confidence in the client's ability to cope and to carry out life tasks, guides the client, and provides needed structure for the client's work.

Problems can arise from the inappropriate use of support. For one thing, there is always a danger that the client will become overly dependent on the worker. Thus, the worker must guard against unrealistic expectations on the part of the client and avoid helping when the client can help himself or when the environment can provide the support. Workers need to be aware of their tendencies to be overly protective or to make up for the wrongs clients have suffered. The worker also needs to be aware that an evaluative tone can create resistance in the client and thus be counterproductive.

While worker support is an important component of the social work endeavor, the worker also should focus on helping the client build an adequate support system within the client's natural environment. Support from relatives, friends, family, ministers, churches, and so on is essential to healthy functioning. If these systems have not been adequate or have broken down, the worker should assist the client in rebuilding or strengthening these relationships as a means of resolving the current situation as well as meeting future needs.

In the past, many social workers have become accustomed to spending extra time in a supportive role with clients. However, managed care and limitations on services have reduced the time available for such extra support services. Social workers need to be certain from the beginning that adequate support systems are in place for the client, especially in a situation in which time limits are placed on the service. If support is needed from more formal support systems, then developing a relationship with those systems must be a priority.

Small groups have been found to be effective for providing support. These support groups are of particular value for use with caregivers,[21] those who have family members suffering from chronic or life-threatening conditions,[22] and those who have had a common debilitating experience.[23] The worker should be aware of support groups and self-help groups that are available in the client's area. If a group is needed, the worker may initiate setting up a group through her own agency if appropriate or may approach another agency whose services might potentially include such a group. In the era of managed care and limited services, agencies may need to sponsor these groups as a means of providing support beyond the time limits of service. If agencies can collaborate and share this task, then the burden of committing staff and resources will not be overwhelming. For instance, a health care agency might agree to sponsor a group for caregivers of cancer patients, the local senior agency may sponsor a support group for caregivers of people with dementia, and the local substance abuse program may sponsor an AA group.

Properly used, support can produce growth, not just maintain the status quo. It provides positive reinforcement and can give clients strength to live and to grow in difficult situations. Support should be a part of the generalist social worker's interventive repertoire.

Case Example

Mrs. Gold is a sixty-year-old widow who has no children. She recently found out that the cancer she suffers from is terminal and that she probably has about eight months left to live; she has been referred to a hospice team. The social worker on the team has determined three foci for work with Mrs. Gold: (1) to see that the resources she needs are provided in such a way that the highest quality of life can be maintained, (2) to help Mrs. Gold problem solve and decide how she wants to live the life left to her and what she wants to happen after she dies (funeral arrangements and disposal of her material possessions), and (3) to provide the support that she so badly needs. In fact, supportive action is the primary focus of the work to be done.

The worker develops a relationship with Mrs. Gold and is careful to let her know what they can do together to make her life more comfortable. She explains the purpose of hospice and how volunteers will be assigned to visit with her and help her with both the activities of daily living and her task of bringing her life to a satisfying close. The worker will also be available to the volunteers to give them support as they provide service to Mrs. Gold.

Use of Activity as an Interventive Strategy

Activity is doing something or performing tasks as opposed to talking about what to do or about feelings and ideas. Activity can take the form of helping clients carry out normal life tasks. It can also take the form of activity constructed by the worker to enhance the helping process, such as role-playing a difficult situation or, in a small group, using an activity that requires cooperation.

Activity can be a powerful means for influencing change in the ways systems and individuals function. Through action individuals learn many of the skills needed for adequate social functioning. Socialization of individuals to the ways of their society and culture (that is, life experience) relies heavily on the use of action. Activity is a means for developing social-functioning skills and also for enhancing self-awareness. Activity leads to accomplishment, which in turn enhances self-esteem and a positive sense of self. Activity also has usefulness in developing an assessment. As the worker observes the client in action, the client's interactional and communication patterns become evident. The worker can also assess the client's competence in functioning and the quality of the functioning by observing the person in action.

Traditionally, activity has been used in certain segments of social work, notably in the use of games and crafts in social group work. The use of play therapy with children has been another use of activity. Milieu therapy (use of the setting) in institutions also uses activity. Some family therapists help families plan family activity. Workers dealing with chaotic families have found activity to be very useful.[24] Literature on the ways people learn emphasizes experiential learning involving activity. Activity has been a major technique in working with children and is considered valuable in working with "action-oriented" persons.

Activity is also useful in a variety of other helping situations and can be used as a technique for meeting many needs of clients. It enhances physical development and neuromuscular control and stimulates intellectual growth. Activity can be an acceptable release for feelings and emotions, teach patterns of behavior and provide self-discipline, enable acceptance by peers, and increase status. It can provide opportunity for making and carrying out decisions, for forming relationships, and for resolving conflict. Activity can also encourage the development of new interests, skills, and competencies. It can enhance social functioning by enabling movement along the normal growth processes and can be useful with persons who may be at risk of not developing. This risk is often related to lack of opportunity, and activity can provide needed developmental opportunities. In this sense, it can be a preventive approach.

Activity can be broadly defined as anything that involves action by the client. This includes structured activities that are a part of individual, group, or family meetings. It includes activities that the worker may participate in as a leader or facilitator. It also includes actions that the client needs to take in order to accomplish various tasks associated with the plan. Some practitioners refer to these latter activities as "homework" in that the client agrees to carry out certain tasks between sessions. There may be practice or role-plays that take place within the session to prepare the client for the work to be done outside the session. For example, in assertiveness training the client identifies a situation that requires him to be more assertive. Alternative ways of speaking up for himself are developed with the assistance of the worker (or the group, if it is group training). The situation is acted out during the session with the expectation that the client will practice between sessions. The client then reports back at the next meeting. It is essential to build activity into the work with the client so that the client can "own" the work to be done. The more active a client is in accomplishing the goals in his plan, the more competent he will feel. Activity is especially helpful to clients who are depressed. Movement toward a goal brings hope and a sense of accomplishment.

Care should be taken in how activity is incorporated into work with clients who have been oppressed or experienced discrimination or excessive control from others. If activities are imposed on these clients, it adds to their feeling of being controlled. The type of activity should enhance opportunities for choice, decision making, and empowerment. The way in which the activity is presented and carried out should also include these elements. Of course, clients should be allowed to decline to participate at any time with any activity without fear of negative consequences.

Social workers must plan activity carefully. This calls for an expanded knowledge of the nature of action and skill in its use. Robert Vinter has identified three aspects of activity: (1) the physical space and social objects involved in the activity, (2) the behaviors essential to carry out the activity, and (3) the expected respondent behavior because of the activity.[25] Before deciding to use any activity, a worker should assess these three aspects as they relate to the specific activity. Some dimensions discussed by Vinter that influence the action include (1) its prescriptiveness as to what the actors are expected to do, (2) the kinds of rules and other controls that govern the activity, (3) the provision the activity makes for physical activity, (4) the competence required for persons to engage in the activity, (5) the nature of participation and interaction required, and (6) the nature of rewards that are inherent in the activity.

It is also important to assess clients' capacity and use of activity. Areas particularly important to consider include:

1. *The client's particular need and interests*—Need should be identified before deciding to use activity. Interest can be identified by considering the client's stated desires, skills, and interests.

2. *The capacity of the particular client to perform the tasks required in the activity*—An understanding of age-group characteristics is important, as is understanding of the usual activities of a client's cultural or other diversity subgroup.

3. *The client's motivation and readiness to use the particular activity*—Some clients cannot use certain activities because of cultural taboos. Others, who are work oriented, may not be able to use activity that appears to be play. Clients need to have an opportunity to make choices among possible alternatives. Activity that is relevant to the client's lifestyle is usually the activity most useful to the client.

4. *The ability of the client's support system and community to accept and support the activity being used*—Consideration should also be given to these factors.

A third kind of analysis that workers using activity should carry out is related to its use in a specific situation and includes:

1. The materials, equipment, and resources needed to carry out the activity

2. The time and capacity required of the worker to help the client carry out the activity
3. The climate and environment in which the activity will be carried out (the environment's ability to allow the activity and its support for carrying out the activity)
4. Directions for carrying out the activity
5. Precautions and safety measures that need to be taken in carrying out the activity
6. Adaptations of the activity that may be needed

Based on the three kinds of assessments discussed above, a decision is made to use a particular activity. In preparing to implement the activity, the following tasks may need to be carried out:

1. *An activity may need to be tested or carried out to determine if all aspects are understood.* It is usually best not to use an activity with clients that the worker has not pretested. Adaptations should be made as necessary.

2. *All supplies and equipment must be obtained.* Rooms or other areas must be obtained. Responsibility is allocated for specific tasks to either the worker, other staff, or clients.

As the activity takes place, the worker should be supportive and positive, show rather than tell, and set appropriate limits. It is also important to discuss the process and outcome of the activity with the client after its conclusion.

In using activity as an interventive strategy, the criteria for "good activity" should be kept in mind:

1. Good activity grows out of the needs and interests of the client(s).
2. Good activity takes into consideration age, cultural background, and other diversity factors of the clients.
3. Good activity provides experiences that enable or enhance the physical and psychosocial development of clients.
4. Good activity is flexible and offers a maximum opportunity for client participation.

Because the possibilities for the use of activity are vast and varied, it is beyond the scope of this book to provide information about the use of specific activity. Social workers can make use of literature from the field of recreation, structured group experiences, and social group work to gain knowledge about the use of specific activity.[26]

In using activity the worker employs a creative approach and adapts the activity to the particular client's need. The creative use of activity can be a powerful influence for helping clients. Its use calls for skill and understanding on the part of social workers.

Case Examples

A ten-year-old girl is having difficulty expressing feelings. The worker gives her paper and crayons to draw a picture about her feelings. The picture is of a boat that she then destroys with black crayon marks. The worker is then able to help the girl verbalize some of her feelings of fear and insecurity, which the picture represents.

A group of mothers of young children is meeting in a battered women's shelter. The goal is for the mothers to interact with their children in expressing various feelings. The worker chooses as the activity the making of picture books containing illustrations of people expressing various feelings. The mothers will use the books with their children. As the books are worked on, the conversation revolves around appropriateness of pictures and how the books will be used.

A family is having difficulty understanding how family members see themselves in the family group. The social worker uses "family sculpting" to draw out the needed information. Family members place other family members in the physical pattern that most nearly depicts the sense of the family as they see it. This active method gives new understanding and enables the family to discuss desired changes.

Action as Mediation

Sometimes as the worker and client explore the client's needs, concerns, and situation, it becomes apparent that the way in which a client and a system in the client's environment interact is not functional. Often the situation is of a conflictual nature. For example, a mother seems unable to communicate with a probation officer so that they can work together in setting limits for her son. The mother is afraid of the authority represented by the probation officer and does not respond to his suggestions. The probation officer is frustrated and believes the mother is indifferent to her son's need for limits. The worker knows this is not the case. In such a situation a **mediation strategy** can be useful.

William Schwartz describes this strategy as "to mediate the process through which the individual and his society reach out for each other through a mutual need for self-fulfillment."[27] Later he describes it as "helping people negotiate difficult environments."[28] The worker's concern—and the focus of the mediation action—is the social functioning of both the client and the system. The transaction between the two is the concern, the target for change.

Mediation is basic to an ecosystems approach to social work practice. This approach views need as arising out of incongruity between the client and systems in his environment. Restoring or developing a balance between the needs of the client and the needs of systems in his environment is necessary for the situation to be resolved. Thus, a mediating role allows the worker to work with the client and individuals or groups in his environment without taking sides. Mediation bridges the gap between direct practice actions, or work done directly with clients, and indirect practice actions, or work on behalf of clients with systems in the environment.

In the example of the A family earlier in this chapter, the worker used a mediation approach in working with John and his father to increase positive feedback to John for positive behaviors. Mr. A wanted his son to reduce his negative behavior and increase his positive behavior. John wanted to hear that his positive behavior is appreciated. The worker was able to convince Mr. A that giving positive feedback would reinforce positive behavior from John. In working with this situation, the worker also could have inquired if John would be able to accept criticism for negative behaviors if he knew that he would also receive recognition for positive behavior. John might be expected to agree with this, since it is an even-handed approach. The worker did not take sides, but was able to help both John and his father come to a middle ground.

William Schwartz and Serapio Zalba and Lawrence Shulman have written extensively about this type of action and strategy.[29] Shulman has identified three blocks in the interactions of individuals with environmental systems:

1. *The complexity of systems*—The development of institutions and the bureaucratizing of their functioning has made it less possible for individuals to understand how to approach these systems or to use the resources they provide. These complex systems seem strange, impersonal, and often overwhelming to many clients.

2. *Self-interest*—The self-interest of systems often is in conflict with the interests of others or of the larger system of which they are a part. When such self-interest is predominant, it is necessary to make that system aware of the interdependence, and thus of the mutual interest, necessary for the functioning of the larger system.

3. *Communication problems*—Often, the inability of systems to work together is a result of a lack of communication or of inaccurate communication and thus of misconceptions about the other.[30]

In overcoming these blocks or problems the worker and client both have tasks. The purpose of mediation is not for the worker to be an advocate and challenge one or the other system but to help the two systems reach out to each other so that together they can achieve a common goal. The worker helps or enables each of the two systems to accomplish the tasks necessary but does not do the work leading to the goal. That work belongs to the client and the environmental system.

The worker has three major tasks to accomplish: (1) to help the client reach out to the environmental system, (2) to help the environmental system respond to the client, and (3) to "demand" that both the client and the environmental system do the work needed to reach the common goal.

In helping the client to reach out to the environmental system, the worker first points out to the client the common interests and goals of the client and the environmental system. The worker also identifies the blocks that seem to be preventing the client from reaching these goals. The worker challenges these blocks by pointing out ways they can be overcome and the advantages to the client of overcoming them. The worker tries to give the client a vision of what can happen if the client and the environmental system find a means of working together. In doing this, the worker reveals her own commitment and hopes for a society in which people and institutions work together for the common good. Through this the worker gives hope to the client. The worker also helps the client define what needs to be done in the reaching out, and together they decide how the client is to do it. The worker is careful to define the limits of what may be expected so that the client does not develop unrealistic expectations.

When helping the environmental system to respond to the client's reaching out, the worker points out their common interest and concerns and the obstacles that seem to prevent cooperative functioning. The worker tries to help the environmental system mobilize its concern and its resources for helping. Where appropriate, the worker can provide the environmental system with information that will enhance its understanding of the situation. In a sense, both the individual client and the environmental system are clients. In some situations (e.g., divorce) a social worker may be engaged as a mediator on initial contact. Both parties immediately are seen as clients under these circumstances.

In using this strategy, the worker negotiates a contract with the client and, when possible, with the environmental system as to the work (tasks) each will do in attempting to overcome problems. The worker helps both carry out their tasks by helping them adhere to the contract, clarifying what is expected in the situation, and requiring that they do their tasks.

Schwartz and Zalba have identified a four-step process for working with a client when using a mediative strategy:

1. *"Tuning in"*—The worker gets ready to enter the process of transactions in the situation.

2. *Beginning together*—The worker helps the various individuals involved to reach out to one another and identify what needs to be done. Contracts are negotiated.

3. *Work*—This is doing what needs to be done.

4. *Transitions and endings*—This consists of leaving the situation, ending the work together, the worker separating from the situation.[31]

Ernesto Gomez has adapted the four steps or phases of work for use with Chicano clients. He places particular emphasis on the tuning-in phase. He notes that in this phase it is very important to "tune in" to the culture by focusing on how culture may be affecting client in situation. This includes concern for linguistic and other cultural practices as they relate to the specific client's needs in the situation for which help is sought. As worker and client begin together, a cultural assessment helps to pinpoint how cultural factors contribute to the situation and how the culture can provide resources for dealing with the difficulty.[32] This approach can be useful when working with minority group members.

When working in a mediation mode, the units of attention are both the original client and the environmental systems involved. Each is helped to acknowledge the common interests and to become aware of the feelings, needs, and demands of all. This requires that the worker be aware of the rules and roles within the situation. The worker provides focus and structure for the work to be done. Based on his knowledge and understanding, the worker also supplies ideas and suggestions as to how the systems might better work together. Clarification and problem solving are important tools of the endeavor.

Although the mediation strategy was developed to use with small groups, it has proven equally effective in working with individuals and is particularly useful with institutionalized individuals.[33] It can also be used with family groups and is often useful in situations in which empowerment is a goal.

Summary

The choice of which kind of action generalist social workers take with a client should be based on the principles of economy, self-determination, individualization, development, interdependence, and focus on service goals. The choice also depends on the skill of the worker and the worker's interventive repertoire. The dimensions of using action follow:

- Action to enable clients to use available resources requires a thorough knowledge of the service delivery system, skill in use of the referral process, and skill in the use of the broker and advocate roles. The service delivery system contains the informal helping network as well as the formal system.
- Action that enables the clients to bring about change in their environment and its institutions allows for empowerment of powerless people.
- Action that enhances positive thinking and positive actions on the part of clients enables them to utilize strengths in themselves to bring about change.
- Action in response to crisis calls for skill in recognizing a crisis situation. Response to a crisis should be immediate and active.
- Action that is primarily supportive is focused on particular positive behaviors and attitudes. It guards against overdependence and can promote growth.
- Action in the form of activity is especially useful when working with action-oriented persons.
- Action is a tool. When using activity, the worker considers the client's lifestyle and characteristics. Also to be considered are the inherent characteristics of the activity and the process for carrying it out.
- Action can have a mediation purpose, which can be useful when the client and environment are not interacting in a functional manner. The worker helps client and environment reach out to each other so they can fulfill common needs.

QUESTIONS

1. What are some factors you would consider when making a choice about the kind of action to take with a client?

2. As a representative of a formal system (an agency), how would you go about helping a client use an informal system to obtain a resource she needs?

3. Empowerment has been considered of particular importance when working with women, people of color, and populations at risk. Why do you think empowerment is important in such situations?

4. Consider a situation that you are facing and describe a negative thought or feeling you have about it. Change the thought to a positive one that predicts a successful resolution and describe the feeling that accompanies it. How would acting on the positive thought change your behavior in that situation?

5. Describe the crisis process in a situation in which you have been involved. What was most helpful in the resolution of the crisis?

6. Name some situations in which you believe support is an appropriate action for a social worker to take.

7. Choose an activity that you think will be helpful in a specific situation. How did you go about choosing this activity? How should it be structured and presented?

8. In what kinds of situations would the mediating model be appropriate? When would it not be appropriate?

SUGGESTED READINGS

Aguilera, Donna. *Crisis Intervention: Theory and Methodology,* 8th ed. St. Louis: Mosby, 1998.

Auslander, Brian A., and Auslander, Gail K. "Self-Help Groups and the Family Service Agency." *Social Casework* 69 (February 1988): 74–80.

Balcazar, Fabricio E., Seekins, Tom, and Fawcett, Stephen B. "Empowering People with Physical Disabilities Through Advocacy Skills Training." *American Journal of Community Psychology* 18 (April 1990): 281–296.

Beck, Judith. *Cognitive Therapy: Basics and Beyond.* New York: Guilford, 1995.

Breton, Margot. "On the Meaning of Empowerment and Empowerment-Oriented Social Work Practice." *Social Work with Groups* 17 (1994): 23–37.

Brown, James S. Toby, and Furstenberg, Anne-Linda. "Restoring Control: Empowering Older Patients and Their Families During Health Crisis." *Social Work in Health Care* 17, 4 (1992): 81–101.

Brown, Karen Strauch, and Ziefert, Marjorie. "A Feminist Approach to Working with Homeless Women." *Affilia* 5 (Spring 1990): 6–20.

Browne, Colette V. "Empowerment in Social Work Practice with Older Women." *Social Work* 10 (May 1995): 358–361.

Castex, Graciela M. "Providing Services to Hispanic/Latino Populations: Profiles in Diversity." *Social Work* 39 (May 1994): 288–296.

Compton, Beulah Roberts. "An Attempt to Examine the Use of Support in Social Work Practice." In Beulah Roberts Compton and Burt Galaway, Eds., *Social Work Processes,* 6th ed. Belmont, CA: Wadsworth, 1999 (Chapters 12 and 14).

Cox, Enid Opal. "The Critical Role of Social Action in Empowerment Oriented Groups." *Social Work with Groups* 14, 2 (1991): 77–90.

Edwards, Richard L., Ed. *Encyclopedia of Social Work,* 19th ed. Washington, DC: NASW Press, 1995 ("Crisis Intervention: Research Needs," "Self-Help Groups," "Direct Practice Overview," "Natural Helping Networks," and "Women: Direct Practice").

Ell, Eileen. "Crisis Theory and Social Work Practice." In Francis J. Turner, Ed., *Social Work Treatment,* 4th ed. New York: Free Press, 1996.

Ellis, Albert. *Better, Deeper, and More Enduring Brief Therapy: The Rational Emotive Behavioral Therapy Approach.* New York: Brunner/Mazel, 1996.

Epstein, Laura. *Helping People: The Task Centered Approach,* 3rd ed. Boston: Allyn and Bacon, 1992.

Ezell, Mark. "Advocacy Practice of Social Workers." *Families in Society* 75 (January 1994): 36–46.

Gilliland, Burl, and James, Richard. *Crisis Intervention Strategies.* Pacific Grove, CA: Brooks/Cole, 1997.

Gitterman, Alex, and Shulman, Lawrence. *Mutual Aid Groups, Vulnerable Populations and the Life Cycle,* 2nd ed. New York: Columbia University Press, 1994.

Greenstone, James, and Leviton, Sharon. *Elements of Crisis Intervention.* Pacific Grove, CA: Brooks/Cole, 1993.

Gutierrez, Lorraine M. "Working with Women of Color: An Empowerment Perspective." *Social Work* 35 (March 1990): 149–153.

Gutierrez, Lorraine M., DeLois, Kathryn A., and GlenMaye, Linnea. "Understanding Empowerment Practice: Building on Practitioner-Based Knowledge." *Families in Society* 76 (November 1995): 534–542.

Harvey, C. B., et al. "Hopefulness and Empowerment in Minority Help-Seekers." *Guidance and Counseling* 10 (Summer 1995): 42–45.

Hasenfeld, Yeheskel, and Gidron, Benjamin. "Self-Help Groups and Human Service Organizations: An Interorganizational Perspective." *Social Service Review* 67 (June 1993): 217–236.

Hepworth, Dean H., Rooney, Ronald H., and Larsen, Jo Ann. *Direct Social Work Practice: Theory and Skills,* 5th ed. Pacific Grove, CA: Brooks/Cole, 1997 (Chapters 7, 13, 14, 16, 17, and 19).

Hoff, Lee Ann. *People in Crisis: Understanding and Helping,* 4th ed. San Francisco: Jossey-Bass 1995.

Kagan, Sharon L., and Weissbourd, Bernice, Eds. *Putting Families First: America's Family Support Movement and the Challenge of Change.* San Francisco: Jossey-Bass, 1994.

Kelley, James, and Sykes, Pamela. "Helping the Helpers: A Support Group for Family Members of Persons with AIDS." *Social Work* 34 (May 1989): 239–242.

Kingsley, Chris. *A Guide to Case Management for At-Risk Youth,* 2nd. ed. Waltham, MA: Brandeis University Center for Human Resources, 1993.

Klein, Amelia, and Cnaan, Ram A. "Practice with High-Risk Clients." *Families in Society* 76 (April 1995): 203–212.

Land, Helen, and Harangody, George. "A Support Group for Partners of Persons with AIDS." *Families in Society* 71 (October 1990): 471–481.

Lantz, Jim. "Cognitive Theory and Social Work Treatment." In Francis J. Turner, Ed., *Social Work Treatment,* 4th ed. New York: Free Press, 1996.

Lynch, Eleanor W., and Hanson, Marci J., Eds. *Developing Cross-Cultural Competence: A Guide for Working with Young Children and Their Families,* 2nd ed. Baltimore, MD: Paul H. Brookes, 1998.

Mattaini, Mark. *Clinical Practice with Individuals.* Washington, DC: NASW Press, 1997.

Miley, Karla Krogsrud, O'Melia, Michael, and DuBois, Brenda L. *Social Work Practice: An Empowering Approach,* 2nd ed. Boston, MA: Allyn and Bacon, 1998.

Mills, Linda. "Empowering Battered Women Transnationally: The Case for Postmodern Interventions." *Social Work* 41 (May 1996): 261–268.

Parsons, Ruth J. "Empowerment: Purpose and Practice Principle in Social Work." *Social Work with Groups* 14, 2 (1991): 7–21.

———. "The Mediator Role in Social Work Practice." *Social Work* 36 (November 1991): 483–487.

Parsons, Ruth J., and Cox, Enid V. "Family Mediation in Elder Caregiving Decisions: An Empowerment Intervention." *Social Work* 34 (March 1989): 122–126.

Reid, William. *Task Strategies: An Empirical Approach to Clinical Social Work.* New York: Columbia University Press, 1992.

———. *The Task Planner: An Intervention Resource for Human Service Professionals.* New York: Columbia University Press, 2000.

Rose, Stephen M., Ed. *Case Management and Social Work Practice.* New York: Longman, 1992.

Rothman, Jack. *Practice with Highly Vulnerable Clients: Case Management and Community-Based Service.* Englewood Cliffs, NJ: Prentice-Hall, 1994.

Rubenstein, Hiasaura, and Lawler, Sharene K. "Toward the Psychosocial Empowerment of Women." *Affilia* 5 (Fall 1990): 27–38.

Schuyler, Dean. *A Practical Guide to Cognitive Therapy.* New York: Norton, 1991.

Sheafor, Bradford W., Horejsi, Charles R., and Horejsi, Gloria A. *Techniques and Guidelines for Social Work Practice,* 5th ed. Boston: Allyn and Bacon, 2000 (Chapters 6 and 14).

Staub-Bernasconi, Silvia. "Social Action, Empowerment and Social Work—An Integrative Theoretical Framework for Social Work and Social Work with Groups." *Social Work with Groups* 14, 2 (1991): 35–51.

Swigonski, Mary E. "Challenging Privilege Through Africentric Social Work Practice." *Social Work* 41 (March 1996): 153–161.

Thyer, Bruce A. "Effective Psychosocial Treatments for Children: A Selected Review." *Early Child Development and Care* 106 (February 1995): 137–147.

Thyer, Bruce, and Wodarski, John. *Handbook of Empirical Social Work Practice.* New York: Wiley, 1998.

Tobias, Mark. "Validator: A Key Role in Empowering the Chronically Mentally Ill." *Social Work* 35 (July 1990): 357–359.

Wood, Gale Goldberg, and Middleman, Ruth A. "Groups to Empower Battered Women." *Affilia* 7 (Winter 1992): 82–95.

Worell, Judith, and Remer, Pam. *Feminist Perspective in Therapy: An Empowerment Model for Women.* New York: Wiley, 1996.

NOTES

1. Ross V. Speck and Carolyn L. Attneave, *Family Networks* (New York: Pantheon, 1973).

2. Eugene Litwak and Ivan Szelenyi, "Primary Group Structures and Their Function: Kin, Neighbors, and Friends," *American Sociological Review* 34 (August 1969): 465–481.

3. Alice H. Collins and Diane L. Pancoast, *Natural Helping Networks: A Strategy for Intervention* (Washington, DC: National Association of Social Workers, 1974).

4. Alan Gartner and Frank Riessman, *Self-Help in the Human Services* (San Francisco: Jossey-Bass, 1977).

5. Yeheskel Hasenfeld and Benjamin Gidron, "Self-Help Groups and Human Service Organizations: An Interorganizational Perspective," *Social Service Review* 67 (June 1993): 217–236.

6. For a good discussion of effective referral, see Elizabeth Nicholas, *A Primer of Social Casework* (New York: Columbia University Press, 1960), chap. 9, "How to Make an Effective Referral."

7. Teare and McPheeters, *Manpower Utilization,* p. 34.

8. Ibid.

9. Lorraine M. Gutierrez, "Working with Women of Color: An Empowerment Perspective," *Social Work* 35 (March 1990): 149–153.

10. Barbara Bryant Solomon, *Black Empowerment: Social Work in Oppressed Communities* (New York: Columbia University Press, 1976); and "Social Work Values and Skills to Empower Women," in *Women, Power, and Change,* Ann Weick and Susan T. Vandiver, Eds. (Washington, DC: National Association of Social Workers, 1980), pp. 206–214.

11. Ruth J. Parsons, "Empowerment: Purpose and Practice Principle in Social Work," *Social Work with Groups* 14, 2 (1991): 7–21. Also contains an excellent case example.

12. Silvia Staub-Bernasconi, "Social Action, Empowerment and Social Work—An Integrative Theoretical Framework for Social Work and Social Work with Groups," *Social Work with Groups* 14, 2 (1991): 35–51.

13. Karla Krogsrud Miley, Michael O'Melia, and Brenda L. DuBois, *Generalist Social Work Practice: An*

Empowering Approach (Boston: Allyn and Bacon, 1995), p. 31.

14. Good discussions of techniques are found in Gutierrez, "Working with Women," and in Solomon, "Social Work Values."

15. The approach that follows is a simplified version of cognitive and behavioral approaches. See Cognitive Therapy and Behavioral Therapy in Appendix. Also see Albert Ellis, *Better, Deeper, and More Enduring Brief Therapy: The Rational Emotive Behavioral Therapy Approach* (New York: Brunner/Mazel, 1996); Judith Beck, *Cognitive Therapy: Basics and Beyond* (New York: Guilford, 1995); Jim Lantz, "Cognitive Theory and Social Work Treatment," in *Social Work Treatment*, 4th ed., Francis J. Turner, Ed. (New York: Free Press, 1996); Mark Mattaini, *Clinical Practice with Individuals* (Washington, DC: NASW Press, 1997); and Bruce Thyer and John Wodarski, *Handbook of Empirical Social Work Practice* (New York: Wiley, 1998).

16. See the Appendix for an outline of this model.

17. Lois G. Selby, "Supportive Treatment: The Development of a Concept and a Helping Method," *Social Service Review* 30 (December 1956): 400–414.

18. Beulah Roberts Compton, "An Attempt to Examine the Use of Support in Social Work Practice," in *Social Work Processes*, 5th ed., Beulah Roberts Compton and Burt Galaway, Eds. (Pacific Grove, CA: Brooks/Cole, 1994), pp. 472–479.

19. Florence Hollis, *Casework: A Psychosocial Therapy* (New York: Random House, 1972), pp. 89–95.

20. Judith C. Nelson, "Support: A Necessary Condition for Change," *Social Work* 25 (September 1980): 388–392.

21. Patricia Ferris and Catherine A. Marshall, "A Model Project for Families of the Chronically Mentally Ill," *Social Work* 32 (March–April 1987): 110–114.

22. James Kelley and Pamela Sykes, "Helping the Helpers: A Support Group for Family Members of Persons with AIDS," *Social Work* 34 (May 1989): 239–242.

23. Carolyn Knight, "Use of Support Groups with Adult Female Survivors of Child Sexual Abuse," *Social Work* 35 (May 1990): 202–206.

24. See Elizabeth McBroom, "Socialization and Social Casework," in Roberts and Nee, *Theories of Social Casework,* pp. 315–351.

25. Robert Vinter, "Program Activities: An Analysis of Their Effects on Participant Behavior," in *Readings in Group Work Practice*, Robert Vinter, Ed. (Ann Arbor, MI.: Campus Publishers, 1967).

26. See Ruth R. Middleman, "The Use of Program: Review and Update," *Social Work with Groups* 3 (Fall 1980): 5–23. The Suggested Readings in this text contain many important sources for this material as well.

27. William Schwartz, "The Worker in the Group," in *Social Welfare Forum 1961* (New York: Columbia University Press, 1961), p. 154.

28. William Schwartz, "On the Use of Groups in Social Work Practice," in *The Practice of Group Work*, William Schwartz and Serapio R. Zalba (New York: Columbia University Press, 1971), p. 5.

29. See Schwartz and Zalba, *The Practice of Group Work*; and Lawrence Shulman, *A Casebook of Social Work with Groups: The Mediating Model* (New York: Council on Social Work Education, 1968), and *The Skills of Helping Individuals and Groups*, 2nd ed. (Itasca, IL: F. E. Peacock, 1984).

30. See Shulman, *The Skills of Helping Individuals and Groups*, pp. 9–10.

31. Schwartz and Zalba, *The Practice of Group Work.*

32. Ernesto Gomez, "The San Antonio Model: A Culture-Oriented Approach," in *Our Kingdom Stands on Brittle Glass*, Guadalupe Gibson, Ed. (Silver Spring, MD: National Association of Social Workers, 1983), pp. 96–111.

33. See Shulman, *A Casebook of Social Work with Groups.*

CHAPTER

14 Indirect Practice Actions

LEARNING EXPECTATIONS

1. Understanding of the need to engage in action with those other than clients.
2. Understanding of influence and its use.
3. Understanding of action to coordinate services.
4. Appreciation of the usefulness of a program-planning and development strategy.
5. Understanding of environmental manipulation as a strategy.
6. Understanding of the change-from-within (an organization) strategy.
7. Appreciation of the need to engage in cause advocacy.

In the generalist approach to social work practice, the worker is not only involved in direct work with clients (as discussed in Chapter 13) but is also involved in work with individuals, small groups, agencies, and communities on behalf of individual and family clients. This work has often been characterized as indirect practice. It is very often work with the agency and community systems and is sometimes described as *mezzo-* or *macropractice*.

In Chapter 1, the discussion of need pointed out the historic cause-function debate in social work. That discussion also noted two kinds of need: private troubles and public issues. Work with individuals and families usually falls in the function and private-trouble domain of response to need, whereas work focused on agencies and communities tends to fall in the cause and public-issue domain.

One of the identifying characteristics of the generalist social worker is the worker's ability to respond to both private troubles and public issues. Furthermore, the generalist social worker identifies both the private troubles and the public issues inherent in any practice situation and then decides the appropriate focus of the action for change. This focus may be on the private-trouble (individuals and families) or on the social-issue (agency and community) concerns. Often the focus may call for work with both private parties and the public. Thus, the generalist practitioner must possess knowledge and skills for indirect as well as direct practice and be able to combine the two when appropriate.

When working for large-system change, the generalist social worker may be able to engage in assessment and planning with the system of focus and thus use a collaborative strategy. If this is not possible, then bargaining or even conflict resolution strategies may be needed.

This chapter discusses six approaches that may be used in indirect practice:

1. Action designed to change the environment
2. Action that involves influentials
3. Action relative to coordination of services
4. Action for program planning and development
5. Action taken to change organizations
6. Cause advocacy action

Before discussing each of these approaches to action, attention will be given to influence as it relates to action on behalf of clients. As the social worker works with clients, the influence for change is heavily based on the worker-client interaction, particularly on the relationship between worker and client. In indirect practice, the worker often works with individuals and small groups in order to meet needs of clients either as small systems (individuals and families) or as collectives (community segments impacted by a dysfunctional delivery system or a social problem). Relationship remains an important aspect of influence, though other factors (such as the knowledge and expertise of the worker and the material resources and services the worker might have available) are also important. The worker's status and reputation are also important sources of influence. All these influences are used when the work together is collaborative and cooperative in nature. Sometimes persuasive techniques must be used for the other system or systems involved to become convinced that a collaborative or cooperative approach is of value to all concerned. Sometimes cooperation and collaboration are not possible, and confrontation, bargaining, and even coercion are necessary to reach the desired goals.

Sometimes the social worker initiates and participates in the action on behalf of clients. Sometimes mediation between systems is called for. At other times the social worker stimulates others to carry out the action. Regardless of who takes the action, some means of legitimizing any action taken must be sought. The social worker does not act in isolation but as a representative of an agency. Sometimes the social worker can act with or through an organization to which she belongs. Without the support of legitimization, the worker lacks the influence needed to support the change effort. Without legitimization, ethical issues can come into play.

Environmental Change

Environmental manipulation is the strategy that brings about alteration in the environment of a client as a means of enhancing the client's social functioning. Specifically, three factors in the environment are considered as appropriate targets for change: space, time, and relationships.

Environmental change has been a strategy of social work since the time of Mary Richmond. The term *environmental treatment* appears in the work of Florence Hollis, who discusses treatment of the environment as bringing about change in the situation of the client.[1] Max Siporin defines situational intervention as "actions that alter structural, cultural and functional patterns."[2] In discussing "change in behavioral setting," Siporin points out that "an environment has profound effects on the behavior, feelings, and self-images of the people who inhabit or use that setting."[3]

Richard Grinnel and Nancy Kyte report a study of the use of environmental modification by social workers in a large public agency. The authors state that this is a much more intricate technique than is widely believed.[4] This may be related in part to the fact that the environment is a complex system that transacts with clients and impinges on their functioning.

Environmental psychology provides some of the knowledge needed to understand the impact of the environment on individuals.[5] This knowledge relates the effects of crowding on individuals, the need for privacy, distance as it relates to different kinds of relationships, territoriality, and other aspects of individual functioning. As this field develops, social workers should gain more understanding about the use of this strategy.

Carel Germain and Alex Gitterman, in *The Life Model of Social Work Practice*, place considerable emphasis on the ecological aspects of human functioning.[6] They differentiate between the social and physical environments, pointing out that people in the environment not only can provide resources for clients but also can affect the client's behavior by their responses to that behavior. When considering the physical environment, both the "built world" and the "natural world" are included. Although social workers have long used the strategy of environmental manipulation, the knowledge base has remained in the realm of practice wisdom or common sense. Germain and Gitterman have provided a beginning knowledge base to use when manipulating the environment.

In using an ecosystems strengths approach, action takes place to change the transactions between the individual or family and formal and informal systems in the immediate environment. In identifying the immediate environment, both proximity and relationships are important. For an individual, the family is often a primary system in the immediate environment. School or places of employment are important systems for individuals and families, as are the neighborhood, extended family, friends, and other significant individuals or systems. The first choice in working with clients is for the client himself to be able to mobilize these systems to assist him in meeting his needs. Actions regarding this approach were discussed in Chapter 13. However, often the relationship between the client and significant individuals and systems in his environment needs to be developed, enhanced, or restored. This may be the reason that needs are not being met and that the client requires assistance from the social worker. In working on behalf of the client, the worker may need to have contact with these significant individuals or systems and take actions that will develop, enhance, or restore important relationships.

Mediation was covered in Chapter 13 as an important action with systems in the environment. Mediation can be used with both formal and informal systems.

Other important skills are improving communication, bargaining, negotiation, problem solving, and conflict resolution. Either the worker may work jointly with the client and systems in the environment, or she may work separately with each. When working separately, the goal is usually to move toward some kind of joint effort to resolve the situation.

The social worker uses her communication skills to facilitate good communication. These skills were covered in Chapter 9. She models good communication and asks people to change their communication patterns to reflect good communication.

Decision-making and problem-solving skills involve the ability to work together to develop a plan that will resolve the situation. Since the social worker is familiar with various models of problem solving, he can assist clients and members of their ecosystem in doing this. In addition, the worker can assist them to develop an ongoing process of reaching decisions or solving problems.

Bargaining, negotiation, compromise, and conflict resolution are used when unresolved differences persist. These approaches involve identifying the needs and concerns of the parties involved and finding ways to meet those needs. As needs are identified, the worker elicits responses to need from others. She may ask those involved in the situation to give and take in order to have their needs met. She may suggest ways of reciprocally meeting needs between parties. Throughout the process, the worker attempts to reach a mutually beneficial arrangement that can be sustained over time. Some questions that might be used are (1) What would you like to see happen in this situation? What would meet your needs? What would it take to satisfy you? (2) What would you be willing to do to resolve this? (3) Would you be willing to...? (4) If..., then would you be willing to...? (5) What do you want to do with this? These questions are designed to move people toward having their needs met by meeting the needs of others in their ecosystem. When needs are balanced, then the ecosystem is balanced.

When planning for change in the environment, a worker can use the variables of relationship, space, and time as a framework. Relationships should be influenced to enhance the competence of the client. This can be illustrated by considering the situation of a physically disabled person. If those in the disabled person's environment provide care so that the client makes few decisions and little use of the physical capacity she possesses, she will feel less competent. If caregivers encourage appropriate self-reliance, however, her competence will be enhanced.[9]

Changes can be made in the spatial aspects of a client's environment. Space should be appropriate for the person who occupies it. According to Irene Gutheil, some of the factors important when considering physical space are the features of a space and whether they are fixed or can be changed through modifying the design of the building and placement of furniture. Also important are issues of territory, personal space, crowding, and privacy.[10] These concerns are particularly important in residential situations but should also be considered in evaluating offices and other areas where services are provided.

For people with disabilities, physical barriers can be a block to relative self-sufficiency. A sense of competence will be enhanced if the barriers are removed.

Physical environmental features should provide for the privacy a person needs. Also, the effects of color and light in influencing feelings and behavior should be considered.

The activity to take place in the space and the manner in which people interact during the activity are also important considerations. There must be provision for appropriate closeness of people; being too close or too far apart can lead to discomfort and cause people to withdraw.

Spatial arrangement that allows for eye contact is important in some situations. A circle arrangement encourages people to talk to one another, as each can see everyone else. Room arrangements in which all individuals face a speaker discourage group interaction and encourage attention to the speaker only. Social workers can use their understandings of clients and their needs and of spatial arrangements to determine how space can be changed to enable people to function more adequately.[11]

When a social worker working with a group arranges chairs at the meeting space to bring about interpersonal interaction, she has manipulated space and created environmental change. The way the physical environment of a social agency is arranged can make clients feel comfortable or uncomfortable and thus cause undesirable behavior or enable constructive activity. Physical arrangement can sometimes make the difference in whether the client uses the services offered or fails to get needs met.[7]

Placement of a child in a residential treatment facility is a form of environmental change. That facility uses the milieu (the arrangement of the space, program, and staff relationships) to help the child. *Milieu therapy* involves attitudes and relationships of the persons who occupy the space as a therapeutic tool. Hospitals, nursing homes, and other institutions can make use of milieu therapy.[8]

Any environmental change should be preceded by a thorough study and assessment of the situation, with particular emphasis on relationship, space, and time factors that may be impeding the client's social functioning. Attention should be given to how culture and lifestyle prescribe the use of the physical environment and time so that the plan does not conflict with the client's culture and lifestyle.

Time factors can be changed in service of clients by the manner in which social workers schedule activity. There is a time for physical or mental activity and a time for quiet in people's lives. By considering client need at various times, the social worker can use the time allotted in ways that are congruent with the client's need. For example, when children have been in school all day, after school they are usually ready for physical activity rather than for sitting quietly. When working with a mother, the worker should realize that times when family demand is high are not times the mother can reflect on her own needs. The timing of appointments should take into consideration the time rhythms of the client's life. Institutions often develop schedules to meet staff desires rather than considering the daily rhythms of those being served. Social workers can be alert to these time elements and work for changes in schedules so that service to clients can be facilitated.[12]

When using the strategy of environmental manipulation, the worker assesses the situation and plans to bring about change in relationships, space, and the use of time. In planning for change it is essential that the worker use her understandings about relationships, space, and time. The social worker also should be creative in structuring environments to support clients' efforts in social functioning.

Case Example

A social worker in a nursing home notes that some patients, who must share rooms with another resident because of funding policies, need an opportunity to be alone for parts of the day. These same residents seem to need a private place to visit with those who come to see them. The social worker brings this need to the weekly staff meeting. At first the staff takes the attitude that this is just the way it is and states that there is no room for a private space. The social worker makes a tour of the facility to identify space that may not be used 100 percent during the day and early evening hours. She finds a craft facility that is only used two hours each morning and afternoon. She also finds a couple of alcoves in hallways that could hold a couple of comfortable chairs. In addition, she notes that there is outdoor space that in nice weather could be used for visiting if comfortable seating were provided. At the next staff meeting she presents her findings. The administrator then asks who is going to provide the needed furniture. The activities director states that she would welcome a comfortable corner in the craft room. She also says that the auxiliary has been looking for a project and wonders if this would not be a good one for them. Within a couple of months the identified space is converted to comfortable private space, and the residents have been involved in developing guidelines for its use.

Involvement of Influentials

One means of gaining support is through the involvement of influentials—people within a community or an organization who have power and/or authority. Individuals may have power because they have a reputation that assigns power to them. They may have power because they are in a position to make crucial decisions, such as which projects get funded, who reports to top administrators, or how regulations are written. Other individuals have power because their role or function involves control over ideas, information, fiscal resources, and so on.

Influentials have the ability to use power to affect the actions of others. These people can persuade others to act in specific ways, gain support for their point of view or way of functioning, and effect compliance with desired ways of functioning. They often have control of needed resources (money, manpower, etc.), can reward or punish others, and can effectively block action they do not favor. They may be influential in all aspects of an organization or community or only in certain segments of the system's functioning. Influentials relate to one another in patterns; this is called the power structure.

In working for change, social workers can work with influentials in several ways:

1. Approval for projects or programs must be obtained from influentials in order to facilitate development of the projects or programs.
2. An attempt must be made to have an influential initiate the action in order to gain the support of others.
3. Influentials must be informed about what is being planned and why to prevent them blocking a project.

The first step in working with influentials is to identify these persons. This can be done by asking those who know the system well ("system knowledge-ables") which people have the reputation of being influential or who of these must be included in decision making. Influentials are not always the same as those who hold authority positions; often, they are less visible and function behind the scenes in the informal system. An understanding of the community and its power structure is essential when working with influentials.

When social workers work with influentials, they need to be clear about the desired change and why it is needed. They can then present facts in a convincing, logical manner. It is often useful to show the influential how the desired change is in her self-interest. This first step for involving influentials allows them to see that the social worker can be an ally in carrying out community projects. Social workers should remain open and flexible when working with influentials. It is important to incorporate appropriate input from influentials into the plan.

The art of **opportunity seizing** is another important skill useful for working with influentials. This involves a keen sense of timing and a sense of when influentials are ready to become involved and make use of the social worker's help and expertise. Involvement in community activities can provide social workers with opportunities to get to know influentials and for influentials to get to know workers.

Persuasion skills are important when working with influentials and often can be useful in helping an influential understand the desirability of working for change. Social workers need to learn how to work with and utilize the support of influentials to effect change in organizations and communities.

Case Example

Joe, a social worker who is employed in a community residential facility for adults with developmental disabilities, was asked after church one Sunday morning by a community influential why these clients were seen wandering around the streets on Saturday with no supervision. Joe pointed out that they had Saturday off from their sheltered workshop jobs, just as many other people had. He said that the clients were fairly high functioning and able to be on their own; he noted that they experienced difficulty because they felt they were discriminated against by local merchants. He informed the influential that the agency lacked staff who could plan recreational activities over the weekend.

(continued)

Case Example   Continued

Several other people became involved in the conversation and asked Joe if there was anything the church could do about the situation. Joe replied that he felt there were things that could be done and that he would be glad to meet with a group to explore the situation. One of the individuals who was involved in the conversation was the local newspaper editor. He asked Joe to stop in to see him sometime during the week, offering to help by doing a human interest story in his paper.

As a result of this initial contact with these influentials, a program was set up that resulted in weekend activities for the clients. The newspaper gave extensive coverage to the program and ran a series of stories on the agency and its clients. All of this activity resulted in changed attitudes toward those with developmental disabilities in the community.

Coordination of Services

Coordination is the working together of two or more service providers. Coordination of activity can be focused on a client, such as an individual or family (microlevel coordination), or it can be focused on persons in a particular category, such as persons with AIDS or developmental disabilities (macrolevel coordination).

Collaboration and coordination are often used as if they were synonymous, but as used in this book, there is a difference between the two. Collaboration is the working together, or teamwork, of two or more helpers using a common plan of action. Coordination does not imply a common plan of action; in fact, there may be two or more plans of action. Collaboration and teamwork are two kinds of coordination. (See the discussion in Chapter 10.) In this section several other methods of coordination are presented.

For coordination to be effective, there must be a spirit of working together toward a desirable end. For example, this end could be a common goal, such as maintaining in the community a person with chronic mental illness. This would require coordination of different services provided by different agencies, such as socialization and vocational rehabilitation services as well as housing services, medical monitoring services, income maintenance services, and the like. Public social services as well as mental health and vocational rehabilitation units and perhaps other agencies would all need to be involved.

In another example, the end may be the common goal of providing a range of services to a particular community to enable it to meet the needs of its aging members. This might involve coordination of the services of the senior citizens' center, the public health nursing agency, public social services, and the variety of other services available in the community. The goal would be not only to help specific older clients but also to enable existing services to more appropriately respond to the needs of all older persons. The common end would be a network of needed services that would be usable by a broad range of older persons.

An important aspect of coordination is the mutual satisfaction of all concerned. The persons or agencies involved need to believe that it is advantageous to coordinate their services with others. This feeling of common benefit leads to open exchange and feelings of satisfaction, which are necessary for productive relationships. Coordination can involve a range of resources broader than those of formal social service agencies. It can involve professionals from a variety of disciplines: service providers of community institutions such as schools and churches; community self-help group leaders; and the informal resources of friends, family, and work colleagues.

One factor that can hinder coordination relates to the differing perspectives on clients and clients' needs held by those of different professional disciplines. A doctor might see an older person's frail health status as the primary need. A social worker might consider this person's lack of a support system as the main issue. A senior citizens' center director might identify the need for socialization to prevent isolation. Each professional would advocate for a different need for the client. The physician might push for a nursing home placement. The senior citizens' center director might want to involve the client in the activities of the center. The social worker might attempt to develop an individualized support system after ascertaining the client's desires.

Each profession has its own societal task to perform, its own way of functioning, and its own values and knowledge base. When social workers work with other disciplines, it is important to have an understanding of the other professions' perspectives. Issues of concern to other professions and areas of overlapping interest and service should also be identified. The social worker should also be aware of potential tensions among professionals. (Working with other professions was discussed in Chapter 6.)

The expectation that every professional thinks or should think in the same ways about a client or a client's needs is a major block to coordination. Understanding differences is a first step to working together in a coordinated manner. This understanding aids in identifying the distinctive capacities of each professional that can be used in developing a coordinative relationship and can lead to respect and acceptance. Respect for and acceptance of another profession's contribution are necessary components of coordinative action.

When coordinating resources and activities from the informal arena, it is important to be aware of the different ways formal and informal resources function. Eugene Litwak and Henry Meyer have pointed out the differences in functioning of the primary group (natural systems) and the bureaucracy (formal system). *Primary systems* are diffuse, personal, have an affective bond, and call for face-to-face contact. They can best deal with nonuniform, relatively unique events. They are adaptable and flexible and have the capacity to respond quickly. *Formal systems* tend to be impersonal, specific as to what they can do, and operate within rules and regulations. They function with professional and technical expertise and deal with large numbers of people in an impartial manner. Both kinds of service systems are important and should be coordinated.

An important contribution of Litwak and Meyer is what they call the *balance theory of coordination*. They believe that the important aspect of coordination is communication. If the two types of systems (formal and informal) are too far apart, communication does not take place. If they are too close together, their differences hinder each other's functioning. Litwak and Meyer believe that there is a midpoint of social distance between the two systems at which each system can function best.[13] (The midpoint is the point at which the two systems can communicate with each other but are not so close that the functioning of either system is impaired.)

Social workers who get to know community influentials and natural helpers in relatively informal community groups can develop relationships that will facilitate coordination with the informal system. If individuals who function in the informal system know the social worker, they will be more apt to consult with her or to refer someone to her. Social workers in turn can discuss common concerns in the informal settings in which these helpers are more comfortable.

Another consideration is the difference between the ways in which men and women communicate. Traditionally, women tend to seek cooperation when communicating, whereas men tend to be more competitive. Women tend to be more comfortable in relatively less structured settings, whereas men are drawn to settings with more formal lines of communication. The natural helping system seems to be more often a female system. The formal system, although staffed with both men and women, functions in a formalized manner that is more akin to traditional male communication. Male social workers should be particularly aware of differences in communication styles when working with the informal helping system. Additional issues involved in working with natural helpers were discussed in Chapter 13.

Coordination can be carried out through several mechanisms. One is to locate those who serve a similar population in a common setting, often called a multiservice center. This can be done by either locating the agency or the individual service deliverers (e.g., family service worker, a community health nurse, an income maintenance worker) representing a variety of agencies in a common setting close to those needing service. It is assumed not only that this will make services more accessible to clients but also that close proximity will encourage sharing among the professionals.

Another means of linking services has been an information-and-referral service; this can serve as a coordinative mechanism, depending on its means of functioning and on the capacity of those who staff it. If the emphasis is on providing information about services, the coordinative function will probably not be carried out. If the emphasis is on referral and enabling clients to access needed services, then a coordinative service is enhanced by follow-up and evaluation of the service delivered. Evaluation can also lead to identification of unmet needs and of needed services that are not available and thus to program development. Two coordination approaches that merit special consideration are case management and networking.

Case Management

Case management has received considerable attention as a coordinative approach to service delivery. It has been found to be useful in the fields of child welfare, mental health (particularly with the chronically mentally ill), developmental disabilities, and gerontology. Its use is often indicated when a client needs a range of services from several social service or health providers. Provision for such services is supported by federal legislation.[14]

Although the process of case management has been identified in a varying manner from field to field, a common thread has emerged. According to Karen Orloff Kaplan, the process contains five components: (1) case identification; (2) assessment and planning; (3) coordination and referral; (4) implementation of services; and (5) monitoring, evaluation, and reassessment.[15]

Assessment and planning involve consideration not only of client needs but also of the resources available within the client's informal network of relationships and in the immediate community. Assessment is carried out with maximal client input and involves identifying the needed resources and weaving the need-fulfilling resources into a plan that is congruent with the client's desires and life-style. This weaving together can be described as developing a *complementary resource pattern.* That is, the case manager provides an integration so that resources are not duplicated or at cross-purposes and so that the client can sense a holistic concern for need fulfillment.

The case manager reaches out to the various resources to obtain their cooperative input and to provide the information needed for coordinating services. The case manager may need to creatively develop a new resource or modify an existing resource. Often the case manager provides a part of the needed service. Regular monitoring is another task of the case manager.

Several case management models have been developed, usually addressing service in a particular field of practice (e.g., child welfare, services to older adults). One developed by Jack Rothman seems to depict the process most thoroughly and clearly. This model begins with access to the agency through outreach or referral and proceeds through intake and assessment, which may have both short- and long-term psychological, social, and medical components to goal setting. From this point a variety of options are possible: intervention planning, resource identification and indexing, and linking clients to formal agencies or informally to families and others. Counseling, therapy, advocacy, and interagency coordination, including policy considerations, may also be used but are outside the process loop and are used only when needed. Monitoring, reassessment, and outcome evaluation are also within the loop. Rothman notes that the process is meant to be used flexibly and is cyclical in nature.[16]

Two goals are often discussed in relation to case management: continuity of care and maximal level of functioning. *Continuity of care* is important because many of the clients who benefit from the use of this approach need services for an extended period of time, if not for the rest of their lives. This care may need to be provided in a range of different community and institutional settings. A holistic plan for services is considered desirable, and case managers can often provide the desired continuity. *Maximal level of functioning* is important because many clients with whom this approach is used operate at a less-than-independent level of functioning. Because of the multiple needs involved, they may not be functioning at the highest level of which they are capable. A case management approach provides an overview that can lead to planning, which encourages a maximal level of functioning.

Stephen P. Moore notes that case management should be an enabling and facilitating activity. A major thrust is to ensure that formal service complements family care and other informal helping rather than competing with or substituting for such care. This can add to the complexity of the service. The case manager may not only need to consider the current and potential strengths, limitations, and ways of functioning of the informal care system but may also need to develop a potential for help within these systems. He may need to provide support and other services to the informal system to enable it to perform as the needed resource. It is important to be aware of the stresses on the informal system as well as the needs of the helping system.[17]

Case management calls for the social worker to use both direct and indirect approaches. It is truly generalist social work practice in that it weaves together a variety of strategies so that the range of needs of clients with multiple challenges can be met. Coordination is a major concern of the case manager.

Case Example

Larry is a thirty-five-year-old man with a developmental disability who needs to be placed in a group home because his parents' advancing age makes it impossible for them to care for him.

A case manager for the agency to which Larry has been referred for placement carefully conducts a comprehensive assessment. He talks to Larry and sets as a short-term goal that he adjust to community living, with involvement in sheltered work and recreational activities. The worker chooses a group home in a small town with a sheltered workshop. The case manager believes that Larry should not have to adjust to big city life, which might be confusing at this time. The staff of this facility has been very successful in working with individuals like Larry.

The case manager discusses Larry's interests and experiences with the sheltered workshop staff, who make suggestions about work assignments and ways of working with Larry. The community into which Larry is to be placed is particularly rich in recreational activities, as it is a college town and students are available to work with group home residents. The group home director and the case manager make specific plans for using this resource.

During the initial placement stage, the case manager plans to monitor the situation carefully, with weekly contacts with Larry, the group home, and the sheltered workshop. The group home manager will take responsibility for setting up the recreational program. After a period of adjustment, the case manager hopes that monitoring can be less frequent. At such a time, it will be important to set up long-term goals for Larry.

Networking

Networking also is a form of coordination.[18] **Networking** is the development and maintenance of communication and of ways of working together among individuals of diverse interests and orientations. This technique can facilitate macrolevel coordination. Networking holds promise as a means for formal system helpers and natural helpers to work together. The technique of networking calls for developing some means of face-to-face communication among people who have the potential for developing a relationship based on a common interest.

One technique used to develop a network is a "fair." People delivering services in a particular area (such as services for women) are invited to set up displays and provide an informed person to be present to discuss informally the services provided. The fair is usually seen as an opportunity for the community to find out about the services. In informal, open discussion at the fair, professional and other helpers discover commonalities of interest and concern. From this discussion decisions begin to be made about working together. A sensitive facilitator can then encourage further planning for activity that will strengthen the network.

Another technique is a monthly meeting of community agencies that can be expanded to include a wide range of community resources. Agendas for these meetings can consist of various agencies presenting their programs and services. Time should be provided for informal discussion and discussion of current community needs. The long-term goal is for relationships to develop among the participants and for a network to emerge.

Because of the differing patterns of functioning and communicating, formal systems must not expect informal systems to accept their approach. Networking calls for the establishment of innovative patterns that allow both formal and informal systems to function together. Informality must not be stifled but rather respected and encouraged when using this form of coordination.

When coordinating with natural helpers, it is important not to place professional expectations on them. Professionals tend to consider these individuals in a paraprofessional capacity and take a supervisory stance in the relationship. This is not appropriate, for two reasons. First, it may destroy any chance of developing the relationship because the natural helper feels demeaned in such a relationship. Second, it may destroy the natural helper's distinctive way of helping and thus his contribution to the situation.[19] Professionals who use a consultative stance are more likely to develop coordinative relationships with natural helpers.

Blocks to effective coordination include lack of respect for, or confidence in, the other helpers involved; lack of adequate sharing of information among helpers; differing perspectives or values about what is to be done regarding clients; lack of capacity to share and work together; lack of time to develop cooperative relationships; and lack of agency sanction and support for coordination. A productive, satisfying coordination is possible when mutual understanding, shared goals, a feeling that it is advantageous to work cooperatively, a capacity to work together, and the sanction needed to develop cooperative relationships are present.

Three social work skills are useful for social workers in facilitating coordination: (1) skill in sensing commonalities and differences and in communicating them appropriately to those involved in the situation; (2) skill in facilitating communication among the participants; and (3) skill in exciting and motivating helping persons to see the advantages of coordinating services. Underlying these skills is the capacity to develop opportunities creatively for open and relaxed communication.

Much has been said about the need for, and the advantages of, coordination in interorganizational and interprofessional relationships. Less has been identified with respect to the means (skills and techniques) of developing and maintaining those relationships. Applying understandings about the nature of other relationships and about the means for encouraging and maintaining them can enhance this knowledge base. Coordination is needed for providing complex services in complex situations. Coordination depends on functional relationships among helping people.

Case Example

Lucille is a social worker who is a member of a board of directors of an information-and-referral service in a medium-sized city. She becomes aware of the fact that there are a number of groups providing services to senior citizens. There are three senior citizens' centers, an RSVP program, a daycare center, five nursing homes, and two nutrition sites. In addition, the Department of Social Services provides social services and homemaker services to income-eligible persons, and the public health agency provides in-home nursing care. There are two private agencies and a mental health center that have counseling services available to senior citizens. Many of these agencies have transportation services for use in attending that agency's activities. There is, however, no centralized transportation service that can be used for shopping and keeping medical appointments. There is one small low-income housing project for the elderly, but there is a demand for additional such housing. To date, the realtors have been able to prevent additional housing from being provided. They have done this through their influence on the city council because they believe these housing units are not in their best interest.

As a social worker, Lucille is concerned that there is no coordination among these social services. In fact, they seem to be competing with one another. Transportation seems to be a particularly sensitive issue. The groups refuse to use their vans for any programs but their own, yet the vans are parked a good part of the day. Also, several different vans pick up in the same area at about the same time.

Another thing that concerns Lucille and other service providers is an imminent cutback in funding for several of the programs. There is a feeling that services could be maintained if some means could be found to eliminate duplication of administrative costs. Each agency claims that it is willing to take on new services but cannot allow the services it provides to go to another agency. Competition for resources is becoming a big issue.

Lucille believes something must be done to better coordinate the services for the elderly in the community. She is aware of the key persons in each agency and their stance. She also knows several community people who are very interested in doing something about the problem, and she discusses the situation with them. Two are former state legislators, older individuals who are highly respected in the community. One is a natural helper who also is well known. Another is a member of the city council. Lucille calls together a small group of service providers, choosing those who are most inclined to try a cooperative venture. In this group she includes several social workers from the Department of Social Services because she is aware that the department (the agency administering Older Americans Act funds) is interested in encouraging cooperative planning.

At the meeting, a small group of service deliverers decides that a larger meeting to discuss coordination should be called. Invitations should go to all those who provide service to senior citizens and other persons who have been identified as having a special interest in senior citizens. A list of about one hundred persons is made. The group thinks that a structured program should be put forth, with some people from outside the community presenting information about coordination of services. The suggestion is made that the state Office on Aging (Department of Social Services) be consulted. It is also decided (Lucille influences here) that Mr. Black, one of the former legislators, would be a good person to chair the meeting. He knows how to do this, has not been involved heavily in any of the programs, and is respected by all. Lucille agrees to see if the Office on Aging has any ideas for speakers.

Lucille contacts the Office on Aging and finds it to be most helpful. The office is interested in this kind of project as a demonstration project. Personnel there are trying to identify means for developing coordination of services for senior citizens. They are willing to provide funds for having two people speak at the meeting. They suggest the director of a senior citizens' center in a community that has a successful coordinative program. They also suggest a faculty member from the School of Social Work at the state university who is working in the area of coordination of services and has some good ideas. The state program director for aging would also be willing to come and discuss what the state office is doing in the area of coordination.

Lucille decides that her next move is to support Mr. Black in calling a small group together and to help it develop a mechanism to maintain the networking. She also believes that it is important to keep the city council member involved, because the support of senior citizen projects by the council will be needed. Perhaps he can even help counteract the influence of the realtors regarding low-income housing for the elderly.

Program Planning and Resource Development

When individual workers or coordinated groups of workers make a survey of resources, they sometimes discover that needed resources are not available. This may be because the need has never been identified or because financial resources to support the resources are not available. Social workers can sometimes use program planning to mobilize different and creative kinds of resources that are relatively inexpensive financially. Two resources that fall into this category are volunteers and self-help groups.

Program development uses the planning process developed in Chapter 12. As the plan is developed, special attention must be given to means of generating support for the plan. Support must come not only from the agencies involved (both workers and administration) but also from the community. Most programs needing community resources cannot be developed without community support.

Usually, in developing a new program, it is advisable to begin small or to serve at first only a portion of the population that might benefit from the program. It is also advisable to begin with that portion of the population with which the chances of success are the greatest. If done in this way, it is easier to find and correct the deficiencies in the plan. Another point to remember is that it is easier to obtain support for small programs that relate to popular causes.

Jack Rothman, John Erlich, and Joseph Teresa have discussed promoting an innovation in an agency.[20] This idea can be related to planning new community programs. They point out that the literature on the "diffusion of innovations" supports the advisability of beginning small and of demonstrating the new program before planning for widespread use. They give three guidelines that are helpful when planning programs to develop or mobilize new resources:

1. Develop and rely on good relationships.
2. Clarify goals and plans for developing the program.
3. Be realistic about the resources that may be available to the program.

Program planning can take place within an existing agency structure or from a community base. If the program is to function within an existing agency structure, the support and involvement of the agency administration and staff are crucial.

If the program is to develop from a community base, community members will carry primary responsibility for its functioning. These people need to be involved in the planning as early as possible. Usually, it is important to discuss the proposed plan with several community influentials as a first step in planning. This discussion will provide the social worker with information needed for developing the plan. It also involves these important persons in obtaining the support needed for the project. Often, it is advisable for a community person to initiate and conduct a meeting to discuss the project. The social worker may need to identify and motivate a suitable leader. The worker then prepares the leadership person for the meeting by making the arrangements for a meeting place, attending to the meeting details, and evaluating with the leadership person after the meeting.

If the decision is made to develop a program, some kind of structure should be set up to do the work necessary for developing the program. This structure can be a provisional board or a planning committee and should allow for appropriate involvement of community persons in the planning process. This group may find it useful to establish the extent of the need the proposed program will address. A needs assessment is an excellent means for doing this. In addition to individual needs, agency and community factors should be considered. This group should also be involved in the development of the program structure and policy. Other tasks are to obtain support for the proposed program, which may involve grant writing and other fundraising activity, and recruitment and hiring of personnel. Developing volunteer programs and monitoring the planning group process also may be necessary.

Sometimes the program becomes a community effort rather than an agency program. In this situation the social worker can fill the role of enabler by helping the community group reach the goals it has adopted. Also, the worker can fill the role of technical expert by providing information about how to accomplish certain tasks.[21]

Sometimes an already-established community group becomes aware of a need and wishes to do something about it. In this situation a social worker can help the group document the need, obtain support (money, people, etc.), and develop the program or resource. For example, a community group was concerned with services for the elderly. The social worker helped the group carry out a needs assessment that indicated that housing for older single women was a prime need in this community. The group was able to interest a local realtor in focusing on this need and worked with the realtor to develop an understanding of the housing needs of older women and plans for making more suitable housing available for them.

At other times, groups of people interested in a particular problem emerge. Social workers can also work with these groups to develop community resources. For example, a women's group was concerned about battered women. The social worker's function was to provide understanding about battered women and their needs. This group talked to women who had worked on the problem in other communities. The group set up a training program and developed a telephone response service, a safe house, and a self-help group.

As these examples show, grassroots groups can be useful when developing community resources for clients. When working with such groups, social workers should not take over the planning; they should respect the group's way of functioning and facilitate the work of the group. Workers must gain and maintain the trust of the group. They should enable individuals to carry out the necessary tasks, suggest ways of proceeding and resources to be tapped, and mediate the group's difficulties with professionals and other community groups. This latter task is sometimes necessary, because already-established services or other professionals may be threatened by a grassroots group or may be concerned about the ability of a grassroots group to provide quality service. In a time of shrinking federal and state resources, maximizing local resources is necessary if human needs are to be met. Program planning and resource development with grassroots groups thus becomes an important task for social workers.

The social worker who attempts to mobilize the community or a group of concerned individuals to address a particular issue may want to form a **task group.** Task groups are also used within agency settings to address a specific concern. Task groups are groups organized to reach a specific goal. They tend to have clear lines of responsibility and specific tasks. Because task groups often include influentials, potential consumers, and service providers (people with various agendas and varying social statuses), it is important to address both interpersonal and task issues throughout the work of the group. Each member must feel he has something valuable to contribute, and this contribution needs to be perceived by other members. It is important to have members who can offer various skills, resources, or services to achieve the goal. For example, if the goal is to establish a hospice service for persons with AIDS, it would be important to have a member who can raise funds, an influential who can work effectively with the community to allay fears or concerns, and someone who can network with the AIDS population. In task groups, the work is generally divided into subgroups, which then work toward various objectives to reach the goal. This implies that there must be shared leadership, with each leader and subgroup given a specific charge and sufficient autonomy to attain the desired objective. Typically, subgroups meet frequently, with the group as a whole coming together less often to share progress, ensure coordination of efforts, and reevaluate the overall plan.[22]

Case Example

A group of people began to discuss the need for a hospice program for people with AIDS in their community of 40,000 people after several dying patients and their families expressed a need for supportive help. A social worker became involved with this group as a technical expert in group process. The group was able to involve several community influentials in the planning process, including a lawyer, a physician, the superintendent of schools, a representative of the county health department, and two pastors. The group, which also included nurses, family members of people with AIDS, and a representative of the local cancer society, involved about fifteen people.

The worker's first task was to develop a working atmosphere in which each member understood and valued the potential contributions of the others. At the same time, the first business of the group included developing a legal structure and applying for nonprofit status. The group worked with the local hospital and obtained office space in the hospital. During this phase the social worker used her understanding of group process and the technical aspects of forming an organization to function as a contributing member of the group. She also obtained materials from another organization forming a hospice, which provided some guidance in the group's deliberations. A lawyer took major responsibility for the legal aspects of the group's formation.

The next step was to form subgroups charged with various tasks that needed to be accomplished. This included developing a number of working papers, such as job descriptions and forms covering the various aspects of service (e.g., request for service, nursing and psychosocial assessments, doctors' orders, care plan). It also included planning for work with the community at large to educate the residents regarding the need for the service as well as addressing concerns that might exist. Subgroups also worked on fundraising and volunteer structure and recruitment. A service flow chart was developed. The social worker assisted the subgroups to adapt materials that had been developed by other hospices to the local situation.

The social worker was active in working with the cancer society and the family members of persons with AIDS in planning and coordinating a very successful training program, which resulted in an attendance of over fifty persons at each session and a recruitment of thirty individuals as volunteers for the program. The success of the training program was due in part to an excellent public relations campaign. The social worker did not need to be involved, as other members of the board were skilled in this area. Several members of the board were very successful in fundraising. Funds were obtained from several community groups, from individuals as memorials, from the county commissioners, and from the local United Way. One task that proved difficult, but with persistence was accomplished, was the obtaining of liability insurance.

After nine months the program was operational, though still needing refinement of its procedures and policies. Patients were referred and service was provided to patients and their families through the bereavement stage. The social worker served as coordinator of social services and worked with others who provided the service to the patients and their families. The board, composed of several members of the original task group, was functional and planned monthly training sessions for the volunteers. An active public relations program continued to be carried out to heighten community awareness of the service and to recruit additional volunteers. Plans were under way to develop closer ties with the health care network of the community.

Developing a Volunteer Program

Volunteers are a resource that has historically been very important in the delivery of social services. Before the development of the social work profession, most social services were delivered by volunteers. In fact, the early social workers were volunteers. Over time, less emphasis has been placed on this resource, although with the cutbacks in governmental support for social services at all levels it has become increasingly urgent that volunteer efforts be enhanced to fill service gaps. Issues of competence, confidentiality, and dependability have been raised when considering volunteers as a resource. Professionals have believed that they were best suited to deliver services. Also, the type of volunteer has changed. Many women (traditionally the volunteers in the social work domain) are now in the work force and are not available for volunteer roles or during agency work hours. The increasing numbers of retired persons are now seen as an important source of volunteer effort.

Effective use of the volunteer resource calls for the development of a volunteer program. Someone must be responsible for helping identify the roles and tasks suitable for volunteers to carry out in an agency or community. Job descriptions and agency policy must be written. To carry out these tasks a volunteer manager must develop an understanding of clients and the services required and of the factors that motivate people to volunteer. The volunteer manager also should be able to work with staff persons to identify services volunteers can provide. The worker also needs skill in motivating people.

A volunteer program should have a means of recruiting and screening volunteers, matching the volunteer with the job, and orienting and training volunteers. Provision must also be made for supervising and recruiting volunteers.

The volunteer coordinator or manager is not the only person involved in planning the development of a volunteer program. Prior to appointing the coordinator, a group must determine the need and focus of such a program and set goals and objectives for it. The group should represent agency staff, concerned community members, influentials, possible volunteers, and perhaps clients to be served. This group can then serve as a board of directors or advisory group when the program manager is chosen; the group should have input into, and responsibility for, choosing the manager.

When an understanding is developed of what a functional volunteer program entails and of the planning process used in developing such a program, the resource of volunteers can be added to those resources already available to clients. Clients thus can be better served.[23]

Case Example

A local state social service agency having two divisions, child protection and services to older adults, was often called on to help in the distribution of Thanksgiving baskets and Christmas gifts. The agency was located in a small city that had several churches that wanted to help but did not know the best way to contact "needy families." The workers in the agency were already overburdened and found this seasonal demand from the community unreasonable. After considerable discussion, a supervisor of the child protection unit wondered if a volunteer could be used to coordinate this project. A job description was written, and staff discussed how they could best protect the clients' confidentiality. It was decided that workers would identify those who might like to receive this help, determine from the clients if they truly wanted the help, and, if so, then decide what food and gifts would be most suitable.

The staff suggested several people in the community who might be interested in this short-term volunteer project. The supervisor decided to contact one she believed particularly qualified. Using the job description, she carefully described what needed to be done to the prospective volunteer. Together they decided this was a job the individual would like to do. The volunteer director of holiday projects then suggested several individuals who could be assistants, and the supervisor helped in developing job descriptions for them. It was decided to limit the number to four. The director assumed responsibility for recruiting the assistants and for planning the project, which involved communication with churches and other organizations regarding needs and ways to process their donations as well as work with the agency employees in identifying those who needed help. The agency provided office space, a telephone, and space for short-term storage and sorting of donations. Distribution was shared by volunteers and agency workers, depending on the situation and need for worker involvement and client confidentiality.

After the holiday time, the workers and volunteer director evaluated the project. The workers said that it was a big help to them, and the volunteer director, although making several suggestions for improvement, said she would be glad to serve again the following year. In following months, as the staff talked about the success of the project, they began to suggest other areas in which volunteers could be used. The agency then moved to set up a more comprehensive volunteer program.

Self-Help Groups

Self-help groups are another resource social workers can help develop. These voluntary small groups, which often spontaneously develop, have been a component of mutual aid that has always been a part of human functioning. In the modern world, in which people commonly feel alienated and isolated from one another, however, it is not always possible on one's own to find a supportive group. Social workers can help those with similar life situations and challenges find each other and provide mutual aid to one another.

Because people facing a new situation or difficulty often feel helpless, it is advisable to include individuals who have had some opportunity to work on the same issue or adjust to a similar situation. They often are glad to help others, for doing this further facilitates their return to more stable functioning.

The widow-to-widow program is a good example of a useful self-help group. Newly widowed persons can be visited by others who have been widowed for a year or more; the visitor can then encourage participation in a group. In the group, the newly widowed person finds others who can help with the many concerns and decisions they face. Much needed information is also shared.

Brian and Gail Auslander have suggested that a *consultation model* is appropriate when working with self-help groups. They identify three roles for the consultant: (1) discussion of client-related needs and possible interventions, (2) discussion of the self-help group's policies and procedures in the hope of obtaining desired change, and (3) a link between resources that the group or individuals in the group may need.[24] The latter role would include providing information about and consulting on the procedures for accessing needed resources. Information as to how similar groups function could also be provided.

Self-help groups are not the answer for all clients. Some self-help groups foster inappropriate dependence or encourage simplistic solutions to complex situations. Some self-help groups develop a strong antiprofessional bias. Some of these negative characteristics can be avoided if, in the process of development, an ongoing consultative role for the social worker can be planned. Some of the ways social workers can support self-help groups are by helping groups find a meeting place, encouraging them to find needed financial resources, providing them with information and training, referring appropriate persons to them, helping the group develop credibility with the community and with professionals, and providing social and emotional support.

Changing Organizations from Within

Historically, consideration of the organization as a target for change has received little attention in social work literature. Yet in working with clients, workers (particularly in the public sector) are well aware that the functioning of the agency (policy, procedures, etc.) often is a source of blockage to client need fulfillment. It follows that social workers should develop a means for influencing agency change. Organizational change as a strategy can be defined as "a means of enhancing the effectiveness of human service organizations in their relations with clients.... [It] is a set of interrelated activities...for the purpose of modifying the formal policies, programs, procedures, or management practices.... The intended outcome...[is] to increase the effectiveness of the services provided and/or to remove organizational conditions that are deleterious to the client population served."[25] This strategy focuses on means of change that arise from within the organization and is carried out by those in middle or lower levels of the organizational structure.[26]

As with any strategy, the social worker begins with assessment. Some of the understandings a worker must develop when using a *change-from-within strategy* include:

1. The agency as a social system (See Chapter 8 for a discussion of a schema for developing this understanding.)
2. The source of the block for need fulfillment (Is it in policy or procedure? Is it due to lack of agency resources? Is it caused by methods used to deliver service?)
3. The forces within the agency and the community that influence the agency functioning in relation to the need
4. The usual processes used to bring about change in the agency
5. The source of decision making in the areas needing to be changed
6. Any influences to which the decision-making source is particularly sensitive
7. The decision maker's receptivity and resistance to the change sought

The assessment process should identify what requires changing if client needs are to be fulfilled. It is not sufficient to say that change must take place. It is important that both the place where the change should take place and the desirable change at that site be specified. The assessment also should specify what change is possible and what is impossible to change. There should be some consideration of timing factors that need to be taken into account in planning for change.[27] For example, if management is under stress because of changes being imposed from a central office, the chances that management will be receptive to discussing other changes with line staff is doubtful. However, if management is concerned with a problem of service delivery, it may be receptive to discussing change that could result in better service and also alleviate the problem.

Herman Resnick and Rino Patti see the change process as

1. Practitioner's perception of a problem in agency functioning
2. Discussion of problem among practitioner and like-minded colleagues, including an assessment of change potential
3. Commitment to the change effort by persons who have been doing the assessment
4. Formulation of the goal to be sought
5. Analysis of resistance to change
6. Development of an action system and mobilization of resources (needed persons added and group development takes place)
7. Formulation of a plan of action
8. Submission of proposal to the decision makers, with other action taken as needed

At this point the change is either accepted, rejected, or modified. At each step goals may change as new information or input is gained.[28]

An important consideration is which people to include in the change effort. At least some participants should have a good understanding of the agency functioning. Some should be respected, valued members of the agency staff. Some should be those who can influence decision makers; some should have skills in negotiation and mediation and in carrying out the particular change. Agency change can originate from the efforts of one person, but to implement a change-from-within strategy, others who possess the characteristics and skills needed also must be involved.

A number of techniques or methods can be used to bring about change in organizations. Patti and Resnick have identified eight collaborative and nine adversarial activities. Collaborative activities are to (1) provide information, (2) present alternative courses of action, (3) request support for experimentation, (4) establish a study committee, (5) create new opportunities for interaction, (6) make appeals to conscience or professional ethics, (7) use logical argument and data, and (8) point out negative consequences. Adversarial activities are to (1) submit petitions, (2) confront in open meetings, (3) bring sanctions against the agency, (4) engage in public criticism through use of communication media, (5) encourage noncompliance, (6) strike, (7) picket, (8) litigate, and (9) bargain.[29]

Collaborative activities should always be tried first. The use of adversarial activities should be restricted to situations in which collaborative activities have not worked. Before using adversarial activities, workers should determine if such strategies will bring harm to clients and if they are willing to take the personal risks involved.

Rothman, Erlich, and Teresa have identified four means of bringing about change in organizations:

1. *Promoting an innovation*—This is carried out by testing a new way of work with a small group of clients. If it is successful or seems useful in meeting clients' needs, it may later be adopted for use on a larger scale. An example would be using a group approach to deliver a service.

2. *Changing an organization's goals*—One way this can be done is by changing the structure of influence by increasing the power of appropriate groups within the agency. For example, a clients' advisory group could be developed. This would be a structure wherein client input into decision making provides a new source of information or influence.

3. *Fostering participation*—This is a means of encouraging broader participation in the functioning of an agency. For example, a staff group could be involved in the planning for a new program. One means of fostering participation is through providing some kind of benefit for the participation. This benefit could take the form of public recognition.

4. *Increasing the effectiveness of role performance*—This can be carried out by clarifying the role performance expected of those working in an agency. It can also be carried out by encouraging various kinds of staff development.[30]

In-service training for workers can be used to introduce new service delivery ideas. If the social worker is skillful in the use of group interaction, she can sometimes enable a staff group to examine and adopt a new idea. Sometimes social workers are given the opportunity to lead an in-service session; in doing this, the knowledge from adult education and staff development literature can be useful.[31]

Edward Pawlak has pointed out that an ideal time for bringing about change in an organization is when leadership changes. He provides suggestions for workers who wish to engage in organizational change, including influencing the selection of new leadership and altering the manner in which rules are interpreted and enforced. Revising of roles, or role interpretation, is another means for change.[32]

From the foregoing, it should be apparent that a number of approaches and techniques are available for changing organizations. The choice of approach depends on the change being sought and the situation. In making this choice two factors must be considered: risk for the worker seeking the change and resistance of other persons within the organization.

Three kinds of risks may be involved when a social worker engages in changing from within: job loss, restricted upward mobility, and strained working relationships.[33] Not all of these risks are present in every situation, but a careful assessment should indicate which are present and the extent of the risk. Each social worker must then make the decision as to whether he is willing to take the risks involved before using this strategy.

Resistance is almost always present to some degree in change activity. Change upsets the system's functioning and causes uncertainty. Thus, the social worker must be prepared to modify the plan to mitigate resistance. When dealing with resistance, an attitude of compromise is often necessary. Workers who are determined that their plan be accepted are most apt to encounter a negative response. Those who engage in joint consideration of a problem likely will find a solution acceptable to all. Understanding the nature of the resistance and dealing with it are essential skills when using a change-from-within strategy.

Because social work is primarily practiced within organizations, particularly bureaucratic organizations, the change-from-within strategy is important to the social worker's repertoire. It is the social worker's ethical responsibility to work toward the humane delivery of social services in a manner that meets client needs. To do this, it is often necessary to bring about change in organizations. To help bring about change in the organization, the social worker can use the change-from-within strategy.

Case Example

A new social worker in a residential facility for juveniles notices that specific information regarding the residents' visits from family members, which occur during the weekends when she is not at work, is not being given to her. She first discusses the situation with the weekend supervisor. The weekend supervisor states that there is not enough time to record all the interactions noticed and, further, that most of these contacts are irrelevant to the work being done with the residents. The worker then talks to the family services coordinator, who agrees that there should be some changes but who also says that trying to get the weekend staff to change their recording is like "pulling teeth." The family services coordinator says that the administrator does not want to hear about problems unless there are specific solutions.

The social worker and the family services coordinator discuss what specifics they would like to have recorded and agree on three areas they think are significant: general interactional patterns between parent(s) and adolescent; any displays of emotion from the adolescent toward family members; and supportive behaviors/verbal interactions from any family member. A recording chart was developed whereby weekend workers could relatively easily enter observed data regarding these three areas. The social worker and family services supervisor then discuss the plan with the administrator of the facility and enlist his support for the plan as well as his willingness to have the family services coordinator present the plan at a staff meeting. At the staff meeting, the social worker and the family services coordinator discuss the rationale behind needing the information, present the recording chart, listen to the reactions and responses from the weekend supervisor, and respond to her concerns. The weekend supervisor can see the value to the residents of the information requested, suggests a few modifications in the chart, and after these are made agrees to present it to the weekend staff and enlist their support. The weekend supervisor states that it is the first time she could recall when the regular staff listened and responded to her concerns.

Cause Advocacy

Social workers using a systemic approach to assessment should be sensitive to situations in which the block to need fulfillment lies in the functioning of societal institutions. Often these blocks affect not just one person or family but groups of individuals. In these situations a strategy that focuses on change in societal institutions needs to be considered. A cause advocacy strategy is one option.

Cause advocacy has been a concern of social work since its earliest days. Early-twentieth-century social workers in settlement houses were concerned with social conditions as they affected the people with whom they worked. During the unsettled 1960s, cause advocacy was a major focus of some social workers. The cause-function debates of the profession relate to social work's concern with changing social institutions. (See Chapter 1 for a discussion of this issue.)

The literature on advocacy recognizes both *case advocacy* (advocacy in service of a client) and cause advocacy (advocacy in service of a class of persons who are victims of a social problem). George Brager has identified an advocate as the professional who identifies with the victims of social problems and who pursues modification in social conditions.[34] Robert Teare and Harold McPheeters identify the advocate role as helping clients obtain services in situations in which they may be rejected or helping expand services to persons in particular need.[35] (See also Chapter 12 for a discussion of the Teare-McPheeters role classification.)

There are a number of means to use in advocating for a class of persons. Robert MacRae has identified the following:

1. Preparation of carefully worded statements of policy on lively social welfare issues
2. Careful analysis of pending legislation
3. Individual consultation with key legislators on the implications of pending measures
4. Persuasion of influential organizations outside the welfare field to oppose or support pending legislation
5. Creation of an ad hoc citizens' committee composed of representative citizens of influence and prestige
6. Continuous interpretation of social needs[36]

J. Donald Cameron and Esther Talavera discuss an advocacy program in which the emphasis was on participation in "important community planning and development groups, and other community organizations." The goal of this activity was "to keep the community needs of Spanish-speaking people visible and to effect the flow of resources to meet these needs."[37] Almost all the literature on social work with diverse racial groups calls for advocacy as an important component of any service provided to these groups.

Robert Sunley suggests the following as useful in a family advocacy program: (1) studies and surveys, (2) expert testimony, (3) case conferences with other agencies, (4) interagency committees, (5) educational methods, (6) position taking, (7) administrative redress, (8) demonstration projects, (9) direct contact with officials and legislators, (10) coalition groups, (11) client groups, (12) petitions, (13) persistent demands, and (14) demonstrations and protests.[38]

There are two major approaches to cause advocacy. The first is influencing the political process; the second is organizing the people affected, or **social action.** Before discussing each of these major approaches, some issues pertinent to the use of advocacy will be considered. First is the position of an agency employee, particularly an employee of a public agency, in advocacy activity. Constraints in public employment policy make it difficult if not impossible for public employees to engage in cause advocacy. This fact places an additional responsibility on social workers not so constrained to be cause advocates. However, public employees can find some legal means to advocate. These include taking annual leave to testify at legislative hearings, providing factual data on the effects of policy on individuals, and giving clients information about organizations that can help them fight for their rights.

Advocacy activity may cause a backlash. Policy and procedure meant to assist one group of clients may cause additional difficulties for another group of clients. Money used to fund a needed program for one group of clients may be taken from an equally valuable program for another group. All workers who engage in advocacy need to carefully assess the possibility of backlash or the effect of the desired change on other parts of the service delivery system. They then must make interventive decisions in light of ethical considerations.

Another issue is related to the ethics of engaging in cause advocacy for persons who have not asked for or do not want such action. Some clients are afraid of recriminations and feel they have more to lose than gain from advocacy activity on their own behalf. Others do not trust professionals. Does a social worker respond to her own sense of unfairness or outrage, or does the social worker respond to the wishes of clients?

Before engaging in cause advocacy a social worker should carefully assess and thoroughly understand the situation. The worker should also be certain that other means for alleviating the difficulty are not available. The risks involved should be thoroughly explored and seem worth taking for the anticipated outcomes. The expected outcomes should be realistically determined. Resources needed to complete the project should be available. Facts to be used should be verified, appropriate, and to the point. Research techniques should be used when possible, since they strengthen the case for change. With all the facts at hand, the social worker can then decide whether to work to influence the political system or to organize the people affected by the problem.

Community Organization

Community organization is a field of study unto itself and is beyond the scope of this book. Community organizing, however, will be discussed here briefly, so that the student has some awareness of its role in indirect macropractice and how it can be used to bring about change in a community. Rothman and Tropman discuss three models of community organization practice that can be used to address social issues and promote change, as follows:

1. *Locality development*—This model is used when the desired change is to facilitate community cooperation and interaction and foster self-help. It is primarily a process model in that it focuses on efforts to involve large numbers of concerned citizens in an area rather than on a specific change per se.

2. *Social planning*—This model is used when the goal is planned change regarding a specific issue such as improved housing. It utilizes "experts" rather than grassroots planners and is commonly used in governmental, educational, and private institutional settings. There may be very little, if any, community involvement in the process.

3. *Social action*—This model utilizes a coalition of a disadvantaged segment of the population to take action regarding a social problem that affects them directly. This is discussed in more detail in a following section.[39]

Influencing the Political Process

Much of the service delivery system is heavily influenced by actions that take place in the political arena. Public social policy is an outcome of legislative action. Policy determines which programs will be supported and to what extent by governmental funds. Some social workers have always attempted to influence that political process, with varying degrees of success. The political process is heavily influenced by the climate of the times, so in times of a more liberal political climate, social workers tend to have more influence; in times of conservatism, less influence.

Currently, the political climate in the United States has increasingly tended toward conservatism. Nonetheless, it is critical that social workers continue to advocate, especially since there are fewer avenues available for populations at risk to voice their concerns. All social workers, not just those in indirect service positions, must become politically active. Direct service workers are in the best position to fully understand the impact of social and political change on their clients.

As with all social work strategies, influencing the political process takes understanding and skill. A thorough understanding of local, state, and national political processes is a must, as is a thorough understanding of the issues involved. It is important to view political decision makers as individuals and know how they respond to others. Reliable data about how the issue of concern affects people are very important. These data should include not only how the problem affects the client group but also how it affects other segments of the population. The cost of proposals under consideration is important knowledge to have. Also, an assessment should be made of possible sources and nature of resistance to any proposed change.

Gathering the information needed to develop this understanding of the political process takes time and skill. Social workers should learn how to use governmental publications and documents as well as statistical material. These materials are available through state and federal representatives, libraries, and various Internet sources. Participating in political activities and establishing working relationships with key political figures can be a means of gathering other needed information.

After the social worker has gained information and understanding about the political process and the particular issue involved, a decision should be made about the appropriate tactics to use in influencing that process. This decision will depend in part on where that issue is in the political process. If it is still in the discussion stage, then suggestions for possible legislation might be the option to pursue.

Some of the means social workers have used to influence the political process include:

1. Researching issues and providing facts to decision makers
2. Testifying at hearings (using facts whenever possible)
3. Lobbying or being present while the legislative process is taking place and influencing legislative votes when possible
4. Forming coalitions with service providers to present information to legislators regarding the local impact of current policies
5. Sharing disguised anecdotal information regarding the impact policies have on clients with state and national groups concerned with the issues
6. Working for the election of candidates who are sympathetic to social issues and to the needs of people
7. Letter-writing/e-mail campaigns to inform decision makers about facts and attitudes

Influencing the political process is a complex endeavor. Although most social workers are not in a position to be heavily involved, they can and should use the tactics available to them to influence the political process. Workers have an obligation to develop an understanding of the process and of the issues so they can participate in political advocacy in a responsible manner.[40]

Social Action Organizing

This approach has been a part of the social work response to human need from its earliest days. Jane Addams organized for social action when she advocated improved social conditions. The approach was widely used during the period of social unrest in the 1960s. Since that time a theory base has developed that supports the use of this approach to organizing oppressed peoples. The focus is on changing the societal power base and basic institutional change. A theory proposed by Saul Alinsky and Richard Cloward and R. Elman is sometimes referred to as a grassroots approach.[41] It begins with people who see themselves as victims, not with professionals who decide what is needed.

The principal thrust of this approach is the organizing of groups of people so that they can exert pressure on power structures, institutions, and political bodies. Adherents believe that equity in society will come about only when existing power structures recognize the power of oppressed peoples; in other words, when the societal power base is broadened to include new groups of people. Tactics used include (1) crystallization of issues and action against an enemy target; (2) confrontation, conflict, or contest; (3) negotiation when appropriate; and (4) manipulation of mass organizations and political processes.

The social worker's first task is to organize people and get them involved in the action. In many ways, this is a self-help approach in that it relates directly to client empowerment and may be an outgrowth of a mutual aid group. The worker then enables the individuals to carry out the action.

Social workers need to develop advocacy skills if they are to help social institutions become more responsive to the needs of all people. How the individual social worker uses these skills depends on three variables:

1. *The position of the worker in the social welfare system*—Some agencies place constraints on workers' involvement in cause advocacy. Also, workers who work cooperatively with decision makers will probably not want to use conflict tactics.

2. *The client's desires regarding action*—If clients do not wish to take the risks involved in an advocacy action, these desires should be respected.

3. *The risks involved in the action*—If advocacy actions have the potential for bringing about backlash or negative influences on the client or on the social service system, advocacy should be used cautiously and only when the client or service system fully understands the possible negative ramifications.

The worker serves as an expert, an enabler, a negotiator, or whatever is needed by the people who direct the change activity.[42]

Case Example

About a year after Marianne, a family services social worker, had organized community-wide efforts to develop a homeless shelter, the housing issue in her community became the focus of attention. Many homeless people were employed or had income from various social welfare programs but were unable to find affordable housing. During the year since the shelter opened, Marianne and her original task group had gathered information regarding the lack of low-income housing in the community. Many existing low-income housing units had been lost to other purposes or had been torn down for commercial or other housing developments.

The issue came to a head when the city council was asked for a zoning change that would allow a parking ramp to be built on property now containing an apartment that housed many low-income people. Marianne organized and met with a small group, including a member of the city council who showed concern about the homeless, a former state legislator, the director of the county social services agency, a low-income resident housed in the apartment, and several other concerned citizens from the original task group.

This group needed to move quickly because a zoning change proposal was to come before the city council in about two weeks. The group assessed the information Marianne had gathered about affordable housing for low-income people in the city. They asked the newspaper to run a feature article, which aroused some citizen concern. With the help of the city council member, they contacted city council members and city staff who had been involved in planning the zoning proposal and discussed the impact of the loss of housing on low-income people. They planned and carried out public testimony at public hearings regarding the zoning change. They were present with the apartment residents at the council meeting at which the matter was considered.

The outcome was that the city council tabled the zoning change and appointed a committee made up of council members and concerned citizens to study the situation further. Marianne and her committee planned to continue to monitor the work of this committee, to collect and provide them with needed information, and to testify as needed.

Summary

Influence is an important component of the interventive repertoire of a social worker engaging in action with others on behalf of the client. The social worker should be able to use influence and to work with influentials.

Environmental change is a strategy used to alter structural, cultural, and functional patterns in the client's environment. Patterns that are particularly important are those of relationships, space, and time. This strategy calls for creative action by the social worker.

Action relative to the coordination of services calls for a thorough understanding of the service delivery system. Communication is an important ingredient of coordination. The social worker instigates coordination by helping service deliverers communicate with one another. Case management and networking are strategies for developing coordination.

Program planning and development involves the use of the planning process to develop new resources. Program planning may take place within an agency or be used by a community group. Self-help groups and volunteer programs are two means for enhancing the resources available to clients.

Changing organizations from within may be the strategy of choice when agency functioning is the cause of the block to client need fulfillment. To use this strategy the worker first assesses the social system of the agency. Emphasis is placed on decision making and resistance to change. This strategy is important because of the ethical responsibility of social workers to work for humane delivery of social services.

Cause advocacy is concerned with changing societal institutions. Two main approaches are used: influencing the political process and organizing the victims.

The generalist social worker provides service to individuals, families, small groups, organizations, and communities. The focus is on transactions among systems, that is, on social functioning. This approach to social work calls for a wide variety of strategies, including those that do not focus on the client. These strategies involve action with other systems on behalf of clients and focus on situations in the client's environment that affect social functioning. Ethically, a social worker must not only work with the client but also with systems that impinge on the client.

QUESTIONS

1. Discuss the strengths and limitations of the various kinds of coordination.

2. In a community with which you are familiar, identify a need you believe a self-help group can fill. A volunteer program can fill. A grassroots group can fill. Using one of these resources, how would you go about working to provide a needed service?

3. Identify an environment that is nonsupportive of social functioning in some way. Discuss how you would change that environment to more adequately support social functioning.

4. What are the ethical considerations of working in an agency that is not meeting the needs of clients (needs for which it has responsibility)? How much risk would you be willing to take in bringing about needed change in an agency? At what point do you think it would be appropriate for you to use a change-from-within strategy?

5. When engaging in cause advocacy, should the response be to injustice or to client wishes? How can these two perspectives be reconciled?

SUGGESTED READINGS

Biegel, David E., Tracy, Elizabeth M., and Corvo, Kenneth N. "Strengthening Social Networks: Intervention Strategies for Mental Health Case Managers." *Health and Social Work* 19 (August 1994): 206–216.

Bobo, Kimberly A. *Organizing for Social Change: A Manual for Activists in the '90s.* Santa Ana, CA: Seven Locks Press, 1996.

Couto, Richard A. "What's Political About Self-Help?" *Social Policy* 23 (Fall/Winter 1992): 39–43.

Dane, Barbara Oberhofer, and Simon, Barbara L. "Resident Guests: Social Workers in Host Settings." *Social Work* 36 (May 1991): 208–213.

Edwards, Richard L., Ed. *Encyclopedia of Social Work,* 19th ed. Washington, DC: NASW Press, 1995 ("Case Management"; "Citizen Participation"; "Community"; "Community Needs Assessment"; "Community Organization"; "Community Practice Models"; and "Ecological Perspective").

Erlich, John, Rothman, Jack, and Teresa, Joseph G. *Taking Action in Organizations and Communities,* 2nd ed. Dubuque, IA: Eddie Bowers Publishing, 1999.

Ewalt, Patricia L. *Social Policy: Reform, Research, and Practice.* Washington, DC: NASW Press, 1997.

Ewalt, Patricia L., Freeman, Edith M., and Poole, Dennis L. *Community Building: Renewal, Well-Being, and Shared Responsibility.* Washington, DC: NASW Press, 1998.

Fatout, Marian, and Rose, Steven R. *Task Groups in the Social Services.* Newbury Park, CA: Sage Publications, 1995.

Fellin, Phillip. *The Community and the Social Worker,* 2nd ed. Itasca, IL: F. E. Peacock, 1995.

Figueira-McDonough, Josefina. "Policy Practice: The Neglected Side of Social Work Intervention." *Social Work* 38 (March 1993): 179–188.

Fong, Lillian G. W., and Gibbs, Jewelle Taylor. "Facilitating Services to Multicultural Communities in a Dominant Culture Setting: An Organizational Perspective." *Administration in Social Work* 19, 2 (1995): 1–24.

Frey, Gerald A. "A Framework for Promoting Organizational Change." *Families in Society* 71 (March 1990): 143–147.

Grossman, Arnold H., and Silverstein, Charles. "Facilitating Support Groups for Professionals Working with People with AIDS." *Social Work* 38 (March 1993): 144–151.

Gulath, Padi, and Guert, Geoffrey. "The Community-Centered Model: A Garden-Variety Approach or a Radical Transformation of Community Practice?" *Social Work* 35 (January 1990): 63–68.

Gutheil, Irene A. "Considering the Physical Environment: An Essential Component of Good Practice." *Social Work* 37 (September 1992): 391–396.

Gutierrez, Lorraine, GlenMaye, Linnea, and DeLois, Kate. "The Organizational Context of Empowerment Practice: Implications for Social Work Administration." *Social Work* 40 (March 1995): 249–258.

Hagen, Jan L., and Davis, Liane V. "Working with Women: Building a Policy and Practice Agenda." *Social Work* 37 (June 1992): 495–500.

Halfon, Neal, Berkowitz, Gale, and Klee, Linnea. "Development of an Integrated Case Management Program for Vulnerable Children." *Child Welfare* 72 (July–August 1993): 379–396.

Hartman, Ann. "The Professional Is Political." *Social Work* 38 (July 1993): 365–366.

Herbert, Margot D., and Mould, John W. "The Advocacy Role in Public Child Welfare." *Child Welfare* 171 (March–April 1992): 114–130.

Johnson, Louise C. "Networking: A Means of Maximizing Resources in Non-Metropolitan Settings." *Human Services in the Rural Environment* 8, 2: 27–31.

Kingsley, Chris. *A Guide to Case Management for At Risk Youth,* 2nd ed. Waltham, MA: Brandeis University Center for Human Resources, 1993.

Meyer, Carol. "The Ecosystems Perspective: Implications for Social Work Practice." In Carol Meyer and Mark Mattaini, *The Foundations of Social Work Practice.* Washington, DC: NASW Press, 1995 (pp. 16–27).

Mizrahi, Terry. "Managed Care and Managed Competition: A Primer for Social Work." *Health and Social Work* 18 (May 1993): 86–91.

Moore, Stephen T. "A Social Work Practice Model of Case Management: The Case Management Grid." *Social Work* 35 (September 1990): 444–448.

Mordock, John B. "The Road to Survival Revisited: Organizational Adaptation to the Managed Care Environment." *Child Welfare* 75 (May–June 1996): 195–218.

NASW Standards for Social Work Case Management. Washington, DC: NASW Press, 1992.

Netting, Ellen F., Kettner, Peter M., and McMurtry, Steven L. *Social Work Macro Practice,* 2nd ed. New York: Longman, 1998.

Powell, Thomas J., Ed. *Working with Self-Help.* Washington, DC: NASW Press, 1990.

Rapp, Charles A. *The Strengths Model: Case Management with People Suffering from Severe and Persistent Mental Illness.* New York: Oxford University Press, 1998.

Resnick, Cheryl, and Tighe, Ellen Gelhaus. "The Role of Multidisciplinary Community Clinics in Managed Care Systems." *Social Work* 42 (January 1997): 91–98.

Rivera, Felix G., and Erlich, John L., Eds. *Community Organizing in a Diverse Society,* 3rd ed. Boston: Allyn and Bacon, 1998.

Rose, Stephen M., Ed. *Case Management and Social Work Practice.* New York: Longman, 1992.

Rothman, Jack. *Practice with Highly Vulnerable Clients: Case Management and Community-Based Service.* Englewood Cliffs, NJ: Prentice-Hall, 1994.

Rothman, Jack, and Sager, Jon Simon. *Case Management: Integrating Individual and Community Practice.* Boston: Allyn and Bacon, 1998.

Rubin, Herbert J., and Rubin, Irene S. *Community Organization and Development,* 2nd ed. New York: Macmillan, 1992.

Saleeby, Dennis, Ed. *The Strengths Perspective in Social Work Practice,* 2nd ed. New York: Longman, 1997.

Sheafor, Bradford W., Horejsi, Charles R., and Horejsi, Gloria A. *Techniques and Guidelines for Social Work Practice,* 5th ed. Boston: Allyn and Bacon, 2000 (Chapter 14, Section B).

Stevens, Ellen S. "Toward Satisfaction and Retention of Senior Volunteers." *Journal of Gerontological Social Work* 16, 3/4 (1991): 33–41.

Weinbach, Robert. *The Social Worker as Manager,* 3rd ed. Boston: Allyn and Bacon, 1998.

Wilcox, Julie A., and Taber, Merlin A. "Informal Helpers of Elderly Home Care Clients." *Health and Social Work* 16 (November 1991): 258–265.

Wyers, Norman L. "Policy-Practice in Social Work: Models and Issues." *Journal of Social Work Education* 27 (Fall 1991): 241–250.

NOTES

1. Florence Hollis, *Casework: A Psycho-Social Therapy,* 2nd ed. (New York: Random House, 1972), pp. 81–85 and chap. 9.

2. Max Siporin, *Introduction to Social Work Practice* (New York: Macmillan, 1975), p. 302.

3. Ibid., p. 305.

4. Richard M. Grinnel, Jr., and Nancy S. Kyte, "Environmental Modification: A Study," *Social Work* 20 (July 1975): 313–318.

5. See Robert Sommer, *Personal Space* (Englewood Cliffs, NJ: Prentice-Hall, 1969); Edward T. Hall, *The Hidden Dimension* (New York: Doubleday Anchor, 1969); and William H. Itlleson, Harold M. Proshansky, Leanne G. Rivlin, and Gary H. Winkel, *An Introduction to Environmental Psychology* (New York: Holt, Rinehart and Winston, 1974).

6. Carel B. Germain and Alex Gitterman, *The Life Model of Social Work Practice* (New York: Columbia University Press, 1980).

7. For further consideration of this topic, see Brett A. Seabury, "Arrangement of Physical Space in Social Work Settings," *Social Work* 16 (October 1971):

43–49; and Thomas Walz, Georgina Willenberg, and Lane deMoll, "Environmental Design," *Social Work* 19 (January 1974): 38–46.

8. See Richard E. Boettcher and Roger Vander Schie, "Milieu Therapy with Chronic Mental Patients," *Social Work* 20 (March 1975): 130–139.

9. For additional discussion, see Anthony N. Maluccio, "Promoting Competence Through Life Experience," in *Social Work Practice: People and Environments,* Carel B. Germain, Ed. (New York: Columbia University Press, 1979), pp. 282–302.

10. Irene A. Gutheil, "Considering the Physical Environment: An Essential Component of Good Practice," *Social Work* 37 (September 1992): 391–396.

11. See Carel B. Germain, "'Space': An Ecological Variable in Social Work Practice," *Social Casework* 59 (November 1978): 515–529.

12. Carel B. Germain, "Time: An Ecological Variable in Social Work Practice," *Social Casework* 57 (July 1976): 419–426.

13. Eugene Litwak and Henry F. Meyer, "A Balance Theory of Coordination Between Bureaucratic

Organizations and Community Primary Groups," *Administrative Science Quarterly* 11 (March 1966): 31–58; and *School, Family and Neighborhood: The Theory and Practice of School-Community Relations* (New York: Columbia University Press, 1974).

14. Karen Orloff Kaplan, "Recent Trends in Case Management," in *Encyclopedia of Social Work*, 18th ed. (supplement), Leon Ginsberg, Ed. (Silver Spring, MD: NASW Press, 1990), pp. 60–77.

15. Ibid., p. 62.

16. Jack Rothman, "A Model of Case Management: Toward Empirically Based Practice," *Social Work* 36 (November 1991): 520–528.

17. Stephen T. Moore, "A Social Work Practice Model of Case Management: The Case Management Grid," *Social Work* 35 (September 1990): 444–448.

18. For further discussion of this concept, see Seymour B. Sarason, Charles Carroll, Kenneth Maton, Saul Cohen, and Elizabeth Lorentz, *Human Services and Resource Networks* (San Francisco: Jossey-Bass, 1977); and Louise C. Johnson, "Networking: A Means of Maximizing Resources in Non-Metropolitan Settings," *Human Services in the Rural Environment* 8, 2: 27–31.

19. See Alice H. Collins and Diane Pancoast, *Natural Helping Networks: A Strategy for Prevention* (Washington, DC: National Association for Social Workers, 1976).

20. Jack Rothman, John L. Erlich, and Joseph G. Teresa, *Promoting Innovation and Change in Organizations and Communities: A Planning Manual* (New York: John Wiley, 1976), chap. 2.

21. For more information about each of the tasks identified, see Bradford W. Sheafor, Charles R. Horejsi, and Gloria A. Horejsi, *Techniques and Guidelines for Social Work Practice*, 4th ed. (Boston: Allyn and Bacon, 1997), pt. IV, sec. B.

22. Ronald W. Toseland and Robert F. Rivas, "Working with Task Groups: The Middle Phase," in *Strategies of Community Organization*, 4th. ed., Fred Cox, John L. Erlich, Jack Rothman, and John E. Tropman, Eds. (Itasca, IL: F. E. Peacock, 1987), pp. 114–142.

23. Marlene Wilson, *The Effective Management of Volunteer Programs* (Boulder, CO: Volunteer Management Association, 1976), is a good resource on developing volunteer programs.

24. Brian A. Auslander and Gail K. Auslander, "Self-Help Groups and the Family Service Agency," *Social Casework* 69 (February 1988): 74–80.

25. Herman Resnick and Rino J. Patti, Eds., *Change from Within: Humanizing Social Welfare Organizations* (Philadelphia, PA: Temple University Press, 1980), pp. 5–6.

26. This strategy is based on the work of Resnick and Patti, *Change from Within*, and the discussion that follows is heavily influenced by their work. For an early version, see Rino J. Patti and Herman Resnick, "Changing the Agency from Within," *Social Work* 17 (July 1972): 48–57.

27. See Rino J. Patti, "Organizational Resistance and Change: The View from Below," *Social Service Review* 48 (September 1974): 367–383.

28. Resnick and Patti, *Change from Within*, pp. 9–11.

29. Patti and Resnick, "Changing the Agency from Within."

30. Rothman, Erlich, and Teresa, *Promoting Innovation and Change in Organization and Community*, chap. 2.

31. See James D. Jorgensen and Brian W. Klepinger, "The Social Worker as Staff Trainer," *Public Welfare* 37 (Winter 1979): 41–49.

32. Edward J. Pawlak, "Organization Tinkering," *Social Work* 21 (September 1976): 376–380.

33. Resnick and Patti, *Change from Within*, p. 12.

34. George A. Brager, "Advocacy and Political Behavior," *Social Work* 13 (April 1968): 15.

35. Robert J. Teare and Harold L. McPheeters, *Manpower Utilization in Social Welfare* (Atlanta, GA: Southern Regional Education Board, 1970), p. 30.

36. Robert H. MacRae, "Social Work and Social Action," *Social Service Review* 60 (March 1966): 1–7.

37. J. Donald Cameron and Esther Talavera, "Advocacy Program for Spanish-Speaking People," *Social Casework* 57 (July 1976): 427–431.

38. Robert Sunley, "Family Advocacy: From Case to Cause," *Social Casework* 51 (June 1970): 347–357.

39. Jack Rothman, with John E. Tropman, "Models of Community Organization and Macro Pratice Perspectives: Their Mixing and Phasing," in *Strategies of Community Organization*, 4th. ed., Fred Cox, John L. Erlich, Jack Rothman, and John E. Tropman, Eds. (Itasca, IL: F. E. Peacock, 1987), pp. 3–26.

40. It is expected that understandings to carry out these activities will come from political science courses and a course in social welfare policy.

41. Saul D. Alinsky, *Reveille for Radicals* (Chicago: University of Chicago Press, 1946); and Richard Cloward and R. Elman, "Advocacy in the Ghetto," in *Strategies of Community Organization: A Book of Readings*, 1st ed., Fred M. Cox, John L. Erlich, Jack Rothman, and John E. Tropman, Eds. (Itasca, IL: F. E. Peacock, 1970), pp. 209–215.

42. Cox, Erlich, Rothman, and Tropman, *Strategies of Community Organization*, 4th ed. (1987); pt. III, sec. IV, "Social Action," is an excellent source for this approach.

CHAPTER

15 Evaluation

LEARNING EXPECTATIONS

1. Understanding the importance of and skill in the use of evaluation in the social work process.
2. Understanding of accountability as it relates to the client, the profession, the agency, and the community that supports the service.
3. Understanding of the various forms of evaluation and knowledge about when each form is appropriate.
4. Understanding of the various forms of recording and skill in the use of each form.
5. Understanding of the use of research techniques in the evaluation process.
6. Appreciation of the computer to process evaluative data.
7. Understanding of ethical and legal issues relative to evaluation.

As an ongoing part of the social work process, evaluation is the means for determining if the goals and objectives of the social work endeavor are being reached. It also involves looking at the means being used to reach goals and objectives. Evaluation identifies spinoffs (unexpected outcomes), both negative and positive, from the helping activity. Evaluation should be continuous, but it becomes particularly important as each step is completed. Evaluation should occur after assessment to see that all needed information has been collected and that appropriate conclusions about the meaning of the information and about client in situation have been drawn. After planning, there should be evaluation to determine if the plan is complete and feasible. After action has been carried out, evaluation should be used to determine if the desired goals have been reached. Evaluation is also an important part of the termination process.

Evaluation, then, is finding out if what is expected to happen is really happening. It looks at completed work and determines which methods and strategies worked and why. It is an opportunity to check with clients and significant others to see how it is going from their viewpoint. Evaluation of one's work is a professional obligation for every social worker and should be a continuous process. Programs and agencies are obligated to carry out, on an ongoing basis, evaluation of the mission, purpose, and goals of the agency and its programs. Evaluation is necessary if social workers and the agencies for which they work are to be accountable to clients, support sources, and the general public.

This chapter will first consider this concern for accountability and how it relates to evaluation. It will then discuss various kinds of evaluation, techniques used in evaluation, and ethical issues related to evaluation.

Accountability

In recent years, much emphasis has been placed on accountability in the social welfare field. In its simplest form, **accountability** is responsibility. However, the complexity of accountability begins to become apparent when one asks the question, Accountability to whom? The social worker is responsible to the client for upholding his part of any agreements or contracts and for providing the service agreed on. The social worker is also responsible to the profession for upholding social work values and the *NASW Code of Ethics* (see Chapter 3) in delivering services. The social worker is responsible to the agency that employs the worker for delivering the service within guidelines, programs, and policies developed by the agency. The agency, in turn, is responsible to those who provide support and sanction to the agency. This latter responsibility adds considerable complexity to accountability. Those who support the agency are a nebulous mass of individuals (e.g., taxpayers) who have no universally accepted goals for the service. The goals that do exist are often not congruent with the goals set by workers and clients.

Accountability is complex because of the multiple constituency of the social agency and because of the systemic nature of persons in situations. It is very difficult, if not impossible, to identify cause-and-effect relationships or all variables that may be operating in any situation. Thus, adequate hard data are elusive. The complexity of social service organizations further adds to the complexity of accountability. In all its complexity, accountability becomes an ambiguous concept.

Accountability has two components: efficiency and effectiveness. *Efficiency* refers to the cost of service. Because of the nature of human services, accountability involves more than determining numbers of clients, time spent with clients, or cost of service in dollars and cents. Social costs also must be considered, including such things as how the service impacts the client's capacity to parent or function in the work force. Social costs also include how the service affects the functioning of systems in the client's immediate environment or how the quality of life of the client, significant others, and the community in general are affected. *Effectiveness* relates to whether the service leads to the goals for which it was intended. Because of the complexity of the human situation and the involvement of individuals with differing goals in agency programs, it is difficult to measure effectiveness. If measurable goals have been included in the plan of action, however, it is possible to determine if those goals have been reached in a particular service situation. If agencies have well-defined purposes and goals, then evaluation and accountability can be carried out on a sound base. The identification of goals and the evaluation of the service are key factors in accountability. Evaluation is not only important as a part of the social work process but also necessary for agency functioning in the contemporary social and political scene.

Evaluation is of special concern for social workers practicing in medical, mental health, and substance abuse settings because of issues raised by managed care and by capitation of services. Managed care and capitation of services represent part of the response to concerns raised over the cost of medical care, the increased demand on entitlement programs by the "baby boom" generation, and the federal budget deficit. These issues have impacted social work services by reducing resources and changing policies relating to how services are delivered. For the most part, social workers and other human service providers are being required to do much more with much less. Balancing efficiency and effectiveness has become more important than ever before.

Proponents would argue that managed care ensures greater efficiency by eliminating the possibility of unlimited or unending service, while also ensuring quality through the various review processes, such as utilization, retrospective, and peer reviews. At the very least, the argument goes, managed care provides oversight for the service delivery system. Critics see it as overemphasizing efficiency and cost savings with little genuine concern about quality.

Determining if a client will receive a given service is a critical aspect of the overall quality of service. Unfortunately, some managed care plans use nonprofessionals to determine if services will be approved. This practice is being challenged in the courts. Also some plans are structured so that managers of care have a financial stake in the kinds of care the client receives. Some have penalties for managers of care who refer clients to expensive services. As part of their sanction by society, professionals are expected to act in the best interests of their clients. This is problematic when self-interest plays a significant part in the decision-making process. In its best form, managed care can help maximize the efficient use of scarce resources. In its less desirable form, it can be used to ensure profits or capitate expenditures by rationing care based on cost.

In many settings, social workers will have to learn to live with managed care for the foreseeable future. Quality services must be rendered to clients in an efficient manner. Constant evaluation of the effectiveness of each phase of the change process is needed. Evaluation becomes especially imperative in an era of shrinking resources and managed care. Social workers also need to realize that approval for additional or alternative services is available in nearly every managed care plan. Generally, the keys to obtaining these services for clients are good assessment, evaluation, and documentation along with knowledge of the managed care system.

Evaluation has been defined as "collection of data about outcomes of a program of action relative to goals and objectives set in advance of the implementation of that program."[1] An agency is most apt to be held accountable for its programs. The worker is accountable to the individual client and to the agency. In order for the agency to be accountable, it must develop ongoing means of evaluating both the efficiency and the effectiveness of programs. As a part of the agency, the worker must contribute data for the agency to use in this process.

Bernie Jones has said that programs are evaluated for a number of specific reasons. Some of these are:

1. To find out how effectively a program is meeting its goals. (Is it making any difference? To whom?)
2. To obtain information that will help restructure a program or manage it more effectively. (Perhaps the evaluator wants to see if a particular component should be eliminated or replaced.)
3. To identify models for others to follow, or to test a theory or an approach to a problem. (What made the program work? Can any elements be used in other programs?)
4. To find out what staff members need in order to be effective.
5. To find out how well the program is working from the client's point of view and how to make it more effective.
6. To improve public relations and fundraising efforts. (What will help sell a program to those whose funds or endorsements are needed?)
7. To meet the requirements of a funding source. (Is the program operating well enough to justify refunding?)[2]

Most of the concern for accountability comes from sources other than the client, but it is important for clients to be involved in developing accountability responses. Clients can provide useful information that cannot be obtained from other sources. Inclusion of the client's evaluation of service also increases the indexes of effectiveness available, but such inclusion is not without problems. Clients and organizations may differ in their view of what is important in determining accountability. Because they have less power, the views and opinions of clients tend to be overlooked. Clients also may not have the knowledge and experience to evaluate a service in all its complexity. They can, however, be involved in constructing questions to be considered in evaluation and can present their viewpoints as to the ideal service for the agency to provide to meet its goals.

In order to fulfill professional responsibility in contemporary social work practice, all social workers must be concerned about issues of accountability. They must attempt to reconcile the different perspectives of the client, the agency, and the supporting public. They must cooperate with clients and other knowledgeable persons and develop means for evaluating services so that accurate assessments of the service being delivered are possible. They must attempt to ensure that the right questions are asked and that issues of both effectiveness and efficiency are addressed. As social workers carry out evaluative activities, they should be ever mindful of the accountability requirements of contemporary social work practice. These requirements include those of the agency, funding sources, and community as well as the worker's accountability to the client and the profession. Workers should collect adequate and accurate data to fulfill the accountability requirements related to both the worker-client relationship and the relationship of the agency to its supporting bodies and the general public.

Kinds of Evaluation

Planning for evaluation when developing a plan of action is one way of ensuring that the plan of action is carried out in a way that yields maximum information to the worker, the client, and the agency. If the information to be used in evaluation is identified before the social work process begins, there is a better chance that such information will be available for use in evaluation.

In order to plan effectively and efficiently for evaluation, an understanding of the various kinds of evaluation and some of the means for carrying out the evaluative process is useful. Evaluation serves many purposes and takes a variety of forms. In its most simplified form, it is a worker thinking about what has happened and why it happened. During the termination phase of the social work process, the worker and client together determine if the goals set out in the contract have been reached and then discuss what enabled the goal attainment. Evaluation involves discussing what has been helpful to the client and what could have been done differently. Program evaluation is more complex, generally involving statistical data or other research methodology. Evaluation may be summative or formative. **Summative evaluation** is concerned with outcomes and effectiveness. **Formative evaluation** is concerned with looking at the process of the work, at how the work during the various steps in the service influenced the final outcome. Such evaluation would look at such things as the nature of the relationship, the content of sessions, or the setting in which the work took place. Both types are important in social work practice and should be included in the evaluation process.[3] This section will point out a variety of other ways of looking at evaluation. The kind of evaluation employed is in part dependent on the stage of the social work process or on the program or agency need for data related to accountability.

One way to develop an understanding of evaluation is to consider various classification schemes used relative to evaluation. The first classification to be considered is whether the evaluation is of a particular case, of a program within an agency, or of the agency itself. When considering a specific case, evaluation focuses on whether or not the goals set by the worker and client together were attained. Evaluation of the process of the work should focus on how the various components of the plan of action contributed to reaching the goal. Evaluation of the process of work is a joint endeavor of the worker and the client, because the client is usually the best source of information about goal attainment and about the process of the work together. Workers often do some additional thinking about the client in a situation and how the client and his situation relate to other clients they have had. This is done so that the worker can develop an understanding of how to approach future clients who may be in similar situations.

Program and agency evaluations determine effectiveness of agency functioning. These kinds of evaluation are often concerned with efficiency of service provision and usually are not as personalized as a case evaluation is. Different kinds of evaluation require different methods and techniques.

Program evaluations serve four purposes. First, they are necessary to meet the requirements of outside funding and accreditation bodies. Second, they can provide indications of client satisfaction. Third, they can provide information that can be used in developing new practice knowledge and worker competence. Fourth, program evaluations can document the need for new services and/or service effectiveness to other service providers, funding sources, and the general public.

A second classification is qualitative versus quantitative evaluation. With quantitative data, an effort is made to measure satisfaction by using numbers and averaging the responses of those surveyed. The advantage of this procedure is that statistical computations can be used to determine if the outcome is due to random error or is likely to be associated with the service. The disadvantage is that the data may not be very meaningful because they lack the richness of individual experiences. Qualitative data tend to derive from asking people to relate their experiences. This has the advantage of providing a comprehensive picture of service from the client's perspective. However, gathering qualitative data is more time consuming and thus more costly than quantitative data collection. In addition, samples of the client population tend to be smaller, and the data are more difficult to analyze. The contemporary service delivery system has been highly influenced by organizational management trends and the use of a quantitative base for evaluation. Clinical practice has also been influenced by behavioral psychology and its emphasis on measuring behaviors. The trend toward computerization of information and records also supports the demand for quantitative data. However, most social workers maintain that not all information can be dealt with in a quantitative manner owing to the qualitative factor in human functioning. Although behaviors can be measured, feelings and emotions cannot, and qualitative measures are a better mechanism for evaluating these factors. Most client surveys should include both quantitative and qualitative data acquisition in order to tap the advantages of each of these methods.

A third classification is that of clinical versus management evaluation. Although this classification might be closely related to the quantitative-qualitative classification (management generally uses quantitative data; clinical generally uses qualitative data), the application of these two types of evaluation is quite different. Management evaluation is used to make internal staffing and program decisions and to substantiate need for services and resources to support services. Clinical evaluation is limited to use by professional persons (worker and supervisor) and the client involved in the situation being evaluated. Because of the different usage, different information is sought for use in different types of evaluation, and different kinds of outcomes are expected. Sometimes data are used for both types of evaluation, which is more efficient in that it avoids collecting two sets of data. It can be difficult, however, to use the same information for two different purposes. Management evaluation is apt to call for statistical data, data that can be broken down into categories of problems. Clinical evaluation is usually concerned with the type of need or concern dealt with and specific information as to how the need and its resolution is impacted by the client and her situation. This information loses some of its meaning when converted to categories or statistics.

Another classification is that developed by Michael Key, Peter Hudson, and John Armstrong.[4] They discuss evaluation approaches along a hard line–soft line continuum. Hard-line evaluation focuses on aims and objectives that are set before the implementation of programs. Some degree of scientific objectivity is involved in this type of evaluation. Soft-line evaluation is based on impressions and opinions. Each approach yields different kinds of information. The worker needs to determine if hard-line information will adequately provide for the evaluation needs and tell the necessary story. If not, then soft-line information should be used either to tell the story or to supplement the hard-line information.

Each type of classification points out a different dimension of evaluation. Each evaluative effort can be classified along a continuum related to each of the four classifications. When choosing evaluation methods and techniques, it is important to consider the requirements of the situation being evaluated, keeping all four possible classifications in mind (case or program agency, quantitative or qualitative, clinical or management, hard or soft), and to choose methods that match the requirements of the situation.

Techniques for Use in Evaluating

The process of evaluation makes use of many of the same methods and techniques as assessment, such as looking at information collected and determining what has happened in the social work endeavor. The information may be gathered specifically for evaluative purposes, or it may be information developed as part of the social work process. Much of this information gathering is done using an interactive process (see Chapters 9 and 10). Processes, methods, and skills presented in earlier sections of this book can and should be adapted to the needs of the evaluation.

There are, however, some special techniques used to facilitate the evaluative process, including various recording and research techniques. Use of the computer, particularly as related to recording and research, is growing in evaluation. When planning for evaluation, social workers should look at various methods and techniques for collecting information and choose those that can provide information most reliably and efficiently. This requires the same kind of creative planning used in developing the plan of action. This section will present methods of keeping records and ways of using research in evaluation. It will also discuss implications for social work practice, particularly for the evaluation process, as well as information management using computers.

Recording

Social work has always placed considerable emphasis on recording. This recording has taken many forms. **Process recording**—a narrative report of all that happened during a client contact, including the worker's feelings and thinking about what has happened—is a form that at one time received great emphasis and was frequently used in the educational and supervisory processes. In recent years it has not been used as often, in part probably because it is extremely time consuming. Also, the intensive individual supervision of workers, which was once considered essential to social work and which made extensive use of recording important, is no longer considered desirable in many settings. Recording, however, is still a technique that has value for students as they and their field supervisors evaluate their work. It is especially useful to the social worker striving to further develop understanding and skill in difficult situations or in situations in which the worker is developing new skills.

The usefulness of process recording depends to a considerable extent on the ability of the worker to recall exactly what happened and in what order and to look at the facts in an objective manner in order to get at underlying feelings and meanings. The worker must be willing to honestly record the actions and communications of both worker and client. When this technique is used in a supervisory process, the worker must have a trusting relationship with the supervisor. Because of its time-consuming nature, process recording probably should not be used with every case or situation but only with carefully selected cases particularly applicable to the worker's development and learning. Process recording is most often used when working with individuals but can also be used when working with larger systems. When process recording is used, confidentiality must be preserved. The written record must be kept in a secure place and only seen by those directly involved in the situation or supervising the worker. If a record is to be used for other purposes, such as teaching or as a case example, it must be completely disguised so that neither the person nor the situation can be identified. The purpose of process recording is to aid the worker in understanding the situation and to serve as a tool for learning. After it is used, the process recording should be destroyed. It should not be made part of the permanent record.

A technique used for purposes similar to process recording is taping, either in audio or video format, of interviews, group sessions, or other interactional encounters. This technique can allow the worker to see himself in action with the client. Sometimes it is also useful for the client to view what has happened as a means of evaluating behaviors and interactions. Unless the time is taken to evaluate the underlying elements of the situation (the feeling elements and the reasons behind behaviors), some of the learning potential of this technique is lost. When using the taping technique of recording, workers must obtain written permission from the client to tape sessions. Sometimes taping may inhibit the client and have a negative effect on the work of the session. Again, confidentiality is an important consideration. Tapes should be destroyed or erased after they have served their purpose.

Another type of recording often used by social workers is the *summary record*. Though this type of record takes various forms depending on agency policy, it essentially includes entry data, often the social history, a plan of action, periodic summaries of significant information and actions taken by the worker, and a statement of what was accomplished as the case was closed. The periodic summaries may be made at specified periods of time (e.g., every week), or they may be made when it is necessary to document some fact or action. The summary record is shorter and easier to use when considering the total service process. It is focused more on what happens with the client than on the worker's input and sifts out the important elements, discarding the superfluous.

Summary records are most important in situations in which long-term, ongoing contact with a client and a series of workers may be involved. These records provide a picture of what has happened in the past with a particular client. Agency policy often specifies the form and content of such records. This policy reflects the agency's need for information both to protect itself when questions about the handling of a particular case are raised and to provide the specific information needed for accountability purposes. As summary records may be subject to review by a number of people, questions of how to deal with confidentiality are important. It is usually good practice to include in summary recording only that which is required to be in the record and only verifiable information, not impressions, feelings, or information that can be misinterpreted.

A commonly used kind of recording is the **problem-oriented record,** which is often used in health care settings. This method is used not just by social workers but also by all health care professionals. This system has advantages when working in an interdisciplinary setting. It is easily translated to computer data bases and is succinct and focused.

Problem-oriented records contain four parts. First is a data base that contains information pertinent to the client and work with the client. This includes such things as age, sex, marital status, functioning limitations, persons involved (family and other professionals), financial situation, or any test results. Second is a problem list that includes a statement of initial complaints and assessment of the concerned staff. Third are plans and goals related to each identified problem. Fourth are follow-up notes about what was done and the outcome of that activity.

Problem-oriented records take several forms. Usually, they consist at least in part of checklists that can be converted into data on a computer. One often-used form is *soaping* (subjective, objective, assessment, plan). In this form, for each identified problem, subjective (the patient's report), objective (the facts as determined by clinical activity), assessment (a statement about the nature of the problem), and a plan for dealing with the problem are stated.

The use of the term *problem-oriented record* is inconsistent with the ecosystems strengths approach. However, a similar format is generally used and might be referred to as a *change-oriented record* or *needs-based record* in that it is driven by the identification and meeting of needs. This record should consist of the identification of needs or concerns and an assessment of the person in environment or ecosystem. A plan is developed that is built on the strengths and resources of the ecosystem and designed to meet the needs of the client and the ecosystem. Progress notes are kept that describe the progress toward goals and objectives. Periodic (generally quarterly) reports summarize the progress made and document the need for further service. A termination summary identifies the reasons for ending the service and the outcomes.

Recent research carried out by Jill Doner Kagle indicates that workers have some difficulty in using what she terms as "new records." The *new record* is narrowly focused on defining the need for service, service goals and plans, service activities, and the impact of service on the client situation. She found that many workers felt this kind of recording did not supply all the information needed in providing service. Her work suggests that workers believe they need information on the dynamics of the situation and perhaps on the context of the client. Another difficulty workers encountered with new records was that they did not provide for the "over-documentation" called for in a world in which all professions are more often threatened with legal actions. The answer to these issues may lie in determining which cases need to have in-depth recording and which can use a new record approach.[5]

Record keeping has always been an important part of the social worker's job and has changed over time due to new practice demands and new technologies. Records have many different purposes that range from improving the worker's competence to obtaining data for accountability and research. It is important that social workers develop the capacity to accurately and efficiently maintain records required by any agency in which they are employed. They also should discover what records are needed for their personal and professional growth.

Case Example

This example illustrates three ways in which the same case material might be handled when recording and evaluating. The three techniques are process recording, summary recording, and problem-oriented recording.

Process Recording

On February 4, 2000, the nurse on surgery called to refer Mrs. Heart to me. She said that Mrs. Heart had been brought in for an emergency appendectomy two days ago. Yesterday afternoon she became very upset and showed much concern about how her children were being cared for. Nurses on the evening shift discussed the situation with Mr. Heart when he came to visit. The children, a boy age 4 and a girl age 2, have been cared for by a neighbor during the day. Mr. Heart left them with a babysitter last night. He, too, showed some concern, saying that neither he nor his wife wanted the children with the neighbor, as they questioned some of her childcare practices, but he didn't know what he could do right now. The request is for me to see Mrs. Heart to see if I can find suitable childcare.

I immediately obtained the medical chart and found that she is medically doing well postsurgically. There is concern that her emotional state may affect her recovery rate. I then went to talk with Mrs. Heart in her room. I found an attractive, twenty-eight-year-old woman who was having some postoperative pain. I quietly introduced myself as the medical social worker. She began to say, "Please don't take my children away." She then began to cry and say, "I can't help it. Why did this have to happen? I love my children." I put my hand on hers and looked her in the eye and quietly said that I had not come to take her children away, that I could not do that as I am not a child welfare social worker. I explained that it was my job to help with problems that arose because people were sick and in the hospital. I told her that I was there because she seemed very concerned about her children and might need some help in finding care for the children while she was in the hospital and for a while when she got home. She again expressed concern that the children would be taken out of the home, although she was not as agitated as at first. I told her that usually children should remain in their familiar surroundings when parents are hospitalized, as they are less apt to be upset about the situation if they stay in the home. Mrs. Heart then said, "I don't know what we can do. There are no relatives we can call on. Mr. Heart might lose his job if he stays home to take care of the children."

I then said I'd like to get to understand the situation better. I thought she could help me. Mrs. Heart by this time seemed quieter and more able to listen. I asked her to tell me about the children. [The recording would then continue to describe the interaction as the worker and client explore the situation and decide together what to do. The actual verbatim dialogue of the interview is recorded when possible. The record could end with a summary section that identifies the salient aspects of the situation, the plan developed, the next tasks for the worker and client, and the worker's evaluation of the interview.]

Summary Recording

February 4, 2000, social work services requested by Nurse Brown because Mrs. Heart is upset about childcare for her two children, a boy age 4 and a girl age 2. Saw Mrs. Heart and developed with her a plan for the care of the children. We identified a friend who will care for children during the day until she is discharged. A babysitter will continue to be used in evenings when Mr. Heart visits. Worker will contact homemaker's service to set up plans for use of a homemaker when Mrs. Heart returns home until she is physically able to care for the children.

Problem-Oriented Recording

Name: Mrs. Linda Heart   Age: 28
Referral from: Nurse Brown   Date: February 4, 2000
Medical condition: Emergency appendectomy February 2, 2000
Subjective: Patient upset about care of her children while she is in hospital. Seems an appropriately concerned mother. Has good intelligence. Seems to have good relationship with husband.
Objective: Children are now being cared for by a neighbor during the day and father and babysitters at night. Parents do not feel comfortable with daytime arrangement. Mother will be in hospital three more days and needs some help with childcare for at least two weeks after she returns home.
Assessment: Alternative childcare arrangements should be explored with family to see if plans more in keeping with their desires can be found. The Hearts are unaware of community resources that might be of help to them. Mrs. Heart is verbal and able to discuss plans, but Mr. Heart should also be included in planning.
Plan: Obtain a list of community resources that may be of help to the Hearts. During visiting hours on February 4, 2000, discuss with both Mr. and Mrs. Heart possible solutions and set up a childcare plan for the next three weeks.

Research

Many research techniques are very useful in carrying out evaluations because evaluation and research share common considerations and concerns. The main reasons that social workers need to be familiar with research and evaluation techniques in practice are (1) to be able to evaluate the success or failure of their services; (2) to be able to evaluate themselves and their strengths and limitations as practitioners; (3) to be able to evaluate the potential use of various approaches and techniques found in professional literature or obtained through training programs; (4) to evaluate programs in order to make them more effective while maximizing the efficient use of resources and to report these results as a part of accountability. This last area will be covered in the next section.

The purpose of this discussion is to point out the relationship of practice and research when evaluating social work practice and to discuss a few research methods and techniques that are particularly suited for evaluation of practice. The research techniques chosen for discussion are single-system design, goal-attainment scaling, and the use of questionnaires, interviews, and observation.*

Single-system design is a research method that fits very well with problem solving or any solution-oriented approach. It is a natural follow-up to the measurable goals and objectives that were identified in Chapter 12. It is important that the worker and the client have developed a plan in which progress toward meeting needs and overcoming barriers can be measured. Otherwise, the work can seem aimless rather than being focused on suitable outcomes. An essential ingredient for change is hope. As the client is able to see progress, she is able to feel more hope that the situation will change for the better. If the plan is based on strengths the client possesses, then progress will be made sooner and the overall plan will have greater chance of success. The client will feel more empowered since she is acting on abilities and capacities she already has. As the client is able to see progress, she will experience positive reinforcement for change. Even the completion of tasks can be very uplifting for the client.

Single-system design can be used with any size client system. It is a variation of what is called time series design, in which a series of measurements are made over time. With single-system design, the same system is measured over time. The system can be an individual, a family, a group, a program, an organization, or a community.

The simplest traditional experimental design uses a control group and an experimental group. Participants are randomly assigned to each group in order to avoid biasing the outcome. The experimental group receives services, and the control group does not. Differences between the two groups at the end of the experiment are assumed to be caused by the service. Statistical methods are typically used to estimate the probability that the results were due to error rather than the service. The problem with this approach is that it is unethical for a social worker to withhold services to clients, especially if the client would benefit from the service.

Occasionally, social work evaluators can develop a research project using a traditional experimental design in which the control group consists of clients on a waiting list for service. The control group might also be offered service at a later time. However, it is nearly impossible to randomly assign clients to a waiting list, and so these designs are considered quasi-experimental.

---

*Other variations of single-system design are not covered here. A more comprehensive study of single-system research should be covered in the required research course for social work students.

In single-system design, no one is refused service for experimental purposes. There is no need to apply statistical methods or to use random assignment to ensure that the control and experimental groups are equivalent. Instead, the client system serves as its own control group by measuring a target behavior, condition, or event before the intervention or service begins and then measuring the same thing during and or after the intervention or service.

In single-system design, clients can be informed and can consent to the evaluation by participating in the process itself. Throughout the change process, the client participates as a partner in change efforts. Including clients in measuring and evaluating change is essential to sound ethical practice. Researchers who are "purists" would be highly critical of this approach. Their concern would be that one would have difficulty in determining whether the intervention or some other influence brought about the change. They would be especially concerned that clients would "contaminate" the results by doing something out of the ordinary that would either enhance or sabotage the results. However, practitioners are interested in assisting clients in changing their circumstances rather than in maintaining purity in research design. If the purpose is to measure client goals, then the concerns of the "purists" are irrelevant.

If the worker needs to generalize the results to answer questions about the effectiveness of an intervention method, a service, a program, or the like, then greater care needs to be taken to control for bias. For most purposes it is sufficient for the worker to limit claims of success or failure to the situation at hand. Another option is to be scrupulous in describing how the evaluation was designed and carried out, allowing others to decide for themselves the validity or reliability of the results.

For an individual client, the research technique of **single-subject design** is used. During the assessment phase a baseline is established for the client's behavior. Interventive methods, goals, and measurable objectives related to a desired change in the behavior are identified. At varying points during the intervention, the target behavior is measured to determine the progress toward reaching the goal. After completion of the intervention, a final measurement is made to determine the extent to which the goal has been reached. The proponents of this method claim that measurable results or outcomes of the intervention can be obtained. It is felt that use of single-subject design provides a reliable means of validating practice. It is also a critical part of developing what is called "practice wisdom," which consists of benefits gained through experience in the field. The more the social worker adds empirical evidence to her experience, the greater her confidence in practice decisions.

Critics of single-subject design believe that the range of applicability is very limited because the technique is only useful within a behavioral framework for social work practice. They also believe that there are qualitative questions that are not addressed by this methodology. Questions also are raised as to the lasting quality of the change when measurements are made during and directly after intervention. Is the planned intervention the cause of the desired change, or have other factors, either in the treatment situation or in the environment, contributed to the change?[6] The major contribution of single-subject design is its focus on goals and outcomes and the provision of a methodology for measuring outcomes, which moves evaluation toward the hard end of the soft-hard continuum.

The simplest single-system design involves a pretest before intervention and a posttest afterward. Another variation involves several measurements during the baseline period, with continued measurement during the intervention. This is called AB design, where A represents time when the intervention is not taking place and B represents time when it is.

Careful attention should be paid to measurement in all single-system designs. In order to ensure validity and internal reliability, measurement must be as consistent as possible. A good way to monitor this is to pay attention to the who, what, where, when, and how of measurement. To be consistent, the same person or group (who) needs to measure the same thing (what) at the same place (where) and time (when) using the same instruments or observation techniques (how). Any variation in any of these circumstances will raise doubts about the validity and reliability of the data or information; that is, whatever is being observed or measured may change because the person sees or interprets it differently or because the time and place are different. If what gets measured or how it gets measured changes, then the worker is actually comparing two different things that may be not be related at all. The worker will have to prove that the relationship exists before the results can be used with any confidence.

It should be noted that measuring lack of progress is as important as measuring progress. Evaluation is not just a matter of measuring success but also of measuring failure. Finding out that something is not working allows the client and the worker to change the plan. If the worker finds that certain techniques or approaches do not work in certain situations or with certain groups, she has added important information to her practice wisdom. In addition, with managed care it is essential that the worker be as effective and efficient as possible. There may be little if any room for error before the client's benefits or reimbursement are cut off or exhausted. To prevent financial hardship for the client or the agency, the worker must be focused on resolving the situation and will need to establish time frames and track progress quickly and with a minimum of effort.

Case Example

Implementation of a Single-System Research Project in Field Placement

Sue is in the senior year of a BSW program and is in field placement at a family service agency. She is required to design and implement a single-system research project in her field placement as an assignment for her senior-level practice class. Sue consulted with her field instructor and decided to do her report on Mrs. Smith, who came to the agency for assistance in controlling her seven-year-old son, Jimmy. He misbehaves, and she is not able to get him to follow through with chores. Sue has met with Mrs. Smith and discussed the use of a reward system for positive behaviors. Mrs. Smith is willing to try it. She has been told about Sue's project and has consented to participating. The following is Sue's final project report.

I. **Identifying Information**
   A. Name: Mrs. S (disguised for confidentiality) and her son, Jimmy
   B. Age: Mrs. S is 30 years of age and Jimmy is 7.
   C. Occupation: Mrs. S is a homemaker. Jimmy is in the second grade.
   D. Presenting problem: Mrs. S sought services due to difficulty with getting Jimmy to respond to her as a parent. At times he refuses to do what he is told and is inconsistent in doing his chores.
   E. Significant others in the client system: Mr. S is a salesman who travels out of town frequently. As a result, Mrs. S is the primary parenting influence. Mr. S is generally able to get Jimmy to respond to him, but he is not at home enough to have an impact on a daily basis.
   F. Targeted behavior to be altered: Mrs. S will be successful in having Jimmy respond to her as a parent when she makes appropriate requests of him.

II. **Intervention Chosen and Rationale**
   The intervention that was chosen by Mrs. S and the worker was a "star chart" reward system. This is a form of behavior modification. Each time Mrs. S asked Jimmy to do something and he responded appropriately, he was given a gold star to put on his chart. The chart had squares for each day of the week and was placed on the refrigerator. At the end of the week, Jimmy was rewarded with a game, a toy, or an activity based on the number of stars he had collected. The rationale for using this intervention was to give Mrs. S a way of recognizing positive behavior. Jimmy was able to experience positive recognition more immediately.

III. **Outcome Desired for the Intervention**
   A. Goal and objectives
      1. Goal A: Jimmy will respond to his mother's first request at least five times each day for one week by April 15.
         a. Objective 1: Mrs. S will ask Jimmy to respond to her expectations and will reward him with a gold star each time he responds to her first request.
         b. Objective 2: Jimmy will accumulate at least five gold stars each day for an entire week by April 15.

IV. **Measurement Method Used to Monitor Client Outcomes**
   A daily behavior chart was constructed that tracked appropriate responses to Mrs. S's requests. Jimmy was given a gold star for each positive response to her first request. Each Saturday, Mrs. S and Jimmy counted up the stars to see if he was able to get a toy, game, or activity. Mrs. S and Jimmy had developed an agreement about the value of each star. Mrs. S brought the weekly charts to sessions with the worker.

V. **Baseline Data Report**
   During the assessment phase, the worker had Mrs. S keep track of the times when Jimmy responded appropriately to her requests. For the baseline period, Mrs. S noted a positive response to her first request on an average of one or two times each day.

(continued)

Case Example   Continued

VI. Intervention Data Report

During the intervention phase, there was a gradual improvement in Jimmy's response to Mrs. S. During the first week, he earned a total of thirteen gold stars, which represented an average of about two stars per day. The range was one to three gold stars each day. The second week resulted in twenty-one gold stars, with an average of three stars per day and a range of two to five stars. The five gold stars were earned on one day. The third week resulted in thirty-one gold stars, with a range of three to seven stars and a minimum of five stars on three days. The fourth and fifth weeks resulted in a minimum of five stars each day of the week and represented a successful completion of the intervention for Goal A.

VII. Assessment of Change in the Targeted Behaviors

There were significant changes that occurred from the baseline period through the intervention period that resulted in the successful achievement of Goal A. The results should be interpreted with some caution, since the baseline period consisted of only one week. Goal A was successfully achieved by the fourth week of intervention and was sustained during the fifth week.

VIII. Conclusions Regarding Intervention Based on Data and Subjective Observations

It appears that the use of behavior charting and positive reinforcement was very successful with Mrs. S and her son. In the absence of any remarkable events during the intervention phase, it is assumed that the intervention was responsible for the changes that were identified. As mentioned above, the results should be interpreted with some caution, since the baseline period consisted of only one week. However, it was reported by Mrs. S that the baseline week was a typical week. It is assumed that Mrs. S did not have any reasons for bias in her reporting of this, especially since she had some fears that the intervention might not work.

Goal A was successfully achieved by the fourth week of intervention and was sustained during the fifth week. Mrs. S and Jimmy felt good about how they were relating to each other, and they decided to continue using the chart. This response gives the worker great confidence that the intervention was the cause of the changes that were made.

It is not known whether the positive results would be sustained beyond the use of the intervention, since the clients plan to continue using it. When they decide to stop, it will probably be important for them to experience continuing satisfaction with their relationship as a natural reward for their newly found, successful interaction.

As mentioned above, single-system design can be used with any size client system. As long as what is being examined can be observed and measured, change can also be measured. Indications of the effectiveness of an intervention, service, or program can be determined, with some caution regarding the generalizability of the results. Extra caution should be used to protect the consistency of measurement when larger client systems are being evaluated and when ongoing or long-term evaluation is planned.

A technique often used with the single-subject design is **goal-attainment scaling.** When using this technique, the goals are set so that the outcomes can be measured on a five-point scale. The five points on the scale are (1) most unfavorable outcome thought likely, (2) less-than-expected outcome, (3) expected outcome, (4) more-than-expected outcome, and (5) most favorable outcome thought likely. Allowance for recording several goals is made by the development of a grid, with goals on one axis and levels of predicted attainment on the other axis.[7]

The major strength of goal-attainment scaling is that it allows for several measurements of success and failure to reach an outcome. By specifying a continuum of outcomes, the technique includes a growth factor. It also offers an evaluative mechanism (the five points on the scale) that can be converted to symbolic codes needed for computerization of data. The grid provides a quickly read summary of the outcomes of a specific episode of service.

The major limitations of goal-attainment scaling relate to the time needed to set up the scales for measurement. Some social workers believe the time spent in setting up the scales would better be used in working with the client. Also, some desired outcomes are very difficult to specify in the manner needed in this technique. Goal-attainment scaling also has some of the same limitations of single-subject design, such as questions about the relationship of the change to the intervention, the emphasis on the outcome of goals, and the sustainment of the change over time.

Other forms of evaluating practice outcomes include *task-achievement scaling (TAS)*. Two of the major contributors to this approach are William Reid and Laura Epstein, who have written about task-centered practice.[8] Joel Fischer and Kevin Corcoran have compiled a sourcebook of over 320 *rapid-assessment instruments (RAIs)* that can be used quickly in assessing numerous client conditions. RAIs generally have the additional advantage of being able to be used over and over with the same client while retaining their validity and reliability.[9] *Individualized rating scales (IRSs)* can be used for developing what are called self-anchoring scales.[10]

One of the most common uses of research for practitioners is for professional development activities. Professional social workers must increase their professional knowledge and skills and should aspire to contribute to the knowledge base of the profession. This means that social workers must be committed to continuing education throughout their careers. Usually, this takes the form of attending in-service events, workshops, conferences, and training programs along with researching and reading professional literature. To be a competent consumer and user of new techniques, the social worker must be able to evaluate the quality of the material presented and its applicability to various clients, practice settings, and circumstances. A solid foundation and knowledge base in the area of research and evaluation is required in order to accomplish this. In addition, competent and appropriate supervision is needed when trying new approaches or techniques.

In aspiring to contribute to the knowledge base of the profession, not every social worker will have an opportunity to write or publish an article or a book. However, opportunities to make contributions occur on a daily basis. These include sharing articles and educational materials with colleagues and other professionals, conducting in-service training and workshops, sharing "practice wisdom" through peer or formal supervision, and networking with other social workers and human service professionals. These daily contributions are fundamental to how social workers have functioned from the very beginning of the profession.

Program Evaluation

When designing and carrying out a program evaluation, collection of data is a most important step, as it is in all research. In order to evaluate a program, it is necessary to first determine what data are needed. Some of the data that might be useful include measures of client satisfaction, measures of success in meeting goals in a valid sample of clients served, cost-effectiveness measures, determinations of the extent to which the need is being addressed by the program, worker effort and satisfaction, and community attitudes toward the program. It is best to collect data related to several indicators of program effectiveness and efficiency.

Important techniques used for collecting the data are research interviews, questionnaires, and observations. When used for research or evaluative purposes, the *interview* is usually more structured than the interventive interview used in the social work process. Usually, there is a schedule, or questions in a specific order, that the interviewer is asked to follow. The interviewer is seeking specific information and should not engage in discussion that might change the interviewee's thinking about the situation being studied.

Social workers have knowledge and skill that can enhance the collection of information. They have knowledge of which information might be important for evaluative purposes and of how to seek and deal with particularly sensitive information. They have basic interviewing skills for engaging individuals in the work at hand, questioning techniques for obtaining needed information, and skill in observing and assessing the nonverbal communication of the interviewee. When a social worker is interviewing for evaluative purposes, the differences between an interventive interview and an evaluative interview should be kept in mind. When those not involved in a program are doing the interviewing, social workers involved in the program can be of help in developing the schedule and giving insight about the information to be obtained.

Questionnaires are another valuable tool in program evaluation. For example, a simple closed-question instrument to gather information about client satisfaction is used by some agencies. This instrument needs to be brief and yet elicit the attitudes and feelings of clients about the service they receive. The questionnaire should be constructed so that the respondent will understand the questions in the way intended. Care should also be taken to ensure an adequate response rate. When an agency is carrying out an evaluation of its programs, workers may be asked to help in the construction and administration of questionnaires. It is also useful to test the questionnaire before administering it to make sure that it is clear and understandable and that it is likely to obtain the data that are sought. The best way to do this is by using a small sample of clients. An alternative is to ask people to respond who have similar backgrounds and education levels as the client population. Another alternative is to have staff at the agency use it and give feedback.

Observation is another way of collecting needed data. Workers may be asked to contribute their observations to the data base. The worker should be clear about the information that is desired and the structure the evaluator has designed for the observation and the recording of the data. Often workers believe that, because of their knowledge of the situation, they may have a better way of structuring the observations and recording related to the observations. If this is the case, it is appropriate for them to discuss their concerns with the evaluator. However, if the evaluator decides not to incorporate the worker's suggestions, it is important for the worker to follow the evaluator's instructions and provide the information obtained in the desired form.

Use of Computers

The computer is often an important tool in the evaluative process. It can record and analyze large amounts of information and can facilitate the storing and retrieval of data to document accountability.

Social workers need to be aware of what computers can do and what their limitations are. They should know how to process information so it can be computerized, how to enter information, how to access existing data, and how to evaluate the usefulness of both hardware and software for social work purposes. They need to know enough about how computers operate in order to communicate with the computer expert or programmer about problems with a piece of equipment or a program. They need to be able to communicate about the tasks they want the computer to perform so that programs can be suggested, written, or modified.

It is also important to understand who can be expected to have access to the information and the purposes for which the information will be used. This helps the worker evaluate whether the most pertinent information is being requested and whether client identification and confidentiality are being protected. If social workers have reason to question whether the information being sought will provide the answers or whether client identification or confidentiality are at risk, they have an ethical responsibility to inform those responsible for the operation of the programs and to ensure that needed modifications are made.

In addition to their use in program evaluation, computers are being used by some agencies to maintain case records. Software has been developed and continues to be refined that will allow for an entire case record to be entered into the system, a big advantage over maintaining handwritten paper records. Interactive programs are available that allow the client (with assistance, if necessary) or the worker to answer questions about the situation and the needs or concerns. The program then produces a narrative assessment. Some programs are designed to suggest a plan, complete with goals and objectives. Whatever is selected can be modified or new goals added. The computer will then elicit feedback regarding goals when progress notes are entered and will produce quarterly, annual, and termination summaries. With the development of voice recognition programs that receive dictation and of powerful laptop computers, it is likely that in the future nearly all social workers will be using some form of computerized record keeping. Technology has the potential for considerably increasing worker efficiency in meeting "paperwork" demands, which could leave more time available to work with clients.

Issues Related to Evaluation

Accountability and evaluation techniques have raised issues related to client rights, confidentiality, and protection of information, which this section will address more completely. The areas to be discussed are client participation in the evaluation process, confidentiality of records, and the effect of privacy and open-access laws on the evaluation process.

Client Participation

When evaluating a particular episode of service there should be a strong element of client involvement. As the worker and client evaluate together what has happened and why it might have happened, plans can be adjusted when needed and contracts modified. If clients are to be involved in assessment, in planning, and in carrying out various tasks, then they are important sources for the information used in evaluation and must be a part of the evaluative endeavor so they can also be involved in making decisions to modify plans and contracts.

As the social work process with a particular client nears the end, or as goals have been met, evaluation becomes important for both worker and client. As a part of the termination process, evaluation provides opportunity for growth for both worker and client. Evaluation at termination will be discussed in Chapter 16.

The involvement of the client in program and agency evaluation is seldom considered because the techniques used require training. The focus is primarily on accountability to funding sources or on administrative functioning. Clients who are already overburdened with their personal needs and concerns usually have little energy to use in this evaluative process.

However, clients are important in this process. The basic purpose of the service or agency should be to meet client needs. Clients have a perspective on the agency's functioning that is important to any evaluation of that agency or program. Thus, social workers must see that the client perspective is included as a part of any program or agency evaluation. Also clients should have knowledge that such evaluation is taking place, of the information relative to them that is being used, and how that information is being used. The worker must make decisions as to how and when to involve the client.

Confidentiality

Responsible evaluation requires substantiating information. In order to be certain that information is available, it is essential that records be kept. The use of records raises concerns about confidentiality of sensitive information about clients, identification of specific clients, and information about the work with the client. The social worker has two responsibilities if the principle of confidentiality is to be maintained: (1) to be sure the client is aware of the records that are to be kept and of the nature of information sharing that will be required of the worker, so that client and worker can make an informed decision about the sharing of sensitive information; and (2) to do all that is possible to ensure that information and records are maintained and used only in ways that protect client identification and confidentiality.

One of the concerns with computerized records is maintaining confidentiality. Systems can be configured so as to limit access to records, but this can become complicated in large systems having many different workers and clients. One of the advantages of a computerized system is that records can be secured in one place. Another advantage is that the computer can keep track of who has opened the file, and a breach of security can be identified more easily. This is something that cannot be done with a paper record. One disadvantage is that in a good security system, access is limited and someone with the ability to access the record may not be available in an emergency. However, having emergency access to a computerized record means that files can be located quickly and are unlikely to be lost. A computerized system must be secure while allowing access to records on a need-to-know basis.

Whenever computers are used to maintain records, a secure, reliable backup system must be used to ensure that records are not lost or destroyed. Mainframe systems should be backed up on a tape system at the end of every day at minimum. Personal computers should use a disk, CD-rom, or zip drive to back up information on the hard drive. The backup system should be kept in a secure area separated from the main information system in case of a fire, flood, or similar disaster. Having two systems in separate places presents some additional challenges to maintaining confidentiality.

Clients need to understand not only the confidential nature of their work with a social worker but the limits of that confidentiality—that is, that information will be discussed with a supervisor or a professional team. Clients should be told what will be recorded, who will have access to their records, and how long these records will be kept. They need to know that records used in agency and program evaluation are depersonalized so that the identity of clients is protected. They need to know what information is shared with whom and why it is shared.

Workers also need to be sure that clients have given informed consent for the use of information in their records. A client should not be asked to give consent when he is desperate for service; at such a time making an informed decision is difficult. It is wise for the worker to discuss the use of information at several points during the work together. If the client decides not to share information and knows the consequences of not sharing that information, then the worker should respect the client's right to withhold information to protect her privacy.

The sharing of information about clients often requires written consent of the client. This consent should be specific; that is, it should state the purpose for the sharing of the information, an expiration date, and the persons with whom the information will be shared. Clients should be helped to understand their rights in signing or not signing such consents for release of information. Usually, it is wise to have someone witness the client's signature. Because the release of information could become a part of a legal action, the advice of a legal expert should be obtained in developing a form for the release of information.

Workers should monitor the use of client records to see that information contained in records is not used improperly. When they detect improper or questionable use of records, it is their responsibility to alert supervisors or other responsible persons to the situation. They can suggest ways in which the client's rights can be protected, such as depersonalizing information. If the improper use continues, workers must decide what action needs to be taken to prevent unethical use.

Effect of Privacy and Open-Access Laws

Federal and state legislation regulates the use of various kinds of records, including those used for evaluative purposes. This legislation has generated a growing body of interpretation and judicial decisions regarding the application of these laws, which has further complicated issues of record keeping.

The Federal Privacy Act of 1974 (PL 93-579) in essence gives the client the right to see any record containing information about that client. It requires that no disclosure of information in any record be made without written consent from the client and that a record be kept indicating any disclosures of information to other persons.

Other laws have been enacted that call for open access to public records. In some cases these laws have been interpreted to mean that the records of public agencies and, in some cases, of situations in which governmental funds have been involved are a matter of public record and can be disclosed in a variety of situations, including court proceedings. There seems to be a conflict between privacy and open-access laws that has not been fully resolved.

Another implication of these two sets of laws is that they seem to discourage confidentiality. It is essential for social workers and social work agencies to determine exactly what records must be kept and how to best manage those records so that the client's, agency's, and the general public's best interests are met. Social workers should involve themselves in serious discussions to resolve these issues.

Three issues relating to evaluation—client participation, confidentiality, and the effect of privacy and open-access laws—have been raised. These issues need to be addressed by ongoing dialogue, creative thinking, and an ever-present sense of the ethics of the profession of social work. These are not the only issues that have or will arise regarding evaluation. Every social worker should be alert to identify other issues and to engage in discussions to resolve them.

Summary

This chapter has considered evaluation as an ongoing part of the social work process. It has pointed out the growing demand for accountability to the client, agency, funding source, and general public and has discussed various kinds of evaluation and their usefulness. Several tools used in the evaluative process were explained. Some important issues that exist for the social worker when engaging in the evaluation process were explored. Evaluation is a skill that all social workers must possess and a process that all social workers must engage in if they are to adhere to the ethical principles of the social work profession.

QUESTIONS

1. What do you see as the positive outcomes of appropriate evaluation?

2. When a worker faces conflicting demands regarding accountability to clients (e.g., meeting client need) or agency accountability expectations, what thinking should go into resolving such conflicts?

3. What are the advantages of using a summative approach to evaluation? A formative approach?

4. What do you see as the similarities and the differences between case evaluation and program evaluation?

5. When should the various forms of recording be used? What are the strengths and limitations of each?

6. What research techniques, other than those discussed in this chapter, do you think might be helpful in the evaluation process?

7. What are the advantages of using the computer to process evaluative information? The disadvantages?

8. What can a social worker do when she finds that required recording is not being used within the guidelines for professional accountability?

9. How can a social worker address the open-access and right-to-privacy laws at the same time?

10. How do the problem-solving approach and single-system research design fit with each other?

11. What are some ethical concerns that social workers might have with respect to the use of the traditional experimental method and with other research designs?

SUGGESTED READINGS

Bloom, Martin, Fischer, Joel, and Orme, John G. *Evaluating Practice: Guidelines for the Accountable Professional,* 3rd ed. Boston: Allyn and Bacon, 1999.

Blythe, Betty J., and Tripodi, Tony. *Measurement in Direct Practice.* Beverly Hills, CA: Sage Publications, 1989.

Blythe, Betty J., Tripodi, Tony, and Briar, Scott. *Direct Practice Research in Human Service Agencies.* New York: Columbia University Press, 1994.

Compton, Beulah Roberts, and Galaway, Burt. *Social Work Processes,* 5th ed. Homewood, IL: Dorsey Press, 1994 (Chapter 16, "Evaluation").

Finn, Jerry. "Security, Privacy, and Confidentiality in Agency Microcomputer Use." *Families in Society* 71 (May 1990): 283–295.

Gabor, Peter, and Grinnell, Richard M. *Evaluation and Quality Improvement in the Human Services.* Boston: Allyn and Bacon, 1994.

Gabor, Peter, Unrau, Yvonne A., and Grinnell, Richard M. *Evaluation for Social Workers: A Quality Improvement Approach for the Social Services.* Boston: Allyn and Bacon, 1998.

Gelman, Sheldon R., Pollack, Daniel, and Weiner, Adele. "Confidentiality of Social Work Records in the Computer Age." *Social Work* 44 (May 1999).

Gingerich, Wallace J. "Expert Systems and Their Potential Use in Social Work." *Family in Society* 71 (April 1990): 221–228.

Grinnell, Richard M., Jr. *Social Work Research and Evaluation,* 4th ed. Itasca, IL: F. E. Peacock, 1993.

Kagle, Jill Doner. "Record Keeping: Direction for the 1990's." *Social Work* 38 (March 1993): 190–196.

———. *Social Work Records,* 2nd ed. Prospect Heights, IL: Waveland Press, 1996.

Karger, Howard Jacob, and Levine, Joanne. *The Internet and Technology for the Human Services.* Boston: Allyn and Bacon, 1999.

Nurius, Paula S., and Hudson, Walter W. *Human Services Practice, Evaluation, and Computers: A Practical Guide for Today and Beyond.* Pacific Grove, CA: Brooks/Cole, 1993.

Patterson, David A. *Personal Computer Applications in the Social Services.* Boston: Allyn and Bacon, 2000.

Potocky-Tripodi, Miriam, and Tripodi, Tony. *New Directions for Social Work Practice Research.* Washington, DC: NASW Press, 1999.

Rafferty, Jackie, Steyaert, Jan, and Colombi, David. *Human Services in the Information Age.* New York: Haworth Press, 1995.

Rubin, Allen, and Babbie, Earl. *Research Methods for Social Work,* 3rd ed. Pacific Grove, CA: Brooks/Cole, 1997.

Sheafor, Bradford W., Horejsi, Charles R., and Horejsi, Gloria A. *Techniques and Guidelines for Social Work Practice.* Boston: Allyn and Bacon, 1997 (Chapter 20).

Tebb, Susan. "Client-Focused Recording: Linking Theory and Practice." *Families in Society* 72 (September 1991): 425–432.

Tripodi, Tony. *A Primer on Single-Subject Design for Clinical Social Workers.* Washington, DC: NASW Press, 1994.

Tutty, Leslie M., Rothery, M. A., Grinnell, Richard M., and Austin, Carol D. *Qualitative Research for Social Workers: Phases, Steps, and Tasks.* Boston: Allyn and Bacon, 1996.

Videka-Sherman, L., and Reid, William J., Eds. *Advances in Clinical Social Work Research.* Silver Springs, MD: NASW Press, 1990.

Weinbach, Robert W. *Statistics for Social Workers,* 4th ed. New York: Longman, 1998.

———. *Applying Research Knowledge: A Workbook for Social Work Students,* 3rd ed. Boston: Allyn and Bacon, 1999.

Williams, Margaret, Tutty, Leslie M., and Grinnell, Richard M. *Research in Social Work: An Introduction,* 2nd ed. Itasca, IL: F. E. Peacock, 1995.

Yaffe, Joanne, and Gotthoffer, Doug, Eds. *Allyn and Bacon Quick Guide to the Internet for Social Work, 1999 Edition.* Boston: Allyn and Bacon, 1998.

Yates, Fred E. *Creative Computing in Health and Social Care.* New York: Wiley, 1996.

NOTES

1. Michael Key, Peter Hudson, and John Armstrong, "Evaluation Theory and Community Work," in *Strategies of Community Organization: A Book of Readings,* 3rd ed., Fred M. Cox, John L. Erlich, Jack Rothman, and John E. Tropman, Eds. (Itasca, IL: F. E. Peacock, 1979), pp. 159–175.

2. Bernie Jones, "Evaluating Social Service Programs," in *Grassroots Administration: A Handbook for*

Staff and Directors of Small Community Based Social Service Agencies, Robert Clifton and Alan Dahms, Eds. (Monterey, CA: Brooks/Cole, 1980), p. 51.

3. For further discussion of this balance, see Beulah Compton and Burt Galaway, *Social Work Processes,* 5th ed. (Homewood, IL: Dorsey Press, 1994), chap. 16, "Evaluation."

4. Michael Key, Peter Hudson, and John Armstrong, "Evaluation Theory and Community Work," in *Strategies of Community Organization,* 3rd ed., Fred M. Cox, John L. Erlich, Jack Rothman, and John E. Tropman, Eds. (Itasca, IL: F. E. Peacock, 1979), pp. 159–175.

5. Jill Doner Kagel, "Record Keeping: Direction for the 1990's," *Social Work* 38 (March 1993): 190–196.

6. See Roy A. Ruckdeschel and Buford E. Farris, "Assessing Practice: A Critical Look at the Single-Case Design," *Social Casework* 62 (September 1981): 413–419.

7. Thomas J. Kiresuk and Geoffrey Garwick, "Basic Goal Attainment Scaling Procedures," in *Social Work Processes,* 2nd ed., Beulah Roberts Compton and Burt Galaway, Eds. (Homewood, IL: Dorsey Press, 1979), pp. 412–421.

8. See William Reid and Laura Epstein, Eds., *Task Centered Practice* (New York: Columbia University Press, 1977); Sharon Berlin and Jeanne Marsh, *Informing Practice Decisions* (New York: Macmillan, 1993); and Catherine Alder and Wayne Evens, *Evaluating Your Practice: A Guide to Self-Assessment* (New York: Springer, 1990).

9. See Joel Fischer and Kevin Corcoran, *Measures for Clinical Practice,* 2nd ed., two vols. (New York: Free Press, 1995). There are also several reference texts available containing assessments for families, groups, organizations, and the like.

10. See Martin Bloom, Joel Fischer, and John Orme, *Evaluating Practice: Guidelines for the Accountable Professional* (Boston: Allyn and Bacon, 1995); and Joel Fischer and Kevin Corcoran, *Measures for Clinical Practice,* 2nd ed., two vols. (New York: Free Press, 1995).

CHAPTER

16 Termination

LEARNING EXPECTATIONS

1. Understanding of the place of the termination process in the social work process.
2. Understanding of the kinds of termination.
3. Understanding of the worker's possible feelings about termination and of the need to recognize and deal with these feelings.
4. Understanding of the components of the termination process.
5. Understanding of the importance of ending and separation to clients and of possible reactions to termination.
6. Understanding of both the transfer and the referral processes.
7. Understanding of some techniques and skills used in the termination process.
8. Understanding of termination with client systems of various sizes, such as individuals, families, and groups.

The final stage of the social work process is **termination,** or the ending stage. Although ending the process is often slighted, it is nevertheless an important aspect of the social work endeavor. Termination is planned from the beginning of the work together. A social work relationship that focuses on meeting the needs of the client terminates when those needs are met. The time line that is a part of the plan of action specifies the anticipated time for termination.

In termination, it is important to consider the background and size of the client system along with the reasons for termination. Life is full of beginnings and endings. The end of one experience usually signals the beginning of another. Termination work can enhance the client's social functioning and can add to the understanding developed by both client and worker as they worked together. Any ending can arouse strong feelings. These feelings can be used as a means for growth, or they can be denied or suppressed, perhaps to arise and interfere with later social functioning.

For clients who are successful at achieving their goals, ending their work with the worker signals a resolution of their difficulties and greater independence. It may also trigger anxiety over the ability to succeed without the worker's assistance. For workers leaving an agency for another job or for students graduating from college, the end of an experience in one setting can be accompanied by excitement and anxiety at the prospect of a new phase in their career path. This represents the ambivalence frequently related to termination.

Because human beings are mortal, it is the nature of all relationships to end. Dwelling on this fact might lead some clients to avoid relationships for fear of the pain or loss associated with the ending. This fear can obscure the need to be free to enjoy relationships with others and go on to other phases in life. Many clients have experienced pain, loss, abandonment, or rejection in some of their significant relationships. Often patterns of loss have been handed down from one generation to the next. Overcoming the results of these experiences may be the central issue that needs to be resolved in the social work process. Thus, termination issues can be a focus of the change process itself. Termination of the worker's involvement is inevitable. Helping clients to successfully terminate is essential to solidifying any change that has taken place. Thus, handling a termination is an important skill for social workers to develop.

Evaluation is closely related to termination. Evaluation takes place during the entire social work process, but it is an important aspect of any planned termination.

In considering termination, three areas will be discussed: (1) kinds of termination and reasons for clients' and workers' terminating a helping relationship, (2) termination with various client systems, and (3) content of the termination process—dealing with feelings, stabilizing change, and evaluating with clients.

Kinds of Termination

Termination is an aspect of social work that is often given inadequate consideration. Endings can be painful for workers as well as for clients. Workers sometimes make decisions about the desired goals of service that prolong the time of service beyond what the client desires.[1] This has resulted in many unplanned terminations (those in which the client fails to keep appointments). According to William Reid, research has shown that:

1. Recipients of brief, time-limited treatment show at least as much durable improvement as recipients of long-term, open-ended treatment.
2. Most of the improvement associated with long-term treatment occurs relatively soon after treatment has begun.
3. Regardless of their intended length, most courses of treatment turn out to be relatively brief.[2]

In recent years an emphasis on short-term service has developed. This service considers the client's desires and expectations in the planning to a greater extent than in long-term service. Plans are much more specific, with specific goals and time frames for reaching those goals. Goals are also measurable, making it easier to know when the purpose of the service has been fulfilled, the goals met, and the contract satisfied. The ending is more apt to be planned by the worker and the client rather than the client deciding that the worker's help is no longer needed.

Termination can take place at any point in the process: when the goals set by the worker and client have been reached and the client feels comfortable in carrying out those goals without help from the worker; when clients feel that sufficient help has been given so they can meet the need or deal with the problem on their own; when it becomes apparent that no progress is being made or that the potential for change is poor; or when a worker or an agency does not have the resources needed by the client or does not have the sanction of the agency to deliver the service needed. This last condition may result in a referral, which was discussed in Chapter 13. Sometimes clients terminate because the systems on which they depend are threatened by the possibility of change.

If a worker is leaving an agency, termination activity may result in transfer to another worker within an agency or referral to another agency for continued service. It may result in a decision by the new worker and the client to work on another goal or use another strategy in reaching an elusive goal and thus continue with a new plan of action. However, termination usually results in separation of the client from both the worker and the agency.

Termination is an expectation discussed with clients from the beginning of the work together; it is planned for by the worker and the client together. When a worker senses that the client is not using the help being offered, or when the client is missing appointments or in other ways is indicating that termination may be advisable, it is time to discuss the possibility of termination. This is done to maximize the benefit that can come from a planned termination and to minimize feelings of anger and guilt that might interfere with seeking help in the future. Many times what a client wants is someone to talk to about his need. This discussion can lead to a better understanding of the need, identification of resources, or planning what can be done about the need. The client does not always need or want any other interventive activity from a social worker or a social agency. Figure 16.1 shows the place of termination in the social work process.

When the worker-client relationship is terminated because the worker is ending employment or being transferred to a new position, special consideration should be given to the client's feelings. In some cases this is also a good time for the client to terminate with the agency as well. At other times, the decision is made to transfer the client to a new worker. The client may be angry because the worker is breaking a contract. The client may feel deserted or may have a reawakening of old feelings about previous separations. The worker may experience feelings of guilt about leaving the client and breaking the contract. The worker also may be absorbed in plans for a new job or in the demands of a new situation. When transfer becomes necessary, it is important to recognize and deal with feelings that may impede the continuation of service to the client.

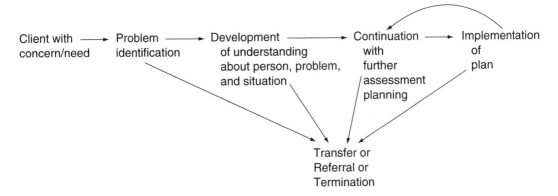

FIGURE 16.1 Termination and its Place in the Social Work Process

When a worker engages in the termination process with a client because of his own plans to leave his current position, it is important to bring the client's feelings into the open, however painful. Sometimes clients can also deal with previous painful separations in this process. The worker should be prepared to accept the client's anger and resentment and, whenever possible, should also help the client accept the new worker. A useful technique is for the worker to introduce the client to the new worker and for all three to discuss the work that has been done and the possibilities for future work. After this session, it is often important for the previous worker and the client to have a last session alone so that they can terminate their relationship.

Whenever a worker takes over a case from a former worker, feelings about termination should be discussed with the individual, family, or group. Clients often need time to adjust; if they are rushed, they will not be ready to accept help from the new worker. Beginnings and endings occur together. How the last relationship ended will determine whether unresolved issues will create barriers or negative expectations for the next relationship. Allowing the client to talk through these feelings can be a strong bridge to building a new helping relationship. For this reason, the worker should discuss with a new client any previous experiences the client may have had and his feelings about that experience.

In order for a social worker to be effective in terminating with clients, she needs to be aware of some blocks to effective termination that arise because of her feelings and attitudes. There may be a tendency for the worker to hang on to clients. This may arise because the worker is reluctant to terminate a relationship that she has enjoyed. Other reasons for hanging on may be that the worker expects more of the client or the situation than is warranted or that she is ambitious and is seeking "the perfect case." Sometimes a worker wants to compensate for what the client may have suffered. Awareness of these feelings and a focus on the client's needs and goals can prevent these blocks to effective termination.

The nature of the worker-client relationship is another factor. Any time a close working relationship develops, both the worker and the client are apt to have strong reactions to termination. When this is the case, more time must be allowed for the termination process so that feelings of loss can be handled.

It should not be assumed that all clients view termination as loss; some, especially those mandated to service, may view termination with relief. Other clients view the work together as a necessary interlude in their lives but are pleased that they have gained understanding and coping skills so they can get on with the business of living without further help from the worker.

Research by Anne E. Fortune, Bill Pearlingi, and Cherie D. Rochell indicates clients can have positive feelings about termination. They can feel pride and a sense of accomplishment in what they have been able to do. This study has limitations, as it was carried out with a small group of voluntary practitioners in a small geographic area. Also, case selection may have been limited to those for whom there was success.[3]

Howard Hess and Peg McCartt Hess have pointed out differences in termination, depending on context.[4] The nature of the relationship required in the work and the expected ongoing relationships with others who have been a part of the process affect the impact of termination. Hess and Hess discuss the difference between termination of the one-to-one relationship and the formed group, in which the loss is not only of the worker but of other group members. In the family and the friendship group, the only person terminating is the worker. The authors also note the differences in termination when the strategy has been counseling, education, or resource mobilization. The nature of attachment and the impact of termination are different in each of these situations. The content of the termination phase will be different in each situation.

If worker and client have developed the habit of consciously terminating each session together, they have developed a good base on which to develop the final termination of work together. Summarizing each session—what has been done and what is to be done—should give the client a good sense of the process and how much time there is before the work is completed and termination takes place. Planning termination should help avoid a surprise ending and the feelings of desertion that go with such endings. Evaluating at the end of each session should give the worker an understanding of the client's sense of the work together and allow for corrections so that unplanned or precipitous termination does not take place. What has been done in a small way at the end of each session can then be done in a more complete manner at the end of the work together.

Issues related to diversity need to be included in termination. Individual values and experiences as well as cultural values, attitudes, and beliefs play an important role. The ultimate termination is death, and individual and cultural attitudes and beliefs about death often reflect attitudes and beliefs about termination in general. The worker should be aware of the stages of termination and be sensitive about individual experiences with termination and about cultural mores.

In many cultures, there are customs such as gift giving when termination occurs. Even without this, some clients will want to give the worker a gift as a sign of appreciation. This presents some ethical dilemmas for the worker, since the social worker should not benefit from her service to the client except through compensation from her agency or through the financial arrangements that were made ahead of time. Gift giving can also signify "the repayment of a debt" by the client, which would be a misunderstanding of the social work relationship. Expensive gifts should clearly not be accepted. Inexpensive ones might be allowed by an agency's policies. In either case, the worker should discuss the situation with the client and with her supervisor to ensure an ethical outcome.

For individuals at risk, termination can represent a crisis in their quest for power and control over their lives and for acceptance and recognition. Empowerment that was gained during the intervention may be ascribed to the worker, and inner doubts and anxieties about the client's own abilities may arise again. Helping clients solidify their gains and assert and advocate for themselves without the support of the worker are major issues during termination with people who have experienced discrimination or oppression. Clients need to know that the fight against discrimination and oppression is both personal and collective. Efforts to connect clients to groups engaged in this cause should be made during the intervention to ensure continuation of support.

Continued success by the client after termination rests to a great degree on the extent to which the plan was based on clients' strengths and their environment and on building strength in areas in which limitations and barriers exist. Client success also rests on the degree to which the worker helped clients learn new skills while resolving their situation and was able to assist clients to experience social work values as a part of the helping relationship and as something integral to their everyday lives. This is what represents true social work and differentiates it from other human service professions. If clients feel more valuable as human beings based on inherent worth, if they are able to exercise greater self-determination and control over their lives, and if they can access appropriate resources to meet socially accepted needs, then they have truly been empowered. This means that the social work intervention has been successful not only on a short-term basis but at a deeper, more significant, and long-term level.

Planned Termination

Individuals

The size of the client system is another variable to consider in termination. Individual clients may experience termination in a very personal way. They may have derived a great deal of satisfaction from the relationship. They may also be vulnerable to feeling pain, loss, abandonment, or rejection. Helping them to resolve these issues is important in determining how permanent any changes might be. Throughout the intervention, the worker should be aware of the impact of relationships and termination on the client. He should note how clients handle termination in other areas of their lives. Sensitivity to the client's attitude toward termination is fundamental to planning for successful termination. The use of a change process that includes termination for each session can be helpful in changing clients' attitudes toward termination and in preparing them for the end of the intervention.

When the worker has been able to support independence and interdependence instead of dependence, she has already begun to prepare the client for termination and for life without the social worker's involvement. However, clients may want to give credit to the worker for the work that was done. Statements that the client may make can be extremely flattering, such as "You were wonderful. Thank goodness that I found you. I don't know how I could have made it without you." The worker should resist the temptation to accept accolades or credit. To do so will undermine the client's sense of empowerment and the need to recognize who did the work. The social work plan identifies clients as the primary force behind change, and clients deserve credit and recognition when they are successful at achieving their goals and objectives. If they had not done what they needed to do, then no real change would have taken place.

At its worst, crediting the worker with the change is a form of magical thinking in which the client makes the worker "the savior" by so defining her in this way. The worker should quickly dispel the myth that she is the only one who could have helped the client. She should credit the client for his courage in facing his difficulty and for the hard work he did in resolving the situation. If there were things that the worker did that were especially helpful, she should point out that such help is available from other social workers who practice the way she does.

Planned termination with individuals should allow enough time to resolve issues related to feelings of termination. These may be similar to, and as intense as, a grief process. Thus, the worker should plan for at least three or four sessions to work through unresolved issues. In the end, the client should have access to positive feelings and a sense of accomplishment as opposed to feeling abandoned or rejected. Some clients stop meeting rather than face the feelings associated with termination. In these instances, the worker should follow up with the client and offer an opportunity to experience an appropriate termination process. If the client refuses, the worker should at least make a follow-up contact at a later date to ensure that the client is still open to receiving help if needed. Unplanned termination initiated prematurely by clients should be handled similarly, except that clients should be offered a transfer or a referral if it is feasible.

Planned termination can include time-limited services imposed by design, regulations, funding sources, limited resources, or other circumstances. The advent of managed care has resulted in limitations on the amount of services that are reimbursed by insurance companies. Although this is viewed by those companies as a form of efficiency and cost savings, in essence it is rationing services for the benefit of the insurer. It ensures profitability for profit-making corporations or capitates expenses for tax-supported programs by limiting the liability for services. Managed care can place social workers in the awkward position of either denying continuation of services when they believe continued service is needed or continuing services without receiving reimbursement. At times, the existence of the agency can be threatened by reduction in revenue. Refusing needed services is a violation of the *NASW Code of Ethics*. Social workers should consider becoming active in organizations that advocate for providing services based on client needs or for decision making on services by those without a financial stake in limiting services. Allowing service decisions to be made by bureaucrats or to be arbitrarily set by diagnosis is not acceptable for clients or social workers.

In the era of managed care, termination is an issue from the onset of service. Social workers need to become proficient in providing brief and time-limited services. Clients are not as likely to invest themselves as significantly in a relationship when termination is an ever-present issue. When there is a significant investment, some form of brief follow-up may be needed to smooth the client's transition. Thus, workers need to develop extensive referral networks for posttermination services. Social workers should be aware of the benefits and rights of clients and ensure that clients are so informed. Workers should be prepared to advocate for needed services and to assist clients in appeals processes and other advocacy actions. Finally, social workers should be open to greater use of natural helpers and nontraditional services, such as self-help and support groups.

Families

Termination with families is likely to be much different from individual termination, although individuals in the family may express feelings similar to those of individual clients. For families, termination generally represents the end of the social work process experience but not the end of their relationship with one another. This is especially true if the worker has been successful at reinforcing and strengthening the positive functioning of the family system by supporting appropriate family roles and relationships and positive interaction with the family's environment. At such times, successful termination brings good feelings as well as a desire to terminate. It is not unusual for family members themselves to conclude that they are ready to try things on their own. They may announce at the beginning or at the end of a meeting that they do not intend to return. If the worker has been tuned in to the family, he may be able to plan for it.

Because the family goes on after termination, less time may be needed to resolve any remaining issues. At the least, members should be given an opportunity to express how they feel about terminating. For children, this might be structured in terms of what they liked best and least about meeting and what they will miss most and least about not meeting. Sometimes an informal celebration may take place, such as going out to dinner or having a picnic, to mark this significant event in the life of the family. Generally, the worker does not participate in these events.

Small Groups

Successful termination in small groups depends on whether the group is an ongoing group or one that is time limited. If an individual is leaving, as in the case of an ongoing group, the individual may have ambivalent feelings. He may feel good about achieving his goals but sad at the prospect of leaving those who have assisted him. The degree to which the group has been cohesive represents a bond or a sense of belonging that is now being left behind. This may be similar to what young adults feel when they become emancipated. Termination by an individual is a reminder for everyone in the group that some day they will also leave or that the group may come to an end. Each member wonders when termination will happen for them. Some may be spurred on to achieve their goals. Others may shrink from the prospect and even regress out of fear or anxiety.

Termination for individuals leaving an ongoing group may include some kind of graduation ceremony, certificate, and/or ritual. At the least, a member needs to be able to say his good-byes so that he can go on with his own work. This is also essential in order for the group to become ready for the new members who will follow. Members should be encouraged to allow for two or three sessions before finalizing their termination from the group. If members drop out without notice or suddenly announce their termination, the group may need time to work out their feelings before they can trust one another again or are ready for a new member.

In time-limited groups, termination is an issue from beginning to end, and members choose how much to invest themselves based on this fact. Those who remain with the group will experience termination together. Often, a celebration or graduation should be planned to mark the occasion and to highlight the success of the group and its members. For some groups, certificates of achievement may be appropriate. At the least, members should be given an opportunity to express their feelings about the group experience.

In both types of groups, members may drop out prematurely. When this occurs, the worker should contact those members to see if they will return to the group. The worker may be called on to help overcome a barrier or to negotiate a problem between the absent member and the group or one of the other members. If a member cannot be convinced to return or if a return is not appropriate, the worker should arrange for alternate services. Since the group has invested time and energy in the absent member, they need feedback after the follow-up contact.

Task groups usually end when the task has been completed, when the group gives up its efforts to effect a change, or when its authority to operate ends, as might be the case for a time-limited task group. Generally, a celebration of some sort is in order when the task is completed. If the group fails to complete its task, some sort of debriefing may be necessary and/or a report may be generated outlining its accomplishments and analyzing the reasons that the effort failed. This may help group members resolve some of their disappointment and can help future groups avoid some of the same difficulties. Such a report may also be needed for accountability to various authorities with an interest in the outcome.

Unlike small groups in which relationships are important, task groups are focused on the task itself, and relationships are secondary to the group's purpose. When individual members drop out, the decision regarding follow-up is generally made based on how critical the person or their organization is to the task at hand and whether they are likely to support or oppose the group's efforts. Follow-up can be done by any member.

Components of Termination

Allen Pincus and Anne Minahan identify three major components of the termination process: disengagement, stabilization of change, and evaluation.[5] As with other aspects of the social work endeavor, these are intermingled in practice and are separated only for purposes of discussion and study.

Disengagement

Endings bring about a cessation of relationships. If relationships have been meaningful, feelings are aroused. An unplanned termination leaves the client to deal with these feelings on her own, which results in a sense of unfinished business. It is assumed that the client is aware that termination will take place when goals have been reached. Nevertheless, when faced with actual termination, the client and the worker should acknowledge the reality of their feelings.

These feelings will vary from situation to situation; however, some common expectations about feelings at termination have been identified. The initial reaction is often one of denial, either of the reality of termination or of the feelings associated with it. Denial is a defense mechanism used to avoid painful feelings. An indication of this mechanism is the phenomenon of flight. This phenomenon is manifested by a client not keeping appointments after termination is discussed or by group members not being as involved in the group process as the time to terminate approaches. The temptation is for the worker to let the client go and to assume that he wants to deal or not deal with the termination feelings in this manner. However, it is important for the worker to elicit feelings at this point so that client and worker can move through the termination process.

The next stage of termination is usually a period of emotional reaction. Feelings or emotions may arise from fear of loss or of the unknown. There may be feelings of sadness or grief over the impending loss as well as anger. There may be a return of feelings associated with old wounds from previous disappointments and separations. There can be regression to old patterns of behavior. Regression may be a client's attempt to say that she is not ready for termination. At this stage it is important for the worker to accept the client's feelings and to help her examine these feelings and the fears, anxieties, and past experiences that are the source of the feelings. Acceptance and help in examining feelings enables the client to work through the feelings. In a sense, the client is helped to go through a process of mourning and is enabled to disengage from the relationship in a helpful manner.

Another means of dealing with disengagement is reminiscing about or reviewing what has been done in the work together. Doing this can help clients see the positive aspects of the work together and develop the understanding that growth often has pain associated with it. At this time, workers also should try to minimize any guilt the client may have about the work together.

Clients sometimes regress when termination approaches; sometimes they also introduce new problems. The worker and client together need to examine why these new problems have been introduced and whether there is a valid reason for continuing the service with a focus on the new problems or whether the client can work on these problems in other ways.

Clients' feelings about termination vary as to intensity and nature. If the intensity of the relationship or the period of time involved has been minimal, the feelings about termination will usually be less than if the relationship has been intense or of fairly long duration. Clients with feelings of success or satisfaction about the service will have different kinds of feelings about termination than those whose service experience has not been as positive. Clients who have had significant losses or separations in their lives—particularly if they have not had opportunities to deal with feelings about those losses—will have different feelings about separation than those clients for whom loss has not been as significant. The client's capacity for independence or need for dependence will also influence feelings. A significant factor in the way a client deals with termination is what is happening in his life as a whole at that point in time. If a client is called on to cope with many changes or other demands, termination may either be more difficult or may come as a relief.

The social worker needs to develop skill in disengaging from relationships with clients. This should be done with consideration for, and sensitivity to, a client's feelings and needs. A useful technique for disengagement is to taper off involvement with the client as feelings are dealt with and other work of termination is completed. Appointments may be set further apart or more emphasis placed on what the client is to do for herself.

The worker needs to develop self-awareness about his own reactions to separation and loss. If the worker has difficulty with these tasks, he will be less able to help the client deal with the tasks of separation. The worker may wonder how to react to the intense feelings of the client that may arise in the process of termination. These feelings may be related not only to loss or grief but to dissatisfaction about what the worker and client have been able to do together. Everyone tends to ignore or downplay feelings that are uncomfortable. If, because of their own discomfort, workers do not adequately encourage the client's feelings about termination and about their work together, they will fail to allow the client to learn management of feelings in coping with life tasks.

The work of disengagement, then, is related not only to the immediate social work situation but also to past and future losses of the client and social worker. In helping the client disengage, the worker is helping the client deal with past losses and unresolved feelings about those losses. Also, the client is being provided with coping mechanisms for dealing with future loss, with understandings for dealing with grief and loss that are part of human functioning. To bypass or minimize the disengagement process is to lose an opportunity for client growth.

Stabilization of Change

In helping a client deal with the feelings of termination and disengagement from the relationship, the client and the worker often review what has happened in the work together. This is useful in stabilizing the change that has taken place and helps clients understand how they have grown and what has led to the growth.

This also gives clients guidelines on how future problems might be approached and dealt with. It enables clients to know that they have resources that can help them to make it on their own and what those resources are.

One way to work on stabilization of change is to review what has occurred. The time together should be seen as one step, an important step, of the growth that results in better coping with life tasks. This view implies there are other steps to be taken, not with the worker but through new relationships or in ongoing responses to life situations. Continued growth is one way of stabilizing the change that has taken place. Worker and client discuss the next steps and how the client can go about taking these steps. They then plan ways of obtaining needed supports and resources the client can use in taking these steps.

Together, the worker and the client explore possible ways for dealing with situations similar to the one that brought the client to the agency for help. They consider how the learning that has taken place can be transferred to other situations. The worker and client may also identify other resources in the client's environment that would be useful in coping with life situations. These may be natural helpers or other community systems, such as recreation programs, groups of people with similar concerns, and the like. These resources can be substitute or replacement support systems.

Usually, the worker offers the client the option of returning to the agency if future problems become overwhelming. It is important for the client to know that the agency makes the service possible and that even if the worker is no longer available, the agency will provide someone else to help. The client needs to be aware that workers come and go but that the agency continues to provide the service. This awareness is particularly important for the client who may be terminating service against the advice of the worker.

Stabilization of change can also be encouraged by discussing possible goals for further growth and resources that can be used to enable growth. This discussion can examine how change took place as the worker and client worked together. The process that was used can be examined, and the worker can maximize the client's understanding of this process. Through the work of stabilizing the change, the worker supports within the client a sense of accomplishment and competence. The client's fears are recognized and examined, and suggestions are made about how to deal with them.

Stabilization of the change is an important stage in growth and change. Without conscious efforts to carry out the tasks involved in stabilization, the client's capacity to sustain the desired change may be lessened.

Evaluation

The third component of termination is evaluation. Evaluation does not take place only at termination but is an ongoing part of the social work endeavor. It is, however, a particularly important component of the termination phase.

As the worker and client engage in evaluation during termination, the major focus is on the goal or goals set as a part of the plan of action and on the client's need or needs, as identified in the assessment process. The major question to be answered is, Did we accomplish what we set out to do? If the goal was achieved and the need met, then the purpose of the service has been accomplished. If the goal was met but the need remains troublesome, then the goal may not have been the right goal or other goals must be met as well.

When considering the outcome of service, it is useful to look at the process of reaching the goal and to identify what has and has not been useful. Any spinoffs or unexpected consequences of the work together should be noted. This aspect of evaluation is useful for both worker and client in that it helps the client better understand how to meet needs in the future. It helps the worker gain greater understanding of the helping process and of means for working with clients.

The worker's openness to evaluating what has happened involves a certain amount of risk, because the worker's mistakes and limitations may come to light. The client may be overly critical or display undue dissatisfaction, which may be one way the client expresses negative feelings related to termination. The worker needs to accept these feelings without becoming defensive and carefully examine with the client the negative feelings and sort out current feelings from past feelings of abandonment or unrealistic dissatisfaction. Perhaps one of the reasons workers have not put sufficient emphasis on the termination process is that it is a time for examining the performance of the worker. This is a threatening experience but one that is essential for good social work practice.

Competence in guiding the termination process is one way of influencing client satisfaction over the work together. The client reviews what has happened, acknowledges improvement or progress, discovers his part in the process and how the experience may be transferred to other life experiences, and assesses how he can continue his growth.

The social work endeavor is terminated through the interwoven activities aimed at disengagement, stabilization of change, and evaluation. Through these activities the client is helped to deal with feelings so that these feelings will not inhibit future social functioning. The client is readied to continue to grow and to cope with activities of living and with the environment and its expectations.

Case Example

A Student's Thinking on Terminating Field Experience

A dictionary defines *termination* as "to come to a limit in time; to end." I have known since the beginning of the semester that my time at the home was limited, but now that the time is actually coming to an end I feel a great loss. I have come to think of the residents as "my" people and am very protective of them. I care and worry about each and every one of them as if they were my own grandmothers and grandfathers and feel that they care about me also. Yet I have nevertheless worked toward this termination all semester by trying to get the residents to fend for themselves. One example of this is my card group. I have made great progress with this group of people, and they have responded by becoming more and more independent to the point that they no longer need me there. They can now organize, keep score, and play together without a referee; and they do play. It gives me a great feeling of accomplishment knowing that this group of people can and will entertain themselves once I am gone.

However, I have learned that there is another aspect to termination—a selfish one on my part. As I said, I am no longer needed there. True, I feel great accomplishment in knowing that I created this independent group, but my price was the loss of authority and the sense of need and importance I felt as head of the group. I guess it is a little like what a parent must feel when sending a child out into the world. True, you feel proud and would want it no other way, but nevertheless there is a selfish feeling of loss that enters in also. I would expect that any time a social worker has a success such as I have had and the client has become more self-sufficient and less dependent, he or she will feel these pride/selfish loss feelings. It is something one must learn to deal with by realizing the importance of the success and the insignificance of the loss. In my case, I am extremely excited that my card group has progressed to the point that they can function without me. Many of the residents in the home have gotten to the point that they will not socialize, entertain themselves, or even consider doing something without supervision or leadership. They seem to refuse to think for themselves and will instead wait to be entertained by someone else. Obviously, this leads to decreased socialization due to their never mixing with others except when there is a planned activity. This also leads to reduced mental stimulation, which I feel is very closely related to the confusion and forgetfulness often typical of the elderly. Therefore, my success at gaining some independence with these people has made me very proud.

I have discovered that talking about termination as being "someday" is very different from saying "I will be leaving here in two weeks." Suddenly it is not only very real but it is also very close. I have had mixed reactions from the residents. Some have taken it quite nonchalantly. I suspect this is due to the fact that they have been through this before with other students and are getting used to people coming and going. However, some of the residents have taken it fairly hard, especially those who are forgetful and cannot remember my telling them I will be leaving; they act surprised every time I tell them. Some of the other residents are already asking me when I will be back and about who will they talk to when I am gone. I have tried to prevent this from happening as much as possible by encouraging residents to talk to Jane, too. However, once a relationship is established it is sometimes hard to get them to talk to someone else; talking to me was often the basis for our good relationship in the first place. I guess all of these things are what make termination in a nursing home setting hard. This is not to imply that termination anywhere else is easy. I would imagine termination is hard no matter what. I can only judge what termination is like for me in my situation.

I have learned that termination is a much more delicate situation than I first anticipated. I can see how a resident could easily get hurt and thus soured toward opening up and sharing with another person. They could easily become leery of developing a relationship for fear it will be cut off at the end of a semester. They could easily feel they were used and discarded by students only out for personal gain and credit toward their graduation. I can recall one such resident when I first worked at the home. She obviously had had a bad experience with someone and had thus decided she would not be vulnerable again. She informed me during our first visit that she wanted to be left alone; besides, she did not think I cared anyway. She said she thought I was only doing my duty by being nice to her. Although I tried all semester to break through that barrier by always waving, smiling, or speaking to her, I never succeeded in breaking down those walls she had built

(continued)

Case Example   Continued

around herself. Therefore, I am being very careful to tell residents early and as gently as possible that I am soon finished at the home. I am also being careful to avoid any promises about the future. Although I plan to visit as often as I can, many times those well-intentioned plans get smothered by other obligations. I do not want anyone sitting and waiting for my visits.

There is another aspect of termination that I have not yet discussed. That is termination with the staff. Jane and I have become very close and help each other with many complicated issues concerning residents. The old saying that two heads are better than one really applies with us. I feel we have truly become a team, even though I am a student. I realize Jane got along quite well without me and will again get along quite well after I am gone. However, we do work well together, and I know I will miss her. We have started new projects, such as our new social history, that I wish I could help her put into use. The new comprehensive care plans are almost finished and now will become most helpful for use with the residents. I regret having to miss being a part of their use.

As is obvious, I really enjoyed my semester at the nursing home and have let it become a part of me. I have learned much from those sometimes funny, sometimes ornery residents and will miss them. Termination is hard and not finished yet, but I can be happy that I will take a little from and give a little to each resident, and I can look forward to joyous reunions.

Summary

The last stage of the social work process is termination. It is planned from the beginning of the process. Termination may lead to transfer of the client to another worker.

There are three components of termination work: disengagement, stabilization of change, and evaluation.

Social workers who engage the client in a well-thought-out termination process strengthen the client's capacity for social functioning in the future. They also enhance their own professional capacity through evaluating with the client what led to the desired outcome. Termination is an integral part of the total social work process.

QUESTIONS

1. What do you believe to be some reasons why "time-limited" social work has become popular?

2. Discuss your feeling about a termination with someone who has been important to you.

3. Discuss some of the reasons why clients may terminate prematurely.

4. When a social worker receives a client through transfer, what should be kept in mind?

5. How does the nature of the client-worker relationship affect the termination process?

6. How can a worker appropriately deal with the threat of evaluation?

7. What kind of reactions might one expect to see in termination with individuals, families, or groups?

SUGGESTED READINGS

Compton, Beulah Roberts, and Galaway, Burt. *Social Work Processes,* 5th ed. Belmont, CA: Wadsworth, 1994 (Chapter 15).

Fortune, Anne E. "Planning Duration and Termination of Treatment." *Social Service Review* 59 (December 1985): 647–661.

———. "Grief Only? Client and Social Worker Reactions to Termination." *Clinical Social Work Journal* 15 (Summer 1987): 159–171.

———. "Termination in Direct Practice." In Richard L. Edwards, Ed., *Encyclopedia of Social Work,* 19th ed. Washington, DC: NASW Press, 1995 (pp. 2398–2404).

Fortune, Anne E., Pearlingi, Bill, and Rochell, Cherie D. "Criteria for Terminating Treatment." *Families in Society* 72 (1991): 366–370.

———. "Reactions to Termination of Individual Treatment." *Social Work* 37 (March 1992): 171–178.

Goldstein, Eda G., and Noonan, Maryellen. *Short-Term Treatment and Social Work Practice: An Integrative Perspective.* New York: Free Press, 1999 (Chapter 7, "The Ending Phase").

Hepworth, Dean H., Rooney, Ronald, and Larsen, Jo Ann. *Direct Social Work Practice,* 5th ed. Pacific Grove, CA: Brooks/Cole, 1997 (Chapter 20, "The Final Phase: Termination and Evaluation").

Miley, Karla Krogsrud, O'Melia, Michael, and DuBois, Brenda L. *Social Work Practice: An Empowering Approach,* 2nd ed. Boston: Allyn and Bacon, 1998 (Chapter 16, "Integrating Gains").

Shulman, Lawrence. *The Skills of Helping: Individuals, Families and Groups,* 3rd ed. Itasca, IL: F. E. Peacock, 1992.

Siebold, Cathy. "Termination: When the Therapist Leaves." *Clinical Social Work Journal* 19 (Summer 1991): 191–204.

NOTES

1. See William J. Reid and Anne Shyne, *Brief and Extended Casework* (New York: Columbia University Press, 1969).

2. William J. Reid, *The Task Centered System* (New York: Columbia University Press, 1978), p. 5.

3. Anne E. Fortune, Bill Pearlingi, and Cherie D. Rochell, "Reactions to Termination of Individual Treatment," *Social Work* 37 (March 1992): 171–178.

4. Howard Hess and Peg McCartt Hess, "Termination in Context," in *Social Work Processes,* 5th ed., Beulah Compton and Burt Galaway, Eds. (Belmont, CA: Wadsworth, 1994), pp. 529–539.

5. See Allen Pincus and Anne Minahan, *Social Work Practice: Model and Method* (Itasca, IL: F. E. Peacock, 1973), chap. 13, "Terminating the Change Effort."

APPENDIX

Models of Social Work Practice

Social work practice theory has been developed in a manner that gives a rich variety of approaches to practice. The various models or practice theories available have been developed in different situations, based on various underlying assumptions, for use in many types of circumstances. Thorough study of each model is needed in order to use it with clients. The summaries presented here can be used to gain a preliminary understanding of the salient points of the various models of practice and to help the student decide on those models in which he or she desires to develop further understanding. Specification of models is primarily based on those appearing in:

Robert W. Roberts and Robert H. Nee, Eds., *Theories of Social Casework* (Chicago: University of Chicago Press, 1970).

Catherine P. Papell and Beulah Roberts Rothman, "Social Group Work Models: Possession and Heritage," *Education for Social Work* 2 (Fall (1966): 66–77.

Joan Stein, *The Family as a Unit of Study and Treatment*, Monograph One (Seattle: Regional Rehabilitation Institute, University of Washington, School of Social Work, 1969).

Jack Rothman, "Three Models of Community Organization," in Fred M. Cox, John L. Erlich, Jack Rothman, and John E. Tropman, Eds., *Strategies of Community Organization* (Itasca, IL: F. E. Peacock, 1970), pp. 20–36.

Francis J. Turner, Ed., *Social Work Treatment: Interlocking Theoretical Approaches*, 3rd ed. (New York: Free Press, 1986).

Robert W. Roberts and Helen Northen, Eds., *Theories of Social Work with Groups* (New York: Columbia University Press, 1976).

Eleanor Reardon Tolson and William J. Reid, Eds., *Models of Family Treatment* (New York: Columbia University Press, 1981).

Jack Rothman with John E. Tropman, "Models of Community Organization and Macro Practice Perspectives: Their Mixing and Matching," in Fred M. Cox, John L. Erlich, Jack Rothman, and John E. Tropman, Eds., *Strategies of Community Organization*, 4th ed. (Itasca, IL: F. E. Peacock, 1987).

Behavior Therapy (Sociobehavioral)

Source: Edwin Thomas, University of Michigan, School of Social Work, based on behavioral psychology. Developed as a reaction to the lack of specificity in traditional methods. Proponents of this model include Sheldon Rose (groups), John Wodarski (families), Richard Stuart (families), and Ray Thomison (families).

Underlying Theory: All behavior is learned. Behavior is sometimes controlled by consequences; at other times, it is controlled by stimuli (stimulus-response). Behavioral psychology.

Practice Theory: Assessment specifies behaviors; defines baselines; and specifies stimulus, antecedents, and consequences. Frequency, magnitude, and direction of problem behavior are monitored during and following intervention. Goals are very specific to behavioral change.

Practice Usage: In situations in which behavioral change is the goal.

References:

Edwin J. Thomas, "Behavioral Modification and Casework," in Robert W. Roberts and Robert H. Nee, Eds., *Theories of Social Casework* (Chicago: University of Chicago Press, 1970), pp. 181–218.
Eileen Gambrill, "Behavioral Theory," in Richard L. Edwards, Ed., *Encyclopedia of Social Work*, 19th ed. (Washington, DC: NASW Press, 1995), pp. 46–57.
Mark Mattaini, *Clinical Practice with Individuals* (Washington, DC: NASW Press, 1997).
Bruce A. Thyer, "Behavioral Social Work Is Not What You Think," *Arete* 16 (Winter 1991): 1–9.
Bruce Thyer and John Wodarski, *Handbook of Empirical Social Work Practice* (New York: Wiley, 1998).

Cognitive (Rational, Reality Therapy)

Source: General category includes Alfred Adler's individual psychology, Albert Ellis's rational-emotive psychotherapy, William Glasser's reality therapy, and Harold Werner's rational casework. An alternative to Freudian psychotherapy, which concerns itself with conscious thinking and behavior.

Underlying Theory: Behavior is mainly determined by a person's thinking and willing. Intensity of acts depends on strength of will. Cognitive theory important. Perceptions, goals, and patterns are principal concerns.

Practice Theory: Assessment focuses on present thinking, feeling, and behavior. The goal is to change the client's consciousness (the sum of thoughts, emotions, and behavior). The interaction focuses on problem solving and having client examine way he or she thinks and behaves in the living situation. Emphasis on "accurate thinking."

Practice Usage: Can be used with individuals, groups, families, and communities when resolution of problems is a focus. Should not be used to treat phobias, addictions, or psychoses.

References:

Harold D. Werner, *Rational Approach to Social Casework* (New York: Association Press, 1965).
William Glasser, *Reality Therapy* (New York: Harper and Row, 1965).
Judith Beck, *Cognitive Therapy: Basics and Beyond* (New York: Guilford, 1995).

Albert Ellis, *Better, Deeper, and More Enduring Brief Therapy: The Rational Emotive Behavioral Therapy Approach* (New York: Brunner/Mazel, 1996).

Jim Lantz, "Cognitive Theory and Social Work Treatment," in Francis J. Turner, Ed., *Social Work Treatment*, 4th ed. (New York: Free Press, 1996).

Dean Schuyler, *A Practical Guide to Cognitive Therapy* (New York: W. W. Norton, 1991).

Communication (Communicative-Interactive)

Source: Work of Don Jackson and Jay Haley in the project on "Family Therapy in Schizophrenia" at the Palo Alto Research Foundation (initiated (1954). Virginia Satir exemplifies social work of this model. Judith C. Nelson has expanded understanding of the use of communication theory in social work practice with particular emphasis on work with individuals and families.

Underlying Theory: Broad communication and transactional base. "Double-bind" communication, metacommunication, and family homeostasis are important concepts. Emphasis is on improved family functioning, particularly improved communication.

Practice Theory: Analysis of family functioning with emphasis on role functioning, rules, and communication modes. Often uses a "Family Life Chronology." Worker is seen as therapist and modeler of communication. Techniques include showing how a person looks to other family members, building self-esteem, making explicit roles and rules, and pointing out nonverbal communication.

Practice Usage: With family group with verbal orientation and willingness to make a time investment. Particularly useful when communication is problematic.

References:

Virginia Satir, *Con-Joint Family Therapy* (Palo Alto, CA: Science and Behavior Books, 1967).

Judith C. Nelson, "Communication Theory and Social Work Treatment," in Francis J. Turner, Ed., *Social Work Treatment: Interlocking Theoretical Approaches*, 3rd ed. (New York: Free Press, 1986), pp. 219–244.

Crisis Intervention

Source: Study of a natural disaster and work of Erich Linderman and Gerald Caplan. Concepts of brief treatment. Work of Lydia Rapoport and Howard J. Parad, Smith College, School of Social Work (1962). The leading proponent is Naomi Golan.

Underlying Theory: Eclectic theory base with emphasis on ego psychology and stress theory. Concerned with cognitive process. Uses public health model. Goal is the restoration of social functioning and enhancement of coping capacity.

Practice Theory: Assessment of client's personality structure, basic defenses, habitual adaptive patterns, the nature of the upset, potential for adaptive response, and resources available. Makes maximal use of the period of upset, reduces client tension and anxiety, gives hope, gives support, and helps with crisis situation. Teaches new patterns of problem solving and coping and corrects perceptions. Short-term service.

Practice Usage: In situations in which developmental or situational crisis is limiting adequate social functioning. Can be used with individuals, families, or groups of individuals in crisis.

References:

Lydia Rapoport, "Crisis Intervention as a Mode of Brief Treatment," in Robert W. Roberts and Robert H. Nee, Eds., *Theories of Social Casework* (Chicago: University of Chicago Press, 1970), pp. 267–311.

Howard J. Parad, Lola Selby, and James Quinlan, "Crisis Intervention with Families and Groups," in Robert W. Roberts and Helen Northen, Eds., *Theories of Social Work with Groups* (New York: Columbia University Press, 1976), pp. 304–330.

Eileen Ell, "Crisis Theory and Social Work Practice," in Francis J. Turner, Ed., *Social Work Treatment,* 4th ed. (New York: Free Press, 1996).

Burl Gilliland and Richard James, *Crisis Intervention Strategies* (Pacific Grove, CA: Brooks/Cole, 1997).

Lee Ann Hoff, *People in Crisis: Understanding and Helping,* 4th ed. (San Francisco: Jossey-Bass, 1995).

Developmental

Source: Developed from work of Grace Coyle (group self-direction), Gertrude Wilson and Gladys Ryland (group autonomy and group decision making), and Helen Phillips (member importance and here-and-now emphasis). Articulated by Emanual Tropp, Virginia Commonwealth University (1969), in part as a reaction to the infiltration of social work by group psychotherapy.

Underlying Theory: Uses an existential-humanistic philosophy. Human beings are seen as free, responsible, and capable of self-realization. Individuals should be treated with respect for their dignity and expected to be responsible. Purpose is to help individuals enhance social functioning through functioning in groups centered around common interests and concerns and to help groups function effectively and responsively.

Practice Theory: Assessment focused on the commonality of members. Uses release of feelings, support for individuals from the group, reality orientation, and self-reappraisal. Uses program content, member planning, group process, and worker use of self as means for achieving members' purposes.

Practical Usage: In voluntary situation with peer groups or formed groups.

References:

Emanual Tropp, *A Humanistic Foundation for Social Group Work Practice: A Collection of Writings by Emanual Tropp* (New York: Selected Academic Readings, 1969).

Emanual Tropp, "A Developmental Theory," in Robert W. Roberts and Helen Northen, Eds., *Theories of Social Work with Groups* (New York: Columbia University Press, 1976), pp. 198–237.

Ecological (Life Model)

Source: Carel B. Germain, Columbia School of Social Work (1970).

Underlying Theory: Ecological approach. Concepts about transactions between people and their environment, adaptation, reciprocity, mutuality, stress, and coping. Also considers growth and development, identity, competence, autonomy, and relatedness. Uses Erikson. Concerned with environmental quality, organizations, and social networks.

Practice Theory: Assessment carried out by worker and client together seeking to understand meaning; focus on person and problem in order to set objectives and devise appropriate action. Engages positive forces in client and environment. Attempts to remove environmental obstacles and change negative transactions. Uses a process of engagement, exploration, contracting, ongoing, ending. Concerned with client need and vulnerability. Focus on life transitions, unresponsiveness of environments, crisis events, and communication-relationship difficulties. Action designed to increase self-esteem and problem-solving and coping skills. Also works to facilitate group functioning and influence organizational structure, social networks, and physical settings.

Practice Usage: For problem in social functioning.

References:

Carel B. Germain and Alex Gitterman, *The Life Model of Social Work Practice* (New York: Columbia University Press, 1980).

Carel B. Germain and Alex Gitterman, "The Life Model Approach to Social Work Practice Revisited," in Francis J. Turner, Ed., *Social Work Treatment: Interlocking Theoretical Approaches*, 3rd ed. (New York: Free Press, 1986), pp. 618–644.

Susan P. Kemp, James K. Whittaker, and Elizabeth M. Tracy, *Person-Environment Practice: The Social Ecology of Interpersonal Helping* (New York: Aldine De Gruyter, 1997).

Carol Meyer, "The Ecosystems Perspective: Implications for Social Work Practice," in Carol Meyer and Mark Mattaini, *The Foundations of Social Work Practice* (Washington, DC: NASW Press, 1995), pp. 16–27.

Existential

Source: Existential psychology and psychiatry. Donald Krill, Denver University, developed use in social work (1969).

Underlying Theory: Basically philosophical. Protests the assumption that reality can be grasped by exclusively intellectual means. Distinguishes between subjective and objective truth. Gives priority to the subjective. Values human choice, self-determination, and individualization. Believes in the capacity for growth and change.

Practice Theory: Assesses only what is going on between people. Uses experience in which reality of how a person thinks of self and relates to others is gradually revealed. Teaches how to choose responses. Brings suffering into the open for understanding and acceptance. Develops a trusting relationship. Helps individuals to make commitments.

Practice Usage: Any situation in which the client is willing to develop self-awareness.

References:

Donald F. Krill, "Existential Social Work," in Francis J. Turner, Ed., *Social Work Treatment: Interlocking Theoretical Approaches,* 3rd ed. (New York: Free Press, 1986), pp. 181–218.
Donald F. Krill, *Existential Social Work* (New York: Free Press, 1978).

Feminist Practice
(material provided by Mary Bricker-Jenkins)

Source: Developed by practitioners as an attempt to integrate feminist theory, commitments, and culture with conventional approaches to social work practice. Goes beyond a "nonsexist" and/or "women's issues" orientation.

Underlying Assumptions: The inherent purpose and goal of human existence is self-actualization, which is a collective endeavor involving the creation of material and ideological conditions that enable it. Systems and ideologies of domination/subordination, exploitation, and oppression are inimical to individual and collective self-actualization. Given the structural and ideological barriers to self-actualization, practice is explicitly political in intent. Women have unique and relatively unknown history, conditions, developmental patterns, and strengths that must be discovered and engaged by practitioners.

Practice Theory: Assessment focuses on preferred and available patterns of strength in intellectual, emotional, social, cultural, physical, and/or spiritual domains; special emphasis given to basic, concrete needs, safety, and perceptions of personal power. Underlying principle informing practice is that healing, health, and growth are functions of validation, consciousness, and transformative action, which are supported and sustained through resources to meet basic human needs, the creation of validating environments and relationships that preserve and nurture uniqueness and wholeness. Uses a range of conventional and nonconventional approaches. Frequent use of groups. Encourages and facilitates individual and collective action. Works for open, egalitarian, and collegial relationships with clients.

Practice Usage: In all kinds of settings, with all populations. Particular attention focused on women.

References:

Affilia: Journal of Women and Social Work.

Mary Bricker-Jenkins and Nancy Hooyman, *Not for Women Only: Social Work Practice for a Feminist Future* (Silver Springs, MD: NASW Press, 1986).

Nan Van Den Bergh and Lynn Cooper, *Feminist Visions for Social Work* (Silver Springs, MD: NASW Press, 1986).

Mary Valentich, "Feminism and Social Work Practice," in Francis J. Turner, Ed., *Social Work Treatment: Interlocking Theoretical Approaches,* 3rd ed. (New York: Free Press, 1986), pp. 564–589.

Mary Bricker-Jenkins, Nancy Hooyman, and Naomi Gottlieb, *Feminist Social Work Practice in Clinical Settings* (Newbury Park, CA: Sage, 1991).

Nan Van Den Bergh, *Feminist Practice in the 21st Century* (Washington, DC: NASW Press, 1995).

Functional

Source: Developed in 1930s at University of Pennsylvania School of Social Work by Jessie Taft and Virginia Robinson. Contemporary source work of Ruth Smalley and others.

Underlying Theory: Uses work of Otto Rank and, to some degree, of John Dewey and of Margaret Mead. Sees individual as defining self from himself or herself, from relationships, and from external conditions of life. Growth orientation. Respect for worth and dignity of persons. Concern that persons have opportunities to realize potential and that human power be released.

Practice Theory: Focus is on release of power for increased social functioning. Principles that guide service are diagnosis (related to nature of service and participated in by client); use of time phases in process (beginnings, middles, endings); use of agency function; use of structure; and use of relationships.

Practice Usage: Can be used in most situations. Has been used with individuals, families, groups, and communities.

References:

Martha M. Dore, "Functional Theory: Its History and Influence on Contemporary Social Work Practice," *Social Service Review* 64 (September 1990): 358–374.

Ruth E. Smalley, *Theory for Social Work Practice* (New York: Columbia University Press, 1967).

Ruth E. Smalley, "The Functional Approach to Casework Practice," in Robert W. Roberts and Robert H. Nee, Eds., *Theories of Social Casework* (Chicago: University of Chicago Press, 1970), pp. 79–128.

Shankar A. Yelajc, "Functional Theory in Social Work Practice," in Francis J. Turner, Ed., *Social Work Treatment: Interlocking Theoretical Approaches,* 3rd ed. (New York: Free Press, 1986), pp. 46–68.

Eleanor L. Ryder, "A Functional Approach," in Robert W. Roberts and Helen Northen, Eds., *Theories of Social Work with Groups* (New York: Columbia University Press, 1976).

Gestalt Therapy

Source: Work of Fritz Perls, adopted by many social workers because of emphasis on "beginning where the client is."

Underlying Theory: Holistic, organismic, emphasis on hunger rather than sexuality, development of self through awareness and responsibility. One must take responsibility for one's own existence. Normal personality characterized by unity, integration, consistency, and coherence. Sovereign drive is self-actualization. Concern for paradoxes.

Practice Theory: Assess what the client is experiencing, what client wants. Process: lay groundwork, establish contact; negotiate consensus between client and therapist; grading, experiment within client's ability; surface client's awareness; locate client's energy; generate self-support; generate theme; choice of experiment; enact experiment; insight and completion.

Practice Usage: In situations in which worker and agency have time and inclination to allow client to develop self-knowledge and to engage in self-exploration. Most effective in oversocialized, restrained, constricted individuals.

Reference:

Michael Blugerman, "Contributions of Gestalt Theory to Social Work Treatment," in Francis J. Turner, Ed., *Social Work Treatment: Interlocking Theoretical Approaches*, 3rd ed. (New York: Free Press, 1986), pp. 69–90.

Integrative

Source: Nathan Ackerman was an early source of basic ideas. Family agencies an important source. Work of Otto Pollak, John Spiegal, Frances Beatman, and Sanford Sherman also influential. Frances Scherz an important contributor (1966).

Underlying Theory: Based in a psychoanalytic frame of reference with particular emphasis on ego psychology and role theory. Eclectic in nature. Incorporates systems theory, small-group theory, family development tasks, and communication concepts. Assumes family is the link between the individual and the larger society.

Practice Theory: Assesses family structure, functioning, and history with emphasis on placement of current problems. Goal is to modify or change aspects of the family relationship system that are not functional. Worker enables and supports family members. Emphasis is on the here and now. Task-oriented. Uses advice, education, and guidance. Demonstrates techniques. Encourages appropriate role development, communication patterns, decision making, and family responsibility. Deals with resistance to change and fears of feelings and of destruction of the family. Helps family members expose hidden feelings and observe themselves.

Practice Usage: In situations in which there is a parent-child, family, or marital problem.

References:

Frances H. Scherz, "Theory and Practice of Family Therapy," in Robert W. Roberts and Robert H. Nee, Eds., *Theories of Social Casework* (Chicago: University of Chicago Press, 1970), pp. 219–264.

Laura Sue Dodson, *Family Counseling: A Systems Approach* (Muncie, IN: Accelerated Development, 1977).

Sonya L. Rhodes, "Family Treatment," in Frances J. Turner, Ed., *Social Work Treatment: Interlocking Theoretical Approaches,* 3rd ed. (New York: Free Press, 1986), pp. 432–453.

Sanford N. Sherman, "A Social Work Frame for Family Therapy," in Eleanor Reardon Tolson and William J. Reid, Eds., *Models of Family Treatment* (New York: Columbia University Press, 1981), pp. 7–32.

Locality Development

Source: William W. Biddle, University of Missouri (1965). Contributing influences include work of United Nations in underdeveloped countries, experimental and demonstration projects of the Ford Foundation, Mobilization for Youth, Peace Corps, and work of settlement houses.

Underlying Theory: Eclectic. Draws from sociology, anthropology, and social psychology. Has an existential leaning. Sees community as eclipsed and lacking relationships. Uses problem-solving capacity of community persons.

Practice Theory: Assessment is problem solving with citizens. Process includes exploration, organization of community persons, discussion of problems, action, new projects, continuation. The goal is the development of community capacity and integration. The worker is an enabler, catalyst, coordinator, and teacher. Citizens participate in interactional problem solving. Involves a broad cross-section of people. Uses small task-oriented groups that seek consensus. Problem solving is primary.

Practice Usage: To involve a total community or neighborhood in discovering and solving problems.

References:

William J. Biddle, *The Community Development Process: The Rediscovery of Local Initiative* (New York: Holt, Rinehart and Winston, 1965).

Fred M. Cox, John L. Erlich, Jack Rothman, and John E. Tropman, Eds., *Strategies of Community Organization,* 4th ed. (Itasca, IL: F. E. Peacock, 1987), pp. 3–26 and Part Three, pp. 351–383.

Mediating

Source: William Schwartz, Columbia University, School of Social Work (1962). Lawrence Shulman also a major contributor. Work of Clara Kaiser and Helen Phillips also suggests this focus. Lawrence Shulman has continued to develop and expand usage with individuals, families, groups, and communities.

Underlying Theory: Social systems theory, symbolic interaction. Sociological understanding about: organizations, institutions, and communities as systems; game theory and small-group theory.

Practice Theory: Assessment is a systems assessment of the blocks to need fulfillment. Focus is on individual in interaction, group process, and impinging environment. Process includes tuning in (worker readies self to move into process), beginning together, work, and transitions and endings. Goals related to mutual need for self-fulfillment as individuals and society reach out to each other. They are specified. Worker is a mediator and enabler, helps client reach out for what he or she needs, demands work, mobilizes healing powers of human association, and mutual aid. Clarifies communication and makes use of problem-solving process.

Practice Usage: Helping people negotiate difficult environments.

References:

William Schwartz and Serapino R. Zalba, *The Practice of Social Group Work* (New York: Columbia University Press, 1971).
Lawrence Shulman, *A Case Book of Social Work with Groups* (New York: Council on Social Work Education, 1968).
Lawrence Shulman, *The Skills of Helping*, 2nd ed. (Itasca, IL: F. E. Peacock, 1984).
William Schwartz, "Between Client and System: Mediating Function," in Robert W. Roberts and Helen Northen, Eds., *Theories of Social Work with Groups* (New York: Columbia University Press, 1976), pp. 171–197.

Organizational (Remedial-Group)

Source: A continuation of a group model known as remedial or preventive rehabilitive. Inception at University of Michigan in mid-1950s in the work of Robert Vinter and colleagues. Outgrowth of use of groups in clinical settings. More recently Paul H. Glasser and Charles D. Garwin have further developed this model, with particular emphasis on the organizational context of practice.

Underlying Theory: An eclectic base with contributions from social role theory, social-behavior theory, ego psychology, group dynamics, systems theory, and organizational theory.

Practice Theory: Assessment of relationship between client's problems, personality, and environment as well as individual's performance in the group and group process. Process includes intake, diagnostic treatment planning, group composition, treatment in the group, evaluation, and termination. Goal is individual change that is a remedy for social dysfunctioning. Focus on individual in the group. Uses direct and indirect influence, including program or activity. Concerned with the context for change, organizational prerequisites needed for change, and targets and strategies for change.

Practice Usage: To help malperforming individuals achieve a more desirable state of social functioning.

References:

Robert Vinter, *Readings in Group Work Practice* (Ann Arbor, MI: Campus Publishers, 1967).

Paul Glasser, Rosemary Sarri, and Robert Vinter, *Individual Change Through Small Groups* (New York: Free Press, 1974).

Paul Glasser and Charles D. Garwin, "An Organizational Model," in Robert W. Roberts and Helen Northen, Eds., *Theories of Social Work with Groups* (New York: Columbia University Press, 1976), pp. 75–115.

Problem Solving

Source: Helen H. Perlman, University of Chicago (1957). Blending of psychosocial and functioning models.

Underlying Theory: All human living is a problem-solving process. Eclectic, using ego psychology, John Dewey's rational problem solving, role theory, and symbolic interaction.

Practice Theory: Assessment identifies and explains the nature of the problem, focuses on aspects of personality involved in the problem. Continuous appraisal of client's motivation, capacity, and opportunity. Goal is to help client cope as effectively as possible in carrying out social tasks and in relationships. Relationship with client of prime concern. Uses time in process. Conceptualized as a *person* with a *problem* comes to a *place* where he or she is offered help through a *process*.

Practice Usage: With individuals motivated to use help in a cognitive and interactive process.

References:

Helen H. Perlman, *Social Casework: A Problem-Solving Process* (Chicago: University of Chicago Press, 1975).

Helen H. Perlman, "The Problem-Solving Model," in Robert W. Roberts and Robert H. Nee, Eds., *Theories of Social Casework* (Chicago: University of Chicago Press, 1970), pp. 129–179.

Helen H. Perlman, "The Problem Solving Model," in Francis J. Turner, Ed., *Social Work Practice: Interlocking Theoretical Approaches*, 3rd ed. (New York: Free Press, 1986), pp. 245–266.

Psychosocial

Source: Florence Hollis, Columbia School of Social Work (1964). Strongly influenced by work of Gordon Hamilton. Outgrowth of traditional diagnostic case work of 1930s.

Underlying Theory: Major source psychoanalytic theory, with emphasis on ego. Uses social science concepts of culture, role, communications theory, and social systems theory. Values acceptance of the client, self-determination, scientific objectivity, and insight.

Practice Theory: Assessment is a differential psychosocial diagnosis. Concerned with personality, etiology, and psychiatric classifications of disorders. Diagnosis very important. Goal is adjustment of the individual through change in perception, response, and communication. Relationship is of prime concern. Uses reflection, interpretation, ventilation, support, and environmental manipulation.

Practice Usage: With motivated verbal client willing to commit long-term involvement and with a desire for self-knowledge or insight.

References:

Florence Hollis and Mary E. Woods, *Casework: A Psychosocial Therapy,* 3rd ed. (New York: Random House, 1981).

Florence Hollis, "The Psychosocial Approach to Casework," in Robert W. Roberts and Robert H. Nee, Eds., *Theories of Social Casework* (Chicago: University of Chicago Press, 1970), pp. 33–75.

Francis J. Turner, "Psychosocial Theory," in Francis J. Turner, Ed., *Social Work Practice: Interlocking Theoretical Approaches,* 3rd ed. (New York: Free Press, 1986), pp. 484–513.

Helen Northen, "Psychosocial Practice in Small Groups," in Robert W. Roberts and Helen Northen, Eds., *Theories of Social Work with Groups* (New York: Columbia University Press, 1976).

Mary E. Woods, *Casework: A Psychosocial Therapy,* 5th ed. (Boston: McGraw-Hill, 2000).

Social Action

Source: Saul Alinsky and Richard Cloward (1960s).

Underlying Theory: Eclectic and selective. Little theory development. Concepts used include disadvantaged population, social injustice, deprivation, inequality. Concerned with power, conflict, confrontation. The community is seen as made up of conflicting interests that are not easily reconcilable and as having scarce resources.

Practice Theory: Goal is the shifting of power relationships and resources as well as basic institutional change that benefits "me and mine." The worker is an advocate, agitator, negotiator, and partisan. Client is seen as victim and employer of worker. Strategy is to crystallize issues and develop organization to take action against enemy target. Also uses conflict, confrontation, and negotiation. Manipulates mass organizations and political processes.

Practice Usage: When individuals are seen as victims of an unjust system.

References:

Saul Alinsky, *Rules for Radicals* (New York: Random House, 1967).

Fred M. Cox, John L. Erlich, Jack Rothman, and John E. Tropman, Eds., *Strategies of Community Organization,* 4th ed. (Itasca, IL: F. E. Peacock, 1987), pp. 3–26 and Part Three, pp. 384–422.

Social Planning

Source: Conventional community organization in planning and funding organizations and governmental planning agencies.

Underlying Theory: Sees the community as an entity with many interacting systems. Particular emphasis on decision making, power control, and the agency system. Political and economic considerations as important as substantive knowledge about social problems. Emphasis is on rationality, objectivity, and professional purposefulness.

Practice Theory: Assessment identifies social problem, its cause, and its possible resolution. The process includes study and assessment of the problematic situation; determining preferences and influences relevant to the problem; examining alternative goals and strategies and their consequences; selection of goals, strategies, and programs; obtaining commitments to desired change; and designing and implementing a feedback-evaluative system. Worker is a fact gatherer and analyst, program designer, implementer, and facilitator. Consumers tend to be power structure of the community.

Practice Usage: Where rational planning toward the alleviation of social problems is desired.

References:

Robert Perlman and Arnold Gurin, *Community Organization and Social Change* (New York: John Wiley, 1972).
Fred M. Cox, John L. Erlich, Jack Rothman, and John E. Tropman, Eds., *Strategies of Community Organization,* 4th ed. (Itasca, IL: F. E. Peacock, 1987), pp. 3–26 and Part Three, pp. 308–350.

Socialization

Source: Developed by Elizabeth McBroom, School of Social Work, University of Southern California, to respond to poverty or "multiproblem" families.

Underlying Theory: Socialization as developed by anthropology, psychology, and sociology. Margaret Mead's use of meaning and selfhood in the "process of interaction." Erik Erikson's epigenetic model. John Dewey's cognitive process. Systems theory, connectiveness of human motivation with events, and feedback.

Practice Theory: Assessment locates client in milieu, looks for "islands of competence," and barriers to competent functioning. Considers external resources and lifestyle of client. Goal is increased competence in areas of work and parenting. Relationship is established by active response to client's request and by explicit communication of acceptance. Worker is an active provider and teacher. Uses contract. Supports client's motivation. Works on time orientation, verbal facility, functioning, and authority relationships. Creates success experiences. Models.

Practice Usage: With individuals and families who have not learned basic socialization skills and who need help of a concrete nature.

References:

Elizabeth McBroom, "Socialization and Social Casework," in Robert W. Roberts and Robert H. Nee, Eds., *Theories of Social Casework* (Chicago: University of Chicago Press, 1970), pp. 313–351.

Elizabeth McBroom, "Socialization Through Small Groups," in Robert W. Roberts and Helen Northen, Eds., *Theories of Social Work with Groups* (New York: Columbia University Press, 1976), pp. 268–303.

Strengths Perspective

Source: Originally developed for working with persons with mental illness but has been extended to other population groups and fields beyond direct practice. Major contributors include Dennis Saleeby, Ann Weick, Richard Rapp, W. Patrick Sullivan, Walter Kisthardt, Charles Cowger, and Julian Rappaport, University of Kansas, School of Social Welfare (1992).

Underlying Assumptions: Respects the unique strengths, abilities, and aspirations of clients and recognizes resources within the client's natural environment. Focuses on people's innate capacity and motivation for growth and change. Views difficulties in life as sources of challenge and opportunity.

Practice Theory: Focuses on regeneration and healing from within and on empowering or discovering the power within people. Respects the resilience of people in overcoming adversity. Builds on the client's knowledge of his or her own situation and aspirations for change. Views the role of the social worker as that of collaborator. Recognizes the role of dialogue, membership, and interrelationships in caring communities in generating resources and contributing to empowerment.

Practice Usage: Applicable to all client systems: individuals, families, small groups, organizations, and communities.

References:

Karla Krosgrud Miley, Michael O'Melia, and Brenda L. DuBois, *Generalist Social Work Practice: An Empowering Approach*, 2nd ed. (Boston: Allyn and Bacon, 1998).

Dennis Saleeby, *The Strengths Perspective in Social Work Practice*, 2nd ed. (New York: Longman, 1997).

Task

Source: William J. Reid and Laura Epstein, University of Chicago (1972). Influenced by Reid and Shyne's work, *Brief and Extended Casework*. Developed as an approach whose results (outcomes) can be empirically researched.

Underlying Theory: Eclectic. Selective. Use of general systems theory, communication theory, role theory, psychoanalytic theory, and certain parts of learning theory.

Practice Theory: Assessment is specification of target problem and desired outcome. Specifies tasks needed to resolve problems. Helps client carry out task as necessary. Goals are specific and limited and related to what the client wants. Uses communication to explore, structure, enhance awareness, and direct.

Practice Usage: For time-limited treatment of problems of living.

References:

William J. Reid and Laura Epstein, *Task-Centered Practice* (New York: Columbia University Press, 1977).

William J. Reid, "Task-Centered Social Work," in Francis J. Turner, Ed., *Social Work Treatment: Interlocking Theoretical Approaches,* 3rd ed. (New York: Free Press, 1986), pp. 267–295.

William J. Reid, "Family Treatment Within a Task-Centered Framework," in Eleanor Reardon Tolson and William J. Reid, Eds., *Models of Family Treatment* (New York: Columbia University Press, 1981), pp. 306–331.

Charles D. Garwin, William Reid, and Laura Epstein, "A Task-Centered Approach," in Robert W. Roberts and Helen Northen, Eds., *Theories of Social Work with Groups* (New York: Columbia University Press, 1976), pp. 238–267.

Laura Epstein, *Helping People: The Task Centered Approach,* 3rd ed. (Boston: Allyn and Bacon, 1992).

GLOSSARY

accountability Evaluation of efficiency and effectiveness factors relating to the delivery of social services.

action The process of carrying out a plan developed through the assessment and action phases of the social work process.

action system System of people and resources involved in carrying out tasks related to goals and strategy of the helping endeavor.

activity Doing something or performing tasks as opposed to talking about what to do or talking about feelings or ideas.

agency The organization that employs the worker and manages resources used to help the client.

assessment Ongoing process of the social work endeavor that develops an understanding of person in situation to use as the basis for action.

blended family A family in which the parents have had previous marriages and have children from those marriages, as well as possibly having children from the present marriage.

bond Emotional tie that determines the cohesiveness of a group; expressed in "we feelings" and commonly held values.

boundary Point at which the interaction around a function no longer has the intensity that interaction of system members or units has. For example, when considering who is a member of a family system, the boundary is the point that divides those who are continually interacting around family concerns and issues and those who have little or no input into family functioning.

broker A social work role in which the worker provides the client with information about available resources and helps link the client with the resource.

burnout A condition that some social workers develop. It is characterized by feelings of lack of appreciation, illness, tiredness, inability to laugh, dreading to go to work, and sleep disturbances.

case advocate A social work role in which the worker pleads or lobbies for services for a client whom a service provider would otherwise reject.

case conference Members of a team or a multiperson helping system in a formal meeting share information and plan for services to individuals and families they are all serving in some manner.

case management A method for coordinating services in which a worker assesses with a client which services are needed and obtains and monitors the delivery of the services.

cause Movement directed toward eliminating a social evil or toward meeting human need in a new way.

cause advocacy Concern about and action on behalf of the victims of social problems that works toward the modification of social conditions.

cause-function debate   Debate about whether to emphasize removal of an evil in community life that impacts the individual's social functioning or to emphasize response to individual malfunctioning.

client   One who has either sought help from a social worker or is served by an agency employing a social worker.

collaboration   The working together of several service providers with a common client toward a common goal.

community   Immediate environment of worker, client, and agency that is manifest as a social system.

community benefits   Organized efforts by the natural helping system to meet needs of a member of the system. Usually the effort is in response to a catastrophic situation.

concern   A feeling that something is not right. Interest in, regard for, and care about the well-being of self and other persons.

conflict   A struggle for something that is scarce or thought to be scarce.

congruity   A situation in which the interactions or transactions within an ecosystem are balanced, resulting in mutual benefit for the person and the environment.

consultation   A way of two or more people working together in which the consultant provides knowledge and expertise but has no power to require the consulted to accept the help or advice. The consulted examines the input from the consultant as to its usefulness in the situation under consideration.

contract   An agreement, verbal or written, between worker and client about the work to be done together. Goals, objectives, and tasks to be carried out by worker and client are specified.

coordination   The working together of two or more service providers in activity focused on a particular client or focused on persons in a particular category (e.g., the aged). Coordinative mechanisms include colocation of services, networking, linking, case management, collaboration, and a team approach.

cope   A person's efforts to deal with some new and often problematic situation or encounter or to deal in some new way with an old problem.

crisis   A state of disequilibrium or a loss of steady state due to stress and precipitating event in the life of a person who usually has a satisfactory level of functioning.

diagnosis   A term borrowed from the medical field. It relates to developing a statement as to the nature of the client's need and the situation related to that need. A more contemporary term is *assessment*.

diagnostic approach   A historic model of social work practice that places a primary emphasis on diagnosis. The contemporary model is usually referred to as the *psychosocial approach*.

direct practice   Action with individuals, families, and small groups focused on change in either the transactions within the family or small group or in the manner in which individuals, families, and small groups function in relation to individuals and social systems in their environment.

dual perspective   Process of consciously perceiving, understanding, and comparing simultaneously the values, attitudes, and behaviors of the larger social system and those of the immediate family and community system.

ecological perspective   A way of thinking about practice that involves a focus on the client's surrounding environment.

ecosystem   A system of systems including the person(s) and all of the interacting systems in the environment along with the transactions among the person(s) and systems.

ecosystems perspective   An approach that examines the exchange of matter, energy, or information over time among all the systems in a person-in-environment approach.

ecosystems strengths approach   A blend of the ecological and strength perspectives with the problem-solving approach to form a process for facilitating growth and change.

empowerment   A process for increasing personal, interpersonal, or political power so that individuals can take action to improve their life situation.

enabling   Making it possible for an individual or system to carry out some activity they might not be able to engage in without support or help.

environmental demands   Expectations that people or social systems in an individual's or social system's environment place on themselves relative to their social functioning.

environmental manipulation   A strategy to bring about change in a client's environment in order to enhance the client's social functioning.

evaluation   Collection and assessment of data about the outcomes of a plan of action relative to goals set in advance of implementing that plan.

extinction   The technique of ignoring undesirable behavior as a way of eliminating it.

facilitation   Enabling others to function effectively.

feeling   An intuitive sense of a situation or solution to a problem. Facts have not been sought. More of an emotional process than a cognitive one.

felt need   A need identified by a client.

feminist perspective   An approach related to redistribution of power that addresses discrimination; useful in working with women and minority groups.

field of practice   A system of policies, agencies, and services that focuses on a social problem, a disabling condition, a particular context, or a particular social system. A major organizing framework for the U.S. social welfare system.

formative evaluation   Evaluation that looks at the process of the work.

functional approach   A historic model of social work practice that places emphasis on the role and tasks of the social worker in the helping situation rather than on a client's deviance or illness.

gemeinshaft   A characteristic of communities that demonstrates a sense of "we-ness" and informal functioning.

generalist practice   Practice in which the client and worker together assess the need in all of its complexity and develop a plan for responding to that need. A strategy is chosen from a repertoire of responses appropriate for work with individuals, families, groups, agencies, and communities. The unit of attention is chosen by considering the system needing to be changed. The plan is carried out and evaluated.

genogram   A pictorial assessment mechanism for showing intergenerational relationships and family characteristics.

gesellschaft   A characteristic of communities in which individuals tend to relate through institutions and other formal structures.

goal   The overall, long-range expected outcome of an endeavor.

goal-attainment scaling   An evaluation technique that not only specifies goals but also specifies outcomes at five levels: expected, more desirable, most desirable, less than desirable, and least desirable.

group-building (group-maintenance) roles   Those roles that focus on the maintenance of the group as a system. The roles may include encourager, harmonizer, or goal keeper.

group task roles   Those roles related to the accomplishment of the functions or tasks of the group. The roles may include initiator, coordinator, or clarifier.

human diversity   A way of viewing persons in situations that considers culture, race, gender, and disabling conditions as they affect human functioning. It views human behavior as highly relative to the social situation in which persons function.

incongruity   A situation in which the interactions or transactions within an ecosystem are out of balance, resulting in unmet needs for the person and/or the environment.

indirect practice   Action taken with persons other than clients in order to help clients.

individual roles   Roles that satisfy individual need but detract from the work of the group. These can include the dominator, the special-interest pleader, and the blocker.

influence   General acts of producing an effect on another person, group, or organization through exercises of a personal or organizational capacity.

influentials   Persons within a community or an organization who have power and/or authority.

interactional skill   The capacity of social workers to relate to both clients and significant others, both individuals and social systems, in such a manner as to be helpful and to support the work at hand.

interface   A point of contact between two systems where transactions occur.

intervention   Specific action by a worker in relation to human systems or processes in order to induce change. The action is guided by knowledge and professional values as well as by the skillfulness of the worker.

interventive repertoire   The package of actions, methods, techniques, and skills a particular social worker has developed for use in response to needs of individuals and social systems.

interview   The structure for operationalizing the interaction between worker and client.

knowledge   Picture of world and the place of humans in it. Ideas and beliefs about reality based on confirmable or probable evidence.

leadership   (in groups) The filling of a number of roles in a group, particularly those needed for group functioning.

life processes   The biological, social, psychological, and spiritual courses of individuals and social systems as they develop and function through the life span.

lifestyle   Manner in which an individual or family functions in meeting needs, in interactions with others, and in patterns of work, play, and rest.

locus of control   The source of an individual's motivation or drive for action or change. The major concern is whether it lies within the individual or within the environment.

mapping   A pictorial assessment mechanism that shows the relationship of subsystems to each other or the relationship of a system to other systems in its environment.

mediation strategy   A strategy in which a worker helps a client and a system in the immediate environment to reach out to each other and find a common concern or interest and to do the work necessary to bring about a desired change.

medical model   Used in medical field and often appropriated by social workers. Characterized by a process of study, diagnosis, and treatment.

moral code   Specification of that which is considered to be right or wrong in terms of behavior.

multiperson helping system   A situation in which more than two persons are involved, such as a social worker working with a small group of clients or several workers (a team) working with a single client.

natural helpers   People who possess helping skills and exercise them in the context of mutual relationships, as opposed to professionals trained in certain helping skills who are not part of a client's immediate community.

natural helping systems   A client's friends, family, and coworkers. Those in an individual's informal environment to whom one turns in time of need.

need   That which is necessary for either a person or a social system to function within reasonable expectations, given the situation that exists.

needs assessment   A process through which needs of a particular population or category of systems are determined.

network   A loose association of systems. Not a social system but an entity that operates through mutual resource sharing.

networking   Development and maintenance of communication and ways of working together among people of diverse interests and orientations. One means of coordination.

norming   The process of setting norms, or expected ways of behaving.

objectives   Intermediate goals that must be reached in order to attain the ultimate goal.

opportunity seizing   A skill that involves use of a keen sense of when the time is right to develop a project or involve an individual or system in a change activity.

patient   An individual treated in a medical setting. Sometimes used in place of the term *client* in clinical social work.

person in situation (or person in environment)   The focus of the social work endeavor. The focus of the social worker is not just on the person or the social situation but on the complex interaction of the two as that interaction affects both person and social situation.

philosophy of life   Beliefs about people and society and about human life, its purposes, and how it should be lived.

plan of action   The way or method for carrying out planned change in the social work endeavor. It is structured and specifies goals and objectives, units of attention, and strategy.

private troubles   Relates to the needs of individuals.

problem   (in social work) A social functioning situation in which need fulfillment of any of the persons or systems involved is blocked and in which the persons involved cannot by themselves remove the block to need fulfillment.

problem-oriented record   A four-point record containing a data base of pertinent information, a problem list, plans and goals, and follow-up notes (including outcomes).

problem-solving process   A tool used by social workers to solve problems in a rational manner. It proceeds through identifiable steps of interaction with clients. These steps include identification of the problem, statement of preliminary assumptions about the problem, selection and collection of information, analysis of information, development of a plan, implementation of the plan, and evaluation.

process   A recurrent patterning of a sequence of change over time in a particular direction.

process recording   Narrative report of all that happened during a client contact, including worker's thinking and feeling about what happened.

profession   A group of people who carry out some societal task. These trained and educated people work from systematic theory, carry authority and community sanction, and have a code of ethics and a culture.

professional relationship   A relationship with an agreed upon purpose, a limited time frame, and in which the professional devotes self to the interest of the client.

psychosocial approach   See *Diagnostic approach.*

public issues   Relates to need from a societal perspective.

referral   The process by which a client is made aware of another service resource and helped to make contact with that resource to receive a needed service.

reframing   Stating a concern or a problem in a new way, from a different point of view.

relationship   Cohesive quality of the action system. Product of interaction between two persons.

role   The way the worker sees self in the specific helping situation.

scientific philanthropy   Systematic, careful investigation of evidence surrounding the need for service before acting on the need.

self-help groups   Voluntary groups in which members with common problems help each other.

significant others   Those persons in an individual's social network who have importance to, or impact on, the system being worked with.

single-subject design   A research method used when the n (number of subjects) is one. The comparisons are made from baseline data, with progress toward goals being measured.

single-system design   A research design in which a single system—individual, family, group, program, organization, or community—is measured over time.

skill   A complex organization of behavior directed toward a particular goal or activity.

small groups   Three or more persons who have something in common and who use face-to-face interaction to share that commonality and work to fulfill needs and solve common problems of their own or others.

social action   A change strategy that organizes people (often oppressed people) so as to bring pressure on societal institutions for change in power distribution.

social functioning   People coping with environmental demands.

social history   A form of assessment of individuals or families. It includes information (historical and current) needed for understanding and working with clients.

social support network analysis   Specification of the nature of an individual's or family's support network. Both pictorial and written depictions are used.

social system   A system composed of interrelated and interdependent parts (persons and subsystems).

social work process   A problem-solving process carried out with clients to solve problems in social functioning that clients cannot solve without help. It is conceptualized as study, assessment, planning, action, and termination.

sociogram   A pictorial assessment technique used with small groups to show the relationships between group members.

solution-based interventions   An approach that focuses on quickly finding a successful solution and empowering clients for change.

special populations   Refers to specific groups of people such as women, members of a particular minority group, those with a particular disabling condition, and so on. These groups may need special consideration when providing services.

strategy   An overall approach to change in a situation. Includes defining roles and tasks of both worker and client.

strengths perspective   An approach to social work practice that emphasizes the strengths and capabilities of the client system and the resources within the client's natural environment.

summative evaluation   Evaluation concerned with outcomes and effectiveness.

support   The use of techniques that help clients feel better, stronger, and more comfortable in some immediate way.

task group   A relatively formal and structured time-limited group of persons involved with or concerned about a particular problem who work together to reach a common goal.

tasks   Steps necessary to achieve a goal.

team   A group of persons, often representative of various professions, who work together toward common goals and plans of action to meet the needs of clients.

termination   The last phase of the social work process when the emphasis is on disengagement, stabilization of change, and evaluation.

thinking   Use of a cognitive process to sort out information or to engage in a problem-solving process.

transaction   The exchange of matter, energy, and/or information among persons or systems within an ecosystem.

treatment   Term used for action segment of the social work process. Very often used in clinical social work.

unit of attention   The system or systems on which the change activity is focused; also called *focal system*.

values   What is held to be desirable and preferred. Guides for behavior.

CREDITS

Material in the following chapters has been adapted and is used by permission: Chapters 2 and 5: Felix P. Biestek, *The Casework Relationship* (Chicago: Loyola University Press, 1957), p. 14. Chapter 6: Florence Rockwood Kluckholm and Fred L. Strodbeck, *Variations in Value Orientations* (Evanston, IL: Row Peterson, 1961), pp. 10–20; Susan Lonsdale, Adrian Webb, and Thomas L. Briggs, *Teamwork in the Personal Social Services and Health Services: British and American Perspectives* (Syracuse, NY: Syracuse University School of Social Work, 1980), p. 1; Thomas L. Briggs, "Social Work Teams in the United States of America," in Lonsdale et al., 1980, p. 72. Chapter 7: Sonya L. Rhodes, "A Developmental Approach to the Life Cycle of the Family," *Social Casework* 58 (May 1977): 301–311; David Landy, "Problems of the Person Seeking Help in Our Culture," in Mayer N. Zald, ed., *Social Welfare Institutions: A Sociological Reader* (New York: Wiley, 1965), 599–574. Chapter 15: Bernie Jones, "Evaluating Social Service Programs," in Robert Clifton and Alan Dahms, *Grassroots Administration: A Handbook for Staff and Directors of Small Community Based Social Service Agencies* (Monterey, CA: Brooks/Cole, 1980), p. 51.

AUTHOR INDEX

Addams, Jane, 377
Aiger, Stephen M., 299–300
Alinsky, Saul D., 377
Allen-Meares, Paula, 278
Ankersmit, Edith, 185
Aptekar, Herbert H., 23, 45, 47
Armstrong, John, 389
Attneave, Carolyn L., 320
Auslander, Brian A., 369
Auslander, Gail K., 369
Avila, Donald, 107

Baer, Betty, 53
Bailey, Royston, 110
Bartlett, Harriet M., 14, 26, 39, 40, 52, 85, 263
Benne, Kenneth D., 228
Biestek, Felix P., 24, 182, 192
Blundell, Joan, 124
Boehm, Werner, 48
Brager, George A., 373
Bramhall, Martha, 176
Briar, Scott, 120
Briggs, Thomas L., 112, 113, 114
Brownlee, Ann T., 194

Cameron, J. Donald, 374
Chau, Kenneth L., 130
Cloward, Richard, 377
Coady, Nick F., 184
Collins, Alice H., 321
Combs, Arthur W., 107
Compton, Beulah R., 54, 108, 191, 335
Cooperrider, David, 63
Corcoran, Kevin, 399
Corniett, Carlton, 101
Crawford, Dale, 195
Croxton, Tom A., 312

Dane, Barbara Oberhofer, 164
Delaney, Anita J., 298
Dewey, John, 22

Elman, R., 377
Epstein, Laura, 399
Erikson, Erik, 8, 99, 101
Erlich, John L., 364, 371
Ezell, Susan, 176

Federico, Ronald C., 10, 53
Feiner, Harriet A., 264
Fischer, Joel, 399
Foren, Robert, 110
Fortune, Anne E., 412
Fowler, James W., 101
Fraley, Yvonne L., 196
Freud, Sigmund, 23

Galaway, Burt, 54, 108, 191
Garvin, Charles D., 252
Germain, Carel B., 12, 271, 351
Ghali, Sonia B., 279
Gidron, Benjamin, 321
Gilchrist, Lewayne D., 28
Gilligan, Carol, 101
Gitterman, Alex, 271, 351
Gold, Nora, 83, 131
Goldstein, Howard, 42
Gomez, Ernesto, 343
Gordon, William E., 39, 40, 47
Greenwood, Ernest, 18
Grinnel, Richard M., Jr., 351
Guest, Geoffrey, 161
Gulati, Padi, 161
Gutheil, Irene A., 353

Hamilton, Gordon, 22–23, 24
Hartman, Ann, 11, 139–140
Hartmen, Carl, 184
Hasenfeld, Yeheskel, 321
Hess, Howard, 412
Hess, Peg McCartt, 412
Hofstein, Sal, 66
Hollis, Florence, 264, 335, 351
Hooyman, Gene, 115
Horejsi, Charles R., 185
Howe, Elizabeth, 18

Hudson, Peter, 389
Hunter, Floyd, 155

Johnson, David W., 108
Johnson, Louise C., 156, 195
Jones, Bernie, 386

Kagel, Jill Doner, 391
Kane, Rosalie A., 114
Kaplan, Karen Orloff, 359
Katz, Harriet, 264
Keith-Lucas, Alan, 48
Key, Michael, 389
Kirk, Stuart A., 260
Kluckholm, Florence R., 96, 97
Kohlberg, Lawrence, 101
Kyte, Nancy S., 351

Laird, Joan, 139–140
Landy, David, 123
Lane, Bruce A., 278
Lee, Porter R., 6
Leighninger, Leslie, 18
Levy, Charles, 47
Litwak, Eugene, 155, 320, 357–358
Longres, John F., 128
Lonsdale, Susan, 112, 113
Lowenberg, F. M., 123

MacRae, Robert H., 374
Maier, Henry W., 227
Maluccio, Anthony N., 108
Martinez-Brawley, Emilia E., 124
Maslach, Christina, 175–176
Maslow, Abraham H., 7, 68, 170, 274
Matson, Floyd W., 202
Mattaini, Mark A., 260
May, Rollo, 55
McPheeters, Harold L., 299, 373
Mermelstein, Joanne, 195
Meyer, Carol H., 12, 26

Meyer, Henry F., 357–358
Miller, Henry, 48, 120
Miller, Pamela, 312
Mills, C. Wright, 6
Minahan, Anne, 27, 114, 120, 417
Mizio, Emelicia, 298
Montagu, Ashley, 202
Moore, Stephen P., 360
Morales, Armando, 47, 52
Morgan, Ralph, 173
Mullen, Edward, 108

Nelson, Judith C., 335
Northen, Helen, 62
Norton, Dolores, 10, 279

Oxley, Genevieve B., 86

Pancoast, Diane L., 321
Parks, Sharon, 101
Parsons, Ruth J., 326
Patti, Rino J., 370, 371
Pawlak, Edward J., 372
Pearlingi, Bill, 412
Perlman, Helen Harris, 24–25,
    61, 83, 190
Piaget, Jean, 8
Pincus, Allen, 27, 114, 120, 417
Poplin, Dennis E., 156
Pray, Jackie E., 133

Pruger, Robert, 173–174
Pumphrey, Murial W., 45
Purkey, William W., 107

Rank, Otto, 23
Rapoport, Lydia, 55
Reid, William J., 399, 409
Resnick, Herman, 370, 371
Reynolds, Diane, 184
Reynolds, Paul D., 41
Rhodes, Sonya L., 141, 253
Richmond, Mary E., 19–20, 351
Rochell, Cherie D., 412
Rodwell, Mary K., 266
Rokeach, Milton, 46
Ross, Murray, 61
Rosseau, Lorraine, 195
Rothman, Jack, 359, 364, 371, 375

Saleeby, Dennis, 13
Schinke, Steven P., 28
Schwartz, William, 6, 86, 341,
    342, 343
Seabury, Brett A., 201, 252
Selby, Lois G., 334, 335
Sheafor, Bradford W., 47, 52
Sheats, Paul, 228
Shulman, Lawrence, 207, 342
Simon, Barbara L., 164
Simons, Ronald L., 299–300

Siporin, Max, 40, 260, 298, 351
Speck, Ross V., 320
Spiegel, John, 80–81
Srivasta, Suresh, 63
Staub-Bernasconi, Silvia, 326
Strodtbeck, Fred L., 96, 97
Studt, Elliot, 307
Sundet, Paul, 195
Sunley, Robert, 374
Szelenyi, Ivan, 320

Taft, Jessie, 23
Talavera, Esther, 374
Teare, Robert J., 299, 373
Teresa, Joseph G., 364, 371
Tönnies, Ferdinand, 154
Towle, Charlotte, 7, 170, 274
Tracy, Elizabeth M., 132, 282
Tropman, John E., 375
Tropp, Emanual, 120

Urry, Amy, 252

Vinter, Robert, 339

Warren, Roland, 48, 49, 155–156
Webb, Adrian, 112, 113
Whittaker, James K., 28, 132, 282

Zalba, Serapio R., 342, 343

SUBJECT INDEX

Accountability
  defined, 384
  efficiency/effectiveness
    and, 384
  evaluation and, 384–387
  managed care and, 385
  worker-client relationship
    and, 385–386
Action. *See also* Plan of action
  for client use of resources,
    319–325
  as mediation, 341–344
  principles for direct
    practice, 319
  in response to crisis, 330–333.
    See also Crisis intervention
  in social work process, 14
  supportive, 334–337
Action system, 181, 188. *See also*
    One-to-one action system
Activity
  analysis of, 339–340
  case example, 341
  criteria for good, 340
  as interventive strategy,
    337–340
  organizational change
    and, 371
  planning/implementation
    of, 339–340
  structuring group, 250
  types of, 338–339
  worker analysis of, 339–340
ADC. *See* Social Security Act
Advocacy. *See* Case advocacy;
    Cause advocacy
Advocate role, 324–325, 373
AFDC. *See* Social Security Act
Agency(ies). *See also*
    Accountability; Cause
    advocacy; Change-from-
    within strategy
  characteristics of, 164–165
  defined, 163

differential aspects of, 164
ecosystems strengths
  approach and, 163
environmental factors
  affecting, 165–166
expectations of, 165
managed care and, 168–169
plan of action and, 306–307
power in, 168
service delivery by, 322–323
as social system, 164–167
structure/functioning of,
  166–167
study of, 250
subsystems in, 167–168
types of, 163
worker understanding of,
  163–169
Aid to Dependent Children
  (ADC), 29
Aid to Families with Dependent
  Children (AFDC), 29
Appreciative inquiry, 63
Assertiveness training, 328
Assessment. *See also* Needs
  assessment; Transactional
  assessment
  analysis and, 259
  case examples, 266–268, 274,
    280–281, 284–286
  change process and, 268–278
  characteristics of, 260–263
  decision making and, 263–264
  defined, 28, 260
  diagnosis and, 259
  ecosystems approach to, 260,
    275–276
  formulation of need and,
    272–274
  historical development of,
    25–28
  identifying blocks to need
    fulfillment and, 270–272
  identifying need and, 269–270

judgment and, 263–266
needs assessment and,
  282–284
planning and, 290–291. *See
  also* Plan of action
of small groups, 277–278
tasks of, 263
use of term, 26, 27, 84
values and, 263–264

Balance theory, of coordination,
  357–358
Behavior, dual perspective and,
  10–11
Blended family, 139, 222
Blending ecosystems strengths
  and problem-solving
  approaches, 62–65
Blending of knowledge/
  values/skills
  case example, 55–56
  creativity and, 54–55
  ecosystems strengths
    approach and, 55
Bond, of groups, 229
Boundaries
  in agencies, 165
  in communities, 154
  in groups, 225, 227
Broker role, 324
  case example, 325
Bureaucracy
  effectiveness in, 174
  managed care and, 175
  worker roles in, 173
  working in, 172–176
Burnout, worker, 175–176

Case advocate, 325, 373
Case conference, 113
Case management, 358–360
  case example, 360
Casework
  change process and, 61

Casework *continued*
  diagnostic approach to, 23
  problem solving and, 25
  process approach to, 25
  relationship principles, 24,
    192–193
  theory. *See* Theory(ies)
Cause advocacy. *See also*
    Organizational change
  case example, 378
  community organization
    and, 375
  defined, 325, 373
  influencing political process
    and, 375–377
  social action organizing
    and, 377
  worker issues and, 376–377
Cause, 6
Cause-function debate, 6–7, 12
Change, ecosystems perspective
    and, 12. *See also* Change
    process; Environmental
    change
Change-from-within strategy,
    370. *See also* Organizational
    change
Change-oriented record, 391
Change process. *See also* Growth
    and change
  assessment and, 268–278
  case examples, 72–73, 274
  casework and, 61
  ecosystems strengths
    approach and, 62, 68–71
  in groups, 241
  social work practice and,
    73–74
  stages of, 66–72
Client(s). *See also* Worker-client
    relationship
  assuming role of, 122–124
  capacity, 131
  case examples, 133–136,
    143–148, 224–225
  definitions of, 119–121
  determination of stress/crisis
    of, 132

ecosystem balance and, 171,
    180–181
ecosystems strengths
    approach and, 64, 65–66
empowerment of, 64
evaluation, 402
family, 143–148 (case
    example), 220–224, 224–225
    (case example), 251–253
fears, 186
gender/sexuality and, 130,
    194–195
human diversity and, 126–130
individual (case example),
    133–136
managed care and, 29–30
minority, 172, 279–280, 343
motivation, 131–132
multiperson, 137
needs, 121–122, 182. *See
    also* Need(s)
nonvoluntary, 187
opportunity, 131
planning and, 291–292,
    299–300, 309–310
roles, 126
self-determination, 64, 110
social history, 126
social responsibility, 110–111
strengths/uniqueness,
    132–133
stress of, 132
termination of service and,
    410–413. *See also*
    Termination
terms for, 122
types, 121
welfare reform and, 29
women, 130
worker understanding of,
    120, 124–133
Climate, interview, 210–211. *See
    also* Environment
Climate-setting skills, 210–211
Clinical evaluation, 388–389
Cognitive skills, 53
Cognitive-behavioral approach,
    328–329

Collaboration. *See also*
    Coordination, of services
  coordination versus, 356
  defined, 113
  in multiperson helping
    system, 113
Communication
  balance theory and, 357–358
  case example, 202–203
  coordination versus, 356
  cultural differences and, 200
  ecosystems strengths
    approach and, 199
  effective, 200–201
  in groups, 230, 238–239
  networking and, 360–362
  problems, 201–202
  process of, 199–200
  purposes of, 199
  in worker-client relationships,
    199–202
Communications theory, 26
Community
  case example, 162
  defined, 153
  ecosystems strengths
    approach and, 70
  model of practice, 161–162
  neighborhood and, 155
  organization and cause
    advocacy, 375
  patterns of, 155–156
  plan of action and, 305–306
  power in, 155
  social agencies and, 164
  as social system, 153–162
  sociological view of, 154–155
  structure/function of,
    155–156
  study of, 158, 161–162
  types of, 156
  worker understanding of,
    157–162
Community benefits, 321
Community organization
  work, 26
Community system, 154
Community units, 154, 155–156

Computers
confidentiality and, 403
in program evaluation,
401–402
record keeping and, 391,
401–402
Concern, 4, 272–274. *See
also* Need(s)
Confidentiality, 402–404
Conflict, 230, 243
Congruity, 12
Consciousness raising, 326–327
Consultation, 113, 243–244
Consultation task, 243
Continuity of care, 359
Contract, of worker-client in
planning, 312–313
Coordination
aspects of, 356–357
balance theory of, 357–358
case examples, 360, 362–363
case management and, 358–360
defined, 356
mechanisms for, 358
networking and, 360–362
resource systems and, 357
Coordination task, 244
Coordinative team, 114
Coping, 24, 123
Council on Social Work
Education, Curriculum
Policy Statement, 53
Creativity, 54–55
Crisis, 132, 330–333
Crisis intervention, 332–333
case example, 333–334
Cultural differences
communication and, 200
interview and, 206
Cultural factors
in assessment, 279–280
ecosystems strengths
approach and, 194
families and, 223
helping relationship and,
193–194
one-to-one action system
and, 183

plan of action and, 292, 298
termination and, 412–413
understanding clients and,
126–130

Decision making
in assessment, 263–264
in families, 252
in groups, 230, 237, 241
Development, in groups,
230–232, 253
Diagnosis
approaches to, 23
assessment as, 259
problem-solving process
and, 24
use of term, 19, 22–23, 77
*Diagnostic and Statistical Manual
of Mental Disorders (DSM-
IV)*, 273
Diagnostic approach, 22–23
Direct practice
activity as interventive
strategy and, 337–340
broker/advocate roles, 324–325
case examples, 325, 329–330,
333–334, 337, 341
categories of, 318
defined, 318
empowerment, 326–329
enabling client access to
resources and, 319–325
mediation and, 341–344
principles for action and, 319
referral and, 323–324
response to crisis and,
330–333. *See also* Crisis
service delivery system and,
320–323
support and, 334–337
Discussion leadership, in
groups, 249–250
Diversity perspective, 78
Diversity, human. *See also*
Special populations
in community, 157–158
gender/sexuality and, 130
human behavior and, 10–11

need and, 9–11
planning and, 310–311
termination and, 412–413
understanding client and,
126–130
valuing of, 51
Dual perspective, 10, 279–280

Eco-map, 140, 146
Ecological perspective. *See also*
Ecosystems perspective;
Ecosystems strengths
approach
assessment and, 260,
275–276, 278
cause-function debate
and, 12
congruity/incongruity
and, 12
defined, 12
historical development of,
28, 30
need and, 12
Ecosystem(s)
case example, 171–172
person in environment
and, 153
transactions in, 170–171
Ecosystems perspective. *See also*
Ecological perspective;
Ecosystems strengths
approach
change and, 16
defined, 16
Ecosystems strengths approach.
See also Ecological
perspective
agency and, 163
change process and, 62, 67–71
defined, 30
ecosystem balance and, 171,
180–181, 275–276
environmental change and,
351–352
expanded focus of, 55
growth and change and,
65–66, 211
historical development of, 30

Ecosystems strengths approach
continued
interventions and, 63–64, 78
mediation and, 341–342, 351
multiperson interaction and,
215–218
needs assessment and,
275–276, 277
person in environment
and, 153
planning and, 71, 125
problem-solving process and,
30, 62–65
service delivery and, 309
transactions and, 76
worker creativity and, 55
worker stress and, 175–176
Effectiveness, 384
Efficiency, 384
Empowerment. *See also*
Assertiveness training;
Enabling; Positive
reinforcement; Positive
thinking
case example, 329–330
direct practice and, 326–327
discriminated-against groups
and, 7
strengths perspective
and, 64
Enabling. *See also*
Empowerment
case example, 329–330
direct practice and,
319–325, 327
group, 237–240
Energy use, 229
Entitlement program, 29
Environment. *See also* Climate
agency as, 163
change in, 350–354
community as, 153–154, 162
Environmental change
case example, 354
ecosystems strengths
approach and, 351–352
environmental manipulation
and, 350, 352–354
Environmental demands, 11

Environmental manipulation, 350
Environmental psychology, 351
Environmental treatment, 351
Erikson's life-stage theory, 8,
99–101
Ethics
influence and, 84–85
NASW *Code of Ethics*, 19, 48,
49, 308, 318, 384
values and, 48–50
Evaluation
accountability and, 384–387
case examples, 392–393,
396–398
client participation and, 402
computers and, 391,
401–402, 403
confidentiality and, 402–404
defined, 385
hard-line/soft-line, 389
issues related to, 402–404
managed care and, 385
privacy laws and, 404
program, 400–401
recording, 389–392
research and, 393–396
summative versus
formative, 387
techniques/methods for,
389–402
termination and, 419–420
types of, 387–389
Extinction, 328

Facilitation, 244
Facilitation task, 244
Family
blended, 139, 222
case examples, 143–148,
224–225
change in, 141–142
cohesiveness of, 140
decision making in, 252
development, 253
environment of, 140
function, 252–253
genogram, 98, 140, 147
as group, 218–224. *See also*
Group(s)

life stages, 141–142
mapping of, 280
as multiperson client system,
137–142, 218–224, 303–305
multiperson interaction and,
218–220
planning and, 303–305
roles, 252–253
social history of, 137, 220, 223
as social system, 220, 251–253
structure, 251–252
subsystems of, 139–140
termination with, 415
transactional nature of, 80–82
working with, 220–224
Federal Privacy Act of 1974, 404
Felt need, 4–5
Feminist perspective, 30, 252,
430–431
Field of practice, 164
Focusing skills, 210
Formative evaluation, 387
Function, group, 229–230,
252–253. *See also* Group(s);
Social function
Functional approach, 23
Functioning, worker's personal,
102–104

Gemeinshaft, 154
Gender
communication and, 358
family power imbalances
and, 252
helping relationship and,
194–195
Generalist practice
contemporary, 1, 31
emergence of, 27–28
meaning of, 14
planning and, 291
Genogram
case example, 105
defined, 98
family, 98, 140, 147
Gesellshaft, 154
Goal-attainment scaling, 399
Goals
defined, 292

development of, in
 groups, 238
plan in planning, 292–296
Group(s). *See also* Family;
 Self-help groups; Small
 groups
activity of, 250
case examples, 232–237, 251
commonality, 248
conflict, 230, 243
decision making in, 230, 238
development, 230–232, 253
discussion in, 249–250
ecosystems strengths
 approach and, 225, 229
enabling for, 237–240
family as, 251–253. *See also*
 Family
formation, 247–249
function, 229–230, 252–253
goal development in, 238
information exchange
 in, 230
interaction, 245–247
leadership, 229, 242
membership of, 237–238,
 248–249
participation issues, 240–243
planning in, 303–305
relationship roles in, 228–229
role definition in, 238
self-help, 321
situations for use of, 215–216
as social system, 225–232,
 251–253
structure, 225–229, 251–252
worker as member of, 237–244.
 See also Worker-multiclient
 relationship(s)
Group-building (group
 maintenance) roles, 228
Group task roles, 228–229
Group work, 26
Growth and change. *See also*
 Change process
ecosystems strengths
 approach and, 65–66, 211
need and, 65–66
process of, 66

Help-seeking process, 123–124
Helping. *See* Helping person(s);
 Multiperson helping
 system; Natural helping
 system; Self-help groups
Helping person(s). *See*
 also Worker(s)
case example, 112
characteristics of, 107–109
responsibility/authority of,
 109–111
skills of, 111–112
Helping relationship, 24,
 190–197
Helping skills, 111–112
Host setting, 163
Human development
environmental factors and,
 10–11
Erikson's psychosocial needs
 of, 8, 99–101
need and, 8–9
Human diversity. *See* Diversity,
 human

Incongruity, 12
Indigenous helpers, 320. *See also*
 Natural helpers
Indirect practice
case management and,
 358–360, 360 (case example)
cause advocacy and, 373–377,
 378 (case example)
community organization
 and, 375
defined, 318
environmental change and,
 350–354, 354 (case example)
influencing political process
 and, 375–377
influentials involved in,
 354–355, 355–356 (case
 example)
networking and, 360–362,
 362–363 (case example)
organizational change
 from within and,
 369–372, 372–373 (case
 example)

program planning/resource
 development, 363–369,
 366–367 (case example)
self-help groups and, 368–369
service coordination and,
 356–362
social action organizing
 and, 377
volunteers and, 367–368, 368
 (case example)
Individual client, 133–136 (case
 example). *See also* One-to-
 one action system
Individualized rating scales
 (IRSs), 399
Influence
bases of, 83
case example, 85
ethical considerations and,
 84–85
indirect practice and, 354–355
problem assessment and, 27
resistance to, 83
Influentials, 354–355
case example, 354
Information exchange, 170,
 181, 230
Instrumental values, 46
Integrated methods, 27. *See also*
 Generalist practice
Integrative team, 114
Interaction. *See also* Multiperson
 interaction; One-to-one
 action system; Worker-
 client relationship(s)
one-to-one, 181–188. *See also*
 One-to-one action system
process of, 92
transactions and, 80–82
Interactional skill, 26
Interactive skills, 53
Interdisciplinary practice, 114
Interface, 153
Interpreting skills, 210
Intervention(s)
activity as, 337–340
case examples, 79–80, 337
changes sought in, 85–87
deficit approach to, 64

Intervention(s) *continued*
  defined, 77–79
  ecosystems strengths
    approach and, 64, 78
  historical development of,
    25–26
  influence of worker on, 82–85
  solution-based, 13, 30
  transactions and, 80–82
  use of term, 77
Interventive repertoire, 26, 52.
    See also Skills
Interview
  cultural differences and, 206
  defined, 203
  preparation for, 205
  program evaluation and, 400
  purpose of, 203–204
  stages of, 205–207
  worker skills in, 207–211

Judgment, 263–266
  case example, 266–268

Knowledge. *See also* Knowledge
    base; Self-knowledge,
    worker
  blending of, with values/
    skills, 54–57
  case example, 44–45, 55–56
  definitions of, 40
  scientific, 41
  values and, 45
Knowledge base
  assessment and, 264–265
  elements of, 43–44
  historical development of,
    19–31
  practice wisdom and, 42
  problems associated with,
    42–43
  social work, 40–44

Leadership, group, 229, 242
Licensing, of social work
    professionals, 18
Life processes, 86
Lifestyle, 95

Listening skills, 208–209
Locus of control, 131. *See also*
    Motivation

Macropractice, 341. *See also*
    Indirect practice
Managed care
  agencies and, 168–169
  brief solution-based
    interventions and, 13, 30
  bureaucracies and, 175
  cost control goal of, 29
  evaluation and, 385
  planning and, 308–309
  social work practice and, 29–30
  support services and, 336
  worker stress and, 175–176
Mapping, 280
  case example, 280–281
Maslow's hierarchy of needs, 7,
    68, 170, 274
Maximal level of functioning, 359
Mediation
  ecosystems strengths approach
    and, 341, 351
  strategy, 341–344
Medical model, 19
Mezzopractice, 349. *See also*
    Indirect practice
Milieu therapy, 352
Minorities. *See* Client(s),
    minority; Diversity, human
Models/approaches, social
    work. *See also* Direct
    practice; Indirect practice
  behavior therapy (socio-
    behavioral), 425–426
  case management, 358–360
  cognitive (rational, reality
    therapy), 426–427
  communication
    (communicative-
    interactive), 1, 427
  community-based, 161–162
  crisis intervention, 332–333,
    427–428
  developmental, 428–429
  diagnostic, 22–23

diversity perspective, 78
  ecological (lifemodel),
    30, 429
  ecosystems, 30, 260, 278
  existential, 429–430
  feminist practice, 30, 252,
    430–431
  functional, 23, 431
  generalist, 1, 27, 31, 291, 299
  Gestalt therapy, 432
  integrative, 27, 432–433
  internationalist, 31
  locality development, 433
  mediating, 341–344, 433–434
  medical, 19
  organizational (remedial-
    group), 434–435
  problem-solving, 435
  psychosocial, 435–436
  social action, 436
  social planning, 437
  socialization, 437–438
  strengths perspective, 438
  task, 438–439
Moral code, 95–98
Motivation, 131–132. *See also*
    Locus of control
Multiclient systems, 137–142.
    See also Family; Group(s);
    Multiperson helping
    system; Worker-multiclient
    relationship(s)
Multiperson helping system. *See
    also* Worker-multiclient
    relationship(s)
  collaboration/consultation/
    referral and, 113
  defined, 93–94, 112–113
  problems in, 115–116
  as team, 113
  types of, 114
Multiperson interaction. *See also*
    Multiperson helping
    system; worker-multiclient
    relationship(s)
  ecosystems strengths
    approach and, 215–218
  family and, 218–220

National Association of Social
Workers (NASW), 19, 27,
39, 308
Code of Ethics, 19, 48, 49, 308,
318, 384
Natural helpers, 320–321
Natural helping system
defined, 171
ecosystem strengths approach
and, 103, 115
service delivery and, 320–322
Need(s). *See also* Concern;
Needs assessment
case example, 5–6
cause-function debate, 6–7
client, 182
common human, 7–8
defined, 4
ecological perspective and, 12
ecosystems strengths
approach and, 65–66
felt, 4–5
formulation of, 272, 274
fulfillment, 270–272
hierarchies of, 5–6, 68, 170, 274
human development
perspective, 8–9, 99, 101
human diversity perspective
and, 9–11
identification of, 269–270
personal, 99–102
private troubles and public
issues, 6
psychosocial, 99, 101
strengths perspective and, 13
systems approach to, 11–12
transactions and, 170
unmet, 12, 65–66, 132–133
want versus, 4
Needs assessment. *See also*
Assessment
analyzing information,
276–277
assumptions about concern/
need, 274–275
assumptions about ecosystem
strengths/resources,
275–276

case example, 284–286
ecosystems strengths
approach and, 275–276, 277
formulating concern/need,
272–274, 274 (case example)
identifying blocks to need
fulfillment, 270–272
identifying need, 269–270
selecting/collecting
information, 276
Needs-based record, 391
Neighborhood, types, 155
Network, 320
Networking, 360–362
case example, 362–363
New record, 391–392

Objectives, in planning,
292–296
Observation, and program
evaluation, 401
One-to-one action system. *See
also* Worker-client
relationship(s)
blocks to, 186–187
case example, 189–190
client needs and, 182
communication in, 199–202
ecosystems strengths
approach and, 181–184,
186–188
exploratory phase of, 182–184
formation of, 182–188
interviewing and, 203–211
negotiation/contract phase
in, 184–185
relationship in, 190–197
Open access laws, 404
Opportunity seizing, 355
Organizational change
case example, 372–373
change-from-within strategy
for, 369–370
methods for, 371
problems with, 372
process of, 370
from within, 369–372. *See also*
Cause advocacy

Patient, client as, 122
Person in environment
(situation). *See also*
Ecological perspective;
Ecosystems strengths
approach
as ecosystem, 153
historical development of, 28
Personal Responsibility and
Work Opportunity Act, 29
Philosophy of life, 95
Plan of action
agency and, 306–307
case example, 301–303
characteristics of, 291–292
client and, 291–292, 299–300,
309–310
as client-centered, 291
community and, 305–306
components of, 292–301
defined, 291–292
diversity and, 310–311
factors affecting, 305–312
goals and objectives, 292–296
social issue and, 307–308
strategies, 296–301
system strengths/limitations,
311–312
tasks and, 300
units of attention and, 296
worker and, 298–299, 308–309
worker-client agreement and,
312–313
Planning. *See also* Plan of action
assessment and, 290–291
characteristics/process of,
291–292
client role in, 300
defined, 291
ecosystems strengths
approach and, 71, 125
managed care and, 308–309
with multiperson client
systems, 303–305
program, 363–369
self-help groups, 368–369
volunteer program, 367–368
worker role in, 299–300

Populations at risk, 310–311. *See also* Diversity
Positive feedback, 329
Positive reinforcement, 329
Positive thinking, 328–329. *See also* Empowerment
Power/control model, of profession, 18
Practice. *See* Direct practice; Indirect practice; Model(s) of practice
Practice wisdom, 42
Privacy laws, 404
Private practice model, of profession, 18
Private troubles, 6
Problem solving
    casework and, 25
    defined, 62
    in groups, 230, 243
Problem(s)
    defined, 63
    in problem-solving process, 63
Problem-oriented record, ecosystems strengths approach and, 391. *See also* Needs-based record
Problem-solving process
    defined, 62
    ecosystems strengths approach and, 13, 30, 62–65
    negative focus of, 63
Process approach, to casework, 25
Process model, of profession, 18
Process recording, 389–390. *See also* Record keeping
    case example, 392–393
Process, 28, 66. *See also* Social work process
Profession, social work and, 18–19
Professional relationships, 190
Program development. *See* Planning, program
Program evaluation, 400–401. *See also* Evaluation
Proximate values, 46
Psychosocial approach, 25. *See also* Diagnostic approach

Public issues, 6
Public model, 18
Public sector, 163

Qualitative data, 388
Quantitative data, 388
Questioning skills, 209–210
Questionnaires, 400

Rapid-assessment instruments (RAIs), 399
Rationality, value conflicts and, 97–98
Record keeping. *See also* Process recording
    computer use in, 391, 401–402
    confidentiality and, 403
Referral, 68, 74, 113, 323–324
Relationship(s). *See also* Helping relationship; One-to-one action system; Worker-client relationship(s); Worker-multiclient relationship(s); Termination
    case example, 197–199
    changes in, 85–86
    in communities, 155–156
    concept of, 26, 28
    defined, 190
    helping, 190–197
    principles of casework, 24, 192–193
    professional, 190
    transactional nature of, 80–82
    value system and view of, 96–97
Research
    qualitative/quantitative data in, 388
    scaling and, 399
    single-system design, 394–398, 396–398 (case example)
Resistance
    to influence, 83
    one-to-one action system and, 184, 187–188
    to systemic change, 372
Resources
    complementary pattern of, 359

coordination of, 356–362
enabling client use of, 319–325
program planning and development of, 363–369
systems of, 357
Role(s)
    in agencies, 167
    bureaucratic worker, 173
    of clients in planning, 300
    family, 252–253
    in groups, 238
    of worker in planning, 299–300
Role definition, 238

Scaling, evaluative, 399
Scientific philanthropy, 20
Secondary setting, of agency, 163
Self-help groups, 321, 368–369
Self-knowledge, worker
    case example, 104–106
    development of, 94–95
    ecological systems approach and, 103
    life experience and, 98–99
    lifestyle/philosophy and, 95
    moral code/value system and, 95–98
    personal functioning and, 102–104
    personal needs and, 99–102
    positive/negative self-worth and, 103
    roots and, 98
Service delivery systems. *See also* Coordination, of services; Social services settings
    dimensions of, 91
    ecosystems strengths approach and, 309
    forms of, 322–323
    natural helping system and, 320–321
Single-subject design, 395–396
Single-system design, 394–398
    case example, 396–398
Skillfulness, 53–54
Skills
    advocacy, 377

blending of, with
knowledge/values, 54–57
bureaucratic, 173–174
case examples, 54, 55–56
defined, 52
in direct practice, 319–320
group discussion, 249–250
guiding, 210
helping, 111–112
interviewing, 207–211
observation, 208
social work practice, 53
types of, 53
Small group(s). *See also* Family;
Group(s)
in agency, 168
assessment of, 277–278
case example, 232–237
defined, 225
as social system, 225–232
termination with, 415–416
Soaping, 391
Social action organizing, 374.
See also Cause advocacy
Social agency. *See* Agency
Social function
defined, 14
in groups, 229–230, 252–253
maximal level of, 359
planning and, 291
problems in, 270–272
worker-client roles and, 14
Social history
ecosystems strengths
approach and, 132–133
of family, 137, 223
of individual, 126
Social issue, planning and,
307–308
Social Security Act (ADC,
AFDC), 29
Social services settings, 163–164
Social support network
analysis, 281–282
Social system(s)
agency as, 164–165
community and, 153–162
defined, 11–12
family as, 220, 251–253

small group as, 225–232
transaction and, 80–82
Social systems theory, 11–12, 26
Social value system, 46
Social welfare, evolution of,
35–38
Social work. *See also* Models/
approaches, social work
ethics. *See* Ethics
historical development of,
19–31, 35–38
knowledge. *See*
Knowledge base
licensing. *See* Licensing
as profession, 18–19
purpose of, 86–87
values, 47–48, 51, 70, 103, 211.
See also Value(s)
Social work knowledge.
See Knowledge;
Knowledge base
Social work practice
change process and, 73–74
context and, 195
influences on contemporary,
77–78
international, 31
managed care and, 29–30
perspectives of, 1–2. *See also*
Models/approaches,
social work
skills. *See* Skills
social systems theory and,
11–12
theory, 21
values. *See* Value(s)
welfare reform and, 29
Social work principle, 5
Social work process, 1, 14, 257.
See also Assessment;
Direct practice; Evaluation;
Indirect practice; Plan
of action; Social work
practice; Termination
Social work team, 114. *See
also* Team(s)
Social worker. *See* Worker
Sociogram, 228
Solution-based intervention, 30

Special populations, 11. *See also*
Human diversity
Stabilization of change, 418–419
Steady state, 229
Strategic thinking, 291
Strategy, in planning, 296–301.
See also Change-from-
within strategy; Mediation
strategy
Strengths perspective. *See also*
Ecosystems strengths
approach
basic tenets of, 13
defined, 13, 63
need and, 13
positive focus of, 63
Summary record, 390–391
Summative evaluation, 387
Support, 334–337
case example, 337

TANF. *See* Temporary Assistance
to Needy Families
Task-achievement scaling
(TAS), 399
Task group, 305, 365–366
case example, 366–367
Task implementation process, in
groups, 230
Tasks
mediation, 342–343
in planning, 300
for working in groups, 243–244
Team(s). *See also* Group(s)
case conference and, 113
change agent system and,
114–115
coordinative, 114
integrative, 114
in multipurpose helping
system, 113
social work, 114
use of, 240–242
Teamwork, 115
Temporary Assistance to Needy
Families (TANF), 29
Termination
case example, 420–422
components of, 417–420

Termination *continued*
  context and, 412
  cultural issues and, 412–413
  defined, 408
  disengagement and, 417–418
  evaluation and, 419–420
  with families, 415
  with individuals, 413–415
  planned, 413–416
  with small groups, 415–416
  social work process and, 410
  stabilization of change and,
    418–419
  types of, 409–413
  worker-client relationship
    and, 410–413
Theory(ies). *See also* Models/
    approaches, social work
  casework, 21–28
  communications, 26
  social systems, 11–12
  social work practice, 21.
    See also Direct practice;
    Indirect practice
Thinking, in social work
    process, 14
Time line, 300
Time orientation, 97
Towle's hierarchy of needs, 7,
    170, 274
Trait-attribute approach, to
    profession, 18
Transaction(s)
  case example, 82
  change and, 85–87
  defined, 80
  in ecosystems, 170–171,
    171–172 (case example)
  ecosystems strengths
    approach and, 76
  as focus for change, 80–82
  information exchange and,
    170, 181
  interaction and, 80–81
  needs and, 170
  social systems and, 80–81
Transactional assessment,
    278–282

Treatment, 21–22, 23, 77

Ultimate values, 46
Unit of attention, 1, 296

Value(s)
  blending of, with
    knowledge/skills, 54–57
  case examples, 51–52, 55–56
  definitions of, 45–46
  ethics and, 48–50
  factors influencing, 46
  knowledge and, 45,
    263–264
  problems, 48–50
  social work, 47–48, 51,
    70, 103, 211
  social work practice and,
    48–51
  types of, 46
Value conflicts, 46–47, 96–98
Value system, 46–47, 95–98
Valuing, 50–51
Volunteer programs, 367–368
  case example, 368

Welfare reform, 29
Worker(s). *See also* Helping
    persons; Self-knowledge,
    worker; Worker-client
    relationship(s); Worker-
    multiclient relationship(s);
    Worker-nonclient
    relationship(s)
  accountability and, 385–387
  advocacy issues and,
    376–377
  bureaucratic settings and,
    172–176
  changes sought by, 85–87
  community environment and,
    153–157
  creativity of, 55
  direct practice skills of,
    319–320
  ecosystem balance and,
    171, 181
  family and, 220–224

  as group member, 237–244.
    See also Worker-multiclient
    relationship(s)
  as helping person, 107–112
  influence of, 82–85
  interviewing skills of,
    207–211
  judgment of, 263–266
  mediator role of, 86
  in multiperson helping
    system, 112–116
  needs, 99–102
  planning and, 298–299,
    308–309
  problem-solving process and,
    67–72
  stress/burnout, 175–176
  tasks in groups, 243–244
  understanding of agency,
    163–169
  understanding of clients, 120,
    124–133
  understanding of community,
    157–162
  value conflicts of, 96–98
Worker-client relationship(s). *See
    also* Communication;
    Cultural factors; Evaluation;
    Intervention(s); One-to-one
    action system; Referral;
    Termination; Worker-
    multiclient relationship(s)
  accountability and, 385–386
  ecosystems strengths
    approach and, 64, 65–66
  obstacles to, 73–74
  plan of action and, 298–301,
    303–305
  in planning, 291–292. *See also*
    Plan of action
  principles of, 24, 192–193
  termination and, 410–413
  trust and, 70
Worker-multiclient
    relationship(s). *See also*
    Group(s); Multiperson
    helping system
  case examples, 232–237, 251

discussion leadership and, 249–250

ecosystems strengths approach and, 246

family and, 220–224

group formation and, 247–249

group membership and, 248–249

interaction and, 245–247

planning and, 303–305

social work tasks and, 243–244

worker understanding/role and, 217–218, 227

Worker-nonclient relationship(s), 188, 196